The Spirit
of Reform

The fear of democracy in 1867: Matt Morgan in *Tomahawk*.

THE SPIRIT OF REFORM

British Literature and
Politics, 1832-1867

Patrick Brantlinger

Harvard University Press
Cambridge, Massachusetts
London, England
1977

Publication of this book has been aided by a grant from the
Andrew W. Mellon Foundation

Library of Congress Cataloging in Publication Data
Brantlinger, Patrick, 1941-
   The spirit of reform.

   Includes bibliographical references and index.
   1. English literature—19th century—History
and criticism.   2. Politics and literature.
I. Title.
PR469.P6B65   820'.9'008   76-30537
ISBN 0-674-83315-5

For Ellen, Andrew,
Susan, and Jeremy

Acknowledgments

I am grateful for ideas and help to more people than I can mention here. My first debts are to two excellent teachers: Jerome Buckley of Harvard and the late Milton Goldberg of Antioch College. Pieces of the dissertation that I wrote under Professor Buckley's wise direction are still afloat in these essays. Don Gray not only read and commented on parts of this study, but also, during his term as Chairman of the Department of English at Indiana, gave me much assistance—a generosity which Ken Gros Louis has continued. Lee Sterrenburg helped me to improve the chapter on Carlyle, and in more general ways has led me to think theoretically about literary studies. Patrick J. McCarthy of the University of California at Santa Barbara read the manuscript and made many suggestions that were helpful in revising it. And I am grateful to other friends and colleagues, particularly to Dan Granger, Martha Vicinus, and Scott Sanders, but also to many of the students who have taken my L645 and L743 courses at Indiana. They have all helped me to get ''beyond aestheticism.'' Tony Shipps and the staff of the Indiana University Library have helped in many ways, and so has Susan Wallace of Harvard University Press. For the illustration by Matt Morgan from *Tomahawk,* I am indebted to Tom Kemnitz of the University of New Hampshire. Finally, for parts of chapters I and IV, I have drawn on materials that I originally published in *Criticism, Nineteenth-Century Fiction,* and *Victorian Newsletter,* and I wish to thank the editors of those journals for allowing me to do so.

Contents

Introduction   1

  I. The Literature of the 1830s   11

 II. Benthamite and Anti-Benthamite Fiction   35

III. The Lessons of Revolution   61

 IV. Two Responses to Chartism: Dickens and Disraeli   81

  V. The Entrepreneurial Ideal   109

 VI. Christian Socialism   129

VII. Liberal Individualism: The Brownings   151

VIII. The Ambiguities of Progress   181

 IX. Realisms   205

  X. 1867 and the Idea of Culture   237

Notes   261

Index   285

THE CRIPPLED STREET BIRD-SELLER.

From Henry Mayhew's *London Labour and the London Poor.*

Introduction

One of the first conditions of any institution being altered is that
people should come to imagine it as conceivably altered. The
great difficulty of the reformer is to get people to exert their
imagination to that extent.

D. G. Ritchie, *Darwinism and Politics*

The leading theme of this study of British literature and liberalism between the Reform Bills of 1832 and 1867 may
seem uncontroversial, partly because it is one which Victorian writers
themselves never tire of repeating: that literature is or can be an instrument of social amelioration, at the same time that it is shaped by social
events.[1] The utilitarians, the Coleridgeans, Dickens, Carlyle, Ruskin,
Arnold, and Eliot all present us with some version of this double thesis.
"The spirit of reform" means the belief that social improvement, and
especially the improvement of the condition of the working class, can be
brought about by some form of political action, whether through legislative and administrative channels, or through social work and private charity. It thus embraces what Louis Cazamian called "sentimental interven-
tionism" in his pioneering study, *Le roman social en Angleterre,* but it
also embraces the Benthamite "scientific" and bureaucratic social planning of the 1830s and after. Used in this way, "reform" may refer to
attempts to improve any social institution, from poor law workhouses to
Parliament.

The spirit of reform in the early 1830s involved evangelical and humanitarian protest, the advocacy of limited government intervention to
correct social abuses and to refurbish outmoded institutions, and Benthamite and Owenite schemes for improving mankind itself. As the first
Chartist petition shows, members of the working class felt cut off from
political influence and betrayed by the middle-class radicals who had
used them to gain the Reform Bill of 1832. But working men in large
numbers joined with middle-class reformers in the Ten Hours Movement
and in the agitation against the New Poor Law. Disillusionment with
Benthamite and with other theories of social reform grew during the depression of 1836-1842 and was reinforced by Carlyle and Dickens, who

1

were advocates of social reform but who, in contrast to the Benthamites and the Owenites, believed that moral reform has to come first—that human nature cannot be changed by changing institutions, but that institutions may be changed by first changing human nature.[2] This is a theme that recurs throughout the period, perhaps most insistently during the second Reform Bill crisis in the 1860s, where it appears, among many other places, in *Culture and Anarchy, Time and Tide,* Felix Holt's "Address to the Working Men," and F. D. Maurice's *The Workman and the Franchise.*

During the 1840s reform tended to be identified less and less with legislation and with bureaucratic social planning than with voluntary humanitarian activity, typified by the Christian Socialism of Maurice, Ludlow, and Kingsley. Ideas of social reform through politics were gradually supplanted by ideas of social progress in spite of politics. This shift was due partly to the successes of the Anti-Corn Law League in 1846 and of the Ten Hours Movement in 1847, partly to dissatisfaction with the New Poor Law, the major piece of Benthamite legislation in the 1830s, and partly to fear of Chartism, which put middle-class liberals on the defensive and made them more wary of tampering with the machinery of society than they had been from 1832 to 1836. Social legislation continued to be enacted, of course, as is evident from the Public Health Act of 1848, but the language of the liberal intelligentsia concerning social issues changed: there was more talk of progress as a built-in function of industrial growth and less talk of controlling or reforming industrialism itself.

During the "age of equipoise," when free trade and industrialism seemed triumphant after 1848, the Benthamite, the "sentimental radical," and the Tory-radical versions of social reform all tended to give way to ideas of inevitable progress through industry and self-help (one version of moral reform). Britain settled down into a period of relative social stability and security in the 1850s and 1860s,[3] and Victorian literature reflects the consequences of this large transition from an era characterized by "social cleavage" (to adopt Asa Briggs's terms) to an era characterized by "the cult of progress." The economic factors underlying this transition include the effects of free trade after 1846; the railroad boom of the middle 1840s; the upsurge in agricultural production after 1846; the discovery of gold in California and Australia; and such enabling legislation as the Limited Liability Act of 1855.[4] To these economic factors may be added at least five related political factors: the partial victory of factory reform in 1847; the demise of Chartism after 1848; the failure of the continental revolutions of the same year; the growth of the New Model Trade Unions and of cooperative societies as focuses of working-class political energy starting in the 1850s; and the dominance in Parliament of liberals and conservatives alike who may be described as believers in Palmerstonian expediency. S. G. Checkland describes the impact of these changes on businessmen and the working class:

> It was between the fifties and the seventies that the absolute increase in production in Britain became so staggering, with all the accompanying effects upon social life and outlook. Moreover the new wealth came forward in an atmosphere of exhilaration among men of business, in rosy contrast to the long struggle against falling prices. By 1853 the general trend of prices, downward since 1819, was reversed; prices mounted all the way to 1873. On the workers' side, too, things were brighter, with real wages rising convincingly from the sixties. Attention could switch from the attempt to offer an alternative formula for society, to organizing to secure a larger share of expansion.[5]

The shift of attention among the workers from Chartism to the trade union movement and cooperation was paralleled in a variety of ways in middle-class literature. The combination of all of these factors, producing a surge of industrial expansion and relative prosperity, made it increasingly difficult for middle-class liberals to maintain reformist ideals. The Great Exhibition of 1851 may be interpreted, as indeed it was by many Victorians, as marking the border between two ages: the past one bleak, hostile, rent with class warfare and political vituperation, and the future one hopeful, golden, ever-advancing on well-oiled wheels down "the ringing grooves of change." This is true even though both Carlyle and Dickens kept up their social criticism in the 1850s and after, and even though as late as 1860, Ruskin was just beginning his forays against the Manchester School and the esthetic atrocities of industrialism.

More indicative of middle-class opinion in 1860 than *Unto This Last* is the manner in which it was received. Ruskin said little in it that Carlyle had not already said in *Chartism* and *Past and Present*. But according to George Smith, one of the publishers of the *Cornhill Magazine* in which *Unto This Last* first appeared, it was "too deeply tainted with socialistic heresy to conciliate subscribers." And even if it was not socialistic in the modern sense of advocating the abolition or the nationalization of property, its humanitarianism alone made it threatening to the *Manchester Examiner and Times:* "His wild words will touch the spring of action in some hearts, and ere we are aware, a moral floodgate may fly open and drown us all."[6] Such a moral spillway was exactly what Dickens and Carlyle wanted to pry open. But to some observers in the 1860s, even a little charity seemed like a dangerous thing. Ruskin was out of step with the times. If he had written *Unto This Last* in 1843, it would have appeared as a reinforcement of *Past and Present.* On the other hand, socialism did not take root in middle-class circles in Britain until the 1870s and after, when Ruskin's disciples—among them William Morris—began to read Marx and Engels as well as Ruskin and Carlyle. The growth of corporate capitalism and of the trade unions, and the series of depressions starting in 1873, rendered the old liberal, reformist attitudes increasingly obsolete and opened the way for the revolutionary socialism of Morris and Hyndman, the pragmatic socialism of the Fabians, and the welfare state liberalism of L. T. Hobhouse.

The public rejection of *Unto This Last* in 1860 is evidence of the mid-Victorian dominance of the idea of progress through unrestricted industrial growth as opposed to the idea of activist reform working to control industry. And even the idea of progress, which in most versions still involved individual initiative as its motive force, was giving place by 1860 to the idea of progressive evolution, with its characteristic dwarfing of the individual in a landscape of cosmic proportions. The radical activism of the Benthamites culminates ironically in Herbert Spencer, with his extreme, contradictory theories of laissez-faire individualism and social organicism. The Benthamite political economists—Ricardo, James Mill, Senior, and McCulloch—presented economic relations in the guise of unalterable laws of nature, but still viewed political relations as open and fluid, subject to rational decision. By the time of the second Reform Bill, in Spencer, Bagehot, and the other social Darwinists, both political and economic relations are reified: only through gradual, inevitable evolution will social progress in any field take place.

The extreme limits of this gradual transition in public attitudes may be suggested by juxtaposing a passage from Sir Robert Peel's "Tamworth Manifesto" with two later statements. Peel's declaration reveals the extent to which a cautious reformism could be assimilated even to conservatism in 1834:

> Then, as to the spirit of the Reform Bill, and the willingness to adopt and enforce it as a rule of government: if, by adopting the spirit of the Reform Bill, it be meant that we are to live in a perpetual vortex of agitation; that public men can only support themselves in public estimation by adopting every popular impression of the day,—by promising the instant redress of anything which anybody may call an abuse,—by abandoning altogether that great aid of government—more powerful than either law or reason—the respect for

ancient rights, and the deference to prescriptive authority; if this be the spirit of the Reform Bill, I will not undertake to adopt it. But if the spirit of the Reform Bill implies merely a careful review of institutions, civil and ecclesiastical, undertaken in a friendly temper, combining, with the firm maintenance of established rights, the correction of proved abuses and the redress of real grievances,—in that case, I can for myself and colleagues undertake to act in such a spirit and with such intentions.[7]

It was as a cautious reformer that Peel did act throughout his career, although sometimes reluctantly. Peel recognized that the reform of institutions had become a leading impulse in the new age; he wished not to stop it, but to give it wise guidance.

In contrast, a writer in *Chambers's Journal* in 1851 advised would-be reformers to be resigned, much as Dorothea Brooke learns the wisdom of resignation in *Middlemarch*. Progress is inevitable, but gradual; individuals cannot expect to have much influence upon its course: "It is given to few such spaces of time [generations] to see great revolutions . . . in the plan of society. The individual must be content to see only his small part of some of those grand movements, the issues of which form landmarks in history." It is better, therefore, not to seek to hurry the divine plan along, for haste in matters of social change is dangerous: "It were well for the most forward class of minds to see and resign themselves to this view of their lot. Seeing with tolerable fulness and clearness what society is working towards, they are apt to chafe themselves in vain efforts to realise what only shall be vouchsafed to their children's children . . . Minds of this class, by their vehemence, often retard the movement they desire to promote."[8] It was this sort of argument, increasing in frequency from perhaps 1846 on, which led a more radical writer in *Hogg's Weekly Instructor* for 1848 to complain about "The Cant of 'Progress.' " The idea of progress, he said, was being used to forestall demands for reform: "The deluded mass is told it is on the advance to a better condition— helping itself on—informed that in every point of view it is reaching the acme of perfection—taught that it is only to struggle and strive a little longer as it is now doing, and the 'good time' will arrive."[9] Certainly for the writer in *Chambers's Journal*, society is to be its own reformer: it is a self-acting mechanism, beyond the influence of individuals (although they may interfere with it), and the spring that drives it is called "progress." So the idea of progress gradually emerges in liberal thinking as the antithesis of the idea of reform, even though they appeared to many to be nearly synonymous.

But both to Peel's statement and to the essay in *Chambers's Journal* may be contrasted one more statement about social change, typical of the 1860s, after the appearance of *Origin of Species*. In his *History of the Intellectual Development of Europe* (1863), J. W. Draper argues that the "equilibrium and movement of humanity are altogether physiological phenomena," and he produces an analysis of the progress of western civilization in terms of "natural law." The reader is to go away from Draper's history believing "that the civilization of Europe has not taken place fortuitously, but in a definite manner, and under the control of natural law; that the procession of nations does not move forward like a dream, without reason or order, but that there is a predetermined, a solemn march, in which all must join, ever moving, ever resistlessly advancing, encountering and enduring an inevitable succession of events; that individual life and its advancement through successive stages is the model of social life and its secular variations."[10] Even the conservative statesman of 1834 appears in the role of reformer. But for the positivist historian of 1863, social change is a matter of evolutionary process and "natural law," and individuals can have little or no influence on the progress of nations. And there is a similar difference between Carlyle's theory of hero worship and Herbert Spencer's attacks on what he called "the great man theory of history" in *The Study of Sociology* and elsewhere in the 1860s.

The passages from Peel and Draper may be taken as the outside limits of the large transition in public attitudes which this study traces. There were obviously many exceptions to the general pattern: Macaulay in the 1830s established many of the themes of the "cult of progress"; Dickens, Mill, John Bright, and others continued to call for specific institutional reforms in the 1850s and after; Tennyson began writing the *Idylls of the King* in the 1830s; and so on. But that many works and writers were responsive to particular phases and crises of social and economic development needs, I think, no elaborate demonstration. Dickens and Carlyle, for instance, are manifestly "topical" authors. To suggest that all writers are always responsive to social change in some manner (whether consciously or unconsciously, contemporaneously or anachronistically, negatively or positively) needs perhaps more demonstration. My main purpose is to show how each of the writers I examine responds to social change in quite specific and characteristic ways. And from a very approximate addition of the particular instances, I have tried to extract the more general pattern or movement away from the reform idealism of the 1830s towards modes of social thinking which, even while calling themselves "liberal," were decidedly more conservative than the radicalisms of the Bentham-

The free-trade hat of the Anti-Corn Law League. (Reproduced by permission of the Radio-Times Hulton Picture Library.)

ites, of the early *Punch* satirists, and of the younger Carlyle, Dickens, and even Disraeli.

A history of the spirit of reform in middle-class literature between 1832 and 1867, then, must be largely a history of its disappearance, as it becomes absorbed either by assumptions of inevitable progress or by theories of progressive evolution. Like all "spirits" in a world of market values and vested interests, the "spirit of reform" was not remarkable for its sturdiness or its longevity. And yet that it did enter the sphere of practice and did influence events for the better is undeniable. Even in the years when it seemed most quiescent, at least in literature, it was clearly at work, and in powerful ways. In the 1860s, when middle-class literature was dominated by the antireform realism of Trollope and by the social Darwinism of Spencer and Bagehot, middle-class liberals—John Bright, John Stuart Mill, William Gladstone—set about passing the second Reform Bill, with help from their Tory rivals.[11]

The weakening of the spirit of reform after 1850 is especially evident in the contrast between middle-class responses to the reform bills of 1832 and 1867. Whereas the first Reform Bill was largely the work of middle-class liberalism and radicalism, and looked to many observers like the British version of storming the Bastille, the second Reform Bill—also largely the work of middle-class liberalism—seemed to threaten an end to the hegemony of the middle class. As a result, 1867 prompted from many middle-class writers apocalyptic warnings like Carlyle's "Shooting Niagara," and patronizing, cautionary notices like Felix Holt's "Address to the Working Men." "We have reason to be discontented with many things," says Felix to his imaginary audience. "But the more bitterly we feel this . . . the stronger is the obligation we lay on ourselves to beware, lest we also, by a too hasty wrestling of measures which seem to promise an immediate partial relief, make a worse time of it for our own generation, and leave a bad inheritance to our children." Perhaps Felix has been reading *Chambers's Journal* on the idea of progress. Nowhere is the transformation of the idea of reform into progress and progressive evolution more strikingly registered than in George Eliot's novels. In *Felix Holt* itself, she traces the decline from the liberal ferment and optimism of 1832 to the cautious disillusionment of 1868:

> At that time, when faith in the efficiency of political change was at fever-heat in ardent Reformers, many measures which men are still discussing with little confidence on either side were then talked about and disposed of like property in near reversion. Crying abuses —"bloated paupers," "bloated pluralists," and other corruptions hindering men from being wise and happy—had to be fought against and slain. Such a time is a time of hope. Afterwards, when the corpses of those monsters have been held up to the public wonder and abhorrence, and yet wisdom and happiness do not follow, but rather a more abundant breeding of the foolish and unhappy, comes a time of doubt and despondency. But in the great Reform-year Hope was mighty.[12]

This declension from a time of faith in political action to one of "doubt and despondency" frames the more specific examinations of writers in this study. The primary causal factor underlying it appears to have been the increasing economic and political power of middle-class industrialism. That power blunted reform idealism and left would-be reformers like Clough and Dickens with a feeling of helplessness, astray in a wilderness of smokestacks and locomotive yards. The "young hopefulness of immediate good" that characterized the 1830s, George Eliot says at the end of *Middlemarch,* "has been much checked in our days."

The language of social class used in this study is not meant to be reductive, crudely deterministic, or judgmental, but rather to help describe ideological limitations and preconceptions in literary culture. The terms "working class," "middle class," and "aristocracy," with such variants as "lower middle class" and "gentry," seem to me to be the logical ones because they are those which the Victorians themselves use most frequently in defining their own class identities. In saying so, I may claim as a precedent such an able social historian as Geoffrey Best, who in his *Mid-Victorian Britain* declares: "I have used the language of class more as it was used by mid-Victorians than as it is used by any ancient or modern school of social theorists; i.e. I have used it continually and confusedly."[13]

The chapters are self-contained essays, at the same time that they are arranged chronologically and are meant to follow the broad outlines of social and cultural history. They do not, however, constitute a complete literary history of the period. As studies of the idea of reform in literature, they necessarily skip over some writers and give greater emphasis to others, especially to political and economic theorists, who are not makers of literature in a traditional sense. But it is my hope that these essays constitute history of a deeper, more genuine sort than standard literary surveys and chronicles. As Lucien Goldmann suggests, literary histories that behave as if one book follows another in a sequence set apart from economic, political, and social circumstances are not genuinely historical. And Tocqueville suggested something like this when he wrote: "The relations which exist between the social and political condition of a people and the genius of its authors are always numerous: whoever knows the one, is never completely ignorant of the other."[14]

Political corruption, from *George Cruikshank's Omnibus*, 1842.

I.   The Literature of the 1830s

Literary historians sometimes consider the 1830s a barren interlude between the Romantic and Victorian periods. Byron, Shelley, and Keats had passed from the scene. Coleridge, who died in 1834, had not written much poetry for years; and Wordsworth was no longer writing great poetry. "A strange pause followed their departure," says G. M. Young, "and the great Victorian lights rose into a sky which, but for the rapid blaze of Bulwer Lytton, was vacant."[1] The number of literary works from the 1830s which are still much read is small: *Sartor Resartus* and *The French Revolution;* Tennyson's first volume; Macaulay's essays; and *Sketches by Boz, Pickwick Papers,* and *Oliver Twist.* Certainly many contemporary witnesses felt that history had reached a crisis in the 1830s and that the arts were not cultivated as they had been in the past or as they would be in the future. In the St. Simonian phrase adopted by Mill, it was "an age of transition."

Of course throughout the century, liberal, middle-class writers never ceased to declare their betweenness, their transitional character. But the 1830s was a time of especially rapid and critical social change, when writers spoke the Pentecostal tongues of utopia and apocalypse. Catholic Emancipation in 1829, agitation for parliamentary reform, the July Revolution in France in 1830, and the Reform Bill itself aroused intense excitement and expectations of further radical changes or of social dissolution. Halévy points to the Irvingites in 1831 with their "mysterious prophecies" and says, "Never had the book of Daniel and the Revelations been studied more diligently."[2] And Carlyle, who shared an apocalyptic rhetoric with his friend Irving, wrote in "Signs of the Times" (1829): "At such a period, it was to be expected that the rage of prophecy should be more than usually excited. Accordingly, the Millennarians have come forth on the right hand, and the Millites on the left. The Fifth-monarchy men prophesy from the Bible, and the Utilitarians from Bentham. The one announces that the last of the seals is to be opened, positively, in the year 1860; and the other assures us that 'the greatest-happiness principle' is to make a heaven of earth, in a still shorter time.''[3] On the level of rhetoric, at least, there was not much difference between the ''millenarians'' and the ''Millites.'' In his *Extraordinary Black Book or Reformer's Bible* of 1831, John Wade wrote that ''we are on the eve of as great a social regeneration as the destruction of feudality, the abasement of Popery, or any other of the memorable epochs which have signalized the progress of nations.''[4] And as late as 1836, the great Birmingham radical, Joseph Parkes, still looked forward to seeing ''the Scythe of Reform'' mow down long-standing abuses.[5] When they were not busily proferring warnings against undue haste, Whigs expressed expectations milder than the radical ones of Wade and Parkes, and conservatives like Keble and Lyndhurst expressed fears of social change in general. But whether hopeful or dangerous, the early 1830s seemed to all observers to represent an especially crucial, apocalyptic turning point in ''the progress of nations.''

By 1836 or 1837, however, utopian expectations were yielding to disillusionment and, especially in the area of Church reform, to conservative expressions of relief. The bright prospects of 1832 suddenly darkened. In large part the change was due to the economic depression of 1836-1842, the worst in the history of early industrialism. In part, too, it was due to the failure of the Benthamite radicals to capture more seats in Parliament and to win more public support for the New Poor Law of 1834. Nowhere does the disillusionment of the late 1830s get expressed more forcefully than in Carlyle, whose *French Revolution, Chartism,* and *Past and Present* are all warnings to do-nothing aristocrats and to ''scientific'' radicals alike to reform themselves before the night cometh. In a letter written in the spring of 1837 to his brother John, Carlyle says:

> Commercial crash coming on, spreading wider and wider; the Paupers of Manchester *helping themselves* out of shops, great bands of them parading with signals of want of bread! On the one hand, Miss Martineau and Secretary Chadwick celebrating their New Poor Law Bill as the miracle of recent Legislation; on the other, the poor Nottingham Peasant hanging all his four children and giving himself up to be hanged that they may not go to the Hunger-Tower of Dante, here called *'Bastille,'* or Parish-Workhouse. It is a clatter of formulistic jargon, of quackery, cruelty and hunger, that my soul is sick of . . . No man in such a case can calculate the hour and the year; but to me it is very clear, all this cursed *pluister* of Lies and Misery is coming

12

tumbling into incoherent ruin, and will grow a great deal more miserable than it ever was.[6]

Having apparently done nothing except exacerbate poverty through the bitter pill of the New Poor Law, and certainly having done nothing to avert economic depression, Chadwick and his ilk are a source only of a "cursed *pluister* of Lies." In *Chartism* and *Past and Present,* Carlyle turns to "the Condition-of-England Question" to show the way back to the truth.

In less apocalyptic language, Mill speaks of the disappointment of the "great hopes" that he and his fellow Benthamites had placed in their allies in Parliament after 1832: "They were in unfavourable circumstances. Their lot was cast in the ten years of inevitable reaction, when the Reform excitement being over, and the few legislative improvements which the public really called for having been rapidly effected, power gravitated back in its natural direction, to those who were for keeping things as they were; when the public mind desired rest, and was less disposed than at any other period since the peace, to let itself be moved by attempts to work up the reform feeling into fresh activity in favour of new things."[7] Certainly the Whig governments of Grey and Melbourne were disappointing to all who hoped to see rapid social improvement flow from legislation. Apart from the Benthamite reforms embodied in the New Poor Law and the Municipal Corporations Act of 1835, the most urgent calls for social change came actually from Tory-radicals like Michael Sadler and Richard Oastler, and from Tory-evangelicals like Lord Ashley. The Tory-radical Ten Hours Movement, moreover, flowed into the agitation against the New Poor Law led by Oastler and Joseph Raynor Stephens, the renegade Methodist preacher, and the anti-Benthamite attitudes underlying both of these movements found new voices at the end of the decade in Carlyle and in the "sentimental radicalism" of Dickens and *Punch.* As long as Chadwick and Mill remained on the scene, the force of Benthamism was far from spent after the 1830s, but the idea of improving society by altering its external machinery through legislative intervention seemed increasingly discredited. The voices of Carlyle and Dickens were the most powerful on the literary scene in the 1840s; they spoke against the main Benthamite achievements and insisted that moral reform must precede social reform. It is important to recognize that some of the strongest pressures for reform through legislation in the 1830s came from Benthamism and Tory evangelicalism, and that the idea that the Benthamites stood for laissez-faire against all legislative interference with society is inaccurate.

Carlyle and Dickens are largely responsible for this inaccurate view; paradoxically, their attacks on Benthamism may have reinforced laissez-faire attitudes by undermining faith in the power of legislation to effect meaningful reforms.

But if the Benthamites, the Tory-radicals, and the "sentimental radicals" were all disappointed with the results of 1832, working-class radicals were bitterly disillusioned. More fully than any other source from the 1830s, the first Chartist Petition reveals the failure of middle-class reform measures to benefit the working class and so to stave off class conflict: "It was the fond expectation of the friends of the people, that a remedy for the greater part, if not for the whole of their grievances, would be found in the Reform Act of 1832 . . . They have been bitterly and basely deceived. The fruit which looked so fair to the eye, has turned to dust and ashes when gathered. The Reform Act has effected a transfer of power from one domineering faction to another, and left the people as helpless as before."[8] Throughout the 1840s, the strength of Chartism revealed the hollowness of the liberal belief in an identity of interests between labor and capital.

In the optimistic atmosphere of the early 1830s, literature and the other arts seemed to yield to politics as the center of cultural activity. As Bulwer-Lytton says in *England and the English,* itself an example of the new emphasis on politics: "Just at the time when with George the Fourth an *old* era expired, the excitement of a popular election at home concurred with the three days of July in France, to give a decisive tone to the *new.* The question of Reform came on, and, to the astonishment of the nation itself, it was hailed at once by the national heart. From that moment, the intellectual spirit hitherto partially directed to, became *wholly* aborbed in, politics; and whatever lighter works have since attained a warm and general hearing, have either developed the errors of the social system, or the vices of the legislative."[9] Bulwer suggests that in order to succeed in the new era, literature must become propaganda; it must present arguments either for or against specific social changes. No doubt the new emphasis on politics will mean that interest in literature will decline no matter how writers respond. Bulwer says that the "political agitation of the times is peculiarly unfavourable to the arts," and also that in the 1820s "politics . . . gradually and commonly absorbed our attention, and we grew to identify ourselves, our feelings, and our cause, with statesmen and economists, instead of with poets and refiners." But he also believes that literature can best serve the times by being responsive to politics. Arguing against political censorship of the drama, he says: "The great reason why the Athenians, always in a sea of politics, were nevertheless always willing to crowd the theatre, was this—*the theatre with them was political* . . . Thus theatrical performance was to the Athenian a newspaper as well as a play. We banish the Political from the stage, and we therefore deprive the stage of the most vivid of its actual sources of interest. At present the English, instead of finding politics on the stage, find their stage in politics."[10] Needless to say, Bulwer's view of Greek drama is very different from Matthew Arnold's two decades later, for Arnold finds in it "disinterested objectivity" rather than the topical relevance of journalism. In the excited atmosphere of the early 1830s, even the great, apparently calm and universal works of antiquity could take on the appearance of tracts and broadsides. At any rate, Bulwer believes that in a political age, literature must be political. And in his own writings, not only in *England and the English,* but also in his novels and plays, politics moves onto center stage.

Bulwer's likening of Greek drama to newspapers suggests a further fact about the 1830s—that it was an age of journalism. "The true Church of England, at this moment, lies in the Editors of its Newspapers," says Carlyle in "Signs of the Times."[11] Many writers besides Bulwer spoke of the growth of periodical and newspaper literature as one of the most striking features of early nineteenth-century culture, and associated journalism with living in a period of especially rapid social transition or of especially dangerous political turbulence. The term "journalism" was imported from France and carried with it overtones of 1789, as Carlyle's emphasis upon it in *The French Revolution* demonstrates. In an article called "Journalism in France" that appeared in the *British Quarterly Review* for 1846, the author says: "Every Frenchman, high or low, is more or less of a politician, and therefore newspapers are in greater number, and circulate through infinitely more hands than in England."[12] Agreeing with Bulwer, the author points out that journalism has two main effects, one good and one bad. On the one hand, it raises political consciousness and thus contributes to the cause of social progress. But on the other hand, because of the tendency of the journals to absorb all literary activity in search of profit, it has a ruinous effect upon the standards of literary culture: "Romances are now ordered by the wholesale houses, in the journal line, by the square yard or the square foot, with so many pounds of abuse of priestcraft; so many grains of double adultery; so many drachms of incest; so many ounces of poisoning; so many scruples of simple fornication or seductions of soubrettes; and so many pennyweights of common sense to knead together the horrid and disjointed masses of parricide, fratricide, incest, murder, seduction, suicide, fraud, covin, gambling, robbery, and rouerie of all sorts, of which the odious whole is compounded."[13] It is a familiar complaint. What this writer says about the effects of journalism on literature in France is said with equal vigor by Bulwer and others about the state of literature in England. It seemed to many observers in the 1830s that the disappearance of patronage and the use of poetry and fiction for profit and temporary political controversy would spell the end of high culture.

Of course the major Romantic writers had used literature as a political instrument—Blake, Shelley, and Byron from radical motives, and Coleridge, Wordsworth, and Southey from conservative ones. As William Howitt argued, "the great modern poets," including Scott, Southey, Wordsworth, and Coleridge, were also "great reformers," "and must forever be numbered amongst the greatest promoters of the freedom of opinion, and the spirit of liberty, that so much distinguish this age."[14] What is different about the political literature of the 1830s derives primarily from Benthamism, from evangelicalism, and from the careful focus of literary works on specific targets for reform. Before 1829-1832, the tools of gradual social improvement seemed out of reach to most writers. Middle-class radicals therefore frequently adopted revolutionary positions, and even the conservatism of a Coleridge or a Southey is utopian. Blake's lament, "I am hid," or Shelley's definition of poets as "the unacknowledged legislators of the world," are partly responses to their political isolation. After 1832 the basic structure of society seemed to have been altered so that access to the tools of reform looked possible. Writers began to feel that they might be, at least in small ways, acknowledged legislators. There were more public forums for them. And the governments of Grey, Melbourne, and Peel were more open to public opinion than the Tory regimes of the previous decades had been. Like the middle class as a whole, liberal writers now had an interest in promoting gradual social improvement at the same time that they also had an interest in preserving the basic structure of society against the threats of revolution, utopian socialism, and working-class radicalism. Despite their apocalyptic rhetoric, most of them subscribed to Macaulay's advice to parliament in 1831: "Reform, that you may preserve." Macaulay's idea of conservative reform, moreover, echoes no less an antirevolutionary authority than Burke. "A state without the means of some change is without the means of its conservation," says Burke. "Without such means it might even risk the loss of that part of the constitution which it wished the most religiously to preserve."[15] And Burke goes on to point out how "the two principles of conservation and correction" have operated at the most critical junctures of British history.

The sharpened, limited, and practical focuses of the literature of reform in the 1830s and after, which contradict the apocalyptic rhetoric in which much of it is cast, is evident in Harriet Martineau's *Illustrations of Political Economy*, in Dickens's attack on the New Poor Law in *Oliver Twist*, and in such free trade propaganda as Dr. John Bowring's revision of Shelley's "Mask of Anarchy," which he wrote in 1841 for the Anti-Corn Law League:

> I met Famine on my way,
> Prowling for human prey,
> Clogg'd with filth, and clad in rags,
> Ugliest of all ugly hags.
> Lo! a sceptre wreathed with snakes
> In her withered hand she shakes;
> And I heard the hag proclaim—
> '*Bread Tax*, is my sceptre's name.'[16]

The specific figures in Shelley's poem—Castlereagh and the other murderers of Peterloo—are types of social oppression in general. The movement of Shelley's poem is outward, to the conflict between freedom and oppression which makes up all of history. Dr. Bowring, Bentham's lieutenant and the first editor of the *Westminster Review*, reverses Shelley's generalizing movement: he is not interested in abolishing all tyranny everywhere; abolishing the "Bread Tax" is cause enough to call forth his Muse. At the same time, Bowring sees nothing contradictory about applying Shelley's apocalyptic rhetoric to the corn law problem. Bowring's poem shares with Ebenezer Elliott's earlier *Corn-Law Rhymes*, with R. H. Horne's *Orion*, and with countless other works written in the 1830s and the 1840s the tendency to place free trade, or some other isolable social issue, at the center of history, at "the still point of the turning world." As Carlyle says in his review of Elliott, "Thus for our keen-hearted singer, and sufferer, has the 'Bread-tax,' in itself a considerable but no immeasurable smoke-pillar, swoln out to be a world-embracing Darkness, that darkens and suffocates the whole earth, and has blotted out the heavenly stars."[17] No doubt apocalyptic rhetoric is an attribute of much propaganda. Certainly it is an attribute of much of the literature of the 1830s. As Joseph Hamburger has shown, James Mill and his hard-headed Benthamite allies helped push the Reform Bill through Parliament partly by playing on the apocalyptic fears of Whigs and Tories: they deliberately magnified the threat of revolution in their public rhetoric in order to bring on reform.[18]

Despite its apocalyptic tone, much of the literature of the 1830s may be described as antirevolutionary, broadly Benthamite, and militantly middle-class. These qualities come together in Macaulay, whose essays and speeches bristle with his aggressive faith in things English, things modern, and things middle-class. "The history of England is emphatically the history of progress," he says in his essay on Mackintosh. And the bearers of progress, endowed with Baconian pragmatism, are the middle class, who stand midway between the destructive extremes of aristocracy and the poor, and midway between past and future, forever at the right place at the right time. For Macaulay, the middle class is literally a third party, identifiable with the Whigs and with liberal reform, which alone has it in its power to save England from revolution:

> It is difficult, Sir, to conceive any spectacle more alarming than that which presents itself to us, when we look at the two extreme parties in this country; a narrow oligarchy above; an infuriated multitude below; on the one side the vices engendered by power; on the other side the vices engendered by distress; one party blindly averse to improvement; the other party blindly clamouring for destruction . . . God forbid that the State should ever be at the mercy of either . . . ! I anticipate no such horrible event. For, between those two parties stands a third party . . . destined . . . to save both from the fatal effects of their own folly . . . That party is the middle class of England, with the flower of the aristocracy at its head, and the flower of the working classes bringing up its rear.[19]

Macaulay agrees with James Mill that the members of the middle class are "the natural representatives of the human race," whose interest is "identical with that of the innumerable generations to follow."[20] This is the heroic myth of the bourgeoisie, shared in one form or another by all reform-minded liberals and middle-class radicals in the 1830s and after. The middle class itself is seen as the acme of history and the incarnation of the spirit of reform, preserving the social order at the same time that it maximizes freedom and radiates prosperity to the "lower orders." Its messianic role is the liberal equivalent of the messianic role of the proletariat in Marxism, with the difference that, after 1832, it seemed to be fulfilling its role—or failing to fulfill it—in the here-and-now. This difference lends an ambiguous quality to much of the language of reform. Insofar as progress is endless, so must social imperfection be endless, and the middle class continue to be the bearer of the future. But insofar as the middle class has achieved both economic power and a measure of political power in the present, the main struggle is over, and "an acre in Middlesex is better than a principality in Utopia." As Macaulay says in his great *History of England*, it is simply "unreasonable and ungrateful in us to be

18

constantly discontented with a condition that is constantly improving.''[21] Once the forces of progress are installed in office, perfection becomes an attribute of the present as well as of the future, and, as Podsnap might reason, there is nothing left to do except to enjoy the infinite vista of improvement which spreads before us. And just as perfection ambiguously becomes an attribute of both present and future, so does truth become an attribute of both: it exists in an absolute form in the radiant heaven towards which we are constantly advancing, and it exists in a temporal form all about us in the present, as that series of compromises which the empirical wisdom of the middle class, "standing midway in the gulf" between all false extremes, is able to effect in its march towards perfection.

For Macaulay, the lessons of history are as plain as day and night, and it is only a wonder that they are not so plain to everyone. The tools of "the two extreme parties" are ignorance and prejudice; the tools of middle-class reform are reason and Baconian empiricism, which, independently of governmental interference, find out the laws of nature and apply them to the affairs of mankind. As in Bentham, there is in Macaulay an easy connection between the truths of science and the increasing happiness of the people, both of which are set over against the errors of the past. The missions of the scientist and the political reformer are the same, though one may produce a new application of steam and the other a new piece of legislation. In any case, the dark ages are defunct and the future is in the hands of the right people, so the main law of the social sciences is simply progress. "We rely on the natural tendency of the human intellect to truth," says Macaulay in his essay on Southey, "and on the natural tendency of society to improvement." And he continues: "History is full of the signs of this natural progress of society. We see in almost every part of the annals of mankind how the industry of individuals, struggling up against wars, taxes, famines, conflagrations, mischievous prohibitions, and more mischievous protections, creates faster than governments can squander, and repairs whatever invaders can destroy. We see the wealth of nations increasing, and all the arts of life approaching nearer and nearer to perfection, in spite of the grossest corruption and the wildest profusion on the part of rulers." Macaulay acknowledges that "the present moment is one of great distress," but it is also a time of rapid and inevitable improvement. "Now and then there has been a stoppage, now and then a short retrogression; but as to the general tendency there can be no doubt. A single breaker may recede; but the tide is evidently coming in.''[22]

And the tide did come in, at least in the form of a veritable "sea of faith" in and of the middle class, evident throughout the literature of the 1830s. It was a self-consciously "improving" literature, sometimes seeking further institutional reforms, sometimes celebrating the triumphs of 1832 and of middle-class industry, and sometimes disseminating "useful knowledge" so that, through self-help, individuals in the working and middle classes could "better themselves." The years between 1827 and 1836 were the heyday of "the march of mind" and of what one of its pioneers, William Chambers, was to call "the cheap literature movement of 1832." In her *History of the Thirty Years' Peace,* Harriet Martineau, who contributed to that movement throughout her career, writes: "As a winding-up of the improvements of this period [1824-1834], and in rank the very first, we must mention the systematic introduction of cheap literature, for the benefit of the working-classes. A series or two of cheap works had been issued before, chiefly of entertaining books meant for the middle classes; and there was never any deficiency of infamous half-penny trash, hawked about the streets, and sold in low shops. The time had now arrived for something very different from either of these kinds of literature to appear."[23] Landmarks in the cheap literature movement include the first use of steam printing presses by *The Times* in 1814, the founding of the Society for the Diffusion of Useful Knowledge in 1827, and the commencement of *Chambers's Journal* and of Charles Knight's *Penny Magazine* in 1832.

Whether through the SDUK or through other efforts, the aim of the cheap literature movement was to improve the mental and moral condition of the working and middle classes and also to counteract the worst effects of the unstamped radical press. As early as 1821, Charles Knight, who later superintended the publications of the SDUK and edited the *Penny Magazine* under its auspices, predicted the rise of a middle-class but still "popular" journalism to counteract the working-class radical press:

> A general view of the influence of the Press would lead us to judge that very much of that influence is injurious to the safety of the Government . . . It is the half-knowledge of the people that has created the host of ephemeral writers who address themselves to the popular passions. If the firmness of the Government, and, what is better, the good sense of the upper and middle classes who have property at stake, can succeed for a few years in preserving tranquillity, the ignorant disseminators of sedition and discontent will be beaten out of the field by opponents of [sic] better principles, who will direct the secret of popular writing to a useful and a righteous purpose.[24]

Although "the ignorant disseminators of sedition and discontent" were never "beaten out of the field" (the cheap literature movement in fact coincided with the war of "the great unstamped" waged by and against *The Poor Man's Guardian* and the working-class radical press in the early 1830s), their voices were matched in volume by a triumphant chorus of liberal and yet intentionally popular journalism that sought both to limit the powers of the aristocracy and to inculcate the virtues of deference, industry, and moderation in the working class. According to Lord Brougham's pregnant phrase, "the schoolmaster was abroad in the land" and mighty was the power of his reforming zeal.

Chambers's Journal boasted that it "has done more to wean the people from trash, cultivate their minds, and excite curiosity, than all the Tract Societies that ever existed."[25] The last phrase suggests that, although intended to counteract working-class radicalism, the cheap literature of the SDUK and the Chambers brothers was also intended to counteract the reactionary values of evangelical tract writing, which it in many ways imitated. The secular cheap literature movement had in fact been preceded by a religious cheap literature movement, stemming from the Methodist revival of the eighteenth century. The SDUK followed the Society for the Promotion of Christian Knowledge, adopting many of its tactics; and Harriet Martineau's political economy tracts are close in form, feeling, and even purpose to Hannah More's *Cheap Repository Tracts,* only with God replaced in the scheme of things by Adam Smith's Invisible Hand (as Douglas Jerrold put it, "There is no God, and Harriet Martineau is his prophet").[26] If secular cheap literature was antirevolutionary and opposed to almost all manifestations of working-class political activity, it was also progressive, scientific, and concerned both with the material betterment and the enlightenment of all classes—or what it deemed enlightenment. In any case, the inoffensive, studiously nonpartisan writing in the *Penny Magazine* and *Chambers's Journal* disguises how controversial they seemed at the time. To working-class radicals like the readers of Cobbett's *Political Register,* they were pabulum rather than solid food, and obnoxiously bourgeois pabulum at that.[27] To conservatives, they were dangerous organs of discontent and religious skepticism.

Something of the controversial quality of the cheap literature movement emerges in Peacock's *Crotchet Castle* (1831), where the Rev. Dr. Folliott tells the utilitarian economist Mr. Mac Quedy ("son of a Q.E.D.") that he has seen too much of "the march of mind":

It has marched into my rick-yard, and set my stacks on fire, with chemical materials, most scientifically compounded . . . It has marched in through my back-parlour shutters, and out again with my silver spoons, in the dead of the night. The policeman who was sent down to examine, says my house has been broken open on the most scientific principles. All this comes of education.

Mr. Mac Quedy. I rather think it comes of poverty.

The Rev. Dr. Folliott. No, sir. Robbery perhaps comes of poverty, but scientific principles of robbery come of education. I suppose the learned friend has written a sixpenny treatise on mechanics, and the rascals who robbed me have been reading it.

Their argument resumes shortly after this, when they assemble at Chainmail Hall to celebrate Christmas. A noisy crowd is heard outside the door, whom the Rev. Dr. Folliott at first thinks may be mummers. But the crowd announces itself as "Captain Swing," and demands to be armed with Mr. Chainmail's antique weapons.

The Rev. Dr. Folliott. Ho, ho! here is a piece of the dark ages we did not bargain for. Here is the Jacquerie. Here is the march of mind with a witness.

Mr. Mac Quedy. Do you not see that you have brought disparates together? The Jacquerie and the march of mind.

The Rev. Dr. Folliott. Not at all, sir. They are the same thing, under different names. Πολλῶν ονομάτων μορΦὴ μία. What was Jacquerie in the dark ages, is the march of mind in this very enlightened one—very enlightened one.[28]

But this time Mr. Mac Quedy coolly agrees with him: "Discontent increases with the increase of information," he says. "That is all."

Of course the leaders of "the march of mind" did not think they were sowing the seeds of discontent but rather nipping it in the bud. The Chambers brothers believed that they had created "a powerful moral engine for the regeneration of the middle and lower orders of society."[29] (Just why they needed to be "regenerated" instead of educated from scratch is not clear.) And they and many others looked to the spread of "wholesome and instructive literature" as one of the causes of social peace in the Victorian period, despite occasional "Jacqueries." In 1872, William Chambers wrote: "The mass of cheap and respectably conducted periodical literature . . . has proved one of the many engines of social improvement in the nineteenth century. Referring to the example of patience which was set by the operatives of Lancashire under the agonizing calamity of [the cotton famine of the early 1860s] a minister of the crown did not hesitate to declare 'that to the information contained in the excellent cheap papers of this country he attributed much of the calm forbearance with which the distressed had borne their privations.' "[30]

Whether *Chambers's Journal,* the *Penny Magazine,* and similar cheap papers written by middle-class teachers of the working class had any such pacifying effect may be doubted, because it is not clear that they reached into the working class as far as their creators thought that they did. And even if they did, their apolitical politics and their lessons of resignation based on Malthus and Ricardo do not seem to have hampered the growth of Chartism, trade unionism, and socialism (and perhaps one should add the growth of the working-class population as well).

Still, that *Chambers's Journal* and the others constituted a mighty "moral engine" in the 1830s and after is true enough, although that phrase reveals more than it was intended to. Peacock poked fun at "the Steam Intellect Society," and it almost seemed as if the SDUK, the Chambers brothers, and other middle-class educators had set out to manufacture enlightenment in the same way that the millers of Lancashire were manufacturing textiles. In fact, the real historical importance of the Chambers brothers is not that they helped to bring on a reign of social peace by convincing the working class of the folly of discontent but that they were pioneers in the creation of modern mass culture. The immense success of their journal led them into related cheap literature ventures—almanacs, encyclopedias, popular histories, albums, and anthologies good for all occasions and for everyone, oozing with platitudinous non-controversies—and they were soon managing what was quite literally a knowledge factory, mass producing books and periodicals by steam, like bolts of cloth: "With twelve printing machines set to work, there was at length [by the 1850s] a fair average produce of fifty thousand sheets of one kind or other daily. Under one roof were combined the operations of editors, compositors, stereotypers, wood-engravers, printers, book-binders, and other laborers, all engaged in the preparation and dispersal of books and periodicals."[31] The Chambers brothers were perhaps the first to show how Coketown factories could produce Coketown facts. It is only fair to notice, however, that they were not Bounderbys but benevolent employers who always gave their workers an annual party (and it is also fair to notice that these fetes were as militantly respectable as *Chambers's Journal:* William describes the first annual party in 1838 as "a temperance *soirée*").

So intent is cheap literature of all sorts on individual and social improvement that it almost ceases to be literature. As Bulwer says, politics in the 1830s overshadows art as an activity. Martineau's *Illustrations of Political Economy,* for example, are fiction almost by accident. James Mill and the other members of the SDUK felt that it was a mistake to wrap sober, instructive fact up in fiction, and rejected Martineau's plan when she first applied to them. She had to produce her economical tracts independently, through Charles Fox, and only after their initial great success did the SDUK reverse itself and offer to publish the series after all.[32] Referring to the SDUK's rejection of Martineau's tales, Charles Knight complains that they ''were then as opposed to works of imagination, as if they had been 'budge doctors of the Stoic fur,' whose vocation was to despise everything not of direct utility.''[33] Push-pin, it seemed, really might be as good as poetry—as useful or as useless, depending on your point of view. Utilitarian hostility to fiction and poetry was one of the reasons for the comparative lack of success of the *Penny Magazine*. *Chambers's Journal* always included a story (''no ordinary trash about Italian castles, and daggers, and ghosts in the blue chamber . . . but something really good''[34]) at least as a sop to its readers. The *Penny Magazine* was made of sterner stuff, and although it was illustrated, its antifictional policy seems to have kept down its circulation.

There is no lack of evidence of utilitarian hostility to imaginative literature: Mill's account of what went wrong with his education and of how ''the cultivation of the feelings'' that he found in poetry helped him over his mental crisis is the best-known example. But evangelicals were at least as hostile to fiction as the utilitarians.[35] For both groups, literature had to be turned to practical, didactic account to be worthwhile, and the result throughout the first half of the century was a literature of cheap tracts which might be either scientific or religious, but which was uniformly stuffy, moral, and uplifting. Even in the case of the dourest Methodist tract, however, the literature of the 1830s still aims at improvement—albeit improvement not of this world. Implicit within the tract writing of the 1830s is the fact of a new, expanding, and self-improving readership. In the midst of its stuffiness and its contradictions, and despite its naive assumption that it can shape the new readership in its own image (whether Benthamite or evangelical), there is also the assumption of progress, and a recognition—however tentative and tangled—of the existence and aspirations of the working class. Literary didacticism is rooted in a basic optimism about human nature and the future: the writer as schoolmaster, armed with simple reason or with simple revelation, believes that he can change his readers' lives and, hence, bring on some sort of millennial regime of virtue, however modest.

At the same time, the working class had no more reason to look favorably upon imaginative literature than the Benthamites or the evangelicals. Cobbett felt that it made more sense to put cheese and bacon into people's stomachs than to stuff their heads with useful knowledge, let alone with useless novels and poetry. In the preface for Platt's *Poetry of Common Life* in 1831, Thomas Arnold urged that poetry should be read by everyone, and argued against the emphasis upon the merely "useful," much as his son was to argue in *Culture and Anarchy* and elsewhere: "Mr. Cobbett would go along with the highest aristocrat in laughing at the notion of the poor reading poetry; not because he would think them not fit to enjoy it, but because he would consider it as not fit to be studied by them: he would regard it as a mere rich man's toy, which none but the idle, or the silly, would hold it worth their while to study."[36] But Arnold himself gave emphasis to the "useful" in his own writings on social conditions and on history. And in language which Cobbett might not have objected to, Arnold claimed that "the object . . . of every honest public writer at this moment [in 1831] should be to calm and to enlighten the poor; to interest and to arouse the rich."[37]

Any writer who agreed with Arnold was liable to be drawn away from merely esthetic considerations into utilitarian and scientific ones. Even in literature intended merely to be amusing, the aims of enlightening the poor and arousing the rich served as theme and moral. Arnold's statement suggests, for example, the direction in which *Pickwick Papers* moved while Dickens was writing it, although he started it as pure entertainment. In pursuit of the improvement of the working class, Martineau stumbled upon fiction; in pursuit of amusing his readers through fiction, Dickens stumbled upon the improvement of the working class and the reform of institutions, which were to be his lifelong goals. When Dickens looked back upon *Pickwick Papers* in the preface that he wrote for it in 1847, he did not view it merely as a piece of humorous writing but as an appeal for legal and penal reform, the equivalent of *Oliver Twist* on the New Poor Law and of *Nicholas Nickleby* on Yorkshire schools:

> I have found it curious and interesting, looking over the sheets of this reprint, to mark what important social improvements have taken place about us, almost imperceptibly, since they were originally written . . . Legal reforms have pared the claws of Messrs. Dodson and Fogg; a spirit of self-respect, mutual forbearance, education, and co-operation . . . has diffused itself among their clerks; places far apart are brought together, to the present convenience and advantage of the Public, and to the certain destruction, in time, of a host of petty jealousies, blindnesses, and prejudices, by which the Public alone have always been the sufferers; the laws relating to imprisonment for debt are altered; and the Fleet Prison is pulled down![38]

25

Throughout the 1830s and into the 1840s, writings the least likely to be serious, like *Figaro in London, Punch in London,* and their more famous offspring, *Punch,* followed the *Pickwick* pattern and took on the grave task of promoting reforms. Clearly, Dickens and the *Punch* radicals did not share the Benthamite and evangelical hostility to fiction. But they did share the Benthamite aim of using literature to promote social improvement, and they were therefore just as concerned about the discovery and accurate presentation of social facts as James Mill and Harriet Martineau.

The effects of the aim of improvement are as evident in the theater as in the fiction and periodical literature of the 1830s. Jerrold was writing plays on radical themes as early as the mid-1820s. In 1829 appeared what is today his only well-known play, *Black-eyed Susan,* and he followed it with a flurry of political melodramas, obviously inspired by the reform agitation. These include *The Mutiny at the Nore, The Press Gang,* and *The Devil's Ducat, or the Gift of Mammon,* all in 1830. In 1832, Jerrold wrote *The Golden Calf,* "ridiculing . . . the blind homage that wealth and high station receive from their votaries";[39] *The Factory Girl,* based on the findings of Sadler's Committee; and *The Rent-Day,* based on Sir David Willkie's painting, which provided the set design for the opening scene. As is true generally of Victorian melodrama, and of much Victorian fiction as well, including Dickens's, in Jerrold's plays, villainous aristocrats try to victimize innocent petit-bourgeois and working-class characters. The good characters are often saved at the last minute by the discovery of obscure wills or deeds, which transfer the privileges and wealth of the aristocrats to the common people, their rightful owners.[40] And Jerrold carried over the same reformist, democratic themes into his humorous writings for *Punch* and for his own journals in the 1840s. Jerrold and Dickens, moreover, are only two members of what was virtually a school of new writers which emerged in the 1830s to fill the void made by the departures of the great Romantics. These were the men who gathered around *Punch*—the Mayhew brothers, Mark Lemon, Tom Hood, Lamon Blanchard, and Thackeray—most of whom came from the lower middle class and had known poverty at first hand at some point in their lives. Perhaps nothing undermined Macaulay's optimism as a factor in middle-class culture so much as the experience of bankruptcy and debt which most of the *Punch* radicals shared with Dickens.

Even for men like Jerrold and Dickens, who had no scientific training and whose instincts ran against reducing experience to numerical tables, the 1830s was an age of sociological and statistical investigation. The Pickwickian aim of exploring tittlebats extended itself to penal conditions and, indeed, to society at large, as in G. R. Porter's *Progress of the Na-*

tion. The development of cheap literature and "useful knowledge" (that is, knowledge productive of social happiness) coincided with the development of statistical societies and with the publication of the findings of parliamentary committees and royal commissions, whose number and activities increased enormously after 1832.[41] The Manchester Statistical Society was founded in 1833 and its London counterpart in 1834. The reading of bluebooks became almost as popular as the reading of novels, as the success of Chadwick's *Sanitary Condition of the Labouring Population* (1842) attests. Carlyle complained in *Chartism* that statistics could be used to prove anything and to impede reform: "With what serene conclusiveness a member of some Useful-Knowledge Society stops your mouth with a figure of arithmetic!"[42] But while statistics were often used to show the progress of the nation, as in Porter or as in Macaulay's rebuff to Southey, they were just as often used for the purpose of revealing how little progress had been made in many areas of social life, as in Chadwick's report. The Manchester Statistical Society was founded "to assist in promoting the progress of social improvements in the manufacturing population by which they are surrounded."[43] The experience of the hero of Kingsley's *Yeast* is indicative of what happened to many middle-class Victorians, ardent in their desire to believe in progress but baffled by revelations of poverty, ignorance, and filth: "So Lancelot buried himself up to the eyes in the Condition-of-the-Poor question—that is, in blue books, red books, sanitary reports, mine reports, factory reports; and came to the conclusion, which is now pretty generally entertained, that something was the matter—but what, no man knew, or, if they knew, thought proper to declare."[44]

Nevertheless, Carlyle's suspicion of statistics is also common in the 1830s and after, and is shared by Dickens and the *Punch* radicals, who associate it with political economy and the New Poor Law. Dickens was at least a desultory reader of bluebooks, and he could count among his friends a Benthamite reformer like Dr. Southwood Smith. At the same time, he could create Mr. Slug of "The Mudfog Association," stern statistical censor of children's storybooks, and the first in a long line of mad social scientists.[45] So deeply rooted was suspicion of statistical investigation in some minds that as late as 1864 a writer in the *Cornhill Magazine,* William Cyples, could argue, with only a tinge of irony, that "an enthusiasm for statistics" would result in the "wholesale ruin of the human world." About one thing, at least, Cyples was correct: he recognized that "this modern notion of averages introduces a habit of thought and a state of feeling which set off the present age from all that have preceded it, and will not fail ever increasingly to modify human experience in the future.

The feeling which it induces may broadly be stated as something *unique* in the history of the world.'' But far from thinking that the unique "feeling" induced by social statistics was the deep-rooted, if often contradictory, desire for social improvement expressed by writers like Carlyle and Dickens, Cyples identified this "feeling" with a dismal loss of individuality: "Love will certainly lose its bloom when it is known we can only look for it in a per-centage degree; prayers will most irreligiously be chilled at the thought of their being offered but with the spontaneity of a ratio; and we question if our hearths would be greatly worth sitting by when it was fully understood that our wives were only statistically kind, and the little children smiled by averages.''[46] Perhaps Cyples was not far off the mark, however. In Charles Bray's *Philosophy of Necessity* (1841), we learn that statistics prove—at least to the satisfaction of scientific "Necessarians" and insurance actuaries—that "the number of marriages are not regulated as is ordinarily supposed by Love, but by the price of corn, that is, by the cheapness of provisions and by the rate of wages!''[47]

With even love regulated by science, it is no wonder that Carlyle complained about the transformation of the universe into a steam engine. But his resistance and that of Dickens and the *Punch* radicals to statistics and political economy obscure their full impact on Victorian culture. Although no *Origin of Species* looms out of the dense underbrush of Victorian sociological reporting to mark their influence, the social sciences were at least as significant for the shape of the arts in the nineteenth century as Darwinism, and nowhere are their effects more visible than in fiction. Stated most broadly, the history of the Victorian novel parallels the history of the social sciences, and the images of human nature and society characteristically projected by Dickens, Mrs. Gaskell, George Eliot, and even Trollope and Thackeray are in many respects those also projected by bluebooks. Put another way, Victorian fiction aspires to the condition of bluebooks—and vice versa, for bluebooks were very often treated like novels. A writer in the *Quarterly Review* said of the Report on Women and Children in the Mines of 1842 that it "disclosed . . . modes of existence . . . as strange and as new as the wildest dreams of fiction." And of the same report, the *Spectator* said that "it discloses scenes of suffering and infamy which will come upon many well-informed people like the fictions or tales of distant lands.''[48]

The debt of several early Victorian writers to parliamentary bluebooks and social investigations is well known. Mrs. Trollope in *Michael Armstrong,* Disraeli in *Sybil,* and Elizabeth Barrett in "The Cry of the Children" drew both inspiration and subject matter from bluebooks.[49] In the "Advertisement" to *Sybil,* Disraeli claims that "there is not a trait in this work for which he has not the authority of his own observation, or the authentic evidence which has been received by Royal Commissions and Parliamentary Committees." *Sybil* is a strange hybrid of bluebook and silverfork romance in which whole chapters lifted almost verbatim from the Reports of the Children's Employment Commission of 1842-1843 are wedged between drawing room scenes that Mrs. Gore might have written —the two sorts of fiction corresponding to "the two nations" of rich and poor. Similarly, Mrs. Trollope based the most excruciating episodes in *Michael Armstrong* upon the Sadler Committee report, while Miss Barrett made her "bluebook in verse" echo part of the work of her friend R. H. Horne, who was one of the investigators for the Children's Employment Commission.

These are familiar examples of direct reliance upon bluebooks, but such obvious indebtedness is only a symptom of the much more profound and pervasive influence that the Victorian social sciences had on Victorian culture. Even those writers who seem most resistant to them were affected by them. Despite his antistatistical grumbling, Carlyle could lament his "want of statistics" for writing *Chartism* and could even send to Chadwick for information. All that he finally claims—and here he is surely correct—is that statistics must be used sensibly: "Statistics is a science which ought to be honourable, the basis of many most important sciences; but it is not to be carried on by steam, this science, any more than others are; a wise head is requisite for carrying it on."[50] At the same time, just as much as any Benthamite or evangelical, Carlyle is hostile to fiction and insistent upon grounding the arts in social and historical fact. In his essay called "Biography," Carlyle says that fiction is merely "mimic Biography" and that genuine biography is to be preferred, especially to "froth Prose in the Fashionable Novel." Fiction, Carlyle proceeds, "partakes . . . of the nature of *lying*," and whereas "here and there, a *Tom Jones*, a *Meister*, a *Crusoe* . . . will yield no little solacement to the minds of men," nevertheless they will yield "immeasurably less than a *Reality* would." With the exception of some early attempts at fiction like *Wotton Reinfred*, everything that Carlyle wrote, including *Sartor*, can be related either to his theory of biography or to social criticism, like *Chartism*. "In all Art . . . Biography is almost the one thing needful," because biography is the closest thing to the actual experience of individuals.[51] And if biography in some measure contradicts the collective information of statistics, it does so by weighing the lived facts of individuals against the mechanical addition of facts in tables and census reports.

The most obvious trait that many novels, bluebooks, and statistical society reports share is the motive of arousing concern for the poor. The

Royal Cornwall Polytechnic Society might have been referring to the writings of Dickens or Carlyle when it claimed that through statistics "the public attention has been fastened, with an intensity never before given to the subject, upon the physical and moral degradation of the poorer classes in the metropolis and many of our larger towns."[52] And at times even Dickens sounds more like Edwin Chadwick than like an avatar of Christmas Present, as when he says that "in all my writings, I hope I have taken every available opportunity of showing the want of sanitary improvements in the neglected dwellings of the poor."[53] The disagreement between "sentimental radicals" like Dickens and utilitarian radicals like Chadwick is basically only over which sort of radical can be benevolent most effectively. If Dickens can portray an economist like Mr. Slug as a heartless grinder of the poor, Harriet Martineau can criticize Dickens for being a "pseudo-philanthropist." In a similar dispute with Charles Kingsley, W. R. Greg defined political economy as "benevolence under the guidance of science." And as a defense against the anti-Malthusianism of Dickens, Carlyle, and *Punch,* John Stuart Mill argued that "those who most broadly acknowledge the doctrine of Malthus" are those most truly concerned about improving the lot of the poor.[54]

No matter who their authors, bluebooks and novels in the 1830s and beyond often share Thomas Arnold's aim of enlightening the rich about the poor. But they share much else as well, and from about 1832 into the 1850s one can trace a rough pattern of mutual development in subject matter. By the 1860s, all phases of English social life had been subjected to scrutiny by social statisticians, royal commissioners, sanitary reformers, and also novelists. After the Sadler Committee's revelations in 1832 of the horrors of "infant labor" in factories, reams of Ten Hours poetry appeared, Jerrold wrote *The Factory Girl,* Mrs. Trollope wrote *Michael Armstrong, the Factory Boy,* and Mrs. Tonna wrote *Helen Fleetwood.* At the same time, the agitation against the New Poor Law was embodied in *Oliver Twist,* Mrs. Trollope's *Jessie Phillips,* Carlyle's *Chartism* and *Past and Present,* and much workhouse satire in *Punch.* And in both the bluebooks and the novels of the 1830s and early 1840s there is a strange disjunction between childhood and adulthood, stemming partly from the notion that government interference was logical in the case of children, who could not fend for themselves in the marketplace, but illogical in the case of adults, who were "free agents." The bluebooks of the 1830s concentrate on factory and pauper children, and the nightmare worlds of *Oliver Twist, Michael Armstrong,* and Jerrold's *St. Giles and St. James,* in which helpless children fall into the clutches of monstrous adults, are reflections of this attitude. Arnold's dual aims of educating the poor and

30

arousing the rich, moreover, suggest two broad categories into which much of the literature of the 1830s can be placed. On the one hand, middle-class literature addressed mainly to the working class, like Martineau's booklets and Charles Knight's *Results of Machinery,* teach lessons of resignation and suggest the futility of political action, at least for the workers. On the other hand, literature addressed to the middle class and the aristocracy, like *Chartism* and Bulwer's *Paul Clifford,* condemn laissez-faire attitudes and call for political action to improve the condition of the workers and of England in general. These two categories are related to a double psychology of victims and free agents which characterizes much of the literature of reform, including Victorian melodrama and Dickens's novels.

In 1842 came Chadwick's best-selling *Sanitary Condition of the Labouring Population,* and novelists increasingly filled their landscapes with the problems of housing, drainage, and ventilation. Through the work of the Health of Towns Association, Dr. John Simon, and the cholera, the way was prepared for the obsessive interest in social filth and cleanliness apparent in *Our Mutual Friend* and Kingsley's *Water Babies.* More significantly, the rising tide of bluebooks through the 1840s led to a growing awareness of the complexity and enormity of social evils, reflected in the wrath of Carlyle's *Latter-day Pamphlets* and the gloom of *Bleak House* and *Little Dorrit.* In Dickens, there is a transition from a sense of isolated social problems like the New Poor Law and the Yorkshire schools to a deepening vision of society as "labyrinth" and of social evil as an insoluble "muddle." Reformism and the Benthamite optimism of the early 1830s give way to despair, or to the melancholy resignation evident in Pre-Raphaelitism and the *Rubaiyat,* as well as to much bumptious declamation about the glories of British industry. Again, writing in the 1830s, Mrs. Trollope could treat child labor in factories as an isolated issue that could easily be cured either by getting rid of factories or by regulating them. But by 1850 no such easy treatment of social problems seemed possible—the world of Coketown or of Mrs. Gaskell's Manchester is far more complex than that of Deep Valley Mill where Michael Armstrong is incarcerated and tortured, or even than that of the slums of Fagin and Bill Sikes. Landmarks in this development are the two reports of 1842-1843 dealing with child labor in mines and in industries other than cotton factories. Instead of the limited focus of the Factory Commission of 1833 or even of the Poor Law Commissioners, the reports of 1842-1843 opened up an enormous vista of social fact, the effects of which are evident in the expansiveness of Disraeli's *Sybil.* Whereas Mrs. Trollope concentrates only upon child labor in cotton mills and scarcely mentions adult labor, Disraeli sweeps across the whole industrial terrain of England, describing conditions among farm laborers, factory workers, handloom weavers, miners, metal workers, and London slum dwellers.

Victorian bluebooks and novels, then, not only frequently deal with the same subjects but also project an increasingly full and complex view of society. The work of the statisticians and the Benthamite political economists made it more and more possible to see society as a gigantic organism—one full of diseases and deformities, no doubt, but still a living, throbbing, interconnected whole. G. R. Porter's *Progress of the Nation*, aiming at a description of "the progress of the whole social system in all its various departments, and as effecting all its various interests," is an early attempt at a complete overview of society, and by the 1850s the notion that one could summarize all existence through social statistics culminated in the formation of the first international statistical congresses.[55] In his inaugural address as President of the Statistical Society for 1872, William Farr suggested the creation of a government agency for the compilation of an enormous statistical summary of the empire. "The statistics of the empire will thus be brought to work together in harmony; science will gain by great generalizations, and the community of statistics will be another bond of union between us all in both hemispheres: the circle will be complete."[56] A similar sense of the feasibility of summarizing all of society by a massive gathering of facts and details and events lies behind novels like *Bleak House* and *The Way We Live Now*. As in census-taking, so in many Victorian novels: one arrives at the truth not by digging below the surface of things, but "by giving an exhaustive inventory of the surface itself."[57]

Out of the increasingly comprehensive and organic vision of society shared by the social sciences and by novels arises a further vision of the individual lost in the urban maze like Oliver Twist, or engulfed, warped, and defined by his environment. "Middlemarch," says George Eliot, "counted on swallowing Lydgate and assimilating him very comfortably," and it succeeds. The organicist vision of society, which received its fullest expression in Eliot's fiction and in the social Darwinism of Herbert Spencer, was both the culmination and the contradiction of Benthamism and the reform-minded social sciences of the 1830s. There are only traces of it in the early fiction of writers like Bulwer and Dickens, who in the 1830s were declaring themselves to be either for or against Benthamism. Their attitudes define the limits of the spirit of reform, and suggest how mercurial it proved to be—how quickly the heady optimism of Macaulay and "the march of mind" was contradicted by Chartism and the Jeremiads of Carlyle. Of course liberal optimism did not vanish from middle-class culture. But faith in the betterment of life through institutional reform did decline, while a very different faith in the inevitable, organic growth of middle-class industry increased. The laissez-faire optimism of the Manchester School superseded the Benthamite faith in progress through government action. Only in the late 1820s and early 1830s was it possible to feel a buoyant confidence in both steam and legislation:

> I have whistled up sprites to bestow my new lights
>   On all that is ancient, exclusive, and dark;—
> I have spread around knowledge—I build London College—
>   I have steam on the Thames, I have gas in the Park.
> No longer a minister frowns and looks sinister,
>   When philosophy mingles with maxims of state;
> Economical squires deride their grand-sires,
>   And reasoning citizens lead the debate.[58]

After the depression of 1836-1842 and the rise of Chartism, the full spirit of reform of the Benthamites and "the march of mind" became itself a part of the dark ages, lost in a past which, for better or worse, was being rapidly left behind.

"He drew nearer to the extremest verge."

Factory reform melodrama: Michael Armstrong contemplating suicide.

II.   Benthamite and Anti-Benthamite Fiction

Although hardly a masterpiece, Bulwer's *Paul Clifford* (1830) is a notable creation, a Benthamite novel calling for specific reforms in criminal law and satirizing many of the leading politicians of the day, and it stands at the threshold of an era in which literature was used consciously and constantly as an instrument of social reform. It has been well-described as a "hodge podge" and also as a "jeu d'esprit" marred by "paradoxical dilettantism."[1] But it was an original and influential work, the prototype of the "Newgate novels" written between 1830 and 1847, and indeed of all the "social problem novels" in the Victorian era. As such, it opened a debate about crime and punishment that is central to the nineteenth-century novel and especially to Dickens, who read it and brought some of its dry ideas to life in *Oliver Twist*. Bulwer comes down on the Benthamite side of the debate, and draws also from the theories of Godwin, whose friend he was and whose own fiction, especially *Caleb Williams*, served Bulwer as a model.

Bulwer's theme is that oppressive laws, bad prison conditions, and corruption in high places are the causes of crime. The criminal is the victim of an unjust society. Law is the result of class legislation, good for the rich and bad for the poor. And the poor man is trapped by circumstances that push him inevitably in the direction of crime. "What is crime?" says Paul to Lucy Brandon, the squire's daughter with whom he falls in love: " 'Men embody their worst prejudices, their most evil passions, in a heterogeneous and contradictory code; and whatever breaks this code they term a crime. When they make no distinction in the penalty—that is to say, in the estimation—awarded both to murder and to a petty theft imposed on the weak will by famine, we ask nothing else to convince us that they are ignorant of the very nature of guilt, and that they make up in ferocity for the want of wisdom.' "[2] Criminals should be rehabilitated, not hung. That much of Bulwer's message is forceful and may well have helped to produce the reforms of criminal law and of prison conditions that actually took place in the 1830s. According to Bulwer's son: "The publication of 'Paul Clifford' did much to stimulate public opinion in favour of carrying Criminal Law Reform far beyond the point at which it had been left by the labours of Romilly: and the book itself was an incident in my father's constant course of endeavour to improve the condition of that large portion of the population which is most tempted to crime through poverty and ignorance,—not by the proclamation of utopian promises, or recourse to violent constitutional changes, but through a better intellectual training facilitated by timely administrative reforms."[3] The last part of this passage suggests a contradiction between the utopian and pragmatic aims of Benthamism. Although not claiming so great an impact for his novel himself, Bulwer saw it in retrospect as at least a "foresign" of the main tendency of the years from 1830 to 1848, which he took to be the promotion of gradual social progress through reform. In the preface to the 1848 edition of *Paul Clifford,* he says: "Since this work was written, society has been busy with the evils in which it was then silently acquiescent. The true movement of the last fifteen years has been the progress of one idea,—Social Reform . . . in books the lightest, the Grand Idea colours the page, and bequeaths the moral" (x).

Throughout *Paul Clifford,* Bulwer argues that man is the creature of "circumstances" or environment, for which society is responsible. "The tragic truths which lie hid in what I may call the Philosophy of Circumstance strike through our philanthropy upon our imagination. We see masses of our fellow-creatures the victims of circumstances over which they had no control" (ix). But at the same time, as in Bentham's "doctrine of circumstances" and also in Godwin and Robert Owen, circumstances for Bulwer are highly malleable, and so is human nature. His thinking is like that which John Stuart Mill attributes to his father: "In psychology, his fundamental doctrine was the formation of all human character by circumstances, through the universal Principle of Association, and the consequent unlimited possibility of improving the moral and intellectual condition of mankind by education."[4] What looks at first like an ironclad determinism in which circumstances make men what they are turns out to be a nearly utopian faith in man's capacity to alter both himself and his environment. This is in fact one of the weaknesses of *Paul Clifford,* as it is also of Benthamism, Owenism, and some other varieties of early nineteenth-century radicalism. Bulwer wants to show how environment (destitution, the slums, prison) makes his hero into a highwayman. But he also wants to show that all of the evils he depicts can be easily remedied and that crime can be cured by softening the penal code and improving prison conditions. The result is that these evils are not felt to be very serious. They lie on the surface of his novel as they seem to lie on the surface of his vision of society. It is a vision that is witty, cynical, and yet optimistic, lacking the tragic dimension of *Caleb Williams*. (Bulwer gives his novel, in fact, a happy ending in which the hero escapes from the hangman, turns over a new leaf, marries the heroine, and settles down into respectability.)

Because he seems to change his opinions lightly, as Pelham changes his clothes, Bulwer may be accused of insincerity. But such a criticism may arise as much from contradictions inherent in the form of *Paul Clifford* as from any actual hypocrisy or even lack of seriousness on Bulwer's part. Bulwer sees the social problems that he wants changed as objects for satire, and he proceeds along eighteenth-century lines, taking Hogarth and John Gay's *Beggar's Opera* as his models, as well as *Caleb Williams*. So he relies throughout his novel on mock-epic conventions, as in his invocation to ambition: "O Thou divine spirit that burnest in every breast, inciting each with the sublime desire to be *fine;* that stirrest up the great to become little in order to seem greater, and that makest a duchess woo insult for a voucher . . . spirit that makest the high despicable, and the lord meaner than his valet" (256-257). In such a passage, social analysis turns into moral analysis: Bulwer lashes the vices and praises the virtues of mankind, which means partly that he cannot see the issues he raises in consistently political and economic terms. The language of moral satire, which implies individual free will, contradicts the idea of social or environmental causation. In a novel that is ostensibly about its powerful effects, environment is constantly being overruled.

For all that Paul Clifford and his partners in crime talk about poverty, for example, they do not suffer from it. They rob from the rich and give to themselves, which Bulwer makes out to be as reasonable as the other way around—the rich battening off of the labor of the poor. And so far from having been rendered evil by their "circumstances," Bulwer's highwaymen are noble rogues. In his *New Spirit of the Age,* R. H. Horne unintentionally indicates the central rift in the novel when he writes that Bulwer "does not make his hero admired for any one bad quality, but for naturally high qualities independent of the worst circumstances."[5]

The *Beggar's Opera* element of *Paul Clifford* also runs counter to Bulwer's chosen theme. On one level, the novel is a roman à clef in which we are asked to think of Paul and his comrades as the leading politicians of the day.[6] Their gang meetings are analogies for sessions of Parliament, and their differing attitudes and personalities are defined as Whiggism or as Toryism. And of course if the thieves are like the ruling class, the ruling class is like the world of the thieves: dishonest from top to bottom. The only difference is that the thieves have the excuse of "circumstances" or environment for their roguery, and the ruling class have not. As the philosophical, Whiggish highwayman Augustus Tomlinson says: "We enter our career . . . as your embryo ministers enter parliament,—by bribery and corruption. There is this difference, indeed, between the two cases: *we* are enticed to enter by the bribery and corruptions of *others; they* enter spontaneously by dint of their *own*" (361). The distinction Tomlinson makes serves only to emphasize the similarities between rich and poor, not the differences. In a corrupt society, everyone is corrupt together. Society is an "organized disorder for picking pockets" (500), whether by taxation, by cheating, or by armed robbery. Bulwer says that his novel is "a treatise on Social Frauds," a phrase which goes back to the idea of moral satire and which rules out the possibility of a documentary study of the lives of the poor or of class conflict. "Fraud" implies intention and free will on the part of all the actors, although some, because of wealth or social status, are better able to make their frauds succeed than others. Bulwer's conception of human nature suffers from the same limitation that John Stuart Mill found in his father's overemphasis upon reason: his characters are all good Benthamites, free agents acting rationally in their own self-interest. Into such a completely individualistic and moralistic world view, the idea of environmental causation intrudes as at best an anomaly and at worst a contradiction.

In his pioneering work on the social novel, Louis Cazamian paired *Paul Clifford* with Harriet Martineau's *Illustrations of Political Economy* as utilitarian fictions, both flawed by reductive rationalism. While his assessment of these works remains valuable, there are, nevertheless, substantial differences between them, besides the obvious one that Bulwer's novel is lighthearted satire and that Martineau's tales are characterized by a spare, puritanical seriousness. Despite Bulwer's "Philosophy of Circumstances," *Paul Clifford* is not an illustration of the inexorable working of economic or social laws but rather an illustration of the absurdity of many human laws. Martineau's booklets are all lessons addressed to the working class to show how economic laws rule them and to demonstrate that it is impossible to change those laws. Supply and demand and the theories of rent and wages impinge on the lives of her characters like Fate in Greek tragedy. Political action (strikes, legislation restricting the free operation of the marketplace, and even private philanthropy) can interfere with these laws and thus can produce more suffering, but it cannot change them. The moral of each tale is the same: we must practice resignation in the face of inevitable scarcity and hardship.

As lessons in resignation addressed to the working class, *Illustrations of Political Economy* seems hardly to fit into the optimistic atmosphere of the early 1830s. But Martineau believed that prosperity for all was within reach if all were willing to make sacrifices over the short run for the sake of production, of technological innovation, and of limiting the size of the labor force. In any case, it would be a mistake to interpret her economic dogmatism either as hard-hearted hypocrisy or as a representative sample of what the bourgeoisie as a whole believed. John Stuart Mill, differing at second hand from his father who was one of her main sources, wrote to Carlyle that "she reduces the laissez-faire system to absurdity as far as the principle goes, by merely carrying it out to all its consequences."[7] At the same time, she herself was entirely sincere and benevolent, and she could write: "I have been awakened from a state of aristocratic prejudice, to a clear conviction of the *Equality of Human Rights,* and of the paramount duty of society, to provide for the support, comfort, and enlightenment of every member born into it."[8] But Martineau's democratic sympathies, arising from her radical, Unitarian, manufacturing background, are curiously paralyzed, snarled in a tragic vision of society which she acquired from Malthus and Ricardo. She is aware of the hardships of the poor and depicts economic distress with great feeling (her own family had suffered bankruptcy and poverty in the late 1820s, and like Frances Trollope she had started writing to make ends meet). But hard work, birth control, obedience to middle-class employers, and patience in the face of adversity are all that she can propose to improve the condition of the workers.

Perhaps the thorniest problem encountered by the sympathetic Malthusian who wished, like Martineau, "to enlighten the people," arose from the vicious circle of population and charity. It was a terrible paradox of political economy that charity, however well-intentioned, was more apt to create distress than to relieve it, for charity fostered improvidence and overpopulation.[9] Yet how could one oppose charity and still claim to feel sympathy for the people? Martineau, "teacher of the people," had the painful duty of illustrating the principle that "all arbitrary distribution of the necessaries of life is injurious to society, whether in the form of private almsgiving, public charitable institutions, or a legal pauper-system."[10] She shows something of her own difficulty in the character of Mr. Burke in *Cousin Marshall,* who, after much internal debate, resigns his position at a charity hospital, because he feels he has been acting against the true interests of society: "The question is whether I am not doing more harm than good by officiating at the Dispensary and Lying-in Hospital, while it is clear to me that the absence of these charities would be an absence of evil to society?'' Distress is created by the attempt to relieve it; the same economic laws that cause poverty also cause progress, and, although Martineau does not realize it, her vision of society inexorably binds one to the other. She and her family, as well as much of the rest of the middle class, had both prospered and suffered through early industrial capitalism, and she expected the working class to do the same. That the suffering was real she knew by experience. But she also knew, or thought she knew, that violations of economic laws only produced worse suffering, while obedience to them would ultimately bring prosperity to both ''men and masters.'' The only kind of charity which is not ''injurious to society'' is that ''directed to the enlightenment of the mind, instead of to the relief of bodily wants,'' and that charity, of course, she generously extends through her tales.

Except that both think the machinery of society is governed by rational principles, nothing could be farther from Bulwer's satiric optimism than Martineau's rigorous, sobering tales of hard work and hardship. Bulwer is writing to demand change in the legal sphere, and Martineau is writing to show why change is impossible in the economic sphere. Together they represent the two sides of Benthamism very clearly: on the one hand, the demand for radical alterations in political and legal arrangements, and on the other hand, the reification of economic arrangements into the unalterable patterns of natural law. Certainly Martineau may be accused of aiding and abetting the policy of laissez-faire; but just as certainly it would make no sense to accuse Bulwer of the same thing—and yet both were Benthamites. Furthermore, what Bulwer fails to demonstrate, Martineau demonstrates very clearly, and vice versa. Economic law impinges on Martineau's characters just as Bulwer says that environment impinges on Paul Clifford. The lives of her workers and her small middle-class employers are hemmed in and completely governed by the tyranny of the marketplace, even though what she is conscious of defending is self-help and free enterprise. The lives of Bulwer's thieves and rogues, on the other hand, are as free as the wind, or as his own aristocratic caprice chose to make them, even though what he tells us he is showing is how they are the puppets of their social environment.

It needed greater strength of imagination than either Bulwer or Martineau possessed to bring the two sides of the Benthamite dichotomy together, in metaphor and symbol if not in intellectual system. In the 1830s, the only writers able to do so with much authority were Carlyle and Dickens, who rejected Benthamism. At the same time, what Carlyle and Dickens offer in the way of imaginative synthesis seems also to involve a loss of that intellectual coherence which is one of the virtues of Benthamism. It is as if the ability to see social problems whole involved for the middle class a sacrifice of the ability to think about them clearly, and vice versa. The central discovery which Mill made during his mental breakdown in 1826 was that he had been trained to think and not feel, and when he came to describe how he wrote his great chapter on "The Probable Futurity of the Labouring Classes," he attributed it entirely to the humanizing influence of Harriet Taylor. "What was abstract and purely scientific [in *The Principles of Political Economy*] was generally mine; the properly human element came from her."[11] And Mill says of his friendship with Carlyle: "I did not . . . deem myself a competent judge of Carlyle. I felt that he was a poet, and that I was not . . . and that as such, he not only saw many things long before me, which I could only, when they were pointed out to me, hobble after and prove, but that it was highly probable he could see many things which were not visible to me even after they were pointed out."[12] Of course Carlyle and Dickens were not deficient in intellectual power, which was therefore all on the side of the Benthamites—of Bulwer, Martineau, and James Mill and Son. But the Benthamites tried to be systematic in their social thinking, while Carlyle and Dickens did not. At the same time, as in all ideological constructions, Benthamism and political economy ruled out much, made much invisible. Carlyle and Dickens could see some of what Benthamism rendered invisible—in particular, they could see the new, raw class inequities built into early industrialism, the potentially revolutionary hostility of the working class towards the middle class because of these inequities, and the break-up of local, communal patterns caused by the factories and by urbanization. Mill's *Principles* comes close to an adequate synthesis of intellectual clarity and humanitarian sympathy, as do also the later novels of Dickens. And perhaps Carlyle's early works, through *Past and Present,* approximate these later ones, although the intellectual coherence that he provides is moral and religious rather than economic and political. But the central fact about the history of middle-class culture in the early Victorian period is the splits that open in the ranks of liberalism after 1832. Benthamite radicalism, Tory-radicalism, and "the sentimental radicalism" of Dickens and *Punch* seem almost to be the fragments of a whole vision of society which, if they could have been united as they perhaps had been in Blake, Paine, and Shelley, might have reached some of the conclusions about injustice that made Chartism and Owenism seem explosive.

At least the raw materials for an explosion are present in Dickens's early writings. Whereas Bulwer writes about "social fraud" and Martineau about the eternal and immutable laws of political economy, Dickens from the outset of his career writes about what it means to be "unekal," as in this passage from *Pickwick Papers*:

> "It strikes me, Sam," said Mr. Pickwick, leaning over the iron-rail at the stairhead, "it strikes me, Sam, that imprisonment for debt is scarcely any punishment at all."
> "Think not, sir?" inquired Mr. Weller.
> "You see how these fellows drink, and smoke, and roar," replied Mr. Pickwick. "It's quite impossible that they can mind it much."
> "Ah, that's just the wery thing, sir," rejoined Sam, "*they* don't mind it; it's a regular holiday to them—all porter and skittles. It's the t'other vuns as gets done over, vith this sort o'thing: them down-hearted fellers as can't svig away at the beer, nor play at skittles neither; them as vould pay if they could, and gets low by being boxed up. I'll tell you wot it is, sir: them as is always a idlin' in public houses it don't damage at all, and them as is always a workin' wen they can, it damages too much. 'It's unekal,' as my father used to say wen his grog warn't made half-and-half: 'It's unekal, and that's the fault on it.' " (576)

Although his viewpoint in *Pickwick* is comic, Dickens's theme becomes injustice and social exploitation. And part of the strength of his vision of "unekality" lies in making Pickwick himself a victim of injustice, the innocent bourgeois precipitated into an abyss of social "degradation." Through the ordeal of Bardell versus Pickwick and his subsequent incarceration, Pickwick ceases to be a mere observer of the social scene—the amateur clubman and tourist who travels through life looking for "novelty"—and becomes embroiled in a situation in which he himself is suddenly "unekal." Of course Pickwick does not turn into a tragic figure—a happy ending is in store for him—but he also learns that a happy ending is not in store for everyone. When he leaves prison, he carries with him a new consciousness: "Alas! how many sad unhappy beings had he left behind!" (667).

At the same time, Sam Weller's talk about being "unekal" does not translate readily into the language of class exploitation. As Dickens was to do throughout his career, Sam effects a division between the deserving poor and the undeserving poor.[13] There are those who belong in prison and those who do not, and Pickwick finds out to his sorrow that laws and lawyers are incapable of making this distinction. In fact, the Dodsons and Foggs of the world seem to exist mainly to confound it. Still, Dickens begins from the consciousness of inequality. It is the rock upon which he builds his fictions. And if he could not manage to be intellectually systematic about it, he was nevertheless able to do something better: to fashion out of his own bitter experience stories rich with the knowledge of injustice.

In his treatise on *Popular Government,* the great legal historian Sir Henry Maine writes, ''It does not seem to me a fantastic assertion that the ideas of one of the great novelists of the last generation may be traced to Bentham.''[14] This is a puzzling judgment, since in *Oliver Twist,* the Christmas stories, and *Hard Times,* Dickens places himself in conscious opposition to Benthamism and political economy. But Dickens's attacks on official institutions and the delays of the law are at least as important and certainly more frequent than his attacks on Benthamism, which are never very logical or thorough.

It has been well-said that Benthamism emphasizes the ''getting'' of early industrial capitalism more than the ''spending.'' Without questioning other aspects of it on any very fundamental level, Dickens reverses its emphasis by insisting upon spending in all the areas where utilitarian political economy preaches thrift, hard work, and prudence. In terms of money, Dickens calls for the spending involved in charity, generosity, and public good works. In terms of time, he calls for the spending of it in the pursuit of jolly good fun rather than in work, self-improvement, or rigorous Sunday observances. And in terms of the private lives of workers and of ''ordinary people'' like himself, Dickens calls for a kind of emotional spending—not just the rejection of ''cash-nexus'' calculation in the name of brotherly love, but also the rejection of the Malthusian calculation that would raise wages by, apparently, inhibiting love and marriage among the working class.

But important as the emphasis on benevolent generosity is in Dickens, Sir Henry Maine is still able to find much to connect him with Benthamism: ''Dickens, who spent his early manhood among the politicians of 1832 trained in Bentham's school, hardly ever wrote a novel without attacking an abuse. The procedure of the Court of Chancery and of the Ecclesiastical Courts, the delays of the Public Offices, the costliness of divorce, the state of the dwellings of the poor, and the condition of the cheap schools in the North of England, furnished him with what he seemed to consider, in all sincerity, the true moral of a series of fictions.''[15] Of course what Dickens learned as a parliamentary reporter did not make him a Benthamite in any strict sense of that term. Whatever new attitudes he acquired by listening to reform-minded radicals in Parliament (like Daniel O'Connell, whose speech on the disturbances in Ireland in 1832 reduced him to tears) were fueled by the deep distrust of existing institutions which he had learned in the Marshalsea and the blacking warehouse. It was a distrust that he could apply to new Benthamite institutions just as easily as he could to ones that, like Chancery, were a snarled heritage from "the Good Old Days." And this is what happens in *Oliver Twist:* it is a reformist novel attacking an abuse, only the abuse happens to have originated in a Benthamite reform.

In several ways *Oliver Twist* is a fuller expression of the broadly Benthamite, reformist culture of the 1830s than either *Paul Clifford* or *Illustrations of Political Economy.* For one thing, Bulwer and Martineau were not "Philosophic Radicals" in any strict sense either. Bulwer shed his rather shallow Benthamism after *Paul Clifford* and adopted a Tory-radicalism close to Disraeli's. His historical and occultist novels of the 1840s, like *Zanoni* and *The Last of the Barons,* he conceived as reactions against the democratic goals of the French Revolution and Chartism. And R. K. Webb says that Martineau was never an orthodox Benthamite, partly because she was too "doctrinaire, utopian, and woolly" to be a reformer by the patient application of the "Felicific Calculus." In any case, in *Paul Clifford,* Bulwer tries to adapt an old literary form—eighteenth-century moral satire—to the new issues of social reform in the 1830s, and runs into contradictions. And Martineau's "improving" tales, which share more traits with religious tracts than with Dickens's novels, are meant to serve the cause of self-reform or self-help more clearly than the reform of laws and institutions. With *Oliver Twist,* Dickens achieves a synthesis of appropriate form with new content that gives full and energetic expression to a middle-class, radical, reformist viewpoint—one that Bulwer and Martineau reflect only imperfectly or in fragments.

Plenty of novels in the 1830s and 1840s attacked abuses, but many of these could not be called Benthamite by any stretch of logic. Factory reform novels like Mrs. Tonna's *Helen Fleetwood* and Mrs. Trollope's *Michael Armstrong* (an imitation of *Oliver Twist*) express a Tory and Christian reaction against utilitarianism, political economy, and, indeed, against liberalism and industrialism in general. Despite much urging, Dickens did not chime in with the Ten Hours Movement that Mrs. Trollope was writing to support. And he would never have agreed with Mrs. Tonna that the factory system was the work of the devil; he was much more inclined to believe that her brand of religion was the work of the devil, as per the Rev. Mr. Stiggins and the Murdstones. But Sir Henry Maine emphasizes that Dickens "in all sincerity" found "the true moral" of his novels in the reform of particular social evils and that he was therefore doing something original in fiction. Dickens's lessons are to be applied not just to changing individuals in the manner of Scrooge but to effecting improvements in the structure of society as well. This is true also of Bulwer in *Paul Clifford,* but more superficially. Bulwer's treatment of the theme of environmental causation does not clearly shift the burden of moral agency away from individuals, as he says it does. But Dickens is able to dramatize the ruinous effects of bad environment—and, therefore, the responsibility of society for crime—in the boldest, most terrifying fashion. *Oliver Twist* is melodrama, true—but one that rises to the level of a powerful social nightmare by asking us to look on as the workhouse and the demonic world of the thieves crush their innocent victim. Oliver's escape does not offset either the terror or the reality of the dangers that assail him. And even the fact that he is not transformed into a thief like Paul Clifford is no contradiction. Dickens understands the nightmares and the longings of childhood and could never have written, as Bulwer does in skipping over the life of his hero until he is twelve, that "there is little to interest in a narrative of early childhood, unless, indeed, one were writing on education" (8). Such an assertion prompts one to wonder what Bulwer thinks he is writing about, if not education?

Oliver is the archetypal hero of melodrama and also of countless folktales and fairy tales, the sacrificial lamb snatched just at the right moment from the jaws of hell. To make him develop—to make him grow or regress either one—would rather spoil the effect than aid it. In fact, it is his very unchanging helplessness that makes him appear to be the pawn of environment. To show him growing more like the thieves would both diminish our sympathy for him and, paradoxically, give us a sense of his independence. The Artful Dodger does not represent the final stage of "the parish boy's progress" that threatens Oliver, because the Dodger knows how to help himself. If he is a product of his environment, he is also a highly independent, impudent entrepreneur, albeit on the small scale of watch chains and pocket handkerchiefs. It is not adaptation to environment that Dickens wants to show, but a failure to adapt, and the annihilation of a life which that failure threatens.

Oliver is a symbolic version of the Lockean tabula rasa. He is the white paper of innocence upon which anything may be written by "circumstances" or environment: "In short, the wily old Jew had the boy in his toils. Having prepared his mind, by solitude and gloom, to prefer any society to the companionship of his own sad thoughts in such a dreary place, he was now slowly instilling into his soul the poison which he hoped would blacken it, and change its hue for ever."[16] Again, it is true that

Fagin does not poison Oliver's soul, but the danger is meant to be and felt to be real. As Dickens said of his own childhood experience in the blacking warehouse and on the streets of London, "I know that, but for the mercy of God, I might easily have been, for any care that was taken for me, a little robber or a little vagabond."[17] How did Dickens escape that fate? Apparently, in much the same nearly miraculous way that Oliver escapes: so he must have felt after his father quarreled by letter with James Lamert, and he was sent home "with a relief so strange that it was like oppression."[18] At any rate, Oliver's innocence is not of a positive, assertive kind—he is not the saintly prig he is sometimes made out to be—but of a negative, passive kind. Dickens wants us to believe in his malleability at the same time that he wants to preserve him unscathed for the world of Mr. Brownlow and Rose Maylie, and into that world of middle-class sweetness and light Oliver eventually ascends, as by a miracle. But because we also know that miracles are infrequent, we remain aware that others—Nancy, Charlie Bates, the Dodger, and even Fagin and Sikes—are not so fortunate. Although it is easier to think of children and women as the victims of circumstance, towards the end of the novel, after Oliver is safe, Fagin and Sikes become caught up in powerful undercurrents of sympathy. As Arnold Kettle puts it, "Sikes is gathered into the world that has begotten him and the image of that world makes us understand him and even pity him, not with an easy sentimentality, but through a sense of all the hideous forces that have made him what he is."[19]

The novel that commences with the helpless orphan trapped in the workhouse ends with the helpless villain trapped in the condemned cell. Workhouse and prison frame the story, with Saffron Hill in between. It is as fitting a symbolic expression as one can find in the 1830s of the Benthamite theory that institutions determine conduct, and that to change conduct one must first change the institutions. That theory is one of the reasons why the problem of crime and punishment is as central to Bentham's thinking as it is to Dickens's. Both make penology their constant study. At the same time, at least one major difference separates them. For Dickens, prison is the symbol for all that is wrong with society, and utopia for him would be a place without prisons because without the injustices that breed crime. But Bentham is that contradictory monster, a utopian penologist. He spent much time and (rational) zeal in designing his ideal prison, the Panopticon. And his emphasis on crime and punishment comes about in designing the future, or the ideal constitutional and legal code, rather than in worrying about crime and injustice in actual society. Crime occupies such a large portion of Bentham's thinking because it is almost the only thing that legislators and judges will have to deal with in the ideal state. Bentham's ideal governors will have very little to do except to design appropriate punishments to curtail the various mischiefs that men will, in their blindness to general utility, continue to perpetrate: "It remains to be considered, what the exciting causes are with which the legislator has to do. These may . . . be any whatsoever: but those which he has principally to do [with] are those of the painful or afflictive kind. With pleasurable ones he has little to do, except now and then by accident . . . The exciting causes with which he has principally to do, are, on the one hand, the mischievous acts, which it is his business to prevent; on the other hand, the punishments, by the terror of which it is his endeavour to prevent them."[20] Bentham, in short, emphasizes crime because he is an incurable optimist. Everything else in a rational society —everything "pleasurable"—can take care of itself without the interference of government. But Dickens emphasizes crime because his vision is rooted in actual society and in its great distance from the ideals of justice and equality. Although a believer in industrial and democratic progress, he is no utopian. In his depictions of social evils is always a sad sense of their great stubbornness, their resistance to change, which makes his prisons loom all the darker and colder in the midst of his fictions. Although he took a keen interest in prison reform and design, he could not be called a utopian penologist in any sense.

Dickens's attack upon the New Poor Law workhouse comes at the start of the novel and seems logically disconnected from the rest of what happens, despite the rather awkward transitions back to Mr. Bumble's love life. But the underlying feeling is that everything terrible that happens— the entire demonic world of the London slums—flows directly out of the workhouse. It is the primum mobile of Oliver's life, at once his birthplace and the adumbration of his death. After Oliver's daring raid on the kettle of gruel, one of the Poor Law guardians prophesies with an ironic truth that he will be hanged. The workhouse keeps the hangman busy, and a direct route leads from it to prison even for such an innocent child as Oliver. Between the supposedly benevolent institution and the penal one there is little to choose. And they do not merely frame the story. In an important way they form, along with the London slums, the main elements of the environment that is always closing in on Oliver, always threatening to destroy him, claustrophobically cutting off the air and the light of middle-class freedom and virtue, like one of Mr. Sowerberry's coffins or like the dark coal bin in which Oliver is shut after his combat with Noah Claypole. As in his later novels, Dickens is concerned to show the symbiotic relationship between the world of official institutions and the world of poverty and crime: workhouse and prison help to cause the conditions which they are meant to correct.

But in a sense the workhouse seems merely tacked on, not an integral part of what happens in the rest of the story. As with Yorkshire schools in *Nicholas Nickleby,* or with Chancery in *Bleak House,* or with divorce law or industrial pollution in *Hard Times,* the workhouse in *Oliver Twist* seems to be a merely local evil, a wen on the body politic that can be easily cut away, at the same time that it is a center from which enormous and nearly all-engulfing evil spreads. So Benthamite optimism seems to clash with a deeper pessimism. The reformer must always feel the urge to make a specific evil seem important, dangerous, universally threatening, and he must always feel the contrary urge as well—to make it seem inorganic, unnecessary, and correctible by obvious, practical measures. Dickens portrays whatever abuse he takes in hand as larger than life, gives it universal and almost (as with Fagin's diabolism) supernatural properties, so that it becomes a symbol of all of the abuses and injustices in the world. And on the other hand, he circumscribes the abuse, makes it appear to be the work of a few selfish individuals, or suggests that it is a minor and temporary ailment that can be cured by some Morrison's Pill or other. (Dickens never shared Carlyle's rejection of politics but rather was a strenuous advocate of Morrison's Pills of all sorts, especially in *Household Worlds* and *All the Year Round.* What he did share with Carlyle was a healthy distrust in the ability of "the National Dustheap" of Parliament and of other official institutions to effect needed reforms.) In one direction, Dickens is led almost to the denial of the possibility of social progress; in the other, he is led to the rosy belief that the evils which he depicts are minor and temporary and can be corrected by a little good will applied in the right ways, either through private charity or through benevolent legislation.

This dialectic of reform, corresponding to class structure, is the main source of the polarized quality of Oliver's experience. Just as social evil in the form of Fagin and Sikes is about to extinguish all hope of freedom, Oliver is whisked off to the middle-class world of Mr. Brownlow and the Maylies. Terror and certain destruction are canceled by easy rescues and by the untangling of the history of Monks and Oliver or of the conventional inheritance plot, which seems like such an unnecessary excrescence on an otherwise powerful story. Moreover, as the world of the thieves is likened to hell, so the world of Mr. Brownlow is likened to heaven—it is the apotheosis of middle-class comfort and benevolence: "They were happy days, those of Oliver's recovery. Everything was so quiet, and neat, and orderly; everybody was kind and gentle; that after the noise and turbulence in the midst of which he had always lived, it seemed like Heaven itself'' (94). In the middle-class world, everything is easy and orderly; in the slums, everything is difficult, terrifying, turbulent. These values are implicit in the idea of reform itself: against terrific social evils are ranged the means to correct them, easy, obvious, and readily available to benevolent members of the middle class. Fundamental changes in economic or even political structure are unnecessary, if only the middle class would get about the business of reform. These attitudes are under-lying assumptions throughout Dickens's early fiction, and in the litera-ture of reform in general.

But despite the falseness of the plot that converts a pauper boy into a respectable young bourgeois, there is no falseness about what Brownlow means to Dickens. Benevolent middle-class individualism is quite simply the only solution that Dickens sees to the social problems that he raises. It is the one institution—if it can be called that—which is incorruptible. Certainly no solution is going to come from the world of official institu-tions in the novel—the courts, the lawyers, and perhaps even Blathers and Duff are, like workhouse and prison, sources of evil or at least of incompetent bungling rather than of social improvement—and that leaves only Mr. Brownlow, Mr. Losberne, and their like to rescue the Olivers of the world through their private initiatives. Brownlow's impor-tance in the novel, then, comes as much from Dickens's having nowhere else to turn to for social improvement as from his desire to celebrate the bourgeois virtues à la Podsnap. All the same, as Brownlow sets about single-handedly to undo Monks and Fagin and magically to transform Oliver's future from workhouse and prison to middle-class freedom, Dickens expresses his faith in the ability of middle-class individualism to banish evil and darkness from the world and to remodel it in its own image. The characterization of Brownlow is related to the novel's narra-tive structure: he is the type of Dickens's ideal reader—a member of the honest, hard-working middle class in whom alone in the 1830s history seemed to have invested the power of social redemption.

The sharp antithesis that the novel effects between what Brownlow represents and what Fagin represents is not entirely reducible either to the categories of class difference or to the categories of good and evil. The novel from beginning to end is about the glaring contrast between rich and poor, but Fagin does not stand for the deserving poor and Brownlow does not stand for the oppressing rich. On the contrary, Oliver is the chief representative of the deserving poor, and the Poor Law guardians are per-haps the clearest representatives of the oppressing rich. And although the bourgeois world of Brownlow is heaven to Fagin's underworld, a direct

translation of these metaphors into moral terms is not possible either, because of the feeling that Fagin himself is not a free agent but a dehuman-
ized creature of the slum world he inhabits: "As he glided stealthily
along, creeping beneath the shelter of the walls and doorways, the hideous old man seemed like some loathsome reptile, engendered in the
slime and darkness through which he moved: crawling forth, by night, in
search of some rich offal for a meal'' (135). While Fagin is never openly
an object of pity, and Oliver's forgiveness of him at the end of the novel
therefore rings false, he is what he would make Oliver, a creature "of
slime and darkness.'' The price of a life of crime is imprisonment and the
gallows; but more than these, it is the loss of freedom and of the possibility of fulfillment outside of prison as well. Dickens divides experience
into two irreconcilable categories, not based directly upon good and evil
but upon freedom (identified with middle-class benevolence and respectability) and upon grinding necessity and death (identified with the lives
of the poor, the outcast, and the "criminal refuse" of London).

The contradictory results of the antithesis between freedom and necessity can be seen perhaps most clearly in Nancy. Fagin and Sikes have
made a complete forfeit of their humanity and, hence, of their free will.
But Nancy, like Oliver, is somehow resistant to the corrosive effects of
environment. "The girl's life had been squandered in the streets, and
among the most noisome of the stews and dens of London, but there was
something of the woman's original nature left in her still'' (301). Despite
being "the fallen outcast of low haunts,'' says Dickens, Nancy still retains "a feeble gleam of the womanly feeling . . . which alone connected
her with that humanity, of which her wasting life had obliterated so
many, many traces when a very child'' (301). Nancy, however, disagrees
with this favorable assessment of herself, and, when Mr. Losberne tries to
persuade her to reject her old life in favor of a life of middle-class freedom
and virtue, she says she is "past all hope."

> "You put yourself beyond its pale,'' said the gentleman. "The past
> has been a dreary waste with you, of youthful energies mis-spent,
> and such priceless treasures lavished, as the Creator bestows but once
> and never grants again, but, for the future, you may hope. I do not
> say that it is in our power to offer you peace of heart and mind, for
> that must come as you seek it; but a quiet asylum, either in England,
> or, if you fear to remain here, in some foreign country, it is not only
> within the compass of our ability but our most anxious wish to secure
> you . . . Come! I would not have you go back to exchange one word
> with any old companion, or take one look at any old haunt, or

breathe the very air which is pestilence and death to you. Quit them all, while there is time and opportunity!'' (353-354)

One hears in Mr. Losberne's language the echo of countless scenes of ''social reclamation'' that took place during the nineteenth century (Gladstone's nocturnal perambulations come immediately to mind). There is enough false sentiment in Dickens's characterization of Nancy and of ''fallen women'' in other novels to swamp the works of lesser writers. But to his credit, Nancy is not ''reclaimed.'' Although as a creature of environment she should not be capable of exercising free choice, she chooses—apparently freely—to stick with Bill and the ''wasting life'' she has always known. At the same time, the inconsistent characterization of Nancy reveals a greater inconsistency: Dickens's treatment of the effect of environment on character is operative only part of the time, through one half of the social experience that he depicts, and the division follows class lines. The poor, it seems, are always in danger of ceasing to be human— but by becoming victims of their environment. The point at which they become morally culpable is also the point at which they cease to be morally culpable.

The division between freedom and necessity that marks Oliver's experience is basic to the middle-class consciousness that created the literature of reform. It is as much a feature of utilitarian radicalism as of Dickens's ''sentimental radicalism'' and is implicit in Bentham's ''doctrine of circumstances.'' For example, both Mr. Losberne's language to Nancy and James Mill's essay on ''Education'' (1818) are governed by the same antithesis. Mill writes: ''It is now almost universally acknowledged that on all conceivable accounts it is desirable that the great body of the people should not be wretchedly poor; that when the people are wretchedly poor, all classes are vicious, all are hateful, and all are unhappy. If so far raised above wretched poverty as to be capable of being virtuous, though it is still necessary for them to earn their bread by the sweat of their brow, they are not bound down to such incessant toil as to have no time for the acquisition of knowledge and the exercise of intellect.''[21] Vice and poverty are linked, although poverty makes vice involuntary. There is a kind of double robbery of ''the poor'' in Mill's language, well-intended though it is, that makes them incapable of being virtuous and also incapable of free moral choice. At the same time, the path upward to freedom from the bondage of environment, or of necessity and vice, lies through an education that would give to ''the poor'' the middle-class virtues of industry and self-reliance, but without making them middle class. It is obviously not an argument for equality. Godwin and Paine remained far in advance of Bentham and James Mill on the issue of economic equality, and middle-class political theory in the Victorian years did not recapture their ground until the 1870s and 1880s.

Melodrama was a natural form for the expression of middle-class reforming zeal because it could contain a double psychology of free agents and victims, or of actions that are to be judged by traditional moral standards and actions that are to be forgiven on the grounds of environmental causation, without seeming contradictory. This double psychology is evident in the social melodramas written by Douglas Jerrold from the late 1820s into the 1840s, and it is also evident in *St. Giles and St. James* (1845), his imitation of *Paul Clifford* and *Oliver Twist.* In the preface he writes: "It has been my endeavour to show in the person of St. Giles the victim of an ignorant disregard of the social claims of the poor upon the rich; of the governed million upon the governing few; to present . . . the picture of the infant pauper reared in brutish ignorance; a human waif of dirt and darkness. Since the original appearance of this story, the reality of this picture, in all its vital and appalling horror, has forced itself upon the legislature . . . and will ultimately triumph in its humanising sympathies."[22] In novels and melodramas that focus upon "the infant pauper reared in brutish ignorance," there is no real question of extending democracy down to the "governed million": not much attention is paid in them to such troubling manifestations of working-class political consciousness as Chartism and trade unionism. They aim rather at arousing "humanising sympathy" in the "governing few," who are thus responsible both for creating social evils and for rectifying them (the Poor Law guardians versus Mr. Brownlow). The double psychology of victims and free agents allows for a thorough exposé of at least the symptoms of social injustice at the same time that it undermines the threat of meaningful political response on the part of "the poor."

The portrayal of an oppressed group as victims in need of external help is always slippery, double-edged. Dickens's attacks on false benevolence, as in Mrs. Jellyby and Mrs. Pardiggle in *Bleak House,* show that he was aware of this problem. He did not fall into the error of treating adult workers as victims, along with orphans and "fallen women," unless they were unemployed or in sweated industries. But the opposite tactic of well-meaning utilitarian radicals like James Mill, Harriet Martineau, and W. R. Greg (and, frequently, of "sentimental radicals" like Dickens and Jerrold as well), which involved rejecting the antithesis between freedom and necessity and treating the working class as manly free agents on a par with their employers, was equally ambiguous.[23] The reductio ad absurdum of the latter position may be found in Samuel Smiles's *Self-Help*, which reverses the Benthamite "doctrine of circumstances": "My object . . . has been merely to show that adverse circumstances—even the barrenest poverty—cannot repress the human intellect and character, if it be determined to rise; that man can triumph over circumstances, and subject them to his will."[24] With Smiles's negation of environmental and economic determinism, we reach the other extreme of the contradictory attitudes toward the working class in middle-class radicalism, whether Benthamite or Dickensian. Quite simply, both the sentimental radicals and the Benthamites tend to view the working class as victims when arguing for legal and political reforms, and as free agents when arguing against economic reforms (for example, trade unions, socialism, and Ten Hours legislation). Stephen Blackpool in *Hard Times* combines both attitudes: he is a manly free agent when he defies Slackbridge and the "tyranny" of the trade union; but he is also a helpless victim, ground down by divorce laws and other pieces of class legislation, and his politics is summed up in his maudlin catchword: "It's aw a muddle."

Because the working class never consisted either of helpless victims in need only of more soup kitchens and benevolent coal societies, or of free agents in the utilitarian sense, there is a falseness in the middle-class literature of reform which vitiates even so late and sophisticated an example as *Felix Holt*. Only a few middle-class writers in the 1840s and 1850s—perhaps most notably Mill and Mrs. Gaskell—were able to treat working-class politics as offering serious alternatives to their own liberalism. The zone of free moral agency, moreover, did not get moved downward in fiction. Many middle-class radicals in the 1830s and 1840s looked forward to the time when free trade would eliminate the tyranny of environment over the poor and make everyone free agents. But such optimism gradually disappeared, at least in fiction and poetry. Through *Middlemarch* to Hardy and Gissing, the zone of free moral agency gradually vanishes, so that both the working class and the middle class come to be viewed as the creatures of environment or of sheer misfortune (Hardy's "chance").

In much of his writing Dickens escapes the charge of what might be called victimizing the poor for charitable purposes partly because he is able to expand the class of victims until it encompasses himself and much of the middle class as well as the working class. He would have disliked James Mill's language, close as it is to Mr. Losberne's, because it sets the dividing line between victims and free agents at "wretched poverty." Mill, in fact, is anticipating the judgment of the New Poor Law commissioners, who created the rule of least eligibility: to receive relief, the pauper should not be in a situation "really or apparently so eligible as the situation of the independent labourer of the lowest class."[25] That rule limited the victims of economic injustice to those who could not work and considered everyone else able to fend for himself in the marketplace. Dickens knew better. His own experience had made him aware of the disasters that could befall anyone, in any station of life. Further, like Jerrold and many other middle-class radicals, he harbored a free-trade militancy that helped him to identify politically with everyone below the level of the aristocracy or the rich or the governing class. He felt that there was more in common politically between small middle-class shopkeepers, clerks, and manufacturers on the one hand and the working class on the other than there in fact was. Jerrold's attitudes are similar: the passage from the preface to *St. Giles and St. James* actually contains two dividing lines, two versions of the class of victims. Jerrold sets "the infant pauper raised in brutish ignorance" over against all the rich, including the middle class. But he also sets "the governed million" over against "the governing few," and he clearly considers himself a member of the former. The imprecision of their categories—the sliding scale, as it were, between free agents and victims—enabled Dickens, Jerrold, and the *Punch* radicals like the Mayhews and Mark Lemon to write forceful and yet ambiguous social criticism, often close to Chartism although not of it. And the hard-boiled rigor with which the line between paupers and "the independent labourer of the lowest" class was drawn in the Benthamite New Poor Law inevitably set the sentimental radicals against it. "Pray tell Mr. Chadwick," Dickens wrote to Austin in 1842, that "I *do* differ from him, to the death, on his crack topic—the New Poor Law."[26] And he continued to oppose the New Poor Law throughout his career, down to the writing of *Our Mutual Friend,* in which Betty Higden takes up the story where Oliver leaves it after he is resurrected into the heaven of Mr. Brownlow and the Maylies. "In my social experiences since Mrs. Betty Higden came upon the scene and left it, I have found Circumlocutional champions disposed to be warm with me on the subject of my view of the Poor Law. My friend Mr. Bounderby could never see any difference between leaving the Coketown 'hands' exactly as they were, and requiring them to be fed with turtle soup and venison out of gold spoons. Idiotic propositions of a parallel nature have been freely offered for my acceptance, and I have been called upon to admit that I would give Poor Law relief to anybody, anywhere, anyhow."[27] Against the extremes of Josiah Bounderby—the working class all left to starve or the working class fed with gold spoons—Dickens contended for a humane, sensible system of relief and social insurance. The New Poor Law provided neither of these things, so Dickens declared it to be the worst conceived and the worst managed law "since the days of the Stuarts." Between them, therefore, Oliver Twist and Betty Higden establish a case for social generosity that is limited and practical, but also unambiguously persuasive.

If Dickens cannot be called a Benthamite, neither can he be called an anti-Benthamite, except in certain respects and on particular issues. But the reaction against Benthamism was a powerful force in the late 1830s and after, emerging most strongly in the Tory-evangelical side of the Ten Hours Movement, in the High Church literature of the Oxford Movement, and, although with some qualifications, in the Tory-radicalisms of Carlyle and Disraeli. A less directly political reaction to the reforming tendencies of the period may also be seen in writers like Thackeray and Samuel Warren, who object to what they see as the snobbish pretensions to social equality of the working and lower middle classes. Thackeray's *Book of Snobs* (1846-1847) is the best-known example of this attitude, the social implications of which he seems later to have regretted.[28] But just as noteworthy is Samuel Warren's best-selling *Ten Thousand a-Year* (1841), which tells the story of a nasty little Cockney clerk, Tittlebat Titmouse, who, through a legal loophole in a will, usurps the place and title of the good Squire Aubrey, everybody's ideal country gentleman. So Warren reverses the pattern to be found in Jerrold's melodramas: the innocent squire is now the victim of a villainous crew of lawyers and of petit-bourgeois swindlers from London, involved in poaching on the property rights of the gentry. Titmouse is almost as vividly repelling as Uriah Heep; Warren sees no good in him or his kind and likens them to voracious worms and rats swarming out of London and infesting the once untroubled countryside. Readers who may have been offended by Warren's class bias may also have been attracted by his nostalgic evocation of a pastoral England where Chartists and Benthamites alike were unheard of. Some of Warren's stories in *The Diary of a Late Physician* (1838), however, typify the literature of the 1830s perhaps better than the anti-Cockney plot of *Ten Thousand a-Year*. There are some entertaining pieces of graveyard Gothic in the *Blackwood's* tradition; in "Grave Doings," for example, the physician-narrator turns "resurrectionist." And the story "Rich and Poor" and a few others contain the sort of general social commentary that is to be found in Dickens and *Punch*. The physician first witnesses the death of "the haughty Earl of ____," who goes "where rank and riches availed him nothing—to be *alone with God.*" He is then called on a charitable mission to the garret of Tim O'Hurdle, who also dies, leaving his family in a desperate condition. "Dives and Lazarus!" exclaims the physician; he meditates on the human lot: "The dispensations of Providence are fearful levellers of the factitious distinctions among men! Little boots it to our common foe, whether he pluck his prey from the downy satin-curtained couch, or the wretched pallet of a prison or a workhouse!''[29]

Apart from existential considerations about wealth and poverty, and from the class bias that informs *Ten Thousand a-Year,* Warren is not much concerned with politics. To find the anti-Benthamite reaction at its clearest, therefore, it is necessary to turn to the evangelical writings of Charlotte Elizabeth Tonna and to the High Church writings of the Rev. William Gresley. Louis Cazamian writes appreciatively of *Helen Fleetwood,* Mrs. Tonna's contribution to the Ten Hours Movement, but it is hard to see why. It is a piece of social hysteria written by a rabid fan of Lord Ashley's, who was known in her time in evangelical circles as the author of such tracts as *The Rockite* and as the editor of the *Christian Lady's Magazine.* But she was never a novelist. After her father's death, she tells us, ''A small annuity was all that my mother could depend on, and I resolved to become a novel-writer, for which I was just qualified . . . and in which I should probably have succeeded very well, but it pleased God to save me from this snare.''[30] She became instead a writer of religious tracts after the manner of Hannah More, whose acquaintance she made and whose techniques she admired.

Mrs. Tonna came to her concern for the poor through her love of Ireland, which took the form of a yearning to convert the ''heathen'' Irish. Unfortunately she had to leave Ireland before she could complete that great work. One day, in 1830, she attended a meeting of the Irish Society in London, where she heard a rousing speech by the Rev. Charles Seymour. ''Suddenly,'' she writes, ''reverting to the state of the many thousands of his poor countrymen congregated in London, he drew a most affecting picture of their destitute, degraded condition . . . 'Open,' he said, 'a bread-shop in St. Giles's; deal forth a little of the bread of life to their starving souls. Ye English Christians, I appeal to you for them: oh, pity my poor lost countrymen, open but a bread-shop in St. Giles's!' '' Mrs. Tonna was electrified. ''So God help me as I will open you a breadshop in St. Giles's, if He does but permit,'' she replied, and she repeated her vow many times. The result was the opening, after much solicitation and fund raising, of an evangelical Church in the slums of St. Giles's, where the Word was preached to the Irish ''heathen'' in their own tongue.

> Victorious Faith the promise sees
> And looks to God alone;
> Laughs at impossibilities
> And says, ''IT SHALL BE DONE.''

"A bread shop indeed it was."[31]

Mrs. Tonna may or may not have succeeded in multiplying loaves in the heart of St. Giles's, but she wrote ardently on behalf of the poor in her factory tract, *Helen Fleetwood*. One may even say that, judged as a tract, it is a masterpiece, though judged as a novel, it is a wretched production because of the artistic naiveté and the religious fanaticism that make it a good tract. In any case, she comes out strongly not just against child labor, but against the factory system itself: "On the system, the vile, the cruel, the body-and-soul-murdering system of factory labor, we cannot charge the innate depravity of the human heart; but we do denounce it as being in itself a foul fruit of that depravity under its hateful form of covetousness, and of being in turn the prolific root of every ill that can inhumanize man, and render an enlightened Christian country the mark of God's most just and holy indignation, provoking Him even to blot its place and name from among the nations of the earth."[32] Without realizing it, Mrs. Tonna comes close to the views of her Chartist character, Tom South, who belongs to a party that seeks "to overturn all right government" (251). Nothing spoken at the Ten Hours meeting that she describes approaches the pious Richard Oastler's recommending knitting needles as a means of sabotaging factory machinery, and she would have been horrified to hear that God-fearing, ex-Wesleyan minister, J. R. Stephens, describe himself as "a revolutionist by fire, a revolutionist by blood, to the knife, to the death."[33] But she approaches them in her own statements, and her revolution will come as surely as that which cast down the Bastille: "Very terrible will be the day of public inquisition and divine retribution. God keeps silence now . . . [but] He hath appointed a day for the open vindication alike of His justice and His faithfulness" (38).

More conscious both of political alternatives and of social facts than Mrs. Tonna, the Rev. William Gresley is not opposed to industrialism. But virtually everything else modern comes under his High Church interdiction. Like his Puseyite mentors, he is the enemy of liberalism in all of its disguises, "for they who acknowledge not God's authority as exercised by His Church are not likely to yield a willing obedience to any other government."[34] His High Church tract, *Charles Lever* (1841), is subtitled *The Man of the Nineteenth Century*, by which he means someone who has lost his roots in the ancient, apostolic principles of Christianity. Charles Lever has left the Church for a Dissenting chapel, but one bad thing leads to another: "When a man once takes it into his head that he may choose his own religion, what is there to hinder him from choosing one form of error any more than another . . . ? He may be a Dissenter today, a Socialist to-morrow" (206). That is in fact what happens to

Lever. When Scipio Suttle, the socialist lecturer, comes to town, Lever is among his converts, and thereafter he becomes embroiled in a trade union assassination, based on an actual incident at Ashton-under-Lyne, and in a Chartist insurrection, based on the Newport rising in 1839. One disaster follows another, all because the hero has ventured beyond the sheltering authority of the Church. The moral is plain on page one, but Gresley leaves nothing to the imagination of his wayward readers, and the penitent hero returns to the High Church fold at the end of the story, a sadder but a wiser man.

Charles Lever reads like a catalogue of conservative nightmares in an age of political upheaval. Although less subtle, Gresley's opinions are not different in kind from those of Newman and the other authors of the *Lyra Apostolica,* or for that matter from those of Wordsworth in his *Ecclesiastical Sonnets* and in the political poems that he wrote in the 1830s:

> Men, who have ceased to reverence, soon defy
> Their forefathers; lo! sects are formed, and split
> With morbid restlessness:—the ecstatic fit
> Spreads wide . . .[35]

Like Gresley, Wordsworth looks out from the shade of his orthodoxy and sees a world in tumult, in vain pursuit of unnecessary liberties:

> Alas! with most, who weigh futurity
> Against time present, passion holds the scales:
> Hence equal ignorance of both prevails,
> And nations sink; or, struggling to be free,
> Are doomed to flounder on, like wounded whales
> Tossed on the bosom of a stormy sea.[36]

Placing the events of 1832 against the timeless backdrop of Church history and apostolic truth, Wordsworth can see little but "the pestilence / Of revolution, impiously unbound."[37] Similarly, for Gresley, Dissent, the Reform Bill, the Municipal Corporations Act, Owenism, working-class drunkenness, trade unionism, and Chartism are parts of a pattern of modern life that he rejects in its entirety. At the same time, economic distress, although a cause of the ignorant discontent of the working class, is not part of the rejected pattern, as it is in Mrs. Tonna's attack on industrialism. For both Gresley and Wordsworth, economic distress is rather a dispensation from on high: "To remove or greatly mitigate this evil is clearly hopeless . . . Alternate prosperity and depression is an essential feature of a wide-extended commerce . . . It may be looked on as a dispensation of Providence analogous to those fluctuations of natural supplies which we find in many other countries'' (184). This is close to Wordsworth's rebuff to the discontented:

What, is there then no space for golden mean
And gradual progress?
. . .

Think not that Prudence dwells in dark abodes,
She scans the future with the eye of gods.[38]

Neither Gresley nor Wordsworth share the extreme anti-industrial attitudes of Mrs. Tonna and some of the factory reformers. But for all their preachments against rashness, they themselves fall into a kind of hysteria in which liberal reform is translated into bloody revolution. Thus, Gresley's rage against Owenism, which he abhors more because it poses a threat to the sacrament of marriage than because it poses a threat to private property, leads him to portray his socialist lecturer as a bloodthirsty madman who, knowing that he cannot win many converts to his irrational creed, proposes to deal with his opponents by means of a remarkable invention. "Suttle . . . suggested, that which alone is the practicable means . . . the wholesale murder of those who opposed their schemes; and with a fiendish look spoke of Maximilian Robespierre, and a guillotine by steam'' (137). Into the image of the steam guillotine Gresley compresses all of his reactionary nightmares. But hysterical as that image appears, it is not different in kind from the rhetoric of fear employed by a much greater preacher against things modern and liberal. In Carlyle's *French Revolution,* the reaction against Benthamism and the spirit of reform achieves its most influential expression.

CAPITAL AND LABOUR.

From *Punch*, 1843.

III. The Lessons of Revolution

Toward the end of *The French Revolution,* Carlyle writes: "That 'if the gods of this lower world will sit on their glittering thrones, indolent as Epicurus' gods, with the living Chaos of Ignorance and Hunger weltering uncared-for at their feet, and smooth Parasites preaching, Peace, peace, when there is no peace,' then the dark Chaos, it would seem, will rise;—has risen, and, O Heavens, has it not tanned their skins into breeches for itself? That there be no second Sansculottism in our Earth for a thousand years, let us understand well what the first was; and let Rich and Poor of us go and do *otherwise.*"[1] History here as elsewhere in his works is "didactic": we must learn from it those lessons of reform that will keep us from producing a "second Sansculottism," with all its attendant horrors of chaos, bloodshed, and "tanneries of Meudon."

In more than one sense, however, the effort is futile: no reform of any sort will help us. The first lesson that *The French Revolution* teaches us is that history—and especially the history of revolutions— does not end: we cannot properly say that even the first Sansculottism is a thing of the past. This is one of Carlyle's central, most original, and at the same time apparently most platitudinous messages: history is unending—there are no safe ways to limit it—it spills over into the present and on into the future. The disease of change cannot be cured by the Morrison's Pills of reform, for the disease is the human condition itself.

In the case of the first French Revolution, Carlyle tells us and shows us in many ways that it is not over, despite Thermidor, Napoleon, and Waterloo. It will go on, in one way or another, for at least two centuries (the amount of time that, Teufelsdröckh declares in *Sartor,* it will take for the "World Phoenix" to consume itself). "What a work, O Earth and Heavens, what a work! Battles and bloodshed, September Massacres,

Bridges of Lodi, retreats of Moscow, Waterloos, Peterloos, Tenpound Franchises, Tarbarrels and Guillotines;—and from this present date, if one might prophesy, some two centuries of it still to fight! Two centuries; hardly less; before Democracy go through its due, most baleful, stages of *Quack*ocracy; and a pestilential World be burnt up, and have begun to grow green and young again" (II, 133). The list of events at the beginning of the passage, which concludes significantly enough with "Tarbarrels and Guillotines" after "Tenpound Franchises," represents a progression down to the 1830s and beyond, and connects the French Revolution with English reform—a connection which Carlyle hammers away at throughout his history. It is not clear whether the working through of democracy and "quackocracy" will produce a world conflagration at the end of two centuries, or whether the two centuries themselves are the conflagration, but it does not matter. During some periods the "World Phoenix" burns more brightly and destructively than during others, and it is these periods of great heat and light that we call "revolutionary," but in fact all of history is "revolutionary"—a mighty progress or a mighty bonfire or both at once, depending on your point of view. From Carlyle's point of view it is usually both at once, for "in that Fire-whirlwind, Creation and Destruction proceed together; ever as the ashes of the Old are blown about, do organic filaments of the New mysteriously spin themselves" (I, 195). Again, as Carlyle puts it in his study of Sansculottism, expanding the concept of revolution until it is synonymous with history itself: "All things are in revolution . . . in this Time-World of ours there is properly nothing else but revolution and mutation, and even nothing else conceivable. Revolution, you answer, means *speedier* change. Whereupon one has still to ask: How speedy? At what degree of speed; in what particular points of this variable course . . . does revolution begin and end . . . ? It is a thing that will depend on definition more or less arbitrary" (II, 211). As fully and acutely as any writer in the 1830s, Carlyle registers the sense of living in "an age of transition"—an age in which, in fact, there is nothing but transition.

Carlyle employs a number of rhetorical devices that reinforce the idea of the continuation of the French Revolution into the 1830s and into English politics. Besides the qualities of grand scale, chaotic energy, dramatization, and highly figurative language that John Holloway analyzes in *The Victorian Sage,* there is the dialectic of romantic historiography in general, which results in "the experience-made-present of the French Revolution"—an experience as much for Carlyle and for the reader as for the participants in the Revolution itself.[2] Carlyle's use of the present tense, for example, is part of a stylistic structure that places us inside events and that also makes them seem contemporary and on-going. He shows that he is conscious of the effects of tense when he says, "For indeed it is a most lying thing that same Past Tense always . . . For observe, always one most important element is surreptitiously . . . withdrawn from the Past Time: the haggard element of Fear! Not *there* does Fear dwell, nor Uncertainty, nor Anxiety; but it dwells *here;* haunting us, tracking us; running like an accursed ground-discord through all the music-tones of our Existence;—making the Tense a mere Present one!" (IV, 81). Related to Carlyle's use of the present tense to place us inside events and to make us experience the anxieties and terrors of them are his frequent uses of rhetorical questions and of what might be called retrospective prophecies. Carlyle often describes events in series of rhetorical questions which suggest the doubts and anxieties that the original actors might have experienced, but the questions lead to prophetic assertions—or to what seem to be prophecies but which are of course assertions about past events: "Where this will end? In the Abyss, one may prophesy" (II, 228). When this kind of thing occurs often enough—virtually on every page, in every paragraph—one is tempted to accuse Carlyle the prophet of hedging his bets, for nothing could be safer than prophecy by hindsight. But Carlyle is writing about the present and the future as well as about the past—he is writing, in short, in a paradoxical mode that might be called prophetic history. The rhetorical questions, the present tense, and the retrospective prophecies all underscore Carlyle's main theme that the events of the first French Revolution are not only repeatable but are repeating themselves now and will go on doing so in the future.

Carlyle has the fact of the French Revolution of 1830 to support his theme. As he says in *Heroes and Hero-Worship,* "The Three Days told all mortals that the old French Revolution, mad as it might look, was not a transitory ebullition of Bedlam, but a genuine product of this Earth where we all live; that it was verily a Fact" (V, 201). And he has also the political turbulence of the reform decade in England, which is his real subject, always in the wings. The essays on "the condition of England question" which he wrote after *The French Revolution—Chartism* and *Past and Present*—are natural sequels to it. Moreover, the first French Revolution was only a little over forty years old when Carlyle wrote and was still as much a matter of lived experience for many as of the dead, hoary past. Histories of it—as opposed to memoirs and to polemical essays like those by Burke and Paine—were new in the 1830s. Thiers's *Histoire de la Révolution française* appeared between 1822-1827, and Mignet's in 1824. In England, Archibald Alison's series of essays on the Revolution started in *Blackwood's* in 1830, stimulated by the July Revolution and by Alison's opposition to reform. In the way of a history published in England before Alison, there was only Scott's biography of Napoleon (1827). Carlyle comes to the subject of the French Revolution, then, when it is particularly fluid and ambiguous—hovering dangerously between history and lived experience, and between past politics and present controversy—and he stresses the fluidity and ambiguity of it in every conceivable way, if only in order to make "the haggard element of Fear" ever present to us.

Of course everyone in the 1830s spoke or wrote about the French Revolution in terms of the present, extracting lessons and "signs of the times" from it, and in this Carlyle is far from original. "Prophetic history" is in at least one way similar to Macaulay's "Whig version of history," for both involve judging the past in terms of the present—although Carlyle's is also a form of history in which Whiggism is rejected. Alison's Tory essays in *Blackwood's* had drawn elaborate analogies between the French Revolution and the prospects of reform which were intended to warn politicians not to make any concessions to democracy. The results of peaceful reform, Alison argued, would inevitably be violent revolution. And John Wilson Croker argued along similar lines in Parliament, thus countering Macaulay and the Whigs, who drew opposite conclusions from the French examples of 1789 and 1830. According to Macaulay, and indeed to all pro-reform Whigs and radicals, it was obviously the failure to grant reform—not the granting of it—that would lead to revolutionary violence.[3]

Carlyle's position, five years after the passing of the Reform Bill and at the start of the period of economic depression and political disillusionment that ran from 1836 to at least 1846, cannot be identified with Tory, Whig, or radical interpretations of the French Revolution. In his estimation, neither reform nor the failure to grant reform have much bearing on the creation of revolutionary violence. Or, rather, they both have a bearing upon it, for while it is necessary to grant reforms in order to avoid revolutionary violence, the granting of them will also lead to such violence.

Carlyle's failure to follow party lines in *The French Revolution* suggests the second lesson that it teaches, after the continuing nature of the Revolution itself. And that is the inability of all politicians to cope with the revolutionary situation. Mirabeau and Danton are the only politicians singled out for much praise by Carlyle, but both failed. And in *The French Revolution,* at least, Napoleon is no exception any more than Necker, because Carlyle so defines the Revolution that Napoleon comes on the scene only after it has (temporarily and in one place in the world) burned itself out. Carlyle's ambivalent treatment of Napoleon in *Heroes and Hero-Worship,* in which Napoleon emerges as a hybrid of quack and hero, does not add much to this assessment, although Carlyle there views him as the great man who brought the Revolution under control, as Cromwell brought the English Revolution under control. "To bridle-in that great devouring, self-devouring French Revolution . . . is not this . . . what he actually managed to do?" (V, 240). Still, according to Carlyle, Sansculottism ran amuck between Necker and Napoleon, and no man was able to tame it.

Carlyle's version of the French Revolution is a strangely dichotomized one: outside the walls of French institutions, no matter whether aristocratic or revolutionary, the storm of Sansculottism rages; inside those walls, a mad succession of politicians takes place, from Royalist through Girondin to Jacobin, all of them trying to allay or at least to guide the storm, and none of them succeeding until it has blown itself out. Thus the main Jacobin revolutionaries are themselves helpless before the Revolution, as much the victims of it as the leaders:

> They ride this Whirlwind; they, raised by force of circumstances, insensibly, very strangely, thither to that dread height;—and guide it, and seem to guide it. Stranger set of Cloud-Compellers the Earth never saw. A Robespierre, a Billaud, a Collot, Couthon, Saint-Just . . . these are your Cloud-Compellers. Small intellectual talent is necessary . . . The talent is one of instinct rather. It is that of divining aright what this great dumb Whirlwind wishes and wills . . . With this one spiritual endowment, and so few others, it is strange to see how a dumb inarticulately storming Whirlwind of things puts, as it were, its reins into your hand, and invites and compels you to be leader of it. (IV, 231-232)

The storm of the Revolution, with all the power and unpredictability of a great natural force, cries out for leaders but destroys those whom it finds —it "devours its own children." Carlyle implies that even Robespierre is not to blame for events and may be forgiven, for the Revolution was never in his control. Because "it went hard with them all," Carlyle says, "History" will "pity them all": "Not even the seagreen Incorruptible but shall have some pity, some human love, though it takes an effort" (IV, 120).

So Carlyle reinforces the second lesson of the Revolution: the helplessness of all politicians, struggling within the walls of palaces, National Assemblies, and Committees of Public Safety, who tried to harness the whirlwind of Sansculottism raging out of doors. It is a lesson that runs directly counter to certain conservative theories of the Revolution, including those of Alison and Croker. A favorite tactic of conservative historians from the time of the Abbé Barruel forward has been to attribute the Revolution to a radical, antireligious, and masonic conspiracy. But a conspiracy involves planning, and it is exactly the element of logical planning which Carlyle sees overridden at all points by Sansculottism. Further, conservative historians necessarily object to analyses that make the events of the Revolution seem inevitable, for that implies the rightness of the democratic future and of the demolition of the past. To liken the Revolution to a great natural force such as a whirlwind (or a deluge, or a volcanic eruption, or an ocean tide) suggests its inevitability and thereby grants the future to democracy (although, as we have seen already, democracy will turn into "quackocracy" before the revolutionary process has burned itself out).

But there are features of *The French Revolution* that are as disquieting to liberals as to conservatives, and not the least of these is again Carlyle's insistence on the futility of political measures to affect the course of the Revolution, for it suggests the futility of actively working for reform (in the two-hundred year cycle, Carlyle thinks, "ten-pound franchises" may very well be followed by "tarbarrels and guillotines," although he does not suggest guillotines by steam). Carlyle's distrust of democracy and representative government is painted all over *The French Revolution.* Representatives in national assemblies and parliaments are "like the fabulous Kilkenny Cats; and produce, for net-result, *zero;*—the country meanwhile *governing* or guiding *itself,* by such wisdom . . . as may exist in individual heads here and there" (II, 216). As in *Past and Present,* the British Parliament is here the "National Palaver" (III, 26), and is no better than French Parlements and National Assemblies, a mere "hubbub" of senseless "motion and countermotion" while the real action of history takes place elsewhere, in the streets and on the barricades.

Carlyle's portrayal of aristocracy and royalty before and during the Revolution shows them to be corrupt: "do-nothing aristocracies," as later in *Past and Present,* are the main source of misgovernment, which is in turn the main cause of revolution. Although Carlyle was deeply influenced by the "Great Burke" (III, 228), nothing could be farther from Burke than Carlyle's portrayal of prerevolutionary France as a society founded upon a sham. Carlyle can even tell us, in one of his more dogmatic moods, that the cause of the Revolution was nothing less than "quackery" which had been built up "from the time of Charlemagne and earlier" and which was bound to explode one day in honest Sansculottism (II, 58). But Carlyle's portrayals of the many versions of liberalism, with the partial exception of the constitutional monarchism of Mirabeau, are no more favorable than his treatment of the ancien régime. No group other than corrupt aristocrats comes in for more abuse by Carlyle than the Girondins, whom, with their faith in free trade, political economy, and their own "moneybags," Carlyle interprets as the forerunners of British liberals and free trade radicals in the 1830s. Carlyle gloats over the insistence of the Paris populace on price controls as against the Girondin advocacy of free trade, and says, "The Trade and Finance of Sansculottism; and how, with Maximum and Bakers' queues . . . it led its galvanic-life . . . remains the most interesting of all Chapters in Political Economy: still to be written" (IV, 143). Meanwhile, the Girondins themselves are the "Pedants of the Revolution, if not Jesuits of it," because of their reliance on "formulas": "They are as strangers to the People they would govern; to the thing they have come to work in. Formulas, Philosophies, Respectabilities, what has been written in Books, and admitted by the Cultivated Classes: *this* inadequate *Scheme* of Nature's working is all that Nature . . . can reveal to these men" (IV, 137).

Carlyle treats the Jacobin Mountain more favorably than the Girondins, because it is closer to "Nature," or else closer to the real center and meaning of the Revolution for him, which is Sansculottism. It may also be that Carlyle gives them his highly qualified approval because they were more successful at whirlwind-riding than the Girondins. There is a good deal of truth to the notion that Carlyle grants his approval to those who succeed in history, for their success means that they "have an honesty in them," and that they are somehow doing the bidding of God. In any case, from Carlyle's perspective, whatever success the Jacobins had came partly from their being unprincipled, free from the cant of formulas, and from their having "Nature" on their side—a most powerful ally: "The weapons of the Girondins are Political Philosophy, Respectability and Eloquence . . . The weapons of the Mountain are those of mere Nature: Audacity and Impetuosity which may become Ferocity, as of men complete in their determination, in their conviction; nay of men, in some cases, who as Septemberers must either prevail or perish" (IV, 122). But the Jacobins themselves—including that would-be "Cloud-compeller," Robespierre—are also doomed to defeat and the guillotine, so Carlyle's approval of their honest "ferocity" is merely relative. At least they are not formulistic "pedants" and "Jesuits" (in comparing them with the Girondins, Carlyle momentarily ignores the fact that the Jacobins were as much infected with "philosophedom" as any group).

Carlyle's Royalists, Girondins, and Jacobins are the Tories, Whigs, and radicals of the Reform Bill decade. Despite being prophetic history, Carlyle's account is not inaccurate in any major way, however: the Girondins were indeed advocates of free trade and "spokesmen for business interests," while the Jacobins "were closer to the people, more flexible in their attitudes, and more able and willing to yield gracefully to popular pressure and to adapt their views to meet the needs and exigencies of the moment."[4] But Carlyle wants to drive home the point that at no time during the Revolution did France get anything like adequate government (the Revolution would have ended if it had), and he also suggests that Britain is close to the same condition in the 1830s. All the French Revolution managed to do was to overthrow one form of misgovernment (aristocracy or royalism) and replace it with another form of misgovernment (democracy or liberalism). Meanwhile the French people—the misgoverned "twenty-five millions"—raged and rampaged: "This huge Insurrectionary Movement, which we liken to a breaking-out of Tophet and the Abyss, has swept away Royalty, Aristocracy, and a King's life. The question is, What will it next do; how will it henceforth shape itself? Settle down into a reign of Law and Liberty; according as the habits, persuasions and endeavours of the educated, moneyed, respectable class prescribe?" (IV, 114). The answer (which takes the form of retrospective prophecy and, hence, suggests a modern parallel) is clearly no. "Girondin Formula" will be no more successful at governing than corrupt aristocracy; indeed, if anything, it will be less so:

> As for the Girondin Formula, of a respectable Republic for the Middle Classes, all manner of Aristocracies being now sufficiently demolished, there seems little reason to expect that the business will stop there . . . Hunger and nakedness, and nightmare oppression lying heavy on Twenty-five million hearts; this, not the wounded vanities or contradicted philosophies of philosophical Advocates, rich Shopkeepers, rural Noblesse, was the prime mover in the French Revolution; as the like will be in all such Revolutions, in all countries. Feudal Fleur-de-lys had become an insupportably bad marching-banner, and needed to be torn and trampled: but Moneybag of Mammon (for that, in these times, is what the respectable Republic for the Middle Classes will signify) is a still worse, while it lasts. (IV, 115)

This passage is a microcosm of *The French Revolution* and also of the social criticism in *Chartism* and *Past and Present*. As the tense shift in the last sentence implies, Reform Bill and French Revolution are similar, for they both represent an end to aristocratic government and the beginning of the "Republic for the respectable washed Middle Classes." But they are also similar because, while altering the political structure, they do not alter the social structure: the masses of poor go on as they always have, in "hunger and nakedness."

Carlyle makes hunger "the prime mover" of the Revolution, which finds its true locus in the suffering of the Sansculottes rather than in the rising expectations of the liberal middle class. As later in Michelet, Carlyle's is a "révolution de la misère": "Troops of ragged Lackalls" with their "fierce cries of starvation . . . become a whole Brigand World; and, like a kind of Supernatural Machinery, woundrously move the Epos of the Revolution" (II, 126). In his shrewd review of the *French Revolution*, Henry Merivale complains that Carlyle's emphasis on hunger is illogical.[5] How can it be, says Merivale, following Malthus, that hunger is always with us as long as population keeps pace with progress, and yet we are not always in a state of revolution? Carlyle might have replied to this that we are always in a state of near revolution, and that it takes only a few minor causes besides the major one of hunger to set the whirlwind going—minor causes like the callous calculations of Malthusian political economy with its New Poor Law "Bastilles," for example, or like franchises that are good for those who can afford ten-pound dwellings, but not for the poor. Twenty years later, Tocqueville would argue that the French Revolution, far from being caused by the grinding misery of the masses—Carlyle's "Hunger and Nakedness"—was instead caused by the progress of middle-class enlightenment and industry. According to Tocqueville, in the years before 1789 the whole nation was better off than it ever had been before. Furthermore, "a study of comparative statistics makes it clear that in none of the decades immediately following the Revolution did our national prosperity make such rapid forward strides as in the two preceding it."[6] Tocqueville's thesis is a more sophisticated version of arguments offered by Macaulay (as in his response to Southey), Brougham, and other leading Whigs and radicals at the time of the Reform Bill crisis. According to Macaulay, for example, the "great cause of revolutions" is certainly not hunger, but progress. If, "while nations move onward, constitutions stand still," the result will be revolution. Macaulay implies that the rising wealth and intelligence of the middle class entitle it to a greater share of political power, and that if the aristocracy does not make room for it, then what happened in France will happen in England.[7]

Modern studies have borne out both the Carlyle-Michelet thesis and the Macaulay-Tocqueville thesis. The researches of C.-E. Labrousse and others after him have made it clear that the growth of middle-class economic power coupled with periodic economic distress—especially the bad harvests and shortages of 1787-1789—were both main factors in creating the revolutionary situation.[8] But Macaulay in 1831 was claiming what Carlyle in 1837 could not or would not grant: the political victory and historical validity of middle-class economic power. Carlyle's emphasis on hunger is a means of demonstrating the bankruptcy of both defunct "Feudal Fleur-de-lys" and "Moneybag of Mammon," for the economic grievances of the populace, and hence the Revolution itself, continue through both sorts of misrule. The rise of Chartism proved Carlyle's case, at least to his satisfaction: here was a second Sansculottism, with a vengeance! At the end of the 1830s Carlyle repeats Southey's case against Macaulay, and insists that the progress of middle-class industry has so far been for the few, not for the many.

On the basis of his emphasis on hunger and of his dislike of both aristocratic and middle-class government, one might expect Carlyle to adopt some form of utopian socialism (Owenism, St. Simonianism) or of working-class radicalism, prefiguring Chartism. But of course he is no more willing to do that than to be a Benthamite, a Whig, or a Tory. He comes closer to identifying himself with hungry Sansculottism than with anything else, but Sansculottism contains more heat than light—more incendiary energy than the wisdom needed to govern a nation. It is a force of nature—deluge, whirlwind, or volcanic eruption—morally neutral but powerful in its moral effects: "Sansculottism will burn much; but what is incombustible it will not burn. Fear not Sansculottism; recognise it for what it is, the portentous inevitable end of much, the miraculous beginning of much" (II, 213). In this sense, Sansculottism is identified simply with mob violence, and it seems to have Carlyle's unambiguous approval: "Your mob is a genuine outburst of Nature; issuing from, or communicating with, the deepest deep of Nature" (II, 251). Carlyle likens Sansculottism more often to a raging fire, however, than to a storm, and that has overtones of something other than moral neutrality and approval. For example, Carlyle refers to the September Massacres as "this dim Phantasmagory of the Pit" (IV, 27), and repeatedly the whole Revolution is a "huge Insurrectionary Movement, which we liken to a breaking-out of Tophet and the Abyss" (IV, 114). Again, Carlyle says that the "very implement of rule and restraint . . . has become precisely the frightfullest immeasurable implement of misrule; like the element of Fire, our indispensable all-ministering servant, when it gets the *mastery,* and becomes conflagration" (III, 73). To control the fire, says Carlyle, demands a hero-magician who can speak the "magic-word" of command. "Which magic-word . . . if it be once *forgotten;* the spell of it once broken! The legions of assiduous ministering spirits rise on you now as menacing ‧

fiends; your free orderly arena becomes a tumult-place of the Nether Pit, and the hapless magician is rent limb from limb" (III, 73-74). Like his use of the present tense, Carlyle's fiery language of demonic outbreaks is calculated to inspire fear, and certainly not to aid us in an assessment of the particular motives or of the conscious politics of the different participants in the Revolution.

Nothing is more characteristic of Carlyle than the wedding of highly inflammatory rhetoric with what has seemed to many to be the virtue of impartiality. According to one recent student of the English historiography of the Revolution: "His *French Revolution* is the only original product of the shaking-up of history in England in the 1830s. It divested the history of the French Revolution of the conventional political approach. This was partly connected also with the loosening of the party boundaries . . . A generation was growing up between 1830 and 1840 used to change and reform as the habitual course. Carlyle influenced this questioning attitude. He detached himself from the old party lines before detachment became the fashion in history."[9] Carlyle's contemporaries often praised his impartiality. Thackeray, for example, writes that "he is not a party historian like Scott, who could not, in his benevolent respect for rank and royalty, see duly the faults of either: he is as impartial as Thiers, but with a far loftier and nobler impartiality."[10] And at the end of the century, Alphonse Aulard described Carlyle's portrayal of the Revolution as "impartial . . . mais non calme ni insensible."[11] So far from being "insensible," of course, Carlyle's history is full of sound and fury, but it is sound and fury which, if not precisely signifying nothing, at least does not add up to an assessment of the Revolution in terms of the values of English party politics. On the contrary, the efficacy of party politics of any sort is denied in *The French Revolution,* and when Carlyle passes judgment on individuals or groups, he does so in the language of moral and religious praise or condemnation. And at its most extreme, his "impartiality" takes the form of equating all political activity with delirious fanaticism:

> For a man, once committed headlong to republican or any other Transcendentalism, and fighting and fanaticising amid a Nation of his like, becomes as it were enveloped in an ambient atmosphere of Transcendentalism and Delirium: his individual self is lost in something that is not himself, but foreign though inseparable from him. Strange to think of, the man's cloak still seems to hold the same man: and yet the man is not there, his volition is not there; nor the source of what he will do and devise; instead of the man and his voli-

tion there is a piece of Fanaticism and Fatalism incarnated in the shape of him. He, the hapless incarnated Fanaticism, goes his road; no man can help him, he himself least of all. (IV, 121-122)

Carlyle's "impartiality," then, does not involve a judicious measurement of the faults and merits of different political positions, but a rejection of politics altogether. It is all false, all misgovernment, and deserves to be burned up in the flames of Sansculottic wrath, like the spontaneous combustion that consumes the red-tape trash in Krook's shop in *Bleak House*. So we arrive at a point in Carlyle's thinking where the one possible way out of revolutionary chaos and the insanity of politics appears to lie not in identification with any group—social class or political party— but only in the rule of the strong, who can succeed in whirlwind-riding. The negation of politics leads to hero worship. Just how the hero differs from the mad fanatic is hard to see, except that the hero does not succumb to insanity and chaos, but strives manfully against them. To return to Carlyle's inflammatory rhetoric, the hero is the magician who can remember the "magic-word" of command, whatever that may be, and so ward off the demons who would rend him "limb from limb."

This is the third major lesson of revolution. Democracy will run its "baleful" course, but at the end of it the true, fundamental principle of government—hero worship—will assert itself. "While man is man, some Cromwell or Napoleon is the necessary finish of a Sansculottism" (V, 204). Hero worship for Carlyle is not tantamount to an advocacy of despotism as a form of government but is rather a declaration of the inevitability of the rule of the stronger over the weaker. This is the safest prophecy of all, a kind of early version of the iron law of oligarchy of Robert Michels, and on one level amounts only to saying that *somebody* must govern. Having rejected both "Feudal Fleur-de-lys" and "Moneybag of Mammon," Carlyle does not ask what should go in their place: that part of the future was a blank to him. The seer can see only the inevitability of an end to democracy, and the advent of someone—some hero or other—who will bring order out of chaos.

At the same time, hero worship is Carlyle's version of the social contract—his attempt to reduce all social and political relations to their most fundamental level. It is also his attempt to counteract rationalistic explanations of social organization, whether these are based on a theory of natural rights and social contract as in Rousseau, or on the principle of utility as in Bentham: "Had all traditions, arrangements, creeds, societies that men ever instituted, sunk away, this would remain. The certainty of Heroes being sent us; our faculty, our necessity, to reverence

Heroes when sent: it shines like a polestar through smoke-clouds, dust-clouds, and all manner of down-rushing and conflagration" (V, 202). Hero worship reduces history to the completely individualistic level of one man's response to another. Our most fundamental choice is always between faith or doubt, respect or disrespect, obedience or disobedience, towards some other individual whose decisions affect us and who poses as our leader. Carlyle's model of social organization, moreover, precludes rational assessment by worshippers of the hero's alternatives before he makes his decisions. It is a matter of faith, not reason. The hero acts in our stead; his mission among us is to make the decisions that we have already proved incapable of making ourselves. Politics for Carlyle thus acquires something of the illogicality of waiting for Godot: we live in a world from which the heroes have vanished; we can do nothing ourselves; we must wait for the heroes to return. If Carlyle's call for heroes is not quite as illogical as his friend Irving's prophecies of the Second Coming, it is close to it—a translation of the apocalyptic imagination of Scottish Calvinism into the language of earthly politics.

A comparison of Irving and Carlyle helps to illustrate their common Scotch Calvinist background and the ways in which it influenced their attitudes toward English politics. Hazlitt has given us a witty, jaundiced description of Irving's preaching in the 1820s, much of which can be applied to Carlyle. In accounting for Irving's success, Hazlitt points to the element of social criticism in his sermons by which he has "converted the Caledonian Chapel into a Westminster Forum or Debating Society, with the sanctity of religion added to it." According to Hazlitt:

> Mr. Irving keeps the public in awe by insulting all their favourite idols. He does not spare their politicians, their rulers, their moralists, their poets, their players, their critics . . . he levels their resorts of business, their places of amusement, at a blow—their cities, churches, palaces, ranks and professions, refinements, and elegances —and leaves nothing standing but himself . . . He literally sends a challenge to all London in the name of the KING of HEAVEN, to evacuate its streets . . . to burn its wealth, to renounce its vanities and pomp; and for what?—that he may . . . reduce the British metropolis to a Scottish heath, with a few miserable hovels upon it, where they may worship God according to *the root of the matter,* and where an old man with a blue bonnet, a fair-haired girl, and a little child would form the flower of his flock! Such is the pretension and the boast of this new Peter the Hermit, who would get rid of all we have done in the way of improvement . . . in order to begin again on a *tabula rasa* of Calvinism.[12]

Perhaps Irving was a Scotch John the Baptist who unintentionally paved the way for the true Scotch Messiah, author of such notable prophetic works as *Sartor Resartus* and *The French Revolution*. Irving's "hyperbolical tone" and his apocalyptic condemnation of "all we have done in the way of improvement" are characteristic of Carlyle as well. And besides the obvious religious factors they share, there is a pastoral factor: the emigrant Scotchman's rejection of the modern Babylon, and his nostalgia for simple Annandale. Such a pastoral factor is evident in everything Carlyle wrote, from his description of Teufelsdröckh's childhood and of Abbott Samson's monastery to the blame that he lays on London in *The Reminiscences* for the downfall of Irving: "What a falling of the curtain; upon what a Drama! Rustic Annandale begins it, with its homely honesties, rough vernacularities, safe, innocently kind, ruggedly mother-like, cheery, wholesome, like its airy hills and clear-rushing streams; prurient corrupted London is the middle part, with its volcanic stupidities and bottomless confusions."[13]

In several ways, Carlyle's *French Revolution* reveals its social origins; he offers us a Scotch peasant rebellion translated into Parisian Sansculottism. It has sometimes been remarked that Carlyle envisions the Revolution in terms of the urban, industrial proletariat of 1837 instead of the shopkeepers, craftsmen, and apprentices of late eighteenth-century Paris.[14] Certainly Carlyle emphasizes and perhaps exaggerates the effects of economic scarcity and unemployment on the "lower classes": like *Chartism* and *Past and Present*, *The French Revolution* should be read as an essay written in hard times about the politics of hard times. But it is less accurate to say that his Sansculottes and Lackalls are the industrial proletariat in disguise, for Carlyle renders them in ambiguous terms. At one time Sansculottism may be the general citizenry of Paris, storming the Bastille; at another time, it may be a horde of sharp-tongued women crying out for bread or for blood; and at still another, it may be the whole twenty-five million misgoverned populace of France. Sansculottism in Carlyle tends to lose its original class reference to the artisans and small shopkeepers of Paris, which is clear in this definition of 1793:

> A *Sans-Culotte* you rogues? He is someone who always goes on foot, who has no millions as you would all like to have, no *chateaux*, no valets to serve him, and who lives simply with his wife and children, if he has any, on a fourth or fifth storey.
>
> He is useful, because he knows how to work in the field, to forge iron, to use a saw, to use a file, to roof a house, to make shoes and to shed his last drop of blood for the safety of the Republic.[15]

74

Carlyle uses the term "Sansculottism" to apply to whatever is outside the walls of institutions, whipping up the storm of revolution. And what is outside is usually an amorphous, broiling mob that he is less concerned to analyze sociologically than to liken to an "outburst of Nature"—whirlwind, deluge, or volcanic eruption. One of the features of Carlyle's version of the Revolution, then, is that it lacks a specific class consciousness, despite all that he says about rich versus poor, and about "Feudal Fleur-de-lys" and "Moneybag of Mammon." This lack of class consciousness, coupled with Carlyle's rejection of institutional politics, renders *The French Revolution* "impartial." And together with his completely individualistic, yet antidemocratic emphasis upon hero worship, these attitudes are ones that fit well with the political attitudes of the peasantry throughout nineteenth-century Europe.[16]

The social status of Carlyle's family was ambiguous—of "the poor," but not of the urban or factory proletariat that swelled the ranks of Chartism and the trade unions in the 1840s. With these Carlyle had no personal connection. His father was originally a stone mason—really an independent craftsman and small building contractor—and then, when trade grew bad at the end of the war, an independent farmer. Carlyle speaks of his "peasant father," a designation that matches his political attitudes. These consisted mainly of reverence for his social superiors, at least when they were honest, coupled with concern for the state of the poor, including "common folk" like himself. When occasion demanded, he could speak out forcefully for what was just, even against his superiors: "More than once has he lifted up his strong voice in Tax Courts and the like before 'the Gentlemen' (what he knew of Highest among men) and, rending asunder official sophisms, thundered even into their deaf ears the indignant sentence of natural justice to the conviction of all" (6). But Carlyle also says that the only time his father took an interest in more than local affairs was when he followed the rise and fall of Napoleon. "For the rest, he never meddled with Politics: he was not there to govern, but to be governed; could still *live,* and therefore did not *revolt*" (31). Not only as a peasant but also as a Scotchman, and perhaps especially as a borderer from Cameronian stock, it must have seemed natural for James Carlyle and his famous son after him to think of institutionalized politics as worthless and to reduce social issues to a kind of realpolitik structure consisting of those who are "there to govern" and of the generalized poor, who either prosper or suffer until the point of blind rebellion is reached. Carlyle goes on to tell us that he has heard his father "say in late years, with an impressiveness which all his perceptions carried with them: 'that the lot of a poor man was growing worse and worse; that the world could not and would not last as it was; but mighty changes, of which none saw the end, were on the way' '' (31). And he concludes his description of his father's politics by saying that ''he was looking towards 'a city that *had* foundations.' ''

Behind all existing political institutions, both James and Thomas Carlyle can discern the lineaments of an apocalyptic ''natural justice,'' whose workings are in heaven: for both, beyond earthly cities of sand there is a ''city that has foundations.'' From such a perspective, democracy is beside the point, and so is any kind of collective action, except for the generalized wrath of the Sansculottic poor. In contrast to institutionalized politics, blind rebellion, although equally futile in worldly terms, appears to be a working-out of God's will against the shams of false government. Froude sums up these attitudes when he says, ''In its hard fight for spiritual freedom Scotch Protestantism lost respect for kings and nobles, and looked to Christ rather than to earthly rulers.''[17] Carlyle merely substitutes earthly heroes for Christ and otherwise retains many of the social attitudes of Scotch Calvinism, which show up as fire-and-brimstone ''impartiality'' in his analyses of English and French politics.

In its farthest extension, Sansculottism is synonymous with humanity itself, stripped of its ''garnitures'': ''And yet a meaning lay in it: Sansculottism verily was alive, a New-Birth of TIME; nay it still lives, and is not dead but changed. The *soul* of it still lives; still works far and wide . . . till, in some perfected shape, it embrace the whole circuit of the world! For the wise man may now everywhere discern that he must found on his manhood, not on the garnitures of his manhood. He who, in these Epochs of our Europe, founds on garnitures, formulas, culottisms of what sort soever, is founding on old cloth and sheepskin, and cannot endure'' (IV, 311). Sansculottism here is identified with ''manhood''—the naked, essential man or ''Adamite'' of *Sartor Resartus*. Carlyle plays on the word and on the idea of clothes just as he does in *Sartor*, with something like the same ''bewildering'' results. In *Sartor*, the ''Editor'' attributes to Teufelsdröckh a ''deep Sansculottism'' (I, 169), and cites his radical sympathies for the poor, but he also insists that Teufelsdröckh, ''though a Sansculottist, is no Adamite'' (I, 47). In elaborating the ''Clothes Philosophy,'' Teufelsdröckh spends as much time dressing the world up as undressing it—or insisting on the need for ''garnitures'' at the same time that he argues that only ''true'' garnitures will do: ''The utility of Clothes is altogether apparent to him'' (I, 47). Teufelsdröckh's Sansculottism does not involve advocating the actual stripping of mankind down to nakedness (which would mean, in political terms, revolution), but rather the imagination of nakedness, and the recognition of clothes as clothes. Both Teufelsdröckh and Carlyle call themselves "speculative radicals," which comes to mean something like the ability to imagine the world in flames or the world without clothes, but without their recommending that result. A "speculative radical" is one who creates hypothetical revolutions by meditating, for example, on "the political effects of Nudity." As Carlyle described *Sartor* to Fraser: "The ultimate result . . . is a deep religious speculative-radicalism (so I call it for want of a better name), with which you are already well enough acquainted in me."[18] Carlyle's trouble in naming his politics suggests his unwillingness or inability to identify himself with any actual political group, while the fact that his stance is as much "religious" as political suggests its main source in Scottish Calvinism. And on one level, "speculative radicalism" means no more than the desire for revolution held in check by the fear of it—the essential ambivalence of all preachers who announce the imminence of a day of doom.

Although Carlyle identifies more closely with Sansculottism than with any other factor in the Revolution and defines it as equivalent to "the people" or mankind, it has nothing creative about it—it is only an honest chaos crying out for order. The hero's function is to produce that order by first abolishing or at least seizing control of parliaments, committees, and the many-voiced hubbub of Sansculottism. Carlyle's vision is so polarized between Sansculottic disorder and heroic order that all mediating terms, including the ideas of social reform and of political institutions, are eliminated, or are at best merely thrown over to the side of disorder. In his review of *The French Revolution,* Joseph Mazzini writes that Carlyle fails to consider the positive results of the Revolution, and also that he falsely rejects all the mediating terms "between the infinite and the individual." Politics, Mazzini suggests, is what fills up the space between those two extremes; politics is the interactions between human decisions and providential design which compose all of history. In ignoring the fruits of the Revolution and also in rejecting politics, says Mazzini, Carlyle is actually denying the role of Providence in history, which for Mazzini means the progressive realization of individual and national liberty. If Carlyle read Mazzini's essay, he must have been surprised to find himself charged with multiplying doubt instead of faith, but such was the conclusion of the great Italian liberator: "The times are serious. Frigid skepticism has eaten but too much into youthful souls born for better things. No writer of Mr. Carlyle's genius, above all no historian, can henceforth add to the stock of doubt, without condemning himself to remorse.''[19] No doubt Carlyle never felt remorse for his ''frigid skepticism.'' But *The French Revolution* does not teach the need for political faith and activism, except in the form of greater concern on the part of the rich for the state of the poor. On the contrary, it teaches the insanity of political commitment in the guise of the Revolution itself: ''What, then, is this Thing called *La Revolution,* which, like an Angel of Death, hangs over France . . . ? It is the Madness that dwells in the hearts of men'' (IV, 248). ''Frigid skepticism'' is a good term for Carlyle's dilemma, albeit a paradoxical one, for Carlyle seems to have reached it at exactly the same time that his conversion experience of 1825 led him to the transcendentalist faith that he expresses in *Sartor.* As he describes it in *The Reminiscences,* his state of grace seems oddly tangled up in a paralyzing sense of the worthlessness of human affairs:

> This year [1825] I found that I had conquered all my skepticisms, agonising doubtings, fearful wrestlings with the foul and vile and soul-murdering Mud-gods of my Epoch; had escaped, as from a worse than Tartarus . . . and was emerging, free in spirit, into the eternal blue of ether,—where, blessed be Heaven, I have, for the spiritual part, ever since lived; looking down upon the welterings of my poor fellow-creatures, in such multitudes and millions, still stuck in that fatal element; and have had no concern whatever in their Puseyisms, Ritualisms, Metaphysical controversies and cobwebberies; and no feeling of my own, except honest silent pity for the serious or religious part of them, and occasional indignation, for the poor world's sake, at the frivolous, *secular* and impious part, with their Universal Suffrages, their Nigger Emancipations, Sluggard-and-Scoundrel Protection Societies, and ''Unexampled Prosperities,'' for the time being! . . . I understood well what the old Christian people meant by their ''Conversion,'' by God's Infinite Mercy to them. (281-282)

Mazzini is right: Carlyle's religious rhetoric camouflages the fact that he has no faith in human affairs and that he only clings to the idea of providential design in history without really believing it. All of Carlyle's language of ''World Phoenixes'' and ''transcendentalisms'' and cycles of growth and decay is a kind of mighty fireworks rattling over an abyss— the abyss that some of his readers have called ''impartiality'' but that appears in this passage as an arrogant disdain for the ''Mud-gods'' of mere people. The lessons of the French Revolution, which are the lessons of gradual democratic reform as well, cancel each other out until we are left only with hero worship and with an equally individualistic, antisocial belief in the reform of the self: "To reform a world, to reform a nation, no wise man will undertake; and all but foolish men know, that the only solid, though a far slower reformation, is what each begins and perfects on *himself*" (XXVII, 82).

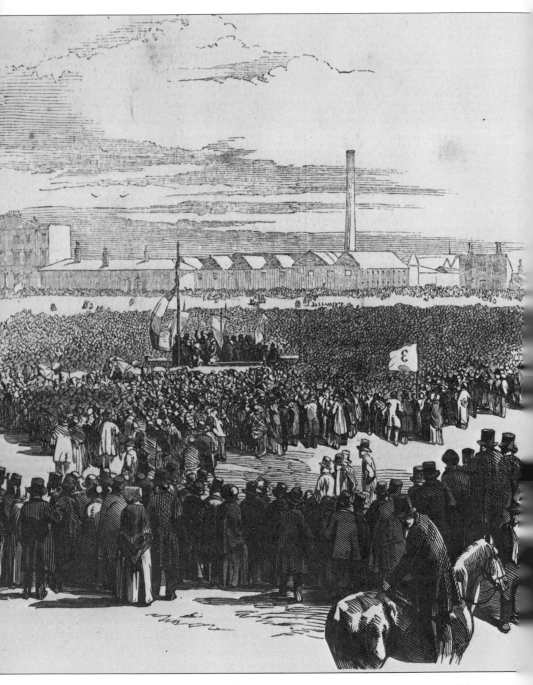

The Chartist demonstration on Kennington Common, April 10, 1848. From *The Illustrated London News*.

IV.   Two Responses
to Chartism:
Dickens and Disraeli

Given his rejection of politics, it is ironic that, in *Chartism* and *Past and Present,* Carlyle appears as an advocate of social reform partly through legislative intervention. But while he expends much rhetoric in condemning "laissez-faire Benthamism" and "do-nothing Aristocracies," he expends just as much rhetoric in condemning Morrison's Pills and the activities of Parliament. Nothing suits him. Heroes, no doubt, will eventually arise to show the way to genuine reform. But meanwhile, when the question is put to Carlyle as to what should be done until the heroes come, he has no very adequate or original reply. As Henry Merivale pointed out: "He seems to believe in the power of government to raise the poorer class altogether out of its present position by legislation. When asked, what are the remedies which he proposes—he answers, very much in the tone of a man forced to say *something*—emigration—and education. The first, in the sense of a general measure, the merest of all delusions. The second, doubtless in its ultimate effects, a lightener of many of the evils which afflict humanity; but even were it attainable . . . still of very indirect and distant influence upon this particular disorder."[1] Agreeing with Merivale, R. H. Horne and Elizabeth Barrett say that Carlyle's only positive proposals (besides the impossibly vague one of "Work")—"universal education" and "general emigration"—are "rather an evasion of Chartism and its causes; for the Chartists say, 'We have enough education to see the injustice of people being starved in a land of plenty; and as for emigration, we do not choose to go. Go yourselves.' "[2]

Carlyle, then, did not succeed very well in answering "the condition of England question." But he did provide an analysis of the causes of revolution in the past and a scenario for revolution in the future which helped to transform the optimistic politics of 1832 into a politics of fear in the 1840s. The parallels between the French Revolution and the reform decade in England that the prophetic historian stresses seem to prove the bankruptcy of middle-class values. Whether liberal reform works and therefore opens the floodgates to Chartist democracy, or whether it fails to work and therefore opens the floodgates to Chartist democracy, the result is the same. Carlyle declares that the halfway measures of liberalism cannot last and that what the second Sansculottism of Chartism represents—the demand for the political and economic equality of the working class—must ultimately triumph. In condemning liberal half-measures and in predicting the fulfillment of Chartist democracy, Carlyle's vision is both strong and true. But he sees no more good in the fulfillment of working-class aspirations than he does in bankrupt liberalism or in equally bankrupt conservatism. The near future for him is entirely bleak and smoky—"Tartarean," in short—and is prefigured in the eschatological violence of the French Revolution, which will repeat itself until the cry for democracy turns into the cry for strong government and the "right to obey," and a green world of natural law and order be reborn from the ashes of industrial and democratic chaos.

In order to bear out his eschatological version of history, Carlyle is prepared to agree both with "physical force" Chartists, who like to magnify the revolutionary potential of their movement, and with upper-class opponents of Chartism, who also like to magnify its threat the sooner to get it repressed. Certainly there is little rhetorical difference between Bronterre O'Brien, Julian Harney, and Friedrich Engels on the one hand, and Carlyle, Macaulay, and Thomas Arnold on the other. Engels writes that the six points of the Charter will be "sufficient to overthrow the whole English Constitution, Queen and Lords included," and also that "the vengeance of the people will come down with a wrath of which the rage of 1793 gives no true idea. The war of the poor against the rich will be the bloodiest ever waged."[3] Almost as extravagantly, Macaulay speaks against the second Chartist petition of 1842 on the grounds that it poses a threat to "the institution of property" and hence to "the wellbeing of society." Give power to the Chartists, says Macaulay, and "the first use which they will make of it will be to plunder every man in the kingdom who has a good coat on his back and a good roof over his head."[4] And Thomas Arnold sees an analogy between the destitute and perilously ignorant English masses of the late 1830s and the slave rebellions and barbarian invasions that undermined Rome. "Has the world ever yet seen a population so dangerous in every respect to the society in which it existed as the manufacturing population of Great Britain?" Despite his liberal sympathies, Arnold advocates a policy of stern repression toward the Chartists, in words that crop up later, at the end of the first edition of his son's *Culture and Anarchy:* "As for rioting, the old Roman way of dealing with *that* is always the right one; flog the rank and file, and fling the ring-leaders from the Tarpeian Rock!"[5] As in Rugby classrooms, so in society at large: occasional flogging seems necessary to help sweetness and light get on in the world. Like Carlyle's French ones, Arnold's Roman analogies suggest the enormity of the threat Chartism seems to pose—for Arnold, nothing less than the existence of civilization is at stake.

Other writers at the end of the 1830s were finding similar historical analogies for Chartism, most often in the French Revolution, as in Bulwer's bizarre Rosicrucian novel, *Zanoni* (1842), but occasionally in more improbable events, like the Wars of the Roses, as in Bulwer's equally bizarre *The Last of the Barons* (1843). Here Bulwer says that the steam engine, the Reform Bill, and Chartism, rather than spelling the end of aristocratic rule, were actually spawned by feudalism long before 1832 or 1789 or even 1688. In the reign of Edward IV, it seems, the alchemist-inventor Adam Warner has nearly perfected the steam engine: a safety valve is all that he lacks, and then, presto!—the world will be transmogrified into the age of factories and railways, thus collapsing some four centuries into no time at all. Meanwhile, Warner is having trouble with exploding boilers. Similarly, industrial capitalism is almost ripe in the age of Warwick the Kingmaker; its spirit is fermenting in the good burgherly merchants of London. And even Chartism, Bulwer suggests, had its original in the fifteenth century, in Robin Hilyard and his merry men who remind us of Robin Hood. In fairness to Bulwer, it should be stated that he does not exactly mean that the industrial revolution and Chartism originated in the 1400s; he explains in his preface that he is indulging in a form of poetic license: "To Fiction is permitted that liberal use of Analogical Hypothesis which is denied to History."[6] If the use of "Analogical Hypothesis" does not explain history, however, then what is its purpose? As in the case of Carlyle's prophetic history, its purpose is rather to explain the present in terms of the past. It is a procedure that involves finding precedents for what seems to be quite unprecedented, a clean break from the past. The result is a kind of historical fiction that violates any conceivable rationale for the writing of actual history; *The Last of the Barons* is almost as much an example of science fiction based on future shock—like Bulwer's later fantasy, *The Coming Race*—as it is of historical fiction after the sober model of Scott.

Equally topical but more reasonable in its dealings with history is Dickens's portrayal of the "No Popery" Gordon riots in *Barnaby Rudge*. Dickens sees religious fanaticism as the main cause of the Gordon riots, but underlying religion is working-class discontent, which connects the events of 1780 to the Chartism and trade unionism of 1836-1841. While religious fanaticism motivates Lord George Gordon, the rioters themselves give indications of another purpose. Maypole Hugh is converted to the Protestant cause by Dennis the hangman and by Gashford, Gordon's villainous secretary, on the following terms:

> "No Popery, brother!" cried the hangman.
> "No Property, brother!" responded Hugh.
> "Popery, Popery," said the secretary with his usual mildness.
> "It's all the same!" cried Dennis. "It's all right. Down with him, Muster Gashford. Down with everybody, down with everything! Hurrah for the Protestant religion! That's the time of day, Muster Gashford!"[7]

Similarly, on the last night of the riots, blind Stagg tells the murderer, Barnaby Rudge's father, how to make a living:

> "How!" repeated the blind man. "By eating and drinking. And how get meat and drink, but by paying for it! Money!" he cried, slapping his pocket. "Is money the word? Why, the streets have been running money. Devil send that the sport's not over yet, for these are jolly times; golden, rare, roaring, scrambling times." (531)

Plunder is the lure that moves many of the rioters, and this fact more than any other is meant to connect them with the Chartists. At the same time, there was much evidence in Dickens's sources for his interpretation of the rioters' motives: George Crabbe described encountering a mob made up of "vile-looking fellows, ragged, dirty, and insolent, armed with clubs going to join their companions," and Mrs. Elizabeth Montagu said, "I am convinced it is zeal for plunder that sets the mob at work."[8] Although Dickens did not realize it, the Gordon riots were one of the earliest disorders stemming from the industrial revolution, so that by accident the topicality of his historical novel makes a good deal more sense than Bulwer's far-fetched analogies. The "No Popery" animus of the rioters was a reaction partly against the tide of Irish workers who were already lowering wages and living standards by adding their competition to the London labor market.

The parallel between the violence to life and property of the Gordon rioters in 1780 and Chartist violence in 1839-1840 is made all the more obvious by the similar ways in which both commenced. On June 2, 1780, a large number of Protestants gathered before the Houses of Parliament to witness the presentation of their petition for abolition of the Catholic Relief Act, and violence started when it became apparent that the government was not quick to favor it.[9] Similarly, the Newport Rising of November 1839, certainly the most serious and possibly the only planned attempt at revolution throughout the early Victorian period, followed the rejection of the first Chartist petition in the summer of that year. And as if this likeness were not enough, one has only to refer to the way Dickens describes the mobs throughout *Barnaby Rudge* to connect them with the Chartists: "They had torches among them . . . Thus, a vision of coarse faces, with here and there a blot of flaring, smoky light; a dream of demon heads and savage eyes . . . a bewildering horror" (385-386). The torchlight mobs in this novel are like another torchlight mob in *The Old Curiosity Shop,* where Dickens quite clearly has in mind the Chartist torchlight meetings on Kersal Moor and elsewhere in 1838: "But, night-time in this dreadful spot!—night, when the smoke was changed to fire . . . and places, that had been dark vaults all day, now shone red-hot, with figures moving to and fro within their blazing jaws . . . when bands of unemployed labourers paraded the roads, or clustered by torch-light round their leaders, who told them, in stern language, of their wrongs, and urged them on to frightful cries and threats; when maddened men, armed with sword and firebrand . . . rushed forth on errands of terror and destruction, to work no ruin half so surely as their own . . . " (336). With reference to this passage, Humphry House writes that "there is nothing more surprising in all [Dickens's] work than the sudden irruption of his fears of Chartism into *The Old Curiosity Shop.*"[10] In context, the firebrands of the Chartists are the symbolic complement to the fiery furnaces and chimneys built and owned by their middle-class adversaries; both are diabolical and both are terrifying to Nell: "Who shall tell the terrors of the night to that young wandering child!" But Chartism and the demonic industrial landscape that Nell and her grandfather wander through are not much more than elements in an evocation of childhood terror, the nightmare thrust upon them by Quilp's villainy, and it is not apparent that Dickens is doing more than applying to Chartism a rhetoric of fear often used by Chartists themselves.[11] In *Barnaby Rudge,* however, Dickens's account of the Gordon riots amounts to an analysis of Chartism, his first full treatment of the problem of class conflict.

It is worth stressing this fact, because the topicality of *Barnaby Rudge* has sometimes been understated and because the novel itself has sometimes been conveniently ignored as less satisfactory than his other early ones.[12] A letter written by Dickens to Lamon Blanchard is occasionally cited to suggest that Dickens did not mean his novel to be as topical as it

actually is: "Barnaby Rudge has nothing to do with factories, or negroes
—white, black, or parti-coloured. It is a tale of the riots of Eighty, before
factories flourished as they did thirty years afterwards, and containing—
or intended to contain—no allusion to cotton lords, cotton slaves, or anything that is cotton."[13] But Dickens is writing to reject a comparison
between *Barnaby Rudge* and Mrs. Trollope's Ten Hours novel, *Michael
Armstrong,* and he is right in saying that his story has nothing to do
either with factory "slaves" or with West Indian slaves—two prominent
concerns of the better side of evangelicalism (he is in fact writing against
the worse side of it in *Barnaby Rudge*). Further, Dickens's letter to Blanchard came before he had fleshed out the links with Chartism that the
finished novel contains. As John Butt and Kathleen Tillotson observe,
"The five years' delay between design and publication . . . increased the
novel's topicality."[14] At the same time, Dickens's letter to Blanchard
does suggest one of the weaknesses of the novel as an attempt to account
for contemporary working-class discontent. Although he gives his rioters
a clear economic motivation, he does not suggest a link between their
privations and "anything that is cotton." To see Chartism prefigured in
the Gordon riots is in fact to disconnect it from industrialism, which did
not flourish until "thirty years afterwards." That connection is at least
symbolically acknowledged in the fire imagery in the industrial scenes of
The Old Curiosity Shop. But in *Barnaby Rudge,* Dickens appears to find
it as logical to associate Chartism with the religious fanaticism of Gordon
or, more to the point, of the Protestant Association of 1839 as he does to
associate it with the growth of middle-class industry.

Dickens's letter to Blanchard and, with it, his early attitudes toward
industrialism and Chartism can only be understood by considering his
complex relations with three social reform movements: the Ten Hours
Movement, which Mrs. Trollope was writing to support, the agitation
against the New Poor Law, which Dickens himself wrote to support in
Oliver Twist and elsewhere, and the Anti-Corn Law League. Through the
encouragement of Ten Hours reformers Dickens made his first tours of
factories in 1838, and his initial response was entirely hostile to "the
enemy," "the factory system advocates," and entirely favorable to Lord
Ashley's drive to shorten the hours of factory children. "With that nobleman's most benevolent and excellent exertions, and with the evidence
which he was the means of bringing forward, I am well acquainted."[15]
Even before his tours Dickens was sympathetic to factory reform. In *Pickwick Papers* he mocks the Christian and commercial citizens of Muggle-
ton, who have presented to Parliament "no fewer than one thousand four
hundred and twenty petitions against the continuance of negro slavery

abroad, and an equal number against any interference with the factory system at home'' (88). But it took a journey through "miles of cinder-paths and blazing furnaces and roaring steam engines, and such a mass of dirt gloom and misery as I never before witnessed''[16] to stir Dickens deeply against the factories, and at the end of his first industrial tour he wrote to E. M. Fitzgerald: "So far as seeing goes, I have seen enough for my purpose, and what I have seen has disgusted and astonished me beyond all measure. I mean to strike the heaviest blow in my power for these unfortunate creatures, but whether I shall do so in the 'Nickleby', or wait some other opportunity, I have not yet determined.''[17]

No task could have seemed more suited to Dickens than writing about "these unfortunate creatures," the factory children; that he planned to join Mrs. Trollope, Douglas Jerrold, and other writers in an already loud chorus of Ten Hours protest is clear. There were certainly strong pressures on him to do so; as early as October 1838 a writer in *Fraser's Magazine* pointed to Dickens's subjects as proof of "his desire to do good":

> The orphan in the workhouse—the exiled child at a Yorkshire school —the poor milliner's slave,—all show the bent of his mind . . . The worst of it is, that after all our sympathy, little can we, the million who read his sketches, do to reform *these* evils. But there is a public crime more vast than either of these, and capable, from its peculiar character, of being put down, in whole or in part by legislative enactment. I mean, *the working little boys and girls to death in the factories.* There is another mischief, too, of great and increasing amount,—the demoralization of our agricultural labourers in the beer-shops of our hamlets, the seminaries of poaching, smuggling and all manner of licentiousness.
>
> In these matters, and in some others which might be named, Mr. Dickens might, without diverging into the thorny path of politics, be of incalculable service to his fellowmen.[18]

While the *Fraser's* essayist believes that factory reform does not lie in "the thorny path of politics"—a sanguine claim if there ever was one— Dickens found plenty of brambles in the roadway to slow him in his Ten Hours travels, and just as many to keep him from blaming working-class discontent on intemperance. But it is clear that his powers as a propagandist were in high demand and that he was being pressured to write for factory reform. Except for one brief, moving paragraph in *Nicholas Nickleby* (653), however, there are few signs of his concern in that novel, and he has no more to say about factory children in *The Old Curiosity Shop,* although the furnace man's story and the opinions of Miss Monflathers are swipes in that direction. But the fact is that Dickens never did "strike the heaviest blow in my power for these unfortunate creatures," for apart from the brief passages noted, there is no word about factory children in any of his novels. As late as the summer of 1841 the theme was still on his mind, although he postponed handling it until he could get the first report of Lord Ashley's Children's Employment Commission. On August 16, he wrote to Forster: "I had a letter from Napier on Saturday, urging the children's-labor subject upon me. But, as I hear from Southwood Smith that the report cannot be printed until the new Parliament has sat at the least six weeks, it will be impossible to produce it before the January number."[19] In 1838, on the basis of his trips to the North and his reading of parliamentary reports, Dickens planned to attack "the factory system" in one of his novels. In 1841, he waited for more information, and his projected article for the *Edinburgh Review* was never written, if only because his American journey intervened. Dickens did eventually write a strongly worded letter to the *Morning Chronicle* in July 1842, signed "B.," in which he attacked Lord Londonderry and other owners of mines and collieries on the basis of the information gathered by the Children's Employment Commission. But criticizing aristocratic mineowners was not at all the same as criticizing middle-class manufacturers.[20]

It is possible that Dickens's trips to the north as a Ten Hours supporter did not affect him in quite the simple, negative way his letters imply. His statement to E. M. Fitzgerald in 1838 that he had seen "the *worst* cotton mill" as well as "the *best*"[21] must be taken as doubtful, for his tours of factories probably took him inside only the model establishments run by Ten Hours advocates, like that of William and Daniel Grant, the Cheeryble Brothers of *Nicholas Nickleby*. Why would the owner of "the *worst* cotton mill" in Manchester open its doors to a Londoner armed with letters of introduction from Lord Ashley? Millowners both benevolent and otherwise had already proved extremely reluctant to admit official inspectors after the passage of Althorp's Factory Act of 1833, so the truth is probably that Dickens got past the doors of only those factories owned by friends of Lord Ashley and the factory children. *Nicholas Nickleby* shows the result of this difficulty clearly enough. As a Ten Hours advocate, Dickens inserts a paragraph contrasting the blighted lives of factory children with the happy lives of gypsy children (653), but the main result of his trips north turns out to be the Cheerybles. Dickens knew that barbarous things went on in some factories, but the few manufacturers he met were probably all paragons of bourgeois virtue who supported factory reform, and perhaps between these extremes his plan to "strike the heaviest blow" in his power for the factory children was left dangling.

Dickens's visit to America seems to have served as a watershed for his opinions about industrialism. Before 1842 he was sympathetic towards the Ten Hours Movement and at least planned to support it in his novels. After 1842 the subject of child labor in factories vanishes from his writings, and his speeches become paeans to British industry and ingenuity. If he knew little about the industrial North early in his career, his growing acquaintance with it seems to have made him more friendly towards it rather than more hostile, despite *Hard Times*. Dickens toured several factories in Lowell, Massachusetts, and wrote about them in *American Notes*. Again, these factories were probably all model establishments, but he was willing to accept them as typical. The places he toured included "a woollen factory, a carpet factory, and a cotton factory . . . I may add that I am well acquainted with our manufacturing towns in England, and have visited many mills in Manchester and elsewhere in the same manner." [22] Dickens paints a rosy picture of life among the young women who work in one factory. They are clean, well-dressed, and prosperous. There are pianos in their boarding houses, they subscribe to circulating libraries, and they produce their own journal, *The Lowell Offering*. How different this is from factory life in Manchester! Dickens insists that he has "carefully abstained from drawing a comparison between these factories and those of our own land" (69), but his abstention is only rhetorical: "The contrast would be a strong one, for it would be between the Good and Evil, the living light and deepest shadow. I abstain from it, because I deem it just to do so. But I only the more earnestly adjure all those whose eyes may rest on these pages, to pause and reflect upon the difference between this town and those great haunts of desperate misery: to call to mind, if they can in the midst of party strife and squabble, the efforts that must be made to purge them of their suffering and danger" (70). These are strong sentiments, no doubt, but they are ambiguously expressed. For one thing, Dickens does not mention child labor in England but speaks in general terms about "desperate misery"—certainly he does not object to young women working in the factories of Lowell. And although the difference between factory life in Lowell and in Manchester is as great as that between "Good and Evil," Dickens does not "deem it just" to point out that difference, giving as his sole reason that there are "many . . . circumstances whose strong influence has been at work for years in our manufacturing towns" from which Lowell is free. Evidently Dickens would like to pass a categorical judgment on the English industrial scene, but his awareness of unnamed "circumstances" makes him draw back. The strangely cautious rhetoric of the passage implies that he could not have made the comparison between English and American industry convincing anyway—not nearly as convincing as that between "Good and Evil." For it is by no means a question of the intrinsic goodness or evil of the factory system itself. If English factories are bad, it is because they are badly run, but the factory system works very well in Lowell, and it ought to work very well in Manchester.

Following his return from America, Dickens seems to have found it easier to support the Anti-Corn Law League than to support the Ten Hours Movement. In a letter to Dr. Southwood Smith early in 1843, Dickens objects to limiting the hours of workers for the rather flimsy reason that this would cause a decrease in their wages—an argument which the opponents of the Ten Hours Bill had been using for years.[23] As a reply to this argument, Smith sent Dickens a copy of the second report of the Children's Employment Commission. Dickens was so moved by the report that he thought of "writing, and bringing out, a very cheap pamphlet, called 'An Appeal to the People of England, on behalf of the Poor Man's Child'—with my name attached, of course."[24] Again, however, as in the instances of the *Edinburgh Review* article and the factory novel that did not get written, Dickens postponed his "Appeal," explaining apologetically to Smith that "reasons have presented themselves for deferring the production of that pamphlet till the end of the year. I am not at liberty to explain them further, just now; but *rest assured* that when you know them, and see what I do, and where, and how, you will certainly feel that a Sledge hammer has come down with twenty times the force—twenty thousand times the force—I could exert by following out my first idea."[25] Perhaps Dickens saw either "A Christmas Carol" or "The Chimes" as the "Sledge hammer" substitute for the pamphlet "Appeal," but one cannot avoid the feeling that he promised more than he performed. Neither story is a criticism of industrialism based on the reports of 1842-1843, even though, of course, both can be read as general blows on behalf of the poor.

While Dickens again shied away from unequivocal alignment with the Ten Hours factory reformers in 1843, the Anti-Corn Law League offered an explanation of economic distress that exonerated the manufacturers and blamed the aristocracy and the government, and Dickens and the *Daily News* adopted this formula enthusiastically. Dickens recognized the need for laws to protect factory workers from dangerous working conditions, and he came to advocate a national insurance program for the lower classes,[26] but he was also a free trader in his opposition to the tariff system and in the great importance he placed on its abolition. Further, the portrayal of class conflict in many of his novels is in essential agreement with the class attitudes of the Anti-Corn Law League. The governing class—either aristocrats like Sir Leicester Dedlock or shady millionaires like Mr. Merdle (who do not manufacture anything but merely lend money and "speculate")—misgovern the middle and working classes, which are united at least in their martyrdom. There is little difference between Daniel Doyce and his workers: Doyce is of working-class stock and is as humbly innocent as his men, and together they are victims of the Circumlocution Office and of Merdle's vague crimes. In *Little Dorrit*, therefore, Dickens is following the notions of class conflict to be found among free traders and political economists, according to which factory owners and workers—"the productive classes"—share interests against the upper class. Dickens sympathizes with all of the poor and oppressed, including people like Daniel Doyce, and outside of *Hard Times* and *Household Words* he rarely makes a firm distinction between manufacturers and workers. The story of Doyce's difficulties with patenting is like "A Poor Man's Tale of a Patent" from *Household Words*, with one instructive difference: Dickens's "poor man" is a Chartist worker, while Doyce is a middle-class master. The switch suggests that Dickens does not distinguish clearly between the two roles.

How does Dickens's treatment of Chartism in *Barnaby Rudge* fit into this pattern of free trade radicalism? Although it is complicated by the fact that Dickens originally thought of his story as an attempt to write historical fiction like Scott's (the Porteous riots in *The Heart of Midlothian* are a main literary source for *Barnaby Rudge*) and only allowed it to become topical as it grew, Dickens's novel expresses a latent desire to find some cause for working-class discontent other than the growth of the factory system and of laissez-faire liberalism. Dickens is willing to associate Chartism with Protestant fanaticism, even at the risk of violating history as Bulwer violates it; he is not willing to allow his novel to be compared to *Michael Armstrong,* and is insistent that it contains "no allusion to cotton lords, cotton slaves, or anything that is cotton." This dissociation of contemporary working-class unrest from industrialism becomes even more striking when it is remembered that Dickens means the Gordon riots in *Barnaby Rudge* to allude not only to Chartism but also to the trade union movement of the 1830s.

Participating in the riots in *Barnaby Rudge* is a group calling itself the United Bulldogs, led by Gabriel Varden's redoubtable apprentice, Simon Tappertit. The Bulldogs used to be the 'Prentice Knights, and in their meetings and doings Dickens ridicules trade unions. Tappertit "had a mighty notion of his order; and had been heard by the servant-maid openly expressing his regret that the 'prentices no longer carried clubs wherewith to mace the citizens'' (34). This is trade unionism after the model of George Barnwell, the murderous apprentice in Lillo's play of 1731, which Wopsle enacts for Pip's edification in *Great Expectations*. Fortunately for Gabriel Varden, Simon is more impotently malicious than dangerous: his part in the riots consists primarily of kidnapping Dolly Varden and Emma Haredale, which he can accomplish only with Hugh's assistance. But Dickens has a greater threat to law and order in mind than Simon: he is thinking of the same phenomenon that prompted William Gresley to write of a trade union assassination brought about by ''a conspiracy of hundreds'' and that kindled Carlyle's wrath in *Chartism:* ''Glasgow Thuggery speaks aloud . . . in a language we may well call infernal. What kind of 'wild-justice' must it be in the hearts of these men that prompts them, with cold deliberation, in conclave assembled, to doom their brother workman, as the deserter of his order and his order's cause, to die as a traitor . . . ?'' (XXIX, 148). Both Dickens and Carlyle can sympathize to some extent with Chartism, which is at least out in the open; but they have no sympathy for trade unions, which they see as characterized by conspiratorial violence.

Dickens describes Simon presiding over an initiation ceremony, sitting on a ''chair of state'' decorated with a couple of skulls and wielding a thigh-bone ''as a sceptre and staff of authority'' (63). In a windy speech to a blindfolded novice, Simon refers to the happy times when the Constitution guaranteed the rights of apprentices, whereby their order had ''had frequent holidays of right, broken people's heads by scores, defied their masters, nay, even achieved some glorious murders in the streets'' (65). Simon proceeds to swear in the novice by a secret oath ''of a dreadful and impressive kind; binding him . . . to resist and obstruct the Lord Mayor, sword-bearer, and chaplain; to despise the authority of the sheriffs; and to hold the court of aldermen as nought'' (66). Dickens based his picture of trade union ritual on various reports of trials of striking union members charged with conspiracy or with administering illegal oaths. *The Annual Register* for 1838 summarizes what was discovered about union rituals from the union trials of the 1830s and the Select Committee on Combinations of 1837-1838:

> Like all secret associations, they begin with the institution of certain mystic and superstitious rites, which . . . impose upon the imagination of their neophytes . . . The apartments in which their nocturnal conclaves assemble, are often . . . decorated with battle-axes, drawn

swords, skeletons, and other *insignia* of terror . . . The novice is introduced with his eyes bandaged—prayers and hymns are recited —and certain mystic rhymes pronounced; after which an oath is administered, of which the imprecatory form, may be easily conceived, and the new member, his eyes being again bandaged, is led out.[27]

Dickens reproduces this description of union ritual in such detail that his allusion is unmistakable. So also is his attitude unmistakable: he is completely hostile to trade unionism, at least insofar as he understands it through the reports of trials and sensational crimes during strikes that filled the middle-class press in the 1830s.

The most famous of the union trials in the 1830s is that of the Dorchester Tolpuddle Martyrs in 1834, but another occurred in 1838 in Glasgow when, after the murder of a strikebreaker, five members of the Glasgow cotton spinners' union were tried for conspiracy.[28] The original crime, never solved, is perhaps reflected in Simon's bluster about "glorious murders in the streets," as it is also in Carlyle's diatribe against "Glasgow Thuggery." The problem of union oath-taking (and, with it, union solidarity) was crucial in both the Dorchester and Glasgow cases: it was above all this practice which, in the eyes of the law, made unions conspiratorial. Trade union oaths were said to bind members to do anything —to commit any crime, no matter how terrific—for the sake of the union. According to Sir Archibald Alison, a chief witness in the Glasgow affair, trade union oaths affected the minds of union members "even more than the terror of vitriol or of pistol-balls."[29] His mistaken loyalty to a trade union oath helps to turn John Barton into a murderer in Mrs. Gaskell's otherwise humane novel, *Mary Barton,* and trade union oaths figure prominently also in *Sybil.* The drawing of lots at which John Barton is chosen to assassinate Mr. Carson is opened by "one of those fierce terrible oaths which bind members of Trades' Unions to any given purpose."[30]

Dickens's condemnation of trade unionism is understandable in view of the hostility towards it in the middle-class press. But it is strange that he should attack it in a context that so completely divorces unionism from its roots in industrialism. True, the 'Prentice Knights figure in a historical novel about the 1780s, and there is therefore no particular reason why they should be shown in relation to the social conditions of the 1830s. But then there is also no reason why Dickens should have transplanted the unionism of the 1830s to the 1780s. The fact that he does so without sensing a violation of logic suggests some sort of blindness to the causes of unionism, and the further fact that the reflection of "Glasgow Thuggery'' in the 'Prentice Knights is one of the most detailed topical allusions in *Barnaby Rudge* suggests the importance of that blindness for an understanding of Dickens's social attitudes.

Simon Tappertit is the nastiest if not the most dangerous working-class character in *Barnaby Rudge*. He is vain and spiteful, two qualities which are intended to suggest that his wants are unreasonable. He is an almost allegorical figure for the overweening desire of working-class radicals and trade unionists for social equality. Gabriel Varden, after all, is a good master, so why should Simon chafe at the bit? In *Barnaby Rudge* Dickens rather than an early version of Bounderby condemns bad workers like Simon (and, with him, all trade unionists) for wanting to be fed turtle soup and venison with gold spoons. Although Dickens's treatment of trade unionism in *Hard Times* is also negative, he is at least willing to grant the justice of union economic demands while condemning union tactics, and the association of unionism with conspiratorial violence has dropped away. In the later novel, Dickens still falls into the pattern of blaming unionism on ''outside agitators,'' represented by Slackbridge, but the workers have real grievances against Bounderby, whereas Simon has only selfish and made-up grievances against Gabriel Varden.

The relationship between Tappertit and Varden involves a kind of wishful thinking that recurs often in Dickens's novels, in other portrayals of employers and workers. The Cheeryble Brothers and Tim Linkinwater, Scrooge and Cratchit, and Daniel Doyce and his workers are all expressions of the free trade radical theory of the natural identity of interests between the middle class and the working class.[31] At the same time, these patterns of personalized work also express Dickens's critical rejection of the dehumanizing tendencies of large-scale industries, joint-stock companies, and ''cash-nexus'' as the main link between employers and workers. In *Hard Times,* the clearest grievance of the unionists involves their reification into ''Hands.'' Little conscious social analysis and much wishful thinking underlies figures like the Cheerybles and Daniel Doyce, and they are vaguely nostalgic, no matter in what time period Dickens places them. The ideal economy is made up of independent master craftsmen or merchants and their apprentices, virtually parts of their families, as Tappertit is part of the Varden household. In *Barnaby Rudge,* where the eighteenth-century setting turns this nostalgic ideal of personalized work into an apparent reality, rebellious trade unionism is totally unjustifiable. When the conflict between labor and capital is reduced to personal or even family relations between fatherly master and apprentice son, what possible cause for complaint can there be, so long as the father is honest and generous? Simon is a monster of ingratitude, and the only surprising thing about his case is that Dickens allows him to mend his ways at the end of the novel. The other members of the 'Prentice Knights "were to a man all killed, imprisoned, or transported" (630). True, Simon loses his legs in the rioting (he has been particularly proud of them, so Dickens amputates them by way of moral surgery), but with the generous help of Varden, he sets up as a shoe-black and is soon an independent business-man himself, employing two apprentices!

As in his treatment of the 'Prentice Knights, in portraying the riots themselves Dickens tries to locate the causes of social unrest somewhere other than in economic conflict between the working class and the middle class. Dickens does not deliberately set out to explain Chartism on some other basis than class conflict, but the analogy he draws between the Gordon riots and Chartism seems to involve a latent wish to divorce Chartism and unionism from the factory system and to preserve intact the idea of the identity of interests between the middle and working classes. Nor is Dickens divorcing Chartism and unionism from industrialism merely by distancing them in time—natural enough in a historical novel that is also topical—although that is partly the case. But the religious character of the Gordon riots makes them particularly irrational to Dickens. Poverty may be a reasonable motive for insurrection, but zealotry is ridiculous. And this irrationality rubs off by implication on Chartism: viewed in the dark glass of *Barnaby Rudge,* it takes on the appearance of a tumult in a void. Further, the rioters themselves are not responsible for their actions, but are manipulated from above by Gashford and Sir John Chester and are also encouraged by the laxness of the Lord Mayor and of Parliament. "The great mass never reasoned or thought at all, but were stimulated by their own headlong passions, by poverty, by ignorance, by the love of mischief, and the hope of plunder" (402). Dickens wanted to have his rioters led by three Bedlamites, but Forster talked him out of this idea. So the rioters are led instead by Barnaby the idiot, by the illegitimate "cen-taur" Hugh, and by Dennis the hangman, who are themselves the pup-pets of Gashford and Chester.

The machinations of Gashford and Chester, moreover, connect the riots with a dark web of personal crime and vengeance, starting long ago with the murder committed by Barnaby's father. Even without the scenes of the rioters breaking into Newgate and Fleet Prison, *Barnaby Rudge* would qualify as Dickens's second Newgate novel. Dickens continues to render class conflict in terms of the pattern of crime and punishment established in *Oliver Twist.* He is not primarily interested in the religious fanaticism behind the riots, and he is not much more interested in the political and economic issues behind Chartism and trade unionism.

Neither "Popery" nor "property" are fully open to analysis for him. Repeatedly his novels indicate that the crimes of the poor are the result of the crimes of the rich. They are crimes nonetheless, rather than politics; as in *Great Expectations,* mankind is bound together by chains of silver and gold, a symbol suggesting bondage to the economic status quo in more senses than one.

When Dickens turns his attention away from "Popery" to the question of "property" (or, rather, poverty), the answers he gives are the familiar ones of benevolence and legal reform. Gabriel Varden, honest tradesman, is the main embodiment of benevolence in the novel: so far from being a cause of working-class discontent, his generosity ought to spell the end of it, and it would if it were not for the absurd vanity of Simon and for the evil machinations of a corrupt governing class. True, Gabriel is a locksmith, and he manfully refuses to pick the lock of Newgate for the mob; but if he represents law and order, he is also a cheerful locksmith, in whose shop "the very locks that hung around had something jovial in their rust . . . It seemed impossible that any one of the innumerable keys could fit a churlish strong-box or a prison-door" (307). The question of why locks are necessary if middle-class benevolence works apparently does not occur to Dickens, although he is never far from asking it. But Gabriel Varden is only one man, a virtuous individual "standing midway in the gulf" between insane mob and corrupt aristocracy, and even though he refuses to pick the lock of Newgate, the rioters break into it anyway. What can one man do, no matter how virtuous, against a host of working-class maniacs and upper-class Machiavels? Dickens, however, does not look only to the example of Gabriel Varden's benevolence for the cure of working-class discontent. He looks also to a reform of the criminal code and the prisons, after the manner of the greatest of middleclass, benevolent locksmiths, Jeremy Bentham. The mob, says Dickens, was "sprinkled doubtless here and there with honest zealots, but composed for the most part of the very scum and refuse of London, whose growth was fostered by bad criminal laws, bad prison regulations, and the worst conceivable police" (374).

While Dickens finds in history causes for working-class discontent that deflect blame from the middle class and allow him to continue to believe in the identity of interests of labor and capital, Benjamin Disraeli rewrites the Whig version of history in order to place the blame for Chartism and trade unionism squarely upon the middle class, or at least upon middleclass liberalism. "Young Hengland," as Thackeray's C. Jeames De La Pluche called it, was an attempt to bring people and aristocracy together under a single "Tory-radical" banner, and thus to outflank the Whigs and the "pseudo-Tories," or Peelites. In *Sybil* Disraeli goes farthest in his attempt to weld Toryism and radicalism together; there he focuses on "the condition of the people" and recommends a political union of the working class and the aristocracy against the middle class. He symbolizes this union by the standard strategy of an interclass marriage, joining his aristocratic hero, Egremont, with his working-class heroine, Sybil Gerard. As some of Disraeli's first readers noted, however, this symbolic union of "the two nations" of rich and poor turns into tommyrot when it is learned that Sybil is not a working-class girl at all but an aristocrat.[32] An equivalent turn of the screw, one imagines, might be changing Blake's tiger into Mehitabel. But if Disraeli is contradictory, he is not stupid, and Sybil's transmogrification from a Chartist working-class girl into a fine lady cannot be in total violation of reason.

Sybil's metamorphosis is matched by a series of historical digressions that reveal Egremont's family to be less aristocratic than it claims. The antiquarian revelations proving Sybil to be of noble ancestry are paralleled by Disraeli's accounts of the modern, felonious origins of the great Whig families. Of Egremont's family, Disraeli tells us that "the founder . . . had been a confidential domestic of one of the favourites of Henry VIII., and had contrived to be appointed one of the commissioners for 'visiting and taking the surrenders of divers religious houses.' "[33] Upon the basis of property pirated from the Church, "honest Baldwin Greymount" boosted his descendants into the peerage. Such are the histories, Disraeli tells us, of most of the "ancient" families who make up the "Venetian oligarchy" of the Whigs and the "pseudo-Tories." And such, too, is one basis for the Tory-radical version of history running throughout Disraeli's novels and speeches, for the Church was the first victim of "the spirit of utility," and upon her former property modern liberalism sprang up, wresting power from the Stuarts along the way. By the same process of spoliation and fraud, the poor were losing their rights. Sybil claims that "the people" have been "driven from the soil" (95), and Philip Warner, the handloom weaver, that he and the rest of the poor "have lost our estates" (134). Although it seems to get Disraeli out of a jam, Sybil's metamorphosis also symbolizes the restoration of the rights and estates of the poor, many of whom are more truly aristocratic than the modern nobility. Not only is the family tree of Egremont and Lord Marney of dubious and recent origin, but so are those of Lord de Mowbray (88-93), the Duke of Fitz-Aquitaine (146-147), and Lord Deloraine (239-240). On the other hand, as Millbank says in *Coningsby,* "The real old families of this country are to be found among the peasantry; the gentry, too, may lay some claim to old blood. I can point you out Saxon families in this country who can trace their pedigrees beyond the Conquest" (169). Walter Gerard, Mr. Trafford, Aubrey St. Lys, and even Sybil's blood-hound, Harold, are "of the ancient breed" (139). Through the shoddy machinations of Baptist Hatton, the powerful quack antiquarian who "has made more peers of the realm than our gracious Sovereign" (273) and who elevates Sybil to a station of doubtful value, Disraeli ridicules the whole concept of the hereditary nobility. "There is no longer in fact an aristocracy in England, for the superiority of the animal man is an essential quality of aristocracy" (123). To think in terms of class at all, an apparently radical Disraeli implies, is nowadays absurd, for blue blood has become thin blood. A person ought to be judged by his talents and not by his birth—look at Disraeli as an example.

The trouble is that having satirized the hereditary basis of the class structure, Disraeli still insists on giving Sybil aristocratic status. Further-more, while he is ridiculing the modern aristocracy out of one side of his mouth, out of the other issues nothing like the sort of sympathy for the poor that we expect from someone who claims to champion them. On the contrary, while Disraeli satirizes the Whigs and the pseudo-Tories, he also satirizes the radicals, the Chartists, and, perhaps unintentionally, the poor as a "nation."

Parallel to the history of upper-class politics since 1832 that forms the subject of the whole Young England trilogy, *Sybil* contains a history of Chartism from its beginnings in 1838 through the Plug Plot riots in the summer of 1842. When the first Chartist petition was presented to the House of Commons in 1839, Disraeli made a speech which, while argu-ing against its official consideration, argued for a sympathetic rejection of it.[34] It is typical of the wily ambiguities that appear in *Sybil,* where this speech is echoed, when the heroine discovers one day that the Charter has been defended in Parliament by an aristocrat: "Yes! there was one voice that had sounded in that proud Parliament, that, free from the slang of faction, had dared to express immortal truths: the voice of a noble, who without being a demagogue, had upheld the popular cause . . . With . . . eyes suffused with tears, Sybil read the speech of Egremont. She ceased . . . Before her stood the orator himself" (337). Besides this noteworthy piece of egotism, Disraeli's history of Chartism in *Sybil* shows its decline from the early, glowing idealism of Walter Gerard and his daughter through the failure of the first petition, the encroachments of factional strife, and the fiascoes of "physical force"—the riots in the Birmingham Bullring, the Newport Rising of 1839, and the Plug Plot violence of 1842. As Sybil sadly tells Stephen Morley, "I believed that we had on our side

God and Truth." " 'They know neither of them in the National Convention,' said Morley. 'Our career will be a vulgar caricature of the bad passions and the low intrigues, the factions and the failures, of our oppressors' '' (289-290). Walter Gerard's "moral force" idealism succumbs to the influence of "the party of violence," and this is seen as the tragedy of Chartism as a whole. Gerard takes part in a conspiracy aiming at a national insurrection, but this leads only to the abortive Newport Rising of 1839 and to his arrest along with numerous other leaders of the movement. By revealing the bankruptcy of both Chartism and Whiggery, of both the radical and the liberal political alternatives, Disraeli tries to demonstrate the need for a third alternative—the Tory-radicalism of Young England.

But while Disraeli's presentation of Chartism is unsympathetic, his presentation of the nation of the poor generally is so riddled with irony that it is difficult to think of him as even approximately their champion. The failure of logic that leads to Sybil's transformation reveals itself again in the fact that there are two distinct kinds of poor people in the novel— the good ones (who are aristocrats anyway in the case of the Gerards), and the riffraff. Thus, while Gerard and his daughter both seem noble and are noble, the mobs of miners and mechanics who fill the background of the tale are hardly idealized. Like Oliver Twist in the clutches of Sikes and Fagin, the angelic Sybil is constantly forced to rub elbows with working-class villains. At least as important symbolically as the union of Egremont and Sybil is the fact that Egremont snatches Sybil from the grasp of a working-class mob during the Plug Plot riots:

> One ruffian had grasped the arm of Sybil, another had clenched her garments, when an officer, covered with dust and gore, sabre in hand, jumped from the terrace, and hurried to the rescue. He cut down one man, thrust away another, and, placing his left arm round Sybil, he defended her with his sword . . . Her assailants were routed, they made a staggering flight! The officer turned round and pressed Sybil to his heart.
> "We will never part again," said Egremont.
> "Never," murmured Sybil. (484)

Scenes like this led Arnold Kettle to describe *Sybil* as "operatic"; he might have added that Disraeli, and not Sybil, is the prima donna.[35] At any rate, if Sybil begins life as a "daughter of the people" who turns out to be blue blooded, she is also brought into rough contact with "the people" at several points in the novel. Her terrifying venture into Seven Dials in search of her father presents us with a contrast between her unconscious gentility and the violence of the slum dwellers (362-366), and the nightmare that she has after her arrest continues the pattern: "She woke . . . in terror from a dream in which she had been dragged through a mob, and carried before a tribunal. The coarse jeers, the brutal threats, still echoed in her ears" (382-383). Before uniting Egremont and Sybil, Disraeli weans her from her "moral force" Chartism by showing her just how degraded, ignorant, and violent "the people" can be, giving her doses of revolutionary chaos and of the lower depths in order to teach her that the tenants in the social cellar need governors, and not that they need to govern themselves.

Disraeli is not much interested in making us feel sorry for the poor; he is much more intent on proving the poor to be mistaken. Thus, the two chief factory workers in *Sybil,* Dandy Mick and Devilsdust, are shown to be adolescent malcontents with only the negligence of their superiors as a real motive for rebellion. They are well-paid enough to entertain two girl friends with drinks and hot sausages in that swank gin palace, "The Cat and the Fiddle." Further, in sketching in their backgrounds, Disraeli avoids evidence that would support Lord Ashley's Ten Hours Bill, even though he voted for it in 1847. The story of Devilsdust's childhood does not present us with arguments for saving children from the horrors of the mill by passing the Ten Hours Bill, and in fact it weighs against that bill. Abandoned by his mother and cared for only by a brutal "nurse" who sends him "out in the street to 'play,' in order to be run over," partly by miracle and partly by tenacity Devilsdust survives. Neglect is what almost kills him, and opposed to neglect is the order and security of the factory system. His salvation comes when good luck guides him, still only an infant, through the gates of a factory and into a job. "A child was wanting in the Wadding Hole . . . The nameless one was preferred to the vacant post, received even a salary, more than that, a name; for as he had none, he was christened on the spot DEVILSDUST" (114). "Fortune had guided him." Disraeli suggests that the factories afford protection to children who would otherwise be neglected and abused by their working-class parents, an idea often expressed by the defenders of child labor.[36]

The most startling scene among the poor occurs when the Owenite, Stephen Morley, travels to Wodgate in search of the antiquarian, Mr. Hatton. There he discovers Hatton's brother, who is the "Bishop" or head man of a town which, though a slough of filth and degradation, is an entirely independent community run by the workers themselves—proletarian blacksmiths and their apprentices.[37] The inhabitants of Wodgate are the most brutalized and violent characters whom Disraeli describes. Morley learns about the Bishop from an apprentice, Thomas, and at the same time he learns how illiterate and deprived some of the citizens of England are, for Thomas's fiancée believes in "our Lord and Saviour Pontius Pilate, who was crucified to save our sins" (192-193). Backward as the Wodgate metal workers are, they are also, Disraeli stresses, free, for they are under the control neither of a laissez-faire government nor of upper-class capitalists, but of masters like the Bishop who belong to their own class. They form a natural society, and they present Morley with two possible lessons, although he comes away from Wodgate as staunchly socialistic as ever. In the first place, Morley might learn that the workers, if left to govern themselves, would increase rather than diminish their degradation. Disraeli exposes the neglect from which the poor suffer, but he also exposes their unfitness to manage their own affairs. And in the second place, Morley might learn that, if left alone, the workers would form a government along aristocratic rather than democratic lines, for Wodgate is ruled by an aristocracy that "is by no means so unpopular as the aristocracy of most other places. In the first place, it is a real aristocracy; it is privileged, but it does something for its privileges. It is distinguished from the main body not merely by name. It is the most knowing class at Wodgate; it possesses indeed in its way complete knowledge; and it imparts in its manner a certain quantity of it to those whom it guides. Thus it is an aristocracy that leads, and therefore a fact" (188). Between the misrule of Bishop Hatton and the misrule of Lord Marney, Disraeli sees a damnable similarity. Between either of these and an aristocracy as it ought to be—as Young England would make it or even as the "Captains of Industry" should make it—there is no similarity.

In the Wodgate episode, Disraeli's satire is both consistent and to the point. His aim all along has been to show the bankruptcy of all potential sources of government save one—a revitalized aristocracy led by Young England. By exposing the absurdity of Bishop Hatton's rule, he simultaneously exposes the neglect of the Church and the post-1832 governments of Grey, Melbourne, and Peel. Chartism and trade unionism are also failures, but their very existence is symptomatic of the bungling of the Whigs and the pseudo-Tories. Having pointed out the inadequacy of all current political programs, Disraeli implies that a group of idealistic young social saviors are waiting in the wings, led by an inscrutable, oriental prophet named Disraeli. The program of this saving remnant, however, remains cloudy, for instead of containing a pattern of genuine paradoxes leading to Tory-radicalism as a climactic oxymoron, *Sybil* contains only a skein of contradictions, growing out of its conflicting plots of the educations of hero and heroine.

Sybil describes the disillusionment of its Chartist characters at the same time that it describes the introduction of Egremont to "the condition of England question." Even more than the discovery of Sybil's aristocratic lineage, this double plot stirs up contradictions and causes consternation in its readers. As Egremont is acquiring some sympathy for the poor, Sybil is losing part of hers, and the Tory-radical compromise that should emerge between them does not materialize. Contradiction arises where there should be compromise; the most glaring instance of this is what happens to the central theme of the novel. This theme is that Queen Victoria rules over "two nations," "the rich and the poor." As Monypenny says, Disraeli's main purpose is to show the difference "between riches and poverty, luxury and suffering."[38] As a description of *Sybil,* this is perfectly reasonable as far as it goes, but it does not go far enough, for Disraeli's other main purpose is to show that the difference "between riches and poverty, luxury and suffering" is blown out of all proportion by Chartists and radicals. The idea that the Queen rules over two distinct nations with a great gulf fixed between them is one of Disraeli's arguments, but it is also an erroneous belief of Sybil's that is stripped away from her during the process of her disillusionment. Significantly, the idea of the two nations is first presented to Egremont and the reader, in the most famous "operatic" set-piece of the novel (76-77), by Stephen Morley, for Morley is a godless Owenite who later tries to murder Egremont out of jealousy (shades of the steam guillotine in *Charles Lever*). Disraeli treats the two nations theme as a paradox that he hopes will startle his readers into some awareness of the problems of the poor, but he also treats it as a dangerous illusion and a cliché of radicals like Morley.

The idea of the two nations comes as a revelation to Egremont; it is the beginning of his acceptance of social responsibility as an aristocrat. On the other hand, the idea of the two nations is an illusion from which Sybil must be won before she can find Egremont acceptable as a suitor. When Egremont undergoes his pastoral education in the humble abode of the Gerards, he does not reveal his social rank but adopts the democratic alias, Mr. Franklin. He quickly discovers that disguise is necessary, for so thoroughly is Sybil a "daughter of the people" and a Chartist that, when she discovers who he is, she spurns him:

> "The brother of Lord Marney!" repeated Sybil, with an air almost of stupor.
> "Yes," said Egremont; "a member of that family of sacrilege, of those oppressors of the people, whom you have denounced to me with such withering scorn." (284)

When Egremont pleads with Sybil not to cast him off because he is an aristocrat, she says, "haughtily": "I am one of those who believe the gulf is impassable. Yes . . . utterly impassable."

Disraeli's prince cleans the hearth while Cinderella snubs him. It is a situation similar to one in *Coningsby,* wherein that young aristocrat falls in love with the daughter of the rich manufacturer Millbank, whose dislike for the "factitious" nobility makes marriage unthinkable. But just as Millbank eventually abandons his class prejudice, so Sybil learns that the gulf between rich and poor is not "impassable." Disraeli's irony is clever, but it is also superficial, because it has never made sense to tell the oppressed (in this case, Chartist workers) that they should be more tolerant and less tyrannical towards their oppressors. That, however, is the lesson that Disraeli teaches Sybil, while he is also making Egremont aware of the existence of the poor.

Sybil has led a sheltered and privileged life, and nothing has taught her to abandon the illusion of the impassable gulf between the two nations until she encounters two very different forces—handsome Egremont and working-class violence. "Educated in solitude and exchanging thoughts only with individuals of the same sympathies," Sybil has reached the view "that the world was divided only between the oppressors and the oppressed."

> With her, to be one of the people was to be miserable and innocent; one of the privileged, a luxurious tyrant. In the cloister, in her garden . . . she had raised up two phantoms which with her represented human nature.
>
> But the experience of the last few months had operated a great change in these impressions. She had seen enough to suspect that the world was a more complicated system than she had preconceived . . . The characters were more various, the motives more mixed, the classes more blended, the elements of each more subtle and diversified, than she had imagined. (335)

The two nations, then, are no more than "two phantoms" of Sybil's imagination that do not describe society realistically, and Egremont is right when he taxes her with being "prejudiced" (318).

Disraeli's contradictory attitude toward his two nations theme affects the structure of his novel in at least two ways. First, it keeps him from offering a straightforward contrast between rich and poor and leads him instead into a series of ambiguous contrasts between a multiplicity of classes, in which factory workers and miners and farm laborers are juxtaposed, while manufacturers disagree with landlords and Chartists disagree with each other. And second, it causes him to make odd, ambiguous assertions about each of the social groups he describes, like Millbank's claim that many of the poor have noble blood in their veins. Working more from bluebooks than from personal knowledge, Disraeli describes conditions among miners, farm workers, cotton operatives, handloom weavers, metal workers, and the Irish poor of London, and he shows with some sympathy and much colorful detail the roots of social rebellion in those conditions. But in the process he demonstrates that the poor are not at all a unified nation confronting the rich. The poor are rather a congeries of quarreling factions, and the same is true of the rich, who split up into at least two major groups, landlords and manufacturers. And while there may be various classes in a society that is nevertheless divided between the haves and the have-nots, Disraeli points to the diversity of the class system as a refutation of the two nations theory held by his Chartist characters.

Disraeli's social panorama is remarkable for its range and its vividness; he often makes the dead bones of the bluebooks come to life. But it is marred by spurious paradoxes and flashy riddles, and perhaps it must finally be regarded as only a colorful "muddle," to use Stephen Blackpool's word. Walter Bagehot said of Disraeli that "nothing has really impeded his progress more than his efforts after originality," and this is exactly the trouble with *Sybil*.[39] Disraeli is so in love with irony that he allows it to undermine even the central thesis of *Sybil*. His irony is so pervasive that he mocks his own Young England comrades, as when Lord Everingham laughs at Lord Henry Sidney in *Coningsby* for his notion that "the people are to be fed by dancing round a May-pole." Disraeli offers the standard Burkean arguments about custom and faith as opposed to theory and reason, and about society as an organism, and this helps to give his rhetoric a prophetic ring. But his portrait of social England reveals so many complexities and shatters so many clichés—not least of which is the two nations idea—that finally the only logical program appears to be the one described by the heroine: " 'It sometimes seems to me,' said Sybil despondingly, 'that nothing short of the descent of angels can save the people of this kingdom' " (199). When Disraeli beat Peel on the corn law issue and irreparably broke the old Tory party, one wonders how many astonished and grateful Saxons realized that the first of the angels had arrived among them.

For both Dickens and Disraeli, the main problem posed by Chartism and trade unionism is that of class conflict, disrupting whatever short-

The Secret Society of 'Prentice Knights

From Dickens, *Barnaby Rudge.*

lived hopes of unity and progress the settlement of 1832 inspired. In the wishful fictional structures that Dickens creates, at least in his early novels, the conflict between the working and middle classes is understated or resolved in various ways, while the conflict between both of these and the aristocracy or the governing class is emphasized, after the manner of the Anti-Corn Law League. Dickens displaces working-class hostility toward industry and toward middle-class employers onto the aristocracy and makes working-class movements out to be misguided, understandable but also irrational. Between good workers and good masters there can be no quarrel; civil disorders originate both further down and further up the social scale, in "the very scum and refuse of London" on the one hand, and in the corrupt, misgoverning aristocracy on the other. Disraeli is intent on reversing the middle-class radical pattern of Dickens's novels, and for this reason he is much clearer about the industrial roots of Chartism and trade unionism than is Dickens. Even in *Hard Times,* Dickens does not recognize class conflict between workers and middle-class masters as inevitable, although he does present it there as a major kind of social unrest. The harmony between Daniel Doyce and his workers, whether real or ideal, is the primary pattern for industrial relations even in Dickens's later novels, and it is perfectly natural and easily practiced. Not recognizing this natural identity of interests, Bounderby unwittingly encourages discontent and strikes. Dickens's criticism of industrialism in *Hard Times,* therefore, does not go much beyond the fact that millowners too often fall short of their moral and legal obligations. "Surely there never was such fragile china-ware as that of which the millers of Coketown were made . . . They were ruined, when they were required to send labouring children to school; they were ruined when inspectors were appointed to look into their works; they were ruined, when such inspectors considered it doubtful whether they were quite justified in chopping people up with their machinery; they were utterly undone, when it was hinted that perhaps they need not always make quite so much smoke" (110). Dickens's satire, here and throughout *Hard Times,* does not suggest (as some of the early Ten Hours zealots did suggest) the destruction of the factories, the establishment of any new economic system, nor even the passage of more factory laws. It only suggests that the factory owners should scrap their plea of laissez-faire and abide by existing laws—laws prescribing the education of factory children, the appointment of inspectors "to look into their works," the fencing of dangerous machinery to avoid "chopping people up," and smoke abatement. Dickens's criticism of industrialism in *Hard Times* is generally specific rather than abstractly ideological, unless one is willing to interpret "the Sleary philosophy" and Stephen Blackpool's martyrdom as expressions of a theoretical stance. When Stephen falls down Old Hell Shaft, one of the lessons has to do with the negligence of mine owners who do not close up abandoned pits.

The story of the trade union in *Hard Times,* moreover, does not illustrate the justice of working-class demands for better wages, shorter hours, more benefits. Dickens offers only generalized descriptions of working conditions within the factories, and he does not describe a strike. He does not even describe, at least in much detail, working-class poverty. Bounderby's narrow-minded selfishness is deplorable, but so is trade unionism, although it is a natural response to Bounderby's bullying lack of sympathy for his workers. As George Orwell says, Dickens believes "that capitalists ought to be kind, not that workers ought to be rebellious."[40] The war between capital and labor is simply an unfortunate mistake, to be corrected by better feelings on both sides.

All the same, even after these reservations have been noted, Dickens's sentimental radicalism obviously places him in closer touch with "the people" and even with working-class radicalism than Disraeli's Tory-radicalism. If his vision blurs in proximity to Chartism and trade union-ism, that is because it is a real proximity, and even the blurring seems to lead him to create powerful symbols for his desire for social justice. Such a process is evident in *Oliver Twist,* for example, where his personal close-ness to and fear of poverty are transmuted not into logical analysis but into the nightmare of the thieves' world. Gissing noted that Dickens's work-ing-class characters rarely entertain political opinions or social theories—they know themselves to be in "a muddle," and that is all—but the same is true of his virtuous middle-class characters as well, and it is true also of Dickens, whose most consistent social theory has to do with the limita-tions of social theories.[41] And it is a simple fact—perhaps his greatest strength as a novelist—that "at no time in his career did he forget the na-ture of human participation in industry."[42]

In contrast, despite the intellectual acuteness and accuracy of much of his social observation in *Coningsby* and *Sybil,* Disraeli is unconvincing. In light of his later political achievements, including the real "dishing of the Whigs" in 1867, the assessment of Marx and Engels looks premature, but it is still understandable. The "feudal socialism" of Young England, they write, is "half lamentation, half lampoon," not to be taken seri-ously as a political theory.[43] It is clear at least that Young England was more purely wishful—less realistic—than Dickens's middle-class radical-ism, despite Disraeli's brilliant paradoxicality. C. Jeames De La Pluche cites "a bewtifle poim" by "the Lord Southdown" which laments the passing of chivalry and the advent of the factory system, facts that no amount of Tory and Tractarian resistance could cancel out:

Our ancient castles echo to the clumsy feet of churls,
The spinning Jenny houses in the mansion of our Earls.

COBDEN, THE FREE TRADE PROSPERO.

A SCENE FROM "THE TEMPEST." ADAPTED TO 1846.

I here abjure :

"But this rough magic
* * * *
I'll break my staff,

Bury it certain fathoms in the earth,
And, deeper than did ever plummet sound,
I'll drown my————newspaper."

[*Solemn music.*

As Cobden abjures the rough magic of the Anti-Corn Law League, Ariel (Sir Robert Peel) punishes Caliban (Disraeli). From *Punch*.

V. The Entrepreneurial Ideal

Wherefore all the grain
From friendly islands they, with scorn, sent back.
A famine soon in Ithaca spread wide,
And hungry people prowled about at night,
Then clamoured, and took arms—their war-cry, "Bread!"
Thus was the dormant evil of their hearts
Attested, and the King his people knew,
And bitterly their want of reverence felt.

R. H. Horne, *Orion*

"The trade of Anti-Corn-Law Lecturer in these days, still an indispensable, is a highly tragic one" (X, 181). So writes Carlyle in *Past and Present,* four years before the repeal of the corn laws in 1846. And although Carlyle is not himself an Anti-Corn Law lecturer, he is the next best thing to one because, in *Chartism* and *Past and Present,* repeal of the corn laws, along with emigration and education, is one of the few practical, legislatible measures he recommends. He is not averse to employing the sort of apocalyptic rhetoric on behalf of free trade that is characteristic of League propaganda; thus, the corn laws have their French Revolutionary parallel: "Good God! did not a French Donothing Aristocracy . . . declare in like manner . . . 'We cannot exist, and continue to dress and parade ourselves, on the just rent of the soil of France; but we must have farther payment . . . we must be exempted from taxes too,'—we must have a Corn-Law to extend our rent? This was in 1789: in four years more—Did you look into the Tanneries of Meudon, and the long-naked making for themselves breeches of human skins!" (X, 178-179). Despite the religious and romantic caste of his thought that leads him to attack Mammonism and "devil take the hindmost" free enterprise as well as parliamentary democracy, many of Carlyle's values fall squarely within what Harold Perkin has called "the entrepreneurial ideal." This is especially apparent in Carlyle's elaboration of the "Gospel of Work," which amounts to a belief in self-help on the individual level and in progress through middle-class industry on the social level. In a time of mass unemployment, a central image for Carlyle is "our poor Workhouse Workmen" sitting enchanted in "Poor-Law Bastilles," and his emphasis on finding real work for people to do is both practical and natural. But it is not just the unemployed workman who figures prominently in *Chartism* and *Past and Present;* it is middle-class industry itself,

held in bondage both by its own Mammonism and—more correctibly—
by the corn laws. "Labour is ever an imprisoned god" (X, 207).

Carlyle's most emphatic message throughout *Chartism* and *Past and
Present* is thus close to that of the Anti-Corn-Law lecturer: only rid labor
of the trammels of antiquated and selfish legislation, and the future prosperity of the nation will be assured. Work is the one unfailing source of
reform (perhaps the only source, since legislation is so untrustworthy); it
is the cure for whatever ails both individuals and nations:

> It has been written, 'an endless significance lies in Work'; a man
> perfects himself by working. Foul jungles are cleared away, fair seed-
> fields rise instead, and stately cities; and withal the man himself first
> ceases to be a jungle and foul unwholesome desert thereby. Consider
> how, even in the meanest sorts of Labour, the whole soul of a man is
> composed into a kind of real harmony, the instant he sets himself to
> work! Doubt, Desire, Sorrow, Remorse, Indignation, Despair itself,
> all these like helldogs lie beleaguering the soul of the poor day-
> worker, as of every man: but he bends himself with free valour
> against his task, and all these are stilled, all these shrink murmuring
> far off into their caves. The man is now a man. The blessed glow of
> Labour in him, is it not as purifying fire, wherein all poison is burnt
> up, and of sour smoke itself there is made bright blessed flame! (X,
> 196)

Labor is the way we are to fulfill Carlyle's injunction to reform ourselves.
It is also the surest way for nations to reform themselves—not through
ten-pound franchises and Morrison's Pills, but through free industry,
under the guidance of free "Captains of Industry." True, Carlyle agrees
that legislative "remedial measures" should be taken—sanitary reform,
factory reform, education bills, emigration bills—but the most important
measure of all, to which he returns again and again, is abolition of the
corn laws, which will set labor free.

In *Past and Present,* which has sometimes been read as a straightforward condemnation of middle-class liberalism and which is indeed a central document in the medievalist reaction against industrial and democratic change, many of the elements of liberalism are affirmed. The main
reservation is Carlyle's refusal to think of democracy as a viable form of
government. But his rejection of democracy also means that, if anything,
he has only slightly less distrust of legislative measures than Anti-Corn
Law lecturers. And his main variance from economic liberalism is his call
for true "Captains of Industry" to arise who will establish industrial relations on a better foundation than "cash-nexus" Mammonism. This vari-

ance is another version of Dickens's ideal of personalized work, which is in turn related to the liberal theory that the interests of the working and middle classes are (or ought to be—a crucial ambiguity) identical. Carlyle wants the captains of industry to cease being "Buccaneers" and "Chactaw Indians" and to establish an industrial chivalry based on social interest rather than self-interest. He wants employers to be "noble Workers," and to provide their employees with some of the communal—and necessarily heirarchic—protection that he sees in feudalism. But this is a message which, like abolition of the corn laws, almost everyone could agree with, except for a few selfish industrialists: Scrooge ought not to treat Cratchit so badly—Scrooge ought to be generous and to look after the welfare of the Tiny Tims of the world. Carlyle, of course, puts the matter in less sentimental terms; his version of economic welfare partakes less of the Christmas spirit than of the bellicose spirit of leading the industrial armies into battle against the forces of chaos. "Look around you," he says to his captains of industry: "Your world-hosts are all in mutiny, in confusion, destitution; on the eve of fiery wreck and madness! They will not march farther for you, on the sixpence a day and supply-and-demand principle . . . Ye shall reduce them to order . . . to just subordination; noble loyalty in return for noble guidance . . . Not as a bewildered bewildering mob; but as a firm regimented mass, with real captains over them, will these men march any more" (X, 275).

Carlyle's call to the captains of industry to be true governors and guardians of their workers is one which, with variations, is repeated throughout the 1840s by writers as different as Dickens and Disraeli and which becomes a main theme in the Christian Socialism of Maurice and Ludlow in the 1850s. In his sensible little book, *The Claims of Labour* (1845), for example, Arthur Helps picks up Carlyle's message to the captains of industry and develops it in the direction of Christian Socialism. He quotes *Past and Present:* "The Leaders of Industry, if Industry is ever to be led, are virtually the Captains of the World," and continues: "Can a man, who has this destiny entrusted to him, imagine that his vocation consists merely in getting together a large lump of gold, and then being off with it, to enjoy it, as he fancies, in some other place: as if that which is but a small part of his business in life, were all in all to him . . . ?"[1] For Helps, as also for Carlyle and Dickens, the best industrial relations are personal relations, and his analogies are to feudalism and to family life: the conduct of employers should be as "conduct in a family and towards dependents" (61). "I believe that the paternal relation will be found the best model on which to form the duties of the employer to the employed; calling, as it does, for active exertion, requiring the most watchful tenderness, and yet limited by the strictest rules of prudence from intrenching on that freedom of thought and action which is necessary for all spontaneous development'' (157). And Helps gives this paternalistic ideal a specifically religious interpretation that moves it in the direction of Christian Socialism. At the same time, there is little in Helps's essay to contradict the basic assumptions of free traders like Cobden and Bright. Helps does not join in the Anti-Corn Law League assault on the aristocracy, and he insists on the need for legislative interference in the affairs of industry, for without such interference, ''the responsibilities of individuals would be left overwhelming'' (247). But, as in Carlyle, the way to achieve prosperity is through rightly organized—and rightly unrestricted—industrial development. Further, the paternalistic model for industrial relations that Helps shares with writers as different as Carlyle, Dickens, and Disraeli is based on the assumption that the interests of workers and masters are the same and that class reconciliation rather than class conflict is what all right-thinking men should seek.[2] This is true even though many political economists and free traders dislike overt calls for paternalism, which, they feel, reduce the independence of the working class. That is the reason for Helps's qualification about limiting paternalism ''by the strictest rules of prudence.'' But the main quality that sets Carlyle and Helps in opposition to political economists and to more thorough-going free traders is that they do not claim the identity of interests between labor and capital as an established fact. They see it rather as an ideal that too many captains of industry fail to live up to. Whitewashing class conflict between labor and capital, along with its corollary of blaming economic distress entirely on the aristocratic ''bread tax,'' was one of the main functions of Anti-Corn Law League propaganda. But Carlyle and Helps, and also Dickens and Disraeli, at least start from the plain fact of class conflict.

Dickens wishes for nothing more strongly than for a rapprochement between classes, but he is only occasionally guilty of following the extreme pattern of Anti-Corn Law propaganda, which presents the identity of interests between labor and capital as a reality. More often than not he perceives it as an ideal—the ideal of personalized work in *Barnaby Rudge* —although industrial relations throughout his novels are usually ambiguous. This is apparent in the factory of Doyce and Clennam in *Little Dorrit*, for example, which is a place of light and hope in the midst of the social wilderness. Its workers perform their tasks with a ''vigorous clink of iron upon iron.''[3] It forms the real ''heart'' of ''Bleeding Heart Yard'' (135), a vital contrast to the death-dealing jumbles of red tape and high society hemming it in. And far from describing "the workman at war with capital" in *Little Dorrit,* Dickens describes just the opposite, for the relations between Doyce and his men are entirely harmonious. When Doyce is lured away by a "barbaric" nation that has sense enough to recognize his value as an inventor and manufacturer, he is seen off by a band of loyal workers, all of whom are "mightily proud of him": " 'Good luck to you, Mr. Doyce!' said one of the number. 'Wherever you go, they'll find as they've got a man among 'em, a man as knows his tools and as his tools knows, a man as is willing and a man as is able, and if that's not a man where is a man!' This oration . . . was received with three loud cheers . . . In the midst of the three loud cheers, Daniel gave them all a hearty 'Good Bye, Men!' and the coach disappeared from sight, as if the concussion of the air had blown it out of Bleeding Heart Yard" (674-675). "The concussion of the air" from the cheers, no doubt, contrasts with the suffocating airlessness of the prisons and of the houses of Mrs. Clennam and the Merdles, just as the comradeship between men and master contrasts with the hollow lovelessness in higher circles. But is Doyce an ideal exception, a model of the benevolent employer, or is he meant to typify actual industrial relations? There is no way of deciding. Certainly if we count the Cheerybles with Doyce and with Rouncewell in *Bleak House,* good industrialists outnumber bad ones in Dickens's novels (Bounderby is in fact the only bad one, although he is also pretty clearly the representative of all "the millers of Coketown"). But whether they are typical or exceptional, Doyce and Bounderby do not contradict each other: Doyce shows how good industrial relations can be and Bounderby how bad they can be, and that is that.

At the time of the Glasgow Cotton Spinners' trial in 1838, Archibald Prentice, the historian of the Anti-Corn Law League, stated the case for free trade against both working-class radicalism and aristocratic monopoly:

> Let the working classes consider the ceaseless labour and the enormous expense they have incurred within the last dozen years to get rid of the Combination Laws, to destroy the truck system, to establish Co-operative Societies . . . to shorten the hours of labour, to bolster up the wages of some particular class of workmen by unions, to fill the country with a cry against the New Poor Law . . . while, during all the time, the Corn Laws are grinding down the reward of their labour on the one hand, and raising the price of their food on the other;—let them . . . reflect in what a different position they

would have stood now, had there been, throughout all these years, *one* combined and energetic effort against the landowners' monopoly . . . England might have been a garden in all its length and breadth, had the energies of its people been employed in the right direction.[4]

As in Dickens's version of the Gordon riots, the energy for class conflict comes from beneath, while the main cause of it comes from above the middle class on the social scale. Meanwhile, middle-class industry is eager to shake off the shackles placed upon it by aristocratic misgovernment, after which the interests of the whole nation will be secured by the middle class following its Promethean partial interest.

Dickens expresses this sanguine view of class conflict in much of his writing before *Hard Times,* most explicitly in the free trade propaganda he wrote as editor of the *Daily News.* In his "Hymn of the Wiltshire Labourers" and his editorial introduction to the *Daily News* in 1845, Dickens appears as a vigorous champion of the Anti-Corn Law League program (the *Daily News* was in fact funded by free traders and staffed by some of the *Punch* radicals and by Anti-Corn Law lecturers like W. J. Fox). In the first issue of the *Daily News,* Dickens declares that it is "impossible rationally to consider the true interests of the people as a class question, or to separate them from the interests of the merchant and manufacturer. Therefore it will be no part of our function to widen any breach that may unhappily subsist or may arise between employer and employed; but it will rather be our effort to show their true relations, their mutual dependence, and their mutual power of adding to the sum of general happiness and prosperity."[5] This apparently impartial, conciliatory position is repeated when Dickens declares it to be the policy of the *Daily News* not to engage in party politics. The principles it supports are above party; they are the "principles of progress and improvement, of education, civil and religious liberty, and equal legislation—principles such as its conductors believe the advancing spirit of the time requires." All that stands in the way of the free operation of these principles is the corn laws. For Dickens and for men like Douglas Jerrold and Mark Lemon —even for the leaders of the Anti-Corn Law League itself—free trade was a partisan cause only because aristocratic obstructionism made it so. During the Reform Bill crisis, the middle class was, according to its members, the bearer of the future and of the universal interest of mankind. And during the 1840s, even in the face of Chartism and trade unionism, it was middle-class industry which, imprisoned by aristocratic misgovernment, yet held the promise of the future and rose above party and class as the universal interest. Quite simply, in the words of John Bright, only do away with the corn laws and "we shall see no more ragged men and women and children parading our streets . . . but we shall have the people happy, 'every man sitting under his own vine and fig tree.' "[6]

Although perhaps not many middle-class writers saw the "bread tax" as the single cause of economic distress and of the supposedly mistaken class conflict based upon it, many were prepared to see it as the main cause, and to look to free trade as the main way out of "the hungry forties." The list of writers who believed in free trade as at least the principal solution to economic distress and class conflict would include most of those mentioned in this study, except for conservatives like Disraeli and Gresley and for the Christian Socialists. Although most of them were not as dogmatic about it as Ebenezer Elliott or Harriet Martineau, Dickens, Mill, Carlyle, Thackeray, Hood, the *Punch* radicals, R. H. Horne, Elizabeth Barrett, and Robert Browning were all among the free trade faithful. And after 1846 it was possible for middle-class liberals to feel that the most important reform of all had been achieved and to look forward to a regime of industrial prosperity that would leave Chartism and trade unionism with no ground to stand on. Class conflict, party conflict, and eventually international conflict will all vanish with the realization of the promise of free trade, which is nothing less than the promise of human nature, rooted in labor. As R. H. Horne describes his hero Orion, based on the Carlylean dictum that the modern epic will concern not arms and the man, but tools and the man:

> The Worker he,
> The builder-up of things, and of himself.[7]

And in John Bright's industrial-pastoral future, there will be no need for partisan politics—everyone will be usefully employed in the mechanical vineyards and will enjoy the fruits of British industry fully, if not exactly equally, and, under the reign of universal labor, there will be no more "Workhouse Workmen" and no more "Unworking Aristocrats." Such was the utopian expectation that many saw reflected in the Crystal Palace in 1851. Referring to the Great Exhibition, a writer in *The Economist* declared: "All who have read, and can think, must now have full confidence that the 'endless progression,' ever increasing in rapidity, of which the poet sang, is the destined lot of the human race."[8]

In the context of the political wrangling and class conflict of the 1840s, free trade utopianism can look either extremely hypocritical or extremely naive or both at once. But images of a conflict-free future seem to increase as actual conflict increases. With this in mind, it is instructive to contrast Dickens's wishful assertion of nonpartisanship in the *Daily News* with the actual contents of that paper, or with other examples of Anti-Corn Law League "nonpartisan" propaganda. In 1839 Richard Cobden sent to Henry Cole the plan for an Anti-Corn Law League woodcut to be executed by Thackeray and to be called "The Landowner and the Factory Child": "This is my idea for the Factory Child and Lord Ashley. A tall mill & high chimney in back—clock at 5 a.m. Two or three pale & starved children going to work with large bits of bread in their hands. Lord Ashley has taken the bread from the first child & has broken it in two, & whilst putting the larger share in his pocket & returning the smaller to the child, he lifts up his eyes & in a very sanctimonious tone says 'I will never rest until the poor factory child is protected by a ten hours bill from the tyranny of the *merciless* & *griping millowners*.' "[9] At about the time that Thackeray was being sought after as a propagandist by the Anti-Corn Law League, Dickens was traveling to Manchester armed with letters of introduction from Lord Ashley. "With that nobleman's most benevolent and excellent exertions . . . I am well acquainted."[10] It is no wonder that Dickens drew back in confusion from the issue of factory reform; the difficulty of committing oneself to a partisan cause in a nonpartisan manner is plain to see, although it was a difficulty that he thought he had surmounted in the case of free trade.

The desires to rise above party and to transcend the barriers of class, evident in free trade propaganda and in middle-class liberalism as a whole, led many writers in the 1840s and after into patterns of wishful thinking related to the entrepreneurial ideal. As in Disraeli's contradictory treatment of the two nations of rich and poor, it is a literature that declares the existence of class conflict at the same time that it seeks to overcome it or to deny its existence in various ways. In Mrs. Gore's *The Two Aristocracies* (1857), Lord Ullesmere rather grudgingly says, "In these times, it [is] the dooty of every man whose position in life renders him an example, to promote to the utmost the fusion of classes."[11] But the more imperative a duty may seem, the harder it may be to fulfill. No matter how desirable the "fusion of classes" might appear to upper-class writers, it was also unimaginable to most of them—including Mrs. Gore, as the very title of her novel suggests. Although interclass marriages—as in the case of Jane Eyre and Mr. Rochester—became a more frequent symbol of the desire for a "fusion of classes," in the literature of the 1840s marriages between proletarians and members of the upper classes are rare. The marriage of Philip Hewson and Elspie Mackaye in Clough's

Bothie of Tober-na-Vuolich (1848) is an honorable exception; the marriage of Sybil and Egremont is a dishonorable one, and there are only a few others. In contrast, Mrs. Gaskell's treatment of the liaison between Harry Carson and Mary Barton is at least based on an honest rejection of wishful thinking. In *Mary Barton,* Mrs. Gaskell gives us an accurate portrayal of a common pattern of class antagonism, rather than the portrayal of a distant or of an insincerely held ideal.

For many middle-class writers, the desire for a rapprochement between classes places them in the awkward position of stressing the very thing they wish to overcome. Harriet Martineau is not alone in accusing Dickens of being a "humanity monger" and of making the poor hate the rich instead of love them.[12] But Dickens sees himself as an advocate of social peace, and criticisms like Martineau's must be balanced by the assessment of the Hammonds, who declare that Dickens did "more to draw English people together than any other influence in the time."[13] In any case, when "humanity mongers" can be perceived as dangers to the state, it may be fairly assumed that the state is ailing. Charles Greville wrote of Shaftesbury in 1844 that "a philanthropic agitator is more dangerous than a repealer either of the Union or of the Corn Laws. We are just now overrun with philanthropy, and God knows where it will stop, or whither it will lead us."[14]

The opposition to "humanity mongering" of both Martineau, with her faith in political economy, and Greville, with his Tory dislike of all agitation, is understandable. But expressions of the danger of excessive philanthropy come sometimes from less understandable sources, and even from some of the "philanthropic agitators" themselves. When Hood's "Song of the Shirt," which was later claimed as a piece of Anti-Corn Law League propaganda, appeared in *Punch* in 1843, it was an immediate popular success. It was set to music and made a text for sermons. It was dramatized as *The Sempstress* by Mark Lemon, who was largely responsible for its original publication, and staged on May 25, 1844, at the Theatre Royal. It was printed on broadsides and even on souvenir handkerchiefs that were hawked about the streets, and it is said to have nearly tripled the circulation of *Punch.*[15] Hood himself was suddenly a successful, serious poet, elevated from his status as "punster" to serve as "the poet laureate of the poor." Given both his success and the sentimental nature of his radicalism, according to which he does little more than attempt to prick the consciences of the rich on behalf of the poor, it is difficult to see how Hood could feel uneasy about the effects of his poetry. But he managed it. In a letter written shortly before his death to Sir Robert Peel, Hood confesses that "The Song of the Shirt" and his other humanitarian poems may have stirred up class conflict rather than allayed it:

> My physical debility finds no tonic virtue in a steel pen, otherwise I would have written one more paper—a forewarning one—against an evil, or the danger of it, arising from a literary movement in which I have had some share, a one-sided humanity, opposite to that Catholic Shaksperian sympathy, which felt with King as well as Peasant, and duly estimated the mortal temptations of both stations. Certain classes at the poles of Society are already too far asunder; it should be the duty of our writers to draw them nearer by kindly attraction, not to aggravate the existing repulsion, and place a wider moral gulf between Rich and Poor, with Hate on the one side and Fear on the other. But I am too weak for this task, the last I had set myself.[16]

But while Hood is afraid that his poems may have widened rather than narrowed the "gulf between Rich and Poor," there were others who disagreed with him. Commenting in the *Edinburgh Review* on Hood's *Poems* of 1846, Leigh Hunt says that Hood "seeks not to influence one class of society against the other by a gloomy poetical Chartism": "his aim is only to point out existing evils; to appeal to the better feelings of men: for their removal or relief; and to unite society, not by the ties of fear or force, but by the bond of kindness on the part of the rich, repaid by gratitude on that of the poor."[17] Hunt's statement, of course, does not contradict Hood's in the sense that it accurately describes Hood's aim, which is to draw classes together rather than to drive them apart. According to Hood's confession to the Prime Minister, however, this admirably pacific and humane purpose has had an opposite result, which appears plainly enough in the interpretation of Hood's poetry by the Chartist poet, Gerald Massey, who writes: "The 'Song of the Shirt' was the first summons of the army of the poor which had besieged the citadel of wealth. The very music of it was like the march of ten thousand men, who come, with dogged step, set teeth, and flashing eyes, to demand redress for their long sufferings and wrongs. It had an ominous sound. Men looked at one another, and, for every poor one pale with want, there was a rich one white with fear."[18] And, as if this were not enough, in an elegy on the poet "Who Sang the Song of the Shirt," Massey delcares that from the "cloud" of Hood's life came

> thunder-voices, with their words of fire,
> To melt the Slave's chain, and the Tyrant's crown.

All along poor Hood had not wanted to speak thunder but had instead wanted to contribute to social peace. But Massey will not let him have his way; he sees even Hood's conciliatory humor as no dampener of his "words of fire": "His wit?—a kind smile just to hearten us" as we go about the work of dethroning tyrants and freeing slaves.[19]

It would be easy to tax Hood with political timidity and even—at least in his letter to Peel—hypocrisy. But for Hood and for the other sentimental radicals, the problem of class conflict is a highly vexing one, and they are very uncertain about how to handle it and also about what effects literature may have upon it. Their first impulse is simply to wish it away, along with party politics. And their position is inevitably contradictory—timidly inflammatory, if such a thing is possible—close to a Carlylean vagueness on the hard question of equality. But there is no feeling in Hood any stronger than his desire for a rapprochement between classes and an end to political controversy, and about this he is sincere to the point of declaring his own not very inflammatory poetry a failure. If he had been a stronger poet, perhaps he could have turned his desire for social peace into some sort of utopian vision based on the entrepreneurial ideal—free trade, self-help, personalized work, and an end to political and class conflict. But he did not see his way clear to such a result. Of all the middle-class writers in the 1840s, perhaps Dickens comes the closest to producing such a liberal utopian vision, at least by implication, in his novels. And if it is not "the steam-whistle party" vision that Ruskin once declared it to be,[20] that is because Dickens seems to grow increasingly aware of the distance between fact and ideal, or of the failure of the Coketowns of this world to be all that he feels it in their power to become.

After the victory of free trade in 1846 and the defeat of Chartism in 1848, there were many novelists and poets who were prepared to celebrate the coming industrial millennium. The oceans might not turn to lemonade as in some of Fourier's wilder imaginings, but the possibility of steady progress through unrestricted industry and its self-help corollary made for a cheering prospect. At the same time that Dickens was producing his most pessimistic novels, including *Hard Times,* which amounts to a declaration of the failure of industrial England to fulfill the entrepreneurial ideal, other writers were declaring that it was already fulfilled.

One of the most interesting of the midcentury novels celebrating the triumphs of middle-class industry, because it is so unqualified in its rejoicing, is Dinah Mulock's *John Halifax, Gentleman* (1856), which describes the evolution of a working-class orphan into a captain of industry. Her tale is a moral exemplum of the creed of Samuel Smiles, or of that

"Golden Rule" proferred to Sir Daniel Gooch by his mother and recorded for posterity in *Culture and Anarchy:* "Ever remember, my dear Dan, that you should look forward to being some day manager of that concern!"[21] When Phineas Fletcher, who narrates Dinah Mulock's novel, gives John Halifax advice, it usually takes this form: "Try—you can do anything you try."[22] As in Carlyle, "impossible" is a bad word. John tries, and by dint of hard work and his great integrity, John triumphs, over both the obnoxious aristocrats whom he sweeps from his path and the recalcitrant workers whom he tames to his will. Through industry and honesty, John wins the respect of Abel Fletcher, a Quaker tanyard owner who is also a self-made man, and in the process Phineas, Abel's lame son, forms a strong attachment to the hero. John saves Abel's flour mill from rioters, marries the genteel Ursula March, maddens the local aristocracy with his great dignity and his failure to observe class limits, acquires a woolen mill, applies steam to it at a time when steam was new to the woolen industry, quells more riots, refuses to run for Parliament because it is too corrupt for him, rules his poor people like a benevolent feudal baron, and in general proves to all who meet him that he is as much a "gentleman" as anyone with the most respectable of pedigrees: "He was indebted to no forefathers for a family history: the chronicle commenced with himself, and was altogether his own making. No romantic antecedents ever turned up: his lineage remained uninvestigated, and his pedigree began and ended with his own honest name—John Halifax" (11).

It is the pattern of the countless rags-to-riches stories that are part of the folklore of industrialism and that are best represented by Samuel Smiles's *Self-Help* (1859) and *Lives of the Engineers* (1862), democratic versions of Carlyle's *Heroes and Hero-Worship* in which heroism may turn out to be the attribute of anybody, provided that he works at it.[23] The moral behind industrial success literature is a double, contradictory one: first, through honesty and perseverance, the free individual can move mountains; and second, the middle class has a monopoly on honesty and perseverance. As James Mill put it, "that virtuous rank," the middle class, is "the chief source of all that has exalted and refined human nature."[24] The monopoly on virtue exists because, with luck, anybody who exercises honesty and perseverance will automatically ascend into the middle class. And the idea of *descending* into the middle class does not arise, for obvious reasons, the most important one being that the middle class as a whole is seen as progressive and upwardly mobile.

Dinah Mulock gives the old pattern of industrial success literature an interesting twist by equating John's rise with the progress of the middle class. The story spans the crucial years of the Industrial Revolution from

1795 to 1834, and as a reformer, John Halifax takes part in the central events of the age—he introduces steam to the woolen industry, brings peace to the "lower orders," and in general supports all good middle-class causes. As Mrs. Halifax tells him, "What with your improvements at Enderley, and your Catholic Emancipation—your Abolition of Slavery and your Parliamentary Reform—why, there is hardly any scheme for good, public or private, to which you do not lend a helping hand" (295). Although John refuses to run for Parliament because it is too corrupt for him ("until the people are allowed honestly to choose their own honest representatives, I must decline being of that number"), it is understood that he and his class are a saving remnant, standing manfully between the revolutionary masses and the degenerate nobility, preserving England from chaos. John, "with a few more, stood as it were midway in the gulf" (214). It is this "middlingness," this sense of progressive compromise between extremes, that is seen in the novel as both the source and the end of social improvement.[25] For it is also understood that John's rise to wealth, completed at about the time of the Reform Bill of 1832, is part of a movement that has led to a golden age of industrial prosperity and security, so that "the present generation can have no conception of what a terrible time that was" before the middle class gained power (63). It is as if industrial turmoil and the "great gulf fixed" between rich and poor are things of the past; in 1856 it was tempting for middle-class Victorians to believe that they had sailed into a calm harbor. For Dinah Mulock, the struggle for reform is essentially over and the future secure. Although she likes to believe that she is being controversial, issues such as the respectability of the middle class were not burning ones in 1856. *John Halifax* is therefore nostalgic rather than combative, "a Gloucestershire Idyll"[26] with a quaintly anachronistic flavor.

John Halifax's battles for social freedom have strict limits—those embodied in the Reform Bill of 1832. His quest is above all for "respectability," or for the "gentlemanly" status that is denied him by the class structure but that is innately his anyway. Dinah Mulock emphasizes that social status is unimportant and anyone may become a "gentleman" through self-help and honesty; and yet like most other Victorian novelists who deal with the theme of social mobility, what she really succeeds in proving is that social status is all-important. Obviously, Bagehot's system of "removable inequalities" depends on keeping up the supply of inequalities to be removed.[27] John starts life as a penniless orphan driving the tanyard skin cart for Abel Fletcher, which proves to be a job worse than the mark of Cain. Some kinds of employment, like handling skins or pasting labels on blacking bottles, are clearly outside the pale of respectability. John argues that "it isn't the trade that signifies—it's the man" (101), but the point is not that all trades are equally respectable; it is rather that even the most disgusting work cannot taint you if you are spotless within. "Perhaps, someday," John says to Phineas, "neither you nor anyone else will be ashamed of me."

> "No one could, even now, seeing you as you really are."
> "As John Halifax, not as the tanner's 'prentice boy? Oh! lad— there the goad sticks." (131)

And a bit later, John exclaims: "Pah! I could almost fancy the odour of these hides on my hands still." Like Pip in *Great Expectations,* John is ashamed of his lowly status and wishes to be a "gentleman." But unlike Pip, John is never made to see his shame as snobbery, even though his story is ostensibly an attack on snobbery.

On one level, Dinah Mulock's attack on snobbery works fairly well. John confronts several annoying aristocrats in the course of his story and proves himself the best man. True, this is not very difficult—the general decrepitude of Miss Mulock's aristocrats may be indicated by the opinions of one of them, Mr. Brithwood, who says to John: "Wouldn't you be only too thankful to crawl into the houses of your betters, any how, by hook or by crook? Ha! ha! I know you would. It's always the way with you common folk, you rioters, you revolutionists. By the Lord! I wish you were all hanged" (161). "Sir," John replies, with transcendent dignity, "I am neither a rioter nor a revolutionist." And when the "savage" Brithwood strikes him, John confounds him by turning the other cheek. Brithwood, fortunately, is the least believable of Dinah Mulock's lot of corrupt aristocrats, but John's confrontations with all of them are always victories for democracy and the common man, like Rouncewell's confrontations with Sir Leicester Dedlock. Brithwood and Sir Leicester are members of the aristocracy of Victorian melodrama, symbols of corruption and the dead hand of the past.

It is rather when John confronts the "lower orders" that the inconsistency of seeking "respectability" while preaching democracy emerges. When Lord Ravenel exclaims, "What brutes they are—the lower orders!" John replies, "Not altogether—when you know them" (326). John knows "the lower orders" better than anyone in the novel, and yet he is always quelling riots, always turning back the threat of revolution. At the outset, he saves Abel Fletcher's business from the mob, and when he gives the starving rioters food, they wolf it down "like wild beasts" (80). And at the end of the story, he is still threatened by working-class violence, even though he has been ruling the neighborhood benevolently for some time. He must carry a pistol for self-defense, and he sadly exclaims, "My poor people—they might have known me better" (309). The trouble seems to be that, although John knows his poor people well, they do not know him well.

Here arises the central inconsistency of *John Halifax* and of all industrial success literature. Its rags-to-riches plot is a symbol for democratic change, but Dinah Mulock, like most of her middle-class contemporaries, believes only in a limited amount of democratic change and no more. John's progress to the status of "gentleman" does not involve the abolition of that status. On the contrary, John's goal is the antidemocratic, feudal industrialism advocated by Carlyle and Arthur Helps. John aims at "not merely the making a fortune . . . but the position of useful power, the wide range of influence, the infinite opportunities of doing good" (209). And he can tell Phineas, "If there was one point I was anxious over in my youth, it was to keep up through life a name like the Chevalier Bayard—how folk would smile to hear of a tradesman emulating Bayard —*sans peur et sans reproche!*" (309). To extend his "useful power," John eventually moves up to "Beechwood Hall" and governs his region like a wise country squire. John intends to use his power to further the cause of social reform; but the goals of democracy and equality look to be as remote as "one far-off divine event." So we are told that John hopes "not only to lift himself, but his sons after him;—lift them high enough to help on the ever-advancing tide of human improvement, among their own people first, and thence extending outward in the world" (302). The final work of democratic reform will be left to his sons, at the edge of some glimmering but fortunately distant dawn, and John, meanwhile, will continue to enjoy his hard-won respectability.

As in all industrial success stories, social relations that are open and fluid at the beginning of *John Halifax* are closed at the end. The cause of this constriction is the hero's success; the victory of the individual—his acquisition of bourgeois respectability—brings the story to a close but leaves the problem of the masses unresolved. In the process, there is a displacement of focus from social to personal forces, much like that which occurs in *Felix Holt,* where the issue of democratic radicalism gets lost in the personal entanglements of the Transome estate and of Felix's love affair with Esther Lyon.[28] As a general rule, novels by middle-class Victorians which start with a focus upon class conflict and social injustice wind through their labyrinthine plots to resolutions that pertain to the central characters but that leave deeper social questions unanswered. This seems to be not simply an incidental weakness in nineteenth-century fiction but a structural feature closely corresponding to the exact historical situation —"standing midway in the gulf"—of the middle-class believers in the entrepreneurial ideal.

With the application of steam to his mill in 1825, the triumph of John Halifax over circumstances and aristocratic obstructionism is largely complete (272-278). At the same time, some of John's "poor people" fall under the erroneous impression that his "machinery has ruined labour," and there is the threat of "a new set of Luddites" (268) arising to work destruction on his mill. Here *John Halifax* comes close to Charlotte Brontë's *Shirley* (1849), another novel celebrating the rise of middle-class industrialism, and one that probably served as a model for Dinah Mulock. Both *John Halifax* and *Shirley* deal with the heroic struggles of early industrialists, and both equate these struggles with the rise of the middle class to economic and political power. Both show their heroes overcoming aristocratic prejudice and also braving working-class violence, which takes the form of a series of riots in *John Halifax* and more specifically of Luddism in *Shirley* (there is otherwise no hint of a viable working-class politics in either book). And both novels are expressions of middle-class faith in self-help, or that creed of rugged individualism made ludicrous by the self-puffing of Josiah Bounderby.

But while Dinah Mulock treats self-help as an unqualified virtue, Charlotte Brontë is critical of unlimited individualism. Her hero, Robert Moore, is altogether more fallible, and therefore more credible, than John Halifax. In wishing for peace with Napoleon on any terms and for the revocation of the Orders in Council, Moore reveals a selfish lack of patriotism, which Brontë sees as the fault generally of "the mercantile classes." "These classes certainly think too exclusively of making money: they are too oblivious of every national consideration but that of extending England's (*i.e.,* their own) commerce. Chivalrous feeling, disinterestedness, pride in honour, is too dead in their hearts."[29] And she concludes this Carlylean paragraph by exclaiming, "Long may it be ere England really becomes a nation of shopkeepers!"

Robert Moore reveals his want of "chivalrous feeling" not just by wishing for peace at all costs, but also by treating his workers harshly. He is a just man, but he is not a merciful man, at least until experience softens him. In the chapter called "Coriolanus," Caroline Helstone criticizes her future husband for his haughtiness: "you must not be proud to your workpeople; you must not neglect chances of soothing them, and you must not be of an inflexible nature, uttering a request as austerely as if it were a command" (93). When Robert asks her if she would have him "truckle" to his workers, she replies: "No, not for the world: I never wish you to lower yourself; but somehow, I cannot help thinking it unjust to include all poor working people under the general and insulting name of 'the mob,' and continually to think of them and treat them haughtily.'' Much of the novel concerns the effects of Moore's ''haughtiness.'' In particular, the uncompromising way in which he imposes machinery on his workers is seen as creating unemployment and fanning the flames of Luddism. Charlotte Brontë is much more tough-minded than Dinah Mulock about the effects of machinery, for, like Ricardo, she recognizes that there is a causal relationship between automation and unemployment (28), whereas the working-class fear of machinery in *John Halifax* is treated as superstition.[30]

Unlike John Halifax, Moore is mistaken about lots of things, and yet it is impossible to know just how to interpret Brontë's criticism of him and consequently her criticism of middle-class individualism. Moore's very flaws make him a typical Brontean hero, an uncut diamond like Heathcliff and Mr. Rochester, needing to be tamed by the heroines, but full of an admirable, dangerous energy: ''Moore ever wanted to push on: 'Forward' was the device stamped upon his soul; but poverty curbed him: sometimes (figuratively) he foamed at the mouth when the reins were drawn very tight'' (27). The fact that Moore's personal dynamism is both economic and erotic obscures the question of his social wrong-doing, and in any case, for all his rough, selfish nature, he is a cause of progress—a reformer in spite of himself. And when, toward the end of the book, a crazy worker shoots Moore, it is difficult to see this as poetic justice and the inevitable social response to Moore's ''Coriolanian'' haughtiness. In fact, the assassination attempt seems so unnecessary in terms of the politics of the book that it is perhaps better understood psychologically as another version of the blinding of Mr. Rochester and, hence, as an obsessional pattern rather than as a social event.

Also, while Moore's inflexible haste in introducing machinery is criticized by Caroline, Brontë sees it rather as a necessary and courageous act. She acknowledges that machinery creates temporary unemployment, but the workers thus martyred are martyrs to progress: ''As to the sufferers, whose sole inheritance was labour, and who had lost that inheritance— who could not get work, and consequently could not get wages, and consequently could not get bread—they were left to suffer on; perhaps inevitably left: it would not do to stop the progress of invention, to damage science by discouraging its improvements . . . so the unemployed underwent their destiny—ate the bread and drank the waters of affliction'' (28). Robert Moore, ''Coriolanian'' though he is, is a pioneer of progress who quells working-class violence with single-minded bravery and vigor, and when the radical Mr. Yorke makes the same criticism of his haughtiness that Caroline Helstone has made, Shirley defends him: "He came here poor and friendless, with nothing but his own energies to back him; nothing but his honour, his talent, and his industry to make his way for him. A monstrous crime indeed that, under such circumstances, he could not popularise his naturally grave, quiet manners . . . An unpardonable transgression, that when he introduced improvements he did not go about the business in quite the most politic way . . . ! For errors of this sort is he to be the victim of mob-outrage? Is he to be denied even the privilege of defending himself?" (376-377). Seen from Shirley's perspective, Moore is not the cause of Luddism but the victim of it, and he does right to resist it manfully. Shirley herself would fight "like a tigress" to protect her property if it were threatened by working-class "ignorance" and "insolence" (271-272). Shirley would prefer to be charitable, but if the poor respond to charity with "ruffian defiance," she will teach them their place. Moore, then, is "Coriolanian," but he is right to be "Coriolanian," and Charlotte Brontë's criticism of him takes on the kind of ambiguity that characterizes her criticism of the Church. Admitting that the Church has its faults, she proceeds: "Britain would miss her church, if that church fell. God save it! God also reform it!" (308).

As Asa Briggs and E. P. Thompson have shown, the story that *Shirley* relates was a piece of industrial folklore signaling the triumph of the manufacturers over both working-class and upper-class opposition.[31] Moore's courageous but unpopular actions in defending his mill were based on those of William Cartwright of Rawfolds, who was the first mill-owner to offer much resistance to the Luddites. "Altogether he was an unpopular man," Mrs. Gaskell tells us, "even before he took the last step of employing shears, instead of hands, to dress his wool." But she also says that Cartwright was "a very remarkable man," and she notes that his courage was rewarded by his fellow millowners to the tune of 3000 pounds. In "those terrible times of insecurity to life and property," Cartwright and his kind clearly could do nothing better than to forge ahead on the march of progress.[32]

By the end of the novel, with prosperity dropping like peace around him, Moore is ready to deal benevolently with his employees. "I have seen the necessity of doing good," he tells Caroline. "I have learned the downright folly of being selfish" (662). And he proceeds to describe how he shall behave towards the poor in future: "Caroline, the houseless, the starving, the unemployed, shall come to Hollow's-mill from far and near; and Joe Scott shall give them work, and Louis Moore, Esq., shall let them a tenement, and Mrs. Gill shall mete them a portion till the first payday'' (664). Compared to the dark violence that has come earlier, this is indeed a utopian vision, to which Moore adds a Sunday school and a day school. But this vision is not so clearly a function of Moore's conversion from hard-heartedness (he had been secretly charitable anyway) as it is of his having defeated the Luddites and of his turning his mill into a thriving place. As in Dinah Mulock's story, reform will come through industrial success, not in spite of it. Henceforward, Moore will rule his poor people as John Halifax rules his, as a benevolent, feudal "Captain of Industry," *sans peur et sans reproche.*

Shirley ends with a glimpse of Moore's neighborhood forty years later, a glimpse that reveals the triumph of middle-class energy and bravery. Like *John Halifax, Shirley* describes "the terrible times" of poverty and insecurity that preceded the mid-Victorian "age of equipoise," and the rugged individualism of its hero also leads directly to a large bank account and a big house: "I suppose Robert Moore's prophecies were, partially, at least, fulfilled. The other day I passed up the Hollow, which tradition says was once green, and lone, and wild; and there I saw the manufacturer's day-dreams embodied in substantial stone and brick and ashes—the cinder-black highway, the cottages, and the cottage-gardens; there I saw a mighty mill, and a chimney, ambitious as the tower of Babel'' (665). "The tower of Babel" adds an uncertain note to this vision of industrial success, but Moore's "extravagant day-dreams" have come true, and there seems nothing left for "the productive classes" to achieve except to continue forever on their march of improvement into the future.

How swiftly Providence advances thus
Our flag of progress placing in the van![33]

Carlyle and F. D. Maurice contemplating the dignity of labor in Ford Madox Brown's *Work*. (Reproduced by permission of the City of Manchester Art Galleries.)

VI. Christian Socialism

I will defy any one to answer the arguments of a St. Simonist, except on the ground of Christianity.

Coleridge, *Table Talk*, August 1, 1831

In the shadow of the Crystal Palace, surrounded by signs of the triumph of the entrepreneurial ideal, two groups of skeptics arose, both influenced by Coleridge and the first Romantics. Together with Carlyle and Ruskin, the Christian Socialists and the Pre-Raphaelite Brotherhood were the major links between the anticommercial, antiutilitarian thought of Coleridge and Southey and the spread of socialism among middle-class intellectuals in the 1870s and after. Both movements began in 1848, Christian Socialism as a response to the Chartist demonstration of April 10, and the first Pre-Raphaelite Brotherhood during the autumn as an apolitical painters' revolt against the conventions of the Royal Academy. Discounting the second Pre-Raphaelite Brotherhood, which included William Morris and Edward Burne-Jones, and also discounting the later avatars of Christian Socialism, both movements lasted for about five years, and members of both came together on common ground in the Working Men's College established in 1854 by F. D. Maurice and his followers. Among its first art teachers were Ruskin and Dante Gabriel Rossetti, and they were joined later by Woolner, Madox Brown, and Burne-Jones. Instruction in art at the Working Men's College during its early history was thus decidedly Pre-Raphaelite, while instruction in everything else was Christian Socialist and Broad Church liberal.[1]

Despite the later flowering of Ruskin's social criticism and the conversion of William Morris to Marxism, the connections between Christian Socialism and Pre-Raphaelitism may seem more fortuitous than logical. One of Rossetti's students, Thomas Sulman, said of him: "Art was his religion; he never talked Mauriceism."[2] And it is evident that politics had as little to do with Rossetti's decision to teach in the Working Men's College as theology: Ruskin talked him into it, and when Ruskin withdrew from regular teaching in 1858, Rossetti followed shortly after. Ruskin continued to appear intermittently at the Working Men's College in the 1860s, striving as always to help people to see as he saw, but by 1858 he had come to the conclusion that his efforts were a failure. He explained to Maurice that he could no longer serve as a teacher because "I [have] ascertained beyond all question that the faculty which my own method of teaching chiefly regarded was necessarily absent in men trained to mechanical toil, that my words and thoughts respecting beautiful things were unintelligible when the eye had been accustomed to the frightfulness of modern city life."[3]

Maurice and the Christian Socialists were quick to recognize an ally in Ruskin; at the urging of Furnivall, the brilliant chapter on "The Nature of Gothic" from *The Stones of Venice* was reprinted as a pamphlet and distributed during the inaugural ceremonies of the Working Men's College. But Ruskin seems to have been oblivious to the work and ideas of the Christian Socialists, although that movement influenced him profoundly. Self-enclosed and eccentric, Ruskin was as unable as Bentham to recognize the sources of his thinking.[4] The bizarre schemes for slaying the dragon of competition that Ruskin tried almost in a vacuum in the 1870s —the Hincksey dig, the tea shop in Paddington Street, and the Guild of St. George—are caricatures of the earlier and much more realistic efforts of the Christian Socialists to put their religious ideals into practice in cooperative workshops and sanitary reforms. Ruskin undoubtedly absorbed many of the teachings of Maurice, whom he often heard lecture in the Working Men's College. But in Letter 22 of *Fors Clavigera,* Ruskin declares that "I do not think of [Maurice] as one of the great, or even one of the leading, men of the England of his day . . . his amiable sentimentalism . . . has successfully, for a time, promoted the charities of his faith and parried its discussion." Ruskin's refusal to contribute to a fund for a memorial to Maurice on the grounds that Maurice has no more "real right to a niche in Westminster Abbey than any other tender-hearted Christian gentleman" stems not from principle, however, but from the fact that he once disagreed with Maurice about the true meaning of the story of Jael and Sisera.[5] Maurice was being both more generous and more accurate when in 1862 he wrote to a friend: "Anything which makes [Ruskin] doubt his own infallibility will, I am sure, do him good. He is earnest, I am convinced, and will come quite right."[6] Maurice, who made a practice of regularly declaring his own fallibility, and Ruskin, who rarely doubted his own infallibility, followed parallel lines that met at many points, although Ruskin chose to be unaware of this fact. The result is that, despite his relationship with Octavia Hill, who also began her career as a reformer among the Christian Socialists, Ruskin's social work went on in a sort of lavish isolation, and his debt to Maurice and to Christian Socialism has never been fully assessed.[7]

Ruskin was only a defender of the Pre-Raphaelite Brotherhood, however, not a member of it, and in 1848 its members had less concern for politics than he had.[8] On the day of the great Chartist demonstration, April 10, 1848, while the future Christian Socialists signed up as special constables or watched events excitedly, boils kept Rossetti at home.[9] True, he wrote a poem entitled "The English Revolution of 1848," but the concern he displays in it is that of the annoyed artist whose privacy has been invaded by ugly events, rather than that of the political or religious idealist. Rossetti's poem is narrated by an unsavoury Chartist agitator, calling the rabble together from the slums for a revolutionary meeting, where they listen to an incendiary speech by "Mr. A. B. C. D. E. F. G. M. W. Reynolds":

> Silence! Hear, hear! He says that we're the sovereign people, we!
> And now? And now he states the fact that one and one makes three!

After more leaden lines, Reynolds arrives at his peroration:

> Upon what point of London, say, shall our next vengeance burst?
> Shall the Exchange, or Parliament, be immolated first?
> Which of the Squares shall we burn down?—which of the Palaces?
> (*The speaker is nailed by a policeman.*)
> Oh please sir, don't! It isn't me. It's him. Oh don't, sir, please![10]

It is difficult to believe that this was written by the son of a Carbonarist and the leader of an important artistic rebellion, but it shows that rebellion in art and rebellion in politics are not necessarily related. Although what the poem expresses may not be settled political opinion so much as thoughtless annoyance at all the bother about what *Punch*, referring to the weather on April 10, called the Chartist "rain of terror," it is just as well that Rossetti seldom wrote about politics. But that Pre-Raphaelitism had a more vital and radical political dimension is evident in the work of Morris and Swinburne and also in William Michael Rossetti's *Democratic Sonnets,* which range in subject and time from postal reform and free trade in the 1840s to women's rights and the Zulu War in the 1870s and 1880s. It is characteristic of Pre-Raphaelitism in its early stages, however, that one of William Michael's sonnets, on the failure of the Hungarian revolution in 1849, was the only piece of political writing in the four issues of *The Germ,* where it appears at the end of the fourth issue. Furthermore, William Michael changed its title so that its otherwise manifest political content would remain hidden, because, as he tells us, *The Germ* was "a magazine which did not aim at taking any side in politics." Its original title was "For the General Oppression of the Better by the Worse Cause, Autumn 1849," and its later, even "more significant" titles were "Democracy Downtrodden" and "Hungary and Europe." But the title that William Michael gave it for *The Germ* was "The Evil under the Sun: Sonnet," and the language of the poem itself is so vague it could refer to anything "under the sun."[11]

On the surface, at least, the mystical and medieval contents of *The Germ* contrast sharply with the forthright political, economic, and religious contents of the journals produced by the Christian Socialists—the short-lived *Politics for the People* (1848), *The Christian Socialist* (1850-1851), and *The Journal of Association* (1852). While *The Germ* is as far removed from contemporary events as its authors can make it, in the "Prospectus" for *Politics for the People,* Maurice declares that contemporary events are the very things that everyone must confront. Although he rejects party politics, he argues that there is a human and religious politics that everyone participates in, whether willingly or not:

> Politics have been separated from household ties and affections—from art, and science, and literature. While they belong to parties, they have no connexion with what is human and universal; when they become POLITICS FOR THE PEOPLE, they are found to take in a very large field: whatever concerns man as a social being must be included in them.
>
> Politics have been separated from Christianity. But POLITICS FOR THE PEOPLE cannot be separated from religion.[12]

The assumption behind much Pre-Raphaelite art is that whatever is beautiful is inevitably divorced from the ugliness of contemporary reality, including politics; the assumption behind Christian Socialism is that religion has a direct role to play in changing contemporary reality, and that "a Churchman must be a politician."[13]

But what religion and "the Church Universal" are to the Christian Socialists, art is to the Pre-Raphaelites: the major counterweights that they oppose to the entrepreneurial ideal, or to a world rapidly becoming indistinguishable from the stock exchange. "Think of it! Was it all to end in a counting-house on the top of a cinder-heap, with Podsnap's drawing-room in the offing, and a Whig committee dealing out champagne to the rich and margarine to the poor in such convenient proportions as would make all men contented together, though the pleasure of the eyes was gone from the world, and the place of Homer was to be taken by Huxley?'' So writes William Morris in ''How I Became a Socialist.''[14] If the path through art to Marxism for this greatest of the Pre-Raphaelites was longer and more complicated than the path through Broad Church liberalism to Christian Socialism was for Maurice, Ludlow, and Kingsley, it was nevertheless in several respects the same path and can be retraced to the medieval communalism of Pugin's *Contrasts* and of Abbot Samson's monastery in *Past and Present* and to the anticommercial attitudes of Coleridge and Southey:

> Down the river did glide, with wind and tide,
>   A pig with vast celerity;
> And the Devil look'd wise as he saw how the while,
>   It cut its own throat. ''There!'' quoth he with a smile,
>   ''Goes 'England's commercial prosperity.' ''[15]

In *Alton Locke,* Kingsley's ''cockney poet'' tours a cathedral with some upper-class characters, including Eleanor Staunton, who is the voice of Christian Socialism in the later parts of the novel. When Alton declares that cathedrals are for him ''symbols of the superstition which created them'' and of the ''crushing bondage'' of feudalism, Eleanor upbraids him: '' 'You may sneer at them, if you will, Mr. Locke,' said Eleanor . . . 'The working classes would have been badly off without them. They were, in their day, the only democratic institution in the world; and the only socialist one too. The only chance a poor man had of rising by his worth, was by coming to the monastery. And bitterly the working classes felt the want of them, when they fell. Your own Cobbett can tell you that.' ''[16] Unlike some of the other medievalizers, including the Pre-Raphaelites, who found nothing in the present corresponding to the beauty of their dreamy versions of the Middle Ages, the Christian Socialists did have a living embodiment of the ''democratic'' spirit of old cathedrals in the modern Church. And it is quite literally to a new reformation of the Church and to new applications of monastic communalism that they look for the victory of Christ over the forces of Mammonite competition.

Maurice states the historical connection he finds between socialism and the Church very clearly when he says: ''I think they [the Owenites] should be made to feel that Communism, in whatever sense it is a principle of the New Moral World, is a most important principle of the old world, and that every monastic institution—properly so called—was a Communist institution to all intents and purposes. The idea of Christian Communism has been a most vigorous and generative one in all ages, and must be destined to a full development in ours'' (II, 7). To enact the principle of Christian Communism in the present, Maurice looks to an awakening of the clergy to a sense of duty and to their transformation into a "clerisy" after the Coleridgean model. "The day will come when you will find that the clergy are the only class who can help you," Eleanor Staunton says to Alton Locke. "Ah, you may shake your head. I warn you of it. They were the only bulwark of the poor against the mediaeval tyranny of Rank; you will find them the only bulwark against the modern tyranny of Mammon" (193). On the surface, the Christian Socialist idea of the clergy as the workers' allies against middle-class Mammonism looks like the Young England paradox of Tory-radicalism, according to which the aristocracy and the workers ought to unite. But, partly because of the emphasis given to the role of the Church, and partly because of the ambiguity of "gentlemen," the class alignments suggested by the Christian Socialists are different from those advocated by Disraeli in *Sybil*. As Kingsley puts it: "I have never swerved from my one idea of the last seven years, that the real battle of the time is, if England is to be saved from anarchy and unbelief, and utter exhaustion caused by the competitive enslavement of the masses, not Radical or Whig against Peelite or Tory—let the dead bury their dead—but the Church, the gentlemen, and the workman, against the shop-keepers and the Manchester School" (xlv).

Kingsley's pugnacious language in this passage, which merely rearranges the terms of class conflict, is in marked contrast to the central principle of Maurice's theology, which is also the central principle of his version of Christian Socialism. This is the principle, based on the Pauline doctrine of membership, that in the living Christ all differences are reconciled. As in Coleridge, so in Maurice: "Extremes meet." "Ideas" for Coleridge are unions of contraries, dimly perceivable to the higher reason, but not to the understanding: "By Ideas I mean intuitions not sensuous, which can be expressed only by contradictory conceptions, or, to speak more accurately, are themselves necessarily inexpressible and inconceivable, but are suggested by two contradictory positions."[17] Translated into the terms of the Broad Church theology of Thomas Arnold, Julius Hare, and F. D. Maurice, faith or intuition may take the place of Coleridgean reason, and the ultimate idea—the fullest reconciliation of all the contrary and warring fragments of life—is Jesus Christ. Further, the institutional lodging of the ultimate "reconciler of opposites" is the Universal Church, identical with the Universal State or Kingdom of Christ, which all people are members of, whether they know it or not, and which is approximated by, although not identical with, the Church of England.

According to Maurice, hitherto the major reform movements in history, whether religious or political, have worked by conflict and divisiveness. But the future and true reformation, acting first upon the Church and then moving outward until it embraces all of society, will overcome factional and sectarian strife and unite men in the community of Christ. After resigning from the editorship of the *Athenaeum* in 1834, Maurice declared to his friend and fellow Cambridge Apostle, R. C. Trench: "If I should ever write again, it will be, I think, on the subject nearest my heart, and from which I cannot wander long together without finding myself the worse for it—the principles and conditions of union among men. Everything without and within seems driving us to meditation upon this mighty question."[18] And in 1871, Maurice told his son that "the desire for Unity . . . both in the nation and the Church has haunted me all my days" (II, 632). That desire led him to seek the hidden oneness behind all phenomena and to deduce harmonies from the most discordant opposites, as when he writes that, in the nineteenth century, "all sects and factions, religious, political, or philosophical [are] bearing testimonies, sometimes mute, sometimes noisy, occasionally hopeful, oftener reluctant, to the presence of the Church Universal."[19]

In one sense, of course, the problem of "union among men" is the only problem that history presents us with; and for the liberal theologian, Christ, invisible and all-embracing resident of the Church Universal, is the only solution to it. But if this seems like a reduction of history to a ladder with only one rung, the ideal of unity leads Maurice through some extraordinarily complex theorizing to some equally complex and original practical results, the most important of which is Christian Socialism. Not only did Maurice provide the spiritual leadership for the movement, along with Ludlow's more practical leadership, but he also provided it with its name, which is at once a Coleridgean yoking of opposites in a single idea by a kind of political leap of faith, and a declaration of the historical communism of the Church, or of equality in Christ.

At the same time, Maurice's search for the hidden unity in things made him a singularly difficult leader to follow. As a field general, he was always joining the enemy, or else ordering a retreat just when victory was in sight. His son tells us: "Beyond all other things he dreaded becoming the head of a *party* of Christian Socialists. His great wish was to Christianise Socialism, not to Christian-Socialise the universe" (II, 41). Early in the history of the movement, Maurice stated in a letter to Ludlow the difficulty he felt of even being a participant in it: "I cannot enter into a party for the sake of compassing an end which involves the destruction of party" (II, 7). Following the same logic, Maurice was unwilling to use the very name he had invented: he insisted that the title of *The Christian Socialist* be changed to *The Journal of Association* and that its contents be made less political—both less "socialist" and less "Christian."[20] Maurice was acutely aware of his problem: how to be a member of Christ and a member of anything less than Christ at the same time? The search for unity, paradoxically, leads to isolation. Because it proscribes partisanship, Maurice says, "it would separate me from those with whom I should most with to act, and would give me not only the appearance of isolation and self-conceit, but the reality of both" (I, 239). There could be no resolution of these opposites, but Maurice tried to resolve them anyway through a lifelong series of bold equivocations and rigorous vacillations that, he knew, might well lead to "the disgrace of being called milksop or spooney, or via media man—a much more offensive epithet to me than either" (I, 479). Given his theory that all sects and movements are merely partisan splinters from the Universal Church, the remarkable thing is that Maurice got mixed up in Christian Socialism in the first place, and that he contrived to be a leader of it is miraculous.

The Coleridgean yoking of opposites into ideas produces equations that are necessarily two-sided, and that is the case with Christian Socialism, which was intended to be a thorn in the sides of both "the unsocial Christians" and the "unchristian Socialists." For the most part, despite several noble and enduring results in the fields of cooperation, labor legislation, and education, their double reformation fell harmlessly between the two enemy camps. Conservative clergymen damned them, and many "unchristian Socialists" either ignored them or else agreed with Marx and Engels, who declared that "Christian socialism is but the holy water with which the priest consecrates the heartburnings of the aristocrat."[21] The same two-sidedness that was meant to put them in harmony with everybody also put them at odds with everybody. The difficulties of such a position run straight through the writings and deeds of all the Christian Socialists, but they reach their fullest expression in Maurice's thorny political theology. His thinking might be called dialectical, since it works by means of antitheses, or of opposites that are always included in each other, and in political terms this means that he is, like his mentor Coleridge, at once radical and conservative, a democrat and a monarchist, a socialist and a supporter of the institution of private property. So in one of his antitheses, he expects church and state ultimately to form an ideal harmony, in which the church will embody the principles of cooperation and communal ownership, while the state will embody the principles of competition and private property. As he writes to Ludlow in 1849:

> The State, I think, cannot be Communist; never will be; never ought to be. It is by nature and law Conservative of individual rights, individual possessions. To uphold them it may be compelled (it must be) to recognise another principle than that of individual rights and property; but only by accident; only by going out of its own sphere, as it so rightly did in the case of the factory children. But the Church, I hold, is Communist in principle; Conservative of property and individual rights only by accident; bound to recognise them, but not as its own special work; not as the chief object of human society or existence. The union of Church and State, of bodies existing for opposite ends, each necessary to the other, is, it seems to me, precisely that which should accomplish the fusion of the principles of Communism and of property. A Church without a State must proclaim Proudhon's doctrine if it is consistent with itself; a State without a Church is merely supported by Jew brokers and must ultimately become only a stock exchange. (II, 8-9)

Although such reasoning is admirably directed towards a comprehensive and flexible union of opposites, Maurice is so flexible and open-minded that he leaves himself with no solid ground to stand upon, except for the ever-present ideal of union in Christ. After hearing one of Maurice's sermons, Benjamin Jowett exclaimed, "Well, all I can make out is that today was yesterday and this world the same as the next," and Aubrey de Vere said that listening to Maurice was "like eating pea soup with a fork."[22]

It is at least clear that Maurice's logic of unity does not work by simple compromise or by a half-hearted rejection of extremes, but by taking two or more sides of a question and parceling them into paradoxes and startling oxymorons; and on a less sophisticated level, a similar procedure is evident in Kingsley's social problem novels, *Yeast* and *Alton Locke*. The extremes threatening to pull Kingsley's two-sided tailor-poet apart are the desire to be true to the working class and the desire to rise into the middle class. "Tailor and poet" is an oxymoron for Kingsley like "Christian Socialist." Torn between his contradictory ambitions, Alton is able to do almost nothing right until after April 10, 1848, when his conversion by Eleanor Staunton to Christian Socialism ends his "damnéd vacillating state."

When Alton tries to please his upper-class friends with his poetry, he is trapped in the falsehood of denying his radical political beliefs. But when he tries to be true to the working class, he is trapped in the opposite falsehood of "physical force" Chartism, which lands him in jail for three years for his part in an agricultural riot in 1845. Alton gets involved in the riot because he has wanted to prove his solidarity with his Chartist friends. But this has become necessary because of his earlier "flunkeydom" of trying to impress Dean Winnstay and his daughter Lillian and because he has been attacked as a traitor to his class by Mr. O'Flynn (Feargus O'Connor) in the *Weekly Warwhoop* (the *Northern Star*). Simultaneously editing the politics out of his poetry on the advice of the Dean and earning his keep through equally dishonest political hack writing for the *Weekly Warwhoop*, Alton has already shown his ability to be untrue to both sides. The "flunkey" in one chapter becomes the hotheaded radical in the next, and sometimes the change takes place in a single paragraph. When Alton's Chartist friend John Crossthwaite announces that there is a rising among agricultural workers which may be "a great opening for spreading the principles of the Charter," Alton impulsively volunteers to travel there as a lecturer: " 'I will go,' I said, starting up. 'They shall see that I do care for The Cause. If it's a dangerous mission, so much the better. It will prove my sincerity.' " (277). His enthusiasm for "The Cause" is squelched immediately, however, when Crossthwaite tells him that the site of the rising is near the town where Lillian and the Dean live. "My heart sank. If it had been any other spot in England! But it was too late to retract . . . I felt I must keep up my present excitement, or lose my heart, and my caste, for ever." But after still another change of mood, Alton is just beginning to feel that his "triumph" at the meeting has been "complete" "when my eye was caught by a face which there was no mistaking —my cousin's!" (278). The presence of this upper-class "basilisk" spying upon Alton's Chartist plans throws Alton into shame and confusion. Although he is only being true to "The Cause" of the working class and has planned to do nothing illegal, he tells us that, in confronting his cousin, "there was nothing for it but to brazen it out; and, besides, I was in his power . . . I dared not offend him at that moment" (279). The same contrariness dogs Alton into the country and at the scene of the riot. One moment he is pacifically preaching Chartism to the laborers; the next moment he is impulsively inciting them to riot; and finally he assumes the role of special constable, trying to quell the riot: "I was shocked and terrified at their threats. I tried again and again to stop and harangue them. I shouted myself hoarse about the duty of honesty; warned them against pillage and violence; entreated them to take nothing but the corn which they actually needed; but my voice was drowned in the uproar. Still I felt myself in a measure responsible for their conduct; I had helped to excite them, and dare not, in honour, desert them; and trembling, I went on, prepared to see the worst'' (298-299).

As a story about a man whose status is unclear and who is caught up in a perpetual social identity crisis, Kingsley's novel has some virtues that make it roughly comparable to Pip's story of guilt and ambition in *Great Expectations*. Alton's quarrel with his evangelical mother when he is struggling to educate himself; his clumsiness at Cambridge, which prefigures the sorrows of Jude Fawley; his longing for Lillian Winnstay, the Estella of his life; and even his uncertainty about what sort of poet to be and what sort of audience to write for are understandable and at times moving. Too often, however, and especially in the midst of political events like the Chartist meeting and the riot, Alton's doubleness makes him less like a possible working-class poet than like some of the "possessed" characters in Gothic fiction, a political version of Jekyll and Hyde, driven first one way by angels and then the other way by fiends, never in control of events or sure of who he is. On such occasions, which are far too numerous to make *Alton Locke* a satisfactory work of art, what appears on the surface are not the uncertainties of the tailor-poet, but the contradictions of the Christian Socialist; the identity crisis is too much Kingsley's own to be credited as that of a Chartist poet like Thomas Cooper or Gerald Massey.

Kingsley says that "the moral of my book is that the working man who tries to get on, to desert his class and rise above it, enters into a lie, and leaves God's path for his own—with consequences" (xxix). But it is not clear what Kingsley means by this—no more clear than when, at one of the Cranbourne Tavern meetings of the Christian Socialists with a few well-behaved Chartists, Kingsley stood up with folded arms and stammered, "I am a Church of England parson—and a Chartist" (xix). Of course he was not a Chartist—except in a Church of England sense. He was doing no more than being rashly and outspokenly unsure of himself, like Alton Locke addressing the farm laborers. And again like Alton trying to stop the ruckus he has helped to start, Kingsley was always prepared to reverse himself after one of his radical forays, as in the placard to the Chartists which the events of April 10 prompted him to write: "Workers of England, be wise, and then you *must* be free, for you will be *fit* to be free."[23] The moral of Alton Locke's story is not at all that he should shun middle-class values in favor of Chartism, trade unionism, and Owenism. But neither is it that a working man should go humbly along on the treadmill provided him by middle-class industry without seeking to "better himself." What, then, does Parson Kingsley mean? He seems to mean only that a worker should not be ashamed of his status and that he should do whatever he can within legal and Christian boundaries to help the other members of his class.

It is clear that Chartism of the pre-1848 and "unchristianized" variety is not part of Kingsley's program. At the end of his story, Alton Locke tells Eleanor Staunton that he is still a Chartist, but of a new and contrite variety:

> "If by a Chartist you mean one who fancies that a change in mere political circumstances will bring about a millennium, I am no longer one. That dream is gone—with others. But if to be a Chartist is to love my brothers with every faculty of my soul—to wish to live and die struggling for their rights, endeavouring to make them, not electors merely, but fit to be electors, senators, kings, and priests to God and to His Christ—if that be the Chartism of the future, then am I sevenfold a Chartist, and ready to confess it before men, though I were thrust forth from every door in England." (429)

In the language of Christian Socialism, there is a spiritual side to every earthly radicalism that validates it only by removing it from the sphere of practice and by projecting it as an ideal into the future, as in "the Chartism of the future." Practical politics becomes a set of noble wishes; good intentions take the place of deeds; the flaws in earthly kingdoms are corrected in the Kingdom of Christ, which is now and here. Such language is often at odds with the actions of the Christian Socialists, which were frequently bold and original. Maurice understood that his search for unity in Christ might lead people to think him a "milksop," but he defended his ambivalent positions bravely, and in 1853, after the publication of his *Theological Essays,* he was dismissed from his professorship at King's College. After one of his sermons, Kingsley was denounced in church by the clergyman who had invited him to give it, and his own two-sided liberalism lost him more than one opportunity for advancement. But perhaps the courage of their weak convictions can be best illustrated by the actions of Tom Hughes on April 10, 1848, before there was such a thing as Christian Socialism. Hughes signed up as a special constable and went to Trafalgar Square to help keep the peace, only to be arrested by a regular policeman for creating a disturbance![24]

The language of Christian Socialism, as in Alton Locke's definition of his religious version of Chartism, combines in oxymoronic fashion a radical apocalyptic strain reflecting the revolutionary uproar of 1848 with a sense that all is well now that the uproar is over: reality itself is the apocalypse, and good Christians are already in and of the Church Universal, whose doors stand open all about us. "The Charter seems dead, and liberty further off than ever" (405), Eleanor says to Alton and John Crossthwaite. But liberty, fraternity, and equality are alive and well in Christ, she tells them, and the Charter is "realized already for you. You are free; God has made you free" (403). The dark sayings and deeds of Chartism are followed by Christian Socialism; the "lowest depths" and Alton's suicidal mood on April 10 are followed by his escape from typhus and his spiritual rebirth through the hallucinatory apocalypse of his fever-dream, by the discovery of his true identity in Christ and his love for Eleanor, and by his voyage to the New World. Kingsley's aim of exposing the worst evils of sweated labor and of insanitary conditions gives way suddenly to a celebration of Christian unity and love. Despite the long trauma of the 1840s and "the frightful scenes of hopeless misery" Alton has witnessed, the outlook for the future is rosy, for "sunrise, they say, often at first draws up and deepens the very mists which it is about to scatter" (409). This is one more aspect of the doubleness of Kingsley's vision and of Christian Socialism generally: in the midst of dissecting the causes of poverty and disease, it chimes in with its avowed enemies of the Manchester School to proclaim that "there's a good time coming." "Hark! Merry voices on deck are welcoming their future home," writes Alton at the end of his voyage to America and of his life.

> Laugh on, happy ones! —come out of Egypt and the house of bondage, and the waste and howling wilderness of slavery and competition, workhouses and prisons, into a good land and large, a land flowing with milk and honey, where you will sit every one under his own vine and his own fig-tree, and look into the faces of your rosy children—and see in them a blessing and not a curse! Oh, England! stern mother-land, when wilt thou renew thy youth?—Thou wilderness of man's making, not God's! . . . . Is it not written, that the days shall come when the forest shall break forth into singing, and the wilderness shall blossom like the rose? (434-435)

So we arrive once again at the mechanical vineyards of John Bright, only through Christian unity and "association" rather than through free trade and Mammonite "competition."

Although she is less given to apocalyptic generalizations, Mrs. Gaskell's vision in *Mary Barton* and *North and South* is similarly optimistic. Class reconciliation through brotherly love is where her stories lead, and while the terms of reconciliation are strained and less plausible in her earlier industrial novel than in her later one, they are nevertheless the answer even to murder and the laws that punish murder. Mrs. Gaskell began writing *Mary Barton* as early as 1845, and its melodramatic account of trade union violence and of the turning of John Barton into a pariah betrays something of the despair middle-class liberals felt because of class conflict before 1848. But *Mary Barton* was not published until 1848, and Mrs. Gaskell was very much aware of its timeliness. On March 21, 1848, she wrote to Chapman that her novel was highly appropriate for "the present time of struggle on the part of work people to obtain what they esteem their rights."[25] And a month later, three days after the Kennington Common demonstration, she wrote to urge Chapman to seek as wide a circulation as possible for her book because of "my own belief that the tale would bear directly upon the present circumstances."[26] Her hope was that *Mary Barton* would help to promote class reconciliation by showing, through the "tragedy of a poor man's life," why working men become Chartists and trade unionists and what the middle class could do about it. When her story made "half the masters" in Manchester "bitterly angry" with her, she was disappointed. Some of the masters apparently believed that she was actually advocating Chartism and trade unionism. But, as she told Mary Ewart, her aim was only to "represent the subject in the light in which some of the workmen certainly consider to be *true, not* that I dare to say it is the abstract absolute truth."

> That some of the men do view the subject in the way I have tried to represent, I have personal evidence; and I think somewhere in the first volume you may find a sentence stating that my intention was simply to represent the view many of the workpeople take. But independently of any explicit statement of my intention, I do think that we must all acknowledge that there are duties connected with the manufacturing system not fully understood as yet, and evils existing in relation to it which may be remedied in some degree, although we as yet do not see how; but surely there is no harm in directing the attention to the existence of such evils. No one can feel more deeply than I how *wicked* it is to do anything to excite class against class; and the sin has been most unconscious if I have done so.[27]

Certainly the novel ends with a strong plea for class reconciliation, although, because Mr. Carson gives up his desire for legal vengeance, at least one writer believed that Mrs. Gaskell may "have wrought real mischief in the hot heads of angry unionists by granting impunity to murder."[28] After the assassination of young Carson, John Barton pines away from guilt ("the Avenger, the sure Avenger, had found him out"), while old Mr. Carson, his peace of mind shattered by his son's death, lives on only for the sake of revenge through legal punishment. But in a denouement that violates the calm, sympathetic, documentary style of the early parts of the novel, the murderer and the father of the murdered man come together in mutual forgiveness:

> Mr. Carson stood in the doorway. In one instant he comprehended the case.
> He raised up the powerless frame; and the departing soul looked out of the eyes with gratitude. He held the dying man propped in his arms. John Barton folded his hands as if in prayer.
> "Pray for us," said Mary, sinking on her knees, and forgetting in that solemn hour all that had divided her father and Mr. Carson.
> No other words would suggest themselves than some of those he had read only a few hours before.
> "God be merciful to us sinners.—Forgive us our trespasses as we forgive them that trespass against us."
> And when the words were said, John Barton lay a corpse in Mr. Carson's arms.
> So ended the tragedy of a poor man's life.[29]

What makes even this unlikely ending superior to *Alton Locke* is that it remains at the level of a personal event in the lives of Mrs. Gaskell's characters. If she reads the destiny of all society in the embrace of Barton and Carson, she does not say so: the realization of Christian love in the lives of a few individuals is not necessarily the groundwork of the Kingdom of Christ in the present. She comes closer to such a generalization in *North and South,* although there both the violence of class conflict and the scenes of reconciliation to which it leads are less melodramatic than in her earlier novel. Thornton is not a bad man, and his striking workers do not conspire to assassinate him. He is more like Robert Moore in *Shirley* than like Mr. Carson, an incarnation of middle-class vigor and integrity who happens also to be "Coriolanian." In his dealings with his workers, as Margaret Hale puts it, Thornton stands "upon his 'rights' as no human being ought to stand."[30] Margaret helps to convert Thornton from raw economic individualism to the ideal of cooperation, or to Mrs. Gaskell's not very utopian version of Christian Socialism. Margaret expresses this ideal when she tells Thornton that "God has made us so that we must be mutually dependent," and that "the most proudly independent man depends on those around him for their insensible influence on his character—his life" (116-117). The harsh experiences of the strike and of bankruptcy prepare Thornton to practice "industrial chivalry" and a moderate form of cooperation. As he explains to Mr. Colthurst: "I have arrived at the conviction that no mere institutions, however wise, and however much thought may have been required to organize and arrange them, can attach class to class as they should be attached, unless the working out of such institutions bring the individuals of the different classes into actual personal contact. Such intercourse is the very breath of life" (419-420). Like Robert Moore, Thornton has become a true "Captain of Industry" and a promoter of class peace, and if this result seems unrevolutionary, there is something admirable about its modesty. Mrs. Gaskell's industrial stories are written with a calm reasonableness and a general accuracy about working-class attitudes and customs that are in direct contrast to Kingsley's two-sided apocalyptic style, and if she arrives at no new or daring answers to the social problems she depicts, neither is she led to strike bargains with Chartists and socialists that she cannot keep.

Mrs. Gaskell, who knew Maurice and Kingsley and allowed them to reprint "The Sexton's Hero" and "Christmas Storms and Sunshine" in *The Christian Socialist,* sees cooperation as a corrective to free enterprise rather than as an alternative to it. Because of this moderate emphasis, her economic ideas (although she claims to be innocent of them) make more sense than the hyperbolic antithesis between competition and cooperation in "Cheap Clothes and Nasty" and *Alton Locke.* But she admired both Kingsley and Maurice greatly and probably considered herself— from the rather distant vantage point of Manchester Unitarianism—a Christian Socialist. If that is the case, then Christian Socialism for her does not mean much more than the establishment of class peace through prosperity and through the right actions of captains of industry like Thornton and the converted Mr. Carson. Maurice, Kingsley, and Ludlow certainly meant more by Christian Socialism than that, although it is not always clear what. Of the three, only Ludlow seems to have maintained a consistently radical vision of an alternative society, based mainly on Owen, Fourier, and Louis Blanc.[31] Kingsley's impulsive illogicality, on the other hand, is an ironic complement to Maurice's steep Coleridgean logic, which is always veering into theological mist.

But Mrs. Gaskell probably did not see such flaws in Kingsley and Maurice. And while many were not prepared to excuse Kingsley's worst excesses, many others, unlike Benjamin Jowett and Aubrey de Vere, were prepared to testify to the wisdom and subtlety of Maurice's thinking. Ludlow believed that he was the greatest religious teacher since Luther or perhaps even St. Paul. And John Stuart Mill declared that he found Maurice a subtle and profound thinker, whose intellectual power excelled that of Coleridge.[32] Mill's appreciation of Maurice, moreover, which is that of the chief liberal social scientist of Victorian England for its chief liberal theologian, is comprehensible on several counts. Both Mill and Maurice share a number of important qualities that reveal the strengths and weaknesses generally of Victorian liberalism at its best. Both are extremely complex and open-minded intellectuals who are forever assimilating other people's ideas, often at the price of contradicting their own. Mill's circumnavigation from Bentham through St. Simon, Coleridge, Carlyle, Tocqueville, and also Maurice to the synthesis of Benthamite and Coleridgean elements in his later liberalism and cooperative socialism is strikingly similar to Maurice's conversion from his original Unitarian radicalism to the Coleridgean, Broad Church liberalism that leads him also to cooperative socialism. Even their reservations about each other are complementary. Although Mill praises Maurice's intellectual power, he also says that Maurice squandered it in timid adherence to the Church of England; while in 1838, after reading Mill's essay on Bentham, Maurice declared: "The circumference of his thoughts is enlarging continually. I wish they had a centre."[33]

There is a remarkable instance of the Coleridgean dictum that "extremes meet" in the testimony given before the Select Committee on Investments for the Savings of the Middle and Working Classes in 1850, chaired by R. A. Slaney. The committee was important to the Christian Socialists because through it they hoped to obtain legislation favorable to workers' cooperatives; it resulted in the Industrial and Provident Societies Act of 1852, which was drafted by Ludlow. Several of the Christian Socialists testified before Slaney's committee, and so did John Stuart Mill, who as the leading political economist in the land was expected to confirm the old prejudices in favor of competition and laissez-faire and to declare that cooperative socialism was scientifically impracticable. When he did just the reverse, the Christian Socialists were jubilant. Ludlow summarized Mill's testimony in *The Christian Socialist* by announcing that "the first political economist of the day, not only in this country but in Europe," has come down on the side of cooperation. Mill, says Ludlow, has testified

that "hardly anything which the legislature could do in the present state of society . . . would be more useful" than to give facilities to working people associating; that the want of such facilities is "a great cause of discontent, and a very just one." He goes further and states that "he sees no reason why such associations should not succeed" . . . He wishes to see the enterprises in which the working classes are now engaged carried on, not as now "by a capitalist hiring labourers as he wants them, but by the labourers themselves, mental as well as manual, hiring the capital they require at the market rate."[34]

The Christian Socialists were surprised by Mill's testimony, but there is not much reason why they should have been, anymore than he should have been jostled out of his supposed prejudices by the idea of cooperation. After all, in his essay "Civilization" (1836), written long before "Parson Lot" had begun the daring venture of rubbing elbows with ex-Chartists and ex-"red republicans," Mill had declared that cooperation was the basis of society, in language echoed by Maurice. According to Mill, savagery is a state of selfishness marked by lack of the power to combine for mutual benefits. On the other hand, "there is not a more accurate test of the progress of civilization than the progress of the power of cooperation."[35] Of course cooperation can mean many things, from brotherly love and union in Christ all the way down the scale to the contractual relations between the workers, the managers, and the capitalist owners of a factory. Nevertheless Mill does not start from the assumption that men are bound together in society because of selfishness: he would argue that "enlightened self-interest" involves cooperation for mutual gain, rather than the "cannibalistic" competition exposed by Kingsley in "Cheap Clothes and Nasty" and by Ludlow in his *Fraser's Magazine* article "Labour and the Poor."

In any case, Furnivall not only got Ruskin's permission to reprint "The Nature of Gothic" for the opening of the Working Men's College in 1854, but he also sought Mill's permission to reprint the chapter on "The Probable Futurity of the Labouring Classes" from *The Principles of Political Economy*. Mill was surprised by the request, for, as he told Harriet Taylor, "I did not expect the Xtian Socialists would wish to circulate the chapter as it is in the 3d edit[ion] since it stands up for Competition against their one-eyed attacks & denunciations of it."[36] But the chapter in the third edition also stands up for cooperation, and Mill refers in it to the Christian Socialists as "a band of friends, chiefly clergymen and barristers, to whose noble exertions too much praise can scarcely be given" and through whom "the good seed" of cooperation has been "widely sown."[37] Even Kingsley was led to invoke Mill against Mammon. Referring to the chapter on the future of the working class as it appeared in the second edition of the *Principles,* Alton Locke says: "Read it, thou self-satisfied Mammon, and perpend; for it is both a prophecy and a doom!" (336). What really separates Mill from the Christian Socialists is not politics so much as religion, but even this gap was almost bridged by Mill's religious speculations in his later essays. The circle has closed when in 1865 Maurice writes to Kingsley that the seventh chapter of Mill's *Examination of the Philosophy of Sir William Hamilton* "is as masterly as anything which has been written in our day, and . . . the passage in pp. 102-103 is a grand and affecting theological statement, as it proceeds from a man who was bred an Atheist and perhaps takes himself to be one" (II, 498).

As the leading political economist in the land was moving towards socialism, the Christian Socialists were engaging in cooperative business practices that tended to erode their hostility towards the Manchester School and to reconcile them to "England's commercial prosperity." W. R. Greg was certainly wrong when he declared that cooperatives were no advance over ordinary businesses, since both had to compete with themselves and with each other for customers or else become monopolies. But he was right in the more general sense that the cooperative movement would not revolutionize British business practices but would rather find its place in the economy side by side with ordinary concerns.[38] In their attempt to "christianize Socialism," Maurice and his followers succeeded in the sense that they were one of the factors that helped to develop the cooperative movement away from Owenite "community building" to self-help "shopkeeping." In his essay on this aspect of the history of the cooperative movement, Sidney Pollard quotes an article in the *Co-operator* for 1866-1867: "Modern Co-operation . . . means a union of working men for the improvement of the social circumstances of the class to which they belong. As defined by secretaries of certain societies, it is the working man's lever, by which he may rise in the world." As Pollard points out, the ideals of reforming the conditions of the working class and of enabling individual working men to "rise," "unlike those of the earlier socialist-co-operators . . . assumed the continuance of a mainly capitalist economic system."[39] And the initial utopianism of the Christian Socialists themselves waned quickly, partly because most of the cooperatives they sponsored failed or had to be turned into joint stock companies, run on the old principle of "devil take the hindmost." By 1854 Maurice had concluded that the time was not ripe for cooperation, largely because the working class was unprepared for it, and so he turned to education as a means of promoting social unity. In 1857, Kingsley wrote that their cooperative ventures have failed "because the men are not fit for them," although he continued to believe that "association will be the next form of industrial development, I doubt not, for production; but it will require two generations of previous training, both in morality and in *drill*, to make the workmen capable of it."[40] The working class, it seems, were not so prepared as the working clerisy to behave like Christian gentlemen and so to bring on the reign of brotherly love.

Maurice's search for unity in Christ and his studious opposition to partisanship, then, appear to be little more than theological declarations in favor of class peace and of social progress through class "cooperation" and self-help. Although stated in terms of Christian ideals, his position is not radically different from that of the political economists and free trade radicals of the 1840s, who insist that the interests of the working and middle classes are bound up together. As Peter Allen observes: "In the future victory of Christian Socialism Maurice foresaw no great change in the structure of society. Like many Victorians his answer to the class war was not the abolition of class but the establishment of class peace, in which the various classes carried out their respective economic functions in . . . good fellowship, to the benefit of all. Maurice regarded the class structure as a necessary expression of the division of labour according to ability; in a truly Christian society, he would argue, men might be spiritually equal and still perform different tasks."[41] Because of their two-sidedness, the apocalyptic and utopian visions of the Christian Socialists are mirror images of the apocalyptic and utopian visions of progress through class peace and industrial "cooperation" inspired by the victory of free trade, the defeat of Chartism, and the Great Exhibition. Their very noble zeal helped to expose some of the worst effects of competition, like the practice of sweated labor, and of the least sanitary conditions, like the Bermondsey cholera district. And their efforts on behalf of trade unions, cooperatives, and working-class education, particularly through the organizational and legal work of John Malcolm Ludlow, were notable contributions towards the development of the welfare state. But, at least in the early 1850s, they expected to sweep away social evils by putting Christian principles into practice, after which the landscape would look very much like Macaulay's Middlesex on the material side and like Maurice's Kingdom of Christ on the spiritual. When their initial zeal waned because most of their tilting against competition failed, and they discovered that the landscape looked very much like Macaulay's Middlesex anyway (it always had been the Kingdom of Christ), they were not greatly surprised or disappointed. Even Christian communism, which, as embodied in the Church, did not seek to overrule the principle of private ownership embodied in the state, was perhaps safer when projected into the future, along with the vexed question of universal suffrage.[42]

The drawing together of the views of John Stuart Mill and Frederick Denison Maurice in the 1850s, then, is less coincidental than it is the logical outcome of the developing complexity of middle-class liberalism, able to assimilate apparently opposite views. After the long warfare of the 1840s, the advent of a period of relative social stability and prosperity allowed the forces of Bentham and the forces of Coleridge, despite the continued resistance of their generals, to begin to merge into yet another Coleridgean "Idea."

Going to the Great Exhibition. Cruikshank in *1851, or the Adventures of Mr. and Mrs. Sandboys.*

VII. Liberal Individualism: The Brownings

> It is not through ruin that we are to seek prosperity. Therefore we hold, that no aspirations for the future need make us reject a present prosperity.
>
> *The Spectator,* April 22, 1848

"Revolutions go off like pop-guns!" Lord Shaftesbury exclaimed late in March 1848.[1] Probably in the same month, Matthew Arnold composed two sonnets "to a Republican friend," warning "citizen" Clough against the utopian expectations aroused by the February Revolution in France:

> Nor will that day dawn at a human nod,
> When, bursting through the network superposed
> By selfish occupation—plot and plan,
>
> Lust, avarice, envy—liberated man,
> All difference with his fellow-mortal closed,
> Shall be left standing face to face with God.

The program of the French socialists, in other words, seeking to bring on the reign of equality for "liberated man" by eliminating "selfish occupation" and "all difference with his fellow-mortal," is not going to be realized. The "nod" will have to be divine rather than human, but God has removed his headquarters, at least for the occasion of Arnold's sonnets, to the far side of the "high uno'erleaped Mountains of Necessity." On the near side, meanwhile, the likelihood for a radical reformation of society by means of political action is nonexistent.

That Clough was more sympathetic than Arnold to the socialist experiments of the Second Republic and also to Chartism is apparent both from Arnold's cautionary sonnets and from their correspondence. Clough was at first elated by the events in France, and in May he visited Paris with a group of his Oxford friends to view events at first hand. But it was on May 15 that various radical and working-class elements, impatient with the failure of the Lamartine government to cure unemployment and also to aid the revolutionaries in Poland and Italy, broke into the Assembly and marched to the Hotel de Ville to set up a new revolutionary government. The disturbance was halted and some four hundred participants were arrested, but the Lamartine government had been forced into a posture of reaction, and disillusionment was rife. On May 19 Clough sent to Stanley a pseudo-Carlylean letter, which expressed his own growing disillusionment: "Ichabod, Ichabod, the glory is departed. Liberty, Equality, and Fraternity, driven back by shopkeeping bayonet, hides her red cap in dingiest St. Antoine. Well-to-do-ism shakes her Egyptian scourge to the tune of Ye are idle, ye are idle; the tale of bricks will be doubled, and Moses and Aaron of Socialism can at the best only pray for plagues . . . Meantime the glory and the freshness of the dream is departed."[2] Clough saw that the chance for a socialist reconstruction was dwindling. Following the June days, all hope for such a reconstruction died, thus vindicating Arnold's skepticism and leading him to write to Clough: "What a nice state of things in France. The New Gospel is adjourned for this bout. If one had ever hoped any thing from such a set of d——d grimacing liars as their prophets one would be very sick just now."[3]

More than any other factor, the failure of Chartism and of the revolutions of 1848 soured Clough's democratic optimism (which he expresses clearly although still ironically in the character of Philip Hewson in *The Bothie of Tober-na-Vuolich*) and helped to make both his social and his religious poetry of the 1850s sarcastic and irresolute. Although he attacked "devil take the hindmost" competition and bourgeois Podsnappery in poems like "Duty" and "The Latest Decalogue," he did not retain much faith in political action or even in the cooperative experiments that the Christian Socialists, undaunted by the failure of Blanc's projects in France, began in 1850. He supported their efforts, but from a distance. One of his unfinished pieces of prose is an "Address on Socialism," signed by "Citoyen" and directed to the Christian Socialists. "Citoyen" sympathizes with them, says that he is "a fixed customer of two of [their] cooperative establishments," but also questions their utopianism.[4] He paraphrases Carlyle: "Given a world of very half and half Christians, is it not too soon to insist on a Christian Socialism from their united action?" And Clough comes to the satiric defense of competition, as he does in "The Latest Decalogue," although it is not clear how ironic he is being. "Citoyen" is a most unconvincing defender of competition, especially when he cites the Bible to prove that we are not our brothers' keepers, but he also attacks the principle of cooperation as naively maintained by the Christian Socialists. *In utrumque paratus*. Clough admires the idealism of the Christian Socialists, but thinks them unrealistic ("The millennium, as Matt says, won't come this bout,'' he wrote to his sister in 1848). Therefore the palm of victory goes to competition, or to that core of original nastiness in human nature which, Clough seems to believe, makes us inevitably competitors rather than cooperators. But what emerges most distinctly from Clough's ''Address on Socialism'' is his confusion over what to think or to do about social injustice. His political irresolution, moreover, is related to his theological irresolution in poems like the two ''Easter Day in Naples'' pieces, for the way out of both his political and his religious quandaries depends upon his answering not so much the question of the existence of God but the question of the innate goodness or selfishness of mankind. And Clough cannot answer it. The result is a poetry of ''twin-mindedness'' as in ''Dipsychus,'' which looks on the surface like the two-sidedness of Maurice's theology but which, rather than discovering union in opposites, is nakedly and honestly contradictory.

While Clough's ironic defense of competition betrays an underlying sympathy with the Christian Socialists, others were prepared to defend competition more vigorously than ''Citoyen,'' and their opinions of socialism were never equivocal. Elizabeth Barrett Browning, who was always a ''fierce Radical'' of the Anti-Corn Law League variety and who could tell her friend Kenyon that the trouble with the Chartists was that there were not enough of them, expressed her fear of the ''theorists of Paris'' in several of her 1848 letters: ''As to communism, surely the practical part of *that,* the only not dangerous part, is attainable simply by the consent of individuals who may try the experiment of associating their families in order to [gain] the cheaper employment of the means of life, and successfully in many cases. But make a government scheme of *even so much,* and you seem to trench on . . . individual liberty. All such patriarchal planning in a government issues naturally into absolutism, and is adapted to states of society more or less barbaric.''[5] She declared that ''Louis Blanc knows not what he says,'' that the theories of the socialists are ''ideas which kill,'' and that she would prefer to live ''under the feet of the Czar than in those states of perfectibility imagined by Fourier and Cabet.''[6] ''Whatever . . . touches upon property is a wrong, and whatever tends to the production of social equality is absurd and iniquitous.''[7] Again, in the same letter to Kenyon in which she expressed her sympathy for the defeated Chartists, she wrote: ''Nothing can be more hateful to me than this communist idea of quenching individualities in the mass. As if the hope of the world did not always consist in the eliciting of the individual man from the background of the masses, in the evolvement of individual genius, virtue, magnanimity.''[8] Governments are made to promote individuality, not to interfere with it. The aim of life, as in Mill's *On Liberty,* is the fullest and freest development of the potentialities of the individual, and the state is the main threat to this aim.

The antisocialist opinions in Elizabeth Browning's letters are one facet of the liberal individualism or the entrepreneurial ideal that informs all of her writing and that of Robert Browning as well. Her humanitarian poetry, like "The Cry of the Children" and "The Cry of the Human" in the 1844 volume, may seem to contradict this statement. But one way of defining humanitarian poetry like hers and like Hood's would be to say that it is political poetry with the politics removed. It examines isolated problems like child labor and suggests limited measures of governmental interference with trade while criticizing unqualified laissez-faire, but it eschews any larger political theorizing. The wrongs of a few factory owners are not the wrongs of a system. Besides, "The Cry of the Human" is a free trade poem, and "The Cry of the Children" is a versification of some of the findings of R. H. Horne, himself both a free trader and one of the investigators for Ashley's Children's Employment Commission.

Elizabeth Browning was almost as uncomfortable in her role as a humanitarian poet as was Hood, although for a different reason. She felt that the use of poetry to expose social wrongs was unesthetic and contradictory. She told her friend H. S. Boyd that "The Cry of the Children" "wants melody," and that "the subject (the factory miseries) is scarcely an agreeable one to the fancy." And when the musician Henry Russell proposed to set it to music, she wrote to Robert that the prospect was not "endurable." Russell's program, she said, "exhibits all the horrors of the world, I see! Lifeboats . . . madhouses . . . gamblers wives . . . all done to the right sort of moaning. His audiences must go home delightfully miserable, I should fancy. He has set the 'Song of the Shirt' . . . and my 'Cry of the Children' will be acceptable, it is supposed, as a climax of agony."[9] She calls the very notion of humanitarian poetry into question. "The factory miseries" are not a suitable subject for great poetry, which ought to elevate rather than agonize. So she comes close to the reasoning that led Arnold to reject *Empedocles on Etna,* and also to a refutation of Bulwer's insistence that poetry should be political and should contribute to reform. From an Aristotelian perspective, both she and Arnold were right, although neither of them allowed their critical principles to prevent them from writing more of the wrong sort of poetry.

The fullest expression of Elizabeth Browning's liberal individualism comes in *Aurora Leigh* (1856), where the poetic sensibilities of the heroine are contrasted to the dehumanizing theories of Romney, her socialist cousin. Romney's work as a reformer is presented as the antithesis to Aurora's work as a poet; he is made to look emotionally retarded while she is made to look like a budding sage—a natural result, perhaps, in a poem that asserts woman's equality with man as well as the folly of socialism. All of Romney's efforts to mend the world go wrong, and his private life goes wrong as well, because he operates by "ideas which kill" rather than by the life-giving poet's and woman's sense of the individual uniqueness of each of God's creatures. According to Aurora, whose heart Romney misjudges as he does everyone else's, "If I married him,"

> . . . He might cut
> My body into coins to give away
> Among his other paupers; change my sons,
> While I stood dumb as Griseld, for black babes
> Or piteous foundlings; might unquestioned set
> My right hand teaching in the Ragged Schools,
> My left hand washing in the Public Baths.[10]

As Aurora tells Romney in rejecting his proposal of marriage:

> "Sir, you were married long ago.
> You have a wife already whom you love,
> Your social theory."
>
> (2. 408-410)

Romney is a clear instance of "an enthusiasm for statistics" threatening the "wholesale ruin of the human world." He has read too many blue-books filled with suffering en masse, and he has become a new version of that stock figure in early Victorian literature, the mad social scientist, like Dickens's Mr. Slug and Mr. Filer. The chief difference is that he is not a Gradgrindian political economist, keeping the poor down by heartless theories, but a benevolent reformer. He is thus a hybrid of Gradgrind and Mrs. Jellyby, being most like the former in that he

> lives by diagrams,
> And crosses out the spontaneities
> Of all his individual, personal life
> With formal universals. As if man
> Were set upon a high stool at a desk
> To keep God's books for Him in red and black,
> And feel by millions!
>
> (3.744-750)

Romney is guilty mainly of the sin of French socialism after the Fourier-ist model, but he is also associated with statistics, political economy, or-ganized charity, Christian Socialism, and dedication to reform in general. All of these are mixed together in the poem without respect for the differ-ences between them, thus forming a general indictment of the active search for social improvement. *Aurora Leigh* expresses a revulsion against political involvement that derives partly from the failures of 1848 and partly from the author's free trade individualism. Fourierism, Christian Socialism, organized charity, and Gradgrindian political economy are similar only because they entail forming abstract theories about society. Aurora and Elizabeth see theories as a sort of vampirism, draining the life's blood from the veins of individuals; fortunately there are women and poets in the world like Aurora and Elizabeth to administer transfu-sions.

"I too have my vocation," Aurora tells Romney,

> "Most serious work, most necessary work
> As any of the economists'. Reform,
> Make trade a Christian possibility,
> And individual right no general wrong;
> Wipe out earth's furrows of the Thine and Mine,
> And leave one green for men to play at bowls,
> Winnings for them all! . . . What then, indeed,
> If mortals are not greater by the head
> Than any of their prosperities? what then,
> Unless the artist keep up open roads
> Betwixt the seen and unseen . . .?"

(2.459-469)

Aurora does not merely claim equal status for poetry with social reform: her ridicule of Romney's goals is too severe for such balance. She sees even moderate efforts for reform—those of economists and Christian So-cialists—as forming a progression leading to the abolition of property, or of "the Thine and Mine." True, Aurora claims for the poet a high func-tion in the work of social improvement, but it is a function which contra-dicts that of the reformer who works by statistics, by theories, or by direct political action. Aurora says that poets are "the only truth-tellers now left to God, / The only speakers of essential truth" (1.859-860), thus taking upon herself a mighty burden of prophetic wisdom. And later she ex-patiates upon the liberalism of poetry:

> "For poets (bear the word),
> Half-poets even, are still whole democrats,—
> Oh, not that we're disloyal to the high,
> But loyal to the low, and cognizant
> Of the less scrutable majesties."
>
> (4.314-318)

But Aurora does not mean more by "democrats" than Robert Browning does by his association of Shelley's "unacknowledged legislator" idea with the cranky celestial spy whom he presents as the type of the poet in "How it Strikes a Contemporary." It is at least clear that Aurora is not going to be any more political as a poet than Elizabeth. As Romney tells her:

> "The human race
> To you means, such a child, or such a man,
> You saw one morning waiting in the cold,
> Beside that gate, perhaps. You gather up
> A few such cases, and when strong sometimes
> Will write of factories and of slaves, as if
> Your father were a negro, and your son
> A spinner in the mills."
>
> (2.189-196)

This is obviously a reflection on Elizabeth's own social poetry like "Cry of the Children," which we are not to regard as forming generalizations about social problems but as making statements about individual cases of misery. What Romney wants, however, is a sense of universal misery: "Why, I call you hard / To general suffering" (2.198-199).

Perhaps the uniting of Romney and Aurora at the end of the poem involves a merger of what they represent, which would imply that social theorizing and reform need to be infused with the wisdom of poetry. But Romney's experiments in social reform are so disastrous, exploding like dangerous chemicals and blinding him, that they cannot be seen as equivalent to Aurora's poetry, needing only to be synthesized with it. After his rejection by Aurora, Romney decides to wed Marian Erle, whom he has rescued from the slums, as a symbolic protest against class barriers, a union of the two nations as in *Sybil*. But Marian, tricked by Lady Waldemar, leaves Romney waiting at the altar; the rabble from St. Giles's who have come to the wedding are angered by this miscarriage and so riot and try to kill him. Failing to learn the right lesson from this fiasco, Romney continues his experiments in social reform by establishing a phalanstery at Leigh Hall, presumably on Christian Socialist principles. "A Christian socialist / Is Romney Leigh, you understand," says the German student to Sir Blaise Delorme, who replies: "I disbelieve in Christian-pagans, much / As you in women-fishes" (5.737-740). The phalanstery, "christianized from Fourier's own," proves to be even more a disaster than Romney's attempted marriage to Marian Erle. As he tells Aurora at the end of the poem:

"My vain phalanstery dissolved itself;
My men and women of disordered lives
I brought in orderly to dine and sleep,
Broke up those waxen masks I made them wear,
With fierce contortions of the natural face,
And cursed me for my tyrannous constraint
In forcing crooked creatures to live straight."

(8.888-894)

As at the wedding, the poor whom Romney tries to help through the phalanstery are ungrateful and destructive wretches unworthy of his goodness. Neither they nor his neighbors appreciate the Christian element in his Fourierism, and they torment him in various ways.

"I had my windows broken once or twice
By liberal peasants naturally incensed
At such a vexer of Arcadian peace."

(8.917-919)

Little boys stone him when he rides by, and he has even been shot at by a poacher who, he says, was

"tired of springeing game
So long upon my acres, undisturbed,
And restless for the country's virtue."

(8.929-931)

As the last act in the farce of Romney's socialism, his neighbors set fire to what they call "Leigh Hell," and during the fire Romney is blinded. Jilted, cheated, stoned, shot at, burned, and sightless, Romney, by the end of the poem, is prepared to renounce his socialism and cheerfully acknowledge the wisdom of Aurora's liberal individualism. He criticizes the "socialistic troublers of close bonds / Betwixt the generous rich and grateful poor'' (8.901-902); and he repents of his own

> "wicked deed
> Of trying to do good without the church
> Or even the squires,''

language that makes his former Christian Socialism look unchristian even by his own account. A chastened Romney tells Aurora:

> "Fewer programmes, we who have no prescience.
> Fewer systems, we who are held and do not hold.
> Less mapping out of masses to be saved,
> By nations or by sexes. Fourier's void,
> And Comte absurd,—and Cabet puerile.
> Subsist no rules of life outside of life,
> No perfect manners without Christian souls.''

$$(9.865-871)$$

Blinded by his socialistic folly, Romney has at last come to see by the light of the spirit. Playing Jane Eyre to his Rochester, Aurora will be his polestar. Has she not all along, as her name suggests, been one of the children of light? She has at least been a woman and a poet, and therefore capable of being visionary for two, if not exactly for masses: "Shine out for two, Aurora, and fulfil / My falling-short that must be!'' (9.910-911).

Despite the arrant silliness of Elizabeth Browning's portrayal of Romney's socialism, she is not guilty of the hysteria of William Gresley in *Charles Lever*. Romney is not an inventor of steam guillotines. Violence is not associated with him except indirectly through his theories. It is instead associated with the scrofulous beggars and ungrateful pickpockets whom he tries to save. Except for Marian Erle, they turn out to be unworthy of his benevolence; all attempts at social reform through active involvement in politics or in charity are reduced to the level of "moving the masses . . . to a cleaner stye'' (2.481). Elizabeth's treatment of politics is hyperbolic rather than hysterical. And her exaggerations seem to arise as much from the difficulty she feels of distancing her poetry from politics as from her hostility towards socialism. She resorts to melodramatic hyperbole, in other words, partly to extricate herself from the humanitarian implications of poems like "Cry of the Children,'' which she believes deals with a subject—"the factory miseries''—incompatible with great poetry. Even *Aurora Leigh* can be read as an expression of the sort of humanitarian concern that inspired "Cry of the Children." But the kind of reform that its heroine would effect is spiritual rather than political, for all politics involves the same futility as utopian socialism, the antithesis of poetry:

> "Ah, your Fouriers failed,
> Because not poets enough to understand
> That life develops from within."
>
> (2.483-485)

Aurora, who radiates the appropriate sort of wisdom for an age of equipoise, will light the path to spiritual reform through her poetry, after false attempts at external reform have blown away with the smoke of 1848.

Against Romney's quixotic efforts to reform society by tinkering with its external machinery and by herding individuals into masses, Aurora preaches a liberal and comfortably religious individualism that is the central message of the poetry of both the Brownings. " 'Tis impossible," Aurora tells Romney,

> "To get at men excepting through their souls,
> However open their carnivorous jaws;
> And poets get directlier at the soul
> Than any of your oeconomists—for which
> You must not overlook the poet's work
> When scheming for the world's necessities.
> The soul's the way."
>
> (8.537-544)

Agreeing with her, the blind and repentant Romney repeats verbatim her words of wisdom from section 2 (475-483):

> "You will not compass your poor ends
> Of barley-feeding and material ease,
> Without the poet's individualism
> To work your universal. It takes a soul
> To move a body, —it takes a high-souled man
> To move the masses, even to a cleaner stye:
> It takes the ideal, to blow an inch inside
> The dust of the actual."
>
> (8.427-434)

Robert Browning, himself a "high-souled man" in frequent touch with the ideal, did not always agree with his wife's politics, but he did agree with her rejection of French socialism and with her sense of the opposition between political reform and the true, spiritual reform offered by poetry. His writing confronts us on a massive scale with the substitution of history for mythology as the basis for the highest literary art. As an empiricist who thinks of "pure crude fact" and of "charactery" as the sources of truth, Browning chooses to create the voices of "flesh and blood" men and women rooted in historical circumstances. But Browning's sense of history is inadequate in several ways, largely because he is so intensely individualistic that it is impossible for him to think in genuinely historical terms. First, as a historian he is often inaccurate. Second, he usually does not perceive clear connections or even comparisons between past and present. And third, he has no clear ideas about the workings of historical and social processes. Instead, he tends to use history as an indiscriminate source of psychological material and also as a means of escape from the present. In the dedication of *Sordello* to his friend Milsand, Browning writes: "The historical decoration was purposely of no more importance than a background requires; and my stress lay on the incidents in the development of a soul: little else is worth study."[11] This attitude toward history as mere "decoration" carries over into much of his later work and suggests that Browning does not understand that "the development of a soul" and "history" may be causally linked.

Because he persists in acting like one, it is important to consider Browning's deficiencies as a historian. Also, Browning thought of himself as a public figure, as a spokesman for his age and for God, and as a realist grappling with the "pure crude facts" of existence. A would-be Shelleyan poet-legislator, his attitudes toward history and politics necessarily affect his art, and because of this Santayana's criticism remains to be answered: "As soon as Browning is proposed to us as a leader, as soon as we are asked to be not the occasional patrons of his art, but the pupils of his philosophy, we have a right to express the radical dissatisfaction we must feel . . . with his whole attitude and temper of mind."[12] Park Honan may be correct when he says that "as the late-Victorian fiction of his 'message' fades, the poems, of course, remain," but Browning probably would not have understood such a defense.[13] A poetry in which "message" is so fundamental an ingredient as Browning's must be judged partly by the coherence and intelligence of that message. It is not a matter of finding in Milton's puritanism or in Shelley's atheism, let alone in Browning's rather jumbled attitudes, acceptable philosophies of life for today. But it is a matter of acknowledging that the conscious contents and unconscious assumptions expressed in works of literature are at least as important for critical understanding as their purely formal characteristics, and also of acknowledging that artistic form is itself an embodiment of value.

Browning's first deficiency as a historian is that he is often inaccurate, very free, even by Victorian standards, in his interpretations of the past, and sometimes ludicrously anachronistic. This is true even though he often provides the trappings of scholarship for his poems. In the notes to *Paracelsus* Browning insists that "the liberties I have taken with my subject are very trifling," but, as DeVane observes, "the liberties he has taken with his subject are immense."[14] And the same is true of later poems. Browning's Pope, questioning his own infallibility, undermining the doctrine of original sin, and predicting the demise of orthodox Christianity itself, may seem to us more like a pontiff of Unitarianism than like the head of the Roman Catholic Church in 1698.[15] No doubt the hand of irony lies heavily over the treatment of Catholicism in *The Ring and the Book;* but historical accuracy is as much the victim of this irony as the Church. Browning repeatedly presents us with figures who are either genuinely prophetic or who almost see into the future, and who betray their own values in doing so. Cleon just misses St. Paul, the Pope looks forward to an age of salutary doubt when "this torpor of assurance" shall be shaken "from our creed" (10.1854), and St. John, in "A Death in the Desert," explains why miracles, necessary once, will no longer occur in the nineteenth century (455-465). St. John can even foresee, as in a glass darkly, the coming of David Strauss.

Second, although Browning repeatedly judges the past in terms of the present, he does not think clearly or consistently about comparing past and present. He does not employ history either to point out where we have been and are going, or as an instrument of social criticism. He is aware of the Comtean doctrine of the three stages of history, but he rejects it as he rejects the Higher Criticism.[16] As in the Pope's prediction of modern skepticism, doubt is seen as progress within the framework of Christianity and not as the start of a movement beyond the theistic and metaphysical eras. Further, Browning gives us part of Ruskin's theory of Gothic in "the philosophy of the imperfect" but not Ruskin's use of Gothic to point out the alienation of the modern worker. The Greeks, according to Browning, were artists and thinkers who set themselves only finite goals and so achieved a finite perfection, like Andrea del Sarto. But Browning does not point out, with Ruskin, that modern industrial technology has returned us to the condition of the Greeks, the Egyptians, or worse. For Browning, it is not just the age of Gothic but the whole of the

Christian era that has opened up that infinite range of possibility in which a man may always strive and always fail, and yet in failing, succeed. Occasionally one of Browning's poems will suggest a comparison between ages, as do "Cleon," "A Toccata of Galuppi's," and "Pictor Ignotus." But except for the contrast between pre-Christian and Christian times, no consistent patterns emerge.

Browning did not often employ poetry for the purposes of social criticism anyway. Studies of his life and work are often apologetic about his politics—or, rather, about his lack of politics. Helen C. Clarke, for example, says that "in the political affairs of his own age and country Browning as a poet shows little interest. This may at first seem strange, for that he was deeply sympathetic with past historical movements indicating a growth toward democratic ideals in government is abundantly proved by his choice and treatment of historical epochs in which the democratic tendencies were peculiarly evident. Why then did he not give us dramatic pictures of the Victorian era, in which as perhaps in no other era of English history the yeast of political freedom has been steadily and quietly working?"[17] Her question is an important one, but she fails to answer it. The best she can do is to insist that Browning is a staunch liberal anyway, "deeply sympathetic" with the democratic tendencies of his age.

Of course Browning was a staunch liberal, or thought of himself as one. But the fact that he did not often feel moved to deal with liberalism in his poetry does not suggest "deep sympathy" with democratic movements and does suggest a felt incompatibility between poetry and politics. One of Browning's two most explicit statements of his political beliefs is "The Lost Leader"—brief, negative, and later regretted. The other is "Why I Am a Liberal," also brief, also negative in its syntax, and not a clarion call to action. In "Why I Am a Liberal," Browning says "the best of us" can only do a "little" and "that little is achieved through Liberty."

> Who, then, dares hold, emancipated thus,
>   His fellow shall continue bound? Not I,
> Who live, love, labor freely, nor discuss
>   A brother's right to freedom. That is "Why."

It is an odd argument, partly because it is so abstract and so platitudinous. It makes the usual identification of "liberalism" with "Liberty," but in terms of a negation. Browning, free, will *not* "discuss / A brother's right to freedom," but will merely accept that right as a given. There is no sense that liberty is something to be won through political action; there is rather the assumption that liberty is with us and is not to be questioned.

When Browning wrote the poem in 1885, of course, this attitude had some truth in it, if only because the third Reform Bill had just been passed the year before. Browning's poem appeared in an anthology of Liberal Party propaganda, *Why I Am a Liberal* edited by Andrew Reid, and all the contributions are at least implicit testimonies to the existence of liberty as a fait accompli rather than as a remote ideal. Browning's liberalism, then, is not the revolutionary political idealism of his first idol, "sun-treader" Shelley. It is rather a conservative, anarchistic individualism—apparent faith in the individual but none in the state or in politics as a constructive activity—an attitude similar to that of Herbert Spencer and of the Manchester School.[18]

Whereas Shelley seldom wrote anything that was not political, Browning seldom wrote anything that was. This absence of politics from his poetry suggests a third fact about Browning's treatment of history. He does not think of history as a structure of social and political processes but only as a vast container of all the experiences of all the individual men and women who have ever lived. Browning's empiricist assumptions about truth root his vision in the concrete particularities of individual consciousness, and at the same time render historical generalizations difficult or impossible. Fra Lippo Lippi tells us that "the Prior and the learned" who objected to his paintings did so, rather like Santayana objecting to Browning's "barbarism," in these terms:

"Your business is not to catch men with show,
With homage to the perishable clay,
But lift them over it, ignore it all,
Make them forget there's such a thing as flesh.
Your business is to paint the souls of men—
Man's soul, and it's a fire, smoke . . . no, it's not . . . "

(179-184)

If we generalize the Prior's argument, we can see that he stands for abstraction rather than particularity, "being" rather than "becoming," and the absolute truths that Browning's poetry calls into question rather than the specific growths of individual consciousness. The Prior is a dry-as-dust Scholastic, valuing dead forms; Fra Lippo Lippi is a "realist," valuing the creatures and details of "flesh and blood." This is what Langbaum means by calling Browning's poetry "relativist." Only through "experience," or the individual's constantly changing perspective, can truth be approached, and not through revelations of an external scheme of absolutes. But in questioning religious and metaphysical absolutes,

Browning also casts doubt upon historical and political abstractions. Browning called himself an "objective" poet, but with its experiential frame of reference his poetry is as subjective as Blake's—only, instead of one "egotistical sublime," Browning presents us with a multitude.

Browning personalizes history. The dramatic monologue form locates significance in the consciousness of individuals rather than in social or communal processes. The fact that Browning is a superb writer of dramatic monologues but at best only a poor writer of dramas illustrates this, for successful drama requires at least a minimal sense of community and of social interaction. This is the thesis of H. B. Charlton, in what remains one of the best analyses of Browning as a dramatist.[19] Charlton contends that Browning's failure as a dramatist is a function of his extreme individualism. Browning's plays are conditioned by a "temperamental blindness to the group as an organic unit. Physiologically, he looked out on life and saw it as an aggregation of separate human souls seeking their relation to God. He never saw, never felt, the real existence of the something or other besides God and yet not ourselves which gives its vital force to a community." Charlton shows that even a play dealing directly with political attitudes, such as *King Victor and King Charles*, is "entirely unpolitical in its essential theme." In the transfer of power between King Victor and his son, there is no rendering of public consequences; it is a play about four individuals rather than about social processes.

One might suppose that Charlton's argument would be less applicable to *Strafford* than to Browning's other plays, because *Strafford*, without being good drama, is still one of Browning's most adequate renderings of a historical and political situation. It is a play dealing ostensibly with the origins of English liberty, and Browning's choice of royalist Strafford instead of Pym for his hero has not deterred some commentators from seeing in the play an expression of sturdy liberal principles. But *Strafford* is no more about history and politics than *King Victor and King Charles*. History in *Strafford* serves as "decoration" for a tale of conflict between two old friends, Strafford and Pym. Its theme is that of personal loyalty undermined by personal treachery; Strafford is betrayed by unprincipled King Charles as he is confronted by overly principled Pym. Instead of suggesting that one side is right and the other side wrong, the play suggests that politics is dangerous—it destroys friendships and kills both soul and body. The principled spokesman for the people and for Parliament, Pym is a self-acknowledged fanatic, who has ruined his private life through politics and has helped to destroy his best friend Strafford (Wentworth) as well:

Have I done well? Speak, England! Whose sole sake
I still have labored for, with disregard
To my own heart,—for whom my youth was made
Barren, my manhood waste, to offer up
Her sacrifice—this friend, this Wentworth here—
Who walked in youth with me, loved me, it may be,
And whom, for his forsaking England's cause,
I hunted by all means (trusting that she
Would sanctify all means) even to the block
Which waits for him.

                                        (5.2.309-318)

Browning, perhaps, takes for granted that we will assess the historical results of Pym's labors for ourselves. What he shows us instead is the enormous personal cost of those labors. And Strafford may be unintentionally
close to the truth when he tells Charles: "You know / All's between you
and me: what has the world / To do with it?" (5.2.223-225).

After the plays, *The Ring and the Book* is Browning's most complete
portrayal of a total community, like those at the center of the great Victorian novels. But as a depiction of social processes, it does not measure
up to *Bleak House* or *Middlemarch* or even *Barchester Towers*. There is a
vivid sense of social interaction in "Half Rome," "Other Half Rome,"
"Tertium Quid," and the lawyers' books—a sense, at least, of communal
participation in the story—but the dramatic monologue form renders the
voices singular, sometimes entirely private (the lawyers, the Pope), contradictory of each other, and long-winded. Besides, a central theme of
The Ring and the Book is the failure of all social institutions to discover
truth and render justice. The treatment of the law is Dickensian and anarchistic. Archangelis and Bottinius are as much shysters as Dodson and
Fogg. The legal apparatus of society fails to protect Pompilia and to recognize the integrity of Caponsacchi. The major dissimilarity between Browning's treatment of the law and Dickens's is that even when Dickens is
most pessimistic about the prospects of achieving reform, he writes to demand it, while Browning implies that the fumbling legal institutions
which he depicts are irredeemable:

Then, since a Trial ensued, a touch o' the same
To sober us, flustered with frothy talk,
And teach our common sense its helplessness.
For why deal simply with divining-rod,
Scrape where we fancy secret sources flow,

And ignore law, the recognized machine,
Elaborate display of pipe and wheel
Framed to unchoke, pump up and pour apace
Truth till a flowery foam shall wash the world?
The patent truth-extracting process,—ha?
Let us make that grave mystery turn one wheel,
Give you a single grind of law at least!

(1.1105-1116)

The poem demonstrates the "helplessness" of "common sense," and also the folly of collective, institutional judgment in the form of the law. The Pope presumably does not use "common sense" but intuition. At least, his great honesty allows him to arrive at the truth, where numerous collective heads have failed:

There prattled they, discoursed the right and wrong,
Turned wrong to right, proved wolves sheep and sheep wolves,
So that you scarce distinguished fell from fleece;
Till out spoke a great guardian of the fold,
Stood up, put forth his hand that held the crook,
And motioned that the arrested point decline:
Horribly off, the wriggling dead-weight reeled,
Rushed to the bottom and lay ruined there.

(1.645-652)

"I nothing doubt," the Pope tells us—a man of faith in himself, if not clearly of faith in his office. The individual succeeds where institutions fail. It is an assumption that pervades Browning's poetry and that is as true of Hamelin as of Rome. That astonishing entrepreneur of the pest-control business, the Pied Piper, is cheated by the mayor and the town council in just the same way, Browning seems to have felt, that all individuals are cheated when society meddles with their affairs.

At the end of *The Ring and the Book* Browning tells us that a central lesson has been that "our human speech is nought, / Our human testimony false, our fame / And human estimation words and wind" (12.838-840). This is surely a strange thing to demonstrate in one of the longest poems in the language. Browning has given us this enormous edifice of words to demonstrate the uselessness and duplicity of words. His is not a poetry of glossolalia, but of Babel. There are honest voices, of course—those of Pompilia, of Caponsacchi, and of the Pope—but the significance of most of the voices lies in their distortions of the truth.

Therefore these filthy rags of speech, this coil
Of statement, comment, query and response,
Tatters all too contaminate for use,
Have no renewing: He, the Truth, is, too,
The Word.

(10.373-377)

You may have faith in the divine Word, but if you have no faith in "human speech," then you can have little in communal interaction or in social institutions. And Browning had perhaps less than any other major Victorian writer.

Browning distrusts institutions because they are threats to individual liberty, but also because they are made up of individuals. As the Pope says, ironically:

Since all flesh is weak,
Bind weaknesses together, we get strength:
The individual weighed, found wanting, try
Some institution, honest artifice
Whereby the units grow compact and firm!
Each props the other, and so stand is made
By our embodied cowards that grow brave.

(10.1492-1498)

Browning has, then, little faith in either the individual or society. That sort of liberal individualism which is based primarily on distrust of institutions is also based on distrust of individuals. It is better to let society alone altogether, because governmental interference is only likely to make a bad thing worse. The possibility of social reform is narrowed to individual acts of love and charity, precisely because individuals in the mass or gathered up into institutions are incapable of love and charity. Here again, of course, Browning's assumptions about society and human nature are close to Dickens's, at least in Dickens's more pessimistic moods —love is the only means of social reform because love is so rare in the world.

And yet Browning undoubtedly saw his poetry as an optimistic celebration of the lives and incarnate truths of individual men and women, and also saw himself as a Shelleyan poet-legislator, "a recording chief-inquisitor, / The town's true master if the town but knew." One might therefore expect to find in his poetry the ideal embodiment of a democratic literature. For the first time on so large and deliberate a scale, a poet adopts "the language of common men." It is not Wordsworth but Brow-

168

ning who give us "men and women" speaking in their own voices instead of in "poetic diction." (Obviously there is poetic stylization in Browning's language, but the usual effect is that of colloquial spontaneity.) In Browning's dramatic monologues we seem to have an expression of the idea of the common man as inspired spokesman of the truth—an idea prominent in that other "barbarian" poet, Walt Whitman. As Blake puts it, "Every man is a prophet." But while Browning creates common men and women speaking in their own voices, these voices usually do not utter inspired truths. Apart from a few honest souls like Fra Lippo Lippi and Abt Vogler, Browning's characters form a rogue's gallery of self-deceivers, fanatics, swindlers, and psychopaths. Instead of inspired truths, his most characteristic poetry offers us lies and special pleadings, and beneath its surface exuberance it expresses a deep distrust of language and also of the common man, much as Elizabeth expresses distrust of the masses in *Aurora Leigh*. Browning claims for even the most warped of his speakers a core of essential truth, but it is, at best, buried truth, like Arnold's "buried life":

> . . . ask moreover, when they prate
> Of evil men past hope, 'Don't each contrive,
> 'Despite the evil you abuse, to live?—
> 'Keeping, each losel, through a maze of lies,
> 'His own conceit of truth? to which he hies
> 'By obscure windings, tortuous, if you will,
> 'But to himself not inaccessible;
> 'He sees truth, and his lies are for the crowd
> 'Who cannot see.'
>
> (*Sordello*, 3.786-794)

Browning expresses little faith either in "each losel" or in "the crowd." Translated into political terminology, such a statement would read like the reactionary side of one of Maurice's paradoxes, who in his *The Workman and the Franchise* (1867) writes: "If it could be put to the vote of the greatest number what they would have for happiness, I have no security that they would not decide for something profoundly low and swinish."[20]

From the time of *Strafford* and *Sordello* through that of "Prince Hohenstiel Schwangau, Saviour of Society," Browning's treatments of politics and political institutions are uniformly negative. Two motifs are dominant. One shows the fate of the political idealist disillusioned or crushed by the real world (Sordello, Strafford, Chiappino in *A Soul's Tragedy*), and the other shows the maneuvering and chicanery by which the successful politician survives (Ogniben in *A Soul's Tragedy*, Prince

Hohenstiel-Schwangau, George Bubb Dodington). The idealists are failures and the realists are charlatans, and there is no ground between them.
"The Patriot—An Old Story" comes as close to illuminating Browning's
attitudes toward politics as "The Lost Leader" or "Why I Am a Liberal":
the end of any overly energetic "patriotism" is likely to be the scaffold.
But the alternative to the zeal of the patriot is equally unsatisfactory, for
to compromise one's political ideals is to be, with Wordsworth, a "lost
leader."

"The Italian in England" describes a situation of conspiracy and betrayal that exemplifies the conflict between Browning's democratic intentions and his distrust of politics. The Italian revolutionary has been
betrayed by Charles, his boyhood friend, a "perjured traitor" who has
gone over to Metternich. His brothers also "live in Austria's pay." He
can trust no one except the peasant girl who brings him food and carries
his message, and she in her turn cannot trust her fiancé (91-98). Neither
the revolutionary nor the peasant girl have faith in those closest to them;
the revolutionary must turn to a complete stranger and, by a leap of intuition, renew his trust in Italy and mankind, symbolized by the girl. Trust
in men on the level of practical politics is dangerous or impossible; the
peasant girl, innocent of politics, offers the revolutionary a trust in humanity in the abstract.

"The Englishman in Italy" is a companion to "The Italian in England," but it is unclear whether Browning thought of it as a contrast or
as a parallel. The Englishman is not an exile but a tourist, and the poem
is a vivid celebration of the Italian landscape around Sorrento. But the
poem makes a direct political assertion, attacking the corn laws in lines
often cited to demonstrate Browning's active liberal principles:

> —'Such trifles!' you say?
> Fortù, in my England at home,
>   Men meet gravely to-day
> And debate, if abolishing Corn-laws
>   Be righteous and wise
> —If 't were proper, Scirocco should vanish
>   In black from the skies!

Like Browning's other explicit statements about politics, these lines are
brief, negative, and ambiguous. They came as an afterthought. They
were not part of the original poem, although Elizabeth liked them and
thought that they gave "unity to the whole."[21] Further, their logical
structure is as fuzzy as that of "Why I Am a Liberal." The guilty sense

that what the Englishman enjoys in the Italian landscape are "trifles" leads to the response in the last six lines: the real triflers are the politicians back home in England, unable to resolve to abolish the corn laws. Of course Browning was against the corn laws, as were all good liberals in the 1840s; but the tacked-on ending of "The Englishman in Italy" expresses guilt for Browning's own political inertia as well as anger at tariffs and also at politics generally. Browning's Italian revolutionary has fled for his life to safety in England; Browning's English tourist has traveled to Italy to enjoy the scenery. The contrast does not suggest what Browning tries to convey in the lines on the corn laws—an active concern for politics on the part of the Englishman.

Under the influence of Shelley, Browning conceived of his role as that of poet-legislator, bringing the fire of inspiration to the aid of suffering humanity. Browning's earliest longer poems—*Pauline* (1833), *Paracelsus* (1835), and *Sordello* (1840)—are considerations of the poet's role in the world, and his plays, through *Luria* and *A Soul's Tragedy* (1846), are usually concerned with political situations and public figures. Further, the poems in *Dramatic Lyrics* (1842) and *Dramatic Romances and Lyrics* (1845) are often suggestive of political situations and are sometimes largely about politics. The earlier volume contains "Cavalier Tunes," "The Incident of the French Camp," and "Waring"; the later one contains "The Italian in England," "The Englishman in Italy," "The Lost Leader," and a tale of political treachery in "The Confessional." *Pauline,* dedicated to "the sun-treader," establishes the theme of the poet as legislator:

> I was vowed to liberty,
> Men were to be as gods and earth as heaven,
> And I—ah, what a life was mine to prove!
> My whole soul rose to meet it.
>
> (425-428)

But the narrator of *Pauline,* as Mill suggested, suffers from acute narcissism and is as incapable of action in the real world as the narrator of *Alastor.* His vow to liberty suffers a severe setback thirty lines later:

> First went my hopes of perfecting mankind,
> Next—faith in them, and then in freedom's self
> And virtue's self, then my own motives, ends
> And aims and loves, and human love went last.
>
> (458-461)

171

After a series of emotional ups and downs, the narrator arrives at an impeccable faith "in God and truth / And love" (1020-1021) but not clearly in either mankind or liberty, so that his stance as poet-legislator is at best vague.

Both *Paracelsus* and *Sordello* are improvements upon the pattern established by *Pauline,* and in *Sordello* especially there is an attempt to move away from the egotistical sublime of *Pauline* and to grapple with real life and with suffering humanity. After three books on the growth of the poet's soul, Sordello begins to turn outward and to try to realize the Shelleyan idea of the poet. He soon understands that he has no way of achieving his humanitarian goals except through choosing between Guelfs and Ghibbelines, so he decides to become a Guelf. But Salinguerra, his real father, is a Ghibbeline leader. Further, the choice between Guelfs and Ghibbelines is seen to be one of nearly equal evils. Everywhere around him Sordello observes the suffering caused by party strife. Book 4 opens with a description of the ruin that threatens Ferrara because "each party" is "too intent / For noticing, howe'er the battle went, / The conqueror would but have a corpse to kiss" (4.9-11). As Sordello says later in book 4 (939-946):

Two parties take the world up, and allow
No third, yet have one principle, subsist
By the same injustice; whoso shall enlist
With either, ranks with man's inveterate foes.
So there is one less quarrel to compose:
The Guelf, the Ghibellin may be to curse—
I have done nothing, but both sides do worse
Than nothing.

And yet it is only through choosing sides that Sordello can hope to enact his humanitarianism. He cannot remain aloof from action, caught up in the ideal realm of "Mantuan chants":

Not so unwisely does the crowd dispense
On Salinguerras praise in preference
To the Sordellos: men of action, these!
Who, seeing just as little as you please,
Yet turn that little to account,—engage
With, do not gaze at,—carry on, a stage,
The work o' the world, not merely make report
The work existed ere their day!

(3.917-924)

Largely because of the conflict between action and reflection, destructive real politics and impossible ideal politics, Sordello is destroyed. The poem demonstrates the incompatibility of political idealism with political action and seems to prove that poets can be legislators only in an ideal sense. It is apparent, nevertheless, that Browning thought he was demonstrating something else: "A poet must be earth's essential king" (5.506). Sordello has lived before his time and has been caught up in the "accidents" (5.511) of party strife. His true position and mankind's cause rise above party. But why, then, does Sordello persist in choosing sides, and why does the conflict destroy him? *Sordello* can be read as an exposition of the poet as lawgiver in an ideal sense, but it is simultaneously a demonstration of the danger of the poet's engaging in political action in the real world.

After *Sordello,* in the plays that were Browning's main attempts in the 1840s to deal with history, politics, and community, the political idealism necessary for the poet-legislator is repeatedly shown to fail when it comes into contact with reality. What is apparent in *Strafford* is expressed in extreme form in *A Soul's Tragedy,* published with *Luria* as one of the *Bells and Pomegranates* series in 1846. It opens with Chiappino, an idealistic republican in hiding from the tyrannical provost of Faenza, accusing Luitolfo of moral compromise. But Luitolfo kills the provost, an act that Chiappino feels he should have performed himself. Luitolfo flees, and Chiappino, in a gesture of selflessness, announces to "the populace" that he, not Luitolfo, is the assassin. Expecting to be arrested, Chiappino is instead hailed by the fickle populace as a hero, and he then decides to install himself as the new provost, thus compromising his republican ideals. In act 2, Ogniben comes from the Pope to investigate the assassination. He presides over the transformation of Chiappino from republican idealist into despotic cynic. "I had despaired of, what you may call the material instrumentality of life," Chiappino tells Eulalia; "of ever being able to rightly operate on mankind through such a deranged machinery as the existing modes of government" (228-232). Now that he is part of the "deranged machinery" himself, he believes he has a chance of realizing his ideals. But "power tends to corrupt, and absolute power corrupts absolutely," as Lord Acton put it; the temptations of power turn Chiappino into another "lost leader"—ideal prince into real toad—in the space of a few lines. It is not clear whether the tragedy of Chiappino's soul consists in having been infirm in his resolve to stand by his ideals or merely in trying to translate his ideals into action. In either case, Browning has given us a situation in which nothing that the hero can do seems right—neither seizing power nor abstaining from seizing it. *A Soul's Tragedy* is a play about politics which negates political activity altogether. Like so many of Browning's swindling souls, Ogniben seems to come close to Browning's own attitude when he says: "Why, look you, when they tax you with ter-giversation or duplicity, you may answer—you begin to perceive that . . . both great parties in the State, the advocators of change . . . and the opponents of it, patriot and anti-patriot, are found working together for the common good; and that in the midst of their efforts for and against its progress, the world somehow or other still advances" (436-445). The world gets on—Browning has plenty of faith in progress—but it gets on in spite of politics. Both the Brownings tend to view reform through active involvement in politics as impossible, as the antithesis of progress.

After the publication of *In a Balcony* in the second volume of *Men and Women* in 1855, Browning wrote no more plays. So, too, after *Sordello* there are no more long, semiautobiographical descriptions of "the growth of a poet's soul." These two impulses—the one towards writing plays and the other towards writing romantic confessional poetry—may not be opposites, as Browning supposed them to be. They spring from an identical source, for the confessional poetry deals with attempts of the poet-narrators to move beyond their narrow egos and to become poet-legislators, and the plays also attempt to deal with public instead of exclusively individual or private concerns. Browning thought he was moving beyond himself into "real life"—achieving "negative capability"—when he abandoned the confessional mode of *Pauline* and *Sordello*. But just about the time that he declared himself to be a dramatic or "objective" poet in the *Essay on Shelley* (1852), he ceased to be a writer of dramas. To be sure, there are still projections of communities and scattered expressions of interest in public issues throughout his later poetry. *Men and Women*, for instance, contains a humorous description of the poet as legislator in "How It Strikes a Contemporary," as well as "The Patriot—An Old Story," "Instans Tyrannus," and some other glimpses of political characters and actions, although these are brief and negative. But *Men and Women* also contains no important political ideas except for the danger of politics, and not much sense of community—just isolated voices speaking for themselves to silent auditors.

For about fifteen years, then, from the period of *Strafford* and *Sordello* through the *Essay on Shelley* and *In a Balcony*, Browning struggled against the intensely individualistic assumptions about life which hemmed him in. He thought that he had won the struggle when he declared himself to be an "objective" poet, writing about "real" men and women, and he did avoid being merely another spasmodic autobiographer. But the men and women he creates are related to each other by no better fact than that they are men and women. Where there might have been ties between them—of history, of community, of politics, of the sort provided by drama or by fiction—there exists a vacuum. Even when Browning comes closest to being a successful dramatist, in *Pippa Passes*, and closest to writing fiction, in *The Ring and the Book*, the structures he gives us are antisocial. *Pippa* consists of four episodes connected only by the slender thread of Pippa's song (the happy factory child, on holiday), and *The Ring and the Book* is a cacophony of separate voices busily contradicting each other.

The oily papal politician in *A Soul's Tragedy*, Ogniben, gives us a foretaste of the main poems about politics written by Browning late in his career. These are "Prince Hohenstiel-Schwangau, Saviour of Society" (1871), based on Napoleon III, and "A Parleying with George Bubb Dodington" (1887), in which Browning attacks Disraeli. Both the democratic tyrant and the democratic Tory are perfect subjects for Browning's keen sense of self-contradiction. Both are seen as figures who have bowed down to the idol of political expediency and who have bartered away their personal integrity. Both are seen as antidemocratic wielders of power in the name of the people, succeeding through irrational popularity. Neither the dupers of the people nor the people duped come off well in these poems. Of the two, the monologue of the Prince is the better poem. The Prince speaks for himself, while Dodington and Disraeli are more direct targets of Browning's not very subtle "parleying": "Folk see but one / Fool more, as well as knave, in Dodington."[22]

After the debacle of the Franco-Prussian War and the fall of the Second Empire in 1871, Prince Hohenstiel-Schwangau looks back over his long career as the "twenty years' sustainer" and tries to justify most of it. He sees himself as the "savior of society" in the sense that he has held it together against the forces of chaos, the extreme left and the extreme right and all parties in between.

> A conservator, call me, if you please,
> Not a creator nor destroyer: one
> Who keeps the world safe.

(298-300)

His central principle has been that of compromise—really a nonprinciple. He understands that he is not a genius, but he claims he has been called upon by God to maintain the social balance and to keep the wheels of the social machine turning at a comfortable rate.

'Tis part of life, a property to prize,
That those o' the higher sort engaged i' the world,
Should fancy they can change its ill to good,
Wrong to right, ugliness to beauty: find
Enough success in fancy turning fact,
To keep the sanguine kind in countenance
And justify the hope that busies them:
Failure enough,—to who can follow change
Beyond their vision, see new good prove ill
I' the consequence, see blacks and whites of life
Shift square indeed, but leave the chequered face
Unchanged i' the main,—failure enough for such,
To bid ambition keep the whole from change,
As their best service. I hope naught beside.

(1087-1100)

Against all parties and special interest groups, the Prince claims to have championed the cause of the masses, although he sees the masses as irrational and helpless. They are "the poor mean multitude, all mouths and eyes" (1492), who would be as apt to elect Barabbas to rule over them as anyone better (934). Browning implies, of course, that they have elected the next best thing to Barabbas in electing Napoleon III in 1848.

Much of what Prince Hohenstiel-Schwangau has to say for himself, however, does not seem far from attitudes that Browning also holds. At least, Browning elsewhere gives much more affirmative expression to many of the ideas that seem to incriminate the Prince. In some instances, the Prince may be holding acceptable ideas hypocritically, but it is apparent that Browning feels most of the Prince's opinions to be wrongheaded, obnoxious, and dangerous. The Prince claims to be an opponent of party strife in the name of the people; *Sordello* demonstrates the madness of party strife and its incompatibility with humanitarianism. The Prince is a compromiser and an opponent of extremes; Browning everywhere shows the danger of excessive political idealism and, as in the case of Pym, its proximity to fanaticism. The Prince is a realist, valuing the things of this world as much as Fra Lippo Lippi. He is practical and antiintellectual, understanding that the value of a good dinner may be greater than the value of a grand theory:

Be Kant crowned king o' the castle in the air!
Hans Slouch,—his own, and children's mouths to feed

176

Two designs executed by Thackeray for the Anti-Corn Law League. From Sir Henry Cole, *Fifty Years of Public Work.*

I' the hovel on the ground,—wants meat, nor chews
"The Critique of Pure Reason" in exchange.

(1108-1111)

The Prince is aware of the privations suffered by the masses, but he is also
aware of the unfitness of the masses to govern themselves. He has been
the champion of freedom for Italy and a hearty, bourgeois opponent of
utopian socialism: "Let us not risk the whiff of my cigar / For Fourier,
Comte, and all that ends in smoke!" (438-439).

All of these attitudes can be found elsewhere in Browning, in contexts
where they are given more positive expression. And while it is possible to
see the Prince as an inauthentic holder of authentic ideas, it is also possible
to see Browning as a confused holder of some very shaky liberal opinions.
Certainly one of the virtues of the dramatic monologue form is that it allows one to attribute one's own contradictory thinking to somebody else
and to hold it up for praise or for ridicule as one sees fit. This is why, to
answer Thomas Hardy's question to Edmund Gosse, Browning is "so vast
a seer and feeler when on neutral ground," but when expressing his own
opinions directly cannot do much better than "smug Christian optimism
worthy of a dissenting grocer."[23] He understands as well as any poet ever
has the rationalizations, wheedlings, lies, and contradictions that go on
in the dark corners of the mind, and he portrays them with great energy
and psychological penetration. But he understands almost nothing else.
Why make poor Caliban puzzle his head about the nature of God? Because Browning was not much clearer about it himself. Perhaps the ridicule of Prince Hohenstiel-Schwangau's shabby opinions, then, masks an
unconscious self-ridicule. Perhaps Browning heaps scorn on political realists for betraying ideals because he senses that he, too, has betrayed them
—has failed to become the poet-legislator that he once dreamed of
becoming. A sense of guilt seems to have nagged Browning from time to
time, whispering that he had not clearly vowed himself to liberty and that
he, too, was one of the lost leaders whose equivocations and self-justifica-
tions he understood so well.

There is a compensatory quality in the scorn which Browning heaps
upon his political realists, just as there may be in his ironic stance towards
religious equivocators like Bishop Blougram. He knows that Prince Hohenstiel-Schwangau's shabby pragmatism and willingness to compromise
are at the opposite pole from the utopian idealism of "sun-treader" Shelley, but he also suspects that he is no utopian idealist himself. The political attitudes that he expressed with greatest consistency throughout his

career made utopian idealism impossible for him, as they also weakened his sense of history and of community. They are the attitudes expressed in the lines of Strafford (5.2.194-196):

> Put not your trust
> In princes, neither in the sons of men,
> In whom is no salvation.

Stoppage versus Progress: Tory China versus Liberal England according to *Punch*, 1853.

Progress bypassing the slums: "Over London by Rail" from Gustave Doré's *London*.

VIII. The Ambiguities of Progress

> O Nineveh, was this thy God—
> Thine also, mighty Nineveh?
>
> Rossetti, "The Burden of Nineveh"

The optimism of Browning's stated beliefs contradicts the distrust of "princes" and "the sons of men" which is implicit in most of his poetry in patterns of betrayal, mendacity, and disillusionment. A similar contradiction is evident throughout much of the literature of the mid-Victorian period and is summed up in the realism of Trollope, Thackeray, and George Eliot. Realism involves a positing of the given either as truer or as better than alternative dimensions. It reverses the emphasis of romanticism by stressing the primacy of material existence and by rejecting or failing to focus upon the absent, the transcendent, the unreal. Or else, Pangloss-like, it blurs the distinction between real and ideal and ends by identifying them. As Fra Lippo Lippi puts it:

> I always see the garden and God there
> A-making man's wife: and, my lesson learned,
> The value and significance of flesh,
> I can't unlearn ten minutes afterwards.
>
> (266-269)

The substantial world of God's making is best; dreams of better worlds are mirages. It is an attitude at once healthy and vulgar, as clear in Browning as in Trollope and Thackeray. But while realism dominates the culture of the 1850s and 1860s as the chief artistic corollary of the entrepreneurial ideal, its negation is manifest in Christian Socialism, in Pre-Raphaelitism, and in the increased complexity and despair of Dickens's social vision in his later novels. Romantic idealism does not vanish with the triumph of free trade and middle-class industry, but it becomes more cautious, subdued, unsure of itself.

This is the bare outline of a very large historical pattern, and there are numerous exceptions to it. But this pattern has often been traced in relation to factors other than the political ones I am trying to clarify here—for example, in relation to the Higher Criticism and to the theory of evolution. Although the correspondence between them is not simple, the twin growths of scientific and economic materialism created a stranglehold upon romanticism and also upon religious orthodoxy which many Victorians found impossible to break. Thus, while Browning could transform Shelley's radical idealism into the comfortable realism of Fra Lippo Lippi without sensing a contradiction, James Thomson, a truer disciple of Shelley's, despairing of living in a universe where the stars blindly run, could express his bleak vision in "The City of Dreadful Night." And just as Thomson's despair is a more logical continuation of Shelleyan idealism than Browning's realism, so too is his political radicalism: "The City of Dreadful Night," although presenting a case of urban blight which is pretty clearly beyond repair by improved street lights and sewers, was first published in Charles Bradlaugh's *National Reformer* in 1874.

There has been a great deal written about "the decline of the Romantic ideal" or of "the Romantic assertion," most of it focusing on the conflict between religion and science.[1] Romantic prophets and poet-legislators give way to Victorian pilgrims in search of the Holy Grail but, like Tennyson's knight-errants, losing their way in the twin deserts of scientific and economic materialism, and returning baffled and visionless. The decline of prophetic assertiveness in poetry can be given countless illustrations. For one thing, some Victorian poets themselves recognized a falling off of poetic power and began quite early to speak in terms of "decadence." Morris, for example, thought that "English poetry was fast reaching the termination of its long and splendid career, and that Keats represented its final achievement."[2] As an illustration of the approach of "decadence" in one of its aspects, Rossetti's "The Hill Summit" will serve:

This feast-day of the sun, his altar there
   In the broad west has blazed for vesper-song;
   And I have loitered in the vale too long
And gaze now a belated worshipper.
Yet may I not forget that I was 'ware,
   So journeying, of his face at intervals
   Transfigured where the fringed horizon falls,—
A fiery bush with coruscating hair.
And now that I have climbed and won this height,
   I must tread downward through the sloping shade
And travel the bewildered tracks till night.

Yet for this hour I still may here be stayed
And see the gold air and the silver fade
And the last bird fly into the last light.

The poem describes a journey through a symbolic landscape; there are the standard romantic metaphors that give the landscape a religious significance. The poet is a "worshipper," and the sun, "transfigured" as it lowers, is both a god and a burning bush. Mounting the hill, the poet captures a last look at the sun, which gives him a moment of revelation. But instead of enduring even in memory to provide the poet with reassurance, the last glimpse of the setting sun gives place to "the bewildered tracks of night," and its whole significance is contained in the last lines, in the mere beauty of "the gold air and the silver" and "the last bird." As in Wallace Stevens's "Sunday Morning," it is the colors in the landscape and nothing behind it which form the meaning of the revelation; Rossetti's symbolic sunset symbolizes no further world, but perhaps only death. In contrast, Wordsworth's description of crossing the Alps in *The Prelude* (bk. 4, lines 557-640) leads to "the types and symbols of Eternity," an apocalypse apparently not available to Rossetti. Granted that he attributes a quasireligious significance to beauty, his poem is still a Wordsworthian journey from which the transcendental meaning is missing. Wordsworth's experience of crossing the Alps proved the impossibility of getting lost in the universe of nature. But for Rossetti, climbing "the hill summit" leads ultimately back down to "the bewildered tracks of night."

Rossetti's sonnet is a romantic gesture that lacks full romantic significance. Pre-Raphaelite art is less one of assertion than of defiance, aimed at the ugliness, the skepticism, and the complacency of mid-Victorian society. The purpose of much of it is summed up in Burne-Jones's declaration that "the more materialistic Science becomes, the more Angels shall I paint."[3] He was not able to assert, like Blake, that he saw angels, nor even that he believed them to exist, but only that he would paint them as a way of defying science. And when it is not an art of defiance as in the Pre-Raphaelites, mid-Victorian poetry tends to be an art of doubt and melancholy, looking out upon scenes of urban and industrial expansion and seeing wastelands instead of fairy palaces.[4]

The major Victorian poets of doubt and melancholy are Tennyson and Arnold, and of the two, Arnold confronts the social origins of his melancholy more directly. But he does so in terms too vastly metaphysical to make the application of "liberal nostrums" look helpful. The "sick hurry" and "divided aims" that are the symptoms of "this strange disease of modern life" are not responsive to political cures. Instead, they are largely caused by the strife of parties representing class interests rather than the universal interests of church and state. Arnold's poem "The Future," probably written in 1852, illustrates the despondency that he feels in confronting social problems. Even so, it is more optimistic than some of his other poems, because it contains an alternative to the dreary present which is at least forward-looking, in contrast to Empedocles' suicide or to the regressive flight of the Scholar Gipsy:

> This tract which the river of Time
> Now flows through with us, is the plain.
> Gone is the calm of its earlier shore.
> Bordered by cities and hoarse
> With a thousand cries is its stream.
> And we on its breast, our minds
> Are confused as the cries which we hear,
> Changing and shot as the sights which we see.
>
> And we say that repose has fled
> For ever the course of the river of Time.
> That cities will crowd to its edge
> In a blacker, incessanter line;
> That the din will be more on its banks,
> Denser the trade on its stream,
> Flatter the plain where it flows,
> Fiercer the sun overhead.
> That never will those on its breast
> See an ennobling sight,
> Drink of the feeling of quiet again.

Such a future, dominated by urban and industrial ugliness, is merely dismal. But Arnold sees cause for hope in the fact that, just as we find it impossible to know exactly where we have been on the river of time, so we cannot know exactly where it will take us. There may be virtue in ignorance after all. It is possible that the current may take us beyond the cities of the plain to pleasanter sights:

> Haply, the river of Time—
> As it grows, as the towns on its marge
> Fling their wavering lights
> On a wider, statelier stream—

May acquire, if not the calm
Of its early mountainous shore,
Yet a solemn peace of its own.[5]

Things will never again be what they were in the golden age before the coming of the factories and the shopkeepers, but they may get better. At the same time, this hope for the future is not very sturdy, partly because the characters in the poem have no control over events. "We" are adrift on the river of time, and its current determines where we travel and what we pass. Further, we are inert spectators, separated by the river from the scenes of crowded, noisy, vulgar activity that we can feel no part of. History as river works its will on us, rather than we as reformers on it or on the scenes along its banks. And while its course may, we hope, be a sinuous progress *back* towards a calm that we have left behind, its goal is in doubt. In the geographical symbolism dominating all of his poetry, Arnold depicts the shape of history as at best only dubiously progressive. Like the struggling pilgrims in "Rugby Chapel," humanity may strive to march in a straight line, but the world is round and its scenery is craggy, full of obstacles that deflect the marchers from a goal that may be nonexistent anyway. Time itself, moreover, is often not linear but cyclic in Arnold's poetry, as in the wearying ebb and flow of the "Sea of Faith" in "Dover Beach."

Equally doubtful, shrouded in the mists of a sometimes consolatory ignorance, are the direction and goal of history in Tennyson's major poems. It is a curious fact that an age with so many reasons for optimism, looking back to the demise of Chartism and to the victory of free trade and forward to an apparently infinite vista of industrial and imperial expansion, should have had so moody and unpredictable a writer as Tennyson for its poet laureate. But it is a fact that suggests the complexity of both Victorian culture and Tennyson's poetry. His work spans the period from 1832 to 1867 and reflects more fully and brilliantly than that of any other Victorian poet the social and the religious crises of his age. This is true even though his resolutions of the crises he explores tend to be anticlimactic, a mere loose bandaging up of the wounds he opens. If it is the role of the poet not to answer questions but to ask them and to provide a full and faithful record of a sensitive mind confronting the crises of his age, then Tennyson is a major poet. As T. S. Eliot remarked, it is not the quality of Tennyson's faith but the quality of his doubt that is the true measure of his stature. And although later critics have sometimes insisted

185

upon the unity of Tennyson's vision, Eliot suggested that there were two Tennysons, for he was "the most instinctive rebel against the society in which he was the most perfect conformist."[6]

The duality of Tennyson as rebel and conformist is apparent in his major work as laureate, the *Idylls of the King*. It is framed by praise of Prince Albert and Queen Victoria; Swinburne called it the "Morte d'Albert, or Idylls of the Prince Consort."[7] The framing pieces contain admonitory language, based on the lessons that Tennyson himself thought the *Idylls* contained, but they are also standard laureate fare, patriotic, laudatory, hopeful about the future of nation and empire. But the *Idylls* themselves describe the rise and fall of a nation, and the emphasis is on fall: only the first two books are hopeful, full of springtime idealism; waxing through the other ten books, deceit and disillusionment eat away at the foundations of Camelot. And what unsturdy foundations they are! Camelot is a reflection of the heavenly city, but it is founded upon an abyss. In what seems to have been Tennyson's earliest plan for the *Idylls*, he describes "the sacred Mount of Camelot" as "the most beautiful in the world . . . But all underneath it was hollow, and the mountain trembled, when the seas rushed bellowing through the porphyry caves; and there ran a prophecy that the mountain and the city on some wild morning would topple into the abyss and be no more."[8]

Tennyson began with the apocalyptic image of Camelot caving in upon itself, and in the 1830s wrote "Sir Galahad," "Sir Launcelot and Queen Guinevere," "The Lady of Shalott," and the "Morte d'Arthur." The first composed but the last in sequence of the *Idylls*, the mournful description of Arthur's passing was a response to Hallam's death in 1833. It is appropriate to the elegiac mood of the *Idylls* that in its end is its beginning. Recursive both in structure and in the manner in which it was composed, it is the opposite of the energetic and forward-looking epic which we might expect from the poet laureate of a progressive empire. As Tennyson himself explained, the history of Camelot follows the seasonal cycle from spring to winter, and though Arthur himself may sail out of the cycle to Avilion, that is not possible for his earthly realm: "The Coming of Arthur is on the night of the New Year; when he is wedded 'the world is white with May'; on a summer night the vision of the Holy Grail appears; and the 'Last Tournament' is in the 'yellowing autumn-tide.' Guinevere flees through the mists of autumn, and Arthur's death takes place at midnight in mid-winter."[9]

The theme of the fall of a civilization, present as early in Tennyson's work as "Timbuctoo," acquires several disturbing implications in the completed *Idylls* of 1872-1874. Whereas *In Memoriam* leads us away from despair to a new faith in divinely guided progressive evolution, the *Idylls* works its way back towards the despair of "Morte d'Arthur." Furthermore, although he is far nobler and "blameless," Arthur is a failed reformer like Romney Leigh. But just because he is noble and blameless, Arthur's failure is harder to understand than Romney's. Is it inevitable that "Soul" should fail to conquer "Sense"? Are we forever doomed to backslide into the old "life of beasts"? And what are the implications of Arthur's failure for modern Britain? Because of the vagueness of Tennyson's "allegory in the distance," there are no final answers to these questions. One thing at least is clear: even a hero's life may be insufficient to translate the civilizing zeal of the reformer into lasting reality. As John Rosenberg says, the *Idylls* is "the subtlest anatomy of the failure of ideality in our literature."[10] The madness of Pelleas, the fratricide of Balan and Balin, the cynicism of Tristram are types of the whole, and so is Merlin's disillusioned language just before Vivien's treachery removes him from the poem:

> Then fell on Merlin a great melancholy;
> He walked with dreams and darkness, and he found
> A doom that ever poised itself to fall,
> An ever-moaning battle in the mist,
> World-war of dying flesh against the life,
> Death in all life and lying in all love,
> The meanest having power upon the highest,
> And the high purpose broken by the worm.[11]

Even if the temporary victory of soul is possible, backsliding into bestiality is easy. The higher Camelot aspires, the shakier it becomes over its hollow foundations. Merlin himself, a symbol of wisdom, shows us how easy it is to backslide when Vivien seduces him. And his despair is one that recurs often in Tennyson's poetry, contradicting whatever faith in progress Tennyson clings to by suggesting that man is always torn between sense and soul, with sense the victor in this world. Civilization is forever undermined by barbarism; linear time stands side by side in Tennyson's work with cyclical time; the desire for social improvement is subverted by doubt about its possibility; and in *In Memoriam*, Tennyson is forced to base his final hope for mankind on that doctrine which most distresses him, the theory of evolution.

Tennyson's heroes, minor Hamlets all, vacillate between ghosts of the past and lures of the future. The narrator of "Locksley Hall," a gentlemanly misfit in an age of machines and money, is trapped between the contradictory urges to action or to escape, and between past and future. "All things here are out of joint," he says, a modern Hamlet like the narrator of *Maud*. The villain is not a murderous uncle, however, but the commercial energy that "gilds the straitened forehead of the fool" and has robbed the narrator of his sweetheart. At the same time, the progress of middle-class commerce has also opened the pathway to the future that the narrator both dreads and hopes to travel:

> For I dipt into the future, far as human eye could see,
> Saw the Vision of the world, and all the wonder that would be;
>
> Saw the heavens fill with commerce, argosies of magic sails,
> Pilots of the purple twilight, dropping down with costly bales.
>
> (119-122)

Although this vision leads to "the nations' airy navies grappling in the central blue," it also leads beyond warfare to the ultimate triumph of democracy and a reign of peace and international law "in the Parliament of man, the Federation of the world."

The narrator's vision of peace and plenty through commerce might as well have been written by Cobden and Bright, but he does not rest long in it. His "palsied heart" and "jaundiced eye" produce another vision, this time of progress too slow and too little to cure social injustice and to ward off revolution: "Slowly comes a hungry people, as a lion creeping nigher" (135). Such doubt, coupled with his blighted passion, leads the narrator into escapist daydreams of "summer isles of Eden lying in dark-purple spheres of sea."

> There methinks would be enjoyment more than in this march of mind,
> In the steamship, in the railway, in the thoughts that shake man-kind.
>
> (165-166)

The choice now posed by the narrator is one between progressive civilization and a "life of savage ease," a regression into barbarism. The initial antithesis of the poem, between tainted wealth and true love, leads to a fuller, more troubling one between a progress which may override the values of love and honor on the one hand, and savage leisure and sensuality on the other. As in the *Idylls* and *In Memoriam*, Tennyson identifies progress with a movement away from bestiality, upward from the apes.

But the fact remains that the commercial civilization that stands opposed to savage sensuality has also robbed the narrator of his sweetheart, Amy. Progressive civilization appears to be hostile to all manifestations of Eros, the good with the bad, a problem that recurs in its fullest form in the *Idylls,* where "Sense at war with Soul" produces an unequal combat. Like Freud, Tennyson identifies civilization with repression: in the savage world, "the passions cramped no longer shall have scope and breathing space" (167). But unlike Freud, Tennyson cannot make clear to himself the tragic element in this identification and so ultimately sees no harm in repression.

It remains impossible, then, for the narrator of "Locksley Hall" to identify himself fully with the vision of future peace and plenty which he had before his youth was blighted by Amy's infidelity. The structure of the poem, like that of so many of Tennyson's, is one of vacillation between contradictory values that the narrator is unable to reconcile. At the end the narrator is prepared to follow "the mighty wind" "seaward," but "seaward" may mean toward the "summer isles of Eden" as well as toward the goal of "the ringing grooves of change." Anyway, the one thing that is clear at the end of the poem is that the storm which brings the future raining down upon Locksley Hall will mean its destruction, or the destruction of the gentlemanly, antibourgeois values it represents. The poem ends not on a note of affirmation but with a glimpse of the past in the midst of its fall, on a note of melancholy almost as dismal as "the last dim battle in the west" in the *Idylls.* Of course the mighty wind that apparently will crash in the rooftree of Locksley Hall is also the wind of the future, but it is not clearly the harbinger of spring and of hope, like Shelley's revolutionary west wind. Tennyson's emphasis falls on destruction rather than renovation. At the close of the poem, his narrator marches defiantly and perhaps self-destructively into a future that is itself a storm, rather than the spring-like aftermath of storm.

This reading of "Locksley Hall" may seem to underrate the optimism of the narrator's vision of progress, but his vacillation and the fact that he had this vision before losing Amy render it ambiguous. It is an ambiguity repeated many times over in Tennyson's poetry—in "Ulysses" and the other classical monologues, in *Maud,* and above all in *In Memoriam.* Furthermore, we have the evidence of "Locksley Hall Sixty Years After," in which the narrator declares the dismal bankruptcy of the vision of progress that he had as a young man:

Gone the cry of "Forward, Forward," lost within a growing gloom;
Lost, or only heard in silence from the silence of a tomb.

Half the marvels of my morning, triumphs over time and space,
Staled by frequence, shrunk by usage into commonest common-
   place!

"Forward" rang the voices then, and of the many mine was one.
Let us hush this cry of "Forward" till ten thousand years have gone.
                                                                    (73-78)

Tennyson insisted on the difference between his opinions and those of his angry narrator, but he did not explain what it is. Besides, whether or not he shares his narrator's opinions in detail, he obviously shares his social anxiety.

Tennyson makes his social anxiety more explicit in *Maud,* written toward the beginning of his laureateship. His tale of betrayal, violence, and madness, as strange a production for a poet laureate as the *Idylls,* follows the story of "Locksley Hall," but with several changes. One is that there is an increase in *Maud* of melodramatic violence because of the duel and the narrator's insanity. The vacillations of the narrator in "Locksley Hall" are a natural expression of his despondency and do not suggest much more than his inability to make up his mind. In *Maud,* although it is a better poem, everything is more lurid and extreme, as if Tennyson is no longer willing to see the same basic story in terms of compromise. Further, there is no "vision of the future" in *Maud.* Tennyson's treatment of the commercial values that disrupt the love affair has nothing sympathetic about it. The alternative to the narrator's despair does not lie down "the ringing grooves of change" as it did in 1842, but in war and the chance for renewing the aristocratic values of heroic action and honor. And it is explicitly against commercial prosperity that Tennyson ranges patriotism and the martial virtues, somewhat like Charlotte Brontë's berating of Robert Moore for his lack of patriotism in *Shirley:*

No more shall commerce be all in all, and Peace
Pipe on her pastoral hillock a languid note,
And watch her harvest ripen, her herd increase,
Nor the cannon-bullet rust on a slothful shore.

                                                                    (3.23-26)

One of Tennyson's responses to his new position as laureate was the writing of poems whose purpose was to increase patriotism. The "Ode on the Death of the Duke of Wellington" is the most notable of his patriotic poems, but he wrote many others in the 1850s warning against the threat of invasion from France and urging the nation on to victory in the Crimean War. And as poet-patriot Tennyson opposed the "peace party" of John Bright and the Manchester School. Although Tennyson later expressed surprise when accused of attacking John Bright in *Maud,* it makes little difference whether his Quaker peacemonger is anyone in particular:

> Last week came one to the county town,
> To preach our poor little army down,
> And play the game of the despot kings,
> Though the state has done it and thrice as well:
> This broad-brimmed hawker of holy things,
> Whose ear is crammed with his cotton, and rings
> Even in dreams to the chink of his pence,
> This huckster put down war! can he tell
> Whether war be a cause or a consequence?
>
> (1.366-374)

It is not clear that the narrator of *Maud* is better able to tell "whether war be a cause or a consequence." But it is clear that war provides him with a surety of purpose which he cannot get from sources associated with domestic tranquillity and commercial progress. And the same is true of Tennyson, who as laureate must have felt grateful for a theme that allowed him to be unambiguously affirmative, since there was so much about which he felt equivocal or negative. As the narrator says, peace is "full of wrongs and shames, / Horrible, hateful, monstrous, not to be told," although he has already told several of them, especially at the beginning of the poem. The first forty-eight lines of *Maud* are a catalogue of social evils bred by industrialism, based mainly on Carlyle and on Christian Socialist sources like Kingsley's novels and essays. *Alton Locke,* which *Maud* resembles in several ways, has been claimed as one of Tennyson's sources, and F. D. Maurice is never far from Tennyson's thinking in the early 1850s.[12] Rather than the language of social harmony, however, Carlyle's bellicose language is what emerges in *Maud.* War and heroism, not workers' cooperatives and education, are advocated by the narrator as a cure for Mammonism and for his own illness. Against the selfishness of Manchester cotton-spinners he ranges the aristocratic values of honor, courage, loyalty, and self-sacrifice. And that the narrator's opinions are Tennyson's is evident from Tennyson's alarmist poems dealing with the French invasion scare and with the Kaffir war in the early 1850s:

> Though niggard throats of Manchester may bawl,
>   What England was, shall her true sons forget?
> We are not cotton-spinners all,

> But some love England and her honour yet.
> And these in our Thermopylae shall stand,
> And hold against the world this honour of the land.[13]

Rather than the Christian Socialist opposition between cooperation and competition, Tennyson works with an explicitly class-oriented opposition between aristocratic "honour" and bourgeois "niggardliness." As the narrator of "Locksley Hall" sarcastically declares, "But the jingling of the guinea helps the hurt that Honour feels" (105), which implies that the power of money will both heal the wound and make it. The narrator's bitterly felt social marginality, similar to Tennyson's own situation in the 1830s, finds vent in his attack on middle-class Mammonism:

> What is that which I should turn to, lighting upon days like these?
> Every door is barred with gold, and opens but to golden keys.[14]
> (99-100)

At the same time, the narrator's earlier "vision of the future" is based on the progress of industry and middle-class economic power. The narrator is trapped between "Honour" and "the jingling of the guinea"; it seems likely that Tennyson felt trapped in the same way throughout his career.

The difficulty of Tennyson's position is manifest in much of his work. Thus, the storm of the future that concludes "Locksley Hall," based mainly on social anxiety, has as its counterpart the language of natural flux in *In Memoriam*:

> And all is well, though faith and form
>   Be sundered in the night of fear;
>   Well roars the storm to those that hear
> A deeper voice across the storm,
>
> Proclaiming social truth shall spread,
>   And justice, even though thrice again
>   The red fool-fury of the Seine
> Should pile her barricades with dead.
>
> (sec. 127)

The storm of the future, threatening individual life and present values, involves both natural violence and political violence. It is only in spite of these that "social truth" and "justice" will at last prevail. The metaphors in this passage again suggest Shelley, but the message that "all is well'' in spite of the stormy weather is in direct contrast to Shelley's revolutionary delight in natural mutability. Shelley's imagery of crowns and castles dissolving in nature's Heraclitean fire is, nevertheless, echoed by Tennyson:

> But ill for him that wears a crown,
>   And him, the lazar, in his rags:
>   They tremble, the sustaining crags;
> The spires of ice are toppled down,
>
> And molten up, and roar in flood;
>   The fortress crashes from on high,
>   The brute earth lightens to the sky,
> And the great Æon sinks in blood,
>
> And compassed by the fires of Hell;
>   While thou, dear spirit, happy star,
>   O'erlook'st the tumult from afar,
> And smilest, knowing all is well.
>
> (sec. 127)

It is not entirely clear whether "all is well" in this world or only in the calm hereafter with Hallam. But the political strife that Tennyson dreads will be bloody and hellish, and it is only against such strife that "social truth" will win its way. Mutability, natural and social, is both the central fact and one source of fear in *In Memoriam,* and it is ultimately only the prospect of a nobler race, heralded by Hallam, and of the "one far-off divine event, / To which the whole creation moves" that allows Tennyson to conclude that "all is well." Both the remoteness of the "divine event" and the apolitical, evolutionary emergence of the nobler race are poles apart from Shelley, whose apocalyptic radicalism demanded the immediate realization of "social truth" through revolution rather than in spite of it. Tennyson translates the terms of political change into those of biological necessity, for which he also manages to find a theological sanction. Like the narrator's stance toward "the jingling of the guinea" in "Locksley Hall," Tennyson finds in the theory of evolution itself the cure for the hurt it causes.

What Tennyson emphasizes in most of his explicitly political poetry, even when he describes social evils as in the opening lines of *Maud,* is not the need for reform but the need for moderation. So he eulogizes the Duke of Wellington as a bastion of temperance who stood midway be-

193

tween "brainless mobs and lawless Powers." And in the same poem, he prays to England's God (whose existence in such a context is not to be questioned) to save England, thus preserving

> the one true seed of freedom sown
> Betwixt a people and their ancient throne,
> That sober freedom out of which there springs
> Our loyal passion for our temperate kings.
>
> (162-165)

In the midst of the reform agitation in 1830, Tennyson and Hallam traveled to the Pyrenees to help the Spanish revolutionary movement against Ferdinand VII. Shortly afterwards Tennyson was back in England writing poems that weighed against at least the more violent aspects of the reform movement. The political poems of the 1830s all assert that "of old sat Freedom on the heights," and that if Englishmen do not proceed cautiously in matters of social change, then true freedom will be lost instead of gained. "You ask me why," "Of old sat Freedom on the heights," and "Love thou thy land" are all attacks upon "the falsehood of extremes," and, while accepting the inevitability of change ("Meet is it changes should control / Our being"), they are in a general way a rejection of politics as an activity. And just as these conservative attitudes mark the beginning of Tennyson's career, so they are with him at the end:

> Raving politics, never at rest—as this poor earth's pale history runs,—
> What is it all but a trouble of ants in the gleam of a million million of suns?
>
> ("Vastness," 3-4)

Throughout Tennyson's political poetry, the central question is how to move forward down "the ringing grooves of change" without falling into the terrible extremes of revolution or of reactionary tyranny. Tennyson's most frequent political message, therefore, concerns the need for mediation between extremes, between "brainless mobs and lawless Powers," although no more than Arnold does he claim mediation as the function of the middle class. Mediation is rather the function of the Constitution and of such stalwart, cautious statesmen as Wellington. It is true that Tennyson waxes more assertive in the poems of the 1850s which deal with the French invasion scare. However, the rallying cry of "Riflemen Form!" was obviously not written in defense of foreign liberal movements but rather against the French extremes of democracy and tyranny. And typical of Tennyson's political thinking throughout his career are the snippets of bland, unnecessary advice that he penned to Gladstone in the 1880s, like "Compromise":

> Steersman, be not precipitate in thine act
>   Of steering, for the river here, my friend,
>   Parts in two channels, moving to one end—
> This goes straight forward to the cataract:
>   That streams about the bend;
> But though the cataract seem the nearer way,
> Whate'er the crowd on either bank may say,
> Take thou the "bend," 'twill save thee many a day.

The hackneyed geography of the fork in the river in this poem contrasts sharply with the profound vision of natural mutability in *In Memoriam*, but they share at least one result. As in the case of Arnold's imagery of rivers and oceans, Tennyson's likening history to tides and river currents suggests the powerlessness of human action to affect the main course of events. The direction and goal of history are predetermined. The proper art of governing is the art of steering the ship of state along the safest current towards an inevitable future, rather than attempting to mould events or to sail against the current.

In the complex of values that Tennyson expresses in "Locksley Hall," *In Memoriam,* and elsewhere, it is apparent that both his hope and his dread arise from a single source, from that storm of the future that promises both destruction and renewal. And the antithesis to the storm of the future, also a source of dread and of false or deluded hope, is the idea of stagnation, of failing to move towards the future, or of falling into a life of savage ease like that which is rejected in "Locksley Hall." The false luxuriation of the Odyssean sailors in "The Lotos-Eaters" and the mouldering away of grange and girl in "Mariana" are parts of a single nightmare, based on the same anxiety. In "The Palace of Art," the soul's guilt is expressed in terms of stagnation, of being cut off from the main currents of the age and of progress:

> A spot of dull stagnation, without light
>   Or power of movement, seemed my soul,
> 'Mid onward-sloping motions infinite
>   Making for one sure goal.
>
> A still salt pool, locked in with bars of sand,
>   Left on the shore; that hears all night

> The plunging seas draw backward from the land
>   Their moon-led waters white.

(245-252)

The soul's punishment is to fail to move with the tides, to fail to be carried along by progress. Self-marooned in a backwater of aristocratic privilege, here identified with luxurious art-for-art's sake instead of with destitute "Honour," the soul has lost her claim to a meaningful future. That future appears to lie with democracy, shadowed forth at the end of the poem by the penitential cottage. Tennyson said that "The Palace of Art" shows that "the Godlike life is with man and for man," whereas the soul, in the midst of her pride, attacks the common people as "swine."

The soul's isolation, then, is not just antisocial and immoral but antidemocratic and antiprogressive as well. And "The Palace of Art" offers one version of the dread of moral degeneration, of goalless melancholy, or of slothful luxuriance that sits like an incubus over all of Tennyson's poetry, taking forms as various as Lotos-land, the onerous immortality of Tithonus, and the self-indulgent grief that the poet castigates himself for repeatedly in *In Memoriam*. If the dread of social change underlies what might be called Tennyson's conservative nightmare, then the dread of social stagnation underlies what might be called his liberal nightmare. The first is the fear of change, of time, of death: "The hills are shadows, and they flow / From form to form, and nothing stands" (*In Memoriam,* sec. 123). But the second nightmare contradicts the first one, for it expresses the dread of a world stagnant or regressive. This is the horror from which Ulysses wishes to escape and which captivates the Lotos-Eaters. It is the horror of isolation in "Mariana" and "The Lady of Shalott," as well as of moral regression in "The Vision of Sin," "Lucretius," and *Idylls of the King*. In his greatest poetry, Tennyson as conformist-rebel fuses his conservative nightmare with his liberal nightmare into tense, paradoxical structures that are monuments not to the beliefs and prejudices of upper-class Victorians but to the quality of their doubts.

If the idea of living in a state of permanent social upheaval was a threat to many Victorians, the idea of an end to progress seemed worse. The latter danger was frequently expressed in terms of cyclical versus linear shapes of history, as in "Locksley Hall": "Better fifty years of Europe than a cycle of Cathay." This is a piece of Podsnappery typical of much middle-class Victorian thinking, but it is Podsnappery with a technical side to it, reinforced by political economy. In *The Wealth of Nations,* Adam Smith had argued that any society might find itself in one of three conditions: "The progressive state is in reality the cheerful and the hearty state to all the different orders of the society. The stationary state is dull; the declining melancholy."[15] In language echoed by later political economists, Smith referred to China—Tennyson's "Cathay"—as an example of a society in a stationary condition: "China has been long one of the richest, that is, one of the most fertile, best cultivated, most industrious, and most populous countries in the world. It seems, however, to have been long stationary. Marco Polo, who visited it more than five hundred years ago, describes its cultivation, industry, and populousness, almost in the same terms in which they are described by travellers in the present times."[16]

By the mid-nineteenth century, stagnant China was the classic contrast to progressive England, partly because of the public display of the "Royal Chinese Junk," the *Keying,* which was moored at Temple Bar Pier in 1851. Dickens had written about it in 1848, and he and R. H. Horne wrote about it again in *Household Words* for July 5, 1851, in an essay called, "The Great Exhibition and the Little One." Horne and Dickens felt that the *Keying,* or the "Little Exhibition," showed how not to run a nation, while the Great Exhibition showed how to run a nation on progressive principles. "The true Tory spirit would have made a China of England, if it could."[17]

Although Mill is undoubtedly thinking more of Adam Smith than of the *Keying,* in *On Liberty* he says that the Chinese "have become stationary—have remained so for thousands of years; and if they are ever to be farther improved, it must be by foreigners."[18] Through the erosion of individuality by the tyranny of public opinion, Europe itself is threatened with the fate of China. And that such a fate would be "dull" if not "melancholy"—Smith's adjectives—is easy to conclude. The assumptions underlying Mill's argument involve the identification of history with progress, and of progress with the meaning of life. Because it is not progressive, says Mill, "the greater part of the world has, properly speaking, no history."[19] And throughout most of his writings, progress is both means and end, the dynamic of history as well as the goal towards which it moves. To arrive at the goal is to remain in perpetual motion, to continue to climb the Jacob's ladder of social improvement. To arrive at any other place is at best to descend into that state of abject changelessness or circularity exemplified by China.

From time to time in his writings, however, Mill recognizes that progress cannot be the goal of progress, and he is therefore less ready than Adam Smith had been to identify progress with the happiness of all members of society. In the famous chapter on "The Stationary State" in his *Principles of Political Economy,* Mill comes close to reversing the terms established by Smith: "It must always have been seen . . . by political economists, that the increase of wealth is not boundless: that at the end of what they term the progressive state lies the stationary state, that all progress in wealth is but a postponement of this, and that each step in advance is an approach to it."[20] The goal of progress turns out to be a condition of equilibrium; its aim is not itself but its antithesis. "This impossibility of ultimately avoiding the stationary state," Mill says, "this irresistible necessity that the stream of human industry should finally spread itself out into an apparently stagnant sea—must have been, to the political economists of the last two generations, an unpleasing and discouraging prospect." Mill himself finds it hard to accept the prospect of arrested development, however, and in most other contexts—in *On Liberty,* for example—he also is guilty of identifying "all that is economically desirable with the progressive state, and with that alone."[21] But in *Principles of Political Economy,* Mill is temporarily troubled by the idea of goalless progress much as Tennyson is troubled by the idea of goalless evolution. Mill's description of the progressive state is of a mad scramble for wealth, like one of Carlyle's tirades against Mammonism: "I confess I am not charmed with the ideal of life held out by those who think that the normal state of human beings is that of struggling to get on; that the trampling, crushing, elbowing, and treading on each other's heels, which form the existing type of social life, are the most desirable lot of human kind, or anything but the disagreeable symptoms of one of the phases of industrial progress."[22] Because he is disenchanted with the progressive state, at least in its present phase, Mill recommends its opposite as "a very considerable improvement on our present condition."[23] And in what is perhaps the best-known statement in the *Principles,* Mill goes on to suggest what the quality of life might be under the torpid economy of the future:

> It is scarcely necessary to remark that a stationary condition of capital and population implies no stationary state of human improvement. There would be as much scope as ever for all kinds of mental culture, and moral and social progress; as much room for improving the Art of Living, and much more likelihood of its being improved, when minds ceased to be engrossed by the art of getting on. Even the industrial arts might be as earnestly and as successfully cultivated, with this sole difference, that instead of serving no purpose but the increase of wealth, industrial improvements would produce their legitimate effect, that of abridging labour. Hitherto it is question-

able if all the mechanical inventions yet made have lightened the day's toil of any human being. They have enabled a greater population to live the same life of drudgery and imprisonment, and an increased number of manufacturers and others to make fortunes. They have increased the comforts of the middle classes. But they have not yet begun to effect those great changes in human destiny, which it is in their nature and in their futurity to accomplish.[24]

For a man who on most other occasions identifies both history and civilization with progress, the chapter "The Stationary State" represents an astonishing reversal. Mill, it appears, is visited by the same contradictory nightmares as Tennyson, and he, too, finds them strangely interchangeable. Although he is describing a desired condition of economic harmony, Mill falls back on the language of "human improvement." In the stationary state, industrial progress may have slowed down, but there will be just as much opportunity as ever for "moral and social progress." And even industrial progress will continue, although its effect will be to increase leisure by "abridging labour" rather than to increase material wealth.

In describing life in the stationary state, Mill relies upon a qualification of the idea of progress that he had offered in his essay "Civilization." There he pointed out that progress is not a unitary phenomenon. Men may improve in some areas, stand still in some, and regress in others: "We do not regard the age as either equally advanced or equally progressive in many of the other kinds of improvement. In some it appears to us stationary, in some even retrograde."[25] This qualification, which seems at first to be the undoing of the idea of progress because it disconnects moral and social from industrial improvement, is in fact what allows Mill to confront the specter of the stationary state with equanimity. Even when the increase of wealth through industrial expansion ceases, progress will still go forward on many fronts, and these will be the most important in human affairs—the cultural, moral, and psychological fronts—where boundless opportunities await the reformer.

What is not possible for Mill to envisage is a stationary state in which no improvements take place because everything is pretty much as it should be. Such a condition may be only a vagary of the utopian imagination. But so engrained is the work ethic in Mill—so imperative for him is the need "to strive, to seek, to find, and not to yield"—that the idea of an end to all progress seems either impossible or nightmarish, like the backslidings of the Lotos-Eaters and Lucretius. Even the prospect of a cessation of industrial expansion is not clearly a happy one for Mill, because it means the loss of one field of struggle and the need to find others to take its place. On most other occasions in Mill's writings, the stationary state seems as melancholy a place as that described in *The Limits to Growth,* the recent study of the future by the "Club of Rome," in which economic equilibrium is recommended as the only way to avoid the catastrophes that will result from uncontrolled technological development: pollution, overpopulation, the exhaustion of vital resources, and worldwide ecological collapse within seventy years. From Adam Smith's easy identification of progress with happiness, we arrive in the twentieth century at the idea of progress as our undoing and of the stationary state as a temporary reprieve, a sort of Keynesian purgatory.

During Mill's mental crisis of 1826, the threat of an end to progress was part of what dismayed him:

> It was in the autumn of 1826. I was in a dull state of nerves . . . the state, I should think, in which converts to Methodism usually are, when smitten by their first "conviction of sin." In this frame of mind it occurred to me to put the question directly to myself, "Suppose that all your objects in life were realized; that all the changes in institutions and opinions which you are looking forward to, could be completely effected at this very instant: would this be a great joy and happiness to you?" And an irrepressible self-consciousness distinctly answered, "No!" At this my heart sank within me: the whole foundation on which my life was constructed fell down. All my happiness was to have been found in the continual pursuit of this end. The end had ceased to charm, and how could there ever again be any interest in the means? I seemed to have nothing left to live for.[26]

The secret dread of the reformer is to have exhausted the objects of his solicitation. What would Henry Mayhew have done, after all, without mudlarks and ticket-of-leave men? Mill's mental breakdown and recovery, analogous to the pattern of Methodist conversion, are also like Tennyson's experiences after the death of Hallam. This is true even though they occupy opposite ends of the spectrum of middle-class values. Both fell into states of depression in which they questioned the meaning of life and the goal of progress, and both found "a solace and a stay" in poetry. More importantly, both escaped from their "sloughs of despond" through renewed faith in the idea of progress. In *The Autobiography,* Mill recounts how, after reading Marmontel, he came to adopt views similar to Carlyle's "anti-self-consciousness theory": "I never, indeed, wavered in the conviction that happiness is the test of all rules of conduct, and the end of life. But I now thought that this end was only to be attained by not making it the direct end. Those only are happy (I thought) who have their minds fixed on some object other than their own happiness; on the happiness of others, on the improvement of mankind."[27] And Tennyson, in the midst of his grief, began to write the lyrics that would culminate in a Christianized theory of progressive evolution in *In Memoriam*. During the same period, in 1833, Tennyson also wrote "Ulysses," which, he said, "gave my feeling about the need of going forward and braving the struggle of life."

> Yet all experience is an arch wherethrough
> Gleams that untravelled world, whose margin fades
> For ever and for ever when I move.
> How dull it is to pause, to make an end,
> To rust unburnished, not to shine in use!
> As though to breathe were life! Life piled on life
> Were all too little . . .

The threat of an end to action—of old age, of stagnation at home—keeps Ulysses moving. So action becomes the goal of action, and progress of progress.

And so, too, in *In Memoriam*, Tennyson overcomes his fear of evolution because he finds in it a means of counteracting his greater fear of aimless grief and moral degeneration. No more than Mill was he able to envisage a healthy human condition without the need "to strive, to seek, to find, and not to yield." For both, a world in which the bourgeois values of work, renunciation, and progress are supplanted by leisure, abundance, and personal gratification is at best impossibly utopian and at worst a threat to virtue. For Tennyson, the associations of leisure and erotic fulfillment are always with the past, with the old "life of beasts" as in the *Idylls*, or with aristocratic privilege and corruption as in "Palace of Art," and they are always guilt-ridden. Mill can imagine such a condition of leisure in the future—in the stationary state which is the goal of progress at least in *Principles of Political Economy*—but it turns out not to be leisure. For Mill, the abolition of strictly economic labor will mean that the laborers can go forth to the harvest in other vineyards, and make endless mental and moral progress.

Nevertheless, Mill comes close to a genuinely utopian vision. It is a rather pinched vision—Mill would prefer to avoid the stationary state altogether—but it is still in some respects comparable to William Morris's vision of guiltless fulfillment in *News from Nowhere*. And perhaps Tennyson has some such utopian future in mind in "Locksley Hall" and in the idea of "the crowning race" at the end of *In Memoriam*. But Tennyson can describe a life of enjoyment—a life that is pure and Edenic in Morris—only in terms of guilt and degeneration. It may be that Morris understood this when he likened his utopia to Lotos-land, for the analogy sounds ironic. Gliding by pastoral scenes along the upper Thames, Morris's narrator says, "It was the sort of afternoon that Tennyson must have been thinking about, when he said of the Lotos-Eaters' land that it was a land where it was always afternoon."[28] Unlike Tennyson's portrayals of wicked sloth and self-indulgence, and unlike Mill's grudging acceptance of an end to progress, Morris's utopia is entirely guiltless and carefree. It is a stationary state as are most utopias, but that is just as it should be. Progress is necessary only in a world of scarcity and evil, in which there are still objects towards which the reformer can direct his concern, finding his chosen labor among the unredeemed who are eternally to be redeemed.

Just as the goal of progress is more progress even in Mill's version of the stationary state, so the goal of the reformer must be to struggle onward in an endless advance "beyond the baths of all the western stars." King Arthur fails necessarily in his civilizing mission, because to succeed would mean paradoxically to retrogress into the condition of beasts, wallowing in the mire of the senses, or in other words to open the way for the sexual license and adultery that spell the doom of Camelot. Because progress and civilization are based on repression, or the at least temporary conquest of soul over sense, it is impossible for Tennyson to imagine any end to progress that is not a guilt-ridden backsliding into simian self-indulgence. And Mill also finds it impossible to abandon the idea of progress for much the same reason. For it is apparent that Mill's stationary state, unlike Morris's, continues to be based on renunciation. Having acknowledged that wealth is inequitably distributed in the present, Mill suggests that it will be better distributed in the stationary state. It will be so less through governmental adjustment of property relations, however, than through Mill's great social panacea of birth control, regulating the wages fund for the benefit of the working class: "Only when, in addition to just institutions, the increase of mankind shall be under the deliberate guidance of judicious foresight, can the conquests made from the powers of nature . . . become the common property of the species, and the means of improving and elevating the universal lot."[29] This is renunciation with a vengeance. Progress depends largely on how well the working class restricts the erotic energy which dominates it. And so in Mill, as in Tennyson, we are exhorted to

> Arise and fly
> The reeling Faun, the sensual feast;
> Move upward, working out the beast,
> And let the ape and tiger die.
>
> (*In Memoriam,* sec. 118)

Just as progress leads from one stationary state to another one in Mill, so progress in Tennyson—should it ever come to a halt—would end in that bestiality whence it started. For both, the Jacob's ladder of history threatens to become an Ixion's wheel of meaningless circularity. The only way to avoid such a melancholy result is to call for more progress, more action, more objects of solicitation, and more life to drink to the lees. "Labour, wide as the Earth, has its summit in Heaven," says Carlyle. Its goal is infinite, and it hardly matters what it accomplishes, so long as it is on the road of endless improvement. King Arthur will come again, we are told, and Camelot must forever be a-building, in the midst of its fall.

The public health issue and a version of the social organism based on the circulation of sewage. From *Punch*, 1850.

IX.   Realisms

At the start of his satire on "Mr. Popular Sentiment" in *The Warden,* Trollope writes: "In former times great objects were attained by great work. When evils were to be reformed, reformers set about their heavy task with grave decorum and laborious argument . . . We get on now with a lighter step, and quicker . . . Ridicule is found to be more convincing than argument, imaginary agonies touch more than true sorrows, and monthly novels convince, when learned quartos fail to do so. If the world is to be set right, the work will be done by shilling numbers."[1] Reform is no light matter, Trollope suggests, and therefore novelists should not concern themselves with it. Novelists like Dickens who take up the cudgels of reform distort experience by dividing it between false extremes, victims and villains. Mr. Popular Sentiment's novel, *The Almshouse,* is of a piece with John Bold's excessive radicalism in *The Warden* and also with *The Jupiter*'s journalistic lack of scruples. It is difficult to tell whether Trollope thinks that Dickens is motivated by too much moral concern, like John Bold, or too little, like the press. In either case, *The Almshouse* is the sort of thesis or propaganda novel that *The Warden* steadfastly refuses to be, although in its refusal it ironically acts like a thesis novel.

In his *Autobiography,* Trollope tells us that he first conceived of *The Warden* as a thesis novel, exposing social evils much as he had sought to expose the causes of Irish unrest in his first two novels, and much as his mother had exposed them in *Michael Armstrong* and *Jessie Phillips. The Warden* might have been just such a biased exposé as *The Almshouse,* Trollope suggests, if he had tried to attack only one abuse in it instead of two antithetical ones. These "opposite evils" are the misappropriation of charitable funds as "incomes for idle Church dignitaries" and "the undeserved severity of the newspapers towards the recipients of such incomes." "I felt that there had been some tearing to pieces which might have been spared." So *The Warden* is a failed thesis novel, because in it Trollope champions causes that cancel each other out. But Trollope goes on to suggest that to write a good thesis novel would have required him to be less than honest, or at least less than true to life: "Any writer in advocating a cause must do so after the fashion of an advocate,—or his writing will be ineffective. He should take up one side and cling to that, and then he may be powerful. There should be no scruples of conscience. Such scruples make a man impotent for such work."[2] By implication, "Mr. Popular Sentiment" is an unscrupulous writer, or at least an unrealistic one, a Dodson-and-Fogg among novelists. Trollope's confession of failure barely masks his sense of superior realism and superior "scruples of conscience": he implies that from the beginning of his career he understood better than Dickens that every question has at least two sides.

Trollope's view of Dickens as a biased reformer grinding unnecessarily sharp fictional axes was an increasingly common one in the 1850s.[3] At about the same time that Harriet Martineau was accusing Dickens of "pseudo-philanthropy" in the matter of factory machinery, Macaulay was condemning the "sullen socialism" of *Hard Times,* and Mary Russell Mitford was complaining about Dickens's "liberal cant." Repeatedly in the 1850s, reviewers accused Dickens of beating dead horses, and advised him to stay away from politics. Bagehot, for instance, viewed Dickens's "sentimental radicalism" as a "pernicious example" to his imitators: "Mr. Dickens has not unfrequently spoken, and what is worse, he has taught a great number of parrot-like imitators to speak, in what really is, if they knew it, a tone of objection to the necessary constitution of human society."[4] Bagehot argues that Dickens's reform idealism made sense in his early novels, but that by the 1850s it has outlived its time. In the period from 1823 to 1845, reform was the order of the day, and the various brands of radicalism were perhaps justified, although extreme. But after 1845, according to Bagehot, everything in the way of reform that is needful has been done, and Dickens's continued attacks on social abuses are anachronistic and dangerous:

> The unfeeling obtuseness of the early part of this century was to be corrected by an extreme, perhaps an excessive, sensibility to human suffering in the years which have followed. There was most adequate reason for the sentiment in its origin, and it had a great task to perform in ameliorating harsh customs and repealing dreadful penalties; but it has continued to repine at such evils long after they ceased to exist, and when the only facts that at all resemble them are

the necessary painfulness of due punishment and the necessary rigidity of established law.[5]

By the enlightened 1850s the crusades have ended, but Charles Dickens keeps tilting at windmills.

Bagehot's and Trollope's criticisms of Dickens are representative of a widespread attitude in the 1850s and after—an attitude apparent in the bourgeois complacency of *John Halifax,* in the revulsion against Fourierism and philanthropy in *Aurora Leigh,* in Thackeray's "profoundly reasoned pococurantism," in the softening of the hard edges of Maurice's and Kingsley's Christian Socialism, and in the cautionary politics of *Felix Holt* and *Culture and Anarchy.*[6] This attitude, which is given its clearest intellectual exposition in Bagehot's thesis about the "deferential" nature of the English, amounts to a form of political "realism" that is directly related to the fictional "realism" of Trollope, Thackeray, and George Eliot.

"Realism" in this political sense means a rejection of reform idealism, although not necessarily an affirmation of the status quo. It seeks to maintain a balance or stalemate between radicalism and conservatism. It identifies truth if not goodness with the given, with "facts" alone, and substitutes either worldly toleration or a scientific-seeming objectivity for critical ideals. And it tends to displace the responsibility for social change from human agency to "laws" of evolution and organic growth. With the emergence of "social Darwinism" in the theories of Spencer and Bagehot, the free trade and reform-minded radicalism of the period from 1832 to 1846 comes full circle to an organicist conservatism similar in some ways to that of Burke and Coleridge. In the social theories of Spencer, the most negative aspects of both Bentham and Coleridge form a merger completely hostile to social welfare legislation—a merger very different from the one Mill thought desirable.

"Realism" in any of its avatars is a vexing word to define. As Harry Levin observes, artistic realism originates in the rejection of other styles and genres, as in the antiromance of Cervantes and the mock-epic of the Augustans.[7] Realism is thus a kind of parasite without an independent life of its own, apart from the carrion of past forms on which it grows. It is a form of illusion that aims at disillusionment. Whether the realist adopts a scientific stance like Zola's or a more leisurely stance like Thackeray's as puppeteer, his claim of rendering the objective truth about life always has implicit within it a satiric element: he will take what is lofty and grand and show how it rests upon the low. Realism, then, is always reductive: the realist promises to analyze experience into its basic units, to show the animal within man and the chemical machinery within the animal. The latent message in all realistic art is the conversion of people into objects, the metaphoric equivalent of the substitution of exchange value for real value which occurs in modern commercial and industrial relations. Everything can be assigned a monetary value, a weight or a measure, as in Moll Flanders' careful bookkeeping or in Trollope's list of what each of his novels has earned. In the world of fictional realism, every man has his price, no matter how many idealistic "illusions" he may have when he starts out upon life's road. As Pip learns in *Great Expectations,* all of us are bound by chains of silver and gold. And as at least latent satire, the realistic novel can be highly critical of the price-tagged or weighed-and-measured reality it depicts. Thus, realism in France during the 1850s, as exemplified by Courbet and Flaubert, was an affront to the Second Empire and to the bourgeoisie. Although it proposed no new ideals to replace the lost illusions of the pre-1848 world, neither did it temporize with the present. Rather than a realism of the bourgeoisie, it was a realism of *épater le bourgeois.*

In England, on the other hand, the advent of realism in the 1850s (the first use of the term "realism" in English seems to have occurred in 1853) involved both a process of disillusionment and a loss of critical energy.[8] It is Trollope's purpose in *The Warden,* for example, to show that while existing institutions are not all that they should be, attempts to reform them are only likely to make them worse. Institutions of all sorts, whether ancient ones like the Church or modern ones like the press, are perhaps inevitably corrupt, and it is therefore best to let them alone. Trollope and Bagehot both uphold a version of laissez-faire based on an amiable cynicism, which is only slightly less negative than Spencer's hostility to all government "meddling." Experience in Barsetshire teaches us that moral, legal, political, and religious issues are always highly ambiguous affairs, like that of John Hiram's will. Trollope presents us with a microcosmic political drama that negates both the reform idealism of John Bold and the reactionary intransigence of Archdeacon Grantly. Trollope would have us believe that there is a third position, somewhere between the extremes of radicalism and reaction, which we are to associate with Mr. Harding's apolitical integrity and also with Trollope's own moral and stylistic realism. Such a middling position Trollope identifies with a prosaic fidelity to the commonplaces of bourgeois life in fiction and also with the contradictory political labels that he applies to himself in his *Autobiography:* "I consider myself to be an advanced, but still a conservative liberal, which I regard not only as a possible but as a rational and consistent phase of political existence" (251).

Trollope proceeds to show us how his "advanced conservative liberalism" works by taking as his test case the problem of inequality. An extreme liberal, he says, sees inequality as manifestly unjust, and therefore mistakenly tries "to set all things right by a proclaimed equality." But the extreme liberal is "'powerless'" to effect his aim, because "'inequality is the work of God.'" On the other hand, the conservative, seeing the failure of the liberal and also recognizing that "'inequalities are of divine origin, tells himself that it is his duty to preserve them'" (252). Both the liberal and the conservative are wrong, and it remains for the "advanced conservative liberal" to show why, by recognizing both "the divine inequality" and "the equally divine diminution of that inequality": "He is equally aware that these distances [of class and wealth] are of divine origin, equally averse to any sudden disruption of society in quest of some Utopian blessedness;—but he is alive to the fact that these distances are day by day becoming less, and he regards this continual diminution as a series of steps towards that human millennium of which he dreams. He is even willing to help the many to ascend the ladder a little, though he knows, as they come up towards him, he must go down to meet them" (253). Trollope's "advanced conservative liberalism," like so many of the candid clichés that served for political theory in the 1850s and 1860s, is no more than a rationalization for the temporary but nevertheless "divine" right of the middle class to its property and power. Both injustice and its future rectification are the dispensations of a morally easy God, who will not ask us too many questions if we repay the favor. What is remarkable about such pious cant, apart from the fact that someone of Trollope's intelligence takes it seriously, is that it allows for an unblinking acknowledgment of injustice which neither affirms it nor seeks to change it. And it is only a step away from Trollope's assertion of the divine character of inequality to the more severely paradoxical idea of the benevolence of nature in the social Darwinists. As early as *Social Statics* in 1850, for example, Spencer writes: "The poverty of the incapable, the distresses that come upon the imprudent, the starvation of the idle, and those shoulderings aside of the weak by the strong, which leave so many 'in shallows and in miseries,' are the decrees of a large far-seeing benevolence."[9] Thus the poor deserve to be poor and the rich deserve to be rich, and it is all a part of the necessary wisdom of things. As D. G. Ritchie points out, social Darwinism is a "scheme of salvation for the elect by the damnation of the vast majority."[10]

Trollope embodied his "advanced conservative liberalism" in Plantagenet Palliser, Duke of Omnium, the chief character in his political novels, which commenced with *Can You Forgive Her?* in 1864 and extended through *The Duke's Children* in 1880. Palliser is Trollope's ideal statesman and "perfect gentleman."[11] What might be called the Palliser platform is, however, virtually plankless, except for the one timber of his moral style—his dignity, his integrity, and his wish to serve the public. Trollope looked upon being a member of Parliament as the highest calling for an Englishman. But, as the careers of both Palliser and Phineas Finn show, he did not think that this calling required the possession of any definite political ideas. Like Bagehot, he was a believer in political "dullness," the virtuous stupidity of John Bull. Ideas and programs are only apt to interfere with the practical business of running the country. If a politician should "have grand ideas, he must keep them to himself, unless by chance he can work his way to the top of the tree. In short, he must be a practical man."[12] As a result, Trollope's parliamentary novels are quite different from Disraeli's in the 1840s. In *Coningsby* and *Sybil*, Disraeli is interested both in real, "practical" issues and in political theory, although the results may seem more fantastic than solid. Trollope's political fictions, on the other hand, may seem as solid as beef and ale (to paraphrase Hawthorne), but they are hollow in an opposite way. Trollope regards politics as an elaborate game, in which institutional procedures and party maneuvers are more important than theories, legislation, or even public opinion. Though he supported reforms of electioneering practices and the civil service, he did so, as Asa Briggs suggests, not to promote democracy or to end inequality but to help the existing system to function smoothly.

In *Phineas Finn* the central questions of parliamentary reform, the ballot, and Irish tenant rights are not answered by Trollope. Mildmay's parliamentary reform bill—the Reform Bill of 1867 in fictional guise—is passed, but it is hardly clear why. Mr. Monk is the only politician who has any clear theories about it, who supports it (as he later supports the rights of Irish tenants), and whom Trollope respects. The other strongly committed proponents of reform are demagogues like Mr. Turnbull (John Bright), or extraparliamentary agitators like Quintus Slide, the sleazy editor of *The People's Banner*. Except for Monk, Phineas Finn's liberal colleagues are trying to pass Mildmay's reform bill because it seems the thing to do: "There was no strong throb through the country, making men feel that safety was to be had by Reform, and could not be had without Reform. But there was an understanding that the press and the orators were too strong to be ignored, and that some new measure of Reform must be granted to them" (1.332). Moreover, says Trollope, many of the public supporters of a new reform bill are privately opposed to it. "That Reform was in itself odious to many of those who spoke of it freely, who

210

offered themselves willingly to be its promoters, was acknowledged"
(1.332-333). The condition of the country is such that no reform seems
necessary, but "Mr. Turnbull, and the cheap press, and the rising spirit
of the loudest among the people, made it manifest that something must
be conceded." "Workmen were getting full wages. Farmers were paying
their rent. Capitalists by the dozen were creating capitalists by the hundreds. Nothing was wrong in the country, but the over-dominant spirit of
speculative commerce" (1.333). Why then, Trollope wonders, should
anyone want reform? And although he has Mr. Monk state his theory of
true representation as a possible reason (1.334-337), it is not clear that
Trollope agrees with Monk. Trollope may just as well agree with Mr. and
Mrs. Low. According to Mr. Low:

> "My idea of government is this,—that we want to be governed by
> law and not by caprice, and that we must have a legislature to make
> our laws. If I thought that Parliament as at present established made
> the laws badly, I would desire a change; but I doubt whether we
> shall have them better from any change in Parliament which Reform
> will give us."
> "Of course not," said Mrs. Low. "But we shall have a lot of beg-
> gars put on horseback, and we all know where they ride to." (1.338)

Trollope appears to believe that much parliamentary activity, while fascinating to study, is both unnecessary and a trifle silly. Politicians by nature want to do something, although more often than not what they
should really do is nothing. It is not clear that Mildmay's reform bill is
different in kind from some other examples of needless activity, like
Phineas Finn's "potted peas" committee, or Plantagenet Palliser's coinage reform scheme. If it is not dangerous like John Bold's radicalism or
like Mr. Turnbull's program (1.163), Palliser's plan to transform the
coinage to the metric system is viewed by Trollope as a comic crotchet, the
Chancellor of the Exchequer's reform hobbyhorse. In *The Eustace Diamonds,* amid the squabbling of conservative "Lizzieites" and liberal
"anti-Lizzieites," we learn that Palliser "was intending to alter the value
of the penny . . . the future penny was to be made, under his auspices, to
contain five farthings, and the shilling ten pennies. It was thought that if
this could be accomplished, the arithmetic of the whole world would be
so simplified that henceforward the name of Palliser would be blessed by
all school-boys, clerks, shopkeepers, and financiers. But the difficulties
were so great that Mr. Palliser's hair was already grey from toil" (2.68).
Palliser's scheme for the decimalization of the coinage is a minor and

comic piece of fanaticism, which does not interfere with his performance of the daily business of party and state. Besides, as an aspect of his noble character, some quantum of political idealism is necessary to distinguish him from the party hacks, although Trollope treats it as quixotic.

On one of the rare occasions in the political novels where Palliser explains his creed in any detail, in chapter 68 of *The Prime Minister,* his ideas are both noble and tinged with the irrational "enthusiasm" that Trollope attributes to all abstract thought. But they are only the ideas of the "advanced conservative liberal." Trollope has Palliser give almost verbatim his own argument about the divine nature of inequality and the equally divine nature of its diminution. Phineas Finn, for almost the first time in his long career, hears his chief expound a political idea, and he is duly astonished. "Phineas knew that there were stories told of certain bursts of words which had come from him in former days in the House of Commons. These had occasionally surprised men and induced them to declare that Planty Pall . . . was a dark horse" (2.266). There are a number of ironies in the situation, not least of which is Trollope's identification of his own utterly safe "advanced conservative liberalism" with quixotic idealism. Palliser goes beyond Trollope, at least rhetorically, in affirming equality as a distant ideal, but the further he goes, the more we understand that, as Palliser himself declares, we are traveling in "cloudland." "Equality would be a heaven, if we could attain it," he tells Phineas, but of course we cannot attain it. And he warns Phineas not to tell anyone "that I have been preaching equality, or we shall have a pretty mess . . . Equality is a dream. But sometimes one likes to dream,—especially as there is no danger that Matching will fly from me in a dream" (2.267). Property—Palliser's Matching estate—may be a wrong in an ideal sense, but it is also a fact and has therefore a better and more solid truth about it than any mere "dream of justice." Furthermore, it is ironic that Palliser's declaration of his political creed comes so late in the series of political novels and so late in his career, suggesting either that theory, to make any sense, must be the outgrowth of practice, or else that theory does not have any bearing at all upon practice.

Palliser is led to declare his "political creed" to Phineas by ruminating at the start of the chapter on the fact that men are ordinarily liberals or conservatives by tradition and may go through long lives of political work without ever asking what their allegiances mean. Presumably this has happened to both Palliser and Phineas Finn. As Palliser says: "It seems to me that many men . . . embrace the profession of politics not only without political convictions, but without seeing that it is proper that they should entertain them. Chance brings a young man under the guidance of this or that elder man. He has come of a Whig family as was my case,—or from some old Tory stock; and loyalty keeps him true to the interests which have first pushed him forward into the world. There is no conviction there'' (2.261). And when Phineas replies, ''Convictions grow,'' the Prime Minister adds: ''Yes;—the conviction that it is the man's duty to be a staunch Liberal, but not the reason why.'' Political convictions, then, must either emerge out of long experience and tradition, like Palliser's, or else they are dangerous counters in the game of politics, to be strictly avoided. There is nothing more threatening or foreign to Trollope than theories: when they intrude into his realism at all, as in John Bold's reform idealism in *The Warden,* it is only as tempting serpents, the bearers of forbidden and unnecessary knowledge.

Not only does politics go on in the Palliser novels as a largely practical business, with people rarely asking questions about why things are as they are, but religion goes on in much the same way in the Barsetshire novels. *The Warden* is just as much a ''church novel'' as *Charles Lever* and *Helen Fleetwood,* except that it is about the ''sacred wealth'' of the Church rather than about its doctrines. The realist's art of reduction comes so easily to Trollope that we are hardly aware of what is missing from his novels while we are reading them. But in fact he gives us religious novels that contain no religious ideas and political novels that contain very few political ideas. What takes their place is what always takes the place of the ideal and the theoretical in realism: the unanalyzed flow of sensation and event, daily business, material surroundings, and financial interests—life on the installment plan.

Trollope's reductive art, moreover, is not clearly satiric. At the same time that he can criticize Archdeacon Grantly for lacking religion, he himself lacks it, and assumes that we do, too. Grantly is Trollope's main specimen of worldliness in *The Warden:* ''He did not believe in the Gospel with more assurance than he did in the sacred justice of all ecclesiastical revenues'' (55). There is occasion for much irony in Grantly's donning ''his good armour'' in defense of ''the comforts of his creed.'' But if Grantly is worldly, so is Trollope. It is not clear whether worldliness is a charge to be leveled against clergymen like Grantly who ought to be above worldly concerns, or a definition of sanity and honesty. The person who comes nearest to being a model clergyman in *The Warden* is the warden himself, but it is not because he is motivated by faith: Mr. Harding is happy with his eight hundred pounds a year and his music—comfortable with ''the comforts of his creed''—until John Bold disrupts his idyllic life. The unconscious materialism of the archdeacon and Trollope's other clergymen serves as a justification for the unconscious materialism of

Trollope himself. Even Trollope's keenest satire, the attack on "commercial profligacy" in *The Way We Live Now* (which Trollope later felt to be extreme), does not resolve the dilemma of the realist who tries to criticize the worldliness of his characters from the vantage point of his own worldliness. Trollope is not clearly attacking the "profligacy" and "shams" of an entire society in the person of Melmotte but perhaps only "the over-dominant spirit of speculative commerce" in the form of stock market fraud. If Melmotte is to be judged wicked merely because of his self-interested materialism, the way Ralph Nickleby, Scrooge, and Dombey are in Dickens, then Trollope stands open to the same charge. In fact, it was precisely because his *Autobiography* reads like a bank book in which literature is treated as a commercial enterprise that Trollope's own stock fell in the market after it appeared. In the case of the *Autobiography,* at least, the "mirror in the roadway" reflected too faithfully and honestly attitudes that its first readers did not want to see in their popular authors.

Thackeray shares Trollope's dislike of thesis novels and also his dislike of Dickens's fictional politics. As a member of the *Punch* staff in the early 1840s, Thackeray was not so radically insistent on using humor to advocate social reforms as were Jerrold and Mark Lemon. Much of his early fiction, moreover, like *Catherine, Novels by Eminent Hands,* and *The Book of Snobs,* involves satirizing political tendencies in current literature. Reviewing *Sybil* in *The Morning Chronicle,* Thackeray declares that "morals and manners we believe to be the novelist's best themes; and hence prefer romances which do not treat of algebra, religion, or other abstract science." And elsewhere, in a review of Charles Lever's *St. Patrick's Eve,* Thackeray says: "We like to hear sermons from his reverence at church; to get our notions of trade, crime, politics, and other national statistics, from the proper papers and figures; but when suddenly, out of the gilt pages of a pretty picture book, a comic moralist rushes forward, and takes occasion to tell us that society is diseased, the laws unjust, the rich ruthless, the poor martyrs, the world lop-sided, and *vice-versâ*, persons who wish to lead an easy life are inclined to remonstrate against this literary ambuscadoe."[13] In his criticism of the "comic moralist" who tries to reform the world through fiction, Thackeray may have had Dickens in mind as well as Charles Lever, for though he admired Dickens, he clearly shared Bagehot's opinion of the wrong-headedness of Dickens's advocacy of reform in fiction.[14] Further, Thackeray wrote to David Masson, "I quarrel with his Art in many respects: [which] I don't think represents Nature duly."[15]

So we return to the charge that Dickens exaggerates, that he portrays experience in terms of a set of false extremes—victims versus villains, rich versus poor, good versus evil. This was the most serious and most frequent charge made against Dickens during his career, and he deployed a variety of not always consistent arguments to counter it. It is clear, moreover, that even in Thackeray the charge of exaggeration is related to Bagehot's criticism that Dickens's radicalism has outlived its time in the 1850s. Dickens's refutations, therefore, have a political significance beyond their more obvious esthetic significance.

In the *Edinburgh Review* for 1857, Fitzjames Stephen, like Bagehot, complained about Dickens's "injustice to the institutions of English society," with special reference to the Circumlocution Office. Dickens retorted with his own article in *Household Words,* defending both the truthfulness of his fiction and the writing of political fiction in general. The dispute between Stephen and Dickens suggests the political character of the charge of exaggeration. In Stephen, Bagehot, and Trollope, the advice to Dickens "to be realistic" means either to acknowledge the righteousness of the Constitution and the status quo, or else to stop meddling with politics in fiction. As Dickens puts it:

> The *Edinburgh Review* . . . is angry with Mr. Dickens and other modern novelists, for not confining themselves to the mere amusement of their readers, and for testifying in their works that they seriously feel the interest of true Englishmen in the welfare and honour of their country. To them should be left the making of easy occasional books for idle young gentlemen and ladies to take up and lay down on sofas, drawing-room tables and window-seats; to the *Edinburgh Review* should be reserved the settlement of all social and political questions, and the strangulation of all complainers.[16]

By "other modern novelists," Dickens means especially Charles Reade, whom Stephen also criticizes and whom Bagehot may be thinking of when he writes about imitators whom Dickens has led astray. Reade may be viewed along with Dickens, Mill, and Ruskin as a writer pursuing social reform themes in a time of "advanced conservative liberal" retrenchment. His muckraking novels attacking conditions in prisons and insane asylums met with much the same negative reception as *Unto This Last* and as the reform themes in Dickens's fiction from *Bleak House* onwards.[17]

Dickens's increasing insistence through the 1850s on "the romance of familiar things" and on the importance of fancy arises partly from the desire to keep the imagination of real injustice and ideal justice alive despite the encroachments of a false "realism," whether in the form of a theory of art or in the form of "advanced liberal conservatism." Against his critics, Dickens sometimes holds that supposedly "exaggerated" elements in his novels are "true": they are either portraits based on nature, or based on his own experience, or else based on researched facts. So in reference to Nancy, Dickens writes: "It is useless to discuss whether the conduct and character of the girl seems natural or unnatural, probable or improbable, right or wrong. IT IS TRUE."[18] Similarly, when G. H. Lewes criticized Krook's death by spontaneous combustion, Dickens responded in the 1853 preface to *Bleak House* that the description was based on his own investigation, and that "there are about thirty cases on record," of which he gives two in some detail. And on still other occasions, Dickens contends that exaggeration is only in the eye of the beholder, and that "all the Pecksniff family upon earth are quite agreed, I believe, that Mr. Pecksniff is an exaggeration."[19]

Dickens appears in such passages in the guise of a simple literalist, advancing a kind of argument that he elsewhere repudiates. For against the charge of exaggeration, Dickens also erects a defense of caricature, or more generally of the "fanciful" in literature:

> It does not seem to me to be enough to say of any description that it is the exact truth. The exact truth should be there; but the merit or art in the narrator, is the manner of stating the truth . . . And in these times, when the tendency is to be frightfully literal and catalogue-like—to make the thing, in short, a sort of sum in reduction that any miserable creature can do in that way—I have an idea (really founded on the love of what I profess), that the very holding of popular literature through a kind of popular dark age, may depend on such fanciful treatment.[20]

Although it is not clear what Dickens means by "a kind of popular dark age," his statement is almost a miniature version of *Hard Times*. When Dickens attacks the Gradgrindian emphasis upon "Facts," he is also attacking the idea of realism in art. Flowers must not be reproduced on carpets, says Gradgrind's colleague, nor horses on walls. Perhaps Dickens has in mind the vulgar literalism of much mid-Victorian design, but he is also lashing out against a whole worldview that he associates with utilitarianism and the factory system. Symbolically, nearly everyone in *Hard Times* is being "hardened," turned out on the lathes of Coketown schools, churches, and factories or else reduced to a sum in arithmetic like "Girl Number 20." And insofar as Dickens is attacking the Coketown tendency to reduce people to objects, *Hard Times* involves an implicit repudiation of artistic realism, corresponding to its more overt repudiation of political realism in the guise of utilitarianism. As his critics accused him of doing, Dickens in *Hard Times* dichotomizes experience, although his central antithesis is less one of victims and villains than one of fact and fancy, or of real and unreal. *Hard Times* thus can be read as Dickens's attempt to defend an idealized or romanticized vision of human possibility, symbolized especially by Sleary's horse-riding, against the pressures of a realism that would identify the good and the true with the given.

Hard Times is largely an attack on ideological justifications for the factory system, whether in the form of a false scientism or of false rules of political economy or of Bounderby's phony philosophy of self-help. But against "the fictions of Coketown" masquerading as facts, Dickens has no facts of his own to offer except for the very human and specific ones embodied in the experiences of Sissy, Stephen and Rachel, and Louisa and Tom. The main alternative to "the fictions of Coketown," in other words, is in some sense more fictions, rather than superior facts or a truer form of political economy. Apart from the experience of individuals, what Dickens opposes to Gradgrindism is merely "Fancy," and whether he uses the term plaintively or ironically (to suggest how Gradgrindism treats everything important as unreal), it is not an adequate counter to "Facts." To put it another way, *Hard Times* suggests that, in response to the charge that Dickens exaggerates or is being fanciful, Dickens agrees, although he also insists that it is wise and necessary for him to do so. The idea of fancy does not turn into a full-blown epistemological defense of the romantic imagination against the encroachments of science and industrial materialism. It has instead the quality of a sentimental wish on Dickens's part to discover some intellectually valid counter to political economy and its ossification into the "advanced conservative liberalism" of the 1850s. "The Sleary philosophy"—"people mutht be amuthed"—verges on being no philosophy at all, but only a pathetic assertion of the need of the working and middle classes for more fun and less work. The difficulty of Dickens's position can be seen in the first two paragraphs of the chapter in which he introduces Stephen Blackpool. In the first, he says that the common people of England are overworked and that he "would give them a little more play." If this is all his indictment of industrialism in *Hard Times* leads to, it clearly does not lead to much. But in the second paragraph, which consists of a single sentence, Dickens leads us through the urban maze of "narrow courts upon courts, and close streets upon streets, which had come into existence piecemeal, every piece in a violent hurry for some one man's purpose," until we get to "a certain Stephen Blackpool, forty years of age" (63). There is obvious irony in juxtaposing such a complex urban landscape, in which the chaotic shape of the single, enormous sentence mimics the chaotic state of society, with such a simple remedy ("more play"). Dickens senses the inadequacy of all remedies and theories, including his own, to cope with the situation.

Dickens's difficulties in responding to the critics who taxed him with exaggeration may be summed up in the phrase, "romantic realist," which suggests that he is a romantic who distrusts his own romanticism, or else a realist who is constantly on the look-out for some higher form of artistic truth.[21] "Romantic realism" is descriptive of the work of a number of mid-Victorians who struggled to defend some form of romantic idealism (Dickens's "Fancy") against the growing claims of both artistic and political realism (Coketown's "Facts"). Something akin to romantic realism is evident in Christian Socialism, for instance, with its high idealism undermined by the typical Mauricean strategy of the identification of the given with the ideal. The socialism of Maurice and Kingsley turns out to be almost as fragile a counterweight to mid-Victorian capitalism as fancy does to the grim realities of Coketown.

Similarly, Ruskin's esthetic theories may be viewed partly as attempts to combine elements of romanticism with elements of realism, leading to such paradoxes as the notion of the "naturalist ideal" in the third volume of *Modern Painters*. There, Ruskin starts with a puzzle that is central to all versions of realism (romanticism tends rather to posit the existence of an ideal dimension without compromising it): "We now enter on the consideration of that central and highest branch of ideal art which concerns itself simply with things as they ARE, and accepts, in all of them, alike the evil and the good. The question is, therefore, how the art which represents things simply as they are, can be called ideal at all."[22] Ruskin's answer, in volume III of *Modern Painters* and throughout his writings, is very much like Fra Lippo Lippi's defense of painting the good things of this world in Browning's poem. The aim of the artist is always to portray the spiritual, inward, or ideal life of "things as they are," but the best method of doing this seems to be to portray "things as they are." The logic of the naturalist ideal is circular, governed by the tendency to identify the ideal with the real. When Ruskin says that "the whole power, whether of painter or poet, to describe rightly what we call an ideal thing, depends upon its being thus, to him, not an ideal, but a *real* thing," he is not reinventing Platonism, or even the Coleridgean imagination. His notion of the ideal is not far from Dickens's notion of fancy in *Hard*

Times: it is a sort of subcategory of the real and has about it the melancholy quality of an insecure faith.

Dickens feels his radical idealism threatened by laws of political economy and by the facts of Coketown. But the ideal in *Hard Times* is scaled down to the level of mere "fun" and "fairy-tales," the very act of realistic reduction that Dickens is struggling against. This is the dilemma of the romantic realist, striving to erect an alternative, critical, or utopian perspective that is forever collapsing back into the real. It is revealing in this regard that Ruskin entertained such opposite opinions of Dickens. In *Unto This Last,* while wishing that Dickens would "limit his brilliant exaggeration" because it weakens his social analysis, Ruskin says that "the things he tells us are always true," and praises *Hard Times* especially. Ruskin here, as later in *Fors Clavigera,* finds in Dickens a natural ally in his own warfare against Mammonism and political economy. But elsewhere he criticizes Dickens as "a pure modernist—a leader of the steam-whistle party *par excellence*—[because] he had no understanding of any power of antiquity except a sort of jackdaw sentiment for cathedral towers."[23]

It is ironic, in light of Ruskin's criticism of Dickens, that the *Quarterly Review* once attacked Dickens as a Pre-Raphaelite.[24] If he was one, of course, nobody knew it except the *Quarterly.* On the contrary, Dickens himself lashed out against what he felt to be the pretentious and silly worship of the past in the Pre-Raphaelites, as he always lashed out against those whom he suspected of idolizing "the good old days." In "Old Lamps for New Ones" in *Household Words* (June 15, 1850), Dickens condemns the new version of what he calls "the Young England hallucination," or the Pre-Raphaelite rejection of things modern. As often in *Household Words,* Dickens comes on strongly as a member of "the steam-whistle party," just as Ruskin accuses him of doing. Dickens states his opposition to "the retrogressive principle" sarcastically: "There is something so fascinating . . . in the notion of ignoring all that has been done for the happiness and elevation of mankind during three or four centuries of slow and dearly-bought amelioration, that we have always thought it would tend soundly to the improvement of the general public, if any tangible symbol . . . expressive of that admirable conception, could be held up before them. We are happy to have found such a sign at last" (265). Such a sign Dickens finds in Pre-Raphaelitism. But Dickens does not restrict his attack on the Pre-Raphaelite Brotherhood to the one charge of fetishizing the past. He singles out J. E. Millais's painting "Christ in the House of His Parents" for special criticism, not for falsely worshipping the past but for employing a deadening, vulgar realism in the depiction of a sacred subject. It is wonderful to behold with what unfair exaggeration Dickens aims his barbs at Millais's supposedly profane literalism: "Wherever it is possible to express ugliness of feature, limb, or attitude, you have it expressed. Such men as the carpenters might be undressed in any hospital where dirty drunkards, in a high state of varicose veins, are received. Their very toes have walked out of Saint Giles's" (266). Obviously, Dickens fails to perceive the common ground that he shares with the Pre-Raphaelites. From one perspective, they are mirror opposites of each other, for the Pre-Raphaelites offer romantic themes treated realistically (the shavings on the carpenter's floor in Millais's work, Dickens generously acknowledged, were well-painted), while Dickens offers everyday themes treated romantically, or at least heightened by "Fancy" (some of the essays in *Household Words* and *All the Year Round* bear such titles as "The Poetry of Railways" and "The Poetry of Facts").

Both Dickens and Ruskin were concerned in their social criticism to refute the hide-bound "laws" of political economy and to reverse the dehumanizing patterns of modern commerce, industrialism, and urban conditions. For both, "wealth is life" and money is death, at least in large metaphoric and ethical terms. That they were not able to treat their awareness of social injustice systematically may be viewed as a weakness, but it is also another shared trait. Their mutual distrust of social theories makes them at times sound as anti-intellectual and as deliberately "dull" as Trollope and Bagehot, but their distrust springs largely from their awareness of how easily theories turn out to be conservative ideologies. And both Ruskin and Dickens tend to express the idea of wealth as life in terms of an impetuous generosity, a "Christmas philosophy" which, while not taking them beyond the confines of capitalist assumptions about property and social class, prompts them to act like sincere but intellectually primitive Father Noëls. Both of them struggle to convert the emphasis on thrift in political economy into an emphasis on spending, giving, and loving. One might compare symbols of benevolence like Brownlow, the Cheerybles, Fezziwegg, and Boffin with such an extravagant fantasy of generosity as that which Ruskin gives us in *Praeterita:*

> For again and again I must repeat it, my nature is a worker's and a miser's; and I rejoiced, and rejoice still, in the mere quantity of chiselling in marble, and stitches in embroidery; and was never tired of numbering sacks of gold and caskets of jewels in the *Arabian Nights:* and though I am generous too, and love giving, yet my notion of

charity is not at all dividing my last crust with a beggar, but riding through a town like a Commander of the Faithful, having any quantity of sequins and ducats in saddlebags (where cavalry officers have holsters for their pistols), and throwing them round in radiant showers and hailing handfuls; with more bags to brace on when those were empty. (*Works,* XXXV, 538)

The paradox of the generous miser is at the heart of Dickens's social imagination, as Boffin shows; and it is at the heart also of Ruskin's conception of himself as a social reformer. Not only did Ruskin squander much of his inherited wealth in ways both foolish and noble, but he played the role of generous miser in his writings as well. As art critic and social prophet, one to whom much has been revealed, he lavishes his insights and his gorgeous prose on the less fortunate in ways that are both patronizing and generous. Further, despite his insistence that wealth is life, Ruskin never escapes from the antithetical idea of wealth as treasure. Art itself is treasure, as in the passage above or in his explanation in *Modern Painters,* volume IV, of how imagination works in great artists like Dante, Tintoretto, and Turner:

Imagine all that any of these men had seen or heard in the whole course of their lives, laid up accurately in their memories as in vast storehouses, extending, with the poets, even to the slightest intonations of syllables heard in the beginning of their lives, and with the painters, down to minute folds of drapery, and shapes of leaves or stones; and over all this unindexed and immeasurable mass of treasure, the imagination brooding and wandering, but dream-gifted, so as to summon at any moment exactly such groups of ideas as shall justly fit each other: this I conceive to be the real nature of the imaginative mind. (*Works,* VI, 42)

The confusion of reality and ideality evident in the naturalist ideal extends to Ruskin's metaphors. The imagination appears here virtually as an act of capital accumulation, although that is obviously not what Ruskin intends. His predicament—one that characterizes his whole career—is quite simply how to move from the static and death-dealing conception of art as a miser's hoard to the dynamic conception of wealth as life. It is not a matter of giving with one hand and taking away with the other, for Ruskin's impulse is entirely generous. But he can see no way of giving except in the form of gift—of money, time, beauty, and knowledge lavished by those that have them on those that do not. The predicament shows up in all of Ruskin's dealings with art and society. He was an avid collector of beautiful objects, a hoarder of treasure; but he insisted that treasure had to be shared or given away to become truly valuable, and he opened his home and his pocket book to his students at the Working Men's College and to anyone else who struck him as worthy and needy.

Treasure is the result of hoarding, of miserdom; but treasure becomes worth having only when it is dispersed. This is a paradox that Dickens also expresses in his ideal of middle-class benevolence. At the same time, it is a paradox that suggests the limits of romantic realism, or the weakness of the concept of fancy in Dickens and the contradictory quality of the naturalist ideal in Ruskin. Despite the large generosity of their social imaginations, neither of them was able to see beyond these limits. To do so would have involved them in the rejection of realism altogether, at least as it was practiced by Trollope, Thackeray, and George Eliot. This is exactly what happens later in William Morris, who, in following Ruskin's idea of wealth as life to its logical conclusion, rejects more and more emphatically the contrary idea of art as treasure. In *News from Nowhere,* Morris has his utopian character Ellen attack Victorian novels:

> "I say flatly that in spite of all their cleverness and vigour, and capacity for story-telling, there is something loathsome about them. Some of them, indeed, do here and there show some feeling for those whom the history-books call 'poor', and of the misery of whose lives we have some inkling; but presently they give it up, and towards the end of the story we must be contented to see the hero and heroine living happily in an island of bliss on other people's troubles; and that after a long series of sham troubles (or mostly sham) of their own making, illustrated by dreary introspective nonsense about their feelings and aspirations, and all the rest of it; while the world must even then have gone on its way, and dug and sewed and baked and built and carpentered round about these useless—animals."[25]

Against the failure of all art under capitalism, including mid-Victorian realism in the novel and even his own Pre-Raphaelite poetry, Morris erects the ideal of art and true wealth as identical with the labor and experience of common men and women. It is this ideal which he calls "popular art."

In the middling positions of social class and of social compromise preferred by Trollope and Thackeray, everyone comes to be judged very much like everyone else. The attitude that we are all citizens of Vanity Fair allows for a largeness of sympathy, but less for clear moral distinctions than for the acceptance of things as they are: "It is all vanity to be sure: but who will not own to liking a little of it? I should like to know what well-constituted mind, merely because it is transitory, dislikes roast-beef? That is a vanity; but may every man who reads this, have a whole-some portion of it through life.''[26] Along with heroes and heroines, Dick-ensian victims and villains vanish from the realism of Trollope and Thack-eray, and we are left with "mixed characters" and averages. George Eliot's portrayal of Amos Barton suggests this process: "His very faults were middling,—he was not *very* ungrammatical. It was not in his nature to be superlative in anything; unless, indeed, he was superlatively mid-dling, the quintessential extract of mediocrity.''[27] The word "mediocrity" captures a central problem of artistic realism. Is "middlingness" a state to be condemned or at least struggled against in the name of some high-er, ideal, albeit extreme state, or is it paradoxically a state of virtuous wis-dom through compromise, "standing midway in the gulf" between false extremes, as Macaulay, James Mill, and Dinah Mulock claim that the middle class itself stands between aristocracy and democracy? To quote George Eliot again, who takes the problem of mediocrity as one of her special themes:

1st Citizen.	Sir, there's a hurry in the veins of youth, That makes a vice of virtue by excess.
2nd Citizen.	What if the coolness of our tardier veins Be loss of virtue?
1st Citizen.	All things cool with time,— The sun itself, they say, till heat shall find A general level, nowhere in excess.
2nd Citizen.	'Tis a poor climax, to my weaker thought, That future middlingness.

(*Felix Holt*, ch. 5)

If what the future holds in store for us is a condition of middlingness, then is history following a path of progress or of entropy? George Eliot asks this question throughout her fiction; she perhaps wisely does not answer it.

Many Victorian speculations about art and politics, including most realisms, involve an epistemology of middlingness or compromise, as in John Stuart Mill's analyses of the way men arrive at the truth: "Truth, in the great practical concerns of life, is so much a question of the reconcil-ing and combining of opposites, that very few have minds sufficiently capacious and impartial to make the adjustment with an approach to cor-rectness, and it has to be made by the rough process of a struggle between combatants fighting under hostile banners.''[28] Mill gives us a nobler and subtler version of Trollope's suspicion of the two-sidedness of every question. Mill's career, in fact, may be interpreted as the struggle of a single capacious and impartial mind working towards truth through a series of progressive compromises, or finding the half-truths in Bentham and Coleridge and combining them into whole ones. But the conception of truth as compromise (or as the progressive reconciliation of ideas through a free, democratic competition among them) involves a contradiction that Mill struggled with in *On Liberty* and elsewhere without resolving. For if truth is merely an adjustment or moderation of opposites (barring some definite mechanism of progress like the Hegelian dialectic), there is no clear way of climbing towards a higher or fuller understanding. Mill's democracy of ideas is problematic for him in much the same way that actual democracy is. The majority opinion must be temporarily right, but the minority is the vehicle for the new, the original, and hence is the source of the progressive discovery of truth. Thus arises the specter of the tyranny of the majority, doomed to be forever mistaken at the same time that it is right.

Mill understands that truth cannot arise merely out of compromise, although he is not able to explain its progressive discovery on some other basis. His difficulty is an aspect of a larger problem inherent in the belief in progress. Can the given state of the world be somehow ideal (or truth-bearing) merely because it is progressive and is always pointing to something better? If there is some greater truth or greater good in the future, however, then the present cannot be ideal. This is the modern liberal version of Zeno's paradox. The world comes to look very much like *The Ring and the Book:* everyone may be in possession of part of the truth, but there is also a whole truth that nobody possesses—except the poet and the reader, who look on from an omniscient perspective. And the same contradictoriness—a clash between relativist and absolutist assumptions about the truth—is inherent in the Victorian novel. In *Middlemarch,* for example, George Eliot shows us the blindnesses and egoistic limitations of each of her characters, lost in the great labyrinth or web of the social organism, but she shows us these things from an omniscient viewpoint, as if knowing the whole truth herself.

A writer in *The Economist* for 1851, lacking Mill's awareness of the difficulties inherent in any theory of the progressive revelation of the good and the true, blandly said, "We see no reason to be discontented either with our rate of progress or the actual state which we have reached."[29] So we live in the best of all possible worlds, because we are headed towards a future when we will live in the best of all possible worlds. Such language might serve as an epitaph for the idea of reform, for behind it lies the assumption that the machinery of social advance is automatic, in need of no tending or outside intervention by reformers. It is simply part of an ideal state of things that is forever getting better. Mill himself subscribed to no such rosy illogicality, but on the other hand he did not know how to reconcile his idea of truth as derived from middling compromise or majority opinion with his other idea of truth as derived from individual excellence and minority dissent. His epistemological dilemma, moreover, is related to the dilemma of the esthetic realist, for whom reality is truth, and yet for whom reality is also inadequate (mediocre in Trollope and despicable in Flaubert) and is therefore less than the truth. But since the realist dismisses everything else as mere illusion, there is no place outside of reality for its felt deficiencies to be made good. The photograph has to signify or to be truth-bearing all on its own, in its state of one-dimensionality, but the suspicion lingers that truth must reside in some extra dimension, above or below the mere surface of things. And the realist has no way of dispelling this suspicion. Flaubert is savagely critical of the world he depicts, but he has no logical basis for his criticism. His very fidelity to the real involves an ironic epistemological affirmation of it, at the same time that it acts also as a form of narrow, provincial entrapment, cutting the artist himself off from the greater world of ideals and illusions after which both he and his antiheroine are forever hankering. As Flaubert wrote to Louise Colet: "There are in me, literally speaking, two distinct persons: one who is infatuated with bombast, lyricism, eagle flights, sonorities of phrase and the high points of ideas; and another who digs and burrows into the truth as deeply as he can, who likes to treat a humble fact as respectfully as a big one, who would like to make you feel almost *physically* the things he reproduces; this latter person likes to laugh, and enjoys the animal sides of man."[30] Flaubert's realism involves the negation of the first of these "two distinct persons," or the suicide of the romantic idealist within himself.

In the realism of Trollope and Thackeray, on the other hand, there is no clear sense of the beauty and tragedy of romantic illusion and little suspicion that the "realities" they depict are incomplete or inadequate or that they need somehow to be validated by alternative dimensions. If roast beef and ale are good enough for the average Englishman, then they are good enough for everybody. "A sense of satisfaction permeates the country," wrote Bagehot in 1866, "because most of the country feels it has got the precise thing that suits it."[31]

Despite their overtly antidemocratic attitudes, given the choice between majority mediocrity and minority excellence, Trollope and Thackeray opt instinctively for the former. And perhaps the clearest shape that this problem takes in their novels is in their treatment of reformers and reform idealism. The failure of John Bold's radicalism and the difficulties that Palliser has in improving the penny have their counterparts in the worldly liberals and failed reformers whom Thackeray portrays. Arthur Pendennis's disillusionment with politics, for example, is typical of Thackeray's realism. During his political phase, Pendennis tells his friend Warrington that all political ambitions are bound to be thwarted:

> "I see men who begin with ideas of universal reform, and who, before their beards are grown, propound their loud plans for the regeneration of mankind, give up their schemes after a few years of bootless talking and vainglorious attempts to lead their fellows . . . The fiercest reformers grow calm, and are fain to put up with things as they are . . . the most fervent Liberals, when out of power, become humdrum Conservatives, or downright tyrants, or despots in office. Look at Thiers, look at Guizot, in opposition and in place! Look at the Whigs appealing to the country, and the Whigs in power! Would you say that the conduct of these men is an act of treason, as the Radicals bawl,—who would give way in their turn, were their turn ever to come? No, only that they submit to circumstances which are stronger than they,—march as the world marches towards reform, but at the world's pace (and the movements of the vast body of mankind must needs be slow) . . . and [are] compelled finally to submit, and to wait, and to compromise."[32]

Pendennis gives us what can almost be read as a history of the waning of political idealism between 1832 and the 1850s—a history of which his own story is a central instance. Viewed in this drab light, politics may be necessary, but it is hardly a constructive activity. Radicalism is forever being transformed into conservatism, because radicals are forever being forced to "submit to circumstances." True, "the world marches towards reform," but not because of reformers. The world is merely following an inevitable law of progress. And in *Pendennis* itself we find a fidelity to "paltry circumstance," a patient reproduction of long tracts of time and of intricate social relationships snarled in unforeseen complications, which are implicit denials of demands for social amelioration through rational political action.

The literature of the mid-Victorian decades is populated by failed reformers and broken or comic idealists, ranging from the socialist silliness of Romney Leigh to the dreamy nobility of King Arthur. If the *Idylls of the King* is the most beautiful expression of the social disillusionment of the 1850s and 1860s, George Eliot's novels are the most profound investigation of the processes underlying that disillusionment. In much of *Mid-*

dlemarch, Eliot sounds like Arthur Pendennis on politics, only with great reserves of sympathy and analytical subtlety which Thackeray lacks:

> For in the multitude of middle-aged men who go about their vocations in a daily course determined for them much in the same way as the tie of their cravats, there is always a good number who once meant to shape their own deeds and alter the world a little. The story of their coming to be shapen after the average and fit to be packed by the gross, is hardly ever told even in their consciousness; for perhaps their ardour in generous unpaid toil cooled as imperceptibly as the ardour of other youthful loves, till one day their earlier self walked like a ghost in its old home and made the new furniture ghastly. Nothing in the world more subtle than the process of their gradual change![33]

Middlemarch is a novel full of metaphoric ghosts, or of the hauntings caused by lost illusions. "The dead hand" of the past everywhere lays its icy fingers upon the living. As a Comtean positivist or something close to one, Eliot was a believer in progressive evolution and in gradual, inevitable social amelioration. But she was capable of entertaining quite a different view of history, close to Arnold's sense of the great sadness involved in mankind's progressing beyond such comforting illusions as God and immortality. There is a feeling of entropy or decadence in the course of history which *Middlemarch* portrays, as much as an optimistic feeling of advance. Besides the two wills of Casaubon and Featherstone, the dead hand of the past takes such diverse forms as Casaubon's mythological "Key of all Mythologies," Raffles's appearance in Middlemarch, and Rome, ironic honeymoon site for Dorothea and Casaubon. From Dorothea's perspective, Rome is a city of "stupendous fragmentariness" and of the ghostly, "oppressive masquerade of ages." "Ruins and basilicas, palaces and colossi, set in the midst of a sordid present . . . the lost vistas of white forms whose marble eyes seemed to hold the monotonous light of an alien world: all this vast wreck of ambitious ideals, sensuous and spiritual, mixed confusedly with the signs of breathing forgetfulness and degradation, at first jarred her as with an electric shock" (143-144). As haunted city of the past, Rome is a symbol for the disillusioning process of history itself, as well as a symbol for the lost illusions about marriage of two of Eliot's central characters. As Tennyson understands, evolution involves its opposite, progress entails the destruction of the past, and to advance into the future seems always to lead toward a shadowy Avilion and an act of mourning. And while past forms (for example, the "unfit" in social Darwinism, or the theological and metaphysical stages in Comte) perhaps deserve to be left in the dust or shut in the tomb, we may nevertheless grieve for them. Such a double attitude toward the past is a natural result of Eliot's own thoughtful version of "advanced conservative liberalism." She is able to combine liberal faith in the future with a Burkean respect for the greatness of what is being superseded. And in *Middlemarch,* one thing that is being superseded, along with the ambitious ideals of Dorothea and Lydgate, is the radical and youthful reform optimism of the early 1830s.

Middlemarch and *Felix Holt* record the liberal ferment and optimism of 1832, and in both the problematic relationship between reform and progress is a central theme. They show what has happened to that liberal ferment from the vantage point of 1870, and the changes they describe are based on compromise and disillusionment: the radical hopes of 1832 have not been fulfilled, even after 1867. "Some set out, like Crusaders of old, with a glorious equipment of hope and enthusiasm, and get broken by the way, wanting patience with each other and the world." George Eliot's insistence on the need for patience, which becomes the dominant idea in Felix Holt's address to the working class, is her equivalent of Arnold's insistence on the need for stoic resignation: both are natural conclusions from the assumptions that social progress is gradual at best, that the contributions of the individual towards making the future are miniscule at best, and that (at least in Arnold, in a poem like "The Future") the shape of things to come may be totally independent of human wishes and efforts. The heroic acts of a St. Theresa are not possible for Dorothea Brooke, whose noble reformist impulses are compromised, although not completely frustrated, as are Lydgate's, in the course of her story. "A new Theresa will hardly have the opportunity of reforming a conventual life, any more than a new Antigone will spend her heroic piety in daring all for the sake of a brother's burial: the medium in which their ardent deeds took shape is for ever gone." *Middlemarch* opens "in those times when reforms were begun with a young hopefulness of immediate good," but it shows historical and personal circumstances, "the dead hand of the past" and "spots of commonness" in the characters themselves, deflecting the would-be reformers from their paths. The "young hopefulness of immediate good" which characterized the 1830s, George Eliot concludes, "has been much checked in our days."

Many of the characters in *Middlemarch* besides Dorothea and Lydgate are reformers in some sense or other; only two of them escape from the general fate of disillusionment. Even Bulstrode is a reformer, along evangelical lines. He aims at "being an eminent Christian" partly by doing good works with his money, until Raffles and the dead hand of his shady past catch up with him. "The service he could do to the cause of religion had been through life the ground he alleged to himself for his choice of action" (453). Bulstrode's failure follows the pattern of the stories of Dorothea, Lydgate, Mr. Brooke, and even Casaubon, who once sought with his "Key of all Mythologies" (or, as Ladislaw puts it, his "mouldy futilities") to be a sort of reformer and "Higher Critic" in the field of theological scholarship. Bulstrode is "simply a man whose desires had been stronger than his theoretic beliefs." The two reformers in the novel to whom the pattern of disillusionment does not apply are Will Ladislaw and Caleb Garth. But Ladislaw's entry into the politics of reform is itself a declension from his youthful artistic ambitions. And Caleb Garth, a deliberate foil to the politicians in the novel, is a reformer by ironic contrast: his quiet workmanship, making for social progress through private, individual effort rather than through political action, is offered as a counter to Mr. Brooke's half-baked radicalism. Dagley's drunken language shows up Brooke as a political reformer who cannot reform his own gates, let alone promote sobriety and good will among his tenants. But Garth, who "has invented a new pattern of gate" that Brooke could use, knows what he can set straight and what he cannot. He and his daughter Mary both know where their "duty" lies, and they proceed to do it without fuss. Speaking of Sir James Chettam's offer to him to become manager of the Freshitt and Tipton estates, Caleb tells his wife: "It's a fine thing to come to a man when he's seen into the nature of business: to have the chance of getting a bit of the country into good fettle, as they say, and putting men into the right way with their farming, and getting a bit of good contriving and solid building done—that those who are living and those who come after will be the better for" (295).

A favorite saying of Caleb's is "business breeds" (402), which perhaps means not only that good workmanship leads to more openings for the worker but also that progress creates more progress. It is at least clear that so long as "business breeds" there is no reason to complain about it or to interfere with it—it will take care of itself. And the same laissez-faire message underlies Caleb's confrontation with the farm laborers who try to harass a group of railroad agents. "Now, my lads," Caleb tells them, "you can't hinder the railroad: it will be made whether you like it or not. And if you go fighting against it, you'll get yourselves into trouble." Like Dagley, the farm laborers may have real grievances, and Caleb cannot assure them that the railroad will do them any good as individuals. But their politics are mixed up; somebody has been giving them false notions, Caleb suspects, by telling them that "the railroad was a bad thing": "That was a lie. It may do a bit of harm here and there, to this and to that; and so does the sun in heaven. But the railway's a good thing" (408). We are told that "Caleb was in a difficulty known to any person attempting in dark times and unassisted by miracle to reason with rustics who are in possession of an undeniable truth which they know through a hard process of feeling, and can let it fall like a giant's club on your neatly-carved argument for a social benefit which they do *not* feel" (408). Nevertheless, Caleb is right; "business breeds." From the vantage point of 1870, George Eliot can see the railways as part of that long, slow growth of industrial complexity and power which increasingly made political interference with it seem dangerous, if not impossible. Caleb's thinking about social improvement, in the midst of the reform agitation that leads Mr. Vincy to believe that the world is coming to an end, is deliberately apolitical. Progress will come through honesty, hard work, and everyone doing his duty—"for the growing good of the world is partly dependent on unhistoric acts; and that things are not so ill with you and me as they might have been, is half owing to the number who lived faithfully a hidden life, and rest in unvisited tombs" (613). Because of the Caleb Garths and the Dorothea Brookes of the world, the last sentence of the novel is hopeful, even while it sums up the theme of broken ambitions and the impossibility of heroism in modern times.

George Eliot's novels present the reform idealism of her characters as abortive; she sees the period from 1830 to 1870 much as Arthur Pendennis sees it, as a history of the world working towards reform at its own pace. The accumulated actions of numerous obscure individuals constitute a force making for social amelioration; but the actions of a single individual are likely to be insignificant, and perhaps also blind and misguided. Society is a highly complicated organism, which is somehow independent of the individuals who compose it: as in Spencer's evolutionary sociology, it grows and improves at its own rate, according to its own mysterious laws of accretion and diversification. *Middlemarch* is that typical product of mid-Victorian culture, a novel without a hero or a heroine—one in which a group, a community, or a whole society dominates the action. But as in other examples of antiheroic realism—*Vanity Fair, The Way We Live Now, Our Mutual Friend*—the hidden protagonist, the social organism, is not portrayed with unqualified approval. Again, it is the nature of realism not necessarily to affirm the social status quo but to present it as inevitable, an immovable object that will change itself through slow growth but that cannot be much affected (except perhaps for the worse) either by individual effort or by legislative reform.

The most extreme statements of the organic analogy in the Victorian period come from Herbert Spencer, for whom society is less anthropomorphic than like an immense centipede or some other hideous creature bearing no similarity to Blake's "human form divine." In his essay of 1860 called "The Social Organism," Spencer elaborates on the analogy between the "body politic" and the "body physiological," coming to such innocently nightmarish conclusions as that the laboring classes are equivalent to the mucous matter in simple animals, that rudimentary governments are like the rudimentary ganglia "in the higher *Annulosa*," and that highways and railroads are like the circulatory systems in complex creatures: "Lastly, it is to be remarked that there ultimately arise in the higher social organisms, as in the higher individual organisms, main channels of distribution . . . And in railways we also see, for the first time in the social organism, a system of double channels conveying currents in opposite directions, as do the arteries and veins of a well-developed animal."[34] One wonders what sort of "well-developed animal" Spencer has in mind; it is more than likely that his Darwinian bestiary contains some specifiable monster.

In Dickens such protoplasmic characters as the Turveydrops, Mr. Guppy, and the Smallweeds evidently spring from a similar vision of society as a monstrous organism, and in the same novel there is that genial monster Tom, of "Tom-all-Alone's," each corpuscle of whose blood breeds pestilence and each atom of whose slime "shall work its retribution." George Eliot comes closer to Spencer's vision than Dickens, for her metaphors usually invoke biological expertise rather than mythic personification. St. Ogg's, for example, is "one of those old, old towns which impress one as a continuation and outgrowth of nature, as much as the nests of the bower-birds or the winding galleries of the white ants: a town which carries the traces of its long growth and history like a millennial tree." The main difference between Dickens and Eliot is that Dickens always portrays the social organism as monstrous, a sort of immense Caliban whose arteries are clogged sewers and crooked streets and whose head is stuffed with Circumlocution Office red tape. Dickens's Coketown, for example, is "a town of unnatural red and black like the painted face of a savage." There is nothing "millennial," inevitable, or lovely about Dickens's London and Coketown, whereas in Eliot as in Spencer the organic analogy is ambiguous: society like nature may be "red in tooth and claw," but that is only its way of being beneficent. Although always with a sympathetic emphasis upon the sadness of what is being left behind, Eliot interprets history in evolutionary terms and applies the language of biological necessity to the dinosaurs of society. Her humaneness and her insistence on duty save her from the excesses of social Darwinism: she does not subscribe to the atrocious paradox of genocide as a source of progress, or even of conflict as a source of creation, as in Bagehot's praise of war in *Physics and Politics,* or in Darwin's chapter on "The Extinction of Races" in *The Descent of Man,* or again in Spencer: "To the unceasing warfare between species is mainly due both growth and organization. Without universal conflict there would have been no development of the active powers."[35]

The organic analogy in Eliot and Spencer is partly a product of conservative attitudes added to an earlier strain of liberalism. Spencer adapted the language of evolution to the free trade radicalism with which he started his career in the 1840s. And the organic analogy as it emerges from Darwinism bears little similarity to the organicism of Burke and Coleridge, except as an invocation of the authority of nature in defense of the status quo. What Spencer especially clings to from the free trade radicalism of the 1840s is his belief in the hostility between individual and society, which is in a general way a main theme of Eliot's fiction. As in *On Liberty,* the individual and the state continue to be seen as enemies by mid-Victorian "realists" and "conservative liberals," even while the claims of society over the individual are being rendered in terms of organic law. Spencer again puts this contradiction in its most extreme form. Staunch defender of laissez-faire individualism though he is, in "The Social Organism" he suggests that jobs and businesses are permanent fixtures in society, whereas individuals are temporary and, from the viewpoint of "science," at least, expendable: "Just as in a living body, the cells that make up some important organ severally perform their functions for a time and then disappear, leaving others to supply their places; so, in each part of a society the organ remains, though the persons who compose it change" (204).

The idea of the social organism overlaps and contradicts Spencer's extreme individualism. The development of his evolutionary sociology, moreover, is an early version of the history of Darwinism itself as a biological hypothesis founded upon assumptions drawn from political economy. As Gertrude Himmelfarb writes: "From Malthus to Darwin and back to a Malthusian Darwinism: the system seemed to be self-sufficient and self-confirming. The theory of natural selection, it is said, could only have originated in England, because only laissez-faire England provided the atomistic, egotistic mentality necessary to its conception. Only there could Darwin have blandly assumed that the basic unit was the individual, the basic instinct self-interest, and the basic activity struggle."[36]

According to this interpretation, Darwinism provides a seemingly scientific justification for all of the more negative aspects of Ricardian economics. The possibilities of both political and economic change turn out to be governed by inflexible "laws of nature." "In this sense, the very idea of reform is antithetical to Darwinism."[37] As the apotheosis of all that is worst in liberal individualism, social Darwinism is also the negation of liberal individualism. For in Eliot as in Spencer, evolutionary time, biological necessity, and the social organism dwarf and threaten to crush all

TICKET-OF-LEAVE MEN.

From Henry Mayhew's *London Labour and the London Poor.*

individual freedom of action. The contradiction inherent in "advanced conservative liberalism" returns upon itself in the form of the conflict between individual aspirations and the encroaching claims of society. "We look on State action," says Bagehot, "not as our own action, but as alien action."[38]

The fictional realism of Thackeray, Trollope, and Eliot displaces the power of social amelioration from human agency to the slow growth of the social organism, which for liberal individualists is at best only a dubiously benevolent monster. To put it another way, the development of Victorian artistic and political realism from about 1850 on involves the gradual reification of ideas of social reform. This process reaches its limit in social Darwinism, which may be viewed as an attempt to give "scientific" finality to the reductive conversion of people into objects that is basic to all forms of realism. One of the final avatars of this process is the operation of fate or chance in Hardy's novels, in which human agency, stripped of all rational control over circumstances, is viewed as existentially absurd. Hardy reintroduces a radical perspective into the novel, however, because both he and his characters rebel against the cruel forms of entrapment that society and nature create. The theme in *Jude the Obscure* of "nature's law" as "mutual butchery" involves both the acceptance of the logic of social Darwinism and a total, uncompromising moral resistance to it. Hardy's thinking is thus similar to Huxley's in *Evolution and Ethics,* in which nature's law of conflict is seen as antithetical to mankind's law of social cooperation. But neither Hardy nor Huxley escape from the bleak vision of nature—as opposed to human nature—which is central to social Darwinism.

In his 1854 diary Mill writes that the trend of recent literature has been away from reform idealism towards a position of realistic compromise, but that it already seems to be swinging back towards the depiction of life in terms of false extremes: "This change [to realistic compromise] is explained, and partly justified, by the superficiality, and real one-sidedness, of the bold thinkers who preceded. But if I mistake not, the time is now come, or coming, for a change the reverse way."[39] Mill's assessment of the trend towards compromise in the literature of the 1850s is accurate, but his notion that there would be a swing back towards a literature of extremes is premature, although it is possible to see such extremes in the apparently hostile camps of Marxism and social Darwinism in the last two decades of the century, after the long period of "middlingness" and realism from 1850 to 1870. Between the Marxist and utopian writings of Morris and Edward Carpenter and the elaborations of social Darwinism in

Spencer, Benjamin Kidd, and Karl Pearson, a literature based on realistic compromise and liberal moderation gives place to a new literature of ''bold thinkers'' who offer either extreme negations or radical affirmations of human possibility.

"Refuge—Applying for Admittance," from Gustave Doré's *London*.

X.   1867 and the Idea of Culture

> then the maiden aunt
> Took this fair day for text, and from it preach'd
> An universal culture for the crowd,
> And all things great.

> Tennyson, *The Princess*

When W. N. Molesworth, in his *History of the Reform Bill of 1832*, reviewed its results from the perspective of 1865, he expressed a satisfaction felt by most mid-Victorian liberals: "The vast expansion of our trade, commerce, and manufactures, which has since taken place, could not have been effected if the landed interest had continued to possess that virtual monopoly of legislation which was taken from it by the Reform Bill."[1] Such satisfaction with the results of the first Reform Bill could be extended, as in Trollope and Bagehot, into a belief in unending progress through liberated middle-class industry, through more or less aristocratic government, and through the continued "deference" of the "lower orders." For the "advanced conservative liberal," politics thus might appear to involve little more than Palmerstonian expediency. But Molesworth's statement might with equal logic be taken to imply that the destruction of the aristocratic "monopoly of legislation" which had occurred in 1832 would need to be repeated by future generations for newly emergent social groups, until everyone possessed equal rights and obligations as citizens. Progress could thus be seen either as the result of free trade and middle-class industry, needing only to be extended into the future with no end in sight; or else it could be seen as the result of the gradual emergence of the "less fortunate" into prosperity and "respectability." It was progress in this second sense that Gladstone had in mind when in 1864 he "venture[d] to say that every man who is not presumably incapacitated by some consideration of personal unfitness or of political danger is morally entitled to come within the pale of the Constitution."[2] For Gladstone, the gradual admission of the "lower orders" into full citizenship would not mean the eclipse of middle-class liberalism but the fulfillment of its promise. As increasing numbers of "respectable" working men were granted the vote, they would be evidence of the solidification of the nation through the end of class conflict and the realization of the social harmony so often wished for by writers and politicians in the 1840s. As Gladstone declared:

> It has been given to us of this generation to witness . . . the most blessed of all social processes; I mean the process which unites together not the interests only but the feelings of all the several classes of the community, and throws back into the shadows of oblivion those discords by which they were kept apart from one another. I know of nothing which can contribute, in any degree comparable to that union, to the welfare of the commonwealth . . . than that hearts should be bound together by a reasonable extension, at fitting times, and among select portions of the people, of every benefit and every privilege that can justly be conferred upon them.[3]

Gladstone's language marks a parting of the ways for liberals in the 1860s. Robert Lowe, the "Adullamites," and "advanced conservative liberals" like Bagehot saw no reason to extend the franchise much if at all, and saw every reason to withhold it from working men who, no matter how "deferential," were ignorant, irresponsible, and—what was far worse than either—potential socialists. Bagehot thought that the "artisan class" or "labor aristocracy" should have more influence on Parliament, but he feared any wholesale reform that would end "deference" and bring on "democracy." But Gladstone, Bright, and Mill believed that the time had come to admit a fair portion of the working class to full citizenship. Even so, the rhetoric of the proreform liberals in arguing for an extension of the franchise in the 1860s was different from the radical rhetoric of the 1830s. Then it had been the middle class that seemed about to sweep away aristocratic privilege and misrule for the benefit of all classes. In the 1860s the middle class appeared to be the granter of rights and obligations and of the fruits of its industry to the working class. Instead of gaining authority, it was having to share it. The result is that there is a cautionary quality about much of the political rhetoric of the 1860s that frequently masks the opposition between those who are for and those who are against extending the franchise.

The arguments of 1830-1832 for extending the franchise, based on theories of natural rights and of utilitarian benefits to the greatest number, give way in the 1860s to the idea of the franchise as a "trust" or an "obligation" and to the question of the moral and intellectual fitness of the working class for political responsibility. Mill, for example, was prepared to argue that at least "the educated artizans"—men like the leaders of the Amalgamated Society of Engineers—had certain virtues superior to those of the middle class, not least of which was the fact that they were "the most teachable of all our classes." What they lacked in actual knowledge, therefore, might be made up in the great schoolroom of Parliament itself, where the free and full competition of ideas was forever spinning progressive truths vital to the nation: "I can hardly conceive a nobler course of national education than the debates of this House would become, if the notions, right and wrong, which are fermenting in the minds of the working classes, many of which go down very deep into the foundations of society and government, were fairly stated and genuinely discussed within these walls."[4] Mill's idea of Parliament as an educational institution, although shared by Bagehot, was perhaps too paradoxical for many liberals to accept. But members of all parties in the 1860s stressed the urgency of education. "We must educate our masters": that was a sentiment to which everyone could subscribe and which helped to produce Forster's Education Act in 1870.

The idea of culture thus became crucial as a measuring stick of fitness of the working class for political responsibility. One stood for or against a new reform bill, depending partly on one's definition of culture and on one's belief as to whether those who were to be enfranchised had enough of it or not. At one extreme were those who, like Robert Lowe, insisted on the "venality . . . ignorance . . . drunkenness, and facility for being intimidated" of the workers.[5] At the other extreme were the authors of *Essays on Reform,* who went farther than Mill in claiming that the working class (or, at least, the "better elements" of it) had virtues and wisdom of its own.

True, there were the "Sheffield outrages" and the breaking of the Hyde Park railings which could be used as evidence of the irresponsibility of the workers. But these were isolated incidents that posed no massive threat to the establishment, as Chartism had done in the 1840s. On the contrary, the peaceable and respectable behavior of at least "the educated artizans" over the long period from 1850 into the 1860s, coupled with the forbearance of the textile workers during the Lancashire cotton famine, seemed to prove the fitness of much of the working class for inclusion within "the pale of the Constitution." Further, the power of combination through self-sacrifice which the trade union and cooperative movements displayed might be viewed as a virtue that the middle class and the aristocracy, governed by individualism and "territorial interest," could use more of. So R. H. Hutton, in his essay on "The Political Character of the Working Class," found in trade unions and benefit societies a community spirit and experience lacking in the upper classes: "In the other classes we have at last attained a tolerably clear conviction what the liberties are which the individual has a right to keep sacred from the invasion of the State. But I think only the working class have got—partly from their trade organizations—a clear conception how much individuals owe, by way of self-sacrifice, to the larger social organization to which they belong."[6] Hutton points to "that spirit of individual sacrifice for the sake of the greater life of the whole class or nation, which pervades the very heart and imagination of the working class" (42), as a quality which, if given a real influence in government, might be of great benefit to all classes and parties. And Hutton also argues that, because it lacks vested interests like those of the middle class and aristocracy, the working class is freer to form objective judgments about many political issues. The working man's freedom from property "is a condition of things which tends to liberate him from the more selfish prejudices of place and time" (39).

Hutton's argument approximates the idea of the proletariat as universalizing agent in Marxism—as the part that stands for the whole or the one social group whose search for justice makes its interest identical with that of mankind and the future. But Hutton is not claiming so much for the working class. He is only arguing that it has distinct virtues and interests of its own which, added to the virtues and interests of the upper classes in Parliament, would make it a more national, more "popular," and wiser institution. It is not a matter of one class standing for the whole, but of all classes having an influence upon government in a just balance of the interests of the nation. But while Hutton's claims for the workers are modest when compared to those made by Marxism, they stand in obvious contrast to the accusations of Robert Lowe. And Hutton's claims stand also in contrast to Matthew Arnold's thesis in *Culture and Anarchy*.

Arnold believes that no class can stand for the whole, and also that the only universalizing agent present in the 1860s is "culture," rising above the "anarchy" of separate class interests. In general terms, of course, his argument seems unimpeachable. Freedom is worthless unless it is coupled with intelligence—which means, as a minimum, with a consciousness of social alternatives. This is the problem with which Mill struggles in *On Liberty* and elsewhere, the most urgent one in democratic theory. For Mill, the importance of defending minority opinion in a democracy is bound up with the problem of preserving the influence of educated opinion in government, which the events of the 1860s made especially critical. In *Representative Government,* Mill elaborates upon Thomas Hare's electoral scheme, in which it appears that the minority that is most in charge of the truth and most in need of legal protection is the minority of the educated: "The natural tendency of representative government, as of

240

modern civilization, is toward collective mediocrity; and this tendency is increased by all reductions and extensions of the franchise, their effect being to place the principal power in the hands of classes more and more below the highest level of instruction in the community."[7] The problem is how to reverse this process and thereby avoid the "future middling-ness" or the dead-level equality that Mill, following Tocqueville, thought would result from "false democracy."

Arnold's defense of culture, influenced by Mill and Tocqueville, is essentially similar to Mill's search for means of protecting minority opinion against the "tyranny of the majority." Culture, or an education based upon literary and historical studies, is what will provide us with a necessary consciousness of social alternatives. It is towards the development of such a consciousness that Arnold's historicism, including even his ethnic stereotyping of peoples and civilizations, tends. From the Hebrews, we may learn faith and self-sacrifice; from the Greeks, rational self-awareness and objectivity. And although he is unable to recognize the intellectual and liberal heritage of the better side of religious noncon-formity, there is no reason to impugn Arnold for thinking that, in 1867, the English needed to "Hellenize" more than "Hebraize." Further, one may appreciate Arnold's institutionalization of culture in the state as a valid alternative to the laissez-faire individualism of the middle class, and as a vague forecast of the emphasis upon state action in later liberal and socialist theory.

The main difficulty with Arnold's position in *Culture and Anarchy* is that his categories are too general to be clear, let alone practicable. Of course Arnold is refusing to be practicable in *Culture and Anarchy* partly to offset the arguments of such practical men as Frederic Harrison, and his ironic intent needs constantly to be borne in mind. But his irony does not offset what Lionel Trilling has called "the reactionary possibilities of Arnold's vagueness." Trilling shows how these "possibilities" affect Arnold's treatment of the working class:

> Speaking of the workers' relation to the State, Arnold ignored or misrepresented the very real feeling for the State-idea which the pro-letariat possessed. Since the very beginning of the industrial revolu-tion the workers had looked to Parliament for the amelioration of their lot; their innumerable petitions had, of course, been met with indignation or indifference. Arnold speaks of a working class with so little conception of the State that it prefers to hide in abandoned coal mines rather than be drafted for service in the Crimea, but he ignores a working class that had conceived the State as an instrument

for international right-doing and had pressed the Crimean War as a kind of crusade against Russian despotism. Indeed, Arnold passes over the remarkable sense of *Europeanism* of the working class, which, until frightened by the Commune of 1871, was for many years the only class in England that held the idea of internationalism.[8]

And Trilling, echoing the authors of *Essays on Reform,* goes on to point to the responsible behavior of the workers during the Lancashire cotton famine and their apparent support of the Unionists during the Civil War as factors that Arnold overlooks.

In *Essays on Reform,* R. H. Hutton suggests that upper-class culture, or "the highest level of instruction in the community," might hinder as much as help in the formation of wise political judgments. He believes that the record of educated judgment in the past, insofar as that has been reflected in governmental decisions, has hardly been notable for its wisdom or its largeness of sympathy. Here again is something which Arnold, despite his often subtle historicism, fails to perceive. And it might even be the case that the relative ignorance or lack of culture of the working class could keep it from being diverted from main issues by minor and irrelevant ideas. Certainly the working class has never been liable to put poetry before politics. Because the working class is not burdened by "a great *variety* of intellectual considerations," Hutton claims, they are all the more "open to the influence of a few *great* ideas, and so willing to make sacrifices for those ideas" (35). As the working class is unburdened by property, so it is also unburdened by intellectual distractions, or culture in its worst sense. The sympathetic interest of the workers in the cause of freedom abroad, Hutton argues, shows their ability to seize upon a single "great idea" and to make sacrifices in the cause of justice for all. Hutton's chief illustration is the forbearance of the Lancashire operatives during the cotton famine and their support of the American Union against their own immediate economic interest.[9]

Several of Hutton's arguments are repeated later in the series by Arnold's ironical adversary, Frederic Harrison, in his essay "Foreign Policy." Harrison claims that, in regard to the Civil War, "the people were and are as conspicuously right as the classes who wield the political power were and are conspicuously wrong" (292). This suggests again that the "uncultured" sympathies of the working class may be sounder guides than the educated opinions of the upper classes. So the authors of *Essays on Reform* strive to counteract the charges of ignorance and irresponsibility which Robert Lowe and others leveled at the working class. From the

242

essay "Popular Education" by Charles Parker, it even appears that the workers rather than the "educated classes" may be the true champions of culture. Parker argues that the spread of culture to the working class waits upon parliamentary reform. He presents testimony to show that the workers understand the value of education and that, if they were given the opportunity to do so, they would elect representatives who would create a proper school system (something the "educated classes" had obviously not done). The ignorance of the workers is not their fault but that of an unreformed Parliament which has so far failed to provide them with an adequate system of schools. Education thus appears to be an issue, like free trade, involving the destruction of an exclusive monopoly by those who have been unjustly excluded—the "ignorant" workers.

It is easy to see why Arnold's studied impracticality in *Culture and Anarchy* was frustrating to a radical like Harrison. Indeed, in responding satirically to Arnold, Harrison had made impracticality one of his main charges. Harrison's Arminius von Thunder-ten-dronck complains that, seeing the turmoil and suffering of history, "Culture," like Tennyson's "Soul" in "The Palace of Art," sits "high aloft with a pouncet-box to spare her senses aught unpleasant, holding no form of creed, but contemplating all with infinite serenity, sweetly chanting snatches from graceful sages and ecstatic monks, crying out the most pretty shame upon the vulgarity, the provinciality, the impropriety of it all."[10] And much the same complaint about Arnold's theory of culture came from Henry Sidgwick: "All this criticism of action is very valuable; but it is usually given in excess, just because, I think, culture is a little sore in conscience, is uncomfortably eager to excuse its own evident incapacity for action. Culture is always hinting at a convenient season, that rarely seems to arrive." Arnold's culture disdains to mix itself with "social action," Sidgwick believes, because that would entail "losing oneself in a mass of disagreeable, hard, mechanical details, and trying to influence many dull or careless or bigoted people for the sake of ends that were at first of doubtful brilliancy, and are continually being dimmed and dwarfed by the clouds of conflict."[11]

There is surely as much justice in Harrison's and Sidgwick's criticisms of Arnold as in Arnold's criticisms of dissenters, partisans, reformers, and practical men like Frederic Harrison. For in *Culture and Anarchy*, Arnold is indeed less interested in supporting any practical proposals than in turning all proposals into tabled motions. *Culture and Anarchy* is partly a call to reflective inaction in a time of what Arnold sees as furious and headlong action. His version of culture involves a withdrawal from the "sick hurry" and "divided aims" of modern life, like the flight of the

Scholar Gipsy, which is ironic in light of his criticism of brooding modern poetry like his own *Empedocles* for expressing only "suffering" with "no vent in action." His strategy in *Culture and Anarchy* is to show the weakness and one-sidedness of all the main positions during the reform crisis of the 1860s. The "disinterested objectivity" that he claims for his version of culture allows him to see how all practical proposals, like the "liberal nostrums" he ridicules in his sixth chapter, are reflections of class or party interests rather than of the whole community. Arnold believes that everything except culture is ideological or tied to class and party interests, but he does not explain how culture escapes this fate. As an inspector of schools, however, whose long, influential, and admirable career was embroiled in the party strife surrounding education, he must have been more aware than most of how difficult it is to get the schools, and with them the saving influence of culture, out of the tangled thickets of politics. Arnold's detachment of culture from class and factional conflict is, then, very much a product of wishful thinking; it is his version of Abbot Samson's monastery, an expression of the desire for order, authority, and clarity in the midst of their opposites. And once he has detached culture from its social roots, Arnold approaches the conclusion that nobody is right because nobody has consulted culture, which is that which makes "right reason and the will of God prevail." Culture is of some other time and place, an educator's utopia.

Furthermore, what does a phrase like "the will of God" mean as Arnold uses it? His stance is not clearly critical or utopian. Such language suggests that he also is a worshipper of the benign and easy divinity of Trollope's "advanced conservative liberalism" (Stanley describes Thomas Arnold as an "orthodox liberal"). Arnold's call to inaction is framed in the language of inevitable progress, with which it is better to cooperate rather than to interfere. The true "educators," and therefore the true reformers, Arnold concludes, are not the active and pushy politicians like Disraeli, Bright, and Harrison, but those who quietly further the inevitable tendency to improvement in the universe which expresses "the will of God." These are Arnold's Caleb Garths and Dorothea Brookes:

> Docile echoes of the eternal voice, pliant organs of the infinite will, such workers are going along with the essential movement of the world; and this is their strength, and their happy and divine fortune. For if the believers in action, who are so impatient with us and call us effeminate, had had the same good fortune, they would, no doubt, have surpassed us in this sphere of vital influence by all the superiority of their genius and energy over ours. But now we go the way the

244

human race is going, while they abolish the Irish Church by the power of the Nonconformists' antipathy to establishments, or they enable a man to marry his deceased wife's sister.[12]

Such language takes us back to the passive conception of history implicit in Arnold's river and ocean metaphors in poems like "The Future." Although there is an element of ironic hyperbole in phrases like "docile echoes" and "pliant organs," this is a result of the paradoxical stance that Arnold adopts throughout *Culture and Anarchy* of urging the wisdom of inaction in a time of action. Further, such language reflects the fact that Arnold's idea of culture is another version of moral or self-reform. We must learn to be better men before we can be sure of making wise political decisions. But this is such a truism that it seems hardly necessary to insist upon it so elaborately as Arnold does. Culture, according to Arnold, points away from squabbling factions to the whole community or the state. The way to the state lies not through political reforms, however, but through an appeal to our individual "best self" against our "ordinary selves." "We want an authority, and we find nothing but jealous classes, checks, and a deadlock; culture suggests the idea of *the State*. We find no basis for a firm State-power in our ordinary selves; culture suggests one to us in our *best self*" (96).

Arnold's main terms of reference—culture, best self versus ordinary selves, and even the state based on these—are expressions of an apolitical individualism that shows up in several other literary responses to 1867, perhaps most notably in *Felix Holt*. At the same time, both culture and the state are expressions of a desire for true community and wholeness as against anarchy, disunity, the clash of sects and parties and "ignorant armies." As such, Arnold's version of culture is related to the Mauricean ideal of union in Christ or the reconciliation of opposites in his Church and Kingdom. Arnold did not think highly either of Maurice or of Christian Socialism.[13] But his thinking is clearly rooted in the liberal theology of his father, Maurice, and Coleridge, and he is perhaps most like them in the ambiguity of his central ideal of union or harmony through culture and the state. Like Maurice's Kingdom of Christ, Arnold's state may be either an ideal realm, or the established state and Church of England, or both at once. And culture, as both the goal of perfection that all should strive for and the already realized possession of a few well-educated and responsible citizens like Arnold himself, leads the same double life. As Sidgwick said, "I think it clear that Mr. Arnold, when he speaks of culture, is speaking sometimes of an ideal, sometimes of an actual culture, and does not always know which."[14]

But whether culture is the possession of a select minority, or else an ideal that no one can be properly said to possess, it is a rarity in the 1860s. Anarchy is the rule, culture is the exception. Such an attitude inevitably places Arnold in opposition to the authors of *Essays on Reform,* who argue that, although "uncultured" in the sense of lacking formal schooling, the workers have virtues—cooperation, self-sacrifice for communal good, the disinterested appreciation of "great ideas," and so forth— that the other classes lack. Arnold is willing to attribute these virtues only to those who have culture; and it is primarily class and party rivalry that undermines them. Of course the authors of *Essays on Reform* do not say that the working class possesses a culture of its own: they use that term as Arnold does primarily to mean formal schooling, and they also see "popular education" as an urgent and largely unrealized goal. No one in 1867 gainsaid the importance of education. The main difficulty that had stood in the way of such legislation as the Education Act of 1870 had been only "the dissidence of dissent" and the squabbling of various party and religious interests over what the nature of a national school system should be. Arnold was best acquainted with this side of social reform, and for him the problem of culture was perhaps inevitably shaped by his sense of the failure to provide schools and of the inadequacy of the schools which were provided. Given a land of ignorance and anarchy, to produce a land of sweetness and light in which the state would be the reflection of our "best self" might then seem necessarily to hinge on something more fundamental than an act of Parliament. To say that Arnold had as much trouble as everyone else in determining what that fundamental thing might be is only to recognize, as he did, the great and perhaps inevitable persistence of ignorance as a force in history.

Much of the attraction for intellectuals of Arnold's thesis lies, of course, in the importance he gives to intelligence in history, and especially to intelligence as it manifests itself in the nonsciences of poetry, literary criticism, and historical studies. He again essentially agrees with Mill that, although ideas have not shaped events often enough or well enough in the past, they can and should shape events. "It is what men think that determines how they act; and though the persuasions and convictions of average men are in a much greater degree determined by their personal position than by reason, no little power is exercised over them by the persuasions and convictions of those whose personal position is different and by the united authority of the instructed."[15] Although Arnold is not comfortable with radical theorizing and system making, identifying these with the destructive side of Jacobinism, neither would he have been comfortable with Bagehot's praise of dullness, which he would surely have identified with Philistinism. Culture conveniently combines two elements that perhaps every political theorist would like to combine, the established past with the unplanned future. Its etymological associations suggest landed gentility and the aristocratic principle. Its common usage, synonymous with education, suggests the power of reason and the democratic principle. Arnold finds in his key idea the elements of the past most worthy of preservation, and he also finds in it the discriminative power of individual intelligence as the agent of wise change, leading from self-reformation to eventual social reformation (or perhaps the two are identical).[16]

While one may sympathize with Arnold's desire to combine these opposed values into one category, one may still feel that the result is neither very logical nor very helpful. Thus, in the debate with Huxley over literary versus scientific education, when Arnold was very much on his own ground as an educator and an expert on actual schools, the wishfulness and vagueness of his culture concept may have weakened his case. Although there was undoubtedly justice on both sides, and although Huxley misunderstood Arnold just as much as Arnold misunderstood Huxley, Arnold did not see so clearly as Huxley did that democratic conditions demanded a revised, democratic curriculum. In a sense, of course, there was less distance between them than the juxtaposition of the terms "literature" and "science" implies. As Fred Walcott says, "The often-mentioned controversy between Arnold and Huxley was nothing more than an amicable clarification, the shoring up of a basic agreement."[17] Huxley never meant to eliminate literature from the curriculum, and Arnold never meant to eliminate science. And both of them wanted education to be as broadly liberal and humanistic as possible, which meant neither narrowly technical nor narrowly classical. But there can be no doubt that Arnold sees culture, which means for him preeminently poetry and the classics, as an embattled domain, in need of defense against the incursions of democracy and scientific skepticism. Religion has fallen on bad times, and poetry will have to take its place in the future, but poetry itself is in danger of failing in the unhealthy atmosphere of the industrial and democratic modern age. Such an attitude seems hard to square with an awareness of the centuries-long struggle of the sciences and of technical subjects to break into the curriculum. The sheer volume of complaints in the nineteenth century about the narrowness and uselessness of the classical curriculum of the universities and public schools (Arnold added his own complaints in his educational reports) should have made him extremely cautious about even appearing to oppose the admission of new subjects into the curriculum.[18]

The debate over literary versus technical education extended back past the founding of London University, the Society for the Diffusion of Useful Knowledge, and Bentham's Chrestomathia to Adam Smith, Priestley, and Locke in the eighteenth century. Except in Scotland, the main tradition of scientific education had to develop outside the established universities and the public schools, as an important aspect of the heritage of religious nonconformity and middle-class radicalism.[19] For Arnold, of course, at least in *Culture and Anarchy,* religious nonconformity is all of a piece, and it is all "dismal and illiberal," while middle-class radicalisms like Benjamin Franklin's and Jeremy Bentham's are written off as vulgar, "fierce," Jacobinical system making. Against this radical heritage, slowly gaining in its long conflict with aristocratic privilege and the established Church, Arnold opposes his version of culture, shaped by his Rugby and Oxford background and having about it the elegiac quality of a "home of lost causes, and forsaken beliefs."[20]

Out of the heritage of radical nonconformity, coming together in the 1850s and 1860s with positivism and Darwinism, a very different idea of culture arose, which developed into a more suitable one for democratic conditions than Arnold's. This is the anthropological theory of culture. In 1871, four years after "the leap in the dark" of the second Reform Bill, Edward Burnett Tylor published his anthropological classic, *Primitive Culture.* The oxymoronic title suggests the novelty of Tylor's ideas. Although there is no indication that he is thinking of Arnold, he turns Arnold's title inside out: the culture of savagery, the civilization of the uncivilized, light in the heart of darkness. But how can you call the uncultured "cultured?" Or the unwashed "washed?" Arnold, however, might not have found Tylor's attribution of culture to savages and barbarians, as Tylor himself calls primitive men, completely illogical. As a believer in progressive evolution, Tylor works with the idea of three levels or stages of cultural development, from savagery or hunting economies, through barbarism or pastoral economies, up to civilization or urban economies. Tylor does not disagree with Arnold's belief in "high culture"; as an evolutionist, however, he asserts that there is also a low culture, which is the source of the high. For Tylor, primitive culture is the ancestor of Arnoldian high culture, just as apes are the ancestors of men. And Tylor holds forth the paradoxical prospect of understanding the high culture by studying the low, or of understanding civilization by studying savagery.[21]

Furthermore, whereas Arnold gives us a prescriptive moral ideal, or culture as a means of personal and social salvation, Tylor's work points toward the modern assumption of a plurality of cultures, or towards cultural relativism. In terms of implicit political values, at least, the Arnoldian concept of culture appears to be resistant to democracy, while the anthropological concept of culture has helped to create a radical respect for different life styles and systems of belief. This is so even though Arnold's basic sympathies are liberal (at least in the Trollopean sense of "advanced conservative liberalism"), and even though anthropology was originally an offshoot of social Darwinism attuned to imperial expansion. These implicit political values, moreover, are important for understanding the modern forms of the humanities and the social sciences, as well as for understanding Arnold and Tylor. For example, whereas a central concern of much modern literary criticism from Arnold forward has been the definition and defense of "great traditions," the impulse behind much anthropological work has been a contrary one. The great anthropologist Franz Boas has this to say about "traditions": "my whole outlook upon social life is determined by the question: How can we recognize the shackles that tradition has laid upon us? For when we recognize them, we are able to break them."[22]

Boas's statement is very much in the spirit of Tylor's work. Although *Primitive Culture* has no direct bearing on Victorian politics, Tylor nevertheless thinks of himself as a reformer, in the sense of a scientific investigator whose researches will sweep away some of the dark cobwebs that tradition and history have spun around mankind. Tylor does not look upon anthropology as an impartial study of men and societies. Instead, he expects it to sit in judgment upon the customs and beliefs of men, much as Arnold expects the critic, the poet, and the scholar to judge. "Active at once in aiding progress and removing hindrance," says Tylor, "the science of culture is essentially a reformer's science" (II, 539). It is a science, moreover, whose findings directly oppose the Arnoldian concept of culture.

Primitive Culture is mainly a study of the evolution of religion. Tylor devotes a major portion of it to an examination of what he calls "survivals," which are customs and beliefs that have persisted from primitive times into modern times. Most of the "survivals" that he examines fall into the category of religious superstitions, and when all of these superstitions are added together, the result is bold and disturbing. Such an amassing of superstitions implies that religion itself is a "survival," an anachronism carried over from the savage and barbarian stages of history. Of course the mere suggestion that religion evolves is subversive of religious orthodoxy, as the Tractarians perceived. Like Comte, Tylor thinks of human reason as struggling out of the morass of primitive superstitions that he documents, through a stage of higher religious development marked especially by Christianity, towards something higher yet—call it the "disinterested objectivity" of scientific rationality. His three stages of savagery, barbarism, and civilization are thus similar to Comte's three stages of intellectual history. "Physics, Chemistry, Biology, have seized whole provinces of the ancient Animism" or religion, says Tylor, and he, for one, is glad of it (II, 269). Tylor's disciple, Sir James Frazer, makes much the same declaration at the end of *The Golden Bough,* where he says that "the movement of the higher thought, so far as we can trace it, has on the whole been from magic through religion to science," and that this movement has meant the progressive elimination of "error and folly" from the world.[23] For both Frazer and Tylor, then, anthropology is a "reformer's science" whose goal is nothing less than the completion of the religious reformation begun in the sixteenth century. With "modern science and modern criticism as new factors in theological opinion," Tylor writes, he and many others "are eagerly pressing toward a new reformation" (II, 535). And in some lines that he contributed to Andrew Lang's "The Double Ballade of a Primitive Man," Tylor says:

> First epoch, the human began,
> Theologians all to expose,—
> 'Tis the *mission* of primitive man.[24]

Primitive Culture is related to the Higher Criticism, but there is very little of David Strauss's or George Eliot's reverence for the past in Tylor.

The differences between Arnold and Tylor can be understood biographically. Arnold grew up in the established Church, a Rugby and an Oxford man, and he inherited his father's zeal for a unified religion at the center of a unified state. But Tylor came from a middle-class family of nonconformists: his father was a Quaker and the owner of a brass foundry, a man like Rouncewell in *Bleak House.* Because he was a Quaker, Tylor was excluded from Oxford and Cambridge and never received any formal university training, although he eventually became the first professor of anthropology at Oxford. His industrial, dissenting origin makes him similar to Huxley and to Herbert Spencer, who were also puritan levelers and iconoclasts in the temple of culture. Frederic Harrison, in contrast, learned his positivism and liberalism at Oxford in the 1850s, partly from Arnold's friend, Richard Congreve. Wielding science as a democratic weapon, all of them attack the errors of religious orthodoxy and the established Church, and also the errors of Oxford and Cambridge. Though Arnold, in his career as an educator, hoped and struggled to make culture available to the working class, to make it democratic, he did not appreciate the difficulties of acquiring it. He did not have the experience of exclusion in his own background to make him fully sympathetic to those whom the established Church treated as being outside the pale. But Tylor had no reason to look upon Oxford and Cambridge as bastions of sweetness and light in a land of darkness, and he had some very good reasons to look upon all men as having some claim to culture.[25]

As reformers of mankind's intellectual life, then, Arnold and Tylor could hardly be farther apart. In the name of science, Tylor wants to reform out of existence the very thing that Arnold would most like to preserve in some fashion: religion. But the battle is already half lost by Arnold, because of course he does not adhere to an orthodox faith. He does not hold forth religious belief itself as a means of salvation from anarchy but a substitute for religion: poetic culture. And to Arnold's advocacy of poetic culture clings a sense of despair—a sense that if "all the creeds are shaken" and religion has gone from the world, the best we can do is to "console" ourselves through poetry. Arnold repeatedly refers to poetic culture less as an active means of salvation than as a passive mode of consolation, "a stay" against the dismal light of science: "More and more mankind will discover that we have to turn to poetry to interpret life for us, to console us, to sustain us. Without poetry, our science will appear incomplete; and most of what now passes with us for religion and philosophy will be replaced by poetry."[26] Comte would agree with this, and perhaps Tylor would also. But Tylor's attitude toward poetry is at least as unsympathetic as Arnold's attitude toward science. His opinion of it seems not far removed from Bentham's, who said that between pushpin and poetry there could be no moral difference, provided that both give the same amount of pleasure. Tylor shows that poetry is based on myth and that myth is only the fanciful, erratic, and superstitious product of the savage mind. "The mental condition of the lower races is the key to poetry, nor is it a small portion of the poetic realm which these definitions cover" (II, 533). For Tylor, *both* poetry and religion are primitive survivals, anachronisms that have managed to carry their stubborn existence into the modern age of reason and science. He does not think that poetry is harmful, like religious superstition, but he would not have agreed with Arnold in finding in it a means of personal and social salvation.

Besides its positivistic character as demystifier of religion in the name of science, Tylor's version of culture has at least two other qualities that place it at variance with Arnold's. In his opening sentence, Tylor says that "Culture or Civilization, taken in its widest ethnographic sense, is that complex whole which includes knowledge, belief, art, morals, law, custom, and any other capabilities and habits acquired by man as a member of society." The important features of this definition are that it makes culture all-inclusive rather than discriminating, and that it makes it a universal possession of mankind. Clearly one does not need to go to Oxford or Cambridge to get culture of this sort: one can get it just as easily by growing up in a grass hutch in Tierra del Fuego. For Arnold, of course, culture is not everything which any society thinks and produces, and it is not the possession of everybody. His version of culture is only the intellectual, religious, and artistic part of "that complex whole" that makes up his own European heritage. And rather than being the possession of everybody, Arnoldian culture is the possession of almost nobody, or at best only of the weary remnant who struggle on through the blizzard of life in "Rugby Chapel." For modern anthropologists, no human condition exists like the one described by Wordsworth in *The Prelude,* "where grace / Of culture hath been utterly unknown."[27] But for Arnold, that seems to be the most frequent human condition: he looks out upon the darkling plain of the nineteenth century and sees "ignorant armies clashing by night."

Further, Tylor's attribution of some level of culture to everyone obviously pluralizes it. Before 1900 the plural form, "cultures," does not seem to occur at all in English except in the archaic sense of tilled fields. So the eighteenth-century poet, John Dyer, could describe a wagon traveling "through lively spreading cultures, pastures green."[28] Certainly Arnold's culture is always singular, always one thing no matter how inclusive, and this one thing is either the process or the result of a liberal education, just the best sort of education that one could get at Rugby and Oxford during the Victorian period. The intellectual and social meanings of culture began to be used in the plural form only quite recently, as the result of broad developments in intellectual and social history which converge in the 1860s—democratization and imperialism, the theory of evolution and the rise of anthropology.

Although Tylor seems not to have used the plural form of the word "culture," anthropologists were probably the first to do so, and it is perhaps first in the work of Franz Boas, starting in the 1880s, that cultural relativism appears in a fully conscious form.[29] In Boas and in the work of his student, Melville Herskovits, cultural relativism is elevated to the status of a moral ideal, one that can be compared to the very different moral ideal of culture that we find in Arnold. Boas calls the ideal of cultural relativism "a higher tolerance than the one we now profess," and Herskovits, in his book on *Cultural Relativism*, puts it this way: "The very core of cultural relativism is the social discipline that comes of respect for differences—mutual respect. Emphasis on the worth of many ways of life, not one, is an affirmation of the values in each culture. Such emphasis seeks to understand and to harmonize goals, not to judge and destroy those that do not dovetail with our own."[30] It would be difficult to exaggerate the impact of cultural relativism on modern values. It is an extreme extension of the transition to democracy, according to which the life-styles of all groups of men are viewed with respect, and it has been a potent factor in combating racism in all of its guises. At the same time, as Herbert Marcuse contends, democratic tolerance can become "repressive tolerance"; the problem of moral and political judgment is not solved by cultural relativism, no matter how beneficial it has been in breaking down prejudices. This version of the dialectic between democracy and authority is a modern form of the dilemma expressed by Mill in the idea of the "tyranny of the majority" and by Arnold in his anxiety for the preservation and spread of culture, part of the search generally in liberal theory for some union of intelligence with freedom.

In his chapter "Hebraism and Hellenism," Arnold turns to the new science of anthropology for support, but he gets from it something different from cultural relativism. Anthropology began as "ethnology," or a study of racial differences, a main purpose of which was to explain why some races were progressive and civilized, while others had remained stationary, lost in the Stone Age. But the theory that the races of man were distinct, immutable species was upset by Darwinism. From a study of the differences between races, anthropology developed into a study of the unity of human nature despite differences. In *Primitive Culture*, Tylor insists that the differences between human groups derive from historical circumstances rather than from race, and that beneath these differences human nature is everywhere the same.[31] In *Culture and Anarchy*, however, Arnold writes: "Science has now made visible to everybody the great and pregnant elements of difference which lie in race, and in how signal a manner they make the genius and history of an Indo-European people vary from those of a Semitic people" (141). Arnold's categories of "Hebraic" and "Hellenic" are racial ones, as are also the categories of German, French, English, and Celtic.

Although Arnold does not mean to set up his racial categories apart from history, and although his arguments suggest that any nation can adopt the virtues or vices of any other nation, the ahistorical nature of racial thinking tends to convert categories like Hebraic and Hellenic into timeless absolutes. In one sense, culture itself for Arnold stands virtually in opposition to history: the idea of "anarchy" might almost be translated into the idea of "history." Anarchy is quarreling, conflict, the clashing of ignorant armies, the hooting and the marching and the smashing of Hyde Park roughs, and the innumerable bickering and angry voices of democratic change. Culture, on the other hand, is forever rising above the ruck and chaos of change, a massively harmonious union of all "the best that has been known and said in the world," overarching experience like a heaven of pure ideas. In one of his letters to Clough, Arnold expresses his refusal to be "sucked for an hour even into the Time Stream" in which Clough and poets like him "plunge and bellow."[32] And yet Arnold obviously thinks of culture as an instrument of social improvement: culture "moves by the force, not merely or primarily of the scientific passion for pure knowledge, but also of the moral and social passion for doing good" (45). Although he hardly specifies what he means by "doing good," it is related to the "study of perfection" and to making "reason and the will of God prevail."

Despite the differences between Arnold and Tylor, they are similar in at least one respect. Neither Tylor's anthropology nor Arnold's humanism aims directly at solving the problems of democratic and social reform. In a general way, both are attempts to make the reform of ideas precede the reform of institutions. They both reverse the radical emphasis of the Benthamites and Dickens by substituting criticisms of modes of thought for criticisms of social structures. The liberations that Arnold and Tylor thought would result from their versions of intellectual reform, or from the humanities and the positivist social sciences, have been at best incomplete. Neither the Reform Bill of 1867 nor Forster's Education Act of 1870 was the product of a national consciousness illuminated by the positivist triumph over religion or by the hellenization of factories and railroads.

Furthermore, behind both *Culture and Anarchy* and *Primitive Culture* is the wish, familiar to every schoolmaster and perhaps every liberal reformer, to impose intelligent order on those who seem disorderly, unintelligent, "primitive" or "savage," creatures of darkness. Some form of this wish underlies all of the literature of reform. It is there in the Working Men's College and in the attempts of the Christian Socialists to teach the working class cooperation instead of competition; in Carlyle's invocation of heroes, and in Disraeli's remodeled aristocracy; in Mill's Malthusianism, and even in Dickens's innocent victimization of the poor for charitable purposes. Perhaps Mrs. Gaskell managed to appreciate the fact that the workers might have something to teach the other classes, and Mill grew in his awareness of the viability of working-class politics, particularly of trade unionism and the early varieties of socialism. And Dickens, Mayhew, and the *Punch* radicals understood the working-class (indeed, the universal) need for fun, and sympathized with the "low" and "cheap" forms of leisure activity that the workers enjoyed. But the middle-class spirit of reform involved not only the desire to remodel institutions for the benefit of the working class but also the schoolmaster's disposition to remodel other people's lives, and especially the lives of those who seemed to have no authentic values, politics, or culture of their own. The reform crisis of the 1860s brought out the schoolmasterly side of liberalism most strongly in Arnold, Eliot, Ruskin, and Maurice, as it also brought out the most reactionary side of Carlyle (in "Shooting Niagara"). But also during the 1850s and 1860s the trade unions became "respectable," and the "Friends of Labour"—men like J. M. Ludlow and John Stuart Mill as well as the authors of *Essays on Reform*—were learning to appreciate the values and opinions of the working class. Perhaps the working class might even teach the "instructed classes" how raw individualism could be tempered by cooperation and how the state could better express "ordinary selves" if not a "best self."[33]

As an anthropologist, Tylor had no direct hand in these political developments. But his attribution of some level of culture to all groups of men is related to the evolution of the idea of working-class culture, similar to and yet distinct from the earlier idea of folk culture, in the socialist and labor movements of the last third of the century. The authors of *Essays on Reform* approached this idea, and so did J. M. Ludlow and Lloyd Jones in their *Progress of the Working Class* (1867). But at least one other writer in the late 1860s explored it thoroughly, an amateur anthropologist very different from Tylor. In *Culture and Anarchy,* Arnold refers to "the Journeyman Engineer," Thomas Wright, who he says agrees with him about "perfection." According to Arnold, Wright recognizes that perfection "is an idea which the new democracy needs far more than the idea of the blessedness of the franchise, or the wonderfulness of its own industrial performances" (65). Wright does indeed deplore the lack of formal schooling of the working class, and he doubts that many working men are able to exercise the franchise intelligently. But Wright is more interested in showing that they have opinions, values, and "habits and customs" fully as understandable, human, and healthy as the "habits and customs" of the upper classes. His three books explore what may be called working-class culture: *Some Habits and Customs of the Working Classes* (1867), *The Great Unwashed* (1868), and *Our New Masters* (1873). In the preface to the first of these, Wright speaks of previous attempts by writers outside the working class to portray "the working man": "Many of these word-pictures of the working man are, as word-pictures, masterpieces, and are, considering that they are written by men outside of the classes which they treat, surprisingly accurate; but still, to a working man even the best of them plainly show a want of that knowledge of the minutiae of the inner life of the working classes which can only be thoroughly known to members of those classes. And it is . . . with a view to throwing some light upon this inner life . . . that the following papers have been written."[34]

Wright's criticism indicates both the main strength and the main weakness of the literature of reform. Carlyle, Dickens, Mill, and Mrs. Gaskell did create masterpieces of sympathetic observation, at the same time that they observed from a distance. Lesser writers like Disraeli and Kingsley were never much more than tourists in the world of slums and factories, sending home "fictions and tales of distant lands." Apart from Engels' *Condition of the Working Class,* Mill's *Principles of Political Economy,* and perhaps Mrs. Gaskell's industrial novels, most descriptions of the working class by middle-class writers between 1832 and 1867 are in some manner patronizing or reductive. Even in *London Labour and the London Poor,* Henry Mayhew deplores the "brutal" and "savage" mentality of his street people and offers sensational examples of their "benighted" condition. "The notions of morality among these people agree strangely . . . with those of many savage tribes." And, in discussing "the literature of the costermongers": "We have now had an inkling of the London costermonger's notions upon politics and religion. We have seen the brutified state in which he is allowed by society to remain, though possessing the same faculties and susceptibilities as ourselves—the same power to perceive and admire the forms of truth, beauty, and goodness, as even the very highest in the state. We have witnessed how, instinct with all the elements of manhood and beasthood, the qualities of the beast are principally developed in him, while those of the man are stunted in their growth."[35]

Mayhew's metaphor of savagery suggests the most serious limitation of the literature of reform: the inability of most middle-class writers to perceive working-class politics and values as rational alternatives to their own. In the slums or at Chartist meetings, liberal reformers perhaps inevitably felt like foreigners, and many of them write as if at any moment they may be assaulted by a bunch of cannibals. The new science of anthropology did little to dispel their fears. "In our great cities," Tylor writes, "the so-called 'dangerous classes' are sunk in hideous misery and depravity. If we have to strike a balance between the Papuans of New Caledonia and the communities of European beggars and thieves, we may sadly acknowledge that we have in our midst something worse than savagery" (I, 42-43). The likening of the mores of the poor to "something worse than savagery" in Tylor and in Mayhew is frequent also in Carlyle, Disraeli, Kingsley, Eliot, and Arnold. Here is a different sort of savagery in the midst of civilization from the survivals of primitive beliefs with which Tylor is mainly concerned. A similar statement comes from another great Victorian anthropologist, Sir John Lubbock, who in his study of *The Origin of Civilization* expresses the hope that "the blessings of civilization will not only be extended to other countries and to other nations, but that even in our own land they will be rendered more general and more equable; so that we shall not see before us always, as now, countrymen of our own living, in our very midst, a life worse than that of a savage."[36] Arnold is at least not guilty of the contradiction underlying Lubbock's statement. He is not so firm a believer as Tylor and Lubbock in the inevitability of progress, and he is less prone than they are to mistake middle-class Victorian values for "the blessings of civilization," which seem inexplicably to carry the blight of working-class "savagery" with them.

Arnold's and Tylor's concepts of culture represent two very different directions that liberalism took after the 1860s: one towards the cultural relativism of modern anthropology and the other towards the cultural prescriptiveness of modern literary studies. But in the 1850s and 1860s another position emerged in regard to the relationship between culture and reform, appearing first in Ruskin as early as *The Seven Lamps of Architecture* and reaching its fullest development in the socialism of William Morris. This is the position suggested by Morris when he says that "the cause of Art is the cause of the People." Art or culture is identified by Morris and to a large extent by Ruskin not with something that the "instructed classes" must administer to the "uninstructed," nor with something that the common people already possess, however imperfectly. It is identified by them instead with social justice itself. In Morris especially, art is the antithesis to the alienation and ugliness created by industrial capitalism, although it is not the instrument of its own realization.

Ruskin's great merit is to perceive the intimate connection between the quality of art or culture and the conditions of labor in a society. Far from rising free from social forms, as in Arnold, culture for Ruskin depends on social forms. And Morris carries Ruskin's perception of the dependence of culture upon social forms one step farther by identifying art with human freedom and fulfillment. He defines both art and freedom in terms of the utopian concept of nonalienated labor, or "pleasurable work." From Morris's perspective, art cannot promote reform, because the creation of beauty and the creation of social justice are both contingent upon a complete alteration of social relations. The reform of institutions must precede the reform of ideas. Of course the philosophical problem suggested here is not completely resolved by Morris's Marxism any more than it is by Arnold's theory of culture. Institutions do not change for the better without plan. As Marx himself understood, the economic substructure is so entangled with the cultural superstructure that one cannot logically be said to determine the other.

Morris's Marxism is a symptom of the general weakening of liberal attitudes in the last quarter of the century, and it is both akin to and the antithesis of another symptom of the same process: social Darwinism. Marxism and social Darwinism by no means exhaust the set of political theories between 1870 and 1900, but their increasing strength and the relationship between them as theories based upon change through conflict do indicate the loss of energy in the reform-minded liberalism that was dominant between 1832 and 1867.[37] Despite its limitations, the literature of reform expresses a faith in the ability of people to improve themselves and their institutions through rational and peaceful political processes—a faith at least partially realized in the record of welfare and democratic legislation from Althorp's Factory Act of 1833 through Forster's Education Act of 1870. Even the transition from the Benthamite and Dickensian emphasis on reform to the "advanced conservative liberal" emphasis on progress did not spell the end of that faith. If the idea of inevitable progress was often used to forestall demands for reform, it also meant that history itself followed a rational plan of improvement. The idea of progress suggested that the machine tended itself, while the idea of reform suggested that it needed tending, but otherwise both forms of liberal theory were optimistic about society and human nature. Marxism and social Darwinism absorbed and qualified the idea of progress, partly by declaring that the machinery of history could not work smoothly to the advantage of all individuals or all nations. (For Marxism, it could in the future, after the revolution; for social Darwinism, it never could.) Dickens, Mill, and Ruskin knew that it did not, but insisted that it should. Much of their greatness and of the literature of reform generally derives from the belief that there is nothing inevitable about injustice, and that people can end it by restructuring their institutions to match their ideals. Their optimism—critical, reform-minded, and based on people rather than machinery—was the finest product of the culture that the Victorians themselves created.

Notes
Index

Notes

Introduction

1. Two discussions of the relations between literature and society which have influenced this study are Raymond Williams, *Culture and Society, 1780-1950* (1958; New York: Harper and Row, 1966), and Jean-Paul Sartre, *Search for a Method,* tr. Hazel Barnes (New York: Knopf, 1963).

2. For recent surveys of political currents and attitudes in the 1830s, see Alexander Llewellyn, *The Decade of Reform: The 1830s* (Newton Abbot: David and Charles; New York: St. Martin's Press, 1972); Norman Gash, *Reaction and Reconstruction in English Politics, 1832-1852* (New York: Oxford University Press, 1965); J. F. C. Harrison, *The Early Victorians, 1832-1861* (New York: Praeger; London: Weidenfeld and Nicolson, 1971); and G. B. A. M. Finlayson, *Decade of Reform: England in the Eighteen-Thirties* (1969; New York: Norton, 1970).

3. See, for instance, G. M. Young, *Portrait of an Age* (1936; New York: Oxford University Press, 1960); W. L. Burn, *The Age of Equipoise* (London: Allen and Unwin, 1964); Asa Briggs, *The Making of Modern England, 1783-1867* (1959; New York: Harper & Row, 1965); and Geoffrey Best, *Mid-Victorian Britain, 1851-1875* (1971; New York: Schocken Books, 1972). There are also useful surveys of specific reform movements in J. T. Ward, ed., *Popular Movements, c. 1830-1850* (London: Macmillan, 1970), and Derek Fraser, *The Evolution of the British Welfare State* (London: Macmillan, 1973).

4. For an interesting analysis of the impact of the principle of limited liability on the novel, see N. N. Feltes, "Community and the Limits of Liability in Two Mid-Victorian Novels," *Victorian Studies,* June 1974, pp. 355-369.

5. S. G. Checkland, *The Rise of Industrial Society in England, 1815-1885* (London: Longmans, Green, 1964), p. 27.

6. The quotations are from Derrick Leon, *Ruskin, the Great Victorian* (1949; Hamden, Connecticut: Archon Books, 1969), p. 296. See also chapter 9 for what is said about critical responses to Dickens in the 1850s and after.

7. Sir Robert Peel, "The Tamworth Manifesto," in *English Historical Documents, 1833-1874,* ed. G. M. Young and W. D. Handcock (New York: Oxford University Press, 1956), pp. 128-129.

8. "Progress," *Chambers's Edinburgh Journal,* Feb. 1, 1851, pp. 65-66.

9. "The Cant of 'Progress,' " *Hogg's Weekly Instructor,* n.s. 1 (1848), 49.

10. John William Draper, *A History of the Intellectual Development of Europe,* 2 vols. (1863; London: George Bell, 1884), II, 400. I owe this example to Sidney Pollard, *The Idea of Progress* (Harmondsworth and Baltimore: Penguin Books, 1971), p. 146. Compare Spencer's "Development Hypothesis," Bagehot in *Physics and Politics,* and T. H. Buckle in *Civilization in England.*

11. For the contradiction between the antireform quiescence of much middle-

class culture after 1848 and the actual record of legislative activity in the same period, see Burn, *The Age of Equipoise,* ch. 4, and Briggs, *The Making of Modern England, 1784-1867,* pp. 429-445.

12. George Eliot, "Felix Holt's Address to the Working Men," in *The Essays of George Eliot,* ed. Thomas Pinney (London: Routledge and Kegan Paul, 1963), p. 418, and *Felix Holt, the Radical* (Boston: Rosehill Limited Edition, 1893), III, 247.

13. Best, *Mid-Victorian Britain, 1851-1875,* p. ix. While discussing the great difficulties in arriving at empirically verifiable definitions of class terminology, G. Kitson Clark says: "It might almost be said that the best definition of the middle class is that it was made up of those people who thought themselves to be middle class and were allowed by their neighbours to be so, or were accused of it." Clark, *The Making of Victorian England* (1962; New York: Atheneum, 1967), p. 119. For those interested in more rigorous examinations of class consciousness and ideology than mine, see Harold Perkin, *The Origins of Modern English Society, 1780-1880* (London and Toronto: Routledge and Kegan Paul, 1969), and R. S. Neale, *Class and Ideology in the Nineteenth Century* (London and Boston: Routledge and Kegan Paul, 1972). See also the superb brief survey by T. B. Bottomore, *Classes in Modern Society* (London: Allen and Unwin, 1965).

14. Lucien Goldmann, *The Human Sciences and Philosophy* (1969; London and New York: Cape Editions, 1973), p. 63; Alexis de Tocqueville, *Democracy in America,* 2 vols. (New York: Knopf, 1948), II, 60.

Chapter I: The Literature of the 1830s

1. Young, *Portrait of an Age,* p. 12.

2. Elie Halévy, *The Triumph of Reform, 1830-1841,* tr. E. I. Watkin (New York: Barnes & Noble, 1961), p. 51.

3. Thomas Carlyle, "Signs of the Times," in the Centenary Edition of the *Works of Thomas Carlyle,* 30 vols. (London: Chapman & Hall, 1896-1899), XXVII, 58.

4. John Wade, "Dedication to the People," *The Extraordinary Black Book or Reformer's Bible* (London: E. Wilson, 1832), p. xiv.

5. Joseph Parkes in *The English Radical Tradition, 1763-1914,* ed. S. Maccoby (1952; London: Adam and Charles Black, 1966), p. 123.

6. Thomas Carlyle, *New Letters,* ed. Alexander Carlyle, 2 vols. (London: John Lane, 1904), I, 69.

7. John Stuart Mill, *Autobiography, and Other Writings,* ed. Jack Stillinger (Boston: Houghton Mifflin, 1969), pp. 117-118.

8. Reprinted in Maccoby, *The English Radical Tradition,* p. 129.

9. Edward Bulwer-Lytton, *England and the English,* 2 vols. (London: Richard Bentley, 1833), II, 110.

10. Ibid., II, 141.

11. Carlyle, "Signs of the Times," *Works,* XXVII, 77.

12. "Journalism in France," *British Quarterly Review,* 3 (Feb. and May 1846), 500.
13. Ibid., p. 508. See also Bulwer, *England and the English,* II, 62-65: The absence of great works is due to "the revolution that has been effected by Periodical Literature."
14. Howitt quoted by Carl Woodring, *Victorian Samplers: William and Mary Howitt* (Lawrence: Universtiy of Kansas Press, 1952), p. 69.
15. Thomas Babington Macaulay, *The Works of Lord Macaulay,* ed. Lady Trevelyan, 8 vols. (London: Longmans, Green, 1879), VIII, 24 (speech of March 2, 1831). Edmund Burke, *Reflections on the Revolution in France* (1910; London: Everyman's Library, 1964), pp. 19-20.
16. Dr. John Bowring, " 'Died of Starvation'—Coroners' Inquests," in Archibald Prentice, *History of the Anti-Corn Law League,* 2 vols. (London: W. and F. G. Cash, 1853), I, 281-282.
17. Carlyle, "Corn-Law Rhymes," *Works,* XXVIII, 150.
18. Joseph Hamburger, *James Mill and the Art of Revolution* (New Haven: Yale University Press, 1963).
19. Macaulay, *Works,* VIII, 71-72 (Speech of December 16, 1831).
20. Macaulay, "Mill's Essay on Government," *Works,* V, 265. Macaulay disagrees with James Mill about government, but not about the middle class.
21. Macaulay, *Works,* I, 332.
22. Macaulay, "Southey's Colloquies," *Works,* V, 366.
23. Harriet Martineau, *A History of the Thirty Years' Peace, 1816-1846,* 4 vols. (London: George Bell, 1877), II, 344-348. See also Bulwer, *England and the English,* II, ch. 3, and Richard D. Altick, *The English Common Reader* (1957; Chicago: University of Chicago Press, 1963), pp. 332-348.
24. Charles Knight, *Passages in a Working Life,* 3 vols. (1864; Shannon: Irish University Press, 1971), I, 260.
25. *Chambers's Journal* quoted by Altick, *The English Common Reader,* p. 337.
26. Jerrold quoted by R. K. Webb, *Harriet Martineau, a Radical Victorian* (New York: Columbia University Press, 1960), p. 299. On evangelical tracts, see Maurice J. Quinlan, *Victorian Prelude: A History of English Manners, 1700-1830* (New York: Columbia University Press, 1941).
27. G. D. H. Cole, *The Life of William Cobbett* (London: William Collins, 1927), pp. 138-140.
28. *Crotchet Castle,* in *The Works of Thomas Love Peacock,* 10 vols. (London: Constable, 1924), IV, 187, 199-200.
29. William Chambers, *Memoir of Robert Chambers, with Autobiographic Reminiscences of William Chambers* (New York: Scribner's, 1872), p. 237.
30. Ibid., p. 283. See also Altick, *The English Common Reader,* p. 5.
31. Chambers, *Memoir,* p. 242.
32. Webb, *Harriet Martineau,* pp. 113-114.
33. Knight, *Passages in a Working Life,* II, 315.
34. *Chambers's Journal* quoted by Altick, *The English Common Reader,* p. 333.
35. On Benthamite hostility to fiction, see George L. Nesbitt, *Benthamite Re-*

viewing: The First Twelve Years of the Westminster Review, 1824-1836 (New York: Columbia University Press, 1934), pp. 96-129. On evangelical hostility, see Quinlan, *Victorian Prelude*, and John Tinnon Taylor, *Early Opposition to the Novel, 1760-1830* (New York: King's Crown Press, 1943).

36. Thomas Arnold, *The Miscellaneous Works of Thomas Arnold, D.D.* (London: B. Fellowes, 1845), p. 252.

37. Ibid., p. 175.

38. Charles Dickens, preface to the "cheap edition" of *The Posthumous Papers of the Pickwick Club* (1948; New York: Oxford Illustrated Dickens, 1969), p. xiii. Page numbers from the Oxford Illustrated Dickens are given in parentheses throughout the text.

39. Walter Jerrold, *Douglas Jerrold, Dramatist and Wit,* 2 vols. (London: Hodder & Stoughton, 1914), II, 208.

40. Michael Booth, *English Melodrama* (London: Herbert Jenkins, 1965), pp. 123-124.

41. Hugh McDowall Clokie and J. William Robinson, *Royal Commissions of Inquiry* (Stanford: Stanford University Press, 1937), p. 67. In *Portrait of an Age,* G. M. Young says that "no community in history had ever been submitted to so searching an examination." See also the first volume of the *Journal of the Statistical Society,* 1838, especially the introduction and pp. 48-50.

42. Carlyle, *Chartism,* in *Works,* XXIX, 125.

43. Perkin, *The Origins of Modern English Society,* p. 165.

44. Charles Kingsley, *Yeast* (London and New York: Everyman's Library, 1928), p. 103.

45. Charles Dickens, "The Mudfog Association," *Bentley's Miscellany,* 2 (1837), 399.

46. William Cyples, "Morality of the Doctrine of Averages," *Cornhill Magazine,* 10 (1864), 218-224.

47. Charles Bray, *The Philosophy of Necessity* (1841; London: Longmans, Green, 1889), p. 11.

48. *The Quarterly Review,* 70 (1842), 159; *The Spectator,* May 14, 1842, p. 462.

49. For Disraeli, see Sheila M. Smith, "Willenhall and Wodgate: Disraeli's Use of Bluebook Evidence," *Review of English Studies,* 13 (November 1962), 368-384; for Mrs. Trollope, see W. H. Chaloner, "Mrs. Trollope and the Early Factory System," *Victorian Studies,* 4 (1961), 159-166; and for Elizabeth Barrett, see Cyril Pearl, *Always Morning: The Life of R. H. Horne* (Melbourne: F. W. Cheshire, 1960), pp. 60-61.

50. Carlyle, *Chartism,* in *Works,* XXIX, 124-129.

51. Carlyle, "Biography," *Works,* XXVIII, 49-52.

52. Quoted by Harald Westergaard, *Contributions to the History of Statistics* (London: P. S. King, 1932), pp. 141-142.

53. Quoted by John Butt and Kathleen Tillotson, *Dickens at Work* (London: Methuen, 1957), p. 190.

54. William Rathbone Greg, *Essays on Political and Social Science,* 2 vols. (Lon-

don: Longman, 1853), I, 469; Harriet Martineau, *The Factory Controversy: A Warning against Meddling Legislation* (Manchester, 1855), p. 35; and John Stuart Mill, "The Claims of Labour," in *The Collected Works,* ed. J. M. Robson, 13 vols. (Toronto: University of Toronto Press, 1967), IV, 363-390.

55. Porter, introduction to *The Progress of the Nation.* Westergaard, *Contributions to the History of Statistics,* p. 172.

56. William Farr, "Inaugural Address," *Journal of the Statistical Society,* 35 (1872), 427.

57. J. Hillis Miller, *Charles Dickens: The World of His Novels* (1958; Bloomington: Indiana University Press, 1969), pp. xv-xvi.

58. Knight, *Passages in a Working Life,* I, 346. Oliver MacDonagh, David Roberts, G. Kitson Clark, and other recent historians have warned against overestimating the influence of Benthamism in government. But in several respects their revisionist findings may not be applicable to the whole culture. See L. J. Hume, "Jeremy Bentham and the Nineteenth-Century Revolution in Government," *Historical Journal,* 10 (1967), 361-375, for a review of the arguments. Whatever its impact on government, the importance of Benthamism as an item of debate in literature, its more general contemporary usage to cover all forms of "scientific" and "economical" social planning, and the prominence of men at least influenced by it in the politics of the 1830s and after (the Mills, Grote, Roebuck, Austin, Hume, Chadwick, Southwood Smith, Nassau Senior, and others) make it appropriate to refer to Benthamism as a highly important factor in the culture of the period, and especially in the early 1830s.

Chapter II: Benthamite and Anti-Benthamite Fiction

1. Keith Hollingsworth, *The Newgate Novel, 1830-1847* (Detroit: Wayne State University Press, 1963), p. 77; Louis Cazamian, *Le roman social en Angleterre,* 2 vols. (Paris: Didier, n.d.), I, 89.

2. Edward Bulwer-Lytton, *Paul Clifford* (Boston: Knebworth Limited Edition, 1892), p. 226. Page numbers from this edition are given in the text hereafter.

3. Edward Bulwer-Lytton, *The Life, Letters, and Literary Remains of Edward Bulwer, Lord Lytton,* 2 vols. (London: Kegan Paul, 1883), II, 244.

4. Mill, *Autobiography, and Other Writings,* pp. 65-66. See also Frederick Maurice, *The Life of Frederick Denison Maurice, Chiefly Told in His Own Letters,* 2 vols. (New York: Scribner's, 1884), II, 7: "I never heard a stronger witness for the power of the will to regulate and command circumstances than came from those Socialist worshippers of circumstances."

5. R. H. Horne, *New Spirit of the Age,* 2 vols. (London: Smith, Elder, 1844), II, 200.

6. For a list of the characters' identities, see Bulwer-Lytton, *The Life . . . of . . . Lord Lytton,* II, 247-249.

7. Mill quoted by Webb, *Harriet Martineau,* p. 120. Webb (p. 122) also cites John Doherty, the trade unionist, for commending *A Manchester Strike* for its "veracity" in *The Poor Man's Advocate,* September 29, 1832. And see Ivanka Kovačević, *Fact into Fiction: English Literature and the Industrial Scene, 1750-1850* (Leicester: Leicester University Press, 1975), pp. 110-127.

8. Quoted by Webb, *Harriet Martineau,* p. 123.

9. See "Charitable Institutions," *Westminster Review,* July 1824, pp. 97-121.

10. Harriet Martineau, *Cousin Marshall,* vol. VII of *Illustrations of Political Economy* (Boston: Leonard Bowles, 1833), pp. 186-187.

11. Mill, *Autobiography, and Other Writings,* p. 149.

12. Ibid., p. 106.

13. See Humphry House, *The Dickens World* (1941; New York: Oxford University Press, 1965), p. 85, and George Ford, "Self-Help and the Helpless in *Bleak House*," in *From Jane Austen to Joseph Conrad,* ed. Robert C. Rathburn and Martin Steinmann (Minneapolis: University of Minnesota Press, 1958), pp. 92-105.

14. Sir Henry Maine, *Popular Government,* p. 153, quoted by A. V. Dicey, *Lectures on the Relation between Law and Public Opinion in England* (London: Macmillan, 1905), p. 417.

15. Ibid., pp. 417-418.

16. Charles Dickens, *Oliver Twist* (New York: Oxford Illustrated Dickens, 1949), p. 134. Page numbers are given in the text hereafter.

17. Edgar Johnson, *Charles Dickens: His Tragedy and Triumph,* 2 vols. (New York: Simon and Schuster, 1952), I, 39.

18. Ibid., I, 43.

19. Arnold Kettle, *An Introduction to the Novel* (1957; New York: Harper and Row, 1968), p. 128.

20. Jeremy Bentham, *Introduction to the Principles of Morals and Legislation* (London: Athlone Press, 1970), p. 70.

21. James Mill quoted by Eli Halévy, *The Growth of Philosophic Radicalism* (1928; Boston: Beacon Press, 1955), p. 290.

22. *St. Giles and St. James* in *The Writings of Douglas Jerrold,* 8 vols. (London: Bradbury and Evans, 1851), I, iii.

23. Mill starts his chapter "On the Probable Futurity of the Labouring Classes" in *Principles of Political Economy* with a rejection of "the theory of dependence and protection" in favor of "that of self-dependence." "The poor have come out of leading-strings, and cannot any longer be governed or treated like children. To their own qualities must now be commended the care of their destiny." See also Ford, "Self-Help and the Helpless in *Bleak House.*"

24. Samuel Smiles, *Autobiography,* ed. Thomas Mackay (New York: Dutton, 1905), p. 132.

25. On the principle of "least eligibility," see S. E. Finer, *Life and Times of Sir Edwin Chadwick* (London: Methuen, 1952), pp. 80-85; and *Report from His Majesty's Commissioners for Inquiring into . . . the Poor Laws* (1834),

extract in *English Historical Documents, 1833-1874,* ed. Young and Hand-cock, p. 698.

26. Charles Dickens, *Letters,* ed. Madeline House and Graham Storey, 3 vols. (London: Pilgrim Edition, 1965-1974), III, 330.

27. Charles Dickens, "Postscript," *Our Mutual Friend* (New York: Oxford Il-lustrated Dickens, 1952), pp. 821-822.

28. Gordon N. Ray, *Thackeray: The Uses of Adversity, 1811-1846* (New York: McGraw-Hill, 1955), p. 380.

29. Samuel Warren, *Passages from the Diary of a Late Physician,* 2 vols. (Paris: Baudry's European Library, 1838), I, 348-349. See Michael Steig, "Subver-sive Grotesque in Samuel Warren's *Ten Thousand a-Year,*" *Nineteenth-Century Fiction* 24 (1969), 154-168.

30. Mrs. Charlotte Elizabeth Tonna, *Personal Recollections* (New York: John S. Taylor, 1844), p. 78.

31. Ibid., pp. 292-297.

32. Mrs. Tonna, *Helen Fleetwood,* 5th American edition (New York: Scribner's, 1852), p. 127. For more sympathetic readings of Mrs. Tonna's fiction than mine, see Cazamian, *Le roman social en Angleterre,* and Kovačević, *Fact into Fiction,* pp. 101-103, 303-312.

33. Joseph Raynor Stephens quoted by G. D. H. Cole, *Chartist Portraits* (Lon-don: Macmillan, 1941), p. 63.

34. Rev. William Gresley, *Charles Lever: The Man of the Nineteenth Century* (London: James Burn, 1841), p. 34. Page numbers are given in the text hereafter.

35. William Wordsworth, "Distractions," *Ecclesiastical Sonnets* 41, in *The Po-etical Works* (1904; New York: Oxford Standard Authors, 1965), p. 345.

36. Wordsworth, *Sonnets Dedicated to Liberty and Order* 12, in *The Poetical Works,* p. 404.

37. Sonnet 2, p. 402.

38. Sonnet 11, p. 404.

Chapter III: The Lessons of Revolution

1. Thomas Carlyle, *The French Revolution,* in *Works* (London: Centenary Edi-tion, 1896-1899), IV, 313. Volume and page numbers are given in the text hereafter.

2. John Holloway, *The Victorian Sage* (1953; New York: Norton, 1965), pp. 58-75; and H. M. Leicester, "The Dialectic of Romantic Historiography," *Victorian Studies,* 15 (September 1971), 5-17.

3. Hevda Ben-Israel, *English Historians of the French Revolution* (New York: Cambridge University Press, 1968), p. 103. See also the arguments repro-duced in Joseph Hamburger, *James Mill and the Art of Revolution* (New Haven: Yale University Press, 1963), p. 35.

4. George Rudé, *Revolutionary Europe, 1783-1815* (Cleveland and New York: Meridian Books, 1964), pp. 133-134.

5. Henry Merivale in the *Edinburgh Review,* July 1840, reprinted in *Thomas Carlyle: The Critical Heritage,* ed. Jules Paul Seigel (London and Boston: Routledge and Kegan Paul, 1971), p. 81.
6. Alexis de Tocqueville, *The Old Regimé and the French Revolution,* tr. Stuart Gilbert (Garden City, N.Y.: Anchor Books, 1953), p. 174.
7. Macaulay, *Works,* VIII, 30 (speech of July 5, 1831).
8. George Rudé, *Interpretations of the French Revolution* (London: Routledge, 1961), pp. 20-21.
9. Ben-Israel, *English Historians of the French Revolution,* p. 149.
10. Thackeray in *The Times,* August 3, 1837, reprinted in *Thomas Carlyle: The Critical Heritage,* ed. Seigel, p. 69.
11. Quoted by Ben-Israel, *English Historians of the French Revolution,* p. 131 n.
12. William Hazlitt, "Rev. Mr. Irving," in *Lectures on English Poets, and The Spirit of the Age* (London and New York: Everyman's Library, 1910), pp. 207-208.
13. Thomas Carlyle, *Reminiscences* (1932; London: Dent, 1972), pp. 305-306. Page numbers are given in the text hereafter.
14. Alfred Cobban, "Carlyle's French Revolution," *History,* 48 (October 1963), 309.
15. Quoted by Merryn Williams, ed., *Revolutions, 1775-1830* (Harmondsworth: Penguin Books, 1971), p. 100.
16. On peasant class consciousness, see E. J. Hobsbawm, "Class-Consciousness in History," in *Aspects of History and Class Consciousness* (New York: Herder and Herder, 1971), pp. 5-21, and the quotation from Marx on p. 19 n4.
17. James Anthony Froude, *Thomas Carlyle: A History of the First Forty Years of His Life,* 2 vols. (New York: Scribner's, 1906), I, 1.
18. Thomas Carlyle to James Fraser, May 27, 1833, *Letters, 1826-1836,* ed. Charles Eliot Norton, 2 vols. (London: Macmillan, 1888), II, 105-106.
19. Giuseppe Mazzini, "The French Revolution," *Monthly Chronicle,* January 1840, p. 84.

Chapter IV: Two Responses to Chartism: Dickens and Disraeli

1. Henry Merivale in *Thomas Carlyle: The Critical Heritage,* ed. Seigel, pp. 81-82.
2. Horne, *New Spirit of the Age,* II, 273.
3. Friedrich Engels, *The Condition of the Working Class in England,* in *Karl Marx and Frederick Engels on Britain* (Moscow: Foreign Languages Publishing House, 1962), p. 334.
4. Macaulay, *Works,* VIII, 222.
5. Matthew attributes the "Tarpeian Rock" statement to one of his father's unpublished letters, but the Roman slave rebellion analogy is frequent in his published works. See Thomas Arnold, *Miscellaneous Works,* pp. 492-496; and Matthew Arnold, *Culture and Anarchy,* ed. J. Dover Wilson (1932; New York: Cambridge University Press, 1963), p. 203.

6. Edward Bulwer-Lytton, *Last of the Barons* (1843; Philadelphia: Lippincott, 1881), pp. v-vi. See Curtis Dahl, "History on the Hustings: Bulwer-Lytton's Historical Novels of Politics," in *From Jane Austen to Joseph Conrad*, ed. Rathburn and Steinmann, pp. 60-71.

7. Charles Dickens, *Barnaby Rudge: A Tale of the Riots of 'Eighty* (1954; New York: Oxford Illustrated Dickens, 1968), p. 288. Pages are given in the text hereafter.

8. Quoted by J. Paul DeCastro, *The Gordon Riots* (New York: Oxford University Press, 1946), pp. 80, 217.

9. DeCastro, *The Gordon Riots,* pp. 29-30.

10. Humphry House, *The Dickens World,* p. 179.

11. See R. G. Gammage, *History of the Chartist Movement* (1854; Newcastle: Browne and Browne, 1894), pp. 94-95, for a description of the torchlight meetings of 1838.

12. Stephen Marcus, *From Pickwick to Dombey* (New York: Basic Books, 1965), ch. 5.

13. Charles Dickens to S. Lamon Blanchard, February 9, 1839, in *Letters* (Pilgrim Edition), I, 507.

14. John Butt and Kathleen Tillotson, *Dickens at Work* (London: Methuen, 1957), p. 82. Avrom Fleishman quotes the letter to Blanchard to show that "it is not the Chartists or other Victorian mobs that Dickens has in mind but the anarchic tendency in modern civilization at large." *The English Historical Novel* (Baltimore: Johns Hopkins, 1971), p. 106. This is simply not the case.

15. Dickens to Edward Marlborough Fitzgerald, December 29, 1838, *Letters* (Pilgrim Edition), I, 484.

16. Dickens to Mrs. Charles Dickens, November 1, 1838, *Letters* (Pilgrim Edition), I, 447.

17. December 29, 1838, *Letters* (Pilgrim Edition), I, 484.

18. In *Dickens: The Critical Heritage,* ed. Philip Collins (London: Routledge and Kegan Paul, 1971), p. 78.

19. Dickens, *Letters* (Pilgrim Edition), II, 359-360.

20. Dickens, *Letters* (Pilgrim Edition), III, 278-285. There is also Scrooge's glimpse of miners' children in *A Christmas Carol.*

21. Dickens, *Letters* (Pilgrim Edition), I, 483.

22. Dickens, *American Notes and Pictures from Italy* (New York: Oxford Illustrated Dickens, 1957), p. 66. Page numbers are given in the text hereafter.

23. Smith seems to have sent Dickens a preview of the second report of the Children's Employment Commission, apparently in the expectation that he would take up the cause of working children in one of his novels. But Dickens was reluctant to do so. He says that the question of child labor "involves the whole subject of the condition of the mass of people in this country. And I greatly fear that until Governments are honest, and Parliaments pure, and Great men less considered, and small men more so, it is almost a Cruelty to limit, even the dreadful hours and ways [sic] of Labor which at this time

prevail.'' *Letters* (Pilgrim Edition), III, 435-436. See also *Charles Dickens' Uncollected Writings from Household Words, 1850-1859,* ed. Harry Stone, 2 vols. (Bloomington: Indiana University Press, 1968), II, 561.

24. To Southwood Smith, March 6, 1843, *Letters* (Pilgrim Edition), III, 459-460.

25. *Letters* (Pilgrim Edition), March 10, 1843.

26. Monroe Engel, *The Maturity of Dickens* (Cambridge: Harvard University Press, 1959), p. 58.

27. *The Annual Register,* 1838, p. 204.

28. Sidney and Beatrice Webb, *The History of Trade Unionism,* rev. ed. (London and New York: Longmans, Green, 1920), p. 170, and Archibald Swinton, *Report of the Trial of Thomas Hunter* (Edinburgh, 1838).

29. Sir Archibald Alison on trade union oaths, in *Report of the Select Committee on Combinations, Parliamentary Papers, 1837-1838,* VIII, 118.

30. Elizabeth Cleghorn Gaskell, *Mary Barton* (London and New York: Everyman's Library, 1961), p. 179.

31. Humphry House, *The Dickens World,* p. 208.

32. For example, Richard Monckton Milnes, ''The Emancipation of the Jews,'' *Edinburgh Review,* July 1847, p. 75.

33. Disraeli, *Sybil,* pp. 10-11. Quotations from *Sybil* and *Coningsby* are from the Hughenden Edition (London, 1881), VIII and VII. Page numbers are given in the text hereafter.

34. *Hansard's Debates,* June 12, 1839, cols. 246-252.

35. Arnold Kettle, ''The Early Victorian Social-Problem Novel,'' in *From Dickens to Hardy,* ed. Boris Ford (Harmondsworth and Baltimore: Penguin Books, 1968), p. 176. See also John Lucas, ''Mrs. Gaskell and Brotherhood,'' *Tradition and Tolerance in Nineteenth-Century Fiction,* ed. David Howard, John Lucas, and John Goode (New York: Barnes & Noble, 1967), p. 154.

36. Edward Baines, Jr., *History of the Cotton Manufacture in Great Britain* (London: Fisher, 1835), p. 480: ''Very many of the poor have not the means either of educating their children, or of supporting them in idleness . . . therefore, to forbid the admission of such children into mills is, in fact, to consign them to the streets, and to deprive them of that food which their work might procure.''

37. Sheila M. Smith, ''Willenhall and Wodgate: Disraeli's Use of Bluebook Evidence,'' *Review of English Studies,* November 1962, pp. 368-384.

38. William F. Monypenny and G. E. Buckle, *The Life of Benjamin Disraeli,* 2 vols. (London: Murray, 1929), I, 651.

39. ''Mr. Disraeli,'' in *Walter Bagehot,* ed. Norman St. John-Stevas (Bloomington: Indiana University Press, 1959), p. 411.

40. George Orwell, ''Charles Dickens,'' *A Collection of Essays* (Garden City, N.Y.: Anchor Books, 1954), p. 59. John Butt and Kathleen Tillotson show that in the plans for the weekly numbers of *Hard Times* '' 'Mill Pictures' are

indeed mentioned . . . but the subject of principal importance here is 'Law of Divorce' '' (*Dickens at Work,* p. 210).

41. George Gissing, *Charles Dickens: A Critical Study* (New York: Dodd, Mead, 1898), p. 281.

42. K. J. Fielding and Anne Smith, "*Hard Times* and the Factory Controversy," *Nineteenth-Century Fiction,* March 1970, p. 417. This essay is excellent on the industrial background of *Hard Times.*

43. Karl Marx and Friedrich Engels, "Manifesto of the Communist Party," *Basic Writings on Politics and Philosophy,* ed. Lewis S. Feuer (Garden City, N. Y.: Anchor Books, 1959), p. 30.

Chapter V: The Entrepreneurial Ideal

1. Sir Arthur Helps, *The Claims of Labour: An Essay on the Duties of the Employers to the Employed* (1844; London: William Pickering, 1845), p. 34. Page numbers are given in the text hereafter.

2. The theory of the identity of interests between labor and capital is not axiomatic in the writings of political economists. According to Ricardo: "I now . . . see reason to be satisfied that the one fund, from which landlords and capitalists derive their revenue, may increase, while the other, that upon which the labouring class mainly depend, may diminish, and therefore it follows, if I am right, that the same cause which may increase the net revenue of the country may at the same time render the population redundant, and deteriorate the condition of the labourer." Marx and Engels agreed: Ricardo and Malthus demonstrated very clearly how the rich may get richer while the poor get poorer. David Ricardo, *The Principles of Political Economy and Taxation* (London: Everyman's Library, n.d.), p. 264.

3. Charles Dickens, *Little Dorrit* (New York: Oxford Illustrated Dickens, 1953), p. 514. Page numbers are given in the text hereafter.

4. Archibald Prentice, *History of the Anti-Corn Law League,* 2 vols. (London, 1853), I, 57-58.

5. Dickens in *The Daily News,* quoted by Henry Richard Fox Bourne, *English Newspapers: Chapters in the History of Journalism,* 2 vols. (London: Chatto & Windus, 1887), II, 141.

6. John Bright quoted by C. R. Fay, *The Corn Laws and Social England* (New York: Cambridge University Press, 1932), p. 101.

7. R. H. Horne, *Orion,* ed. Eric Partridge (London: Scholartis Press, 1928), I (2), 14.

8. In *Golden Times: Human Documents of the Victorian Age,* ed. E. Royston Pike (New York: Praeger, 1967), p. 45.

9. Quoted by Norman McCord, *The Anti-Corn Law League, 1838-1846* (London: Allen and Unwin, 1958), p. 69.

10. See Chapter IV.

11. Mrs. Catherine Gore, *The Two Aristocracies,* 3 vols. (London: Hurst and Blackett, 1857), III, 65.

12. See Chapter IX. See also George Ford, *Dickens and His Readers* (1955; New York: Norton, 1965), ch. 5.

13. J. L. and Barbara Hammond, *The Age of the Chartists, 1832-1854* (1930; Hamden, Conn.: Archon Books, 1962), p. 257.

14. Charles Greville quoted by Christopher Dawson, "The Humanitarians," in *Ideas and Beliefs of the Victorians* (New York: Dutton, 1966), p. 250.

15. R. G. G. Price, *A History of Punch* (London: Collins, 1957), p. 47; *The Memorials of Thomas Hood,* 2 vols. (London: Edward Moxon, 1860), II, 182.

16. Thomas Hood to Sir Robert Peel, *The Memorials of Thomas Hood,* II, 257.

17. Leigh Hunt, "Hood's *Poems,*" *Edinburgh Review,* April 1846, p. 198.

18. Gerald Massey, "Thomas Hood, Poet and Punster," *Hogg's Instructor,* 3d ser., 4 (January-June 1855), 326.

19. Gerald Massey, *Poems and Ballads* (New York: J. C. Derby, 1854), p. 67.

20. John Ruskin to Charles Eliot Norton, June 19, 1870, reprinted in *Charles Dickens: A Critical Anthology,* ed. Stephen Wall (Harmondsworth and Baltimore: Penguin Books, 1970), p. 191.

21. Arnold, *Culture and Anarchy,* p. 80.

22. Dinah Mulock (Mrs. Craik), *John Halifax, Gentleman* (1906; London and New York: Everyman's Library, 1950), p. 193. Page numbers are given in the text hereafter. There is a useful commentary on *John Halifax,* including a comparison with *Great Expectations,* in Robin Gilmour, "Dickens and the Self-Help Idea," in *The Victorians and Social Protest,* ed. J. Butt and I. F. Clarke (Newton Abbot: David and Charles, 1973), pp. 71-101.

23. See Asa Briggs, *Victorian People* (1955; New York: Harper Colophon Books, 1963), pp. 116-139.

24. For James Mill and the middle class, see Chapter I.

25. See Vincent E. Starzinger, *Middlingness: Juste Milieu Political Theory in France and England, 1815-1848* (Charlottesville: University of Virginia Press, 1965).

26. Joseph Shaylor, introduction to *John Halifax,* p. ix.

27. Walter Bagehot, "Sterne and Thackeray," *Literary Studies,* 2 vols. (1911; London and New York: Everyman's Library, 1950), II, 124-126.

28. See William Myers, "George Eliot: Politics and Personality," in *Literature and Politics in the Nineteenth Century,* ed. John Lucas (London: Methuen, 1971), pp. 105-129.

29. Charlotte Brontë, *Shirley,* vol. II of *The Life and Works of Charlotte Brontë,* ed. Clement Shorter, 7 vols. (London: Smith, Elder, 1905), pp. 171-172. Page numbers are given in the text hereafter. See Terry Eagleton, *Myths of Power: A Marxist Study of the Brontës* (London: Macmillan, 1975), pp. 45-60.

30. Ricardo, *Principles of Political Economy and Taxation,* ch. 31, pp. 263-271.

31. Asa Briggs, "Private and Social Themes in *Shirley*," *Brontë Society Transactions*, 1958, pp. 203-219. E. P. Thompson, *The Making of the English Working Class* (New York: Vintage Books, 1963), pp. 561-563.

32. Elizabeth Gaskell, *The Life of Charlotte Brontë* (1919; New York: Oxford World's Classics, 1966), pp. 85-88.

33. Martin Farquhar Tupper quoted by Briggs, *Victorian People,* p. 15.

Chapter VI: Christian Socialism

1. See Lowes Dickinson and J. P. Emslie, "Art Teaching in the College in its Early Days," in *The Working Men's College, 1854-1904,* ed. John Llewellyn Davies (London: Macmillan, 1904); and E. T. Cook, *The Life of John Ruskin,* 2 vols. (London: Allen, 1911), I, 378-385.

2. Oswald Doughty, *A Victorian Romantic: Dante Gabriel Rossetti* (New York: Oxford University Press, 1960), p. 167.

3. Arthur C. Benson, *Ruskin: A Study in Personality* (New York and London: Putnam's, 1911), p. 77.

4. When Ruskin was accused of imitating him, he wrote a denial to Carlyle: "People are continually accusing me of borrowing other men's thoughts and not confessing the obligation. I don't think there is anything of which I am more utterly incapable than this meanness; but it is very difficult always to know how much one is indebted to other people, and it is always most difficult to explain to others the degree in which a stronger mind may guide you, without your having, at least intentionally, borrowed this or the other definite thought. The fact is, it is very possible for two people to hit *sometimes* on the same thought, and I have over and over again been somewhat vexed as well as surprised that what I really *had,* and *knew* I had, worked out for myself, corresponded very closely to things that you had said much better." Quoted by Joan Evans, *John Ruskin* (London: Jonathan Cape, 1954), pp. 206-207.

5. John Ruskin, *Works,* ed. E. T. Cook and A. Wedderburn, 39 vols. (London: Allen, 1903-1912), XXVII, 389. See also *Praeterita, Works,* XXXV, 486-488.

6. *The Life of Frederick Denison Maurice, Chiefly Told in His Own Letters,* 2 vols. (New York: Scribner's, 1884), II, 421-422. Volume and page numbers are given in the text hereafter.

7. James Clark Sherburne, *John Ruskin, or the Ambiguities of Abundance* (Cambridge: Harvard University Press, 1972), p. 100.

8. Edward Alexander, "Art Amidst Revolution: Ruskin in 1848," *The Victorian Newsletter,* Fall 1971, pp. 8-13.

9. Rossetti to Charlotte Lydia Polidori, April 12, 1848, in *Letters of Dante Gabriel Rossetti,* ed. Oswald Doughty and J. R. Walsh, 4 vols. (New York: Oxford University Press, 1965), I, 37-38.

10. Dante Gabriel Rossetti, *Works,* ed. William Michael Rossetti (London: Ellis, 1911), pp. 261-262.

11. *The Germ: A Pre-Raphaelite Little Magazine,* ed. Robert Stahr Hosman (Coral Gables: University of Miami Press, 1970), p. 258:

> How long, oh Lord?—The voice is sounding still,
>   Not only heard beneath the altar stone,
>   Not heard of John Evangelist alone
> In Patmos. It doth cry aloud and will
> Between the earth's end and earth's end, until
>   The day of the great reckoning, bone for bone,
>   And blood for righteous blood, and groan for groan:
> Then shall it cease on the air with a sudden thrill;
> Not slowly growing fainter if the rod
>   Strikes one or two amid the evil throng,
>   Or one oppressor's hand is stayed and numbs,—
>   Not till the vengeance that is coming comes:
> For shall all hear the voice excepting God?
>   Or God not listen, hearing? —Lord, how long?

See also Leonid Arinshtein and William E. Fredeman, "William Michael Rossetti's 'Democratic Sonnets,' " *Victorian Studies,* 14 (March 1971), 241-274.

12. F. D. Maurice, "Prospectus," *Politics for the People* (May 6, 1848; London: John Parker, 1848), p. 1.

13. Quoted by Alex R. Vidler, *F. D. Maurice and Company* (London: SCM Press, 1966), p. 177.

14. William Morris, "How I Became a Socialist," in *Political Writings,* ed. A. L. Morton (New York: International Publishers, 1973), p. 244.

15. Samuel Taylor Coleridge, "The Devil's Thoughts," in *Complete Poetical Works,* ed. Ernest Hartley Coleridge, 2 vols. (New York: Oxford University Press, 1912), I, 322.

16. Charles Kingsley, *Alton Locke* (New York: Macmillan, 1889), p. 190. Page numbers are given in the text hereafter.

17. Coleridge quoted by Charles Richard Sanders, *Coleridge and the Broad Church Movement* (1942; New York: Russell and Russell, 1972), p. 26.

18. Quoted by Sanders, *Coleridge and the Broad Church Movement,* p. 243.

19. Ibid., p. 246.

20. Torben Christensen, *Origin and History of Christian Socialism, 1848-1854* (Aarhus: Universitetsforlaget I Aarhus, 1962), pp. 211-215.

21. Marx and Engels, "Manifesto of the Communist Party," *Basic Writings on Politics and Philosophy,* p. 31.

22. Both remarks are quoted by Edward C. Mack and W. H. G. Armytage, *Thomas Hughes* (London: Ernest Benn, 1952), pp. 70, 53.

23. Charles E. Raven, *Christian Socialism, 1848-1854* (1920; New York: Kelley, 1968), p. 107.

24. Mack and Armytage, *Thomas Hughes,* p. 55.
25. *The Letters of Mrs. Gaskell,* ed. J. A. V. Chapple and Arthur Pollard (Manchester: Manchester University Press, 1966), p. 54.
26. Ibid., p. 56.
27. Ibid., p. 67.
28. Quoted by Arthur Pollard, *Mrs. Gaskell, Novelist and Biographer* (Manchester: Manchester University Press, 1966), p. 54.
29. Elizabeth Cleghorn Gaskell, *Mary Barton* (London and New York: Everyman's Library, 1961), p. 351.
30. Gaskell, *North and South* (London and New York: Everyman's Library, 1968), p. 160. Page numbers are given in the text hereafter.
31. N. C. Masterman, *John Malcolm Ludlow: The Builder of Christian Socialism* (New York: Cambridge University Press, 1963), pp. 72-78. See also Raven, *Christian Socialism,* p. 62.
32. John Stuart Mill, *Autobiography, and Other Writings,* pp. 92-93.
33. *The Life of Frederick Denison Maurice,* I, 252.
34. Ludlow summarizing Mill, quoted by Raven, *Christian Socialism,* pp. 293-294.
35. Mill, "Civilization," *Dissertations and Discussions,* 4 vols. (London: Longmans, 1859, 1867, and 1874), I, 165-169.
36. Mill, *Principles of Political Economy,* ed. J. M. Robson, 3 vols. (Toronto: University of Toronto Press, 1965), III, 1033.
37. Ibid., p. 786.
38. William Rathbone Greg, *Essays on Political and Social Science,* 2 vols. (London: Longman, 1853), I, 468-469.
39. Sidney Pollard, "Nineteenth-Century Co-Operation: From Community Building to Shopkeeping," in *Essays in Labour History,* ed. Asa Briggs and John Saville (London: Macmillan, 1960), p. 100. Cooperation in one sense seemed antithetical to self-help, but in another it was actually a version of self-help: workers through their own efforts improving their lot. Samuel Smiles saw the self-help value of mutual benefit societies and cooperatives.
40. Kingsley quoted by Guy Kendall, *Charles Kingsley and His Ideas* (London: Hutchinson, 1947), pp. 65-66.
41. Peter Allen, "F. D. Maurice and J. M. Ludlow: A Reassessment of the Leaders of Christian Socialism," *Victorian Studies,* 11 (June 1968), 474.
42. As on other questions, Ludlow was more radical than either Maurice or Kingsley on the issue of democracy. See Masterman, *John Malcolm Ludlow,* pp. 136-139.

Chapter VII: Liberal Individualism: The Brownings

1. Edwin Hodder, *The Life and Work of the Seventh Earl of Shaftesbury, K.G.* (London: Cassell, 1887), p. 393.
2. Arthur Hugh Clough, *Correspondence,* ed. Frederick Mulhauser, 2 vols. (New York: Oxford University Press, 1957), I, 207.

3. *The Letters of Matthew Arnold to Arthur Hugh Clough,* ed. H. F. Lowry (New York: Oxford University Press, 1932), p. 84.

4. Arthur Hugh Clough, "Address on Socialism," in *Selected Prose Works,* ed. Buckner B. Trawick (Tuscaloosa, Ala.: University of Alabama Press, 1964), pp. 243-249. See also Masterman, *John Malcolm Ludlow,* p. 81.

5. Elizabeth Barrett Browning to Mary Russell Mitford, April 15, 1848, *The Letters of Elizabeth Barrett Browning,* ed. Frederic G. Kenyon, 2 vols. (New York: Macmillan, 1897), I, 359.

6. Ibid., and Elizabeth Browning quoted by Gardner B. Taplin, *The Life of Elizabeth Barrett Browning* (New Haven: Yale University Press, 1957), p. 327.

7. Elizabeth Browning quoted by William Irvine and Park Honan, *The Book, the Ring, and the Poet: A Biography of Robert Browning* (New York: McGraw-Hill, 1974), p. 247.

8. Elizabeth Browning to John Kenyon, May 1, 1848, *Letters,* I, 363.

9. Elizabeth Barrett to H. S. Boyd, August 9, 1843, *Letters,* I, 153; and Elizabeth to Robert in *Letters of Robert Browning and Elizabeth Barrett Barrett, 1845-1846,* ed. Elvan Kintner (Cambridge: Harvard University Press, 1969), p. 505.

10. *Aurora Leigh,* in Elizabeth Barrett Browning, *Poems* (Boston: Houghton Mifflin, 1974), 2.785-796. Section and line numbers are given in the text hereafter.

11. All quotations from Browning are taken from *Robert Browning's Works,* ed. F. G. Kenyon (London: Smith, Elder, 1912). Line numbers (and section numbers when applicable) are given in the text hereafter.

12. George Santayana, "The Poetry of Barbarism," in *The Browning Critics,* ed. Boyd Litzinger and K. L. Knickerbocker (Lexington: University of Kentucky Press, 1967), p. 59.

13. Park Honan, "Robert Browning," in *The Victorian Poets: A Guide to Research,* ed. Frederic E. Faverty (Cambridge: Harvard University Press, 1969), p. 120.

14. William C. DeVane, *A Browning Handbook* (1935; New York: Appleton-Century-Crofts, 1955), p. 55.

15. The Pope raises the question of infallibility in the first three hundred lines; he suggests that evil exists to promote moral progress in lines 1369 to 1409; and he comes close to a denial of original sin in lines 1533 to 1540. Finally, he predicts the advent of a healthy skepticism in lines 1844 to 1870. See also R. D. Altick and James F. Loucks, *Browning's Roman Murder Story* (Chicago: University of Chicago Press, 1968), pp. 327-359.

16. E. C. McAleer, "Browning's 'Cleon' and Auguste Comte," *Comparative Literature,* Spring 1956, pp. 142-145.

17. Helen C. Clarke, *Browning and His Century* (Garden City, N.Y.: Doubleday, 1912), p. 118.

18. The best studies of Browning's politics are D. V. Erdman, "Browning's Industrial Nightmare," *Philological Quarterly,* October 1957, pp. 417-435;

James McNally, "Browning's Politics," *Queen's Quarterly*, 1970, pp. 578-590; and Lawrence Poston III, "Browning's Political Skepticism: *Sordello* and the Plays," *PMLA*, March 1973, pp. 260-270. See also Irvine and Honan, *The Book, the Ring, and the Poet*, pp. 290, 511.

19. H. B. Charlton, "Browning as Dramatist," *Bulletin of the John Rylands Library*, April 1939, pp. 33-67.

20. F. D. Maurice, *The Workman and the Franchise* (1866; New York: Kelley, 1970), pp. 201-202.

21. DeVane, *A Browning Handbook*, p. 158.

22. See William Clyde DeVane, *Browning's Parleyings: The Autobiography of a Mind* (1927; New York: Russell and Russell, 1964), pp. 134-166.

23. Thomas Hardy to Edmund Gosse, March 3, 1899, quoted by Betty Miller, *Robert Browning: A Portrait* (London: Murray, 1952), p. 164.

Chapter VIII: The Ambiguities of Progress

1. See, for example, Meyer Howard Abrams, *Natural Supernaturalism* (New York: Norton, 1971); R. A. Foakes, *The Romantic Assertion* (New Haven: Yale University Press, 1958); and James G. Benziger, *Images of Eternity* (Carbondale: Southern Illinois University Press, 1962).

2. William Morris quoted by J. W. Mackail, *The Life of William Morris* (New York: Oxford World's Classics, 1950), p. 113. On the ideas of decadence and progress in Victorian literature generally, see Jerome H. Buckley, *The Triumph of Time: A Study of the Victorian Concepts of Time, History, Progress, and Decadence* (Cambridge: Harvard University Press, 1966).

3. Edward Burne-Jones quoted by Jerome H. Buckley, *The Victorian Temper* (1951; New York: Vintage Books, 1964), p. 164.

4. For wasteland and fairy palace metaphors, see Curtis Dahl, "The Victorian Wasteland," *College English*, 16 (1955), 341-347; Benjamin Disraeli, *Coningsby*, bk. 4, chs. 1 and 2; and Stephen Marcus, *Engels, Manchester, and the Working Class* (1974; New York: Vintage Books, 1975).

5. Matthew Arnold, "The Future," in *Poems*, ed. Kenneth Allott (London and New York: Longman/Norton, 1965), p. 263.

6. T. S. Eliot, *Essays, Ancient and Modern* (New York: Harcourt, Brace, 1936), p. 203.

7. Swinburne, "Under the Microscope," in *Tennyson: The Critical Heritage*, ed. John D. Jump (London: Routledge and Kegan Paul, 1967), p. 339.

8. Tennyson quoted by Christopher Ricks, ed., *The Poems of Tennyson* (London and New York: Longman/Norton, 1972), p. 1461.

9. Ibid., p. 1470.

10. John D. Rosenberg, *The Fall of Camelot: A Study of Tennyson's* Idylls of the King (Cambridge: Harvard University Press, 1973), p. 11.

11. Tennyson, "Merlin and Vivien," *Idylls of the King*, lines 187-194, in *Poems*, ed. Christopher Ricks, pp. 1460-1756. Line numbers (and section numbers when applicable) from this edition are given in the text hereafter.

12. Sir Charles Tennyson says that the social criticism in *Maud* "sprang from his long talks with Charles Kingsley and F. D. Maurice about the terrible conditions in the rapidly growing industrial cities." *Alfred Tennyson* (New York: Macmillan, 1949), p. 281. He also suggests the importance of *Alton Locke* as an influence on *Maud*. And see John Killham, *Tennyson and the Princess* (London: Athlone Press, 1958), pp. 132-133.

13. Tennyson, "The Third of February, 1852," *Poems*, p. 1002.

14. For the social and biographical context of both "Locksley Hall" and *Maud*, see Ralph Rader, *Tennyson's Maud: The Biographical Genesis* (Berkeley: University of California Press, 1963).

15. Adam Smith, *The Wealth of Nations* (1937; New York: Modern Library, 1965), p. 71.

16. Ibid., p. 71.

17. Charles Dickens with R. H. Horne, "The Great Exhibition and the Little One," in *Charles Dickens' Uncollected Writings from Household Words, 1850-1859*, I, 319-329.

18. Mill, *On Liberty*, in *Autobiography, and Other Writings*, p. 419.

19. Ibid., p. 418.

20. Mill, *Principles of Political Economy*, III, 752.

21. Ibid., p. 752.

22. Ibid., p. 754.

23. Ibid., p. 754.

24. Ibid., pp. 756-757.

25. Mill, "Civilization," *Dissertations and Discussions*, I, 161.

26. Mill, *Autobiography, and Other Writings*, p. 81.

27. Ibid., p. 85.

28. William Morris, *News from Nowhere* (London and Boston: Routledge English Texts, 1970), p. 158.

29. Mill, *Principles of Political Economy*, III, 756-757.

Chapter IX: Realisms

1. Anthony Trollope, *The Warden* (New York: The Oxford Trollope, 1952). Page numbers are given in the text, as are also volume and page numbers from *The Eustace Diamonds, Phineas Finn,* and *The Prime Minister* (New York: Oxford University Press, The Palliser Novels, 1973).

2. Anthony Trollope, *Autobiography* (New York: Oxford World's Classics, 1953), pp. 81-82. Page numbers are given in the text hereafter. Trollope's early thesis novels are *The Macdermots of Ballycloran* (1847) and *The Kellys and the O'Kellys* (1848), with which might be included *La Vendée* (1850).

3. George Ford, *Dickens and His Readers* (1957; New York: Norton, 1965), pp. 75-109.

4. Walter Bagehot, *Literary Studies,* 2 vols. (1911; London and New York: Everyman's Library, 1950), II, 191.

5. Ibid., p. 190.

6. On this transition in public attitudes, see the works cited in note 3 of the Introduction. On Trollope and Bagehot as chief exponents of this new "realistic" mood, see Briggs, *Victorian People,* pp. 87-115. See also George Watson, *The English Ideology: Studies in the Language of Victorian Politics* (London: Allen Lane, 1973); Milton Goldberg, "Trollope's *The Warden:* A Commentary on the 'Age of Equipoise,' " *Nineteenth-Century Fiction,* 17 (1962), 381-390; and Trygve R. Tholfsen, "The Intellectual Origins of Mid-Victorian Stability," *Political Science Quarterly,* March 1971, pp. 57-91. "Profoundly reasoned pococurantism" is David Masson's phrase for Thackeray in *British Novelists and Their Styles* (1859; Boston: Willard and Small, 1892), p. 250. Masson says that he means "a skeptical acquiescence to the world as it is."

7. Harry Levin, *The Gates of Horn: A Study of Five French Realists* (New York: Oxford University Press, 1963), p. 56.

8. Robert Gorham Davis, "The Sense of the Real in English Fiction," *Comparative Literature,* 3 (1951), 214; Richard Stang, *The Theory of the Novel in England, 1850-1870* (New York: Columbia University Press, 1959), pp. 148-149; Levin, *The Gates of Horn,* pp. 67-68.

9. Herbert Spencer, *Social Statics* (1850), quoted by Gertrude Himmelfarb, *Darwin and the Darwinian Revolution* (Garden City, N.Y.: Anchor Books, 1959), p. 419.

10. D. G. Ritchie, *Darwinism and Politics* (New York: Scribner and Welford, 1889), p. 7.

11. Trollope, *Autobiography,* p. 310.

12. Ibid., p. 255.

13. W. M. Thackeray, *Contributions to the Morning Chronicle,* ed. Gordon N. Ray (Urbana: University of Illinois Press, 1955), pp. 77-78 and 71.

14. Gordon N. Ray, *Thackeray: The Uses of Adversity, 1811-1846* (New York: McGraw-Hill, 1955), pp. 14-15. Ray quotes Chesterton: Thackeray "seemed to take it for granted that the Victorian compromise would last; while Dickens . . . had already guessed that it would not."

15. Thackeray quoted by Ray, *The Uses of Adversity,* p. 394.

16. Fitzjames Stephen, "The License of Modern Novelists," *Edinburgh Review,* July 1857, pp. 64-81; Charles Dickens, "A Curious Misprint in the Edinburgh Review," *Household Words,* August 1, 1857, pp. 97-100. There is a good account of Stephen's political thinking in John Roach, "Liberalism and the Victorian Intelligentsia," *Cambridge Historical Journal,* 13 (1957), 58-81.

17. Reade's novels sold well, but reviewers like Stephen objected to his political themes. The one novel which the reviewers accepted with least criticism of its politics was *Put Yourself in His Place,* in which Reade attacked trade unions. See Malcolm Elwin, *Charles Reade: A Biography* (London: Jonathan Cape, 1931), pp. 134-135, 206; and Stang, *Theory of the Novel,* pp. 24-29.

18. Dickens, preface, 3d ed. of *Oliver Twist,* p. xvii.

19. Dickens, preface, 1867 ed. of *The Life and Adventures of Martin Chuzzle-*

wit (New York: Oxford Illustrated Dickens, 1951), p. xv.

20. Dickens quoted by John Forster, *Life of Charles Dickens,* ed. J. W. T. Ley (New York: Doubleday, Doran, n.d.) pp. 727-728.

21. For the phrase "romantic realism" applied to Dickens, see Harry Levin, *The Gates of Horn,* p. 67. As Richard Stang notes, "The critical term most often opposed to *realism* was *idealism,* and the most articulate advocate of the latter was Bulwer-Lytton" (*Theory of the Novel,* p. 153). As suggested in chapter 2, the "romantic realism" of both Dickens and Bulwer is superficially opposed to, but still related to, the reform idealism of the Benthamites.

22. John Ruskin, *Modern Painters,* III, in *Works,* V, 111-129. A full account of Ruskin's artistic thought is in George P. Landow, *The Aesthetic and Critical Theories of John Ruskin* (Princeton: Princeton University Press, 1971).

23. Ruskin to Charles Eliot Norton, June 19, 1870, quoted by Ford, *Dickens and His Readers,* pp. 94-95.

24. The *Quarterly* seems to have associated both Ruskin and Dickens with its evaluation of Pre-Raphaelitism as subversive. See F. R. G. Duckworth, *Browning, Background and Conflict* (New York: Dutton, 1932), p. 23.

25. William Morris, *News from Nowhere* (London and Boston: Routledge English Texts, 1970), pp. 129-130.

26. W. M. Thackeray, *Vanity Fair,* ed. Geoffrey and Kathleen Tillotson (Boston: Houghton Mifflin, 1963), p. 485.

27. George Eliot, *Scenes of Clerical Life* (Boston: Rosehill Limited Edition, 1893), VIII, 64.

28. Mill, *On Liberty,* in *Autobiography, and Other Writings,* p. 395.

29. *The Economist* quoted by Pike, *Golden Times,* p. 38.

30. Gustave Flaubert to Louise Colet, January 16, 1852, *The Selected Letters of Gustave Flaubert,* tr. Francis Steegmuller (New York: Farrar, 1953), p. 127.

31. *The English Constitution,* in *Walter Bagehot,* ed. Norman St. John-Stevas (Bloomington: Indiana University Press, 1959), p. 324.

32. W. M. Thackeray, *The History of Pendennis,* 2 vols. (New York: The Oxford Thackeray, n.d.), II, 795-796.

33. George Eliot, *Middlemarch,* ed. Gordon S. Haight (Boston: Houghton Mifflin, 1956), p. 107. Page numbers are given in the text hereafter. See also James Scott, "George Eliot, Positivism, and the Social Vision of *Middlemarch,*" *Victorian Studies,* 16 (September 1972), 59-76.

34. Herbert Spencer, "The Social Organism," in *The Man Versus The State,* ed. Donald MacRae (Harmondsworth and Baltimore: Penguin Books, 1969), pp. 222-223.

35. Herbert Spencer quoted by George Nasmyth, *Social Progress and the Darwinian Theory* (New York and London: Putnam's, 1916), p. 64.

36. Himmelfarb, *Darwin and the Darwinian Revolution,* p. 418. See also Ritchie, *Darwinism and Politics,* p. 3: "In Malthus the idea of struggle for existence was a very uncomfortable one; but, when it comes back to eco-

nomics after passing through biology, it makes a very comfortable doctrine indeed for all those who are quite satisfied with things as they are." And see Thomas Cowles, "Malthus, Darwin, and Bagehot: A Study in the Transference of a Concept," *Isis,* 26 (1936), 341-348.

37. Himmelfarb, *Darwin and the Darwinian Revolution,* p. 424.

38. *The English Constitution,* in *Walter Bagehot,* p. 398.

39. Mill, 1854 diary, in *The Letters of John Stuart Mill,* ed. Hugh Elliot, 2 vols. (London: Longmans, 1910), II, 360 (January 18, 1854).

Chapter X: 1867 and the Idea of Culture

1. W. N. Molesworth, *History of the Reform Bill of 1832* (London: Chapman and Hall, 1865), p. 338.

2. W. E. Gladstone quoted by F. B. Smith, *The Making of the Second Reform Bill* (New York: Cambridge University Press, 1966), p. 27.

3. Ibid., pp. 48-49.

4. John Stuart Mill, speech on the second reading of the bill of 1866, April 13, 1866, *Hansard's Debates,* 3d ser., vol. 182, col. 1261.

5. Robert Lowe quoted by Smith, *The Making of the Second Reform Bill,* p. 80. See also Briggs, *Victorian People,* pp. 232-263.

6. R. H. Hutton, "The Political Character of the Working Class," in *A Plea for Democracy (Essays on Reform* and *Questions for a Reformed Parliament),* ed. W. L. Guttsman (London: MacGibbon and Kee, 1967), p. 42. Page numbers are given in the text hereafter.

7. John Stuart Mill, *Considerations on Representative Government* (New York: Liberal Arts Press, 1958), p. 114.

8. Lionel Trilling, *Matthew Arnold* (1939; Cleveland and New York: Meridian Books, 1955), pp. 252-253.

9. For the position of the working class in regard to the Civil War, see Royden Harrison, *Before the Socialists* (London and Toronto: Routledge and Kegan Paul, 1965), pp. 40-69; and Gertrude Himmelfarb, *Victorian Minds* (New York: Knopf, 1968), pp. 333-392.

10. Frederic Harrison, "Culture: A Dialogue," *Fortnightly Review,* November 1867, p. 610.

11. Henry Sidgwick, "The Prophet of Culture," *Macmillan's Magazine,* August 1867, pp. 279-280.

12. Arnold, *Culture and Anarchy,* p. 212. Page numbers are given in the text hereafter.

13. Patrick J. McCarthy, *Matthew Arnold and the Three Classes* (New York: Columbia University Press, 1964), pp. 45-46; Trilling, *Matthew Arnold,* p. 335.

14. Sidgwick, "The Prophet of Culture," p. 272.

15. Mill, *Considerations on Representative Government,* p. 14.

16. For a full exploration of the meanings of "culture," see Williams, *Culture and Society, 1780-1950.*

17. Fred G. Walcott, *The Origins of Culture and Anarchy* (Toronto: University of Toronto Press, 1970), p. 106.

18. For instance, see Sidney Smith's *Edinburgh Review* essays on education in the 1808-1810 issues, partly reprinted in *The Selected Writings of Sidney Smith,* ed. W. H. Auden (London: Faber and Faber, n.d.), pp. 258-271.

19. A full survey is Brian Simon, *Studies in the History of Education, 1780-1870* (London: Lawrence and Wishart, 1960).

20. This is Arnold's description of Oxford in the preface to his *Essays in Criticism, First Series* (London: Macmillan and Co. and Smith, Elder, 1903), p. xi.

21. Edward Burnett Tylor, *Primitive Culture,* 2 vols., 1871, reprinted as *The Origins of Culture* and *Religion in Primitive Culture,* ed. Paul Radin (New York: Harper and Row, 1958). Volume and page numbers are given in the text. For the anthropological version of culture, see A. L. Kroeber and Clyde Kluckhohn, *Culture: A Review of Concepts and Definitions* (1952; New York: Vintage Books, 1963). For Tylor and the history of anthropology, see George W. Stocking, *Race, Culture, and Evolution* (New York: Free Press, 1968), pp. 195-233; J. W. Burrow, *Evolution and Society* (New York: Cambridge University Press, 1970); Marvin Harris, *The Rise of Anthropological Theory* (New York: Crowell, 1968); and T. K. Penniman, *A Hundred Years of Anthropology,* 3d ed. (1936; London: Duckworth, 1965).

22. Franz Boas quoted by Abram Kardiner and Edward Preble, *They Studied Man* (New York: New American Library, 1963), pp. 121-122.

23. Sir James Frazer, *The Golden Bough,* 12 vols. (London and New York: Macmillan, 1935), "Farewell to Nemi," VIII, 304-309.

24. Quoted by Kardiner and Preble, *They Studied Man,* p. 54. An interesting examination of the links between nineteenth-century social reform and the Protestant reformation is Eugene Goodheart, "English Social Criticism and the Spirit of Reformation," *Clio,* Fall 1975, pp. 73-95.

25. There is biographical information in H. R. Hays, *From Ape to Angel: An Informal History of Social Anthropology* (New York: Knopf, 1958), pp. 58-83; Kardiner and Preble, *They Studied Man,* pp. 50-68; and the article on Tylor by R. R. Marett in *Dictionary of National Biography, Twentieth Century, 1912-1921,* pp. 539-541.

26. Matthew Arnold, "The Study of Poetry," in *Essays in Criticism, Second Series* (London: Macmillan and Co. and Smith, Elder, 1903), p. 2.

27. Wordsworth, *The Prelude,* 13.196-197. The full passage is a rejection of the idea that virtue and love are dependent on education, or on "manners studied and elaborate."

28. Stocking, *Race, Culture, and Evolution,* p. 229. Stocking claims to have found no plural uses of the word "culture" before about 1900; a review of dictionaries and encyclopedias will show that the anthropological definition

of it gains a place in them only after 1900. Dyer's *The Fleece* is quoted in the *Oxford English Dictionary* under "culture."

29. Stocking, *Race, Culture, and Evolution,* pp. 195-233. Boas's criticism of Darwinian categories led him to reject Tylor's idea of levels of culture for the more scientific and much more democratic idea of many cultures.

30. Melville Herskovits, *Cultural Relativism* (New York: Random House, 1972), p. 11.

31. Tylor says that "the character and habit of mankind at once display that similarity and consistency . . . which led the Italian proverb-maker to declare that 'all the world is one country,' 'tutto il mondo è paese.' " And he ironically cites Dr. Johnson as an authority. Having read about Patagonians and South Sea Islanders in Hawkesworth's *Voyages,* Johnson declared in disgust that "one set of savages is like another" (*Primitive Culture,* I, 6).

32. *The Letters of Matthew Arnold to Arthur Hugh Clough,* p. 95.

33. For the "Friends of Labour," see Harrison, *Before the Socialists,* pp. 251-342, and Masterman, *John Malcolm Ludlow,* pp. 180-232.

34. "A Journeyman Engineer" (Thomas Wright), *Some Habits and Customs of the Working Classes* (1867; New York: Augustus M. Kelley, 1967), p. vi.

35. Henry Mayhew, *London Labour and the London Poor,* ed. John D. Rosenberg, 4 vols. (1861; New York: Dover, 1968), I, 43 and 25.

36. Sir John Lubbock, *The Origin of Civilisation and the Primitive Condition of Man,* 7th rev. ed. (London and New York: Longmans, Green, 1912), pp. 394-395.

37. For the emergence of Marxism in the last quarter of the century, see Stanley Pierson, *Marxism and the Origins of British Socialism* (Ithaca: Cornell University Press, 1973).

Index

Albert, Prince, 186
Alison, Archibald, 63-64, 66, 93
Althorp's Factory Act, 88, 258
Amalgamated Society of Engineers, 238
Anti-Corn Law League, 2, 17; and Dickens,
86, 90-91, 105, 112-117; and Carlyle,
109-112; and Elizabeth Browning, 115,
153-154. *See also* Free trade
Anti-slavery movement, 78, 86-87, 121
Arnold, Matthew, 1, 15, 25, 83, 120, 183-
185, 194, 195, 227, 240-258; *Culture
and Anarchy,* 83, 207, 240-249, 253-255;
on Chartism, 151; on socialism, 151-154,
241; sonnets "to a Republican friend,"
151; *Empedocles on Etna,* 154, 184, 244;
on progress, 183-185, 244-245, 257;
"Scholar Gipsy," 183-184, 243-244;
"The Future," 184-185, 245; "Dover
Beach," 185, 252; "Rugby Chapel,"
185, 252; and culture, 240-242, 243-255;
and ethnology, 241, 253-254; and educational reform, 244, 246, 247-248, 251;
and Christian Socialism, 245
Arnold, Thomas, 25, 30, 134, 244, 245,
250; and Chartism, 82-83
Ashley, Lord, seventh Earl of Shaftesbury,
13, 86, 87, 88, 100, 116, 117, 151, 154
Athenaeum, 135
Austin, Henry, 54

Bagehot, Walter, 121, 208, 225; and political economy, 4; and social Darwinism, 4,
8, 32, 207, 209, 232, 233; on Disraeli,
104; on Dickens, 206-207, 214-215; on
political "dullness," 210, 220, 247;
Physics and Politics, 232; on Reform Bill
of 1867, 238, 239
Barruel, Abbé, 66
Beggar's Opera, The, 37
Bentham, Jeremy, 12, 17, 19, 43, 52, 72,
96, 130, 145, 149, 207, 224, 251; Panopticon, 46; and penal reform, 46-47; doctrine of circumstances, 51, 53; Chrestomathia, 248
Benthamism, 1-2, 4, 6-7, 12-14, 16-18, 24,
26, 29, 31, 32-33, 35-59, 70, 81, 145,
216-217, 238, 254, 258

Blackwood's Magazine, 55, 63-64
Blake, William, 16, 41, 97, 165, 169, 183,
231
Blanc, Louis, 144, 152, 153
Blanchard, Lamon, 26, 85, 87
Boas, Franz, 249, 250-251
Bowring, John, 17
Boyd, H. S., 154
Bradlaugh, Charles, 182
Bray, Charles: *The Philosophy of Necessity,*
28
Bright, John, 6, 8, 112, 115, 141, 188, 191,
238, 244
British Quarterly Review, 15
Brontë, Charlotte: *Jane Eyre,* 116, 125,
159; *Shirley,* 124-127, 143-144, 190
Brougham, Lord, 21, 69
Brown, Ford Madox, 129
Browning, Elizabeth Barrett, 169, 170, 187;
"Cry of the Children," 28-29, 154, 157,
159-160; on Carlyle, 81; and Anti-Corn
Law League, 115, 153-154; and Char-
tism, 153; on socialism, 153-161; *Aurora
Leigh,* 154-160, 169, 187, 207, 226;
"Cry of the Human," 154; feminism in,
155
Browning, Robert, 115, 154, 157, 160, 161-
179, 181-182; and democracy, 157, 163-
164, 168-169; "How It Strikes a Contemporary," 157, 174; and Shelley, 157,
161, 164, 168, 171, 174, 178, 182; and
realism, 161, 164, 174, 176, 181-182;
and socialism, 161; *Sordello,* 161, 169,
171, 172-173, 174, 176; "Andrea del
Sarto," 162; "Cleon," 162, 163; "A
Death in the Desert," 162; *Paracelsus,*
162, 171-172; and positivism, 162; *The
Ring and the Book,* 162, 166-168, 175,
224; "The Lost Leader," 163, 170; "Pictor Ignotus," 163; "A Toccata of Galuppi's," 163; "Why I Am a Liberal," 163-
164, 170; "Fra Lippo Lippi," 164, 176,
181-182, 218; as dramatist, 165-166,
169, 173-175; *King Victor and King
Charles,* 165; *Strafford,* 165-166, 169,
173, 174, 179; "The Pied Piper of Hamelin," 167; "Prince Hohenstiel-Schwan-

gau," 169-170, 175-178; *A Soul's Tragedy,* 169, 173-174, 175; "The Englishman in Italy," 170-171; and free trade,
170-171; "The Italian in England," 170-
171; "A Parleying with George Bubb
Dodington," 170, 175; "The Patriot—
An Old Story." 170, 174; *Dramatic
Lyrics,* 171; *Dramatic Romances and
Lyrics,* 171; *Luria,* 171, 173; *Pauline,*
171-172, 174; *Bells and Pomegranates,*
173; "Caliban upon Setebos," 174;
Essay on Shelley, 174; *In a Balcony,*
174; *Men and Women,* 174; *Pippa
Passes,* 175
Bulwer-Lytton, Edward, 11, 14-16, 23, 31,
32, 40-41, 42, 44-45, 84, 154; *England
and the English,* 14-15; *Paul Clifford,*
31, 35-38, 44-45, 52; and legal reform,
35-38; *The Last of the Barons,* 44, 83;
Zanoni, 44, 83; *The Coming Race,* 83
Burke, Edmund, 16, 63, 66, 104, 207, 232
Burne-Jones, Edward, 129, 183
Byron, Lord, 11, 16

Cabet, Étienne, 153, 159
Caleb Williams, 35-36
Carlyle, James, 75-76
Carlyle, John, 12
Carlyle, Thomas, 1, 3-4, 6-7, 11-12, 15, 17,
30-31, 32, 39, 48, 61-79, 119, 120, 123,
124, 129, 133, 145, 152, 191, 198, 200,
203, 255, 256, 257; opposition to Benthamism, 1-2, 13-14, 40-41, 55, 59, 81;
Chartism, 3, 12-13, 27, 29, 30, 31, 63,
68, 74, 81, 92, 109-110; *Past and Present,* 3-4, 12-13, 30, 41, 63, 66, 68, 74,
81, 109-111, 133, 244; and hero worship,
6, 65, 72-73, 77, 81, 120, 254; "Shooting Niagara," 8, 255; *The French Revolution,* 11, 12, 15, 59, 61-79; *Sartor
Resartus,* 11, 29, 61-62, 74, 76-77;
"Signs of the Times," 11, 15; "Corn-
Law Rhymes," 17; on statistics, 27-30;
"Biography," 29; on fiction, 29; *Wotton
Reinfred,* 29; *Latter-day Pamphlets,* 31;
on democracy, 61-62, 66, 67-70, 72, 76-
79, 81, 109-110; on progress, 62, 70, 77-
79, 109; prose style, 62-63, 70-71, 78;
Heroes and Hero-Worship, 63, 65, 120;

on aristocracy, 66, 68, 81; and New Poor
Law, 69, 109; impartiality of, 71-72, 76-
79; Scotch Calvinist background, 73-76;
Reminiscences, 74-78; on trade union-
ism, 92; and Anti-Corn Law League, 109-
112, 115; on "captains of industry,"
110-112, 123
Carpenter, Edward, 234
Cartwright, William, 126
Castlereagh, Lord, 17
Catholic Emancipation Act, 11, 121
Chadwick, Edwin, 12-13, 27, 29-31, 54
Chambers, William, 20-23
Chambers's Journal, 5-6, 8, 20-24
Chapman, John, 142
Chartism, 1, 2-3, 23, 27, 29, 32-33, 41, 44,
52, 54, 55, 57-58, 70, 75, 104, 114-115,
118, 138-142, 144, 146, 148, 151-152,
185, 239, 256; Chartist petition of 1839,
1, 14, 85, 98; Newport rising of 1839, 58,
85, 98, 99; Carlyle on, 81-83 (*see also*
Carlyle, *Chartism*); Thomas Arnold and,
82-83; Chartist petition of 1842, 82;
Macaulay on, 82; Dickens on, 83-96,
104-107; torchlight meetings, 85; Disraeli on, 96-107; Birmingham riots, 98;
Plug Plot disturbances, 98, 99; demonstration of April 10, 1848, 119, 129, 131,
137, 139-142; Rossetti on, 131; Kingsley
on, 137-141; Matthew Arnold and, 151;
Clough on, 151
Cheap literature movement, 20-24, 27
Cheap Repository Tracts, 21
Children's Employment Commission, 28-
29, 31, 88, 90, 154
Christian Lady's Magazine, 56
Christian Socialism, 2, 111-112, 115, 129-
149, 181, 191-192, 207, 218, 254; Cole-
ridge's influence on, 129, 133, 134-136;
and Pre-Raphaelitism, 129-133; and
Working Men's College, 129-130; and
Owenism, 133-134; Clough on, 152-153;
Elizabeth Browning on, 156, 158-159;
and Matthew Arnold, 245
Christian Socialist, The, 132, 136, 144, 145
Civil War (American), 242
Clough, Arthur Hugh, 9, 116-117, 151-
153, 254; *The Bothie of Toberna-Vuol-
ich,* 117, 152; "Address on Socialism,"

286

152-153; "Duty," 152; "The Latest
Decalogue," 152; "Dipsychus," 153;
"Easter Day in Naples," 153
Cobbett, William, 21, 24-25, 133
Cobbett's Weekly Political Register, 21
Cobden, Richard, 112, 116, 188
Cole, Sir Henry, 116
Coleridge, Samuel Taylor, 1, 11, 16, 144-
145, 149, 207, 218, 224, 232, 245; and
Christian Socialism, 129, 133, 134-136
Colet, Louise, 225
Committee on Investments for the Savings
of the Middle and Working Classes, 145-
146
Comte, Auguste, 159, 162, 178, 227, 250,
251
Congreve, Richard, 250
Cooper, Thomas, 139
Cooperative movement, 2-3, 113, 136, 144,
145-149, 191, 239. *See also* Christian
Socialism
Co-operator, The, 147
Cornhill Magazine, 3, 27
Courbet, Gustave, 208
Crabbe, George, 84
Craik, Mrs. *See* Dinah Mulock
Crimean War, 190-191, 241-242
Croker, John Wilson, 64, 66
Culture: and "popular education," 239,
243; working-class, 239-240, 255-257;
Arnoldian, 240-242, 243-255; anthro-
pological, 248-255; cultural relativism,
252-253
Cyples, William, 27-28

Danton, Georges-Jacques, 64
Darwin, Charles, 232-233; *The Origin of
Species,* 6, 28; *The Descent of Man,* 232
Darwinism, 28, 182, 187, 230-234, 248,
252, 253
DeVere, Aubrey, 137, 144
Dickens, Charles, 1, 3, 6-7, 9, 25-26, 31,
32, 35, 55, 111, 155, 181, 197, 254-255,
256, 258; opposition to Benthamism,
1-2, 13-14, 30, 40-55; *Oliver Twist,* 11,
17, 25, 30, 31, 32, 35, 43, 44-55, 95, 99,
107, 216, 220; *Pickwick Papers,* 11, 25-
26, 42-43, 86; *Sketches by Boz,* 11; and
New Poor Law, 17, 25, 31, 54-55, 86;

Hard Times, 23, 31, 43, 48, 53, 54-55,
89, 91, 94, 104, 105-106, 113, 114, 119,
156, 216-219, 231; on legal and penal reform, 25, 96, 166; *Nicholas Nickleby,*
25, 48, 87-88, 113, 214, 220; and statistics, 27-30, 155, 216-217; "The Mudfog
Association," 27; and "sentimental radicalism," 30, 117, 119, 206; *Bleak House,*
31, 48, 52, 72, 113, 122, 166, 215, 216,
231, 250; *Little Dorrit,* 31, 91, 94, 106,
112-113, 215, 231; *Our Mutual Friend,*
31, 54-55, 220-221, 230; and class conflict, 41-43, 48-55, 112-114, 117, 119;
Benthamite tendencies in, 43-55, 96;
Christmas stories, 43, 90, 214, 220; and
political economy, 43, 90, 197, 217,
219, 220; and evangelicalism, 44, 86;
and Ten Hours Movement, 44, 86-91,
116; *All the Year Round,* 48, 220;
Household Words, 48, 91, 197, 215,
219; *Barnaby Rudge,* 83-86, 91-96, 112;
and Chartism, 83-96, 104-107; and industrialism, 84-96, 105-107, 112-114,
116; and trade unionism, 84, 91-95, 104-
107; *The Old Curiosity Shop,* 85-86, 87-
88; and Anti-Corn Law League, 86, 90-
91, 112-117, 119; journey to America,
88-89; *American Notes,* 89; *The Daily
News,* 90, 114, 116; "A Poor Man's Tale
of a Patent," 91; *Great Expectations,* 92,
96, 122, 139, 208; ideal of personalized
work, 94-95, 111; "Hymn of the Wiltshire Labourers," 114; and Browning,
166, 168; "The Great Exhibition and the
Little One," 197; and progress, 197, 219-
220; Trollope on, 205-207; *Dombey and
Son,* 214; and "romantic realism," 214-
223; *Martin Chuzzlewit,* 216; "Old
Lamps for New Ones," 219; and Pre-
Raphaelitism, 219-220; on Young England, 219; and social organicism, 231
Disraeli, Benjamin, 7, 28-29, 31-32, 44, 55,
244, 254, 256, 257; *Sybil,* 28-29, 31-32,
93, 97-104, 107, 117, 134, 157, 210,
214; and trade unionism, 93, 101, 105;
and Chartism, 96-107; and Young England, 96-104, 134; on aristocracy, 97-
98, 101; *Coningsby,* 97-98, 103, 104,
107, 210; and Ten Hours Bill, 100; and

free trade, 104; and Anti-Corn Law League, 111-112, 115; Browning on, 175; Thackeray on, 214

Draper, J. W.: *History of the Intellectual Development of Europe,* 6

Dyer, John, 252

Economic depression: of 1836-1842, 1, 12, 33, 64; of 1870s, 4; and French Revolution, 69-70

Economist, The, 115, 224

Edinburgh Review, 88, 90, 118, 215

Education Act of 1870, 239, 246, 254, 258

Educational reform: Benthamism and, 20-21, 23-24, 248; Carlyle and, 81, 109-110; and Christian Socialism, 129-130, 136, 147, 148; and Reform Bill of 1867, 239, 243, 254, 258; and Arnold, 244, 246, 247-248, 251

Eliot, George, 1, 8-9, 28, 250, 255, 257; Felix Holt's "Address to the Working Men," 2, 8, 228; *Middlemarch,* 5, 9, 32, 53, 166, 224, 226-230, 244; *Felix Holt,* 8, 53, 123, 207, 223, 228, 245; social organicism in, 32, 230-231; realism in, 181, 207, 222, 223, 226-233; *Scenes from Clerical Life,* 223; and positivism, 227; and progress, 227, 229-230; *Mill on the Floss,* 231; and social Darwinism, 231-233

Eliot, T. S., 185-186

Elliott, Ebenezer, 115; *Corn-Law Rhymes,* 17

Engels, Friedrich, 4, 82, 107, 136, 256

Essays on Reform, 239-240, 242-243, 246, 255

Evangelicalism, 13, 16, 24, 55; and hostility to fiction, 26, 29; Dickens on, 44, 86; in Mrs. Tonna, 56-57

Ewart, Mary, 142

Extraordinary Black Book or Reformer's Bible, The, 12

Fabianism, 4

Farr, William, 32

Ferdinand VII of Spain, 194

Figaro in London, 26

Fitzgerald, E. M., 87, 88

Flaubert, Gustave, 208, 225

Forster, John, 88, 95

Forster, W. E., 239

Fourier, Charles, 119, 144, 153, 156, 158, 159, 160, 178, 207

Fox, Charles, 24

Fox, W. J., 114

Franco-Prussian War, 175

Franklin, Benjamin, 248

Fraser's Magazine, 87, 146

Frazer, Sir James, 250

Free trade, 2, 17, 53, 104, 109-119, 131, 156, 170-171, 181, 185, 237; and the Girondins, 67-68; and Dickens, 90-96; and Disraeli, 104; and Christian Socialists, 115, 141, 145-147, 148; and Elizabeth Browning, 153-154; and Herbert Spencer, 232. *See also* Anti-Corn Law League

French Revolution of 1789, 44, 61-79, 82, 83, 109

French Revolution of 1830, 11, 12, 14, 63, 64

Freud, Sigmund, 189

Froude, James Anthony, 76

Furnivall, F. J., 130, 146

Gaskell, Elizabeth Cleghorn, 28, 31, 53, 117, 126, 254, 256; *Mary Barton,* 93, 117, 141-143; on trade unionism, 93, 142-143; and Christian Socialism, 141-144; *North and South,* 141, 143-144; "Christmas Storms and Sunshine," 144; "The Sexton's Hero," 144

Gay, John, 37

Germ, The, 132

Gissing, George, 53, 107

Gladstone, William, 8, 51, 195, 237-238

Godwin, William, 35, 52

Gordon riots. *See* Dickens, *Barnaby Rudge*

Gore, Catherine, 29; *The Two Aristocracies,* 116

Gosse, Edmund, 178

Grant brothers, William and Daniel, 88

Great Exhibition, 3, 115, 129, 148, 197

Greg, W. R., 30, 52, 147

Gresley, Rev. William, 56-59, 92, 115, 159; *Charles Lever,* 57-59, 102, 213

Greville, Charles, 117
Grey, Earl, 13, 16, 101
Guild of St. George, 130

Hallam, Arthur Henry, 193, 194, 200
Hardy, Thomas, 53, 178; *Jude the Obscure*, 139, 233
Hare, Julius, 134
Hare, Thomas, 240
Harney, Julian, 82
Harrison, Frederic, 241, 242, 243, 244, 250
Hawthorne, Nathaniel, 210
Hazlitt, William, 73
Health of Towns Association, 31
Helps, Sir Arthur, 123; *The Claims of Labour*, 111-112
Herskovits, Melville, 252-253
Higher Criticism, 162, 182, 229, 250
Hill, Octavia, 130-131
Hobhouse, L. T., 4
Hogarth, William, 37
Hogg's Weekly Instructor, 5
Hood, Tom, 26, 115; "The Song of the Shirt," 117-119, 154
Horne, R. H., 29, 81, 154, 197; *Orion,* 17, 109, 115; *A New Spirit of the Age,* 37
Howitt, William, 16
Hughes, Tom, 140
Hunt, Leigh, 118
Hutton, R. H., 239-240, 242
Huxley, Thomas Henry, 133, 247, 250; *Evolution and Ethics,* 233
Hyde Park disturbances of 1866, 239, 254
Hyndman, H. M., 4

Industrial and Provident Societies Act of 1852, 145
Industrialism, 2-3, 4, 8-9, 12, 31, 33, 114-116, 154, 181; conservative reaction against, 44, 57-59 (*see also* Ten Hours Movement); Carlyle on, 70, 109-112, 115, 123, 203; Bulwer on, 83; Dickens on, 84-96, 105-107, 112-114, 116; Disraeli on, 100, 104, 107; in *John Halifax,* 119-125; in *Shirley,* 124-127, 143-144; and Christian Socialists, 132-135, 140-141, 145-147; and Mrs. Gaskell, 141-145; and Ruskin, 162; and Arnold, 184-

185; and Tennyson, 191; and Mill, 198-200; and George Eliot, 229-230
Irving, Edward, 11, 73-74

Jerrold, Douglas, 21, 55, 87, 114, 214; plays on reform themes, 26, 30; *St. Giles and St. James,* 30, 52, 54. *See also Punch* radicals
Jones, Lloyd, 255
Journal of Association, The, 132, 136
Journalism, 15-16, 20, 205
Jowett, Benjamin, 137, 144

Keats, John, 11, 182
Keble, John, 12
Kenyon, F. G., 153
Kidd, Benjamin, 234
Kingsley, Charles, 2, 27, 30, 31, 133-134, 137-141, 144, 146-147, 207, 218, 256, 257; *Yeast,* 27, 137; *Water Babies,* 31; *Alton Locke,* 133-134, 137-141, 143, 146, 191; "Cheap Clothes and Nasty," 144, 146; on Mill, 146; and Tennyson, 191
Knight, Charles, 20, 24, 31, 33

Lamartine, Alphonse de, 151-152
Lamert, James, 46
Lancashire cotton famine, 22, 239, 242
Lang, Andrew, 250
Legal reform, 25, 35-38, 43, 46-47, 96, 166-167
Lemon, Mark, 26, 54, 114, 214; *The Sempstress,* 117
Lever, Charles: *St. Patrick's Eve,* 214
Lewes, G. H., 216
Limited Liability Act of 1855, 2
Limits to Growth, The, 200
Locke, John, 248
London Statistical Society, 27
London University, 33, 248
Londonderry, Lord, 88
Lowe, Robert, 238, 239, 240, 242
Lubbock, Sir John: *The Origin of Civilization,* 257
Luddism, 124-127
Ludlow, John Malcolm, 2, 111, 133, 135, 137, 144, 148; on Mill, 145-146; "La-

bour and the Poor,'' 146; *Progress of the Working Class,* 255
Lyndhurst, Lord, 12
Lyra Apostolica, 58

Macaulay, Thomas Babington, 11, 16, 26, 27, 32, 148, 223; on progress, 6, 18-19; *History of England,* 18; on revolution, 64, 69-70; and Chartism, 82; on Dickens, 206
Maine, Sir Henry, 43, 44-45
Malthus, Thomas, 23, 30, 39, 43, 69, 232, 254
Manchester Examiner and Times, 3
Manchester School, 3, 33, 134, 141, 147, 164, 191
Manchester Statistical Society, 27
Martineau, Harriet, 12, 21, 25, 26, 41, 42, 52, 115; *Illustrations of Political Economy,* 17, 23-24, 30, 31, 38-40, 44; *History of the Thirty Yeas' Peace,* 20; and Dickens, 30, 117, 206
Marx, Karl, 4, 107, 136, 258
Marxism, 18, 129, 133, 234, 240, 258
Massey, Gerald, 118-119, 139
Masson, David, 214
Maurice, Frederick Denison, 255; and Christian Socialism, 2, 111, 129-131, 132, 133-137, 140, 144-149, 207, 218; *The Workman and the Franchise,* 2, 169; and Working Men's College, 129-130; on Ruskin, 130; and *Politics for the People,* 132; and Broad Church theology, 133-137, 140, 144-145, 148, 153, 245; *Theological Essays,* 140; on J. S. Mill, 145, 147; and Tennyson, 191
Mayhew, Augustus, 26, 54
Mayhew, Henry, 26, 54, 200, 255; *London Labour and the London Poor,* 256-257. *See also Punch* radicals
Mazzini, Joseph, 77-78
McCulloch, J. R., 4
Melbourne, Lord, 13, 16, 101
Merivale, Henry, 69, 81
Metternich, Prince, 170
Michelet, Jules, 69
Mignet, François, 63
Mill, James, 4, 17, 18, 23, 26, 36, 38, 39, 41, 51-52, 53, 120, 223
Mill, John Stuart, 6, 11, 24, 53, 207, 215, 233-234, 253, 254-255, 256, 258; on Reform Bill of 1867, 8, 238-239; on Reform Bill of 1832, 13; and Benthamism, 13, 145; *Autobiography,* 24, 200-201; and Malthusianism, 30, 202-203, 254; and James Mill, 36, 38, 39; and Harriet Martineau, 39; and Carlyle, 41; and Harriet Taylor, 41, 146; *The Principles of Political Economy,* 41, 146, 197-203, 256; and Anti-Corn Law League, 115; and Christian Socialism, 144-149; and Coleridge, 144-145; "Civilization," 146; *Examination of the Philosophy of Sir William Hamilton,* 147; *On Liberty,* 154, 197, 198, 223-224, 232, 240; on Browning, 171; and stationary state, 197-203; and industrialism, 198-200; mental crisis, 200-201; on democracy, 223-225; *Considerations on Representative Government,* 240-241, 246
Millais, J. E., 219-220
Milsand, J., 161
Mirabeau, Honoré-Gabriel, 64, 67
Mitford, Mary Russell, 206
Molesworth, W. N.: *History of the Reform Bill of 1832,* 237
Montagu, Elizabeth, 84
More, Hannah, 21, 56
Morning Chronicle, 88, 214
Morris, William, 4, 129, 132-133, 182, 201-202, 234, 257-258; *News from Nowhere,* 202, 222
Mulock, Dinah, 223; *John Halifax, Gentleman,* 119-125, 207
Municipal Corporations Act, 13, 58

Napier, Macvey, 88
Napoleon I, 61, 64-65, 75, 124
Napoleon III, 175-176
National Reformer, 182
Necker, Jacques, 64-65
New Poor Law, 2, 12-13, 17, 25, 27, 31, 53-55, 69, 109, 115; agitation against, 1, 13, 30, 86, 113; Dickens on, 44, 46-49, 53-55; and rule of least eligibility, 53-54
Newgate novels, 35, 95

INDEX

Newman, Cardinal, 58
Newport rising of 1839, 58, 85, 98, 99
Northern Star, 138

Oastler, Richard, 13, 57
O'Brien, Bronterre, 82
O'Connell, Daniel, 44
O'Connor, Feargus, 138
Orders in Council, 124
Owen, Robert, 36, 144
Owenism, 1-2, 36, 41, 57-59, 70, 100, 102, 133, 139, 147
Oxford Movement, 55, 57-58, 78, 107, 250

Paine, Thomas, 41, 52, 63
Palmerston, Lord, 3, 237
Paris Commune, 242
Parker, Charles, 243
Parkes, Joseph, 12
Peacock, Thomas Love: *Crotchet Castle,* 21-23
Pearson, Karl, 234
Peel, Sir Robert, 4-6, 16, 101, 104, 118, 119
Penal reform, 25, 35-38, 46-47, 96
Penny Magazine, 20-24
Peterloo Massacre, 17
Plug Plot disturbances, 98, 99
Political economy, 4, 21, 23, 30, 32, 38-40, 41-44, 67, 91, 112, 117, 125, 145, 155-156, 196-203, 217, 219, 220, 232. *See also* Statistics
Politics for the People, 132
Poor Man's Guardian, 21
Porter, G. R., 26-27, 32
Positivism, 6, 162, 227, 248, 250-251, 254
Postal reform, 131
Prentice, Archibald, 113-114
Pre-Raphaelitism, 31, 129-133, 181-183, 219-220, 222
Priestley, Joseph, 248
Progress, 2, 4-8, 114-115, 119, 129, 185, 237, 257-258; progressive evolution, 4, 8, 201; Macaulay on, 6, 18-19; Carlyle on, 62, 70, 77-79, 109, 203; in *John Halifax,* 119-124; in *Shirley,* 124-127; and Christian Socialists, 132-133, 140-141; Mill on, 146, 197-203, 223-225; Robert Browning

and, 174; Arnold on, 183-185; Tennyson on, 186-203; versus stationary state, 196-203; Dickens on, 197, 219-220; Eliot on, 227, 229-230
Progress of the Nation, 26-27, 32
Protestant Association, 86
Proudhon, Pierre Joseph, 137
Public Health Act of 1848, 2
Pugin, A. W., 133
Punch, 13, 26, 30, 41, 55, 117, 131, 214
Punch in London, 26
Punch radicals, 7, 26, 27-28, 54, 114, 115, 255

Quarterly Review, 28, 219

Reade, Charles, 215
Realism: antithetical to reform idealism, 8, 181-182, 205-207; and Carlyle, 29; and Browning, 161, 164, 174, 176, 181-182; and Eliot, 181, 207, 222, 223, 226-233; and Thackeray, 181, 207, 214-215, 222, 223, 226, 233; and Trollope, 181, 205-206, 207, 208-214, 225-226, 233; and Dickens, 205-207, 208, 214-223; and social Darwinism, 207, 209, 233; and Flaubert, 208, 225; and Ruskin, 218-222
Reform Bill of 1832, 1, 4-5, 8, 11, 13, 14, 17, 58, 62, 64, 67-69, 83, 105, 110, 114, 121, 194, 228, 237
Reform Bill of 1867, 1, 2, 4, 8, 107, 210-211, 228, 237-240, 244, 248, 254
Reform Bill of 1884, 164
Reid, Andrew, 164
Revolutions of 1848, 2, 131-132, 140, 151-153, 160
Reynolds, G. M. W., 131
Ricardo, David, 4, 23, 39, 125, 232
Ritchie, D. G., 1, 209
Robespierre, Maximilien, 59, 65
Romanticism, 11, 16, 17, 26, 129, 133, 181-183; "romantic realism," 218-222
Romilly, Samuel, 36
Rossetti, Dante Gabriel, 129-131, 181, 182-183
Rossetti, William Michael: *Democratic Sonnets,* 131-132
Rousseau, Jean-Jacques, 72

291

Royal Cornwall Polytechnic Society, 30
Rubaiyat of Omar Khayyam, The, 31
Ruskin, John, 1, 3-4, 119, 215, 255, 257,
258; *Time and Tide,* 2; *Unto This Last,*
3-4, 215, 219; and Christian Socialism,
129-131, 146; and Working Men's College, 129-130; *Fors Clavigera,* 130, 219;
Guild of St. George, 130; on F. D.
Maurice, 130; "The Nature of Gothic,"
130, 146; and Robert Browning, 162;
Modern Painters, 218, 221; and "romantic realism," 218-222; on Dickens, 219;
and political economy, 220; *Praeterita,*
220-221; *Seven Lamps of Architecture,*
257
Russell, Henry, 154

Sadler, Michael, 13; Sadler Committee, 26,
29, 30
St. Simonism, 11, 70, 129, 145
*Sanitary Condition of the Labouring Popu-
lation,* 27, 31
Sanitary reform, 2, 27, 31, 110, 141, 148
Scott, Sir Walter, 16, 64, 71, 83; *The Heart
of Midlothian,* 91
Second Empire (France), 175, 208
Second Republic (France), 151-152
Senior, Nassau, 4
"Sentimental radicalism," 2, 13, 14, 30,
41, 51, 52-53, 107, 117-119, 206, 214-
223
Seymour, Rev. Charles, 56
Shelley, Percy Bysshe, 11, 16, 17, 41; and
Browning, 157, 161, 164, 168, 171, 174,
178, 182; and Tennyson, 189, 192-193
Sidgwick, Henry, 243, 245
Simon, Dr. John, 31
Slaney, R. A., 145
Smiles, Samuel, 119-120; *Self-Help,* 53,
120; *Lives of the Engineers,* 120
Smith, Adam, 21, 200, 248; *The Wealth of
Nations,* 196-198
Smith, George, 3
Smith, Southwood, 27, 88, 90
Social Darwinism, 4, 8, 32, 207, 209, 227,
230-234, 258; in Bagehot, 4, 8, 207, 209,
232, 233; in Spencer, 4, 8, 32, 207, 209,
231-234; in Eliot, 231-233; and political
economy, 232; and anthropology, 249

Socialism, 3-4, 16, 23, 53, 57-59, 70, 129,
133, 144-145, 151-153, 154-161
Society for the Diffusion of Useful Knowl-
edge, 20-21, 23-24, 27, 248
Society for the Promotion of Christian
Knowledge, 21
Southey, Robert, 16, 19, 27, 69-70, 129,
133
Spectator, The, 28
Spencer, Herbert, 164, 230-234, 250; and
social Darwinism, 4, 8, 32, 207, 209,
231-234; *Social Statics,* 209; "The Social
Organism," 231, 232
Stanley, A. P., 152, 244
Statistics, 26-32, 155-156, 216-217. *See also*
Political economy
Stephen, Fitzjames, 215
Stephens, Joseph Raynor, 13, 57
Stevens, Wallace, 183
Strauss, David, 162, 250
Sulman, Thomas, 129
Swinburne, Charles Algernon, 131, 186

Tamworth Manifesto, 4-6
Taylor, Harriet, 41, 146
Ten Hours Act of 1847, 90, 100
Ten Hours Movement, 1, 2, 13, 30, 44, 53,
55, 56-57, 59, 86-90, 106, 116
Tennyson, Alfred, 6, 11, 182, 183, 185-
197, 198-203, 227, 237, 243; *Idylls of the
King,* 6, 182, 186-189, 190, 196, 202-
203; *In Memoriam,* 186, 188, 189, 192-
193, 195, 201-203; "The Lady of Shalott," 186, 196; "Morte d' Arthur," 186-
187; on progress, 186-203; and evolution, 187, 201, 227; "Locksley Hall,"
187-190, 192, 193, 195, 196-197, 202;
Maud, 188, 189-191, 193; "Locksley Hall
Sixty Years After," 189-190; "Ulysses,"
189, 196; on French invasion scare of the
1850s, 190-192, 194; and industrialism,
190-192; "Ode on the Death of the
Duke of Wellington," 190, 193-194; on
war, 190-191; and Christian Socialism,
191; political poems, 191-192, 194-195;
"Vastness," 194; "The Lotos-Eaters,"
195-196, 199, 202; "Mariana," 195-196;
"The Palace of Art," 195-196, 201, 243;
"Lucretius," 196, 199; *The Princess,* 237

Thackeray, William Makepeace, 26, 28, 55, 181, 225-227, 233; *Book of Snobs*, 55, 214; on Carlyle, 71; on Young England, 96, 107, 214; and Anti-Corn Law League, 115, 116 (*see also* illustrations on p. 177); and realism, 207, 214-215, 222, 223; *Catherine*, 214; on Dickens, 214-215; *Novels by Eminent Hands*, 214; *Vanity Fair*, 222-223, 230; *Pendennis*, 226-227, 230

Thiers, Adolphe: *Histoire de la Révolution française*, 63

Thomson, James, 182

Tocqueville, Alexis de, 9, 69, 145, 241

Tolpuddle Martyrs, 93

Tonna, Charlotte Elizabeth, 56-59; *Helen Fleetwood*, 30, 44, 56-57, 213

Tory-radicalism, 2, 13, 14, 41, 44, 55, 96-107, 134

Trade unionism, 4, 23, 52, 53, 58, 75, 84, 104, 114-115, 139, 142, 239, 255; New Model Trade Unions, 2-3; Dickens on, 91-95, 104-106; trade union rites, 92-93; Disraeli on, 93, 101, 105; Glasgow cotton spinners' union, 93-94, 113; Tolpuddle Martyrs, 93; and Christian Socialism, 148; Amalgamated Society of Engineers, 238; "Sheffield outrages," 239

Trench, R. C., 135

Trollope, Anthony, 8, 28, 181, 205-214, 220, 225-226, 233, 237, 244, 249; *The Way We Live Now*, 32, 214, 230; *Barchester Towers*, 166; *Autobiography*, 205-206, 208-209, 214; on Dickens, 205-207, 215; and realism, 205-206, 207, 208-214, 222, 223; *The Warden*, 205-206, 208, 211, 213; and "advanced conservative liberalism," 208-214; *Can You Forgive Her?*, 209; *The Duke's Children*, 210; *Phineas Finn*, 210-211; and Reform bill of 1867, 210-211; *The Eustace Diamonds*, 211; *The Prime Minister*, 212-213

Trollope, Frances, 39, 86-87; *Michael Armstrong*, 28-29, 30, 31-32, 44, 205; *Jessie Phillips*, 30, 205

Tupper, Martin Farquhar, 127

Turner, J. M. W., 221

Tylor, Edward Burnett, *Primitive Culture*, 248-255, 257

Utilitarianism. *See* Benthamism

Victoria, Queen, 102, 186

Wade, John, 12

Warren, Samuel: *Diary of a Late Physician*, 55; *Ten Thousand a-Year*, 55-56

Wellington, Duke of, 190, 193-194

Westminster Review, 17

Whitman, Walt, 169

Why I Am a Liberal, 164

Willkie, Sir David, 26

Woolner, Thomas, 129

Wordsworth, William, 11, 16, 168, 170; *Ecclesiastical Sonnets*, 58-59; *The Prelude*, 183, 252

Working Men's College, 129-130, 146, 222, 254

Wright, Thomas, 255-256

Young England, 96-107, 134, 219

Zola, Émile, 207

PART
OF A
WINTER

PART OF A WINTER

a memory more like a dream

GEORGE SIBLEY

HARMONY BOOKS/NEW YORK

ACKNOWLEDGMENTS

The author gratefully acknowledges permission to reprint the following excerpts from:

"Dover Beach" by Matthew Arnold from *The Norton Anthology of English Literature, Vol. II.* Copyright © 1974 by W.W. Norton and Co., Inc.

"East Coker" by T.S. Eliot from *Four Quartets.* Copyright, 1943, by T.S. Eliot; Copyright, 1971, by Esme Valerie Eliot. Reprinted by permission of Harcourt Brace Jovanovich, Inc.

Edges by Ray Raphael. Copyright © 1973 by Alfred A. Knopf, Inc.

"For the Time Being, A Christmas Oratorio" by W.H. Auden from *W.H. Auden: Collected Poems* edited by Edward Mendelson. Copyright © 1976 by Random House, Inc.

The Glory and the Dream by William Manchester. Copyright © 1974 by Little, Brown and Co.

"Heigh-ho", lyrics by Larry Morey, music by Frank Churchill. Copyright © 1938 by Bourne Co. Copyright renewed. Used by permission.

Memories, Dreams and Reflections by C.G. Jung, recorded and edited by Aniela Jaffe, translated by Richard and Clara Winston. Copyright © 1963 by Random House, Inc.

"Mythologies" by W.B. Yeats. Copyright © 1959 by Mrs. W.B. Yeats.

"The Tower" by W.B. Yeats. Copyright © 1928 by Macmillan, Inc., renewed 1956 by Georgie Yeats.

Sections of *Part of a Winter* first appeared in a slightly different form in the *Mountain Gazette,* October 1975-January 1976.

Inquiries should be addressed to:
Harmony Books, a division of Crown Publishers, Inc.
One Park Avenue, New York, New York 10016

Published simultaneously in Canada by General Publishing Co., Ltd.
Printed in the United States of America.

Designed by Ken Sansone

Library of Congress Cataloging in Publication Data

Sibley, George.
Part of a winter.

1. Sibley, George.   2. United States—Biography. I. Title.
CT275.S514A35 1978   973.9'092'4 [B]   78-5647
ISBN 0-517-53189-5

For Mike Moore

and his

Mountain Gazette

The human brain is the kernel which the
winter itself matures. . . . The winter is thrown
to us like a bone to a famishing dog, and we
are expected to get the marrow out of it.

—Henry Thoreau

PART ONE

> At six I passed [James Collins] and his family on the road.
> One large bundle held their all—bed, coffee-mill, looking-
> glass, hens—all but the cat; she took to the woods and
> became a wild cat, and, as I learned afterwards, trod in a
> trap set for woodchucks, and so became a dead cat at last.
>   —Thoreau, from *Walden*

James Collins has a very modest place in American history:
an Irish immigrant, gandy-dancer, semi-itinerant squatter,
in 1845 he sold a shanty for $4.25 to Henry Thoreau, who
salvaged the boards for building his own more famous shanty at
Walden Pond.

Since the Collins cat was promptly homeless upon
Thoreau's taking possession of the shanty, it is fair to assume that
Thoreau and the cat took to the woods at about the same time,
albeit independently: Thoreau to study on the wildness there,
and the cat to actively participate in it. And from that basic
difference, we can probably assume that they had different
experiences in the woods, different conditions, considerably
different attitudes toward life in the woods—Thoreau's
statement, for example, that "in wildness is the preservation of
the world" might not have sat well with the cat, who died of it.

I too took to the woods for a time—for four years in the
early Seventies—and I would say that both my reasons for going
and my conclusions from the experience probably lay some-

where between Thoreau's and the cat's. Henry went, in his own words, "to drive life into a corner"; the cat went because life had driven it out of its corner; and I went because I had the feeling that life had more or less driven me into a corner from which a rabbit-hole to the woods was the only exit. If pressed, I would probably have to confess that it came down, as life so discouragingly often does, to a matter of economics: I went to the woods because there was a situation there that I could afford without resorting to steady employment—a mundane kind of consideration that I can only dignify by suggesting that it might have been in the back of Thoreau's mind too.

Nevertheless, it wasn't a decision that made a great deal of sense. It could have, in fact, been called a decision to put off deciding for awhile.

At that point in my life, common sense said it was time to stabilize, throw out the anchor and batten down; with three years invested in one place, time to take out a twenty-year note on the near future and settle in for the thirty-year haul; with a baby in the crib, time for a little family planning; with my thirty-first birthday a receding memory, time to decide, once and for all, what I wanted to be when I grew up.

But instead, I seemed to find myself spending more and more time in my newspaper office, media baron of the mountain town of Crested Butte, Colorado (population 8,410—less than the altitude), imagining that the stranger walking down the street toward my office might be an emissary from some truly unlikely place, perhaps even the future. Not just another Texan, or Georgian, or seaboard expatriate wanting a subscription, or information as to where he might be able to buy a house cheap; not somebody looking for the editor, or the business manager, or the director of advertising, or the copy boy; but finally, somebody looking for me, somebody aware of the fact that all those hats were just a cover.

"Sibley?" he would say, with the perfunctory manner of

one already knowing; and I would nod, and he'd get into it without preamble: "We've searched the files..."

"What files?" Wariness is usually noted.

"*All* the files. We've searched all the files, and narrowed it down to you. You are apparently the only one who might possibly be able to do a certain job we have in mind."

A pause—but I would remain silent. Overeagerness is usually noted.

He would continue. "Other than what I will now burn in your stove"—and he would proceed to do so: the best way to keep a secret is to burn the instructions before reading—"there will be no further instructions, no contacts, no reports, no time limit. The only real requirements for the job are imagination and ingenuity; so far as experience and expertise are concerned— forget it. The idea is to correct the successes of the past, and people who know how to do things right are a drawback. You might as well know—in the event you haven't already guessed— that the chief factor in selecting you for the job is the degree and quality of imagination you've displayed in screwing up your life to this point...."

Well, it filled up the slow afternoons between issues. But as you might expect, no emissary from any place stranger than New York—there were people from Sydney, and London, and Rhodesia, of course—but no emissary from any place stranger than New York ever came by my office, certainly no one from any place so remote as the future. And in fact, so many emissaries from New York, Atlanta, Dallas, and L.A. were coming by, wanting subscriptions, or ads for their new gift shops, that my cover was in danger of being blown. I was at the point where all I needed was a little infusion of American capital and Protestant grit, and I might have been comfortably trapped there forever, my allegiance declared. One more fellow, future in hock to the ways of the past, trying to figure out the best way to do what he hadn't really decided was the best *thing* to do.

Nothing particularly out of the ordinary there, I might call it the life story of at least one generation. But I did feel that there were extenuating circumstances in my case—if nothing else, the amount of time and energy that I had in fact invested in screwing up my life, or at least making it as unnecessarily difficult as possible. To suddenly get squared away at that point would have negated that whole effort, dismissed it as nothing more than youthful folly. And at thirty-one...while I felt I was probably too old to be young anymore, most of the time I felt too young to be old yet.

The upshot of it was that I decided to defer the decision, thought I should think about it all some more. So in the fall I sold the newspaper to an emissary from New York, a guy looking for a village to be voice of; and together with my wife Barbara and our son Sam—then six months old—I moved out to the woods. To think, to wait, whatever. I could have hung out a shingle, like Crested Butte, Aspen, Stowe, and Squaw Valley:

"Open For The Winter"

I went to the woods because I wish to live deliberately, to front only the essential facts of life, and see if I could not learn what it had to teach, and not, when I came to die, discover that I had not lived. I did not wish to live what was not life, living is so dear; nor did I wish to practise resignation, unless it was quite necessary. I wanted to live deep and suck out all the marrow of life, to live so sturdily and Spartan-like as to put to rout all that was not life, to cut a broad swath and shave close, to drive life into a corner, and reduce it to its lowest terms, and, if it proved to be mean, why then to get the whole and genuine meanness of it, and publish its meanness to the world; or if it were sublime, to know it by experience, and be able to give a true account of it in my next excursion.

—Henry Thoreau, from *Walden*

We had actually had no overt intention or expressed desire of going to the woods that winter, Barbara and I. At the time, we were living in the small Colorado mountain resort town of Crested Butte. I was editor of the town's newspaper, a very small weekly; and Barbara was running an equally small wood-carving business. Most of her work was beautifully incised, richly finished designs in walnut, cherry, rosewood, mahogany—signs, wall plaques, anniversary plates and desk sets that could have given a janitor's closet a feel of executive class.

But after four years of carving signs—sometimes for repeat customers who still had the same old names—Barbara was beginning to see alphabets dancing by in her sleep. Stately processions of classic Roman L's and P's, with Q's trailing trains of fine lines; *burgher-bunds* of portly, swarthy Fraktur B's and Schwabacher K's whispering in conclaves; Dionysian riots of Doric and Italic, with a Great Latin T, sly and sinuous, slipping off to perform lewd acts with a wanton, sylphic V.... She was bored with signs, names, *flatwork;* she wanted to try her hand at some full sculpture. Add a dimension—the third—to her work.

I was on a similar plateau with the newspaper. It is not so easy to describe the "dimension" I felt was lacking in my work; but I was, and am, convinced that it was not a problem of personal competence so much as a matter of the general relevance—or lack thereof—of newspapers. Beyond its obvious utility as an aid to communication between people doing things and the people watching them—and that covers all the activities of artists, shysters, criminals, and governments for the most part—the newspaper as a tool for social reform, for significant change on even a local front, began to seem about as effective as a spoon for digging cellars. It was possible, to be sure, to do little things here and there; but I remain unconvinced that a lot of little changes are what the world needs now.

I was worried about the fact that not only was my newspaper having no apparent effect on the way things were going with the community, worse, it was having no discernible effect on the way things were going with me. I didn't seem to be able, in other words, to even take my own editorial advice.

I can get out those old newspapers now and, reading back over the editorial pages, I shake my head in wonder. Who is this rational, eminently sane, witty editor? This font of good sense and generous humor, this wellspring of ideas for a better community, public service and duty, interpersonal relations....

Or more specifically—is this guy who wrote editorials for

nine months straight on the need for town planning the same guy whose wife was spending those same nine months nurturing a baby who represented the Neanderthal ethic in family planning (once you've got the family, you start planning)? Is this champion of reason, honorable compromise, and considerate behavior the same asshole who is as often as not expounding loudly from a barstool pulpit at midnight every third night or so?

Some might call it hypocrisy, this problem of getting along with myself as newspaper editor. But I think the truth turns on the fact that, no matter what it is you want to say, when you say it in a newspaper you start talking like a newspaper. Anyway, I do. And whether you call it hypocrisy or something less insulting, the burden of the dichotomy gets heavy, and I saw no real resolution. I found out, for one thing, that the more I dug in and tried to really grapple with the multiplying facets of issues, the *less* rational and lucid my efforts became.

My problem was that I myself—that's not the newspaper editor, but *I* my schizoid self—did not really care to eliminate the fool on the barstool. Because I was a socially responsible editor with a liberal background, I would support liberal abortion laws in my newspaper—but faced with the minor cataclysm of a child about to come into the world with no visible means of support, the idea of aborting never really came up. The fool on the barstool (alternately panicking and rejoicing those long winter nights before his son's birth) laughed in his beer and said *who am I to say when I'm ready to be a father?* It seemed necessary for me to remain disorganized and untogether enough to keep the possibility of the unexpected alive. But if you put that kind of shit in an editorial, you get a reputation like William F. Buckley, Jr., an intellectual bishop in the ranks of reaction.

So I was basically in the position of writing a good rational newspaper for a good rational society that I wasn't sure I wanted. For the successful control and maintenance of one like myself—and I didn't see myself as all that unique in the world today—I needed, or anyway wanted, something better than just the packaged administration of straight good sense. I needed a world based on some *better, more comprehensive* sense—a whole new dimension added to what is rational, sensible.

With thoughts like that rolling around in my head, and visions of alphabets dancing through Barbara's, we sold the ship and burned the bridges, and prepared to go...well, somewhere.

But where? That was a question. On the surface, our plans were simple enough: we wanted to go someplace cheap and reasonably quiet, where we could buy maybe a year's time on the proceeds from our sale of real estate, fourth estate, et cetera, and lay low while we "practiced our scales."

We thought, naturally, as young would-be artists do, of the city: envisioning a garret in some genteel slum. One room, the baby crying in a corner, me muttering as I picked Barbara's woodchips out of the typewriter—you know the picture. But a shopping tour of a few cities brought us to the realization that we didn't really know what we were getting into, and by the time we found out we would surely be broke. We were, in effect, too poor to be starving artists in the city.

Having burned our bridges though, we had to go somewhere; and that was when we started to look the other direction from Crested Butte—not back the way we'd both come, but a little further on. And as it happened, a summer biological field station eight miles north of Crested Butte agreed that, with the burgeoning backcountry traffic in ski-touring and snowmobiling, a winter caretaker sounded like a good idea.

So there was one winter at least: no rent, no utilities, a forest right out the door liberally laced with dead-standing fuel, as quiet and cheap as life could be. All we needed was enough cash ahead to buy a winter's worth of food.

As you can see, we did not go to the woods so deliberately as Thoreau did; nor did we have any definite intentions toward the woods *per se*.

I did not intend to write about "life in the woods." I knew I would continue writing, of course. A writer is not something I hope to become; a writer is what I *am*—just as I have a friend who is a drinker, another who lives for tennis, and another who is going to smoke his brains out. Writing is a habit I support, like dope or drink; and if it gets so bad that the well-being of the family is threatened—no, say instead, *when* it gets so bad that the well-being of the family is threatened, I go out and get a job for awhile, working construction, hauling garbage, laying rock...I don't really care what, because that isn't my life; it's just what I do to support my habit.

But even though I knew I would keep writing away at something, when friends heard where we were going and (after a pause) said...*Well...that ought to at least give you something to write about*...I ground my teeth a little. After thirty years in the toils and tribulations of Western Civilization, I needed to go out to the unfanged, second-growth, multiple-used, road-laced, over-administered woods to find something to write about?

I made what was close to a solemn vow that I was not going to write another "Life in the Woods." That shelf is full, I told myself. I hadn't turned in the green eyeshade and the Harry Golden cigar just to pick up a pipe and the battered cap of the outhouse philosopher.

But when I got there the woods surrounded me like a dream. I would be out walking or skiing, ostensibly looking for firewood or on my way to town for the mail run, but with my vagrant mind wandering off as far as Pittsburgh or London...when I would be suddenly tugged back, as surely as Natty Bumpo on hearing a twig snap...only I would be unable to recall the snap of a twig, or anything. There was never anything there but the woods, the woods, strange and beautiful, bland, indifferent; the woods were everywhere, like mice. Sometimes, in fact, the woods *were* the mice, or vice versa....

There were weeks at a time when we worried that the mice

might drive us out of our cabin, out of the woods. I spent hours looking around outside the cabin, inside up around the rafters, down on the floor, trying to figure out how the nightly wave of mice was getting in. If we left the butter out, there would be little poppy-seed turds all over it in the morning. They got into my desk drawers somehow, and peed all over my book; they stole Sam's little socks and wove them into their burgeoning nests; they ate part of a dollar bill; and once, when I didn't check the bottom drawer of the desk for a couple of weeks, a fertile little she-mouse shredded some old Crested Butte *Chronicle* stationery for a nest and gave birth to seven babies. I moved them out under the couch. We would wake up at night—*what the hell was that?*—and know that a mouse had featherfooted its way across a face or a hand. We could lie there in the dark listening to them court, fight, and screw, until it got to be ridiculous, at which point we would throw a shoe or book. Then, practically overnight, the assault would cease and we would know that the white weasel was back in the neighborhood. The woods give, and the woods take away.

You get the idea. I can say that I went to the woods solely because it was a cheap, quiet place to work on the salvation of Western Civilization; but no matter how true that might have been at the beginning, it was the woods that came to dominate my mind, to critique my busy little thoughts with the great roaring silence, to evaluate with a kind of blind contempt the ideas parading past my consciousness...well, if I thought I was confused when I *went*....

> I rejoice that there are owls. Let them do the idiotic and maniacal hooting for men. It is a sound admirably suited to swamps and twilight woods which no day illustrates, suggesting a vast and undeveloped nature which men have not recognized.
>
> —Thoreau, from *Walden*

It was an interesting coincidence of our relationship, Barbara's and mine, that it had more or less begun there at the field station, four years earlier.

Not long after she had moved to Crested Butte and was well into her business of carving wooden signs, we'd both been to a kind of pick-up dinner party that ended up in the bars of Crested Butte. Eventually everyone else in the party had drifted off home, but we'd sat on, talking and talking. When the bars closed, we'd taken to the streets, walking and talking. Around four a.m., we got in Barbara's car and headed for Gunnison to get a cup of coffee. Sixty miles round-trip for a lousy cup of highway coffee!—God, the holy nights when you think you'll live forever in plenty and beauty.

But at dawn that morning, we found ourselves back up the valley, north of Crested Butte, parked at the intersection in Gothic waiting for the sunrise. By then, I'm afraid, my feelings about this unfolding situation were either something more or something less than purely platonic. I knew, I mean I *knew,* beyond any shadow of doubt, that with this carver-of-signs it wasn't going to be casual; and I was ready right then to begin a headlong rush into intensity on any and all levels. This soul-baring glut of talk had awakened as many appetites as it had sated. But Barbara was either not so sure or not so impatient—"Things take time" she carved on her bench—and so we did in fact mostly just watch the sunrise that morning. Facing east like a couple of tourists, unaware that the real show was behind us, up on the gray old face of the mountain where the sun's light can be seen moving down over the cliffs some time before it appears over the eastern hills to light the valley.

More than once during the years we lived there, I stopped there in the intersection on my way back from the springbox and recalled that morning. Occasionally, in fact, wishing I could go back to that morning, so I could get out of her car, walk on home, and never see her again. I would never wish to be guilty of fostering the illusion that married life is more idyllic in the woods than it is in town.

And if that intersection had been not just the spatial intersection of two roads, but also an intersection in time, I would have been able to lean down and whisper through the vent window to that earlier self—*Relax! Four winters hence you'll be living with her not two hundred feet from this very spot...and there'll be all the intensity you want, and maybe a little beyond....*

"We don't talk like that anymore," Barbara has said. Sometimes there's a kind of nagging undercurrent to her tone that makes me feel like not answering. But other times she says it in a way both matter-of-fact and gently regretful...and I don't know *what* to answer. Yes, we don't; she's right, we don't talk like that anymore, all evening and on into the night, all night and on into the morning.

Before we were married, one of the old-timers in Frank Starika's Bar in Crested Butte told me, "If you put a penny in a jar everytime you fuck the first year, and take out a penny every time you fuck after that, you'll never empty the jar."

I don't know whether he was trying to be reassuring or discouraging—maybe just factual. At any rate, as it turns out, he was wrong. In the usual case, a certain amount of the first year or so gets spent just mastering the mutual mechanics of fucking—but then you either start to relax and make love or you don't; and if you do, while it may not be a dramatic bankruptcy, you'll empty the jar.

But *talking*—that's something else. If we had put a penny in a jar for every hour we spent in soul-baring talk that first year we knew each other, and taken a penny out for every hour we've spent in the same kind of talk since then, we would still be money ahead in that jar.

When the comment about not talking like we used to rubs me the wrong way, I want to shout *Okay then let's talk dammit!*. That's a sure way of shutting a person up. You get a silence so cold and deadly destructive that it is eventually necessary for someone to cry a little just to restore a human environment. I'll tell any married man right now, if your wife bugs you with the observation *you never talk to me anymore,* if you can't shut her up by sitting down like MacArthur preparing to negotiate an unconditional surrender and saying in a steely quiet voice *Okay then let's talk dammit*—if you can't shut her up that way, you'll have to shoot her.

But if it happens that you think you still love her, in spite of all the dull travesty and tedious farce that inevitably accompanies marriage, especially if there are kids; if in spite of all those daily stupid debates over the same goddam stupid points of order and discipline and finance and neighborhood trauma, you still love her; if in spite of the fact that most of the time you know what she's going to say about what, just from the way she opens her mouth and the look on her face and what went before, you still love her and don't want to shoot her at all—what do you say then? What's there *left* to talk about? We've covered everything—twice. At least. I've told you my past; you've told me your past. Except for an occasional diamond swept out of some cobwebby corner of the soul, a couple of people seven or ten or forty years married are no more capable of presenting each other with real surprises than—well, than they were capable of really, truly making love the first time they fucked.

We reach a point where, in the company of others,

something is said that triggers a memory from *her* past in *my* mind—and I look at her and know that I'm going to get a rerun, whether it's one of my old favorites or not. And vice versa. Sometimes in the middle of recounting one of my own inimitable hilarious experiences, I happen to glance her way—and suddenly I'm hearing myself not with my own forgiving ears but through her more objective auditors, and if the expression of polite semi-attendance on her face means what it seems to mean. . . .

Thus doth familiarity breed silence. Great vines of silence that begin to creep out from under the couch, up the walls, over the table, blooming in leaves. It isn't really that unpleasant, though, that silence. I think of the traditional vine-covered cottage, vines up the chimney, all over the walls and roof, meeting at the peak of the roof and curling down entwined vine in vine, and inside the old couple who sit all day in a silence that is not that uncomfortable: all stories told and retold (the evening news will remind them both of something that happened to one or the other or both). As close as the closeness of making love, they vibrate as a single unit. *Till death do us part.* Does it really matter that the silence is always, to a degree, the mute acknowledgement of a conditional surrender on a fair number of unresolved issues? *If you don't bring it up anymore, I won't either.*

They used to say about the old prospectors who went off into the woods in pairs that they would either come back as lifelong inseparable friends, or only one would come back. And for a fact, often enough only one did come back. Muttering about an "accident," a rock fall, a foot slipped.

In light of that, it seems strange to note that the worst year of our marriage, Barbara's and mine, was the year following our return to civilized life.

I don't mean that we fought more that year—if anything, perhaps we fought less. But there was a kind of. . .drifting apart. It only lasted about a year, and, with no really conscious grunting effort on either of our parts, we seem to have tied it up again.

But I found that subtle drifting apart puzzling. A certain intensity dropped out of our relationship for a while, and rather than making our generally squally mutuality more bearable, it seemed to make it less so. I think the situation must have had something to do with the persistent background of diversionary motion, noise, and light in the civilized world. Our friends were accessible again—and we were accessible to our friends. There was the "village," six minutes instead of six miles away: stores, restaurants, bars. Among other things, it was possible to avoid an argument, not finish a fight. One could stomp off in a righteous, or anyway self-righteous rage; it was easy to dial-a-sympathy.

It was different in the woods. Have you ever tried to stalk off in a dignified display of wounded righteousness on snowshoes?

But the problem was larger than just cutting a figure with the dignity of a duck. To stomp out of the house at half-time in another round of the ongoing child-rearing debate, or some other fight, was a little like the cartoon in which Wile E. Coyote runs straight off a cliff, finds himself standing in midair twenty feet from the cliff's edge, then slowly and ever so carefully begins to tiptoe back on thin air.... I'm not sure why it's like that in the woods, but it is. There is something about standing out in the middle of a predominantly non-human environment at twilight, feeling the piss-off leaking out of one like air out of a rotten tire and being replaced by nothing that has anything to do with the presence of God and His Divine Order in Nature, that makes one realize there is as much practical wisdom as altruism to the notion that one should "never let the sun set on a quarrel."

Finding no reinforcement or sympathy out in all that cold supernal beauty, one might go back indoors—determined to bear the hurt of being misunderstood in stoic silence—only to find the occasionally beloved adversary having the *temerity* (are you *mocking* me?) to pretend to the same stoic silence. Well, so be it: as right as *I* am, as misunderstood as *I* am, if I can't outlast her in being stoical.... But then one thinks about the fact that it is dark already—night comes quickly in the winter, when the sun drops behind the mountain at three o'clock—and there is no other place to sleep but in the same bed with the great stoic pretender. One thinks about the cold depressing sound of the roof creaking as the cabin cools—and suddenly there is nothing to do but finish it off: toe-to-toe and eyeball-to-eyeball, it has to be carried through to some renewed flow of warmth, flow of tears or blood, it's all one and the same. Friction or fusion, heat is heat, and it's necessary on a cold winter night. Never let the sun set on a quarrel; never let the night squat on a silence.

The hurt is not always imagined, of course. There is a mark that occasionally shows up on Barbara's face: a little tic-like fold or wrinkle by the mouth that is part of an expression somewhere between anger and pain. The mark is something between a scar and a flinch, the record and anticipation of a wound, but not a wound from a physical assault. The weapon I've always used on Barbara is logic. It's usually enough. This is not the hard clean logic of formal and theoretical gaming; it is a kind of lumpish and vulgar logic—best compared, maybe, to assault with an old leg of mutton.

I use it on Barbara when she tends to get a little too spontaneous and free in her mental associations. She has a tendency to come out with a thought or an idea that really hasn't been in the oven of the mind long enough—and whap!—right up along the psychological chops with cold mutton logic. It's for her own good, right?—I'm just trying to help her learn to think things through more thoroughly before she opens her mouth.

But now, there must be something of a recognizable expression that comes over my face as I raise the leg of logic for the exemplary blow. I picture it in my own mind as a kind of

Presbyterian look, a Grant Wood Presbyterian. But anyway, there must be a giveaway expression on my face, because she will now sometimes stop in mid-motion, and the little mark will indent about her mouth, not unlike the sudden advent of a dimple under different circumstances.

I saw a self-portrait once of the artist wife of a friend of mine. At first I didn't recognize her at all in her own picture. Then I realized that I had never seen her as she saw herself. I knew her only as my friend's wife. Sometimes when Barbara and I go somewhere, she goes as my wife; sometimes I'm going as her husband. (And sometimes we're going as "the Sibleys," and we each wish we could stay home and read while the couple goes out.) When I'm tagging along as her husband, for dinner or whatever with some of her friends that aren't really my friends, I do my damnedest to be pleasant, charming, mannerly, and modest—hardly myself at all, in other words. And when she is accompanying me as my wife, she wears the mark like a little jewel, close to the surface.

We have each said, antiphonally and in unison, that if anything ever happened to the other of us, we would never marry again. We've looked each other in the eye and said that— only later becoming aware that there's as much backhanded tribute to such a pronouncement as openhanded accusation. The thing that never seems to come up, even in those foul moments, is the idea of calling it off. I might stomp off seething and chewing my cheek, wishing her gone to hell—but if at the moment of so wishing, an angel came down and said *be of good cheer, your wish is granted,* I would be riding the devil's tail as he carried her off. Not to recant and seek her return, not at *that* moment, but to make sure she got what she deserved there. Which would, I am sure, turn out to be me, forever and ever amen. I think the secret of our marriage is that, when love falters, stubbornness picks up the burden.

The biological field station we were committed to protecting from skunks, thieves, badgers, coyotes, vandals, and other local wildlife is located on a patch of private land in the middle of a great sprawling entity mapped as Gunnison National Forest. It is actually on the site of a former town, Gothic, one of those long-shot-and-short-run silver boom towns of the 1880s; as a growing concern, the town of Gothic did not even hold out for a decade, although its last resident, one Garwood Judd, hung on into the late Fifties. Mayor, police chief, clerk and council, dogcatcher, and sole resident.

The field station is located at the junction of two streams. One of these is Copper Creek, a dippy bouncing little thing, noisy as a freeway, that drains a steep and rather narrow valley from the northeast, toward Aspen. High in the valley sits a tiny Bavarian-fantasy lake, replete with island but no Ludwigian castle, its waters held there by old glacial moraines. Above this lake are two high passes, East Maroon and Conundrum, which provide access into the Maroon Bells-Snowmass Wilderness Area for a mind-boggling traffic of summer hiking-tourists. The mines that supported the town of Gothic and its mill were up on the steep slopes at the headwaters of Copper Creek.

By contrast, the other stream, the East River, flows easily through a broad and peaceful mountain valley and must surely be one of the most leisurely streams in the alpine world; it has been so befuddled by beavers over the course of centuries that it can hardly find its way downhill anymore. Coming over the ridge from Crested Butte, you have a sudden splendid look at its meanders in the valley six or eight hundred feet below. In the spring when the water is still high, it looks like nothing so much as a loose coalition of ponds, backwaters, and bends trying to organize a lake. A French parliament of a river.

There are still beaver on this river—or beaver again, as the case may be. There are so many beaver on the river, in fact, that they become a problem. There is a fine damsite just downstream from a bridge across the river, and every so often a beaver with an Army Corps of Engineers complex puts in a dam; these dams go up fast, and a couple of days later the bridge approaches will be flooded. Then the Department of Fish and Game has a ticklish job, even a dangerous job: destroying a beaver dam a few yards away from a well-traveled tourist road.

"Daddy, what's that man doing?"

"Hey man, what're you doing?"

"I'm tearing out this beaver dam. It's flooding the road."

"I thought you guys were supposed to protect the beaver."

"I'm not hurting the beaver; I'm just tearing down his dam; it's flooding the road."

"Why not just elevate the road? I thought beavers were endangered or something."

The only thing presently endangering the beavers on the East River is their own success. The beavers no longer have a natural enemy in the national forests—I exclude man, not because we are not natural, but because we are now such reluctant and conscience-stricken enemies for the most part. So the beavers thrive like people, until they are ripe for some social disease or community plague. For years, Fish and Game men have been live-trapping beaver and transplanting them to less populous—less *beaverous,* I should say—areas. Now, in some places—and the East River valley is one—they are resorting to the steel trap and the rifle for population control, as most of the less beaverous valleys are filling up too. The only hope, to relieve men of such an ugly job, would be to reintroduce something big and intelligent enough to kill beavers, such as the wolf. But no one has figured out how to teach a wolf the difference between a beaver and a beef.

The mountains drained by this generally indolent little river are part of the Elk Range, an accumulation of intrusives from the tertiary age that, less Alpish than the San Juans to the southwest, less plain massive than the Collegiates and other peaks in the central ridge of the Divide, do have a distinctive feel of their own...as what mountains don't, after a few years in their midst? But I think even a casual passerthrough would note in the Elks a certain expansive tranquillity that is not common to all mountains everywhere. This is certainly as much due to the lush and gentle valleys separating the mountains as to the mountains themselves, for some of them—Crested Butte and Gothic Mountain, for sure—would leave different, more overbearing impressions if it weren't for the "roomy" valleys around them.

From the town of Crested Butte, Gothic Mountain is almost mystically symmetrical—the first time I saw it, I thought at once of a small-scale Fuji. But from where we lived in the woods, it was an entirely different mountain. From the back door of our cabin (after a slight descent to the East River) it rises some three thousand feet in less than a mile, which is a decent grade for an aging mountain. The last thousand or so vertical feet of the mountain are nearly bald rock, cliff-like on the side overhanging the field station and our cabin. The wind, frost, and weight of time that exposed this once-buried rock are now at work on the rock itself, and the cliffs have been weatherbeaten into a kind of relief arrangement of steep couloirs separating rock faces that have the rough but unmistakable shape of the gothic arch—whence the mountain's name.

The cabin we lived in there at the foot of Gothic Mountain

did not belong to us; nor did we, like Thoreau at Walden Pond, build it with our own hands. But this in no way diminished its value or importance to us; and while it was nothing on which we could borrow money or be taxed, it was home for four years, and for me, in this restless age, that is a fair amount of home living.

For Barbara and me, it was an episode; but for Sam those four years lacked only a few months of being his whole life, and as "first homes" go, it was a powerful one. And our daughter Sarah—we left Gothic when she was still too young to remember anything in a conscious way, but that cabin was where she was born one summer night, and that must make some difference in the unconscious foundations of a life.

The cabin was not large—sixteen by twenty feet, with a half-loft, for a total of around 450 square feet of usable space. By the time we used the space required for beds, a table, a heating stove, kitchen stuff, Barbara's workbench, my rolltop desk, and nine months' worth of foodstuffs, it was all but necessary to make reservations to use what little space was left. In the middle of the city, it would have amounted to slum conditions; but out there, for instant relief from a sense of overcrowding, one had only to step outside.

There was, in fact, something about the immense, never quite perfectly silent quietude of our estate there that made a small, slightly close and crowded, but very definable *limited* space not only tolerable, but even psychologically desirable.

There are many mountain chalets that make you wonder if the architect isn't maybe getting a kickback from the glass companies. Most of these, it is true, are "second homes," built for short stays and showing off and not really for living in. But I don't think I would ever build a glass house out in the middle of a non-human environment. I would take a look at the other animals already living there: to judge from their homes, the animals that live in the woods all the time consider it sufficient to be able to enter the great world at will, but also necessary to be able to leave it completely too, to be contained within a small, close, comfortable, and familiar space, to be able to put their back up against something solid and watch the entrance if that seems to be the thing to do.

I suppose that sounds a little paranoid. Actually, thinking about it, I am as aware as anyone that there is nothing, demonstrably nothing, in nature to give a rational being any cause for paranoia.

But at the same time, I am also as aware as anyone of what a general strain it is trying to be a rational being all the time, even at home; and for the backslider the night implies that there is nothing in nature, absolutely nothing, to give a paranoid being any sense of rationality.

Through the summer and into the early fall each year, the biological field station was a busy scientific community of 100-150 people from all over the country. They used the station as a base for study and research forays out into an environmental smorgasbord running the gamut from the deserts of the Colorado plateau not all that far off to the south and west, up through the piedmont grass-and-scrub lands, the montane forests and mountain valleys, and finally the high and heady alpine tundra, beyond which it's another science. Due to the spectacular topographical changes, one can head east into the Rockies from the edge of the desert, and in a few hours go through as many "tree zones" and climatological regions as one would in a trip of many thousand miles to the north.

But each year as September wore out, the people at the station returned to their home institutions, and that quiet that is almost substantial settled back over the place. The mountains waited for winter.

Winter came on a schedule of its own: raids and forays, flurries, advances and retreats, in a different pattern every year, as if our front were only one of many under a general command. One year it hardly snowed at all until a week after Thanksgiving. Another year it snowed so hard the day before Halloween that we couldn't get Sam to town for the annual party; and then it didn't snow again until a few days before Christmas.

But giving a week or two either way from Thanksgiving, winter had the region secured. One night the snow would come in a businesslike way, and when it cleared off a day or two later, I would have to shovel the stuff away from the Jeep to drain the radiator; the road was closed and the truck would go nowhere till spring. From then on until sometime in late May, the dominant reality for us was as much that of life on the ocean as life in the woods. Except for an island of tramped-down snow around the cabin (with peninsular extensions to the springbox and outhouse), we were as dependent on "small craft"—skis and snowshoes—as any islander is on his boat.

We could have made do with either skis alone or snowshoes; but as it happened we had both, and we learned that each had its special uses and functions. The difference between snowshoes—or "webs" as some call them—and skis—or "snowshoes," according to those who call snowshoes "webs"— can be compared to the difference between the farmer's tractor and the car he drives to town.

Snowshoes are for working: going to the spring for water, up into the woods for firewood, out to the outhouse with the chamberpot; they are for moving around on deep snow when you need to have your hands free. They are also excellent for tramping out paths that you can walk on without snowshoes after a couple of days.

Skis, on the other hand, are for stepping out and going other places. Skis-and-poles, I should say, because once you begin to get that good coordinated swinging "glide-stride," legs and arms working together to eat up ten or twelve feet with each "step," you realize what an organic unit skis-and-poles (when connected together by a skier) are. Like the sail and boat of a sailboat.

There are those who say you can do anything on skis you can do on snowshoes, and those Alaskan and Canadian trappers and trampers who say you can cover distances just as well on their long drawn-out webs. They are all right, after a fashion. But when you stretch out snowshoes to make them better for running, you lose some of the maneuverability in close woods that is one of their chief values—and no matter how you streamline them for running, you can't get the things to glide, or coast downhill. And if you have ever tried to walk uphill through thick trees on 220-centimeter skis, or carry two five-gallon waterjugs downhill on skis on a slick crusty day, you know that just getting the job done is not the sole criterion. . . .

The first winter we lived in the woods, I spent quite a lot of time on the webs. There was a coal strike that fall, and we hadn't been able to get any coal in before the snow closed the road, which left wood as our only fuel.

That was fine; there was plenty of dead-standing fuel within easy reach of the cabin. But as it was all fast-burning pine, spruce, and aspen, we needed plenty. I hauled down several truckloads in the fall; but, fearing it wouldn't be enough, I supplemented the pile through most of the winter by going out on the snowshoes every day that the weather was halfway decent and bringing down a couple of dead-standing aspen—tying them to a kind of harness rig I made, and harnessing myself in like the old gray mule. It was good exercise: hauling wood that way, then bucking it up, I was twice warmed by the wood before it ever got into the stove.

But that wood-hauling operation became something more, something not really related to the chore itself. As the winter wore on, my search for the daily dead aspen took me further and further out from the cabin in a widening arc. It was of course easier to drag today's trees down over as much of the packed trail left by yesterday's trip as possible, so I worked my way out into the woods like a railroad: a main line from the cabin and the sawbuck, trunk lines breaking away into different parts of the aspen-covered slope, secondaries off from the trunk lines, and finally spurs and sidings to every dead-standing tree with a diameter of more than three or four inches.

January that winter was cold—it got down to -35°F. once, which is pretty cold for that far up the valleys—but it was almost snowless after a few big storms in December, so the tracks leading out of the woods multiplied, until finally one day the inevitable happened: I "laid a new siding" toward a likely firewood-tree and was surprised to come upon a path in the snow that terminated at a fresh stump...just me arriving where I'd been before, from another direction. A new look, in passing, at an old encounter. Like on a tree, when the twigs at the end of different branches meet and mingle, scrape against each other in a breeze.

So, better than the railroad metaphor for those tree-seeking expeditions is the metaphor of the tree itself: in looking for the trees, I'd created the map of a tree among them.

I don't know whether that sounds stupid or irrelevant or merely profound—I like the picture, is all. I mention it here for a couple of reasons, however. For one thing, it seems to shed a favorable light on the generally unappreciated and largely lost art of deliberate digression—which is, when you stop to think about it, intimately related to the also-lost art of exploration.

And, second reason—I offer the image up to the reader as a kind of half-assed excuse for the occasionally deliberate but generally digressionary construction of this book. This is not, as I've said, "My Life in the Woods," it is more like "My Life from the Woods"; and if it should begin to appear that I am going nowhere except off on tangents, well, that approach works well for gathering firewood, so why not for seeking sense out of diverse and varied experience?

What is exploration but the act of going off and—armed to

the teeth with acquired skills, accumulated experiences, beads and mirrors, and a wholesome faith in blind luck—deliberately getting lost? "Old men," said T. S. Eliot, "should be explorers." And I've thought that when I grow up I would like to be an explorer.

Thinking about the map of a tree among trees, I am reminded of an old grade-school riddle: How far can you go into the woods?

The right answer, the socially approved answer, the one they taught us in grade school and high school, through college and a million examples in the organized society all around us, is: "Only to the middle, because after that you're coming out of the woods"—one hopes with a good retirement plan, some sound investments, and the mortgage payments finally eating into the principal.

But if you've been to the woods in winter, with all the paths either covered over or dismissed as predictable six miles back down the road where the plows stopped; if you've lived there long enough to start reading the maps that lead up to the trees rather than between them—then you know that you can go just about as far into the woods as you are willing and able, and you won't run out of woods.

> The forest shimmers in a lovely twofold light; there are new dangers, new initiations. The Celtic forest is not an opposing world, like the hell of the Christian theology, but a realm of the soul itself, which the soul may choose to know, to seek therein its most intimate adventure....All that is dark and tempting in the world is to be found again in the enchanted forest, where it springs from our deepest wishes and the soul's most ancient dreams.
> —Heinrich Zimmer, from *The King and the Corpse*

When I wrote the following pages, or rather the bulk of them, I lived alone, in the woods, a mile from any neighbor, in a house which I had built myself, on the shore of Walden Pond, in Concord, Massachusetts, and earned my living by the labor of my hands only. I lived there two years and two months. At present I am a sojourner in civilized life again.

—Thoreau, from *Walden*

It is difficult to imagine an ex-urbanite from America, or Europe, or any part of the world much touched by Western thought for that matter, going to live for awhile in the woods without at least a peripheral awareness of the precedence there of Henry Thoreau. Different trees, maybe, than the ones around Walden Pond, but the woods are the woods.

I will do more than just acknowledge his prior presence there—pissing on top of his watermark, as it were. I feel pretty certain that had Thoreau not gone out to the woods for two years around 1850—and written down his experience there—I probably wouldn't have gone to live in the woods around 1970.

It's not that I wouldn't have liked the idea; I just doubt that it would have occurred to me. I enjoy being outdoors, and seem to spend a good deal of my time out under the sun, either working or playing; but I am not basically a very woodsy person. I like to go walking or hiking, but not so much as I like to play tennis; and I am a very lukewarm camper at best, even a fair-weather camper. I was not a Boy Scout, I never once slept out in the woods as a kid, and I didn't even own a sleeping bag until I was twenty-two. I now own a fancy down-filled sleeping bag, and I have given it some good outdoor use; but I would guess that for every night I've used it out under the stars, I've spent a night in it in some friend's living room—which is ridiculous: it is built to keep a body warm in temperatures down to 10 above zero (F.) or something like that, and as a result I have spent some of the worst nights of my life in 74° upstairs apartments (usually after too much to drink), gasping and thrashing in a clammy, sticky "mummy's embrace."

But that is beside the point, the point being that I am not cast in the mold of, say, John Muir. My very nature is otherwise; and when both Barbara and I decided that it was time to stop doing what we were doing lest we go to sleep in place, grow old and die without noticing, the idea of "proving that a modern family could survive in the North Woods" did not really enter our thinking; nor did we want to go back to the land in the spirit of the Mother Earth people, to experiment with hydroponics, communalism, and windmill construction. When I think of that kind of either/or commitment to the woods, I am like Henry Miller—"I realize what a terribly civilized person I am—the need I have for people, conversation, books, theatre, music, cafes, drinks and so forth...."

But while Thoreau tended a beanfield at Walden Pond, his two-year effort could hardly be misconstrued as a commitment to the idea of physical self-sufficiency. And it is almost ridiculous to think of Thoreau in an "alternatives" commune. Ralph Waldo Emerson reports a mutual friend saying, "I love Henry, but I cannot like him; and as for taking his arm, I should as soon think of taking the arm of an elm tree." Thoreau was a loner.

There were loners in Thoreau's day going to the woods in a big way; many of those who found "society commonly too cheap" were not bothering to hang around long enough to tell society what they thought of it. Sycophantic journalists—not unlike the network people who venture into Wyoming or Utah or Montana today—gladly sent back East just about any lie the legendmakers like Jim Bridger would tell them. But there is evidence that the Mountain Men we know about were probably no more than the tip of the iceberg: the Rockies and Sierras were as alive with grizzly men as grizzly bears—about matched in disposition and eating habits. *That* was a "life in the woods" ...but Thoreau did not go that far either.

Consider some of what was happening in the woods during Thoreau's lifetime, say between the years of 1837 (when Thoreau graduated from Harvard and returned to Concord) and 1854 (when *Walden* was finally published). The major westward migrations were barely under way, and most of America was unsettled. The almost measureless Louisiana Purchase had been traversed here and there, with a few trails beginning to show, but the real mapping expeditions had not yet happened. Word was coming back of *real woodsmen,* like Bridger, who built his fort on the Oregon Trail in 1843. The Donner Party provided a certain morbidly fascinating perspective on life in the woods in 1847. And in 1848, gold was discovered in California.... When I remember these things, I don't know whether to snicker at the naiveté or admire the bravado of a young man starting a book: "When I wrote the following pages...I lived alone, in the woods, a mile from any neighbor...on the shore of Walden Pond, in Concord, Massachusetts...." America was caught up in a fascination with the woods (and a million more or less exploitative ways in which to "appreciate" them); but not the overrun, surrounded, divided-and-conquered woods a mile outside downtown Concord. The woods America was looking at were forests you could lose the state of Massachusetts in.

Still, it was a large part of Thoreau's creed that, for the person willing to look for it, there was plenty of "wildness" left on a borrowed woodlot—an idea for which he found sufficient evidence. But that part of his "Life in the Woods" I personally find more interesting than compelling. What I find most intriguing is the degree to which Thoreau *didn't* live in the woods while at Walden Pond.

"At present I am a sojourner in civilized life again," he begins—but throughout his account he is so often tripping over, reflecting on, railing against, or visiting the "civilized life" of Concord and all the places the railroad ran to, that it is difficult to say that he was ever away for long, at least not in spirit. By his own admission, he actively sought out what passed for civilized life in Concord the whole time he was living alone at Walden:

> Every day or two I strolled to the village to hear some of the gossip which is incessantly going on there, circulating either from mouth to mouth, or from newspaper to newspaper, and which, taken in homeopathic doses, was really as refreshing in its way as the rustle of leaves and the peeping of frogs. As I walked in the woods to see the birds and the squirrels, so I walked in the village to see the men and boys; instead of the wind among the pines I heard the carts rattle. . . .

But if he wasn't quite all the way into the woods, he certainly didn't have his heart in the village, and the mainstream of society. Emerson summarized Henry's efforts to settle into an "honest job"—

> After leaving the University, he joined his brother in teaching a private school, which he soon renounced. His father was a manufacturer of lead pencils, and Henry applied himself for a time to this craft, believing he could make a better pencil than was then in use. After completing his experiments, he exhibited his work to chemists and artists in Boston, and having obtained their certificates to its excellence and to its equality with the best London manufacture, he returned home contented. His friends congratulated him that he had now opened his way to

fortune. But he replied, that he should never make another pencil. "Why should I? I would not do again what I have done once." He resumed his endless walks and miscellaneous studies....

And thereby renounced his chance to be known forever as "the man who put the lead in the American pencil." So much for the American way.

Another contemporary of Thoreau's was Horace Greeley, and he was telling the "aspiring young men" of the time whereat it was in his New York *Tribune:*

> The best business you can go into you will find on your father's farm or in his workshop. If you have no family or friends to aid you, and no prospect opened to you there, turn your face to the great West, and there build up a home and fortune.

Given this as the common wisdom of the day, Thoreau could hardly have taken a more deliberately uncommitted stance than to go off a mile to sit by the pond, walking out from there to observe in the woods, observe in the village...participating nowhere.

His actions seem to both invite and dismiss the often-offered criticisms of his arrogance, coldness, indolence, of his being a good-for-nothing son of a...well, stop right there—just a son. One of the first truly quintessential, lifelong, dedicated and determined sons since that Sun among Sons, Jesus Christ. A son to be borne as a lifelong trial by his diligent, anxious parents—"He's bright...good with his hands, clever...he's basically a good boy, he just hasn't *found himself....* Give him time, he'll settle down, turn *useful....*"

Eventually in considering Thoreau, I think one has to look up the dictionary definition of "sojourner" and conclude that Thoreau was "sojourning" wherever he was. He never really lived wholeheartedly in the woods or the village either.

Throughout his too brief life, Henry was basically, perhaps deliberately, neither here nor there:

> I went to the woods because...I did not wish to live what was not life, living is so dear; nor did I wish to practice resignation unless it was quite necessary.

and then

> I left the woods for as good a reason as I went there.

But to be neither wholly here nor wholly there is not necessarily to be nowhere at all; one can be both here and there in such a way that a whole new sensibility is being created.

Looking at the picture from a hundred-year perspective, it seems apparent that all those young men who went west at Greeley's exhortation did not end up doing anything very different at all from what they'd left behind. But Thoreau, who only went a mile and kept wandering back every day or two, established a philosophical alternative that really had as little to do with life in the real woods as it did with life in the village, yet was, somehow, gleaned from aspects of both.

Thinking about Thoreau like that brings to mind a concept that biologists came up with: the "ecotone" or edge, most simply defined as "the area of transition between ecological communities." With the possible exception of things like a vertical cliff or the edge of an advancing glacier, there are no sharply delineated borders or boundaries between this place and that in nature. Instead there are border zones, "zones of edge" if you will; where the woods meet the prairie, the prairie meets the lake, or the continent meets the ocean, there are ecotones with their own unique mixture of life from the two areas coming together.

A California writer and teacher, Ray Raphael, gave the biological concept of ecotones a sociological application in an interesting book called *Edges: Backcountry Lives in America Today on the Borderlands between the Old Ways and the New*. Early in the book he speaks of the strange vitality present in the ecotone:

Many of the most interesting things, say the biologists, happen on the Edges—on the interface between the woods and the fields, the land and the sea. There, living organisms encounter dynamic conditions that give rise to untold variety. Scientific studies of bird populations reveal that "forest edge" species are generally more abundant than those which confine their territory to the interior of the forest. The intertidal zone, meanwhile, that thin ribbon which separates the land from the sea, supports a plurality of life uniquely adapted to both air and water. When the tide is high, the flora and fauna of the beaches and tide pools may provide nourishment for fish; when the tide is low, land-bound mammals such as raccoons will claim the zone as their own by feasting on the intertidal creatures. Such ecotones—areas of transition between ecological communities—owe their existence to neighboring environments, yet they seem also to create a world in themselves....

Thoreau at Walden Pond seemed to be a creature of the ecotone, the "edge" between "civilized life" and "life in the woods": walking one of his paths in the evening, he would feel a "strange thrill of savage delight" at "a glimpse of a woodchuck stealing across his path," and perhaps a hundred yards further on he might encounter—usually with less pleasure—some laborer returning home after a day in another man's fields. At the Pond, he sat like Janus.

It was this aspect of Thoreau and his "life in the woods" that I found so attractive, although not really in a conscious way; and when we "went to the woods," we did and didn't go to the woods to about the same extent that Thoreau did and didn't go to the woods...we went into the edge, in other words.

In and out of the edge, over the edge this way, over the edge that way. One morning we left our cabin right after breakfast, skiied to town, got in a car, and drove to Denver; had there been any need we could have hopped on a plane in Denver and flown to New York, Chicago, London. Or we could have left our front door in the opposite direction and spent the night in a snowcave up in the high alpine tundra, as wild and desolate a place in the winter as you'll find anywhere outside the arctic circle. We were edge-dwellers all the way, neither here nor there.

If from the edge of the woods we freely crossed the edge of civilization and penetrated to its centers, many of the effects of civilization as easily reached out to where we were in the woods.

For example—I almost blush to admit it—we had electricity. Back in the Forties and Fifties, when Colorado's West Slope was still getting a little deeper into the Depression Era all the time rather than pulling out of it, one of the only available sources of employment was through the Rural Electrification Administration. Crested Butte's out-of-work coal miners ran lines and poles up and down every hill where there was even the weakest excuse of a need. Some of them were afraid of the height, and lugged ladders all over the countryside rather than using the climbing spikes, but a job was a job. The biological field station we were caretakers of had been there since well before the REA, and a line had been run up the valley in 1951. So we had electricity—and when a tree fell over the line one winter, the Electric Association repairmen came out on snowmobiles to fix it—for one family.

We had a citizen's band radio for communication with Crested Butte. We had an AM radio, on which I was able—barely—to pick up the Texaco Metropolitan Opera Broadcasts every Saturday throughout the winter. "Good afternoon, radio opera fans, this is Milton Cross, live from the Metropolitan Opera House in New York"—Jesus! Life in the woods! Outside the wind scratched at the door like a blind genie....

Let us spend one day as deliberately as Nature....Let us settle ourselves, and work and wedge our feet downward through the mud and slush of opinion, and prejudice, and tradition, and delusion, and appearance, that alluvion which covers the globe...till we come to a hard bottom and rocks in place, which we can call *reality,* and say, This is, and no mistake; and then begin, having a *point d'appui,* below freshet and frost and fire, a place where you might found a wall or a state, or set a lamp-post safely....
　　　　　　　　　—Henry Thoreau, from *Walden*

I like Thoreau's imagery here—what I might call his "sedimental journey." In essence, he is saying that that which we call civilization is but the detritus of time and the accumulating progression of efforts to deal trial and error with problems that are really the alluvial consequence of *prior* efforts to deal with problems that are the alluvial consequence—and so on, back through layer upon layer of symptom-treatments until—bump!—we all at once touch down on the rock-bottom problem that was the seed-irritant for the whole cultural pearl.

To put this to a specific, we might consider the population problem (too many people), and think of it as one of those simplified hardline drawings in the geology textbooks showing the layers of rock in some cliff or mountain.

One major reason we have this population problem is because we have been so successful in solving the problems of infant mortality and epidemic control. But these problems were partially the result of the proximity of people following the agricultural revolution—which in turn was partially an effort to solve the problems endemic to the uncertain and unrelenting lifestyle of the nomadic hunter/forager peoples. So essentially we could say that every time we cover a problem with a solution, the solution seems to engender new problems requiring new solutions.

Thus does the "alluvion" build up, and we have to go on that laborious sedimental journey to even notice the macro-irony of the fact that all our efforts to solve the problems of a precariously small population have suddenly led to a precariously large population. Here we can draw a heavier line in our socio-geology, and so define an age in the geology of civilization. Now we are trying to get a new age under way, in which we define the age's major problem as too many people; we will lay down solution upon solution until (we can imagine) one day we will suddenly discover that again we have a precariously small population. End of another age. It could, of course, be a very short age.

But a problem with Thoreau's sedimental journey has to do with his unverified assumption that it would eventually lead to "a hard bottom and rocks in place, which we can call *reality*." "Let us do this," he says, but in a rhetorical kind of way, sounding more like the Harvard Henry of our own day, picking up the shovel not to use it but to try to talk somebody else into it.

Where, or what, would such a *point d'appui* be? It seems impossible to see it today as any more than a matter of conjecture—or as they say about *passionate* conjecture, a matter of belief. To that extent, Henry's words are definitely rhetorical.

A great deal is said about Thoreau's capabilities as an "observer of Nature"—and rightly so, for the most part. But when it comes down to trying to somehow reconcile his accurate and beautiful observations with his stated conclusions and theses about the world, and especially mankind in the world, I find myself unable to make some of the leaps that he makes—as when he says, "I should be glad if all the meadows on the earth were left in a wild state, if that were the consequence of men's beginning to redeem themselves...."

I don't want to compete with Thoreau in the observations department, but my own modest efforts in that direction lead me to consequences so divergent from Thoreau's that I feel moderately confident in charging him with maybe only observing part-time. I too am a lover of wild meadows, but I recognize my love as an affordable luxury: I don't have to survive in them anymore, but can return as a visitor indulging an ancient nostalgia, who will only pay for the privilege with a few milliliters of blood for the hexapods. I can go on at some length about what I love about those meadows—probably will sooner or later here—but as the present topic is the redemption of mankind through wildness, I really can't kid myself: everything we find discouraging or disgusting about ourselves today can be traced back to the rough behavior which can be witnessed just about any day out in those meadows and the woods. Most of our problems today—population, certainly—stem from the fact that we succeeded too well in doing what obviously comes naturally out in the woods. We defended ourselves so well against our environment, and our neighbors in our environment, that we have effectively defeated them. So great were our defenses against the indifferent and antagonistic aspects of our environment that we occasionally have trouble locating remnants of it under the excesses of our ingenuity. But we kid ourselves, if we imagine that we would learn better manners and habits if put back in the wild meadows and a true wilderness with nothing to wear but our wits....

I remember one snowy day out in the woods—slick, sloppy, and silent—I was riding home from town on my bicycle (the last bicycle trip that winter), when, right near the field station, I came upon a skunk and a badger maintaining the balance of nature out in an open empty field. I say "maintaining the balance of nature"; what in fact was happening was that the badger was killing the skunk, and I assume he meant to eat the skunk when he'd finished.

The skunk, of course—pardon his frantic ignorance—didn't get the big picture, and the air was heavy with his protest. A skunk has a sharp set of teeth, and claws like tenpenny nails, but they are practically useless. His mouth is tiny, his nose in the way, his jaw underslung, and he's as slow and clumsy as a drunken Russian. The awkward assemblage of his frame should be enough to make even the most devoted believer in a master plan want to ask the great *a priori* whether the skunk was a dirty trick or just an honest mistake.

But the badger seemed totally indifferent to the fact that the skunk was pissing perfume by the liter—cousin to the skunk, the badger is no daisy either; all of the mustelids have some power to raise a stink. But the badger was so indifferent to the smell that he was making his prime target the source of that less than divine odor; although badgers are no speedsters, most anything is faster than a skunk, and the badger was just staying behind the swiveling skunk and playing a very literal and vicious kind of "grab-ass." I suppose there was good badger-sense to this particular attack; everywhere else the skunk was covered with thick winter fur, so the badger went for the pink, maybe figuring that in the process of badgering the skunk to death he could take care of half the eating too.

This may sound ridiculous; but it wasn't really very funny or enjoyable; and under the gray imminence of winter, even though this was Nature in the Raw—what the adventure films call a life-and-death struggle in the wilds—it really wasn't even very interesting. It was, in fact, tedious and disgusting; and even though it was none of my business, and was a typical example of man interfering, I broke it up. Sticks, snowballs, and loud noises.

When the badger retreated a little ways, the skunk dragged itself right in my direction, passing me by so closely I could have reached down and petted it, consoled it . . . but what did I have to say to a skunk trailing blood from both ends? Obviously I had done him no great favor: he was leaving a blood trail that probably every predator in our neck of the woods there would be snurfling down by half-past dusk. What solace did I have for him? Buck up, fella—sure it's a hard life, but we're all just links in the great sausage string of the food chain, and if we all do our part, eating and being eaten, it all balances out in the end. . . . *My* end, burbles the skunk through blood, my *ass*.

Actually I don't believe the skunk even saw me. I followed it down to the creek, where it drank through a hole in the ice. Then it trundled off into the thick willows by the creek, where its chances of survival were certainly better than they were out in the open meadow. Whether it actually survived or not, I don't know. And what if it did, that day? Tomorrow is always another day, and for a skunk what is tomorrow and tomorrow and tomorrow but a long procession of badgers, martens, coyotes, martens, coyotes, and badgers—or maybe the swift silent white owl. *There* is the meadow's notion of mercy, no tedious ass-chewing struggle where death is finally a matter of exhaustion, but a sudden back-breaking crunch and clutch. Out of the night.

Leaving the skunk to cool his burning butt in the snow under the willows, I went back to where I had left my bicycle, now a kind of soft geometry under the accumulating snow. The badger was still hanging around waiting for me to leave. He hissed and snarled at me—furious, of course, as I suppose I would be, if I were getting ready for a hot meal and some silly shit came along and took it away because it offended *his* aesthetics.

The badger didn't appear frightened of me at all—even the badger's little cousin, the weasel, is not afraid of a man: I surprised one by the woodpile once, him resplendent in his winter coat of white; we stood looking at each other for a moment, then to my amazement he took a couple of steps *toward* me; it was such an incongruous move that I actually backed up a step—then realizing I was being "tried," took a quick step back in his direction, whereupon he of course yielded the field. Not in fear, but good sense. I had a similar experience with the larger marten one night—the sinuous catlike marten that looks like a cross between a small stretched-out fox and a furry snake. I caught it in the beam of the flashlight, and it started stalking the light. The mustelids are a strange aggressive breed (excepting the "mistake," the skunk), and it is easy to see why the animal most feared by the early trappers and mountain men was not the wolf, or the grizzly, or the cougar, but the smaller wolverine, which is basically only a badger built on a scale to deal with a man. A big mean muscle for dull rage and violence.

I was raised so sheltered, spoiled, and civilized that I can feel regret for the fact that the success of genus *Homo* has meant defeat for so many species in an environment of contention for the same space and food. But it is a considerably more subjective experience to stand in an open field on a winter day being measured by a badger, and knowing that if the badger were a wolverine it would be my ass and not a skunk's, unless I had a little technology to stick in his face. As it was that day—by way of excuse, I plead gray weather and my own naive dismay at the tedious ugliness of the feast I interrupted—I reacted like some fumbling, paranoid neo-ape for whom the erratic, evolving consciousness was only an impediment to smooth reflexive action, and waved a club I didn't really have and acted out in superior rage nature's first and most basic form of defense: the bluff. The badger said the hell with it, and ran under a building at the field station.

But at any rate, when I am drawing conclusions and "consequences" from my observations, I have to balance the extreme beauty of a wild meadow in full flower against all the squalid little daily deaths down amongst all those flowers, and I think that what we might find, if indeed all the meadows of the world were put back in a "wild state," might not be our "redemption." And I doubt very strongly that it would have any of the qualities of stability and centricity that we would associate with "a hard bottom and rocks in place"—I don't believe, in other words, that we would find it to be the Garden.

In a way, isn't that what Henry seemed to be looking for? That ancient center of all creation, that which lies at the bottom of all our historical layers of "sham and appearance," our unrepentant record of prodigality, our debris of sins of ignorance and arrogance, omission and commission: the Garden.

Ah come on, you say, nobody believes in *that* Garden anymore. But it seems to me that it is one thing—a pretty superficial thing—to drop a worn-out legend, and something else entirely to actually cut oneself free on the deepest philosophical and psychological level from the idea of "a hard bottom and rocks in place" at the unknown and unproven "center of existence." And if a person subconsciously accepts—and the acceptance is pure faith, nothing but—subconsciously accepts the existence of this "hard bottom," *point d'appui,* then that person's whole perception of the dynamics of life is grounded on that belief.

And that hard bottom doesn't even have to be specifically the Garden for a number of things to be "explained" in an age that seems to be plagued with the sour fruits of hasty actions, the roosting of unanticipated chickens. We have violated some natural order (we've eaten the forbidden fruit); we are tampering with unknown consequences. And only if we strip away all our illusions of significant toil, squelch our drive to do, and re-affirm the existence of a well-balanced, ecologically sound, and vast eternal plan in which our conscious activity is not only superfluous but disruptive, only then can we again return to the "hard bottom and rocks in place," the Garden, there to move in peaceful harmony with a nature that was peaceful until we started trying to play god.

But without the Garden, the hard bottom, all of this theorizing obviously falls apart; it is a pattern that requires a predicating center: a Pole Star, a zero meridian, and other fixed points of reference. But in the wake of developments that were beginning right where Thoreau left off historically, it becomes more and more difficult to be a "Western navigator."

Even as Henry was sounding the depths and taking the measure of Walden Pond (1845-47) for example, another young man was about halfway through a similar, but grander, venture on the larger ponds, a twenty-year episode of note-taking and journal-keeping that would put cracks all through the foundations of our Judeo-Christian navigation.

That man was Charles Darwin, and just five years after the publication of *Walden,* he brought out the *Origin of Species.* This was—and still is—a serious blow to the nobly tragic view of man and woman as over-reachers fallen from grace, trying to work our way back, and subsequent biologists and paleontologists take us further away from the "sedimental journey" all the time. The earliest conscious perception of "reality" has to be set not at a "hard bottom" but at an arbitrary threshold of consciousness, and any bottom reality lies so far beyond that in the subconscious that it would have to be minuscule and largely immaterial to consequences on this side of the threshold.

But the world had barely begun to assimilate this information on a conscious level when the physicists started exhibiting their heresies about the nature of matter and energy, talking of building blocks so incredibly small for structures so incredibly large that the image of God the Father working with lumps of clay was more of a hindrance than a help. The metaphysical strain approached the limits of psychic elasticity during and after World War I, with the publicity and furor surrounding the publication of Einstein's Theory of General Relativity:

Nature and Nature's law lay hid in night.
God said 'Let Newton be' and all was light.
It did not last: the Devil howling 'Ho!
Let Einstein be!' restored the status quo.

—Sir John Squire

And now, even the static metaphorical beauty of the "sedimental journey" is shattered, even the physical notion of a "hard bottom and rocks in place" is set afloat by the recent revelations of the tectonic geologists: our concern that the world might be falling apart at the seams is countered by evidence indicating that the world was maybe *never really put together at the seams* but is, was, and ever will be a fluxion of growing plates of cooling magma that grind into each other, collide, and ride over one another in an eternally dynamic restructuring.

So the more we learn, the less we know for sure that's any help in charting a course. And—as if all this weren't enough—at the same time that the fixed points were winking out and the illusion of hard bottoms proving to be quicksand in the external world, Freud and Jung and other pioneer explorers in the internal realm were beginning to try to chart the deep invisible currents that have altered our courses since time immemorial.

Where, in this ever-evolving awareness, do we still imagine there might be a hard bottom and rocks in place, a Garden? I might mention in passing that, in the midst of all this, an international gathering of navigators agreed to accept Greenwich as the zero meridian in 1884—but even this seems to make it more of a convention, subject to popular whim (like the Congressional definition of wilderness), than a true fixed point. It has been quite a century, this last hundred years.

But it would be unfair to paint Thoreau entirely as a "fundamentalist." Too much, I think, he saw what he wanted to see out there on the edge between Concord and the woods; but there were other times when he was down off the soapbox and deep, deep in the woods—"the twilight woods which no day illustrates"—and what he saw was no hard-bottom Garden but "a vast and undeveloped nature which men have not recognized":

> All day the sun has shone on the surface of some savage swamp, where the single spruce stands hung with usnea lichens, and small hawks circulate above, and the chickadee lisps amid the evergreens, and the partridge and rabbit skulk beneath; but now a more dismal and fitting day dawns, and a different race of creatures awakes to express the meaning of Nature there.

Yes. And so we come, with Henry, to that zone of edge which we could probably just call modern times. The post-Darwinian, post-Freudian, post-Einsteinian ecotone where we have one foot still back in the Garden and the other tentatively treading the insubstantial squish and glop of the savage swamp.

Back there is that reasonably well-organized, well-lit, well-mapped history with its theocentric points of reference, its just (if harsh) gods, its psychological tremors muted and damped by rational philosophers. . . . But on ahead—well, the swamp, where one grasps at reeds floating by (or is one maybe floating by the reeds?), throws them together into little floating islets, throws the islets together with other islets in a coalition roughly reminiscent of what one used to call "reality," drifts with that possible potential tentative reality until it too drifts apart. Pole Stars for the soul and carrots-on-a-stick are sold from classifieds and streetcorners (installation extra and that's where they get you), but they're all just swamplights, will-o'-the-wisps in bottles, bottled wisps of the one-time will, once so reverenced but now just a joke on the bathroom wall, and they burn out in a month, warranty notwithstanding; *caw caw* laugh dark birds from bare metaphysical trees, or was that *call God;* call God and see who answers, you won't believe it: God isn't dead, he was just picked up cheap by an insurance conglomerate; *we've got the whole world, in our hands* sing the singing commercials from tall barren trees, but it's all slipping away through their fingers (I can't believe we ate the whole thing), slipping away here in the swamp, the savage swamp where the art of survival is learning to tread water for the time being, tread water....

I will tell you—or try to show you, as one who knows from experience—that it is not necessarily like falling over a cliff or getting hit by lightning to make that journey east of Eden from the Garden of the Good Old Days to the near edge of the modern up-to-date swamp-of-the-future. It can as easily—and more likely—be no more than a complacent trudge across the busy bourgeois plains with a downtilt so subtle as to be undetectable. You begin to notice isolated things that don't seem quite right, quite what was promised. Like the "lamps going out all over Europe," this old fixed point fades, a milepost is found to be not quite where it ought to be found, an old chart seems so out-of-date as to be irrelevant. But it's all one-by-one, no sudden catastrophic change—until suddenly you realize that you are up to your knees in sucking sand, up to your neck in questionable water and curious crocodiles. Then you flail out like one getting out from under an unanticipated nightmare, you try to retreat (which way did I come?), but it's no good. You've arrived, is all. Anyway, that's the way it was with me.

All my life, I've come to realize, I have lived on the edge in one way or another. The edge was not where I felt comfortable necessarily, or at home, but I felt *alive* on the edge: that was my habitat.

In terms of physical environment, I grew up on the edge between the human settlement and the woods. From the time I was a small child until I left for college and the city, we lived on the outskirts of a small city on the Allegheny River in western Pennsylvania, north of Pittsburgh. It was a city of ten thousand—10,006 by the 1950 census, and as we'd moved there in 1947, a family of six by 1950, we always claimed to have kept the population from being a nice round number. Eight miles away up the river, there was a larger city of twenty thousand; and a circle with a radius of say thirty miles, with Franklin (where we lived) at its center, would have enclosed maybe a hundred thousand people.

But nature is strong and hardy there. The great virgin forests that had covered the area in pre-Revolutionary days, making the rivers the only real highways (with a fort-town at every junction), had been almost completely logged off for lumber, or just cleared off for farming. An oil boom in "Pennsylvania crude" followed Drake's first oil well there in 1859. But the West Slope of the Allegheny Mountains is a wet region with good thick layers of rich earth from many generations of deciduous trees dropping tons of leaves; and in a matter of decades, abandoned farms lose their boundaries to encroaching woods, old oil roads yield up to berry bushes, scrub growth, and new trees. Everywhere where people weren't constantly active, the renewing woods were. A surprising variety of wildlife practically coexisted with the people when I was growing up there, and still does for all I know. It was nothing to see fifty head of deer down by the narrow twisting highways in the winter.

Our house was a big old shabby frame building up on a hill that literally looked down one of the intersecting main streets of the town. I can best describe the location of that house by noting that one night my father woke me up to watch the burning of a big bakery building downtown, gas explosion after gas explosion hurling loaves of flaming toast high in the air like fireworks. . . and another night my mother woke me to watch, as if in a dream, a fox chasing its tail out in the backyard under the moon. Walking to school one morning, I was startled to see a guardrail post looking back at me—only to find there was a sad looking screechowl sitting there, glum as a drunk at dawn. I hated to mow the grass, not because it was a job but because of all the garter snakes in the lawn—if you have ever gotten a garter snake tangled up in a handmower, you will know exactly what I mean. I would walk all over the lawn before mowing, swishing a stick through the grass, but it seemed like there was always one dull serpent who didn't get the message, until it was too late and his "ass was grass" as we used to say. Rest in pieces.

During the years I was growing up on that hill, the woods were at the peak of a period of "re-infiltration": with the war and war industries, bad times in the coal industry (the machinery for which was the town's principal industry) as gas and oil took over, and the general attrition of the times on the rural lifestyle, the area was gradually losing population and gaining trees and wildlife.

At present, the opposite is the case; times are good in the coal industry, and the town is booming. One-time working farms that all but went for taxes are sprouting real estate developments and trailer parks. Nearly every one of the vacant lots on the hill where we used to roam at will is now occupied with a trailer, two cars, and a lawn with a power mower. And there are no snakes to speak of in the lawns—a few, but nothing like there were; they have retreated with the woods. However, according to my father, the last time I was there with him, the Japanese beetles are something ferocious, with the snakes gone. And so it goes on the edge: back and forth, back and forth.

After graduating from high school, I went on to college in Pittsburgh, and in terms of the physical environment, that is nowhere near the edge between "life in the woods" and "civilized life"; but there are certainly other "zones of edge," places and, maybe more important, stretches of time, that are neither here nor there.

My last two years in high school were washed over with the turbulence following the first Russian satellite—Sputnik I to history, but then, just "the Sputnik," the challenge. The Cold War and the Bomb were as much a part of my "natural environment" as were weather and baseball; it was one of my father's parental fanaticisms that the six o'clock news be ingested with dinner. Every night of my early years we sat down to dinner within a few minutes of the dididah Morse code lead-in to the CBS news over the Youngstown radio station, and there was absolute silence at the table until the news shifted into low gear for sports at 6:15. If somebody accidentally belched or farted, anyone who reacted with more than a snicker quickly swallowed took their plate to the dark kitchen. The fact that my sisters and I ate two of our three daily meals to the news throughout the Fifties without developing young ulcers is a measure of the degree to which tension living has become our "natural environment."

Something else that was part of my natural environment was college. I was a bright kid in school, and I cannot remember ever thinking of doing anything other than going on to college after high school. It was assumed by my parents, all my teachers, and the classmates who eventually voted me the dreary, priggish, alien title of "Most Likely to Succeed" (at what, for godsake, at what?) that I would go on to college, and I came to assume it too.

And after Sputnik the Challenge leapt into the sky, mooning the Free World from apparently unattainable heights every ninety minutes, it was more or less taken for granted by all of the above, including me, that in the name of freedom, America, the human spirit, and all that I held dear, I would become a scientist. I hated chemistry, and didn't understand physics, certainly not twentieth-century physics; but I did well in mathematics, or what I *thought* was mathematics; and I decided that it was there that I would make my contribution. I mean— one and one is two, right? It all starts there, and a guy who is willing to work hard and do his homework and listen to his teachers. . . .

This was a mistake. I was over the edge the wrong way in mathematics—in science in general: I was a fish out of water, a cat in the sea. I went to college thinking that mathematics was Euclidean geometry and Arabian algebra. I had a high school teacher who talked one day about Nikolai Ivanovich Lobachevsky and his ideas about the parallel postulate; but it made no sense, he sounded like a Russian troublemaker to me, and I knew how to add one and one, and Russian and troublemaker in those naive days: you got two and Communist, in that order.

So I entered the School of Engineering and Science at Carnegie Institute of Technology on the eve of the Sixties (fall of 1959) believing: a) that science would save us all from Communism as it had from thunder (the lightning rod, B. Franklin), and b) that the Golden Mean was the scientific equivalent of the Word that Was in the Beginning. This was a lot like going into high school still believing in Santa Claus.

Because I was diligent and not dumb, I worked hard and managed to plug along in good shape for two years. I was a classic example of the fact that grades do not necessarily measure understanding, because I was on the Dean's List at Carnegie Tech those two years—by no means an easy school, then ranked with M.I.T. and Stanford—and I didn't know what the hell I was doing. I felt like a blindman inching my way along a boardwalk, toes sweeping out for something firm, taking a step, but not knowing whether it was forward, backward, or upside sideways.

Then one day—the course was Advanced Calculus—I reached out with one foot, felt this way, that way...over there...there...there was nothing. It wasn't a boardwalk, it was a dock; and it was the end of the line for blind pedestrians. Time to learn flying or swimming.

I remember sitting in the dormitory room of a friend, a senior, one year ahead of me—but that one was a light-year. He was trying to help me adjust to the conventions that had replaced foundations in modern mathematics. "What you have to do for now," he said, "is let the little thing that is never quite nothing go laughably small—then laugh at it." Or something like that: I remember *liking* what he had to say a great deal, even if I didn't remember it right. But I didn't know what he was talking about. He wasn't a fellow student, he was a bird. I would ask him a question; and he would push off the end of the dock, up and away, fly like a bullet toward the sun, go into a power dive, do a few loops and an Immelmann, finish off with a moebius flip, then glide back down to perch beside me on the miserable end of the miserable dock. "You see?" He wasn't showing off; he was showing me what was necessary. I sat there like a bald soggy pelican.

I walked away from it. I don't know if that makes it more of a defeat or less. I got a C in that Advanced Calculus course, which indicates I might have absorbed something, whether I was aware of it or not. Or did I just know how to take tests? In the Calculus of Probabilities and Statistics, where I don't believe we ever even stooped to using a real number all semester, I turned in two tests, not having the foggiest notion how I'd done in either: one came back with a 95 and the other a 36. I got a C in that course too that semester. And walked away from mathematics at the end of it.

To this day, I wonder if, had I maybe stayed with it, I too might not have one day just jumped off the end of that miserable dock, flapping and flailing, falling like a rock for a gutflopping moment—then suddenly found wings and caught air, scooped and cupped and drunk of the invisible ether, and just laughed and laughed. . . .

I transferred to the University of Pittsburgh. It only took one "Educational Psychology" course to convince me that, whatever my dubious instincts for *teaching* might be, I definitely did not belong in *education;* and after that I settled into one of the traditional refuges for the intelligent, clever, but basically aimless and faithless student, English Literature.

I did well in English Literature. As a freshman I'd had some trouble with Composition—mostly a tendency toward embroidery, too much of what a freshman thinks of as "creative writing." But once I got a harness on my syntax, I turned out to have a fair knack for writing good, tight, analytical but also sympathetic papers about other men's agonies. "The Clowns in Shakespeare: Antecedents of Modern Existential Angst." "Don Quixote, Viewed in Light of Jungian Archetypal Theory." "Fire and Ice: Elemental Imagery in the Poetry of Frost." I did well enough to be nominated as a candidate for Woodrow Wilson fellowships, which amounted to an invitation to apply for a lifetime of teaching and literary research and criticism. I was tempted—if for no other reason than that there was someone who thought I might be good for *something.* But I never filled out the applications, partly because they wanted too much privileged information (such as "Future Plans in Approx. 1000 Words"), but mostly because I again found myself at the edge.

If I were to say I was in the edge-zone between the "sciences" and "arts and humanities," I would be exposing myself as a phoney, a tourist, to any true sojourner of edges and ecotones.

No, the edge I was in was the one between science and the arts on the one side, and the humanities and the social sciences on the other.

The edge is a perimeter, a hedge enclosing a garden, if you will; and in the garden are the humanists and economists and essayists and critics and political scientists with their structures and societies and hierarchies and priestcrafts and systems. I was in training to be such a gardener—taking these mysterious bundles of mystery, pain, and discovery, and identifying, classifying, and naming them; planting, pruning, and watering them; preserving them; crossbreeding them; comparing them; contrasting them; cultivating them. If things got a little slow in any section of the garden, we spent the time criticizing each other's criticisms and cross-grafts, pruning jobs, et cetera. Occasionally someone—like Joseph Campbell recently—would discover a whole section of the garden that had been neglected for some time, and there would be a stampede over to comparative mythology or whatever.

But outside the hedge, over the edge and into the everything else, were the artists and the scientists, the anchorites and the nuclearites, the oracles and shamans and blind seers— amoral, egocentric, cantankerous, maniacal lot! They traveled light, no structures, no systems, no priests and no gods...if they felt the lack of the latter, they made one up, kicked it around until ready to move on, then sent it back...they kept their wits about them and that's about all, poking around in the unholy thrashing dark, beating through the unknown night like the nighthawk with its mouth wide open, hoping it won't come up too fast on an elephant's ass. They weren't out there for America, or the forces of freedom, or even the good of all mankind; they were having a good time! Word comes back of moments like this:

> Out of the meeting came something which Edward Teller brought into the meeting with his own head, which was an entirely new way of approaching a thermonuclear weapon....Calculations were made, Dr. Bethe, Dr. Teller, Dr. Fermi participating the most in this. Oppy very actively as well....Everyone around that table without exception, and this included Dr. Oppenheimer, was enthusiastic now that you had something foreseeable....

That one came over the hedge like a dead megacat. It would sully the name of a man with a conscience like Dr. Robert Oppenheimer's to say that the hedge is inviolable, that those outside can never come into the garden or vice versa. Only a few months before that meeting, Oppenheimer had said, "In some crude sense, which no vulgarity, no humor, no overstatement can quite extinguish, the physicists have known sin and this is a knowledge they cannot lose." That is a "garden statement," and Dr. Oppenheimer was both a physicist and a humanist. But—and I'll acknowledge the grounds for argument—when Wildman Teller, Tarzan Teller, Lord of the Abstract Tracts, swung into the garden, Dr. Oppenheimer and others like him showed they were gardeners second and explorers first.

I knew that if there were ever a garden party to which were invited not only all the gardeners but all the creators of the objects they pruned and arranged and grafted onto, once all the compliments had been passed out and it was down to the real talking and drinking, eventually all the gardeners would be talking to each other of Michelangelo. But Michelangelo would be off in a corner with Shakespeare and Einstein, talking with Goethe about where else he *might* have gone to look for the

Urpflanze...and pretty soon Goethe would sneak off to start looking again...back over the hedge, over the edge.

People are a little goofy for the Fifties today; there is the notion that it was somehow an idyllic, laid-back, and quiet time: politically, sexually, economically, environmentally. Generally, an age of relative innocence.

I suppose it depended on where you lived, and how you lived. I grew up—a little bit, here and there—in the Fifties in a home where Eisenhower was not a household word, and we did not have a television. When I was old enough to drive, I didn't get a late-Forties car with a back seat, but instead bought a Vespa motorscooter.

I was as sex-obsessed as most of my contemporaries, although I was a general all-round strikeout. And not just because I only had a Vespa motorscooter. I was the kind of guy who gets such tender words written in his yearbook as—"To a real brain...," "To one whom we're all sure will go far...." ("But not with me," she might have added.)

There were compensations in the social sector to partially balance out what I seemed to lack as a local sex symbol. I served on committees; did a term as president or groupleader or figurehead for practically every local youth organization that needed one; and if I didn't make it in team sports, I was the local tennis champion. I enjoyed those years—but not as they are being remembered today.

I grew up in a different part of the Fifties, maybe. I think my parents were anticipating the early Sixties from 1952 on, and both by nature and immediate environment, I came to do the same.... In the edge-zone again, and from the edge, the Fifties looked different.

There are quiet times, and there are quiet times. A couple of kids sitting in a roadster at a drive-in having a shake is one kind of quiet time. A man sitting quietly at the scene of a wreck, quietly wondering why his leg is still hurting when he can see it fifteen feet away on the road, that's another kind of quiet time.

There are times when the only sensitive reaction to a situation, showing a sufficient awareness of the true gravity of the matter, is to go into shock. I could probably overdo the metaphor, but I don't think it's stretching it to suggest that a lot of the silence of the so-called Silent Generation might have been a kind of massive shock. When a nation or a world is confronted with such incinerations as Dachau and Hiroshima; when millions of young fathers are trying to forget the incongruously bloody and beastly aspects of a righteous war; when containment has replaced victory in strategy because the bomb has made the "all-out effort" suicidal, and the "big picture" shows nothing but the evident possibility of Korea after Korea against a supposedly monolithic worldwide enemy...then a moment, or a decade, or an age of silence, the silence of shock, seems in order. *Humankind can only bear so much reality*—at one time, anyway. Trying to grapple with the postwar world, after half a decade of effort in a world at war, must have been, at the time, like trying to get a drink out of a firehose.

Because they were quiet times on the surface, the Fifties were a time of undercurrents—easy times to get nostalgic about, because currents move on, leaving pictures of the surface that are right out of Rockwell. But if one were in the right places at the right times—in the edge-zones—there were pictures, fragments that showed the undercurrents too.

I was too young to really remember Stevenson making the remark about the stubbed toe in his concession speech in 1952: "I'm too old to cry, but it hurts too much to laugh." But I remember the morning after the second time Eisenhower beat Stevenson, and my mother was looking out the dining room window, listening to the radio and crying to herself.

There was an evening at the dinner table; somehow the talk got around to Roosevelt. I was somewhere in high school at the time, more full of wisdom, or insight, or something, than I've ever been since; and I pressed an attack with some kind of a wise observation about Yalta. And my father said *That's enough.* My father had a way of saying *That's enough* that let you know, truly and certainly, whether you agreed at heart or not, that that was and would be enough. Then he would start to read the paper with an intensity that made you wonder why the words didn't start to curl and smoke on the page. I didn't know what was going on. Weren't we rational people? Couldn't we discuss something without somebody getting mad? *That's* what *he* always told *me* when *he* was winning the discussion....

I didn't—and don't—really know what was going on during the Fifties; I only know it wasn't as easy as it looks today. The pictures and intuitive feelings I carried into the early Sixties were like X-rays of a massive heart problem; everyone hurt, and no one really knew what to do about it, except to keep up a good front and hope it went away. There is a kind of irony to the fact that Ike kept smiling, and relaxing, and so did America, but everyone was very concerned, with good cause, over the state of Ike's heart.

I rejoiced in—and suffered with—Kennedy: he came in like a doctor to a darkened room, turning on the light and saying *Okay, let's see what can be done.* At the time, the fact that the light was at the other end of the tunnel seemed quite acceptable; nobody said it was an easy world, any light was better than none, and it was impossible to know how long the tunnel was, or how easy to get lost inside.

I knew—most everyone knew, I think—that the confident, businesslike manner had to be partly a bluff. How much a bluff, there was no telling at the time; I doubt if Kennedy himself knew. But anyway, one of the great lessons from the history of medicine is the fact that a doctor who *seems* to know what he is doing is better than one who probably does but doesn't appear to.

By 1962, I was still a believer, but my enthusiasm had begun to be tempered by my apprehension of the old undercurrents and undertows of the Fifties. I supported the liberal legislation, the Warren Court, the ACLU—but in a passive way; I couldn't pick up the rational signs and slogans, and I found myself getting in drunken discussions, under cover of the bravery of beer, with liberal friends, on the difference between the treating of symptoms and the curing of causes. Give me three beers, and I always forget what I *ought* to be saying.

"It's better than doing *nothing*," they would say, when I got into my spiel—"You can't legislate brotherhood, can't enforce or force equality. We're being eaten alive by something from the inside out, and the government issues aspirins for the pain...."

It was, I would concede, better than nothing; and although my enthusiasm was diminished, I saw Kennedy, and those with whom he was trying to work in America and the world, as our last best hope against...well, that is part of life in the edge, when it's the edge between pieces of time: one has only intuitions and intimations of what lies ahead—and fragments of feelings from what's past.

One of my favorite pieces of contemporary literature is a longish essay that Norman Cousins wrote for his magazine in 1970, reflecting—nostalgically, to be sure—on events following the Cuban missile crisis of 1962. For several months after that crucial event, Cousins served as a kind of a courier for the "improbable triumvirate," Kennedy, Khrushchev, and Pope John. He felt that that crisis had been a turning point, the point at which everyone involved said, "We've looked into the void, and we have to do something different." While not necessarily a time for much more than cautious optimism, it was an "open" time; a time when anything could maybe be made to happen, and whatever it was would probably be better than what *had* almost happened.

Like everything else in our immediate world, we are both

too close and too far from that moment; it is muddied by too many perspectives, too many opinions, too many damned intrusive irrelevant facts. But I don't read that essay for instruction—and I don't think Cousins wrote it for instruction. I read it because it reminds me how I *felt* then, and I haven't felt that way about the world situation since. I get nostalgic too, but not for the illusion of nothing much happening.

I tell you this with no intention or desire of engaging in a discussion of your "incontrovertible true facts of the matter," which demonstrate beyond all reasonable doubt what a bastard and pretender Kennedy was, what a politico and manipulator Khrushchev was, and what a dippy idealist the Little Father was. I have become the way my father was on the subject of Roosevelt and Yalta: *That's enough* I say. And whenever I'm in a city, feeling lost with some time to kill, I will continue to go occasionally to the public library and pull out that volume of that almost blindly rationalistic magazine of Cousins', and reread "The Improbable Triumvirate," just as another might get down a copy of Shakespeare's king plays, or another Sir Thomas Mallory or Thomas Carlyle. At bottom, all politics is pure faith, the brief formalization and flowering of powerful feelings that flow for a bit, then ebb, and even those who leave the church remember the altar and parts of the service.

In the balance, I was happy at the time that, aspirin legislation or not, Bay of Pigs notwithstanding, misgivings about Laos and Vietnam acknowledged, I would get to cast my first presidential vote as a vote of confidence for Kennedy.

> The Sea of Faith
> Was once, too, at the full, and round earth's shore
> Lay like the folds of a bright girdle furled;
> But now I only hear
> Its melancholy, long, withdrawing roar,

Retreating, to the breath
Of the night wind, down the vast edges drear
And naked shingles of the world.

Ah, love, let us be true
To one another! for the world, which seems
To lie before us like a land of dreams,
So various, so beautiful, so new,
Hath really neither joy, nor love, nor light,
Nor certitude, nor peace, nor help for pain;
And we are here as on a darkling plain
Swept with confused alarms of struggle and flight,
Where ignorant armies clash by night.

      —Matthew Arnold, from "Dover Beach"

B ack in that Pennsylvania town where I grew up, when I would be walking back from downtown to the big shambling old house on the hill, I often indulged in romantic fantasies of returning home after some long and mysterious absence. My return was unexpected, of course; no one would have any idea where I had been or if I were ever coming back. In that fantasy, I was always surprised to see that nothing had changed substantially; everything was still pretty much as it had been when I'd left long years before. I would walk up the long flight of cement steps, up onto the big old creaky porch, and up to the door, where, peering through the screen down the long hallway to the kitchen, I would see my mother, looking older of course than she had that fateful day so long ago when she'd sent me to the store for some oregano and I hadn't returned—looking older, but looking the same too. And then I would walk in, worldworn and wise in experience, and I would say to her *Here's your oregano, sorry I was so long....*

There ought to be bases, centers like that to one's life, don't you think? But who's going to stay at home and man them? As it happens in reality, you can go home anytime you want—but you'll probably find the place full of strangers.

In 1963, my father and my two sisters still living at home moved out of that big old house, into a new and smaller house my father had built. It wasn't a long move: the new house was only a couple of hundred feet up the alley from the old one—up in a formerly vacant lot where for several years I'd had a freeform rambling shack, that had grown and shrunk as a function of the supply and demand situation regarding old boards in the neighborhood. It was also the place where I had buried most of the snakes run over with the lawnmower, all the waxwings "slain by the false azure of the windowpane," the various shoebox foundlings of the animal world that hadn't made it through their orphaning, and a cocker spaniel that had died of civilization. In this graveyard of a boyhood, the only marked grave was the cocker spaniel's, and when my father turned the weedlot into a lawn he put a little concrete around the base of the cross and mowed around it: housebreaking the spaniel had been his job.

My mother and father had always planned to build a smaller, house once we kids were grown and gone off on lives of our own, and had things gone in accord with their plans, I imagine it would have been a satisfactory base for the family, private rooms or no. But their plans didn't work out. While I was still in high school, my mother's health began a serious decline. She developed *lupus erythematosus,* a degenerative disease of the tissues, along with a host of related and consequent problems; and they decided to go ahead with the new house while two of my sisters were still in high school. The old house was too much to take care of, and the new house they designed with the fact in mind that my mother would be at least partially bedridden for the rest of her life.

But as fast as my father was able to work on the house, evenings and weekends and summer vacation time, her condition deteriorated faster. She was in and out of the hospital for several years; then in 1962 she was more in than out, and that November she died there, half a year before the house was ready to move into. In a way, the house was haunted before it was ever inhabited. Nothing nasty or terrible, just the subtle presence of all the might-have-beens—going up the stairs, for instance, one always saw the small door on the wall of the never-finished dumbwaiter she had wanted to help her get things up and down stairs.... It was a *sad* house, even through my father's remarriage and up to his death thirteen years later.

But by our first Thanksgiving in that house—my first and last, the way things were to work out—that sadness was diffused, as much a part of the house as old furniture; and a sharper and more immediate hurt held our attention, a traumatic amputation for America in general: Kennedy had been murdered the week previous.

I'd wanted to talk to my father when it had happened. But at home from the University for Thanksgiving the following weekend, when we talked I found his attitude almost as incomprehensible as the event itself. He was so goddam *rational, philosophical* about it all. "It's not the end of anything," he said. "He was a good man, and trying hard...and sure, it's a terrible thing. But in time to come it won't look so bad...."

So he was trying to put it in perspective. The man was not yet cold in his grave, and my father already had it sewed up in history; just another bad day, but the republic had survived those before—*That's enough!* I wanted to say. The way he'd said it to me. I didn't of course: that's a one-way, father-to-son, over-and-out communication that doesn't work the other way. Unless perhaps punctuated with a heavy object, or the threat of it, and I wasn't ready for that.

People were talking a lot about the "generation gap" then, but this was one of its clearest manifestations for my father and me; I could be rational about his President, he could be rational about mine. Together, we could both be reasonably rational about whether the lawn needed mowing today or whether it could wait till Monday.

Many people, my father included, were taking comfort from the fact that the head of the state could be so totally blown away, and yet the state not only did not fall but seemed hardly weakened, as one would expect had the wound been in a vital spot. Slap, dash, another head was stuck in place, and aside from a flutter in the pulse of the Dow-Jones, a pause for re-orientation and course correction, Monday had been met at the door as usual. "A terrible thing, yes, but...." If the state is a rational state, no part of the state can be so important as to be *vital*—especially no mortal, human part.

But those who could find no comfort in that fact, myself included, seemed to go to the opposite extreme—rather than "Great is the system with replaceable parts," we said "Irrelevant is the system with replaceable parts." Were we really expected to believe, just because he *said* he was picking up the torch, and just because it was all vaguely outlined somewhere as "policy," that Johnson was going to carry on what Kennedy had started? The rational system suddenly seemed to be its own best parody at that moment. It was not a reflection of the strength of the system we were seeing, but a shadow of the strength that uses and manipulates the system—it was, in other words, in our best interests to try to believe that the system was as rational and invulnerable as it was pretending to be at that time, because the alternative was a kind of political paranoia thinly veiling a fairly serious flirtation with chaos and madness.

I tried to believe that it was the way I was supposed to try believe it was, but that terrible weekend the world wobbled on its axis; and after you have first felt your world wobble on its axis, it doesn't matter that it seems to straighten up and fly right, not even if the wobble is brief and the recovery almost immediate. The world has shown itself vulnerable, and time slips out from under all things vulnerable.

I had spent the weekend previous to that Thanksgiving with the rest of America, glued to the networks, not because I was morbid, but because we were all waiting for news. We are still waiting, more or less, for the news we waited for that weekend in 1963; but most of us don't expect much of it.

We cried, or sat dry-eyed and desolate, depending on our

natures, over the pathetic and moving courage of those bearing up in the sights of the cameras, the muzzles of the cameras that would not leave them alone; great personal grief became a kind of national soap-opera as the networks filled up the time, filled up the time, waiting for the news from the thousand agents checking out this, following up that.... We sat and listened to the commentators say the same things over and over, marking time with them in hopes that a slip of paper would be passed on-camera, listened to the prowl and keen of the vagrant organ music hoping for *we interrupt this broadcast...we are switching you to...where...following important announcement....*

There was a brief flurry of excitement Sunday morning over the first nationally broadcast live murder—nothing, of course, to the fast well-executed ballets of violence performed nightly on prime time—but there was excitement because *now there are two, where before there was only one—maybe it's all part of a plot.* It was a letdown to find out that Jack Ruby was just the boozed-up proprietor of a cheap booze parlor in Dallas *but maybe it's just a cover.*

But the real news, the big break, didn't come; we buried the old President, started to try to begin to attempt to get used to the new President, long live the interchangeable Presidency—and by then it was too late for news. There are still those hard at work trying to dig up some semblance of what we were waiting for then; but any "new leads" that might bear fruit at this point would only confirm what we most feared that weekend: that the event had no rationale of its own, was a blow struck as part of no understandable plan, but instead was a mad attack on rationality itself, an assault on sanity.

And it worked. I joined liberal America in grasping at Johnson like a straw—and for a while, it looked like the rational system held the field. Had Kennedy lived to be ninety-five, he would never have seen all the legislation passed that went through Congress all but unanimously during the months following his death. "The Xerox Congress," said Goldwater. But legislation is just legislation: worth the paper it's printed on, and maybe a little more, as it requires more paper to get rid of it, and is always so obtusely and obscurely stated in legalese that neither its would-be friends nor foes can agree on where to start their defense or attack, let alone its implementation. But the letter of the law takes all its momentum from the spirit of the law, and when the spirit loses coherence, the letter of the law has no oomph. And so, as quickly as pop-goes-the-weasel, the period that we should have been remembering now as "the Sixties" was truncated to "the Early Sixties."

I hadn't even got up off my ass. At the time of the assassination, there was a partially completed Peace Corps application on my desk. It had been there, partially completed, since September. I had read Martin Luther King's "Letter from Birmingham Jail" early that summer, and been very moved—but not transported south to march. I still seemed to be at least up to my ankles in the mudsuck of the Fifties.

But after half a year of Texas populism trying to deal with the urban chaos, there didn't seem to be any place to move that made a great deal of sense—not, at any rate, as I, a white, middle-class, naive innocent had been taught to try to make sense. All that cream that seemed to have risen out of the "milk of human kindness" in the Early Sixties was souring and curdling in the jar. The vigorous, future-leaning shape-up of the "New Frontier" slipped easily, all too easily, into the elephantine schlock of the "Great Society." Bread and circuses.

In the period of a few months after the assassination, Vietnam went from an act with a deteriorating rationality to a flaring, blooming psychosis. Those who blame Kennedy for Vietnam tend to forget, or just don't know, that shortly before he went to Texas, Kennedy had signed an order for the withdrawal of the first thousand men from Vietnam; he knew a mistake on its way and was ready to face up to that. Johnson quietly reversed that order in his first days in office. Johnson had called Diem "the Winston Churchill of South Asia."

On the domestic front, even before the unfingered forces of chaos put out a contract on King, the civil rights movement was undergoing its derationalization: SNCC was snapping at King's heels, Uncle Tomming him, but that was nothing to the visceral incoherence coming out of the heart of the ghetto, from Elijah Muhammed and his acolytes; and the rational ecstasy of the black and white brotherhood arm-in-arm against impacted stupidity was falling apart under centrifugal forces. It was back to fighting fire with fire, stupidity with stupidity.

And in those three short but intense years, what appeared to be an all-out, multi-fronted attack on sanity came even to the uncommitted millions who would neither march nor take up axe-handles. As if the assassins with their deliberately chosen targets were not bad enough, there came the mass murderers, whose only discernible message was that the universe was and would be henceforth a random and senseless phenomenon. A random and senseless universe would not even stoop to playing favorites, going only for the "natural" targets, but would have us all in the sights; and no one would know when one of a thousand blank windows, the top of a gray building, might suddenly become a fortress for guerrillas advocating nothing, promising nothing, coming from nothing, working toward nothing, valuing nothing; or when the human mind, rehearsing its visions and plans for a world or a watch that works ("I have a dream—") might in an instant become a gray splash on the pavement, something to be mourned and cleaned up.

And in a weird kind of a way—remember, I'm not a historian, just a guy who was trying to make sense of the newspapers—in a weird kind of a way, the rationale of the times seemed to wind down and curl in toward that "lowest common denominator," that picture of man as ultimately a madness a mess to be cleaned up. The spirit that started the Sixties saying if we all pull together we can save ourselves from our own past madness left the Sixties saying maybe if we work at it we can at least save *the natural world* from our past and present madness.

Memo to Western Civilization:
Please pick up your trash on the way out.

But every time I start trying to look "objectively" and generally on three years or a decade or a week of life in this world, I realize anew what an irrelevant effort objective generalization is. We are fed study after study, poll after poll, and I think they are supposed to help us cope somehow or another; but I swear the only ones that are useful are the ones where the bias is obvious, because then I at least know where the pollster lives. The more objective and comprehensive the study or poll, the less it seems to say about anything in particular; and I lean toward the conclusion that the ultimately thorough and fair study, weighed by no bias or preconception, leaving no stones unturned, would show only that almost everything is happening to one degree or another almost all the time; that the world is consistent only in that it is always, dependably and predictably, going off in all directions. And the decline and fall of this person or group or civilization is balanced by the ascent of another....
I eventually have to come back to confront the fact that it isn't *the* world that is going to hell; it is *my* world that is going to hell, or going mad...and not a block away is a smug fellow who can't understand my consternation, everything is just fine in *his* world.

So if I pick out this fact or that example and these circumstantial assumptions to illustrate my conclusion that things have been falling apart in the world from—well, all the way from Darwin down to now, but most noticeably during the years following the Kennedy assassination...all that I am saying for sure is that *my* world, my perception of the world, more or less fell apart during those years.

Are you familiar with the old term "walking pneumonia"? It was just a folksy way of describing a low-grade infection that had settled in the lungs; you weren't quite up to normal, but not sick enough to be down in bed or wasting time at the doctor's office...but then something happened that diverted some of your defenses, lowered your resistance just a hair—and boom! It was like a revolution where there is already a minuteman or a communist in every household—

> *Sick on Friday*
> *Worse on Saturday*
> *Dead on Sunday*
> *Buried on Monday*
> *So went the life*
> *Of Solomon Grundy.*

There is a similar psychological state, I think, that ought to be called "walking madness." The walking mad are those who are going through life with an outward show of slightly aggressive normalcy, but an inward awareness that they are always, always on the edge of the real, immobilizing, debilitating, catatonizing loss of It All, and one bump or a wobble at the wrong moment.... The best defense for the walking mad is to collect all the evidence they can that it is not just them, alone on the edge of madness, but the world around them, their whole environment. Misery loves company; madness organizes it.

I look around me in the world today, and I don't believe it is just advanced latent paranoia on my part that sniffs out "walking madness" nearly everywhere I go. But no matter how much the condition might be the result of "something in the air," a kind of general propensity in the modern world toward disorientation and disintegration, it is the nature of the disease that the general condition works through different weaknesses in different people, at different times, and in different ways; and thus the madness manifests itself in ways that seem unique, perversely personal, or personally perverse, and therefore alienating. The infestation may be general, but the manifestation is personal and not just a little lonely. We break in different ways in different places; it is usually a little inconvenient and interrupts plans. It is embarrassing.

My own search for evidence that I am not alone in being worried about cracks in the foundation leads me in a closing spiral to a particular weekend in July 1965.

I find bits of evidence—for example, on the weekend in question, Lyndon Johnson and the Joint Chiefs of Staff and selected members of McNamara's Band burned the midnight oil "reaching a consensus" (as Johnson liked to put it) on his desire to up the U.S. troop commitment in Vietnam by 50,000. I didn't know about that bit of madness at the time, of course—no one would know for more than a week, because Johnson was going to prevaricate about it.

Also that weekend, although nothing extraordinary happened, it was very hot in the cities across America; perhaps a slightly higher-than-normal number of citizens of several colors had gone up against the wall for routine police search on general suspicion of this or that; but as I say, nothing particularly out of the ordinary happened. It was still three weeks and three days until Officer Minikus would ask for Marquette Fry's I.D. at the corner of Avalon and Imperial in the Watts district of L.A.

But that and a lot more besides would hardly constitute an epidemic flare-up of social madness, sufficient for one to claim to have merely caught something that was in the air; and I'm left with the enigma of a previously unknown (or anyway un-acknowledged) and still largely unidentified personal element that suddenly presented itself, that balmy evening of July 18 in Chicago, when I arrived at what seemed to be a splendidly rational and well-formulated decision to destroy myself.

What seemed most attractive about the idea was that the destruction was not to be complete; the idea was just to eliminate a great deal of dead weight. I had the instinctive sense that it wasn't life that was intrinsically bad; it was just *my* life that was ridiculous, closed off from real experience, bad not because it was sinful, but bad because it was *safe, niggardly, pale, weak, unimaginatively ordinary, and generally duller than doorknobs.* The idea then was to die and be reborn immediately on my own terms; or to be more specific, I wanted to destroy Lieutenant George Sibley, oh five triple two nine two one, a/k/a one nine three two five two oh four eight, Bachelor of Arts (Master of None), white, Anglo, sometimes Protestant, virgin, middle class, intellectual, innocent, bright, clever, normal; and open up a clear path to the future for—well, for something else.

And so I walked out of a barracks at Fort Sheridan, Illinois, that Sunday evening with a change of clothes rolled up in a tidy bundle, and got into my ordinary, dependable, generally dull, secondhand Rambler, and, as the proceedings under the Code of Uniform Military Justice put it later, "absented myself without proper authority from the place of duty at which I was required to be."

Spiraling up through the ascending freeways from the surface streets of Chicago toward Interstate 80 West, the demented rational exterior with which I had calmly undertaken this act of self-destruction began cracking and splitting like an old chrysalis—laughing and crying, laughing and crying I headed into the night. Days, weeks later it all got sour and tedious; but oh God, I didn't forget, and never will, the mixed adrenal exaltation and despair of leaving the lights of Chicago behind me that night, running west on Interstate 80 into the unholy humid Illinois night, my lights splitting the dark like an ax in old pine. Somewhere along that white-as-death-in-the-lights-against-the-night-dark-as-hell road, my muffler fell off in a great glorious shower of sparks and noise. I backed down the road to pick it up; and while I waited for it to cool down enough to throw it in on the floor until I got to a station where I could wire it on, I just crouched there by the road and listened to that Illinois night. They say you can hear the corn growing those muggy summer nights, but it wasn't just corn I was hearing, that was life, *life*, the whole mothering night was one big womb bearing babies, bats, beastlings, worms, spiders, angels, peons, birds of paradise, hounds of hell, general accountants and countesses, all rustling and skitching around waiting to get out, waiting to get *in*: the night was a big dark bloom unfolding, an event pregnant with all possibilities, and I was finally a part of it, emergent as a soggy wrinkled butterfly from whom the crisp sensible shell was cracking and falling away like last fall's cornshucks. . . . *Thank God* I sobbed and giggled *at last at last I'm doing something totally stupid they'll never forgive me this I'm burning my paperwork behind me I'll bury my wallet and change my name shave my head and grow a beard cross my eyes and cross my heart I'll I'll I'll—*.

The Interstate: These supposedly sane and normal Fifties saw the inauguration of a number of projects of dubious sanity—the thermonuclear bomb, the missiles, the space race—but there were none so subtle and insidious as the Interstate Highway Program. All the others are largely spectator fantasies, but the Interstate Highway System is a truly democratic madness, by, for, and of the people. Part of the rationale for the system was urban evacuation in case of nuclear warfare; but the unspoken rationale was escape of another sort: the system is the logical extension of the private automobile, a concrete unreality for dream machines.

The private automobile, as I'm sure we're all aware, has its Jekyll-and-Hyde aspects. It can be used all day like a horse or an ox or a trolley, for hauling kids, groceries, and garbage; but at night the automobile comes alive in a peculiar way—you can go out at ten o'clock with nothing more on your mind than running down to the 7-11 for the eggs you forgot you need for breakfast; but the moment you start the car, turn on the lights, and pull out into the street (lights cutting a swath through the neighbor's darkness), the muffled engine is talking to you *Is this it? Are we going?*—no no, you say...just down to the 7-11 again...but be patient....The automobile made the Interstate freeway inevitable, for reasons no more sound and sensible than the tenuous rationale of the automobile. The automobile and the night were two-thirds of an incomplete trinity; they needed something to bring them together, a blank detached nonenvironment, a concrete unreality—a *limboid*.

> *lim′ boid* (lĭm boid) n. (L. *limbus* border, edge + *eidos* shape, likeness) *Geom*. A figure with two long parallel sides and no particular ends.

The limboid is the zone along the edge between space and time, distance and duration. In a limboid like Interstate 80, especially at night when there is no visible world to distract you, you can measure your progress as easily by your chronometer as your odometer. One of the big green signs looms up in that immediate future just down the road: *seventy miles to nowhere. Great* you say *in an hour and ten minutes I'll be approaching nowhere. I'm making great time.*

The time-space conversion factor in the limboid could be defined as the white zip—which is what you see if you look down at the dotted white line through the driver's window: zip—zip—zip. The conversion factor is (assuming a relatively constant and nearly legal speed of sixty mph):

$$1 \text{ white zip} = .2 \text{ sec. (approx. enough)}$$

Using that conversion factor and a relatively sensitive foot on the accelerator (or one of those constant-speed governors), by merely counting the white zips and dividing by five you can figure out how long you have been counting how far you have gone. You can also have a terrible accident.

I have never seen Interstate highway being laid out across the fields and hills, but I am a son of Newton and can imagine the machine with no particular trouble. It is about the length of a city block and the width of a limboid right-of-way (adjustable). It is attended by a fleet of hundreds of dumptrucks. The original design called for ten operators, but when it was pointed out that it would only be used on federal projects, the design was changed to accommodate up to seventy-five operators.

The front of the machine is a huge mass of gouging blades: the machine is capable of going into a hill at a grade of twelve percent (the maximum allowable on Interstates) and making a cut two hundred feet wide by fifty feet deep in three or four assaults, depending on the nature of the ground composition. For hills less than fifty feet high, the operators just set the grade bubble at level and eat straight through. *The uneven ground shall become level.*

Meanwhile, another team of operators is busy controlling the dirt being chewed out of the hills by the machine. The machine is capable of storing this dirt for later use as fill— enough for a hundred yards of fill up to nine feet deep—or diverting the dirt into the accompanying fleet of dumptrucks, to be carried off and dumped on a town of under 50,000.

When fill is needed, *Every valley shall be lifted up*, the dirt in the storage bins is moved toward the front of the machine and spread evenly for the built-up roadbed. The machine moves forward on a large number of caterpillar tracks—728, I believe it is—and the weight of the machine packs the fill. In order to adjust the pounds-per-square-foot in packing the fill, half the tracks can be hydraulically raised and lowered to compensate for the emptying of the storage bins.

Where more fill is needed than the storage bins can hold, *the rough places a plain*, a steady stream of huge dumptrucks feed the great augers spreading the fill: these trucks drive up a ramp at the end of the machine, over the top of the concrete factory, and around a track with an open slot through which they dump their loads without even stopping.

The whole rear third of the machine is a huge concrete mixing-and-spreading mechanism, also supplied by large trucks dumping through a slot in another trackway. The mud is mixed and laid immediately in parallel fifty-foot-wide strips, raked and leveled and smoothed by great steel blades and whirling "trowels."

Even the median strip between the great concrete paths is taken care of by a relatively small part of the machine that lays a thick mulch of straw and grass seed between the lanes.

This great machine is capable of laying up to ten miles of standard Interstate super-road a day through relatively uncomplicated terrain, *every mountain and hill be made low*; it moves over bare land, good for nothing but farming and grazing, and within the distance of a city block is followed by a perfect highway, needing only a couple of days to dry and a set of white zips.

As such a machine is necessarily about three stories high—if only to accommodate all the operators—I am still not exactly sure what happens when it comes to one of those overpasses waiting for it like a prophet awaiting the coming of the Messiah. But where there's a will, there's a technology; and the fact that the Interstate system is approaching completion is ample evidence that they "crossed that overpass when they came to it."

> In the wilderness prepare the way of the Lord,
>   make straight in the desert a highway for our God.
> Every valley shall be lifted up,
>   and every mountain and hill be made low;
> The uneven ground shall become level,
>   and the rough places a plain.
> And the glory of the Lord shall be revealed,
> Zip, zip, zip.

Is this it? Are we going at last? Breaking out of these daily disguises moving out like the tiger tiger burning bright up the ramp and into the night into the limboid and out along the last living edge

O where is that immortal and nameless Center
    from which our points of
Definition and death are all equi-distant? Where
The well of our wish to wander, the everlasting fountain
    Of the waters of joy that our sorrow uses for tears?
O where is the garden of Being that is only known in Existence
    As the command to be never there, the sentence by which
Alephs of throbbing fact have been banished into position,
    The clock that dismisses the moment into the turbine of time?
                    —W.H. Auden, "For the Time Being"

PART TWO

In a memory that now seems more like a dream, I am struggling up out of three or four feet of seemingly bottomless snow at dusk. I am floundering in the snow looking for my skis; instead of ski poles, I have a shovel in my hands, and I'm so pissed off that I throw it into the falling snow at the gathering darkness: it flirls through the straight-down, leadfeather fall and sinks without a sound.

But the snow erodes, engulfs my anger. I sit there in the soft and shifty stuff, and the rage trickles out like the snowmelt, or sweat, trickling down my back. The only sound is the sound of me panting; everything else is the small sibilant hiss of the new snow slipping down the sides of the hole I made falling, filling in and smoothing out my rough disorderly contours—but that is less a sound than an eater of sound; if I were to shout, cry out a curse, or sing a psalm, it would be swallowed up in that sibilation before it got fifty feet. Everything visible is similarly made indistinct, as if seen through deep gauze: the woods beside and below are mere shadows, insubstantial, gray on gray. The snow falls so thick and fast and fascinating that for a dizzy moment it becomes the stillness and I am rising through it, swift and silent as smoke....

Viewed dispassionately, and from a perspective of relative recovery, twenty-four is probably not a bad age at which to have what amounts to a nervous breakdown. If your world is going to fall apart, let it happen before a great deal of your world is realized in costly structures and details in which you have too much time and effort invested. Let it crumble when you are still a son or daughter rather than a father or mother, when you are still young, and strong with the apparently boundless energy of youth.

For my purposes here, it is sufficient to say that that seems to be what happened to me—although I don't know if I make a good argument for getting it over with early or not.

When I was twenty-four, after twenty-four years as an apparently dedicated model American son (it seemed apparent even to me), and after one uneventful and unpressured year on active duty as a second-lieutenant in the Army Reserve, I suddenly one night got into my car and went absent without leave. Absent without leave or apparent cause. Those are the facts in the situation, the *only* facts.

I was absent without leave for about four days—four weeks?. . . Say four rubbery, wear-on-forever days, aimless days in which my principal occupation was trying to figure why I'd done what I did. After that, I returned to my post, turned myself in as it were, was examined by psychiatrists, was condemned and scorned by some of my working acquaintances and friends, but was treated with a kind of wary sympathy by most. . .everyone, including myself, was vaguely disturbed by the fact that I seemed to be unchanged, the same person after my strange act as before.

After about four months generally flavored in my memory with the feeling of dead air, uninhabited corners, and backwater stagnancy, I was given a discharge. General, under honorable conditions. An ambiguous affair. In my memory, the period is only faintly tinged with a sense of reality; it is more like one of those dreams that flirts with, but never quite reaches the proportions of, nightmare.

There is a great deal I could say about that period, but in the end it might say nothing at all. It's enough, probably, to say that after six or seven years of increasingly frantic effort to keep an increasingly patchwork sense of the world and of myself in the world together—first plastering over the cracks in the foundation of the mind with rationalizations, then tacking old pictures over the crumbling plaster and widening cracks, and epoxying great gummy wads of mental busyness and familiar mundanity into the growing holes—I just finally let go. Said the hell with it, squatted on my heels in a corner and watched the floor fall away, then grabbing my ankles with my elbows and tucking my head and rolling forward into a region of darkness in the egg-float or fetal position. . . .

I thought of Henry often enough in the year or two following that letting-go, a time of standing by as material witness to the character assassination of myself, by, for, and of myself. I read his famous essay "On the Duty of Civil Disobedience" one night before my discharge—during the early weeks when I might still have at least partially redeemed my act by attaching it to something.

I'd read the essay before, in college; but I read it differently that night. Little things popped out at me that I'd passed over on first reading. "I saw," said Henry, of his night in jail, "that if there was a wall of stone between me and my townsmen, there was a still more difficult one to climb or break through before they could get to be as free as I was."

There were questions I would have put to Henry, those days. "Henry," I wanted to ask him, "I know that 'society is commonly too cheap' and all that—but do you ever get lonely for it all the same? Like tonight, in jail, Henry, separated by those two walls from your townsmen—listen, where the night carries the sound of the fiddle from the tavern down the street there: isn't that a sound as sweet as a cricket or a handful of frogs? And the barn-dance coming up, Henry: isn't there some rebellious part of yourself, a little Irish in the woodpile, that sometimes swells up like the peepfrog's throat and says *I want to dance myself dizzy in an overwarm room get flushed with wine and womanpresence?* I know you'd rather 'be right than be president,' Henry, who wouldn't...and maybe you'd rather be free than be right...but doesn't the question ever arise, tonight, tonight, would you rather be free or be laid?..."

I didn't want to put such questions to Henry by way of being cruel; it's just that the questions asked themselves of me, and I was curious as to whether they ever came to him too. The ironclaw owl of the three o'clock wakening.

The duty of Civil Disobedience. Duty to what, to whom? The eventual improvement of the self, the society? Or the marriage between the self and society? If my act of civil disobedience had any meaning at all to me at the time, it was a formalization, an acknowledgment of a *de facto* dissolution of that marriage at least on the conscious level: self and society were no longer married, and the act was a denial of the notion of duty to civil anything. I would leave the world alone if the world would leave me alone.

After my night of exultation out along the limboid, in the cold gray light of the next day—a rainy day in Nebraska, with a sky that looked like a sick puddle—I knew I was going to go back, face the music whatever it would be, get it over with—but I also knew I wasn't going to be slinking back with my tail between my legs, even though there was no honor in what I'd done. Going AWOL is what privates do, the not-too-bright soldiers with more problems than solutions and a snootful of booze. But I was neither going to try to brazen it out nor be abject about it; I was just going to get it over with. There's no honor in divorce court either.

My disenchantment with my life went beyond and beneath the symptomatic manifestations of the political situation—Vietnam, the betrayal of America by Lyndon Johnson, the fact that writing a letter to your Congressman ran neck-and-neck with pissing in the ocean for futile efforts. There'd been a

breakdown of more than just communications between this part
of the people and the government; the whole damn relationship
between me and the world I moved in had broken down. I of
course got the credit for the breakdown; but that was okay,
because I realized those days how totally untouchable I was. The
government, the Great Society, the lesser societies, the Army,
the psychiatrists—they couldn't touch me. One of the
psychiatrists was giving me a hard time one day, and he was
actually starting to get to me. I was getting mad, I was about to
give it to him: Make a Statement, pick up the burden of Civil
Disobedience—but then I just laughed. Laughed in his face, and
shook my head. He sent me back down the hall to the Spec-4 for
another test of some kind. I was untouchable. They could put me
in jail; they could put me up in front of the firing squad; they
could put me up in front of the laughing squad even; they
wouldn't have touched me. I *know* that wall, Henry, that "still
more difficult one" than even a "wall of stone between." I was
as free sitting in my quarters under house arrest as I've ever
been, or will be, in the wildest place in the world.

I was so free that it no longer mattered to be right, or even
understood. The Army shrinks said it was a tendency toward
masochism; I wanted to be punished, wanted to suffer for the sins
of the world. I won't say that wasn't close to the truth, maybe—
what is truth, after all? A grab-bag full of surprises, an artichoke
without a heart. But if I "wanted to suffer for the sins of the
world," it would only be because I couldn't think of a more
imaginative way to punish the world for its sins, if I wanted to
punish the world for its sins. My motives would have been
Calvinistic, not Christian; my soul lacks the Mediterranean
warmth necessary for benevolent suffering. Knowing that about
myself, whether or not I could ever go ahead and carry out a
good act of social masochism continues to remain an academic
question, as I've so far avoided the temptation.

But in arriving at that conclusion, the psychiatrists became the unwitting accomplices of my freedom. I received a "written reprimand" from the Commanding General of the post for my actions; and I *did* lapse for a bit. I answered his reprimand with a letter that would have got me ten years per word in a more innocent age without psychiatrists. But there was that report: he *wants* to be punished—so the worst thing we can do to him is not punish him. Let him go. Let go. Let go.

They let me go, and I was as free as Henry. I was a proven untouchable: everyone either avoided me or treated me with the wary respect accorded strange dogs with lowered heads. My friends took care of me, let me sleep on their couches and didn't ask embarrassing questions about grocery money. I had to get away from my friends before I lost them.

I found a lover, who was also, it just happened to happen, a nurse. It would, however, be too simple to say that she had nothing more in mind than to help me, make me something ordinary again, save me from too much of myself. That was a strong element in our relationship, but within herself there was also a war that dignified the relationship in our early days together: she halfway wanted the nurse to lose, I think; she wanted the madman to win a little, rework enough of our immediate world to succeed in establishing a separate reality, like a small principality on the edge of a large nation, a Monaco of the soul. But I wasn't working that out, and ultimately our relationship was too much nurse-and-patient for both of us.

Ah freedom! Let it ring! People were announcing from the universities, pulpits, and city-hall steps that it wasn't true, that America wasn't the land of the free. They pointed to residual chronic racism, the draft, Vietnam, economic inequality, sexual chauvinism, and the like, and said that a country plagued with such things could not claim that its people were free. When apologists for America said where else in the world would you be free to bitch so much and still stay out of jail, Marcuse tongued the Doublespeak of "repressive tolerance." And people began hurling themselves against barricades or policemen, to prove they could go to jail and were therefore not free.

But however honorable and brave their efforts were—those of the protestors and apologists alike—the whole thing didn't really have much to do with "freedom." The elimination of racial intolerance requires the instillation of racial tolerance. What's that to do with freedom? The best possible resolution for the Vietnam conflict was eventually chosen: to stop the conflict so Vietnam could get about working on its resolution. Nothing there about freedom. There are certain things we can grant each other: to the oppressed, tolerance; to the peaceful, the right to not fight; to women, access to the same bag of worms that we men are so happy and fulfilled by; to the meek and the weak and other "unequals," a head start and a stacked deck if the strong are feeling especially magnanimous. But nobody gives us *freedom*—because if you want freedom, you just take it; its right there, take all you want, no limit.

And America is one of the few places in the world that will stand behind you all the way: tolerate your mild excesses, take care of you (however reluctantly and half-heartedly) in your major excesses, and call a halt only when you show signs of turning into a major menace to the rest of the populace. That's because freedom is one of the few things that America does in fact genuinely and down-to-the-last-ditch stand for. America might not stand for tolerance, the right to not fight, or equality; when it comes to the role of the woman and what defines proper sex, America might be as lasciviously conservative as Europe. But if you really and truly want freedom, *freedom*, and make it clear to the inquisitors that it really *is* freedom you want and not "freedom from the draft," "freedom from repression," "freedom from regulation," or something else that really isn't freedom at all but is commitment to something...if it's really freedom you want, and you pass all the tests and show yourself untouchable, then that's what the Land of the Free is all about—

as is seen in the testimony of our Boweries, Mission Streets, and the interstate interchanges where the future waits with its thumb hanging out. Freedom!

"I heartily accept the motto," Henry begins his essay "Civil Disobedience," " 'that government is best which governs least;' and I should like to see it acted up to more rapidly and systematically. Carried out, it finally amounts to this, which I also believe—'That government is best which governs not at all;' and when men are prepared for it, that will be the kind of government which they will have."

But from where I stood, just over the edge in a state of apparent freedom even from such duties as civil disobedience, I began to wonder if we in America hadn't maybe gone overboard in establishing an independent reality outside of ourselves that we called "the government." Our bulwark and strawman. It occurred to me that "the government" in this country, and indeed in most countries, is much more representative than we believe—but not in the ways that we perhaps want it to be representative. That is, a government that seems to close its eyes and fart a lot would be representative of a society that collectively doesn't know whether to shit or go blind, to put it in the vernacular. A government that is tidy, efficient, and effective would almost certainly be representative of a society that is tidy, efficient, and effective, marching lockstep toward some bright morrow...and who the hell would want *that*?

The government, it occurred to me, is like the visible ten percent of an iceberg—for every cubic foot of ice you see, there's nine cubic feet you don't see. There must be a similarly consistent ratio between the conscious social structure that is "the government" and the great body of day-in, day-out social interactions and relationships and conflicts that make up the whole structure of a society. A small and relatively uncomplicated government implies a small and relatively uncomplicated society. Like maybe we were once. A large government, on the other hand, so complex it can't turn a corner without running into itself going the other way, implies a large and radically diverse society that could no more get together on a direction than two dogs could get together on a fencepost. When half the society wants to forge on in the grand old tradition of balls-out exponential growth, and the other half wants to put on the brakes, and yet another half—if you don't understand my mathematics, ask the Budget Office—is waiting in its seats picking its collective nose ready to go or not go wherever... then what is an honest representative government to do? Why, just what ours is doing: set the brakes, then give 'er the gas, and off we go lurching with a shriek of metal and a smell of burning rubber. Witness, our Brave New Department of Energy.

But this idea about the ratio of government to underlying social structure gave me second thoughts about the merit of Henry's ideal of "no government at all," because that would imply no social organization at all, beyond the minimal "each man for himself and God against all" society of the Big Stick and piss-on-your-corners territorialism.

Perhaps Henry did have it within himself to be that totally self-sufficient, capable of living with no external social structure at all. Every man to his own beanfield. Would he even have missed the slightly perverse pleasure he took in going to "observe their habits," the men and boys of the village? Maybe not. Had the village suddenly disappeared one day, would he have mourned its passing? Or would he merely have noted it in his journal, one more impassively accurate observation? And then gone in the other direction to see if the same curious accident had befallen the "colony of muskrats in the river meadows...."

I saw that, if there was a wall of stone between me and my townsmen, there was a still more difficult one to climb or break through, before they could get to be as free as I was. Letting go was like falling off the iceberg of reality: slipping and slithering down out of, off of, the visible structure of society—but then, drifting down, sinking, deeper and deeper, and still the shadowy dimension of the iceberg was there, vast bulk of social organization all bound up in the same crystalline structures and forms I thought I'd left behind. People taking a quick look as I drifted past, drifted through, untouched and uncaught, then going back to their business or busyness, and I knew that "still more difficult" wall.

And then finally one day, in a memory that is now more like a dream, I was struggling up out of three or four feet of seemingly bottomless snow at dusk. All sound swallowed up in the thick swaddle of snowfall; everything visible made indistinct as if seen through deep gauze: I might have been the only living thing on earth. I had never so experienced the sense of being perfectly alone. *That which governs not at all*—and there was the near edge of not at all.

A memory more like a dream. I have no trouble placing the memory: it was my first day of real work as a ski patrolman in Crested Butte, Colorado. A day more like a nightmare, that one was. The month was December (early), the day was a Monday, the year was 1966, and a glance at the weather records would show the date, because it hasn't snowed like that on a Monday in early December (not for the third straight day, anyway) in at least the last ten years, if ever. It was one of the worst days of my life—nobody'd told me a ski patrolman had to be able to ski with a shovel.

It was pure coincidence that had driven or drifted me to Crested Butte that winter. I had spent part of the winter previous—the winter after my discharge from the Army—mopping floors and hauling garbage in a ski resort restaurant on Loveland Pass in exchange for room, board, and skiing privileges. The summer following, I'd worked construction in Denver, but I'd decided I wanted to go back to the mountains for the winter.

But where to go, what to do?—I'd wondered that summer in Denver, parboiling in my own sweat on the roof of another exclusive tract home, looking away toward the far floating mirage of the Continental Divide. I wasn't enthusiastic about the idea of another winter of mops and slops. I took a first-aid course, in order to be qualified for ski-patrol work—my first investment in the future since I'd left the Army.

According to the popular mythology of our times, you *have* no future if you have a bad military record; and several months of job-hunting in Pittsburgh had convinced me that, so far as employment in mainstream industrial America was concerned, that was pretty much the situation. With that essentially verified, I lowered my sights and found that there was no particular shortage of futureless jobs—driving taxis, pounding nails on non-union jobs, pearl-diving, and the like. But there were scales and levels in that world too, and ski patrolling sounded like a better way to be futureless than mops and slops.

My problem was finding a ski area that needed a patrolman with less than a year of actual skiing experience. I of course wanted to go to Aspen for the winter, that mountain mecca of hedonism. I went up there and put my application for ski patrolman on the bottom of a stack of ski-patrol applications stored in a wastebasket; then—being realistic about my chances—I found a "backup" job in the mops and slops department of a restaurant. The only affordable places to live were four-to-a-room bunkhouses. The more I looked at a winter in Aspen, the less it looked like what I'd had in mind. I wanted to go to the mountains, and going to Aspen had begun to look like just going to another city.

Nevertheless, I was more or less resigned to the idea until one morning back in Denver, getting ready to pack up for the move. Over coffee at the Super Chef Cafe, I saw a tiny item in the Rocky Mountain *News* saying that a ski area in Crested Butte had just been sold in bankruptcy proceedings the day before, and would be open for the winter.

Open for the winter. My buzzwords, as they say in California. But this time it sounded authentic. Aspen, Sun Valley, Squaw Valley, Vail, Stowe—they were all advertising *open for the winter* too in tasteful ads in magazines like *The New Yorker.* And to get a piece of the New York crowd—even a small percentage of ten million *is* a crowd—they were all competing to see who could be most like an alpish New York...in a *fun* way, of course: New

York like *The New Yorker* sees it. Mohammed had to go to the mountain, but the mountain comes at the thought of Cholly Knickerbocker.

This Crested Butte Ski Area had the ring of authenticity, however. It was bankrupt; and being there myself in a psychic way, I knew that was the best credential of all for truly being open for the winter.

I found the place on the map, and was there the next morning. Employed as a ski patrolman by lunchtime. Nobody even asked if I could ski.

The only reason I was hired for the Crested Butte Professional Ski Patrol that year was because the Forest Service regs said you had to have six ski-mounted bodies on duty every morning in order to turn on the lifts, and the draft was on that year. The ski patrol had been paid late and irregularly the whole year previous, and a ski area just coming out of bankruptcy proceedings when most areas are already half-booked into March doesn't exactly have a running start on the season. Today, if you want to work on the Crested Butte Ski Patrol you have to come out on top of a "Patrol School" to even get a chance to be considered, should there be an opening. But that year, all you had to do was show up—I didn't even own a pair of skis. Just some ancient soggy leather boots. My "forty-pound tennis shoes," as another patrolman put it.

Part of my trouble was not really knowing just how inept a skier I really was. There had been very little snow the previous winter at Loveland Ski Area, and I had learned to negotiate familiar terrain on hardpacked snow reasonably well, although I wasn't as fast and quick as I needed to be on steep and mogully slopes. I had "skiied powder"—about ten times, and never more than a foot, lying on a good base of hard snow on familiar slopes in clear weather.

So I was totally unprepared for what happened.

It didn't snow in time for a Thanksgiving opening that year, and it didn't snow the rest of November after Thanksgiving. A few days into December, faced with a succession of bland sunny skies, people were already starting to worry about Christmas, the fat season. Then, late one Friday afternoon it clouded up, and started to snow late in the evening.

It snowed all day Saturday, all night, and well into Sunday. Sunday afternoon it quit snowing and looked like it might break up, but that was just the eye of the storm; it started in again Sunday night, and was still snowing hard Monday morning; it snowed without letup all day—except for a short burst of rain late in the morning.

By that Monday morning, there were three feet of heavy wet snow on top of a few crusty and highly crystallized inches of old snow; avalanches were running everywhere. Six miles up the road in Gothic, where I would be spending the sixth winter hence, two monstrous avalanches wiped out a cabin and lifted a twenty-foot steel bridge out of its abutments, setting it fifty feet downstream unharmed. I didn't know it could snow like that. And it hadn't really occurred to me that ski patrolmen had to go out in shit like that. A body could get killed!

But there we were. Work to be done. Saturday and Sunday I was assigned to a packing crew. That was before they'd perfected the big flat-footed wide-track packing machines that most areas have now, and the only way to pack the snow down to a ski-able base on the steeper slopes was to go to the top of the slope with a crew of fifteen or twenty people, and sidestep down the hill with skis on in a long diagonal line. The most mindfuckingly boring and thighbusting job in the world, and if it is snowing an inch an hour at thirty-two degrees, so that everything that hits a warm body melts instantly and soaks in to dilute the slippery sweat of strenuous exertion—try walking sideways down a mountain with skis on in three feet of slush sometime—it is also the most uncomfortable job in the world.

But at least it was a job I could do, and I wasn't being exposed for the kind of a skier I was, or wasn't. I looked through the wet curtain of falling snow, down those slopes with their three feet of bottomless snow covering God knew what boulders, fallen trees, growing trees, willow tangles, ghost towns, fallen civilizations—I was *glad* they told me to walk down sideways. The idea of trying to ski in that stuff scared me to death.

By Monday we'd packed the first two feet of snow on all the slopes—not that you'd notice, with another foot or two on top of it—and it was time to get the area ready to open, in case a skier or two heard that the place wasn't bankrupt after all. . . .

There were two major jobs that had to be done that day—the fact that they took most of the day is an indication of how fast things don't move when it's snowing like that. We had to do avalanche control work, and we had to put up all the trail signs and fence off all the dangerous areas.

For some reason, Bachman, the patrol leader, picked me along with a couple of other patrolmen to go with him on avalanche patrol. Perhaps he wanted to see how well I could ski. With a kind of relief, I stayed back while the rest of the patrol picked up trail signs mounted on twelve-foot 2x4s, or armloads of eight-foot bamboo poles, and slipped off into the snow curtain, over the gentle cliffs they called ski trails there. Then Bachman called us back into the warm patrol shack, to make up the charges.

Charges? Yes: two or three pounds of seismographic powder (for the shock wave, rather than the power of dynamite) strung together with primer cord, plugged with a nitro cap crimped onto a forty-five-second fuse. Bachman put these charges in a couple of small backpacks and handed me one.

He wanted me to ski off into that shit with six pounds of blasting powder, all capped and fused and ready to blow up, on my back. The simple thought of that lowered my marginal abilities right down into the absolute zero of quivering total spasticity.

Fortunately some of the avalanche slopes were not too far from the top of the lift. I did a lot of fast traverse-and-kick-turn skiing, and met up with the others only a few minutes behind.

They were peering over a raggedy gash in the otherwise smooth contours at the top of a steep slope angling off one of the main runs: so sensitive were the conditions that a big avalanche had broken off when Bachman had skied up and stopped; his motion had transmitted enough vibrations through the soft snow to trigger the slide. As an old boyhood friend would have said, "That's a gulper."

We skiied on a little further, to a small steep slope right on the edge of one of the trails—part of the trail, actually, but steep enough to slide under the right conditions. I say it was a "small slope"—only big enough to bury a person in eight or ten feet of snow if he happened to get caught in it. I have always privately called that little piece of trail "Sibley's Exposure."

Because it was in the ski-able part of the area, Bachman didn't want to use powder and blow a big black hole in the nice white snow, so he used it as an exercise in teaching us how to "ski off" an avalanche. To ski off an avalanche, you simply ski across the slope fairly high up in its convex tension area, as quickly as possible, using your weight to cause it to break away under you and slide off below. "And whatever you do," boomed Bachman, "don't fall down!"

He skiied across first, to show us what he meant: nothing happened. "Okay," he said, "it's probably okay but let's all ski it just to get the idea." I was next. I pushed off onto the slope. "Faster!" he yelled. I fell down. Fell down downhill. My six pounds of powder didn't go off. But there I was, upside down, head below my feet, in the middle of an avalanche slope. The only way I could get up was to do a sort of a somersault to get my feet below my head again. By the time I was standing up, I was almost to the bottom of the steep part; the slope was virtually "body-packed."

"I guess we'll call that one controlled," said Bachman, turning to ski off.

I spent the rest of the day helping with trail signs. Wrestling up barricades with bamboo poles and tangles of rope. The day was a soggy nightmare; words hardly suffice for describing it. I was ill-equipped: I'd rented a pair of skis that were first of all camber-sprung and half-destroyed, and second of all equipped with cable bindings, which in four feet of soggy slop popped open at the most embarrassing points of the awkward turns I was trying to crank with a sort of a timid high-stepping stem turn. Going into those turns, I probably looked like a bashful dog trying to zero in on a skittery hydrant.

In my own defense, I have to note that I wasn't the only one having trouble that day. I saw some falls, in fact, that were downright cheering to me: misery loves company. But even in good company, misery is still misery.

The ski area was officially opened at noon: there were some hardy skiers from town and the college in Gunnison just champing at the bit. That meant we would have to sweep the mountain at four-thirty—although in my case, the idea of me being responsible for getting skiers off the mountain was laughable: anyone who actually *wanted* to ski on a day like that should have been helping *me* off the mountain. But the sweep run did have one enticement: after a day of thrashing around with twelve-foot 2x4s and jackstraw-loads of bamboo poles, we would get to ski one run with our ski poles, like God meant skiers to ski.

But even as we were all getting our skis on at the top of the mountain that afternoon's-end—still snowing in thick soft windless curtains—the patrol phone rang. Bachman went back in to answer it...and came out shaking his head. The packing machine had slipped off into a ditch down in the flats where the trails converged.

"Everybody grab a shovel."

And that brings me to that moment in the gray-on-gray dusk, that memory more like a dream in which I find myself squatting for the umpteenth time that day in the usual tangle of skis poles cables gloves shovel and slush, finally tired beyond anger, looking into what might be called the Ultimate Alternative.

Over the past decade I've known two people who have gone over that edge and into that most silent of nights. Just lay down in the snow and went to sleep, both of them. The nap that opens up like a doorway between this and the same thing on the other side, only once you go through, the doorway disappears and there's no way back to this side.

Or so I might theorize. Those who have been dragged back from that edge in the nick of time, pulled away by friends into a warm place, slapped and rubbed and cajoled back to life, indicate that it probably wouldn't be a bad way to go. So long as you fight it, you are cold and miserable, soggy with simultaneous sweat and chills. But if you just decide to let go, or continue letting go, if you decide you just don't care any longer if you are ever warm again—then suddenly you do begin to feel warm, as your body, committed to live life to the last bitter calorie, sends out the vital heat in a last piss-in-the-ocean effort against the pervasive omnipotent cold. It's called hypothermia, and the last memory before going to sleep is of finally, finally, being warm.

But that was just about exactly the time and the place when I stopped letting go and started looking around for involvement, commitment, the embrace and embracing of ideas, people, futures, options, the possibility of a new or slightly used set of good operational illusions; and that day, after that quick look at the alternative, I picked myself up from about the umpteenth fall and put myself and my skis back together, found my shovel, and made my way on to where some others as soggy and wornout and pissed as I was were working, waiting for me—shadows against the gathered night, lumpy and out-of-focus with dampness and tiredness, but still capable (as I found myself also) of the casual curse and the laugh that must have struck the storm, with its love of silence, as blasphemous....

When I arrived in Crested Butte, there was a Town of Crested Butte and a Crested Butte Mountain, a little over two and a half miles apart as the raven flies from peak of mountain to center of town.

The mountain, of course, was there first, in fact and in name: one of the surveying expeditions under Ferdinand Hayden coined the name "crested buttes" for some of the mountains in this part of the Elk Range—Crested Butte Mountain, Gothic Mountain, Carbon, Axtel, and the Marcellines, all of which are substantial mountains standing in a relatively isolated butte-like relationship with each other. They are all batholithic intrusives from the tertiary period—big glops of granite that welled up into the earth's crust fifteen or twenty million years ago, and were subsequently uncovered by wind and water erosion.

The Town of Crested Butte, on the other hand, only dates back to 1880, and until 1960 and the advent of skiing on the mountain, the name was the only real connection between the town and the mountain: none of the mines that supported the town were located on or close to Crested Butte Mountain. When skiing did come to the mountain, there was still some question as to whether the mountain and the town had anything in common, even though many people from the town were employed in resort-type activities thereafter. The base area of the ski lifts, where the main resort development occurred, was two and a half miles from the town, five or six hundred feet higher, and about two generations out of phase with the town.

These separations—especially the philosophical antipathies engendered by the last—proved significant enough so that in 1974 the resort development at the ski area finally "declared its independence" and formed yet another variation on the common name, calling the new town Mount Crested Butte. Superficially this might sound like an unnecessary complicaton, but in fact it does seem to represent a significant political and social clarification; and with not too many exceptions, whether you live in Crested Butte (downtown) or Mount Crested Butte (up on the hill) says quite a bit about your brand of America. Despite a heavy degree of interdependence, the two towns are each unique and in many respects antithetical.

But when I arrived there in November 1966, there was only a handful of second-home chalets at the ski area, and nearly everyone who worked at the area lived down in the town.

Crested Butte was a picturesque town when I moved there—and still is, if in a somewhat different way: today nearly everything is painted, and many of the older houses have been restored to a degree that seems to render the term "restoration" inadequate—"rebuilt" is more like it, from the ground up and at no small cost.

Unlike Aspen or Central City or Georgetown or Ouray or any of those other quaint mountain towns in Colorado, Crested Butte has almost no evidence of the silver boom's "Age of Ostentation": no fancy brick buildings in the business district, none of the great "Victorian" frame houses with gables and turrets and gingerbread and all that other cute vulgarity. The first time I drove down Elk Avenue—Crested Butte's main drag—a good fifty percent of the buildings in town (including garages, woodsheds, and residual outhouses) had apparently never seen paint, and fifty percent of the rest had apparently not seen it in twenty years.

There was a decidedly ramshackle quality to the quaintness in Crested Butte: just driving past the big old frame false-front buildings of the two-block business district (and no great show of busyness that day), I could see immediately that strong foundations and structural endurance had not been major preoccupations of the town's early builders: sighting along a wall, running the eye down a ridgeline brought on a mild seasickness. They didn't look like buildings in any great danger of falling down; it wasn't that bad. But they looked like buildings trying to get comfortable. Working their way into their own private compromise with the hard and stony ground—they don't call those the "Rocky Mountains" for nothing, after all. Think of a fat lady on the folding chair in the doctor's waiting room, shifting around with little groans, sagging off to this side a little here, listing that way a little to counter-balance. . . .

At that time, it was possible to rent an entire house in Crested Butte for less than a flophouse bunk in Aspen. The $60 house I lived in that winter wasn't much, of course. Worth its rent, you might say—but over the next five years, the rent would triple, while the house, well, the house just got five years older.

From the front door to the rear bedroom, the floors of that house sloped away like the lawn of an old riverside plantation, although most of the rooms had terrace-like areas here and there that were level enough for a table, a bed. This natural drainage had its advantages, however: one night a pipe froze and broke in the kitchen, and rather than going everywhere, the water simply drained down the hall into the bedroom, and out a small hole in the corner, probably drilled there for that purpose earlier.

Things bumped along the bottom financially that year in Crested Butte, but the situation did seem to illustrate a valuable lesson in economics: if everyone is broke, and everyone knows that everyone else is broke, then nobody suffers nearly as much.

The best example of the "we're all in this together" attitude which seemed to prevail in Crested Butte that winter was the Dinner Special at the Grubstake Restaurant and Bar downtown. At that time, the Grubstake was owned and operated by a couple of West Slopers named Sampson—Jerry and Tina. They sold the Grubstake in 1969 for enough to invest in a Lake Powell marina; then sold that at a substantial enough profit to "retire" to a farm and ranch in Iowa. But in 1966 they were still struggling pretty hard to keep the Grubstake in Crested Butte afloat. Jerry Sampson told me that winter that during the autumn hunting season he had kept the lights on all night and napped behind the counter on a cot, in order to not miss a chance to serve a cup of coffee to a late-arriving hunter who might come back later for dinner.

But in spite of all that, and on account of all that, they were running a nightly Dinner Special that must have been almost a charity operation: all you could eat (within reason) for $1.29. And if you were living in town you could run a tab. It was more like a boarding house than a restaurant. If there happened to be tourists, they were allowed to order the Dinner Special too, but only if the Sampsons were sure all the locals were taken care of.

One might cynically say that they served us the Special at that price just to get us into the place—a "loss leader," I think the supermarkets call it—in hopes that we would stay on and drink all evening. But that argument falls apart when you stop to figure that we would probably have been in there most of the evening anyway—and besides that, the heavy-duty imbibers were always drinking on the tab after the middle of the month: even at 70¢ a shot and 25¢ a bottle of beer, wages weren't high enough to support a real cupman. And while all bar owners so reckless or desperate as to extend credit have different formulae for figuring their anticipated bad-debt percentage, extending credit in a bar amounts to discounting your drinks. There were people who left Crested Butte at the end of every winter owing the Sampsons four, five, six hundred dollars. If they came back in the fall, they paid off the old tab with summer money and started a new one. If they didn't come back in the fall—well, some mailed a check and some didn't. But at any rate—giving away dinner *just* to get the bar business they'd have had anyway doesn't cut it as a "subtle business ploy"; there had to be a little constructive community spirit involved too.

And either way, whatever the intent, the effect was that every evening most of the "unattached" population of Crested Butte was sitting down like a family, to break bread and eat non-fried, unfranchised, home-style food. I wouldn't have found that in Aspen (not in 1966), or Denver or Pittsburgh for sure; and it established for me the fact that, regardless of what Crested Butte wasn't, like a good place to get rich, it *was* something out of that mainstream that I didn't seem to get along in. "Open For The Winter" was fulfilling its promise.

As the winter wore along, I began to be aware of the fact that the Grubstake was only a part of a larger context that was unlike any social scene I had ever witnessed, much less been a part of. Or apart from. My introduction to the greater society of Crested Butte came almost entirely through my patronage of the bars; but that was an entirely legitimate way to get to know Crested Butte, because at the time the town was very much a "cafe society" in a rather European sense.

There seemed to be a large number of older people in the town who came out every morning, afternoon, or evening—or sometimes all three—for a cup of coffee or a beer. They weren't dressed like ski tourists—that was before bib overalls became casual high fashion—and they didn't act like members of that vast and growing semi-nomadic body of retired tourists with their portable pickup-mounted room-and-bath units; so the logical assumption was that they lived in the town, were natives, which implied that the town had a history going back before

1960 and the ski area.

I discovered that these old-timers were willing to talk to just about anyone who was willing to listen at least part-time—not in a compulsive way, like the Ancient Mariner, but simply as fellow beings interested in killing a little time visiting. That was, in fact, why they were there: to talk, visit, tease one another, conduct town business and debate national issues, straighten out the society...and tell stories about Crested Butte to newcomers like me.

For those old-timers I met in the bars—and gradually, for me—the time spent in the bars was not an escape from reality, it was the formalization and focus of reality. The three downtown bars that were open that winter were the town's newspaper, message center, public forum, group therapy, and community center. Once you got acquainted with certain routines and rigamaroles, you could just about predict when you should go where to find almost anyone you needed to see about anything.

I more or less fell in love with all this, that first winter. And who wouldn't have? I had a job that paid me most of the time to do what the customers paid through the nose for. There was, to be sure, a certain amount of plain hard physical labor, and there were days when I would just as soon have had an inside job in a warm dry room—like that first day. And there were occasionally some nasty, sobering accidents to take off the hill in the big toboggans—you don't forget your first look at a good compound fracture. Or the muffled shouts and screams from the wrapped cargo when you hit the inevitable bumps with the toboggan. Although I've never had to be evacuated from the mountain myself, testimony from those who have leads me to believe that probably the only thing worse than coming off the mountain in the sleds with a broken leg is lying out on the mountain freezing to death with a broken leg.

But for the most part, our contracted duty was simply to get out there and ski the trails, make sure there weren't too many rocks showing, watch out for bashers, help people get off slopes they didn't belong on, put up bamboo poles where the rocks were bad, stand around looking like heroic Crusaders with the big red cross on the puffy down parka, et cetera.

And if there was a day when I didn't feel much like skiing, someone else on the patrol probably did and would take my runs while I sat in or (on a sunny day) outside our patrol shack up on one of the world's most beautiful mountains (I'd put it in the top seven hundred) and spend most of the day reading. It's true that I wasn't going to get rich on the pay—but with all that snow, clean air, and easy scheduling, who needed to be rich too?

Then in the evening after work, to go downtown and partake of a community that was truly a community, bound together by the peripheral assaults of the bogey bankruptcy but somehow remote from the major chronic depression such bogeys bring in the city, a community hardly more than a step up from the tribal fire, having just moved the circle indoors and replaced the exposed flame with the liquids that burned a little on the way down and left everyone with their doors unlocked...what more could a person want?

Well, a person could want to be something more than just a passive recipient of all this—especially if that person were by heritage and environment something of a Protestant do-body, estranged and to a degree liberated from his own background but wanting to be an active participant in some alternative something-or-other. Probably the most dangerous kind of person there is.

But anyway—I did want to be more than just a passive recipient in this strange small world. I knew—as did a lot of the other new-timers in town—what lay down the valley and over the hill, in Denver, New York, Chicago, and California. Too many people like myself, is what it was, although I didn't articulate it quite that way. Unfortunately, perhaps. So it is natural that I would see my role in Crested Butte as doing what I could to help protect, propagate, or preserve the town's unique and unspoiled character. Again unfortunately, I wasn't making subtle distinctions between apparently innocuous words like "propagate" and "preserve"—the difference there being like the subtle difference between the kind of transfusion you get at the hospital and the kind you get at the mortuary.

But how was I going to fulfill this role through real action? I gave the question a lot of thought—as did a number of other new-timers in town with whom I had a common bottled-in-bond concern. And one night during my second winter as a ski patrolman in Crested Butte, when a group of us new-timers were sitting around in Bea Norris's Fondue House, pretty well into our cups and talking about what the town needed, the idea of a town newspaper came up. I tentatively cleared my throat. I'd been thinking about that myself.

That was before I knew what a newspaper was. I had never even considered a journalism course in college—too *practical*. My only active experience in newspapering had been as a delivery boy in Franklin, Pennsylvania. Followed by a few guest editorial appearances in the "Letters" column of a few select publications.

Nevertheless—and this was one of the more beautiful things about that town at that time—next thing I knew I was a member of a corporation. "Crested Butte Media, Inc." is what one of our incorporators wanted to call it, but we settled instead for the more traditional "Crested Butte Publishing Company." And in addition, I was the editor, business manager, editorial department, senior reporter, cub reporter, city desk, office boy, weatherman, and janitor of our first and only publication, the Crested Butte *Chronicle*, a four-page weekly that began to double exponentially at about two-and-a-half-year intervals. Just like the town.

The paper did well enough from the start. I don't mean it ever came close to making me very much money. The paper and I arrived at an accommodating agreement—largely because of my overwhelming antipathy for selling advertising—whereby the paper paid its own way, while I odd-jobbed and worked part-time at something else to pay my way. But the paper was never stacked and burned at the base of a stake I was tied to; I was only occasionally threatened, and that usually anonymously; and the paper was thoroughly read—four pages, what the hell—by almost everyone in town: in those ways it did well enough from the start.

What I liked most about the newspaper, however—and the fact that it broke even left me money ahead, as I probably would have paid for the privilege—was the fact that it made just about everything going on in town my business, to some degree or another. It gave me an excuse for listening.

It gradually dawned on me that I was literally, even obviously, born to be a journalist. Before I got into newspapering, I'd thought that a journalist was someone who spent most of his time writing for newspapers. But once I began to get my bearings in the medium, I realized that an honest journalist and editor spends at least as much time listening as he does writing; and if the physical paraphernalia is any indicator at all, I was obviously a born listener, because I have a set of ears like mudflaps.

I grew up more than just a little sensitive about my ears, which seem to be an inherited feature from my mother's side of the family. I have a big nose too, but it was the ears that gave me trouble as a kid. Never mind, said my folks, Abraham Lincoln had big ears too. But so does Bugs Bunny, so does Dumbo the Elephant, so does a Chevrolet coming down the road with both doors open, and it wasn't Abraham Lincoln that my school-buddies thought of when they looked at me. I have wondered sometimes if my drive in high school, my constant effort to get the best grades, write the wittiest themes, come up with the cleverest wisecracks to disrupt a class, wasn't rooted in the fear that the barest evidence of chronic mental mediocrity would be all I would need to show to be really hung with "Dumbo" forever. I wonder if Walt Disney knows how many childhoods that silly little elephant has scarred?

But suddenly, along in 1969 in Crested Butte, it occurred to me that those ridiculous flaps, those cornucopic collectors of noise, dust, bugs, and small birds were perhaps a message from destiny: I was meant to use them. Turn them on and tune in. That didn't mean I was to think, after Isherwood, "I am a taperecorder." It just meant—*listen* a lot. How can you try to be the *vox populi* without also being the *auris populi*?

But what makes the combination of being a born listener and a newspaperman so ideal is the fact that you waste a lot less time listening to chatter and inconsequentia. You can get right to the point with someone else, or they can get right to the point with you, and it doesn't appear impolite or pushy. There's also the undeniable fact that most people make a better effort to keep a conversation interesting when the local Boswell is lurking about, ears revolving like a radar turret.

The newspaper actually gave me an excuse for doing what I most enjoy doing: generally hanging out, talking and listening, talking and listening. If I'd been born rich, I would probably be a "wastrel and idler"; but given the condition that I have to work for a living, and as "my object in living is to unite my avocation and my vocation," newspapering in Crested Butte in 1969 was probably as good as life will ever be.

Among other things, my role as town editor gave me not just the opportunity but almost the duty (once more, a buzz-word) to hang out in Frank Starika's bar afternoons. Every afternoon from twelve on, a kidney klub of retired miners (mostly) would assemble at either Frank and Gal Starika's Bar or Tony Kapushion's Tavern, across the street from each other. These were the old-timer bars: both of them, and their owner-operators, not only predated the advent of the ski area but went back to the coal-mining days in Crested Butte. And the retired miners with their modest pensions had been a mainstay of the two bars' business during the long cold winters between the closing of the last mines and the advent of the winter resort.

These old men—Fritzie Kochevar, the brothers Panion, Emil Lunk, Pitsker Sporcich, Botsie Spritzer, Tommy Snellar, Joe Saya, Frank Hodgsen, Frank Cosetta, Tony Gallowich, Pete Raines, and of course the two hosts, Tony Kapushion and Frank Starika—were either natives of the town, sons of immigrants, or immigrants themselves.

A good indicator of the ethnic background of the town was the reunion of veterans of the First World War on Armistice Day in 1968. Five veterans showed up for that one at Starika's Bar, and they had each fought under a different flag: there was the Englishman Frank Hodgsen who had fought for the King, John Panion who had been with the Yugoslavian army, Ralph

Falsetto who had fought with the Italians, and Anton Danni, another Italian, who had already immigrated and fought with the A.E.F. Then there was Emil Lunk, who had fought for the *Kaiser* until he took a shot in the leg. Emil entertained the troops that night with his bandonium (an accordion-like instrument), just as he had done fifty years earlier on the way to the trenches.

Many of those old men were bachelors—life-long, confirmed: the kind of men who know one good woman in their lives, their mother, and no others need apply. In a generally earthy context, they were wry and subtle in their humor; and they talked like I skiied: slow and easy. I had never realized that the big mirrors behind old bars were something more than decoration until I started sitting in on those afternoon sessions; then it became ridiculously obvious that the mirror was a conversation-facilitator: a line-up of patrons could talk to (and listen to) each other's reflections and thereby avoid a lot of neckbending and craning.

As they sat there in a row at the bar, talking straight ahead to each other's reflections about what was new in town, relating it to what was old in town, telling stories and jokes on each other, debating current events, and formulating judgments on this and that, I was reminded of nothing so much as the chorus in old Greek plays. In that low-key afternoon occupation, they might well have been the model for Aeschylus and Sophocles, whose choruses were often made up of old men or old women who formed a kind of living backdrop of judgment-by-custom against which the action of the play unfolded...

> As for us, our bodies are bankrupt,
> The expedition left us behind
> And we wait, supporting on sticks
>   Our strength...
>   ...[but] age can still
>   Be galvanized to breathe the strength of song...
>   —Aeschylus, from *Agamemnon*

Those afternoons at Starika's were not always rewarding—but what is? Some afternoons would pass with no more than a rambling desultory accumulation of inaccuracies and irrelevancies about the weather, the sex life of hippies, what to do about the dogs (or what they would *like* to do), and what did or didn't look like it would last the winter. That was the final flat condemnation of something or someone new in town from that Greek Chorus: "It won't last the winter."

But most afternoons were good for at least a story or two. Especially if there were someone around who hadn't heard all the stories, like me. Not that the fact that a tale had been something more than twice told prohibited repetition. They all knew each other's stories so well that you could see mouths and minds moving along in silent chorus with the speaker sometimes, but when the general drift of a conversation seemed to roll up to the edge of a particular well-known story, and then stop and wait expectantly.... Where you have a good story-telling tradition, the stories are more like poems or songs, where the presentation is at least as important as the content. I don't want to carry that simile too far: the stories aren't like songs or poems in any other way than that general sense; they aren't art; in fact, most of their appeal lies in an almost deliberate eschewal of style in favor of a special kind of homely and vulgar artlessness. But through many retellings, these stories take on the kind of polished dull-deep patina you see on an old buckeye chestnut carried around in the pocket for a lifetime of warding off rheumatism. And in a way, you could say these people carry around those stories, with their patina of much handling, to ward off anonymity.

But there were other days, rich days...like "Bear Day." "Bear Day" was actually any day that bears happened to come into the conversation legitimately, thereby precipitating the telling of bear stories. But I remember one Bear Day in particular I happened to sit in on. Late the night before—early in the morning actually—Botsie Spritzer had been just getting ready for bed, when a rather dreadful clamor arose on his back porch. He looked out the window and saw a bear, scrounging in his overturned garbage can. Botsie went out the front door at once, jumped in his car, and went downtown, where he found a marshal's deputy watching the bars close down for the night. The deputy went back with him; but by the time they got there, the bear had of course gone on to other garbage cans.

The deputy told of the incident at the breakfast table next morning, and the word got around pretty well; by the time Botsie got to Starika's early in the afternoon, they were ready and waiting for him. No one seriously doubted that a bear had actually been on his back porch, but the fact that no one else had seen the bear was excuse enough for kidding the Bots a little.

As I remember, Fritzie Kochevar started it off. "Frank, I heard there was a big black dog out knocking over garbage cans your way last night." Starika lived across the street and just down the block from Botsie's house and the *Chronicle* office. "Know anything about that?"

"It was a big dog, I guess," adds Pete Raines. "About as big as a bear, they say."

"Sure," says Bots, nodding into the mirror behind the bar, the resignation of a martyr in every line of his face. "Sure. I know all about that dog. You can ask me. You bet."

"Did he give you some trouble too?" asks Fritzie, all innocence and wonder.

Botsie takes the offensive. "You guys—! You want to just come up to my place, look at my back porch which I'm still trying to get straight—I'll show you what that dog, which wasn't no dog but was a bear as sure as it's me standing here, and a big bear too, I'll show you what he done and you tell me if it looks like a dog done it!"

"Have another beer, Bots." Starika slides him one on the house. You don't want the guest of honor leaving in the midst of his tributes.

"I was by your yard just last week," says Joe. "It looked then like it'd been worked over by bears and you never did say nothing about those'ns."

That gets laughs, and Botsie looks heavenward, seeking perhaps the Angel of Truth to come testify.

"You hadn't maybe just closed up the bars when you saw this—bear or whatever?" Pete asks.

"Maybe I had," says Bots. "Why else would I be up at two in the morning? But I wasn't loaded, and anyway the sight of that bear, which wasn't no dogsize bear, would of sobered up anybody."

"Well, some of these dogs get pretty big."

"Not *that* big."

The teasing has apparently more or less run its course for the time being, so Starika steps into the conversation with a new direction: "Well, it wouldn't be the first time there was ever a bear in this town."

The floor is open for bear stories.

"I remember one bear that come to town," says Joe. "You ought to remember too, Frank. Right down there by the school—what was the name of the people lived in that, that hippie house now, that Henry sold to Doc Smith—what was their name, lived there before Henry—"

"Matoski?" volunteers Starika.

"Yeah, Matoski. Big guy, broke-nose miner. Had a couple kids. But one night a bear came down and started rootin' and snorflin' in their garden, and old lady Matoski come out in her nightgown and run it off with a broom—"

"I remember that," puts in Fritzie. "It wasn't no broom drove that bear off—you ever see old lady Matoski in her nightgown?"

"Neither'd you," says Joe.

"That night, I sure did. We heard the commotion all the way uptown and come down."

"Anyway," Joe continues, "that bear either didn't see too

good, or she was so scared she had her eyes closed—"

"She'd just seen old lady Matoski in her nightgown," puts in Fritz.

"—'cause she went tearin' through the schoolyard and run right smack into the backstop at the ball park. Brought the whole thing right down on top of her.

"She started raisin' hell, tryin' to get out, and pretty soon there was half the dogs in Crested Butte raisin' hell too all over town—"

"We heard the commotion clear back uptown, and come down," says Fritzie.

"—pretty soon half the town was out, too. People runnin' around dressed every which way, and watching that bear all wrapped up in chicken wire tryin' to get out with the dogs runnin' in and snappin' at her butt...." He stopped, shook his head, and took a gulp of his beer.

That was the time for someone like myself, apprentice straight man, who hadn't heard the story, to ask, "What happened?"

"They shot that bear," says Joe, matter of factly. "There didn't seem to be anything else to do."

"I remember that," says Fritzie. "How it was that night. At first everybody all excited and jumpin' around...."

"But then it got clear that there wasn't no way of gettin' that bear out'a the backstop and livin' to tell of it," Joe continues, "and that's when the marshal shot him. Then all the kids started cryin' and howlin'—'Why'd he shoot it, daddy, why'd he shoot it!' " Joe shakes his head at the memory. "It was really too bad, the way it come out." He's quiet for a moment—then slides his glass toward Starika's side of the bar. "Better fill me up. And see if these guys need anything."

"I only ever saw one bear around here," says Fritzie, "and it was a just a few years ago. I was up by Smith Hill screenin' coal, and I'd set down for a rest. I got that feeling of being watched, you know how that is? So I gave a careful glance around, and there not further away from me than that booth over there was the biggest black bear I ever seen."

"The *only* one you ever seen," Pete reminds him. "You just said so yourself."

"It was big enough," says Fritzie, unfazed, "so I don't care if I never see one bigger."

"What happened then?" asks the apprentice straight man.

"Nothin'," says Fritzie. "From the time I set eyes on that bear I never twitched so much as a muscle or blinked an eye. I don't know as how I would of been able to move if I'd wanted to, come to think of it. The bear, he just watched me for a minute more, then he must of decided I was just another tree and went snufflin' off to the woods again."

"Lucky he didn't try to climb you, if he thought you was a tree."

"Damn right." Fritzie picks up his new glass, lifts it to Joe in the mirror. "Thanks Joe." Joe nods to the mirror.

Botsie enters the conversation, over being mad. "A guy told me once, if you ever come face-to-face with a bear, what you do is throw a handful of shit in his face."

Everybody stares thoughtfully at the mirror for a moment. I think about it. "What if you don't happen to have a handful of shit?" asks the apprentice straight man.

"Don't worry," says Bots. "You will."

Everybody gets a good laugh. Me too: happy to be of service. "Don't worry," Bots says again. "You'll have all you need!"

"I guess if I could of moved anything that day," says Fritzie, "that would of been the first thing. If that bear'd decided to take a closer look, he'd of needed a clothespin for his nose and chains for traction, the last five feet atween us."

And so it would go, on into the afternoon. Slow and easy. They knew these stories of each others' as well as they knew the scars on the bar their fingers idly traced. Some of those stories I heard more than once, and the telling was always nearly identical—even down to Joe needing somebody to supply Matoski's name. He hadn't forgotten the name; it's just a device for bringing in the audience. It is a form of little theatre, a small art. Buckeyes in the pocket of the soul, to ward off anonymity and other cancers.

I look back over the issues from the first year of the newspaper and blush at a lot of it—the boosterism, the cuteness that was meant to be clever, the corn that was scratching the surface of sentiment. But people enjoyed it—and why not? What stuck out all over it was a desire to Do Something For The Town, and if there were many different ideas as to what was good for the town, then I would try to do something for everybody. I heard a joke once about a man with a donkey who tried that (he lost his ass), but at the time I really had no standards other than the appreciation of readers.

Whatever the merits and demerits of my own work were, however, my one undebatable success as an editor all the way through from the first issue was editing and publishing Botsie Spritzer and his "Sporting Life" column.

Writers are known for their writing, but editors are not remembered for their editorials: rather their claim to fame is what they managed to cajole, flatter, threaten, cheat, and otherwise crank out of writers; and I am content to let my reputation as an editor ride with Botsie and "The Sporting Life."

Botsie was born in Crested Butte, and has lived nearly all his life there. His father and mother were both Croatian immigrants, and he was the "baby" of a family of ten. His father, Martin Spritzer, worked in the mines until bad eyesight forced him to quit; whereupon he was able to get into the saloon business in the building where Botsie grew up and still lives.

Martin Spritzer's real love in life was music, and he had a "string orchestra"—three accordions, two violins, a tamburica and a barda (both native Yugoslavian stringed instruments), and a saxophone—that occasionally traveled as far as Paonia over Kebler Pass to play an engagement. A large part of the string orchestra was made up of his own sons, and, growing up with music like that, Botsie eventually taught himself to play the accordion. My first acquaintance with him was at the Grubstake, where he played frequently for dances.

It didn't take me long to discover that in addition to being a good self-taught musician, Botsie was a fine storyteller; and in addition to that, he had a reputation for being a fine fisherman. There is ongoing lively debate among the old-timers as to exactly who is the best fisherman in Crested Butte, and there are other contenders. But if he doesn't have the title, he generally has the reputation.

When he was a child, he fell and hurt his arm. The local sawbones said it was just a sprained wrist and told him to soak it for a few days. But the arm didn't get better, and when his mother took him back to the doctor, the doctor took another look—this was without X-rays of course—and decided that the big bone in the forearm had been broken. The late diagnosis plus an inept effort to set the arm resulted in a bone infection that nearly did Botsie in and finally necessitated the removal of most of that bone, leaving the arm forever weak. As a result, Bots was unfit for most of the jobs in the mines, and picked up a living wherever and however he could—rodman for surveying parties, cook for cowcamps, and whenever there were enough people in town to warrant a dance, musician.

Being barred from heavy labor did not break Botsie's heart at all. He would confide in a whisper, after a couple of beers, that he didn't much like hard work anyway. Some of us are made to live by our hands and some of us are better suited to living off our wits.

Botsie had come to know many of the regular summer

visitors to Crested Butte, which made his association with the paper invaluable in terms of getting some circulation outside the immediate community—which, with a population still under four hundred, wasn't going to support either a newspaper or the future. Botsie's column—and his downtown promotion of his column—sold so many subscriptions that I started paying him a commission—provided he turned in an address with the money. By the end of each week, I would have a pile of paper napkins, matchbook covers, counter checks, business cards, beerbottle labels, and potato skins with addresses on them. Addresses and no zip codes. And invariably, it seemed, cash for one more subscription than I had addresses for, which meant that sooner or later there'd be a letter: "Several months ago, I subscribed to your newspaper but haven't yet received...."

At first, Botsie was writing his columns out in longhand, but that seemed to take some of the shine off his stories. He wrote like most Americans educated in lackluster public schools: unnaturally for the most part, adequately at best, and not at all when half-loaded, which was his best story-telling mood. So after a while, he began dictating the columns to me, and that worked really well. Occasionally he would get rolling, and next thing we knew, we had a three-week serial in hand. Other times, I would find myself out scouring the bars at midnight on Monday with a printer's deadline the next morning, finally finding him, and hearing *Jeez George is it that time again already?* But I liked to save his column to take down to the printer's the day I made up the paper anyway, because the printer—a crusty guy who'd sooner have died than laughed at any of my jokes—would sometimes get to chuckling and giggling in the middle of setting it on the linotype, and that was the ultimate audience test.

"The Sporting Life" gradually began to evolve into something that was as much "life" as "sporting." Botsie didn't see his duty to the reader ending, for example, with just giving some hints about rabbit-hunting; he took it all the way home to rabbit-cooking too. Although one wouldn't have guessed it from his bachelor eating habits at Starika's (a beer-and-a-chili-hold-the-chili) Botsie was an excellent cook. As he said once, a restaurant cook who can't cook can go from restaurant to restaurant, but a cowcamp cook who can't cook doesn't come back alive.

He'd learned to cook from his mother; and he'd learned from both parents the art of putting up foods, making sausage, smoking meat, souring kraut and turnips, and the like. He has continued to do these things in the autumn, as though it were literally "in his blood." The season of getting ready for winter. All of this gradually found its way into "The Sporting Life"; I would sit in his kitchen like some bumpkin Boswell, taking down his narration of what he was doing, as he did it. Boswell's reward came when, say, after an afternoon of Botsie talking his way through the butchering and packaging of a hindquarter of deermeat, he would set aside a few of the little tenderloin steaks for panbroiling the way his mother had taught him, a process that exalts a piece of meat, rather than disguising it like Europeans do. But of course, you have to start with fresh meat that has nothing to be ashamed of. . . .

One of the most memorable meals I've ever eaten was in that kitchen, and the entree was—can you believe this?—liver. Botsie and Fritzie Kochevar had some nephews in common, who came up each autumn for a week or so of hunting. One year they got a big elk, and I somehow got in on the cooking-up of the vitals—only the heart and the liver, as it turned out, which were more than enough. Before that night I had never liked liver, but ever since that night it has been one of my favorite fruits: I can buy a piece of supermarket beef-liver that cooks up like a shoesole and tastes like last Saturday's urinal cake, but the first bite still has enough of a hint of what the cow used to be before it got technologized and civilized, before it was even a cow and was still something that pissed in the high forest (and didn't shit on its tail) and moved like a shadow among tree shadows, courted by the hunter.... I was kind of catching it second-hand that night, because I hadn't helped kill, clean, and carry out that elk—hadn't seen the liver goosh out, dark purply-brown and still warm. But sitting there whole on the table, vibrating ever so slightly on the plate as someone walked by, bumping the table on the way to the fridge for another beer as we talked laughed drank sweated waiting for the stove to finish the big pan of fried potatoes *Somebody want to slice that* said Bots, turning the potatoes, and yes and no, we did and didn't want to slice it, great purple-brown petal from the dark flowering viscera. While there was no solemnity, there was still something of ritual to that meal *Take eat this is my heart and liver* that did honor to the elk, properly gave thanks. It was not an especially *macho* thing. It was like supping in a cave in the valley of the Dordogne.

It would be inaccurate to say that Crested Butte at that time was a direct and "unpolluted" descendant of the old-country European village culture. The majority of the old-timers were American-born, raised in a mixture of old-country ways and modern American ways. They had televisions in their houses.

Also, by then, they had begun the traumatic shift from being an insular and rather remote "former mining town" to a growing modern resort—in terms of emphasis, the town had gone from a place with a past to a place with a future. The town was being pried open by the twentieth century.

But the point is—if the town in 1966 was no longer what it had been, it was not yet what it has since become; transition was the name of the game in those years. The cafes were the center of the town's life, and they showed the progress of the transition better than anything else. On Saturday afternoon, the Grubstake might be full of old-timers and new-timers alike, watching a baseball or football game. And then Saturday night, much of the same crowd might be back in the place—to dance the polka.

Dancing the polka in Crested Butte! Maybe the way we dance says more about what we are than all we say....

Before I moved to Crested Butte, I had never really danced much. A typical liberal intellectual with a chronic Protestant hangover, I thought it a little vulgar to "have rhythm." How did that improve the rational society? In the town where I grew up, dance night and alley-fight night at the YMCA were one and the same. I was, of course, able to get out on the floor and sway and waver my way through some stage of physical embrace; but I wasn't out there for the *dancing* so much as the opportunity to try to squash a warm body against my own. Maybe get poked in the eye by a foam-encased breast (I was short in high school). When I was in ninth grade, I got invited to the Rainbow Girls' "Formal," and my invitation included a couple evenings of free dancing lessons under tutelage of the girl's mother. A most depressing experience. I learned to prettyfoot it two steps in one direction ("On your toes, George, not your heels") then two steps back the other way in another direction ("Count with your head, not with your mouth"), then around and back again. I later refined the two-step shuffle down to the one-step sway.

I observed that there were two basic ways of dancing. One way was "step" dancing, like the waltz or minuet, where there was a right way to do it, a pattern to follow; and the other way was what we called at the time jitterbugging, and which has before and since been called any number of things, and could maybe just be designated "Twentieth century post-jazz popular dancing." This was the antithesis of step-dancing: there was no real pattern to learn; everyone more or less worked out his or her own variations on some common basic rhythmic movements, and the main idea was self-expression. You could have called the formal dances—especially when you got into the ones where the pattern was all, like the square dance—the dances of the superego; and the things the kids liked best the dances of the id. You could have called them that if you like that kind of thing.

But in Crested Butte, at those polka parties, I began to see that there was a third kind of dancing, between those two extremes. My first year in Crested Butte, I was no more interested in dancing than I'd ever been; but I went to the dances for two reasons: first, that's where the women would be; and second, the dances were in the bars, which is where I usually went every evening anyway.

But, like just about everything else in open-for-the-winter Crested Butte that year, those dances bore no resemblance to the *apres-ski* scene I'd encountered in Vail or Georgetown. The honking reedy wail of the accordion—Botsie Spritzer and his Stomach Steinway—all those old and young people, old dancing with young, spinning and dipping and bouncing and twirling in a fine mist of sweat, smoke, beer smell, and Skoal spray, two-G grins plastered on faces red and dazed from going round and round—*this* was not the authentic reproduction promised in the universal basic ski brochure; these people didn't look either bored enough, or prosperous enough; this looked like it might be the real thing behind the pictures....

I studied it carefully from the bar, trying to figure out which of my two categories it belonged in. I was vaguely aware that in folk-dancing classes they taught a "polka," a form of round dance with steps and all; but if this was the polka, it was a "deteriorated" form. There was no circle, and it didn't look like there was much more of a step than bounce-bounce on this foot, then bounce-bounce on that foot. I naturally assumed, civilized hick that I was with my either-ors, that since it didn't belong in the category of formal dance, it must be a form of do-it-yourself self-expression dancing.

So I had a few beers to get my self-expresser going, grabbed a girl, and went out to make up for my lack of grace with an abundance of exuberance. I got banged around a bit, and banged others around a bit; but that's life, right? I seemed to have a natural advantage: big feet. Size twelve mountain boots with wafflestomper soles and reinforced toes: I created sizable clearings in the wilderness of movement out on the floor. Once I asked a girl to dance, and she said sure, she'd rather dance with me than against me. I thought she was just having her little joke.

But one night at Starika's Bar, Gal Starika took me in tow: she said she was either going to have to teach me to dance right or kick me out. She showed me how to polka with quick little steps rather than my great galumphing lunges: this was the right way, not just because it was safer for everyone else, but because it made it possible to change directions more quickly and easily (taking advantage of openings as opposed to "creating" them), and you could spin like a damned dervish. Any good quarterback would tell you the same.

But these techniques she told me all illustrated a single basic lesson about this "deteriorated" form of the polka: if you aren't dancing according to some formal pattern that tells you where to be when, and if you aren't at the other extreme of staking out a small area in which you express your self and shake your ass—if in other words, you want to be dancing along with everyone else through the common space—the dance will only work out if everyone does his own thing with a total awareness of what everyone around him is doing.... And when a roomful of people are really *dancing*, everyone can be whirling and spinning and moving around at top speed, all over the floor, slipping into and through the narrowest and briefest of openings, spinning off and sliding past each other like greased pigs in a Maytag. There is no formal pattern dictating anyone's movement; yet a kind of dynamic, shimmering, and very, very fragile structure can emerge in the dancing that is entirely dependent on everyone's sensitivity to the movement of everyone around them. It can be very beautiful. It is group dynamics light-years beyond the self-conscious touchie-feelie stage. It is neither a civilized dance, evocative of the desire for order that leads to social structures and organizations, nor is it a primitive expression of simple emotions. It is something from the region between; and, more than a million words, it says in a single metaphor what it was to be in open-for-the-winter Crested Butte for a few years there.

I was talking earlier about "edges"—ecotones, the transitional areas between two environmental entities. Crested Butte is an "outpost" on the outer edge of what we tend to call "civilization as we know it."

But it is the nature of edges, ecotones, that they do not exist between something and nothing. They have to be between something and something else. And living on, or rather *in* the edge, there is always a tendency to want to find out what it is that's "over the edge" the other way. Crested Butte can be said to be in the edge-zone between civilization and winter.

That may sound like an effort to combine two un-combinables—like trying to add up apples and oranges for an answer expressed in bananas. But it isn't. We have managed to come up with such a powerful and extensively pervasive civilization that we are able to carry on business as usual through some excesses in the "natural" environment (better to say "non-human" or "pre-human" environment) that would have stopped us dead in our earlier, less sophisticated ages. To be sure, an unusually hard winter can cripple our cities for a while; but that is because the cities are only set up to deal quickly with the normal winter. Where we have made an all-out effort to anticipate and stay ahead of the harshest winter weather, as in the mountain regions of America, we can usually keep the roads open and the traffic moving. Civilization, in short, effectively is an environment unto itself, with a relative degree of (temporary and expensive) independence from nature.

But this was certainly not always the situation, and the "civilizing of winter" in a place like Crested Butte was more of a job than we might imagine today. And even today, there does seem to be a point beyond which it is simply too expensive to push on into winter's terrain with the full equipage of Western Civilization in America. The "zone of edge" begins about ten miles south of Crested Butte, at a hill called Round Mountain where the weather seems to "break" consistently—heavy snowfall north of the hill, lighter snowfall to the south. "Street-level civilization" continues on to the edge of Mt. Crested Butte, where Barbara and I had to park the car (when we had one) and strap on the "small craft" for the ski trip to the cabin. "Electrical civilization" continued on beyond that to our cabin. On beyond our cabin, winter had dominion: it was nice country to visit, but you wouldn't want to live there. Within that zone, civilization and winter were, and are, engaged in a dynamic contention, which has been a pervasive and important element in the whole life and history of the towns in the area—to include the ones that have failed as well as the ones that survived.

Over the seventy years that weather records have been kept in Crested Butte, however haphazardly, downtown Crested Butte has shown an ability to bear up under an average of around 225 inches of snow a winter, with the biggest winters going to over four hundred inches. The town usually has its snow cover by late October, early November, and the last of the coal-sooty, dog-bepissed, dirt-and-turd-brown stuff is not gone until late May. At the height of winter—or its rotten depths, if you're over forty and not a skier—the snowpack on level ground might be a steady five feet after new-snow settlement; snow sliding off the roofs on low-eaved buildings begins to meet the snow piling up under the eaves; and when the rotary plow comes along, chewing a vertical wall on the plowbanks to allow for car parking, the streets become shallow canyons that, among other drawbacks, trap random packs of claustrophobic dogs at street level where they fight, fuck, chew pedestrians, and generally tie up traffic.

The air at 9000 feet (approximately the altitude of the sundeck on Sancho's Cantina) is thin and dry; it provides little resistance to the sun's rays, but there is also little there to be warmed and retain the heat. Thus, it might be shirt-sleeve weather on that south-facing sundeck in the middle of February, while fifty feet away across the street, in the shadow of the false front of the Princess Theatre, a thermometer would show 17° F.

It has been observed, rightly I think, that although Crested Butte lies geographically in the "four-seasons" temperate zone, the preponderant impact of winter in the high Rockies sets a different schedule of seasons there; and instead of four, there are three seasons, all having to do with winter. There is the season of getting ready for winter, there is the season of winter, and squeezed in between the two (briefest season of all) there is the season of forgetting about winter for a while. "I work all week," said Willard Ruggera, "so I'm always happy when summer comes on a weekend."

In the town's earlier days, survival on something more civilized than the dog-eat-dog level depended entirely on the thin umbilical track of the train. And the narrow-gauge trains were very small to be going up against something as big as the winter in its own territory. Little engines with tippy little cars creeping along ledges carved out of cliffs, switchbacking and looping up the mountains. Sometimes it would snow hard and fast enough to get ahead of the ability of even a double-header with a wing-plow to push its way through. Then the train might back down the track again, disconnect the engine with the plow, and that engine would go screaming up the track full tilt into the accumulating drift, trying to break through. If that didn't work, the train simply didn't get through until the big rotary plow was brought up to chew and spit its way through. Sometimes this meant waiting until the storm was over, and there were periods of a week or more when there would be no train to Crested Butte at all.

Avalanches too threatened that umbilical connection. Occasionally the noise of the train set them off, and once the train was hit by a huge one off the side of Mount Emmons just west of town, and pushed out onto the ice of Peanut Lake. Miraculously, no one was hurt. But the avalanche didn't have to hit the train to disrupt the connection: all it had to do was deposit twenty feet of hard snow on the tracks, and not even the rotary could touch that.

Those were bad times in town. The coal cars waiting to go down the valley would stack up in the yard; there would be no empties to fill. So the work force would be cut to nothing. Miners who needed the money in the worst way knew there would be no relief until the storm ended—and it would just keep snowing and snowing.

The stores would begin running low on food, the bars on beer and whiskey...and it would just snow and snow. People would start going on credit—if they weren't already on it—and as their bills mounted, so would the nervous tension. The snow would just keep on coming. There would be arguments, fights, edginess everywhere; the very social fabric would begin going all threadbare and holey...and still the snow would snow. Winter was on the counter-offensive. *And if it doesn't stop soon* people would begin to mutter....

But these past hundred years, in the end it has always been winter that weakened first; the storms wore out before the towns. And there would come a day—literally overnight—when the morning sun would be gleaming on all that deep snow so white, with only a few residual clouds caught on peaks and slopes of the mountains, gray fluffs obviously innocent of further ill intent.

Then a hundred miners on their long "snowshoes" and webs would head down the valley with Number Two scoops to where the avalanche debris or wind-drifts defied even the rotary plow.

Working in levels, with the shovelers at the bottom of a widening, deepening trench shoveling up onto a bench where other shovelers shoveled it on up over the rim and out, the track would be cleared for the waiting train. Whereupon the miners would climb on to the train and arrive back in town with much whistling and bell-ringing, shouting and cheering and snowballing coming from the crowd come down to greet the first train— the whole thing a moment comparable to the moment in the movies when, just as the fort or the wagon-train is about to go down under the Indian assault, bugles sound and over the ridge, out of the gap, rides the cavalry, and once again the outpost is saved.

It wasn't until well into the early Thirties that the highway department began making a concerted effort to keep the road open all the way into Crested Butte through the winter. Prior to that time, those few who owned autos in Crested Butte put them in storage for the winter, and for the duration the town lived on top of the snow rather than down at street level. Horse-drawn sleighs and pedestrians packed down the snow in the streets, and shoveling was largely a matter of keeping your doorways clear (house-to-street and house-to-outhouse) and doing whatever grading seemed to be necessary or desirable to get up to the level of the street snowpack.

Snow was not the only artillery of the winter, of course; there was the cold too. To a degree, the snow and the cold fight each other: it can actually be too cold to snow, and when the ground is well covered with snow the effects of the cold are cancelled at ground level. But strip off the snow cover....

The people of Crested Butte found out what happens when you strip off the snow cover once they started keeping the streets plowed through the winter. The water lines ran down the streets, until 1952 when a new system of lines was installed in the alleys, six feet down, and eight feet where they crossed the streets.

Before the new water system was installed, the position of Town Clerk was largely an outdoor job through the winter. The town had an electric thawing apparatus on sled runners: heavy-duty wires were hooked to the frozen hydrants and pipes, and the clerk shinnied up the nearest electric pole and hooked other wires directly into the power supply—effectively turning the plumbing system into a big resistance heater. Then the Town Clerk either went back to the office to try to squeeze in some bookwork, or drank coffee until the frozen pipe started running water again or broke from the pressure behind the ice.

This was something more than a matter of inconvenience— although a chronic inconvenience can be a terrible depressant: there is nothing quite so destructive to morale as waking up in a cold house and finding that there isn't even any water to get a pot of coffee going once the stove is lighted. But far more serious was the matter of fire.

Nearly every building in town was a fire hazard from the word go; insulation was a generally unavailable luxury in such places right up to and including World War II, and the only way to get the buildings at a comfortable temperature was to put a cherry-glow on the potbelly stove in the living room and enough fire in the kitchen range to hear it suck air. If your stove wasn't hot enough to turn the metal buttons on your overalls into a set of branding irons at three feet, there was no way it was going to keep the plumbing from freezing at thirty below outside. The water was left running at a trickle: it wasn't the sound that kept you awake, it was listening for the trickle to stop. But under that kind of use, pipes and chimneys burned out, walls behind stoves got heated and reheated day after day until they were dried and primed for a little overheating.

The Town Clerk tried to make certain that there were hydrants thawed in every section of town, so that the volunteer fire department could get hose just about anywhere it might be needed. But the colder the night, the sooner the water in the thawed hydrants began to slush up again, and the hotter everyone had their fires....

Crested Butte didn't really have a fire truck until 1972. The town's basic fire equipment until that year was two hand-pulled hose carts with six-foot wheels. Good on any terrain, I suppose, if you had the heart and lungs to pull them. I was a member of the volunteer fire department from 1969 until we moved to the woods in 1971, and I found it to be work you wanted to stay in shape for. One winter night the siren went off at three a.m., and I had the dubious honor of being one of the first two firemen half-dressed, half-awake, and all-adrenalized at the firehouse; Jim Wallace and I both grabbed the handle of one of those two carts and took off at a dead run down the icy streets toward where we could see the gray smoke blotting the clear black sky. We lasted about a block running. Have you ever tried to run at night with the temperature at minus twenty-five? Adrenalin alone is not enough.

When we had finally trotted, walked, shuffled, and crawled to the hydrant nearest the fire, hooked up our hose, and turned the valve, it was an immeasurable relief to see the hose swell and stiffen with the surge of water.

In my mind's eye that night, I replayed similar scenes from the past—nightmare scenes: *No water! Try the one next block! And off again dragging the damn heavy hose—no water there either.* The great rage of impotent frustration as the building blows up and lights the one next to it.... In 1890 the north side of the business district was lost; in 1893 it was the south side. Both fires were started by overheated stoves in the dead of night in the dead of winter, January both times. Both times, all the hydrants in town were frozen; and both fires were finally stopped by the rather extreme measure of dynamiting buildings at the downwind ends of burning city blocks, to create a gap too wide for the fires to leap. When I was a fireman in Crested Butte, the department motto was "We never saved a building but we never lose the lot." The winter wins the buildings.

If the winter seemed to manifest an almost conscious effort to drive man out of its once-undisputed territory in the Rockies, such spectacular multi-front attacks as a cold night combined with frozen hydrants and overheated stoves leading to a major fire were not its most successful efforts. Western-civilized folk have always had a way of getting their backs up in the face or the wake of disaster—the big fires in Crested Butte apparently had the same unifying and strengthening effect on the people as, say, the bombing of London had on the British. A high price to pay—but who said gumption was cheap?

No, winter was at its best in accumulating a long-run impact through countless small irritations, embarrassments, discouragements, and frustrations. The seemingly eternal confrontation with the snow piling up too deep on the roof, pressing in against the bottom glass of the windows, filling in the doorway with every passing wind, blotting out the path to the outhouse...well, the outhouse alone represents a certain vulnerability to the harsher elements that even now ought to be enough to raise empathetic gooseflesh. On even a moderately cold morning, the Throne of Vulgaria would be delicately rimmed with beautiful but otherwise uninviting frost feathers. And nobody called it "the little boys' room" or the "little girls' room" in those days: if you were big enough to go to the outhouse, you were going to a *man's* place. Or you used the chamber pot in the corner of the kitchen. The popular euphemism Botsie Spritzer taught me for this was, "got to go back away from the icicle."

Basically, the difference the winter made in Crested Butte, up through the Fifties really, meant doing without many of the things already taken for granted in most of the rest of the country. You couldn't take running water for granted, you couldn't take fire protection for granted, you couldn't take the use of the automobile for granted, you really couldn't even take survival itself for granted, at least not above the most minimal level: all that was necessary was the right combination of storms. . . an avalanche off Gibson Ridge big enough to tear out a stretch of track at a time when the town's supplies were already at a vulnerably low level. . . . All it would have taken would have been a winter just a little worse than the worst winter in memory, and the hell with this, everyone would have said.

Or so they said. I've sat in Frank's with natives of the town, sipping beer after beer and watching it snow and snow: they'll talk then about the worst winter they ever saw, and how it wouldn't take one much worse than that and they'd shake the slush of these streets off their heels forever and ever and go down to Arizona or out to California, or even over to Denver where there's still a winter but nothing like these sonsabitches. . . . And many of them do leave: sell their houses to rich hippies in need of a little suffering for prices they can't believe, and head down toward milder winters. To "arrive" is to depart. And some of them have to leave in order to stay alive: the thin dry air is slow death to a man with coal-dust lungs. But despite their predictions and polemics, many of them won't leave until they catch the pinebox express: they will continue to shovel their way out, build their fires against the night, worry about their pipes, and complain their way faithfully through from first snow to final melt and the brief season of forgetting about winter. "You got to be a little bit crazy to live in a place like this," we say, not without a touch of pride.

But things have gradually changed—the position, you might say, has been reinforced, and the lines of supply secured. Civilization has finally reached Crested Butte and places like it. Winter comes, but each year the lives of the people are less affected and altered by it. Schedules can be maintained and routines go uninterrupted by all but the biggest storms.

But that was not enough. The final step was to rub salt in the Old Man's wounds. The people from Kansas came in and built ski lifts on Crested Butte Mountain and the town became a winter resort. So now, life not only goes on *in spite* of winter; to a degree it goes on *on account of* winter. We have finally put even winter into harness for our own use.

Crested Butte natives have always said, "Snow is the only crop that never fails around here." And now it's a cash crop. Now it is the light winter, the easy winter like 1976-77, that's the disaster; and in the midst of all but the most bitter raging storm, people will cheerfully lay down ten or twelve bucks a day to go ride up in unprotected chairlifts and plow around in a thick heavy snowfall. Checking each other for frostbite. "Isn't this fun?" they say. "Isn't this beautiful?"

On the last day of my first winter as a ski patrolman, we had a little party up in the patrol shack—little enough, but it lasted all day. Hot rum punch on a Coleman stove. It was a rather nasty day, windy and sleety but toward the end of the day, for no reason discernible, one of my fellow patrolmen demonstrated his prowess at parallel skiing by dropping his ski pants around his ankles for the last run of the year, and sleet and wind notwithstanding, skiing the mountain bare-assed. He managed to fall toward the bottom of the mountain, spraining his shoulder and greasing the icy snow with about a pound of flesh.

But that act, its tasteless, graceless exuberance, has stuck in my mind as a kind of symbolic gesture in which we all shared by our very presence there where only a madman or an Englishman would have dreamed of spending the winter a century ago—*A moon for your gray sullen skies, winter!*

When I try to weigh the years I spent in Crested Butte and come up with something in the way of—well, something to steer by, something to carry into the future as a talisman of guidance or whatever, I find it most difficult. Maybe it's not even necessary or desirable to try, although I suspect it is.

We've just gone through a period in this nation of trying to somehow see where we've gone and what we have and haven't done in a period of two hundred years. Two hundred years! Jesus, who can weigh an iceberg-size lump of time like a century? Let alone two of them. Ridiculous season. I have enough trouble with just a decade, a baker's-dozen of years at the most. But maybe centuries are easier in a way than decades. The *intimacy* of a decade might make us prefer the remote, cerebral solemnity of centuries, the Bicentennial instead of the "decennial." We can still *feel* a decade; everything is still close enough to revive its own original joy, pain, and confoundedness; we are still all too aware of our own personal presence in the dynamic ballooning profusion of unforeseen consequences.

When I was in Crested Butte (from *within* Crested Butte), I thought I had pretty well recovered from my "breakdown" with the Army and the society in general. Wasn't I keeping it together pretty well? I worked two years for the Ski Area, ski-patrolling; my work was good. I was dependable, trusted, respected to a degree. People enjoyed my company. I occasionally relaxed.

My third year there, I got into business—if you would in fact call a newspaper in a town with 450 inhabitants a "legitimate business." (Keep in mind the growth potential.) I became involved in, somewhat committed to, Crested Butte—as a place, and as an idea: a place where, along with others of a similar background and mind, we might be able to initiate and implement some modest alternatives to the American mainstream. Maybe we did, in modest ways.

My fourth year there, I fell in love and got married.

My fifth year, with the paper doing well, Barbara's sign business doing well (I mean, we were struggling, but were on schedule), I became a father. And then we sold the works and went to the woods. So much for the pretty illusion of normal recovery, recovery of normalcy.

Part of me yearned for the picture I seemed to be painting around myself. Sometimes I wanted it so badly I could have cried for it: family, a dependable job, a well-bounded and clear-cut set of roles to fulfill.... The human spirit must be a gaseous substance, which expands to fill the limits and configurations of its container: take away or blur a person's sense of his obligations, drives, responsibilities, and all the other "limitations" on his total spiritual freedom, and you get a person as generally diffuse and diffusely general as a weak fart in a coliseum. A person going off in all directions at once, someone everywhere and nowhere simultaneously. Like the Grecian urn, we only begin to come into being as we perceive and accept the size and shape of all those "limitations," maybe.

One of the more interesting aspects of life in Crested Butte at the time was the degree to which one could actually *afford* to play at surrounding oneself with the accoutrements of normalcy without much in the way of resources, experience, or training. I, for example, didn't know a thing about newspapering when I decided to become a newspaper editor in Crested Butte. No training, no experience—I wouldn't have been able to get a job carrying coffee on any respectable newspaper in the city, and there I was: editor, business manager, city desk, senior reporter, junior reporter, columnist, editorialist, advertising department, and janitor for the Crested Butte *Chronicle.* And I did just fine too; it wasn't a bad newspaper. But it is difficult to take your success very seriously when it comes that easily. I don't mean that I didn't work hard; I did. But there's something about starting at the top (even in a very small place) and succeeding from there that puts a kind of a surrealistic halo around your efforts.

It is not insignificant that, during the years I was newspapering in Crested Butte—I've got to think of a better way of putting it: "newspapering" sounds too much like "wallpapering"—that during those years the most popular movie in Crested Butte was *King of Hearts,* the Alan Bates classic about the inmates of an asylum in Europe who, after the evacuation of the town near the asylum during World War I, get out and all start playing at the various roles implicit in the abandoned buildings of the town with varying degrees of success and normalcy.

The succession of proprietors of the Princess Theatre— most of them playing at theatre management for the first, and often last, time—brought *King of Hearts* to town twice a year from 1969 on into the early Seventies. For several of those years, the film was given a special local flair by virtue of the fact that it was a Cinemascope film and none of the Princess managers had the scratch for such fancy equipment; so everything in the picture was scrunched up to about half its normal width. This was a drawback with some films—notable films like *Hud* and *The Great Escape*—since it tended to make one laugh at all the wrong things; but it was no problem with *King of Hearts* at all. If anything, it added something.

But at any rate, that was the way many of the new people in Crested Butte felt about Crested Butte those years: that it was a kind of asylum-without-walls where people driven to a state of "walking-madness" by the acceptable insanities of the so-called real world could a) masquerade as normal people engaged in normal enterprises, and b) at the same time constitute our own witty (we thought) commentary on this so-called normalcy.

I think that this attitude has perhaps always been a strong thread running through the history of the American West—how else do you explain the "false-fronts," the big elaborate facades on the shabby little overnight buildings? It was literally the case at times that the false fronts were built first, propped up with boards, and backed up with a tent until the proprietor did enough business out of the tent to afford the rest of the building. Real live theatre. When the circus came to town, it really had to be something to beat the circus that *was* the town.

But, unfortunately or fortunately, the parallel with film did not carry on to the same conclusive ending in what we will call, ignoring for the time being the implications and implicit problems, real life. In the movie, the inmates were having a grand time fulfilling the roles of butcher, baker, and candlestick-maker when the two warring armies simultaneously arrived in town from opposite directions. The friendly outgoing inmates thought this was just great too, the more the merrier; and they turned the thing into two sort of impromptu parades toward the center of town, leading both armies to believe that they were being welcomed as liberators. The parades converged on the town square, and went around a couple times—until the two military leaders saw with a start that they were sharing the honors with the opposition, whereupon they opened fire on each other at close range. Revolted and disgusted, the inmates shed all their external accoutrements of normalcy and trudged back to the asylum. Joined by Bates, our local Everyman. The moral wasn't too obscure for the average viewer.

But what happened in our case, in Crested Butte, lacked all that upfront drama. The major armies of the modern world—the straight, opportunity-oriented, progressive business people; the new barbarians with their backpacks, big dogs, bread-and-circus orientation and money from home; and the regulators with their planning and zoning and control of this and that—they all arrived, but not abruptly. They infiltrated, dribbled in a few at a time, set up their covers and began operations. There was only a subtle and barely distinguishable difference between them and us: we were all secretly mad, practicing the fine art of faking normalcy; they were all secretly normal, and came out at night faking craziness.

And that, of course, is nonsense—not the basic idea, but the judgement that there was actually a "them" and an "us," two definable sides into which we could have been divided. I don't think that any of us were really *faking* anything. We wanted very much to establish ourselves, get something together, build a door against the wolf, achieve the degree of predictability and sufficiency and comfort in our lives that we call, with no contempt whatsoever in our voices, a state of normalcy.

But there was also the fact that we were mostly there because we had been somewhat dissatisfied with things in the mainstream society we'd left. Some of us were dissatisfied with that "real world" because we didn't like the kinds of things there were to do in that world. Some of us were dissatisfied with it because we had seen no good opportunity for working our way into and up through that world. Most of us were somewhere in between. But once we'd set ourselves down in Crested Butte, with nothing on beyond but the woods and the winter, we had to do something, and most of the things we knew how to do were the things we'd done, or tried to do, back in the world we thought we'd left behind. So that's what we did. Even though we thought, when we had the time to think, that we were crazy to come to a new place and do the same old things... In both our normalcy and our craziness, there wasn't really much fakery.

George Santayana held a fairly jaundiced view of civilization, for an early-twentieth century American. Scribbling in the margin of a book of essays called *Civilization in the United States*, he noted that

> ...civilized means citified, trained, faithful to some regimen deliberately instituted. Civilization might be taken as a purely descriptive term, like *Kultur*, rather than a eulogistic one; it might simply indicate the possession of instruments, material and social, for accomplishing all sorts of things, whether those things were worth accomplishing or not.

Certainly one of the more basic instruments of our civilization is the newspaper: a way of disseminating information about certain kinds of things, with a certain intensity, depth of perception, and pervasive regularity. Whether those kinds of things are worth paying attention to or not.

The function of a modern newspaper (not necessarily its intended function but certainly its effective function) seems to be to tie up the senses and the mind in a consideration of abstractions, conventions, and other mind-born structures which have no reality other than that which we grant them. The Dow-Jones. The Executive, Legislative, Judicial, and the Candlemaker. The Federal Reserve, the Floating Dollar—these abstractions and conventions were, once upon a time, conceived of as means for dealing with certain realities around us. But the newspapers make them realities unto themselves: no longer the means of our prevailing but the ends that insulate us from a more real world. We tune our sensibilities to the printed page, where we learn that the big board is slipping, or that recent polls indicate that so-and-so has an edge over whosis in California, and our day is ruined, while all around us a beautiful woman might be walking past, or a Mack truck about to run us over, or a poodle about to piss on our shoe—real things! Tangible, sensible, touchable, real things.

But what began to bother me a great deal, during my newspapering years in Crested Butte, was the almost "gravitational" inevitability with which I found myself beginning to sound more and more like the standard, run-of-the-mill newspaper. The sum and total of my experience there was the conclusion that I wasn't editing the newspaper; I was being edited by what a newspaper is.

I saw a certain progression. In 1968, when I'd only been newspapering a month or two, I neglected one week to mention the monthly meeting of the Town Council. One of the councilmen called me on it. "But nothing *happened* at that meeting," I said. "That doesn't matter," he answered. "The *Chronicle* is the official paper of the town, the paper of record here, and you ought to record such things whether anything happens or not."

I wasn't sure I agreed. But then on the other hand.... If nothing was happening at the Town Council meetings, was that because the Council had nothing to do? Or was it because the Council wasn't doing anything about whatever there was to be done? Your ordinary citizen—which is what I think I am at heart, politically—is, when pressed, generally skeptical about the ability of the government, local to national, to do anything constructive about anything. But it is the nature of governments and newspapers to go hand-in-pocket with each other: governments depend on the newspapers to keep hammering away on the importance of bringing the government into this, into that. Accordingly, while I might feel secretly relieved that the government wasn't too busy, I was gradually "edited"—if only by the need to either take the "easy" news provided by the town government or make up something more interesting to fill the space above my ads—into giving credence to the illusion that the Town Government was the most important game in town.

The "dog problem" was one of the better examples of the tedious folly that comes of taking the role of the government too seriously. Every town in the country has a dog problem to some degree or another, but in Crested Butte it has been exacerbated by the fact that strange dogs on the street were a viable target for old-timers and "new old-timers" and "old new-timers" desirous of striking a blow at the strange people to whom the dogs belonged. And for their part, the new new-timers whose dogs were the focus of the attention made it clear that, while they might not agree that all dogs were created equal or confirm other fine points like that, they would fight to the death, or near there, for the god-given right of dogs to run free and shit where they pleased.

So what was the proposed solution to this situation? Why, a dog ordinance, of course. So the government devoted hours and hours, days overall, to the dog problem—*but treating it as if it were in fact a dog problem.* Trying to figure out equitable leash laws that didn't violate dog rights, a system of fines and penalties that would suitably frighten dog owners, and the like, when all along it was not a dog problem at all, but a cultural gulf between new people and old that was deeper than grief itself. How was the mere government—itself a reflection and manifestation of that gulf by then—going to deal with that? No way. So we picked and parried around in the superficial zone of symptoms, while the causes ripened, festered, supporated, and leaked their poison into us all.

I of course didn't have any idea how else to attack the problem—I suspected, in fact, that there was *no* way to give it a good flashy, visible solution that would make even most of the people happy, let alone everyone. But there is something about a newspaper which simply, absolutely, precludes the consideration of "no solution" as a possible alternative—and if you don't understand that, I probably can't explain. Perhaps the neat lines of type, the nicely justified margins, the compartmentalized nature of the make-up, the crisp finitude of an editorial (I knew I was in trouble when my editorials started consistently spilling over into a second column). . . .I don't know exactly what it is, but there is a tidy illusion of rationality to the large printed sheet that fosters the illusion that life could be like that too: a big spread, but everything in its place, well organized and nicely laid out, *understandable, rational.* Thus are editors edited.

Barbara's sign shop, right down on the main drag next to the Grubstake Bar, was the former Crested Butte barbershop. Barber to Barbara, shaves to shavings. The barber chair and the waiting bench were still there; and perhaps out of ingrained habit a lot of the old-timers, when downtown or on their way to the bars for the afternoon, would stop in there for a short sit on the bench, talking to Barbara. A lot of the younger men about town did that too, such as yours truly before we were married.

To the barbershop furniture she had added a rough-cobbled worktable, a stool, and a small but eminently solid wall-bench built out of a single piece of wood about four inches by eighteen, dried as straight and true as a simple heart. On the front of that, she had carved "Things Take Time"—either a philosophical credo or an admonition to customers; I forgot to ask.

In a row around two walls she had hung plaques, each one a letter of the alphabet carved in a different type of wood. She never finished that alphabet—she ran out of spare ends of exotic woods before she ran out of letters.

In an adjoining room she had a lathe and a sander; as a result the air of the shop was always fresh with the smell of sawdust, the sight of sawdust, the silky-dry feel of sawdust. The afternoon sun coming through the tall windows—her shop faced south— blocked out its beams in the light haze of sawdust always in the air, and lit up the usual light film of sawdust on her hair, brows, eyelashes, and clothes as she worked. The Sawdust Queen.

I liked to watch her work on her wooden signs. I can't stand it, myself, having someone watching me at work, but she didn't seem to mind. I was amused, or anyway *mused*, by the fact that we both dealt in words for a living.

There was a difference, of course: I was a lot more, uh,

productive than she was, cranking out two or three thousand words a week; while in a good week she might work her way painstakingly through a dozen or twenty. There were similarities too: in both instances, much of our work was fairly perfunctory, things we'd done before, things we would do again, things that had become somewhat routine. Chipping away backgrounds for her, typing out meeting notes for me. On the jobs we were each seriously, even passionately, interested in—an editorial on a subject close to my heart, a wedding plate for good friends of hers—we were both able to muster a certain elegance of style, in our own ways.

But I had to concede privately that in terms of durability, the long run—the quality of lastingness—mine seemed like an inferior product. The words fell out of my typewriter like the chips falling around her bench—I might make a thousand words while she was making a thousand chips, for one word.

It wasn't just that "less is more"—and I don't universally accept the maxim that a picture is worth a thousand words. There are arrangements of words, maybe only a phrase or a piece of a sentence, that are more evocative to me, go straighter to the heart, than a thousand pictures—*I did not wish to live what was not life, living is so dear*. . . . I can't begin to conceive of the picture or pictures that would wake up in me what those few words wake up.

No, the difference was not the per-word time factor or anything else so simple, but something about what went on in that time involved.

Barbara did two basic kinds of carving, incised (which was carving the letters down into the background) and relief (which was carving the background down away from the letters). Of the two, my favorite—both in terms of the finished product and for watching her do—was the incised.

She would sketch her letters onto the wood with pencil, but that was mostly for spacing arrangement; it was only when she put her blade to the wood that the letter itself really began to emerge: she would draw the blade down through what was seen, closeup, to be a veritable underbrush of sketch strokes, but it was as if the blade were on tracks, picking out a razor-thin invisible line just ahead of itself. . . .

It draws me back again to the simile of dancing the polka: the times when you instinctively sense that a "moving opening" is going to trace an invisible line from where you almost are, that will curve and swirl all the way across and around the room; but you'll only be able to follow that moving opening if you and your partner are moving neither too fast nor too slowly, spinning and gliding at just the right speed in the right resolved direction—"moving in measure," as Eliot said. In a way, it is "giving yourself up to the occasion," but not in the sense of a passive surrender, not that at all.

And so would that blade seem to pick its smooth uninterrupted path down through the ten-dollar chunk of hard walnut. Have you ever tried to draw a perfect circle freehand? The harder you concentrate, the greater your pains, the more it looks like you're concentrating too hard and making it painful. Whenever I try to letter a poster or anything of the sort, you can almost hear the "G"'s grunt and the "O"'s go *oof*.

A great deal of Barbara's worktime was spent sharpening her chisels and knives, cleaning out the wood in the incised valleys or chipping away the broad plains of relief background, and finishing the piece of work; the actual time right down there on the hard edge of the letters, drawing the knife down those long graceful curves, was short by comparison. But nevertheless, it was in those few relatively quick and sure strokes that the quality of her work lay—no, say instead: the quality of her work lay in the overall attention to every detail, from the properly sharp blade to the right blend of oils and the proper wax for the finish, but the subtle *art* in her work lay in the quick and almost naive confidence with which she executed those few strokes.

Lest you think her too perfect in her work, I will note that occasionally she slipped, either damaging her work or, less consequentially, herself. Usually, she claimed, cursing herself a little, it was because she should have stopped to sharpen a tool but didn't; it is the first law among woodcarvers that "the sharp blade carves the wood and the dull blade carves the carver." Over the years I have done some bandaging, and once we had to make a midnight run to the emergency room for a nicked artery in the thumb that needed some sewing. But better a little flesh wound than a slip that runs a gouge down that ten-dollar chunk of walnut with eight out of twelve letters already done.

It occurred to me that it might improve the game a little if, once a year, every newspaper were required to put out one issue not on newsprint, but tablets of stone. Or blocks of wood, same difference. Sometimes I would sit over in the office, resting between paragraphs or pages, and wonder what I would be saying about the past week and the most recent Council meeting or the proposed suggestions for amending the revised version of the reworked draft of the zoning ordinance, if I had to go down to the printer's and set it all up in handtype. There would have been a few more *Nothing much happened here last week* weeks, you can bet on that.

But more to the point—where was that *organic* feeling that Barbara must have had, drawing her knife down through that walnut, knowing she was on the invisible track of the perfect curve and it was *right*, like nothing in mechanistic, political society is ever right? "In the groove of the Way," as my hippie translation of the I Ching says. That's not a complaint, that's an observation: nothing in mechanical, political society is ever *right*. It is a foregone conclusion that in any specific instance there will be two sides with two lawyers, or two teams of lawyers, and both sides will be right, which means only that either there is no organic truth inherent in the circumstance, or there is no *sense* of the organic truth there, and either way amounts to the same:

either we need more "instruments, material and social" that work in more productive areas, or we need better ones to plumb deeper in the areas now so futilely scratched over...or I don't know, maybe we need less again.

There was a time, wasn't there, when a story or event had to survive the strenuous test of time, being told from father to sons who themselves became fathers and either did or didn't tell their sons. Eventually, if the story passed that test, it was painstakingly scribed on precious parchment with the blood of berries. Even after the invention of the early printing press, the process of broadcasting the stories and events was so comparatively time-consuming that selectivity was still the name of the game. But now with cheap paper—don't tell the trees—and such marvels as Ottmar Mergenthaler's linotype, the need for selectivity has been rendered obsolete. Whether this was a "thing worth doing or not" seems, to me, to be a valid enough question.

But that's getting a little strident, isn't it? I don't think I'd any more waste my time on a campaign to develop a sense of responsibility for selectivity in newspapers than I would waste my time, any more, in reading newspapers. I'll pick up *King Lear*, or *Hamlet*, or Spengler or Santayana first; that's current enough.

Three bound volumes of *Chronicles* stand on my shelves, and I occasionally get one down to thumb through it, here appreciating the achievement and there confronting the accusation. Someday some historian, suffering the illusion that something of significance happened there and then, might find them useful—although nowhere in those volumes is the real event spelled out: *"During these years, and with the help of this instrument, world civilization arrived in Crested Butte with its instruments, material and social, for accomplishing all sorts of things, whether those things were worth accomplishing or not. Ecce, homo."*

In the same room with those volumes, there is a small plaque on the wall—a beautiful piece of walnut, blank except for four words down in one corner. Barbara made it for me one birthday, and the words on it are something I put in the *Chronicle*, not once but many times, as one of those little fillers used to finish out columns of type:

He Who Laughs Lasts

My newspaper career distilled to that one plaque; the rest passed with the time of its writing.

But mentioning it now reminds me--I ought to heed my own advice. It's like a conditioned response: mention newspapers, and I start sounding like an editorial. I'm six years away from the newspaper and I'm *still* trying to break the habit of sounding like an editorial. Time to get on here—get on with something I hope is a little closer to the organic heart of things.

> *So here I am, in the middle way, having had twenty years—*
> *Twenty years largely wasted, the years of* l'entre deux guerres—
> *Trying to learn to use words, and every attempt*
> *Is a wholly new start, and a different kind of failure*
> *Because one has only learnt to get the better of words*
> *For the thing one no longer has to say, or the way in which*
> *One is no longer disposed to say it.*
> —Eliot, from "East Coker"

PART THREE

I pace upon the battlements and stare
On the foundations of a house, or where
Tree, like a sooty finger, starts from the earth;
And send imagination forth
Under the day's declining beam, and call
Images and memories
From ruin or from ancient trees,
For I would ask a question of them all.
                    —W.B. Yeats, from "The Tower"

What am I doing here?" is a question that can sound on a number of different levels all the way from the top of the head to the bottom of the heart, or thereabouts.

It can sound with the dull windy thud of the Cosmic Question—the Abstract I inquiring about the General All-Purpose Here. It can also be a passionately personal (if no less rhetorical) utterance, riding a wave of irritated frustration—as when the midwinter howler has dusted the outhouse throne with half an inch of snow and put little drifts up against the toilet-paper roll. I do not know much about the esoteric art of levitation, but I have become something of a master at the earthier art of the half-inch hover: teeth to teeth with the wind, asking, "What am I doing *here?*"

Between those two—the vague eternal and the temporal personal—there is probably a way of asking "What am I doing here?'' that takes in the full outback approach as well as the immediacy, the long-range getting-here as well as the rootless being-here, and warrants consideration as an important question. Did I fall here or was I pushed? And where is here anyway?...

I want to tell you about my porch.

When Henry went to the woods, he gave a detailed account of the cabin he built there at Walden Pond. I mean "detailed," too. I am almost sorry to say that I did not build the cabin where we lived in the woods—sorry not because it gives Henry one up on me, but because Henry goes a long way toward convincing me that one of the essential ingredients of the owner-built life is an owner-built home at some point in that life. But it will have to be another point in this life, as there was already a cabin waiting for us when we moved to the biological field station to be caretakers for the winter.

However, the directors of the field station were lenient on the matter of cabin improvements and improvisations; we were more or less free to do anything we wanted to make the place more livable, so long as the field station didn't get the bills. Which brings me to my porch.

The cabin had no porch at all, except for a tiny stoop, when we moved in; and that was the situation through the first winter we lived there—a porch was of course hardly a first-order necessity. But there were sunny, immensely clear days, especially toward (but not necessarily during) what passes for "springtime in the Rockies," days when you just wanted to go out and get crisp, sit down in the sun and burn off that old layer of winter skin that felt like a graft of dandruff held together with old potato peels....But with no porch on the cabin, and two or three feet of sodden snow still piled around on into late April, followed by a four-inch layer of mud and wood-ash in May, you soaked up more than just Vitamin D sitting outdoors.

So after the first winter it was apparent that a porch was, if not necessary, at least highly desirable. "A porch sure would be nice this winter," Barbara said off and on through the second fall. "I'm thinking about it," I would reply.

And I was, in a sort of a way. Mostly trying to think how to do it cheaply, or if possible for nothing, as we had no money to speak of.

But there was also the fact that different people in different situations require different kinds of porches. You look at a South Sea islander: his dwelling is mostly porch, a cultural reflection of his environment. Your Eskimo on the other hand, who will not see the sun for months, builds no porch at all.

The city-dweller used to build houses with porches for a double purpose, only indirectly related to the physical environment. The city keeps the sun's heat so well (so much better than forests and grasslands) that the neighborhood stays hot well into the night; and in an earlier day, once supper was cooked and the smell of cabbage and onions and gray hamburger lay over the house like a carpet of wet dogs, everyone went out to sit on the porch where a sufficient number of rocking chairs, swings, gliders, and desultory jaws might start up a local breeze. And since everybody else was out there too, people hollered back and forth, or went visiting on each other's porches...all of which had the *third* function of keeping the streets open for people. How's a mugger going to make it when every porch is full of hecklers? But then the mad scientists, ever the tool of crimes large and small, invented air-conditioning, and the hooded range, and fourteen inane smells to replace cabbage and onion and wet-dog smells, which worked right in with television and the concept of prime-time. There went the porch; there went the neighborhood.

But getting back to my problem...what kind of a porch did *we* need, out in the woods? Certainly not a neighborhood-type porch; there was no immediate neighborhood. A patio? No grill. I really couldn't imagine. And I didn't want to just knock together some plan out of Sunset Magazine's *Book of Deck and Porch Construction*. It had to be, somehow, right for the cabin, right for the woods, and right for us in that cabin in the woods—you see my problem.

That second winter we made do with a kind of a floating-porch design—I got out the shutters the biologists had used for our cabin windows before we created the position of caretaker, and built snow platforms to lay them on. We could have a different porch any time we wanted. I built the snow platforms at different levels, so we could pick our own level in whatever seemed to be the natural hierarchy of the day.

But to my way of thinking, this was far from ideal. There were practical problems, for one thing—the most serious, or ludicrous depending on your point of view, the natural result of a sun growing in strength day by day through the warming months of March and April: the snow would rot and melt under the south edge of the shutter-platforms, and one might carefully carry out a sandwich, two graham crackers, five figs, and a beer—only to have the platform give way and go planing off down toward the outhouse, lunch sinking into the snow in every direction.

But aside from such minor inconveniences, there is something else that a porch should be, which this shifting arrangement of floating platforms was not, and that is a stable, dependable buffer zone between the inside and the outside. Anyone who has ever stepped out of a porchless house on a rainy day will know exactly what I mean; you need a place to stand that is neither still inside out of the rain nor yet outside in the rain, a place to pause for the putting up of umbrellas or flipping up of rainhoods, the cursing of gods and appointments, or the luxuriant decision to just sit down on the glider and what the hell wait till it's over.

But when one is living on a small offshore island on a frozen ocean, a purely *physical* buffer between inside and outside, shelter and exposure, is perhaps less important than a kind of a *spiritual* buffer between what Emerson distinguished as Soul and Nature, what Jung called the Conscious and the great Unconscious—essentially, oneself and everything else.

Finally, the god of porches—it's Janus, I believe, who is also the god of edges—smiled on me.

There are some terrific scavengers affiliated with that biological field station. In fact, probably half the laboratory before 1960 was put together from odds and ends scavenged, borrowed, and according to at least one plaintiff, stolen from the surrounding fifty miles or so. The station, like all successful organizations, is gradually passing into the hands of a younger, more conservative and stuffy set who want to buy everything new from authorized dealers.

But I digress....At any rate, a mammologist and veteran scavenger from the station happened to pass the site of a house-razing in Crested Butte; the work crew had a whole dumptruck load of old wood and general debris ready to take to the dump. In what was regarded (among the older set, not the younger) as one of the all-time coups, he managed to divert the whole load eight miles up the road to the firewood area at the field station.

Most of that load belonged in the firewood area; but the work-crew at the station, of which I was a member that summer, picked through and found some fine boards ranging in length from eighteen inches to six and a half feet...and a porch. A whole, pre-assembled, ready-weathered, nail-in-place, add-a-chair-and-sit-back porch deck.

It wasn't a large porch, only about four feet by eight feet—but then if you're thinking about shovelling between two and three hundred inches of snow off it over the duration of a winter, you don't want a very big porch. And snow presented another problem: the cabin had a steep roof (45°), one side of which unloaded directly on the south side of the cabin. This meant that for both comfort and safety—it could unload at a drip a week or five hundred pounds at once—the porch needed to extend out from the cabin far enough to keep the porch sitter out of the danger zone. Accordingly, I ran the long dimension of this prefab porch unit perpendicular to the cabin wall, rather than parallel as in conventional porching. I nailed the short end to the cabin with big nails, notched out a couple of logs off my firewood pile for supports on the other end, and that was the basic porch. Thinking ahead to the need for seats on the porch, I left the support logs sticking up above the deck fifteen inches, then tacked short boards on top of those for seats. A table made out of a few scrap lengths of two-by-twelve nailed on top of another firewood log, a fat one, completed the rustic picture.

I would give you a complete accounting in the tradition of Thoreau, down to the ha'penny, but I didn't spend anything. The nails were reclaimed—the field station might be one of the few remaining places in America that straightens and reuses old nails. I had a couple of hours of my time invested, but I have different rates for my time, and that day I charged and paid myself at my standard rate for porch-sitting rather than porch-building.

But in installing the porch at right angles to the cabin wall, I had unwittingly given it the exact . . . what should I say—style? Flair? Image? Personality? It was, let me say, the right porch, in the right relationship to the woods, and the cabin, and us in the cabin in the woods. Barbara noticed it first: "That porch," she said, "looks just like a dock."

And indeed it did. It looked exactly like an humble little rowboat dock from which the water had receded long ago with "melancholy, long, withdrawing roar."

And wasn't there a shale bank just up the road with little fossil seashells all through it?

Well, that was fine with me, for the new dimension it added to porch-sitting; to all outward appearances it might have *looked* like I was doing nothing a lot of the time, when in fact it was perfectly evident, upon explanation, that I was engaged in the portentous and quite traditionally respectable business of waiting, as they say, for my ship to come in.

Sometimes out on the porch there, rather than just sitting—"thinking," as I put it, when asked—I would "consult an oracle": the *I Ching,* the old Chinese "Book of Changes."

My Protestant roots rebelled at this—still do, to a degree: they make me want to hasten to add...oh, some kind of a proper disclaimer, dissociating myself from just another one of *that kind.* "We have let the house our fathers built fall into decay, and now we try to break into Oriental palaces that our fathers never knew," said Dr. Jung. Himself something of a devotee of the *I Ching.*

To sit up there on my porch, that little dock on the edge of a frozen sea (although warm in the afternoon sun), and shuffle through the forty-nine stalks of the oracle—Diamond toothpicks, in my case, but the same well-used set of fifty each time (fifty in case one breaks under the strain of consultation perhaps)—was "recreation" in the truest sense of the word. The handful of toothpicks raised, ready to drop—but first the incantation, from the Apocryphal Visions of Esdras:

> Think of the beginning of this earth: the gates of the world had not yet been set up; no winds gathered and blew, no thunder pealed, no lightning flashed; the foundations of paradise were not yet laid, nor were its fair flowers there to see; the powers that move the stars were not yet established, nor the countless hosts of angels assembled, nor the vast tracts of air set up on high; the divisions of the firmaments had not received their names. Zion had not yet been chosen as God's own footstool; the present age had not been planned; the schemes of its sinners had not yet been outlawed, nor had God's seal yet been set on those who have stored up a treasure of fidelity. *Then did I think my thought...*

Then the small thunder on the tabletop—*Chen,* the Arousing—as the forty-nine drop, and the quick nervous fingers, sorting and shuffling, counting...the fingersmith's meditation.

Engaged in that recreational pursuit one brilliant afternoon —a September afternoon *circa* 1973, according to the personal "Book of Changes" I kept of my consultations—I came up with the fourteenth hexagram, "Possession in Great Measure," which had the trigram for "Flame" above, the one for "Heaven" below—the image of "Fire in heaven above." The oracle could hardly have come up with a better description of that very afternoon, one of the earliest and finest days in the season of Getting Ready for Winter.

But the hexagram as I'd cast it had three "moving" lines; and it resolved, or dissolved, or anyway changed into the fourth hexagram: *Youthful Folly*. Or *Immaturity* in another book. Thanks a lot, was my first reaction. Smartass oracle: sucks me in, then slips it to me.

Nevertheless, I read on. You can't always get what you want, but you usually get what you need. The trigrams for *Youthful Folly* were "Mountain" above, "Abysmal" or "Water" below. And the Image for the hexagram began, "A spring wells up at the foot of a mountain....," and I knew we were still connected.

A couple hundred feet from where I sat on the dock or rather the porch, there was a fresh spring from which we got our water. It is not a large spring, running anywhere from one to maybe twelve or fifteen gallons a minute depending on the season. But it runs the year round, is untouched by human institutions, and the water tastes like it might have come from the well at the beginning of the world.

One of the chores on which our survival depended, in a routine kind of a way, was the daily trip to the spring to fill one or two five-gallon containers—we used an average of about seven gallons a day (two flushes, back in town). This wasn't always a pleasant chore; as the snowpack built up through the winter, it required quite a bit of shovelling to keep the spring accessible; and there were blizzardy days with the air full of minute caltrops of blown snow that made even just five minutes of dipping and pouring, dipping and pouring, no fun at all.

But as chores went, it was not one of the worst—not as bad as "mining" a lump of coal out from under a five foot snowpack, or emptying the chamberpot. And on a nice day, even in midwinter, there was no hurry at all; and I could sit there on the edge of the stone springbox until my butt went numb, watching Gothic Mountain. . . .

There were, to be sure, days when no part of the mountain was visible and I didn't even want to raise my head to look. There were days when it was possible to imagine a mountain twice or ten times larger out of the fragments showing through the breaking clouds; days when the snowfields on top of the mountain blended so perfectly into a dirty white sky that there was no way to tell where the mountain left off and the sky began; days when a pale sky and a thin sun and nervous wind made the mountain look gray and old; days when blowing flurries and curtains of snow made it loom ominous and ugly. But I remember it best as I seemed to see it most often: vast but comprehensible in strong sunlight, white with winter, calmly finite and commensurable in space and time—Kên of the Book of Changes, *keeping still.*

A mountain is something you can get to know, in an upfront and straightforward, but at the same time intimate and personal, way. I think I can say that I know Gothic Mountain well enough to know what I would have to do to *really thoroughly know* the mountain—see it in all its moods and tempers, read through its bowls and slopes and ridges like a library, catalogue and characterize its inhabitants, dig into its core, run ropes like a web on its face and feel out its features. . . . I might have to hire a staff, get a government grant—well, don't worry, I won't of course. Like the conceptual artist, I'm just a conceptual scientist; I like the kind of projects you can think about without thinking about having to clean up the mess.

But someday, I tell myself, someday if things get unduly messy, and it's a question of turning myself in or taking myself away, I could maybe duck out to Gothic Mountain, finish what's barely begun, make out a list of things to study—like the universe, finite but boundless—and finish getting to know the mountain. Alone, one-to-one: there is something about a mountain which extends that possibility.

But the spring flowing out of the mountain is something else again.

One December afternoon, a sunny afternoon a few days before the solstice one winter, I flipped up the lid of the springbox to find a dead toad floating on the dark surface of the water. Quite a surprise: where does a dead toad come from on a brilliant but very cold December day? Out of the mud on the bottom of the spring is the logical answer, I suppose, but there is something about the experience that seems to make the logical answer—or worse, *several* logical answers—a little irrelevant, or at any rate a little late. No matter how much explanation and illumination gets thrown on that kind of thing, it's all a running-after, and the experience itself remains at large, moving randomly through the mind and, as likely as not, to just casually drop into a dream some night, belly up and bloated....But a mere dead toad is a mild mystery compared to what the spring seems to promise, or imply.

"The Abysmal," Richard Wilhelm calls it, in the well-known Chinese-to-German-to-English translation of the I Ching. In a more direct but somehow less interesting Chinese-to-Hippiese translation, Gia-Fu Feng calls it simply "The Pit." The more brilliant the light on the mountain, the darker the surface of the water by contrast, in the spring that wells up at the foot of the mountain; on a really sunny day in March or April, looking into the springbox can be like looking into a black hole.

There was a fair amount of life in our springbox, even during the winter: shiny little black bugs, an occasional earthworm off his course, and most interesting, the caddis-fly larvae with their little "mobile stone homes" of glued-together sand and bits of rock.

But most of the organic matter that intruded into the springbox was taken care of by the planaria, small leech-like creatures that indiscriminately latched onto and slowly "disappeared" anything that wandered or fell into the water—leaves, earthworms, everything but the hardshell bugs and the stone-encased fly larvae.

The planaria were doing us a favor by keeping our water clean, but there was something quite creepy about them to me. They were genuine "shape-shifters": when one would get into the dipper by accident, I would watch it for a moment. One second it would be a stubby black comma, maybe a sixteenth or an eighth of an inch long. Then with what can only be described as a flowing motion, it would lengthen out to a quarter-inch and turn from concentrated black to dilute gray as its substance spread. If I happened to be in a bad mood, I would "rub it out." They had the feel and consistency of a little piece of snot. There seems to be very little substance to a planaria, but several of them can take care of an earthworm in a few days. The earthworm just disappears. The springbox was a nice place to visit, but I wouldn't want to live there.

I tried to imagine where our spring comes from, and I would see in my mind's eye the ground water that trickles and filters down the great woody slopes above....I read somewhere that ground water moves in such minute and capillarious passages that it only travels a matter of feet and inches per year in some types of soil. But I also know that this subterranean water eats away great chunks of soluble mineral earth, leaving caverns and labyrinths as vast and tangled as time itself. I have heard of black underground rivers, and lakes that teem with blind albino life, where the subtle splash of anything that moves is a sound at once so muffled, resonant, echoed and penetrating as to be positively chilling. This is a whole new world, beneath our own thin world at the interface of earth and air. This is an underworld, beneath our conscious well-lit world: this is the subconscious, and if planaria guard the entrance, god knows what patrols the halls and chambers.

A spring wells up at the foot of a mountain; so this is where we are living, I said to myself that day.

"Keeping still is the attribute of the upper trigram; that of the lower is the abyss, danger," says Wilhelm. "Stopping in perplexity on the brink of a dangerous abyss is a symbol of the folly of youth."

And according to Gia-Fu Feng, the Protestant Chinese hippie: "Immaturity is groovy. I don't seek the kid, he seeks me out. I answer his first cast, but if he pesters me three times, he gets boring. I don't teach bores...."

Five years before that move to the woods, before my involvements in Crested Butte, I would have resented being called—even by an oracle—an "immature young fool." I would probably have refuted the charge on the basis that "the world hadn't given me a chance yet"; opportunity—or even the Harris polltaker—hadn't knocked, seeking my wisdom; the world was muddling on unaware of the talents for rational analysis, sympathetic mediation, and conciliatory resolution I was capable of exhibiting, at least when dry-running the world and its problems through my mind.

But after three years of intense intimacy with the "surface problems" of a small but increasingly complex and cosmopolitan resort town, in whose streets, like Bethlehem's, "the hopes and fears of all the years were met," I was willing to concede, at whatever cost to my depressed ego, that I did not really have a deep enough, true enough, or total enough grasp of what was going on beneath all this surface stuff: the insane consumption of obviously limited resources while talking a mile a minute about "the need for conservation"; the planning-and-zoning game where everyone wanted and could justify a personal variance; the burgeoning overblown government which no one, not even the government, seemed to want but no one knew what to do about; the totally contradictory tendencies to talk ourselves into an ever-and-ever tighter corner of limitation and regulation at the same time we talked about mind-expansion and the need for spiritual release....It seemed as foolish to go on believing we were somehow going to talk our way through and out of this mess on the purely rational plane of newspapers and governments, as it now seems young and foolish to have once believed that trees made the wind.

Possible new word:

porch-ant (p̄orch ̆ănt) adj. [OF. porche, fr. L. porticus] keeping still on the edge of.

Even when I was a boy I could never walk in a wood
without feeling that at any moment I might find before me
somebody or something I had long looked for without
knowing what I looked for.

—W.B. Yeats, from *Mythologies*

I grew up taking the trees in my environment more or less for
granted. They were simply always there, just as buildings,
phone booths, fire hydrants, and people with watches to give
me the right time were always there.

Occasionally I was able to get off into a place where, for
the time being, my environment would be mostly trees and
nothing else: up into the woods on Flagpole Hill behind our
house in Pennsylvania, the shortcut path down over the
undeveloped slope between us and the town; a once-a-summer
visit to Cook's Forest in the Alleghenies (where there were
usually as many people as trees); and then, after moving to
Colorado, into the abundant National Forests.

But even when I was out in a place where it was just me and
the trees, I was never there long enough to shed all the
relationships with trees that defined them in terms of *my* world,
my environment. And is there really any intrinsic difference in
basic attitude between the timberman who sees trees as a source
of boards and the poet who sees them as a source of inspiration?
There is a big difference to the tree, of course—but in each case,

there is the tendency to pull the trees, woods, and everything else into an auxilliary relationship with our own needs and desires, whether those needs and desires be primarily utilitarian or aesthetic. I'm not complaining about this tendency; it seems quite natural and inevitable that we would eventually describe and define our individual and composite realities in terms of the relationships of use, and yes, abuse, which we develop with the real things around us.

But after a certain amount of steady exposure to something like trees—enough constant and pervasive exposure to get beyond the gee-golly wide-eyed stage of induced appreciation, and down into the more normal and more *honestly* perceptive low-key-but-broad-spectrum consciousness of everyday living— then I think you begin to get subtle hints that it's perhaps not such a "small world, after all," as the one so entirely bounded by your set of relationships with that world....

The woods where we lived were a mixed forest of the broadleaf aspens and various conifers—white pine, yellow (or ponderosa) pine, Douglas fir, balsam fir, blue spruce, Engelmann spruce. And I suppose I shouldn't forget the willow brush, either: scruffy, persistent, occasionally obnoxious stuff (like if you wanted to be on the other side of it), clogging every gully and tiny stream and water-sink in a vaguely pubic way; the willow brush may lack the size of a tree but certainly none of its toughness, and it is the first woody plant to grab onto some mean slopes, holding them against the wind—so long as there is water for them.

But my favorites by far, of those trees, are the aspen. Among aspen, in any season, even when the bare branches are black lace against a grey sky, I just feel good, find myself relaxing, expanding, getting a little goofy even—no particular reason necessary: I just feel good among aspen.

At our altitude—9500 feet at the station—the aspen are not particularly big. Lower down in the mountains, they become a fairly impressive tree, 80 feet or so in height with trunks up to eighteen inches, maybe two feet, in diameter; but above 9000 feet they rarely get taller than fifty feet with eight or twelve inch trunks. They are too small for logging; they aren't particularly strong or durable; nor are they very long-lived; nor are they particularly spreading or shady; nor do they seem to possess in any great measure *any* of the tree-traits that make trees *useful*. Even as firewood, although aspen burns hot and clean and is known as a good chimney de-sooter, it burns quickly and has an unimpressive BTU count—12.5 million to the cord, compared to fifteen million or more for most kinds of pine.

But what the aspen lacks in the way of a sturdy and substantial tree-like constitution, it makes back in a kind of spiritual beauty. Or a pleasing spirituality, something like that. "Poems are made by fools like me," said Kilmer—but the aspen is proof to me that God must have had a bit of the poet in His Highness too.

If I'm out among the aspen and feeling mystical, I might start hypothesizing that, if there is some *spiritual* reincarnation similar to the more empirical material circulation and regeneration in the *physical* cycle of life, then the souls of good trees and plants that die (giving their lives in service to humanity) must eventually get to go to the mountains and be useless, beautiful aspen trees.

I think of the huge beds of coal under the Elk Mountains, and the gross, sweating, tangled masses of vegetation they represent in condensed form: it must have been hell being a plant in the Carboniferous Period, something like being a child laborer in Manchester during the early ugly years of the Industrial Revolution. So thinking, I imagine that the ethereal aspen trees, spreading like a fugal melisma over the sunslopes covering those coal beds today, are the freed spiritual essence of those compacted jungles. The sulphur that stayed in the coal—well, that's an essence of a different entity.

If on the other hand I am not feeling particularly mystical, but am more my usual analytical self, I can readily see through this "spirituality," expose it as just another trick of nature, a well-made but fairly obvious illusion; through the construction of its leaves, the aspen tree is a manipulator of light. That's all there is to it.

The secret lies in the long, supple, and uniquely flattened stem that connects the small broadleaf to the twig. Due to this stem, the smallest movement of air is sufficient to set the leaf to fluttering—hence the nickname, "quakie," for the tree.

The color and texture of the aspen leaves further the illusion of "spirituality." The leaves are smooth, almost but not quite shiny, waxy. They come on in the spring with an unbelievably delicate green, a *feathery* green that drifts up and across the gray-brown slopes of winter like smoke. The green deepens through the summer, but where there is plenty of water—as there usually is above 9000 feet—the leaves do not dull down like most broad-leaves do in their maturity. Each leaf, then, is a small reflector mounted on a long, supple shaft. The least breath of a breeze is sufficient to set the reflector in oscillating motion, "manipulating light."

Thinking in terms of one leaf, of course, this is not an especially impressive illusion. But on one of those incomparable mountain afternoons, when the time after lunch seems to settle like a lake rather than flow like a river, and there is no noticeable wind, though the restless dynamics of air under the influence of sun set up a stirring almost too subtle to be consciously noted, then not one leaf but a million, a hundred million leaves go into motion, and a whole slope will shimmer like a mirage.

In the fall, the aspen go to yellow. One might not be overly impressed with a forest that merely turns yellow in the fall but something a little different goes on that makes it quite worthwhile.

Like all trees and most people, aspen do the same thing in the end but never all at the same time; so a few days into the fall change, there will be some all-yellow trees, and there will still be some all-green trees, but most of the trees will be in some stage between, partly yellow and partly green—and then they are *really* manipulating light, manipulating reality almost. As they shimmer away in the breeze one barely feels, there is the sense of looking at yellow light with green shadows. Or is it green light with yellow shadows? It hardly seems to matter, and on the cloudless days of September Indian Summer, with the sky so transparent a blue that the planets are sometimes still visible even at mid-morning, the blue and yellow, the two primary colors with their secondary green, so dominate the day that they create a sense of organic totality; one feels suddenly giddy, compelled to cast around frantically for something out of the red side of the spectrum, grab onto something brown and solid, maybe pick up a rock and tap it lightly against the skull, as egg against egg, fearful for the moment that the reaction might be fusion and a streaming-off in all directions of just more visible energy, but at the same time needful of reassurance that there is still at least your own substance unbroken by all this silent interpenetrant light.

In such days as those, even the most godless analytical mind must be able to read a chapter in the unwritten prehistory of all religion. I have no trouble at all imagining—remembering, in a way—what it must have been for the earliest men, still struggling to gain some control over the disjointed barrage of sensation, dream, imagination, and memory, to see a great slope of green and yellow trees start to stir and shimmer with a wind not yet felt—*almighty whatchamacallit, something's coming for sure*. . . .

And then, in the disastrous depths of winter, cave-bound, cold, and bored, behind a smoky fire, full enough of food but not yet ready for sleep and peripherally tuned to the restless creep of a different wind in sadder trees—for survival's sake, the Fifth Necessity, something to make it all worthwhile, it must have been necessary to invent the spiritual advent of something other than mere overbearing, indifferent, desolating winter, for that evanescent luminous day in the foggy welter of memories and dreams.

> For speech was born in mute times as a mental language. It was fitting that the matter should be so ordered by divine providence in religious times, for it is an eternal property of religions that they attach more importance to meditation than to speech.
> —Giambattista Vico, from *The New Science*

Laying out the map of a tree among trees in the search for firewood is, if nothing else, a good way to get to know a piece of woods fairly intimately. And while I don't want to get in arguments with the Big Picture people, I think that to really get to know the forest, you have to get down to where you can't see it for the trees. So it was for me on that aspen slope rising away from our cabin on the sunny side of Avery Mountain.

Where I had initially been conscious of just a big expanse of aspen trees—mostly alive and beautiful, some dead and useful—I began to notice some big old burnt stumps among the aspen, too large to have been aspen stumps, and also, here and there among the aspen trees, little groves and clumps of spruce and pine.

I gradually assembled a story that connected up those observations—and checking on it later, found out that my deductions matched those of science. And why not? It was fairly obvious.

It is a story with an unhappy ending for the aspens spreading over the hillside on the sunside of the mountain: that beautiful aspen wood is not, like the Grecian urn, to be a thing of beauty forever. It is a transitional, and therefore transitory, forest. In the scheme of things, as the scheme has evolved, aspen trees (which need lots of light to manipulate and play with, remember) move quickly into an area that has been "opened up" by a fire—or today, logged over and then ignored. In so doing, the aspen perform a very valuable function: because they grow quickly, with lots of new little trees growing right out of the shallow spreading lateral roots of "parent trees," they effectively lace together and hold down a slope that would be otherwise exposed to serious erosion.

For several generations as aspen live and die, they have the hillside, washing it in green and yellow light, each year dropping a new layer of dead leaves to rot into a fertile carpet of rich humus, nurturing the soil they hold together—is it possible to find anything *bad* to say about the beautiful, spiritual aspen? Impossible! BTU count be damned: the house whose heating stove pops and snaps with burning aspen is warmed by a blessed heat. Choosing your wood solely for its BTUs is like choosing grain alcohol over a good brandy because it has a higher alcohol content.

But gradually the evergreen forest begins to take back the hillside. A few conifers here and there that survived the fire which claimed the old forest spread their seeds; and, sheltered by the guileless aspen, which cut the harsh high-altitude sun without blocking it, the pine, spruce and fir trees begin to grow up in their own time frame, new little trees spreading out from older trees in little groves. While a spruce tree is just approaching its maturity, with its old age and vulnerability maybe a century in the future, the short-lived aspen around it grow up, grow old, and die. But when the new little aspens try to grow up among or near the conifers, they find the conifers to be less generous than the aspen were to them. Where aspen reflect light, conifers seem to absorb it, cutting off not only the aspen but, eventually, even their own offspring.

In forests where the transition is almost complete from old sick evergreen forest through the aspen period to new vigorous evergreen forest, I have seen the (to me) sad spectacle of long scrawny aspen trees with only a small crown of leafed limbs near the top, where they can still grab off a little sunlight from the overshadowing conifers. When those aspen die, the evergreens hold the hillside again—until they have pressed on to their own *reductio ad absurdum*: an overgrown, overbearing, topheavy forest full of insufficiently nourished trees crowded together but still growing cones and throwing down seeds which may sprout but will have nowhere to go, nowhere to grow, until finally the "merciful angels of death" creep in. The barkbeetle, the fungi, witches' broom, the diseases, and at last the cleansing fire. Then once again light will reach the forest floor and again the aspen will come in from the edges to hold things together and have their brief place in the sun....

There was a particular grove of conifers on that hillside that...well, it bothered me, is one way of putting it. Its trees put me on guard somehow, as if they had set off a small alarm in an unfamiliar area of my mind.

They were not young trees, like the ones in the new little groves spreading clumpwise through the aspen; they were bigger, and therefore older trees. They sat in a bench niched out of the hillside; and I concluded that they were probably trees that had been young and healthy when the fire had swept the hillside years before, leaving only the great charred and ghostly snags among the aspen as a clue to the scale of the old trees.

During those years in the woods, I picked up part of our grocery money fighting forest fires with a trained suppression crew from town called the "Crested Butte Hotshots." As jobs went, it was hot, dirty work on a totally capricious schedule; you could ruin a pair of boots if you didn't keep looking down and lose your life if you didn't keep looking up; it was dangerous work and, you sometimes suspected, futile; but the pay was decent, we got to travel around a bit—once as far as a big fire in Idaho—and it was the kind of gut labor that leaves even the basically effete and ejjicated easterner like myself feeling like walking as though his cock were fighting his feet for legroom. If you'll pardon my language.

But getting back to the topic.... In the course of that work, we had occasional opportunities to watch forest fires in action—when a fire is really running, there's not much to do *but* try to get in a good flank position out of the way and, if you're lucky, watch it go until it's had its fun for the day and has subsided to a comparatively fightable conflagration. What can you do about a fire that's moving through trees a hundred feet off the ground, raining fire and sucking all available oxygen as it moves uphill in great leaps and gulps? Stay out of the way, is what you can do.

What became evident from watching forest fires in their "eating phase" was the fact that they are selective—or inefficient, whichever you'd rather call it. Unlike a good logical clear-cutting operation, the fire didn't eat everything on a hillside, but raced through taking the easy parts of the forest— the places with diseased, dead and overcrowded areas. Healthier parts of the forest, where trees were young, better spaced, and undiseased, often got no more than a quick once-over by the fire, if that. But even that quick once-over could be harmful to healthy trees, singeing needles and burning holes in bark in a way that made the trees at least temporarily vulnerable to pests. And in or near the unhealthy parts of the forest, the moderately healthy trees were taken along with the dying and dead.

What the fires always seemed to do, however, was leave enough of the old forest to at least regenerate the new forest gradually, over a period of time, during which time something like the aspen keep the terrain together. This is probably how forests managed to perpetuate themselves before there were Principles of Forestry and a Forest Service to administer them.

That grove of older trees, then, was perhaps not so much a part of the returning evergreen forest as it was father to it.

Which fact did nothing in itself, of course, to explain that subtle alarm going off in the back of my mind—not so long, at any rate, as I continued to think of trees as I grew up thinking of trees. Lumber, fuel, shade, poetry, et cetera. Gunnison National Forest, Land of Many Metaphors.

But then I thought: this place hasn't always been Gunnison National Forest, trees by the grace of and for the multiple uses of the people. And these trees here—this grove of trees was young in a great forest ignorant of the ax-bite. There may have been some Ute hunting parties through, maybe a scruffy mountain man trapping some beaver...but essentially, the forest for which these trees are the genetic memory was a forest that knew no men.

Does that mean anything? Does a tree falling in a forest make a noise if there's no one to hear it? Does a tree *not* falling in the forest have a "presence" if there's no one to feel it?

It gradually came over me, out there in those woods, that trees have a subtle but eventually unignorable presence all their own that is so alien to my understanding that I can't even really talk about it—except to say that, ultimately, trees must be something more than just what they are to us; they must be something *like* us...but in their own way.

I noticed this most at night, of course. During the day, in that still and brilliant opacity of over-exposure that makes the noon hours of a clear day almost depressing in the mountains— the same way an overbearingly cheerful and jovial person is vaguely depressing—I found the trees as basically boring as a board-foot estimate, a picture postcard, a Wilderness Society newsletter.

It became apparent to me that trees sleep during the day— never mind that they're grinding away at their photosynthesis work; the guy on the assembly line can both work and sleep too, otherwise he would have to quit.

But toward nightfall, stirred by the subtle flow of cooling

air beginning its slow push down hill and valley, the trees come awake—and I can't say what that means, except to say that, after a couple of years in the woods I knew they were there and awake, not as boards, pictures, or metaphors in my mind, but as whatever they are to themselves.

The evergreens, I was pretty certain, didn't care for my presence there. The aspen didn't mind. The aspen are joyful by nature, blithe spirits, magicians with tricks, and they love an audience, any audience. But the evergreens are not a happy lot; they are the originals that the Protestants tried to copy. I believe they might have envied my mobility as I moved among them (as I might envy them their stability and "rootedness"); and while they couldn't do much by way of active retaliation, they emanated little dreams in which they saw me quite lost, to the point that sometimes I would get nervous even though I knew—didn't I?—exactly where I was. They gave me claustrophobia.

To the modern mind, thinking of trees in the modern context, the idea of our ancestors' "tree-worship" sounds a bit simplistic and, well, childish: but then, man was a child then, right? And now we have grown up, grown civilized.

But, just on the basis of a single disquieting moment in a remnant of a forest that, for all its reduced splendor, managed to convey the impression that it was looking over and past me without really seeing me, I will have to confess that I'm not sure what my reaction would be, if I'd been a poor primitive just trying to get by in prehistoric Europe.

There would have been basically two ways to go. One way would have been to strike out with every weapon at one's disposal: find a decent clearing, then go to war, chop, slice, hack, blast, bulldoze, push back the trees, enlarge the clearing, try to hold the perimeter by whacking off all new seedlings. And the other way would have been appeasement—give the forest something every now and then, a virgin, a hanged man. Don't do anything to aggravate the forest—and if some fool does do something stupid, punish him first, don't let the forest get the idea his foolishness was acceptable—listen to this, from Sir James Frazer's *The Golden Bough* on "tree worship":

> How serious that worship was in former times may be gathered from the ferocious penalty appointed by the old German laws for such as dared to peel the bark of a standing tree. The culprit's navel was to be cut out and nailed to the part of the tree which he had peeled, and he was to be driven round and round the tree till all his guts were wound about its trunk. The intention of the punishment clearly was to replace the dead bark by a living substitute taken from the culprit; it was a life for a life, the life of a man for the life of a tree. . . .

Maybe that sounds like "worship" to you, but to me it sounds like "peace at all costs." Which of course might be more the motivation underlying true worship than we insulated moderns would ever guess. . . .

The San Juan Mountains are not at all like the "crested buttes" in the Elk Mountains among which I lived. They are a much more "Alpish" range, steeper and more crowded together; they are also generally green mountains— green and red, foliage against sandstone—due to the moisture they con out of the cooling air off the deserts. But their great alpen beauty notwithstanding, I don't find them "friendly" mountains. "Friendly," of course, is the wrong word—but there do seem to be mountains that sit in the sun, and mountains that seem to be doing what they can to protect their shadows, and the San Juans are among the latter: they might be haunted.

The towns of the San Juans like Silverton and Ouray, shaped, crowded and shadowed as they are by the mountains, I think of as small oases of dog problems, sign ordinances, economic recessions, and zoning problems, over which, occasionally, dragons swoop. Ouray especially is crowded by the mountains—great cliffs of red rock that literally rise straight out of the city limits. In the summer of 1977, a big rock banged down one of those cliffs and fell through the roof of the theatre, a Main Street building. In Silverton, an occasional avalanche all the way down the long chutes on Mount Kendall blows open the doors and breaks windows on the south side of town with its air blast. You can't get much closer than that to a combination of raw nature and a grocery store.

Some people will try to tell you that the Million Dollar Highway connecting the two towns was so named because it was paved with what they later found to be gold-bearing gravel. The truth, as usual, is more mundane; when a series of hair-raising and back-breaking county and private roads were improved and brought up to state standards—more or less—with state and federal money in the early Twenties, the cost of the project was around a million dollars.

There are roads and highways that seem to deserve recognition as art. Like all true works of art, they reflect, refine, and interpret their surroundings, their environment. The Interstate is not art, because its purpose is the elimination of any real feel of the environment the concrete lawnmower is passing through (with a few exceptions, like pieces of I-80 in Pennsylvania). But the Million Dollar Highway is consummate art. The rigorous terrain makes it a flawed masterpiece—there are places where a smooth flowing curve would obviously be impossible, even for a Billion Dollar Highway. And there are the unavoidable intersections, like the Curran Gulch Intersection, which always have a vaguely nervous and uncomfortable feel to them, even in the summer. But for the most part, the Million Dollar Highway is an absolute triumph of a marriage between rational intent and random nature. Coming up the Mineral Creek Valley from Silverton toward the old Chattanooga townsite, one can see the beautiful line of the road as it snakes left, then flows through the Muleshoe Curve and climbs right in a smooth powerful rise above an old mine working... and on the Ouray side, in the broadening but still steep-walled canyon formed by the Uncompaghre River and Red Mountain Creek, there is one long, long sweeping curve along the cliffs that can be seen in its totality from the time one starts into it: it may well be one of the most beautiful man-made things in the world.

As an elitist, environmentally aware aesthete—a little too

eastern and effete, I sometimes think—I find myself reflexively reacting in favor of "roadless areas" and "wilderness designation"; but when I stop and consider, I realize that all I am saying—to myself—is that there are too many *bad* roads in the world today. Roads that go nowhere, and do a poor job getting there.

Kicking around these mountains in Colorado, I keep having the feeling that the eyes I see with, the ears I hear with, are not entirely my own. That is to say: I hold the lease on them for the time being, but they've been here before and are still looking out and listening on the behalf of people not here with me but nevertheless close in a way....

And why not? My mother's people were all over this West Slope of the Colorado Rockies from the time the government escorted the Utes out in 1881.

Every time, for example, that I see one of those remaining bits of the old railroad grade—all overgrown now, but still distinguishable as low "moraines" either too straight or too smooth in their curves to be "natural"—I find myself trying to look through the eyes of a lanky civil engineer, Del Johnson, who worked most of his life for the Denver and Rio Grande Railroad. He was my grandfather, and he so loved his mountain railroads that when he died he had my grandmother scatter his ashes along a favorite curve of his on the run up through the Glenwood Canyon of the Grand River. He died when I was still a very small boy—and before the D. & R.G. abandoned the whole Third Division, up out of Salida over Marshall Pass, through Gunnison (with a branch to Crested Butte) and down the Black Canyon to the North Fork country where he met my grandmother.

My grandmother was born and raised on a homestead in the beautiful green hilly valley of the North Fork of the Gunnison River—apple and cherry orchards predominating, until recently when the coal boom hit the valley and the orchards started sprouting housing developments and trailer parks.

My mother grew up mostly on the East Slope in Colorado—the "train towns" of Salida and Alamosa, and finally Denver—but nearly every year my grandmother packed her and her brother and sister up for the summer and (freeboarding on my grandfather's family pass) took them over to the North Fork valley for a couple months. The mesa where the Short brothers had homesteaded near Hotchkiss was a very special place to my mother, and she talked about it a lot to my sisters and me. As a result, as a boy growing up in Pennsylvania, I gradually got from her a jigsaw of Western Colorado geography, some of the pieces of which I am still, after a dozen years, trying to fit together.

But the "near ancestor" for whom I feel perhaps the greatest affinity is my grandmother's brother, my great-uncle Harley Short. I don't know him well at all—have only met him a few times, in fact, and only really talked to him once. Nevertheless, I think that I might be walking in his tracks more than anyone else's, most of the time.

Part of that feeling of affinity probably traces to a purely physical resemblance that we could maybe both do without: we both have what is known in my mother's family as "the Short features"—the aforementioned mudflap ears, and a nose you could use to fight eagles or shelter a cigar in a rainstorm.

But beyond that, there must be a kind of a psychological resemblance as well, as in an unconscious way I seem to be doing—and not doing—the same kinds of things with my life as my great-uncle did and didn't do with his.

When he was a young man, for example, Harley Short moved to the mountain town of Silverton, where he proceeded to do, as he so succinctly puts it, "everything." A generalist, a Jack of All Arts. He worked in the silver mines, helped build and maintain the roads, worked in a lumber yard, ran a grocery store, packed goods and people around the mountains by mule.

Talking about that mule-packing gig, he commented on a group of eastern alpinists he packed in once for a climbing adventure. They kept asking him for the names of the peaks around them. He finally told them he didn't know the names of the mountains, had nothing to do with the mountains: "I'm no mountain man; I'm a valley man."

That distinction has become one of my own basic criteria in considering the people, old and new, I meet in Colorado. "Mountain people" garb themselves in all the external trappings of "rugged American individualism," but they are really "city people" at bottom, totally plugged in to the interdependent, specializing, organizing, and ultimately homogenizing structures of civilization—the rigors of the confrontation with winter, as already described, require that kind of massive logistical support. But down in the mountain valleys, sometimes in the towns but mostly out on the homesteads (now just into their second or third generation), you still find a few real "Jeffersonians"—if you want to go back to Constitutional definitions and intentions, the last of the real Americans. They work the basic seven-day seventy-hour week with two days off for fishing every year; they specialize in knowing everything there is to know about everything on their place; they can read, write, and fix anything with balingwire. The Shorts were valley people. I returned to their country as a mountain person wanting to thrash off the filamentous webs of the city while still holding on to the short hours, modest responsibilities, and conveniences. I may learn better.

Harley Short has a sense of humor as dry and pellucid as the Colorado sky, and will put you on with a straighter face than a Republican judge hanging a Democrat. When I asked him how long he'd lived in Silverton doing everything, he said with not so much as the hint of a smile, "Oh...just part of a winter."

My grandmother, who was with us, snorted. "Part of a winter!...It was thirty-six years!"

But nobody is purely this or that, and that goes for mountain people and valley people. Great-uncle Harley had a few jobs that weren't exactly valley-people jobs—such as working in the silver mines—but one in particular can't be written off as just something one does for the money: he drove a snowplow on Red Mountain Pass, and south from Silverton, on Coalbank Pass.

I was talking earlier about the "war" between winter and civilization in the Rocky Mountains, and the standoff or stalemate that seems to have evolved in the Crested Butte vicinity. But it is not all quiet along that western front, and Red Mountain Pass is still a very active war zone. Nowhere more so than at the "Curran Gulch Intersection."

Just this past winter—in February 1978—plowdriver Terry Kishbaugh, of Ouray, was clearing away the debris from an avalanche called the "East Riverside," where it intersects with U.S. 550 on Red Mountain Pass at Curran Gulch. As he was cutting through the piled-up snow with a State rotary plow, the avalanche ran again—the second time in a few hours. It was several days before searchers even found the remains of the plow. His body wasn't recovered until it melted out finally in mid-May.

This almost exactly duplicates the fate of another plowdriver, Bob Miller, who was clearing the same "Curran Gulch Intersection" in 1970, when the East Riverside ran twice in short succession, killing Miller and reducing a D-7 bulldozer to scrap.

But the most disastrous encounter at the Curran Gulch Intersection was the incident that occurred one Sunday morning in March, 1963. It was snowing heavily, and there was a small slip onto the highway near Curran Gulch. Plowdriver Leo Janes cleared one lane through the sluffed snow, then pulled off to the side of the road—a second plow right behind him—to let a car go through. In the car were Reverend Marvin Hudson and his two daughters, on their way to Silverton where Hudson was to conduct the Sunday Service.

Hudson drove around the plows and into the partially cleared lane, but his tires spun out in the snow. Right in the middle of the Curran Gulch Intersection. Hudson got out of the car, apparently to put on his chains; Janes started to get out of the cab of his plow to give the man a hand. But before he could get his door open the whole road appeared to explode in his face: the shock wave literally threw his twenty-ton snowplow ten feet back through the air, where only the other plow kept it from going into the canyon. When he could see again, there was no car, no road, no pieces, nothing but a twenty-five-foot high white wall.

It's only snow—that famous light-and-dry "Colorado Powder," the skier's dream, sometimes less than an inch of water to forty or fifty inches of snow (newfallen). But the East Riverside avalanche has a catchment basin of seventy-five acres, high on the side of Mt. Abrams; it funnels all the snow (or half of it, to bait the trap) from the area into Curran Gulch, which isn't more than a hundred feet wide where it intersects the highway. By the time all that concentrated and focused "powder" reaches the road, it has driven five thousand feet down a 63% grade; it comes at 120 m.p.h. and it all hits at once. Turning over the snow with bulldozers two abreast, it was a week before the remains of the car, the Reverend, and one of his daughters were found. The other daughter, like Kishbaugh, finally melted out in May.

So that is the kind of intersection you find on Red Mountain Pass. Look and listen, but don't stop if you can help it.

As it happens, I had no option about stopping at the Curran Gulch Intersection one night.

The aforementioned Don Bachman, ski patrol leader at Crested Butte and ultimate snow freak, got a four-year research job in the early Seventies collecting avalanche data on Red Mountain Pass for the Institute of Arctic and Alpine Research.

That of course made Bachman as happy as a cat in cream, so much was he into avalanches—occasionally in a literal, if peripheral way. It also made his friends in and around Crested Butte (I was living in the woods by then) happy, because it provided a base of operations for some winter nosing-about in the San Juans. As soon as he had been there long enough to ingratiate himself with the local populace in Silverton and get located in an apartment with a big living room, a few of us tied our skis onto Francie Austin's car and headed down for a visit.

All the way from Crested Butte that day we traveled in fair weather; but as soon as we climbed out of Ouray onto the first switchbacks, just after dark, we ran into a gusty, nervous wind and snow flurries—it's always doing something somewhere in the San Juans. And about a third of the way up the pass we rounded one of Otto Mears' cliffhanger curves to find the road completely blocked by a wall of snow a good twelve feet deep on the cliff side.

We got out of the car and clambered over the snowpile. Ahead of us, on the other side of the avalanche, there were six cars also bound uphill—but they were stopped by another avalanche over the highway, larger than the one blocking us. Parked by that slide was the familiar flashing blue light of a State Highway snowplow, and a bulldozer was working in the plow's lights to break a path through the snow debris. A surrealistic scene.

We asked the man in the last car trapped between the two slides how long he had been there. A few minutes, he said. Which meant that we'd only missed getting buried by twelve feet of snow by a few minutes. He wasn't even aware that the second slide had slipped in behind him, that his retreat was cut off.

We learned the names of our slides from Bachman the next day: the one that had stopped us was a smallish one called the "Mother Cline." The one that had run first, on up the road, was the East Riverside itself.

I stood in the lee of a cliff maybe seventy-five feet down from the Curran Gulch Intersection, and watched the man push at the snow on the road with the little D-7 cat—it *looked* little, there, that night. He was working as fast as he could, given the lack of maneuvering room, but there was a frustrating sense of slowness to it. I found out the next day just how comparatively small that slide was that night: Bachman had a trip-wire strung across the gulch attached to a clock that would stop when an avalanche ripped away the wire, and the avalanche that night was so small it went under the wire without stopping the clock. Yet it still took a D-7 bulldozer half an hour to clear those two little slides enough for traffic to move through.

Obviously, the winter didn't have to put out a very major offensive to stop human traffic in its mountains. An avalanche big enough to flatten a bulldozer is mere overkill; easier to just nickel-dime the dozer and driver into old age or madness with a slip here, another little slip behind him while he's cleaning up the first one, then another back where the first was. . . . Actually, something very like that happened, that same winter, at the "Mother Cline" slide.

Going up the pass one day after a small storm, plowdriver Jim Campbell found that the Mother Cline had slipped a little snow onto the road. He was blading that off, when more snow came down, right on top of the truck, denting in the roof and banging up the flashing blue light. He was able to drive out from under the new snow, and went at it again—only to have the snow slip a third time, this time dumping on the hood and fenders. The plow had depreciated considerably there in about ten minutes, but he finally got that snow off the road and moved on up the pass.

But Mother Cline wasn't finished with him that day. On his return trip down the pass, the slope ambushed him with a fourth load of snow, hitting with sufficient force and quantity to completely bury the plow, breaking out all the glass and packing the cab. The only thing that saved Campbell was his hardhat, which got jammed over the face by the snow and left him a little breathing room. Fortunately for him, there was a car right behind his plow with a man of true quality at the wheel, who jumped out and dug away the glass and snow from Campbell's face with his bare hands so he could breathe. Campbell survived with only face cuts and bruises, but the plow was nearly totaled. Some joker, that Mother Cline.

The morning after our encounter at Curran Gulch, I tagged along with Bachman in a strange parade: his old truck between two orange State Highway pickups, and the one we were following was towing a 75 mm Army howitzer. Back over the pass toward Ouray again, but at the beginning of Red Mountain Creek Canyon, the state truck behind us pulled out across the road to block any further traffic descending into the canyon.

We followed the gun on down to the sharp curve where the road crosses over Bear Creek Falls, a place from which the summit of Mt. Abrams with its big catchment basins is fully exposed. Sid Foster, a retired Army artillery officer, and his Highway Department protege Pete Petersen, unhitched the howitzer, consulted some charts, did some aiming and cranking on the gun's mechanisms. . .then loaded a shell and opened fire on the East Riverside avalanche's starting zones.

Earlier that morning—sunny and clear after the night's snow flurries—I'd watched Bachman make snow measurements, melt the new snow for water content, check the wind charts, and look back into the "recent history" of the snowpack. His analysis had coincided with the Highway Department's intuitions, that the East Riverside and several other Red Mountain avalanches ought to be "shot" to either bring down the potential avalanches on a known empty highway or to at least stabilize the snowfields.

They fired several exploding shells into the known critical loading points—wind cornices, and areas of heavy wind deposit on the lee sides of ridges. They broke loose no avalanches, and it was only possible to assume at best that the big basins had been stabilized for the time being—until winter's next move, which would probably be the storm already forecast for later that week. . . .

The people of the San Juans have been all but begging the State Highway Department for either an avalanche shed or a tunnel at the Curran Gulch Intersection for years—the equivalent, I suppose, of an underpass for a local road under one of the big Interstate Limboids. The answer is always the same: insufficient traffic to warrant the expense. And it would be expensive, at modern construction costs.

After Kishbaugh's death this past winter, the State did appropriate some money to "study the problem" at the Curran Gulch Intersection. But the East Riverside is only one of more than fifty avalanches along the twenty-three miles between Silverton and Ouray with the potential to do as much damage. Just a couple of years ago, the mine bus carrying the day shift down to Silverton from the Idarado Mine was brushed off the road by the very edge of the "Brooklyn" slide—a very close brush in which no one was hurt, although the busdriver apparently suffered a mild heart attack. And a number of years before that, a Continental Trailways bus was pushed off the road south of Silverton by the "Champion" slide—miraculously hanging up on the small tailings pile by somebody's old "Vein Hope No. 4" mine rather than going all the way down to the Animas River. Again nobody hurt. But the buses go up and down the road every day through the winter: a situation not unlike a shooting gallery.

The fact that Great-uncle Harley is not entirely a valley man seems recorded for history: there is a slide on Coalbank Pass, visible from Silverton, that is named after him, because once when he was plowing the road it tried to get him. It pushed his plow right to the edge of the road, and he had to wait for someone to come dig him out, but he was unhurt.

What nobody in Silverton or Ouray suggests, of course, is closing the pass for the winter. There are economic arguments against that—the biggest mine up on the pass, the mail getting through, supplies from Montrose, et cetera. But beyond that...well, the road stays open, that's all. And the men who drive the plows are bought beers and treated in town like soldiers who do what they do for a little more than the money.

I went down to Silverton the summer following that winter visit to Bachman. I was in my old Jeep truck, which meant a couple stops for cooling on the way up Red Mountain Pass, and I made one of them at the pullout by the emergency phone just below the East Riverside. A dark piece of canyon that seems to always be cold, and watched by sentinel breezes. I rocked the wheels so the Jeep wouldn't end up cooling off down in Red Mountain Creek, left the hood up and the engine idling, and walked on up to the Curran Gulch Intersection.

Something in the permanent snowpile down in the canyon there caught my eye. I scrambled down to it, and found the exhaust pipe of a diesel sticking up out of the snow. State Highway orange. I gave it a tentative tug, to see if it was still attached to a truck or a bulldozer. It came loose in my hand: about a foot of pipe, raincap on one end intact, but trailing off in a six-inch spiral of torn metal on the other.

I thought it might have been off Jim Campbell's plow, from his scuffle with the Mother Cline that winter. But the Highway people in Silverton said, no, Campbell's plow hadn't lost its stack. The only thing it could have been part of was Bob Miller's bulldozer. Pieces still melting out five years later.

It's a war zone, is what it is.

There are places that we regard as "unforgettable"; yet in truth they are sometimes literally "unrememberable." Such a place would be just about anywhere above timberline—the alpine tundra, the high grassy meadows and boulder fields with their tiny life and huge spaces. I can sit here and call up mental pictures of such places—Fravert Basin just over Frigidair Pass with its dominance of blue and purple flowers, the reds and yellows of the rolling sloping meadows on the west side of West Maroon Pass in early August (where Barbara and I got totally lost one day), the June view down into Conundrum Basin from the pass with old snow and new green so vividly mixed— but I know that if I went there even a thousand times, the thousand and first would be like the first time because there is something about such places that is unrememberable. Something to do with the dizzying immensity, the openness, the vast slants of bare rock and small life down and away to treeline—not to mention the effect of mild oxygen starvation, which is a little like the best part of being slightly drunk...whatever it is, it's as unrememberable as it is unforgettable; it makes you want to go back again.

In the mountain region where, as I've mentioned, there are not four but three seasons, one would expect that the brief season of "forgetting about winter" would be a pale shadow of the summer season in the more temperate climes, but it isn't so.

Rather, when it's actually summer here—for a month, or a week or a few minutes—there is a giddy excess to the occasion that is not unlike the last days of Sodom and Gomorrah, perhaps.

And it is up in the high and heady tundra, from the tangle of timberline to the lower edge of the summit baldrock and talus, right up to the rough walls of winter's final stronghold, that the brief summer seems to go to the greatest glad excesses in flouting the winter. The plants of the high tundra are small as individual specimens, bred that way for survival, but they are legion in number; and at the peak of a good summer great cirques a quarter mile across and half a mile long are so dominated by massed flowers that the underlying greens of grass, leaf, and stem hardly register to the eye. I have always hated to step on a flower in bloom, and will avoid it if I can; but it is impossible to cross one of those tundra meadows without crushing thousands. I can think of nothing more luxuriant, richer, than to wade calf-deep into those deep purples, delicate violets, small rubies, fire reds, great splashes and dashes of yellow and white, leopard patches of yellow and brown daisies. On a still, blue day, with the sun frying your face in Sea'n'Ski, it's the kind of a place that makes you want to take off your clothes and roll naked, happy as a puppy in a pasture-pie.

But like winter stretching itself to raise hell in the temperate-zone cities, there is an intensity to this summer that can't be sustained; and up on the tundra it only lasts a few weeks—sometimes, it seems like only a few days. And on any day that you might succumb to the temptation to take off your clothes and roll in the flowers (watch out for downwind Sierra Club Outings), you might suddenly find yourself within the hour scurrying for your clothes in a sudden chill breeze, and wondering where the big cloud came from—then running for timberline and the nearest tree big enough to huddle under, out of a sleety rain that is all toothpicks and tacks....

Winter is never any further away than the shady side of the

mountain. Back in the north- and east-facing couloirs and bowls, down at the bottom of avalanche runouts, up in the tangle at the edge of the trees, there are "permanent" patches of snow: dirty, pocky patches, ugly as dead snakes. One can look at these and think of them as the seeds of once and future glaciers. Thinking that always makes me want to kick at them, break them up and spread them out in the sun to dry.

In light of the year-round picture, then, this short glorious summer looks like nothing so much as the brief flaring rebellion of an oppressed populace against some tyrannical authority which lets life run riot for just a little while—to wear it down—then moves back in with the shock troops, the big guns, and wave on wave of blank-eyed, stony-face infantry....

In the face of this, one wonders why the place is not as barren as the sands of the Sahara. That's not an easy question at all. I have been up in that high tundra in the dead of winter; I know that there is life hidden there, but it's the kind of thing you only know in an intellectual way. Under the snow, down through tunnels and passages among the tangle of roots and the rocks that are the mountains' sandbags against the fluid wind, the daily melodramas and terror tales of tundra life go on. But up on the surface, it's all winter: there is no *feel* of life about. There is a compelling beauty to that grand desolate winterscape—one can get lost in the runic legends left on the snow by the passing wind—but it is not a living beauty, and is as indifferent to life as the silent snowfall.

Having been up in that tundra region winter and summer, I never fail to be impressed at the difference: they might be two different worlds, as different as life and death. Or rather than two worlds, maybe I should say the manifestations of two great forces in a see-saw struggle for control of the same world.

There are people who would try to tell me that there is no elemental warfare in nature like that: that nature works harmoniously, life and death in a beautiful balance, except of course where man has intruded his heavy and insensitive hand. They would point to the way that the winter snow blankets the life in those bowls, protecting it from the cold and then, in melting, watering that life. They would point to the fact that life has to adapt everywhere to the conditions of climate: things are rough all over at first, but still everything works toward the balance and affirmation of the harmony.

But then I look at the contour of the bowl itself, the ripped and gouged stone under the thin furze of life, and I wonder if maybe somebody forgot to tell the ice about the harmony of nature. I wonder too if an "objective observer" would have seen the entrenched stalemates of World War I as an affirmation of harmony, since everything was so nicely balanced.

There is a nice balance today to life and death up in that tundra. But four times in the last million years, the ice has simply taken over, not only scouring the mountains of all their life but gouging out a few hundred feet of sterile stone as well. Life has yet to do as well in going "over the top" in the Rockies.

Glaciers are indeed something awesome to contemplate. Avalanches are more exciting—fast, nasty, and morbidly glamorous phenomena that almost seem to invite us to take them on, with howitzers, underpasses, instruments and computers. But glaciers are something else again—too much for us, something on an entirely different plane of being. Or not-being.

I have been in snow deep enough for long enough so that what to do with any more snow got to be a problem. One of the caretaker's responsibilities at the field station where we lived in the woods was making sure that none of the roofs caved in, and this meant that once a year, toward late winter, the valleys on the north side of the roof of the big dining hall had to be cleaned out—a job that required a heavy duty digging shovel rather than a snow shovel, and an ax was occasionally useful too, so compacted was the snow from its own weight.

But the snow I have seen doesn't even begin to touch the

dimensions of a glacier. Chicago had a record snowfall in 1978; I've seen pictures and read stories of what happens in Chicago when one of those Canadian howlers drops a couple feet of snow in the city....But the next time your plane breaks down through the clouds that seem always to be over Chicago, and you see the city spread out a thousand feet or so below—imagine snow and ice piled up from the ground to the level of your plane window, a smooth reach of dazzling snow that stretches as far to the north as you can see, and beyond....And a mere thousand feet of snow wouldn't be much for the ice-sheets that piled up two miles thick over so much of the northern hemisphere during the Pleistocene epoch.

Four times in the last million years, great sheets of snow compacted and crushed to black ice have grown outward from the north polar regions, drawing back each time for "interstadials" longer than what we optimistically call the "post-glacial" modern epoch of the past 50,000 years or so, then advancing again. Four times, each time covering most of Europe north of the Alps to varying degrees and the North American continent about a third of the way down into the present United States.

The conditions created by and accompanying these strange times are so alien-sounding that they might be from another planet. Earth scientists theorize that Hudson Bay is the result of the weight of the Laurentide ice-sheet: so thick and heavy was the ice that the crust of the earth sagged and cracked. So much of the sea's water was "tied up in frozen assets" that sea level dropped between three and four hundred feet.

We usually think of glaciers as moving downward off the mountains, under the influence of gravity—and this is true, I think, for all the glaciers still left in the modern world, except for the polar ice caps, which aren't moving much at all these years. But mountains are not necessary for getting a glacier in motion. As the snow piled up and piled up for centuries in the northern areas—nothing spectacular in our time frame perhaps, just a little more snow falling each year than melted—the snow compacted into deep "black ice" with a kind of plasticity; and as the weight toward the center grew, the pressure translated itself outward, causing the less compacted snow and ice around the edges to squoodge outward. Something like pouring molasses in January on a marble tabletop: the goo piles up at first, until the weight starts forcing it to spread. This begins to happen with an ice-sheet when the snow and ice toward the center is only two hundred feet deep.

When a glacier begins to grow and spread outward, it begins to have certain ominous effects on the general climate that tend to aid and abet the growth and spread of the ice. New snow reflects up to eighty percent of the sunlight striking it: old snow around fifty or sixty percent; this means that, rather than absorbing the radiant energy of the sun, as the earth does, the glacier throws most of it back out into space. The glaciers reject heat—and in so doing, accelerate the cooling of the earth.

Glaciers also create huge masses of cold air, as the warm air coming up from the tropical regions cools over that immense mass of snow and ice—causing the tropical air to drop its load of moisture in the form of snow—then the cooling air begins to sink, and goes booming back down over the uninterrupted monotony of the glacial surface like a kid on a sled, and piling off the edge in a steady wedge of cold dry wind that must have been sheer misery blasting across the open plains of central Europe and the American midwest. The actual edge of the glacial advance must have been a constant war-zone where the warmer, moister air from over land or sea engaged this cold dry-as-death wind off the ice, a region of perpetual violent storms.

And so the glaciers and ice-sheets advanced their own cause. It was in effect a dramatic attempt to reorganize the climate along the lines of winter—not leaving winter just the underlying reality in the polar regions and high montane regions, but the dominant reality of a whole hemisphere. *Whose* attempt?

The are many hypotheses as to what caused the ice to begin its dreadful advance—each hypothesis about as good as the next, each with its flaws, lapses in credibility, and lack of good evidence. The fact is, we don't *know* what caused the ice to come; and there is something vaguely ominous in that.

Under what we regard as "normal" conditions, most of the snow that falls every winter melts every summer. In the high mountain country, sometimes the sun barely gets the old stuff out of the way before the new stuff starts arriving; sometimes it is all gone by the end of July. On the face of Gothic Mountain, above the field station, there has been a persistent pile of avalanche debris—called "The Old Maid" due to its usual late-summer shape. There was so little snowfall the winter of 1976-77 that for the first time in anyone's memory the Old Maid melted out completely in 1977. But it will no doubt be back after the next good winter. The sun simply can't quite take care of it every summer. There is, evidently, a fairly delicate balance between enough sun to prevent glaciers, and the lack of sun which permits the glaciers to begin growing, linking up, throwing the heat back in the teeth of the sun....

We can only presume that the periods of glaciation were precipitated by something abnormal that happened either to the sun itself or somewhere between the sun and the surface of the earth—perhaps in the earth's atmosphere. While the earth scientists are generally cautious about making definite statements about anything—for good enough reason, I suppose—there might be some correlation between sunspot activity and precipitation on earth: perhaps the ice advances were kicked off by some unusual activity of that sort. Maybe a period of tremendous and concentrated earth upheavals and volcanic activity filled the atmosphere with a lot of natural smog, causing a cooling effect (although other scientists argue that that would cause a "greenhouse" warming effect). Maybe a combination of a lot of factors like that, coincidence coming around on the wheel of chance.

The most ominous theory has to do with the expansion of the universe postulated by Einstein and scientists since his time. We know that the life forms that have evolved on earth are as much a factor of our distance from the sun as our closeness to it: a little further away and our atmosphere would be lying on the perpetually cold ground in crystals, sublimating away in the weak sun until, like Mars, we would be down to a planetary desert with a couple of polar ice caps of frozen nitrogen. And a little closer to the sun, our oceans and atmosphere would be one and the same, a steam bath with water water everywhere and nothing cool enough to drink. But we are where we are, and we've evolved on the basis of that: just enough heat arriving and departing to maintain the currents of wind and water that keep the ice at bay and, with a fair degree of predictability, evaporate and carry over the land enough water to maintain life inland.

But if the universe is expanding, as most post-Einsteinian theories predict it to be, then we are slowly but surely getting a little further from the sun. This would account for the fact that the past million years have been colder apparently than any of the billion years previous on earth. And in the past half-million years, only a paltry *ten per cent* of the time has been climatically what we, today, call "normal." The rest of the time has been winter.

Today, the sun seems to be holding its own; it takes care of most of last winter's ice before this winter's snow begins to pile up with its glittering shield of heat-defeating albedo. The fact that the sun might continue to carry the day for the next thirty or forty thousand years, which takes it pretty safely out of my immediate concern, is beside the point, however. The point is this: if human nature is to be taken as a manifestation of nature—and it must, mustn't it?—then the same struggle for control of the human soul might be at the heart of human nature. Or if "soul" offends you—say instead: the same struggle for control of human energy might be at the heart of human nature.

But what is the struggle? I think it eludes conscious definition—every attempt at defining it seems itself a tiny raft of rationalization at the mercy of whatever currents are flowing and ebbing in the struggle. It has to do with the difference between life and death—but cannot be so simply phrased because of the many things, like cancer, that are both life and death.

It has to do with the variety of life in the summer on the one hand, and the homogeneous grinding uniformity of ice in the winter on the other, but it seems insufficient to call it a war between summer and not-summer, winter and not-winter.

It has to do, most of all I think, with the difference between the warm bright light of our own star, and the cold dim glimmer of all the other stars, a struggle between radiant energy and distances between, the things which are and the nothing between the things. The vast gulf of black void which scientists say is the fastest growing thing in the universe. Or *no:* they don't say that; I do. They say the universe is expanding; I say the void between the stars is growing. I think that makes me a pessimist instead of a scientist.

What we hate long enough, we become.

—yogi saying

It was obvious enough to me—after awhile—that we did not
represent any triumph of the self-sufficient individuals over
the harsh elements. If anything, our presence there—from the
Norwegian skis and Italian boots, prime northern goosedown
vests we used for skiing in, and Sam's fiberglass toboggan, to the
coal we burned in our stove (and the coal that burned a couple
hundred miles away to give us electricity whether we needed it
or not)—was more a triumph of technology and the interdependent society. We lived by the efforts of our hands and minds, but
not through growing our own food, shooting our own meat,
making our own candles for light. Barbara with her carvings, me
with my carpent'ring, we made things for sale in the most
energy-consumptive kind of resort area imaginable: a place
where people came to submit themselves to winter in winter's
region of excess. The money we made we took to the grocery
store just like everyone else—the main difference being that we
went nine months between shopping trips.

Thanks to the equipage of civilization, I was able to go up
into the great cirques and bowls in the middle of their winter as
well as their not-winter. I have stood up there as part of the
summer and again as part of the winter, part of the variety of life
and a particle of life capable of surviving nicely in the

homogeneity and uniformity of winter. I marvel at both the upward (if slowing) rush of life and the inexorable grind of the ice that decapitates mountains and creates the bowls. Finally, I cannot be objective about it; I'm curious as to just which side I'm on, or mostly on.

I begin to think of the works of man. I think of the coal stove in our cabin—and I think of the strip mines I've seen. I think of the four of us crawling into the car to go laughing and quarrelling and galumphing off to Denver for Thanksgiving with the relatives—and I think of the molybdenum mine of Fremont Pass near Leadville that we might or might not go past.

That molybdenum mine is probably the best example of what is bothering me. Molybdenum is an additive for steel and grease—hardens the steel and softens the grease, or somesuch. Molybdenum has helped keep steel competitive (say its advocates) with lighter-weight metals like aluminum, because a lighter gauge of moly-hardened steel does the same job as a clunky gauge of steel without molybdenum.

But the recovery rate of molybdenum from its ore is absurd—eight or ten pounds of molybdenum from a *ton* of ore. There are about four pounds of molybdenum in an average-size automobile, which means that every car that drives over Fremont Pass has contributed about half a ton of the chalky-looking sterile shit in the very impressive tailings piles that line the road for a couple miles.

The mine is right at the top of the pass; it is a strip mine; and what it amounts to is a very respectable cirque. Give it a couple hundred years when the company is done, and it will be indistinguishable from the other cirques in the area.

But its terminal moraines will be much further away than average for a glacial cirque; the final debris from that molybdenum mine is already building up in great rusting stacks and ridges of old automobiles way down in Denver.

Yes, great were the glaciers and mighty the ice—but

sometimes we don't do so bad ourselves. It took the glaciers tens of thousands of years to grind out their bowls, but they didn't have such sophisticated technology as we do. We've managed some respectable gouges in a little under three hundred years—counting just the Industrial Revolution; if you want to include all the time it took us to tool up for the work—say eight or ten thousand years. "Civilization is the possession of instruments, material and social, for accomplishing all sorts of things, whether those things were worth accomplishing or not."

But what *are* we accomplishing? That's where I start getting antsy. I am not like Thoreau and the Sierra Club, mooning over some lost Eden, a pastoral paradise I never knew and would not be at home in. But neither am I in there hump, hump, humping for the greater glory of progress and the GNP. I don't think I can be accused of wanting to both have my cake and eat it. I have lived these last ten or fifteen years in a state of genteel poverty that even Henry would probably have grudgingly acknowledged as being on the right track, and it hasn't been so unbearable that I want to change too radically for the better. (Our biggest problem has been not flaunting our poverty, even unconsciously, before friends not quite so bad off, thereby making them feel bad about their relative state and losing them as friends.)

All I want to know is this: are these tremendous accomplishments—the creation of cirques on a par with glacial work, the piling up of great moraines of rubble and rust—somehow worth it in what they bring us in the passing? I have, as I said, largely stopped reading the papers, and I've always avoided the television news like the latent alcoholic obeying a sixth sense to avoid that first drink, so I don't know what good news I've been missing...but the street-talk this year has all been about the incredible fact that the coal-miners don't seem to want to go down and dig the glorious coal for the glorious future achievements of America! And everywhere I go—into stores, into groceries, into the discount temples—I find the set smile or the more honest glumness that seems to whisper behind eyes *Don't tell me about it, I'm just into it for the money.* I hear we're going to get a tax break so we'll all have more money to spend, thereby cranking up the economy: we'll consume more, we just aren't creating those cirques and moraines fast enough. . . . Jesus God, are we on some kind of a *timetable* or something? When we are working at maximum efficiency, this civilization of ours, what will our rate of consumption be? One mountain per decade? One per *year?* *Two* per year?

There is an old mountain just outside Crested Butte— literally beginning its long rise right inside the town limits, in fact. Mt. Emmons, much more the town's mountain than the one across the valley named Crested Butte. I used to watch this mountain from the gondola at the ski area: there is a huge glacial cirque on the side of the mountain facing the town, making the mountain look like some ancient ruined and headless god. The steep head well might be a slumped and caving chest and torso, the side ridges arms lying lax along a wooded throne. It sits musing over the town, a great sculpture carved out by the black ice of the Big Winter: winter's graven image.

But now it appears there will be more carving done on this mountain, for the same company that brought us the new cirque on Fremont Pass, and contributed to the terminal moraines rusting by the river in Denver, has discovered molybdenum in that mountain. American Metals Climax, Inc.—that's the name of the company—has tentative plans to begin mining operations on that mountain in "the mid-1980s, when according to our present forecasts, another source of molybdenum will be required in addition to all other sources presently known. . . . "

American Metals Climax. . . . What a perfect name for a major mining company. Connotations of consummation. But when *do* we consummate; when *is* the big shuddering climax? I wonder if American Metals Climax will ever get to the Big One; I get this image of a level plain as far as the eye can see—but wait! Isn't that a molehill off in the distance? Yes! And immediately the roving advance squads or corebuggers from Consolidated Occidental Mineral Extractors (COME) gallop off, followed by the lumbering clanking machinery of extraculation...just one more quickie, *then* we'll be through....

AMAX says they will have to mine that molybdenum on Mount Emmons, but that this time they aren't going to do such a clumsy and vulgar job as they did up on Fremont Pass, back before the hippies invented the environment.

This time, they won't be so stupid as to put the tailings area out by the road where everyone driving past will be reminded what their car costs in small part; they will hide the tailings—estimated at two square miles by five hundred feet deep—back behind a mountain away from the road. They are aware that, for ninety percent of the people, "environmental awareness" is code for "don't let me see anything ugly that's my fault."

They probably won't strip mine this time, either: they may just go in and hollow out the mountain—between 130 million tons worth (present find) and 300 million tons (what they hope for). The mountain will be as pretty as ever—so long as no wind blows too hard, not too much snow falls, and no Sierra Club outings of more than 236 people step on it at the same moment: the hollow shell might collapse then.

The AMAX corporation is aware that such a project would have a substantial environmental and social impact. They are also aware of the fact that, in this post-NEPA age, a bunch of hard-core conservationists, environmentalists, anarchists, revolutionaries, and other friends of the earth, like you might find in Crested Butte today, can keep a good respectable American company in court for two generations if they want to—"penthouse preservationists" is the local West Slope term for them. And in Crested Butte, there's every indication they might want to. So AMAX is prepared to bend over backward to accommodate all radical complaints and hare-brained idealistic ideas from the start—except for one: forget about mining that mountain. That's too hare-brained; that's un–American. What would the world do without moly-hardened steel?—but that's not a very smart question either come to think of it. No, the mountain must be mined. Remember the Marching Song of the Industry (from *Snow White and the Seven Dwarves):*

> *We dig dig dig dig*
> *dig dig dig from*
> *early morn to night*
> *We dig dig dig dig*
> *dig dig dig up*
> *everything in sight*
> *We don't know what we're*
> *digging for, but we*
> *dig dig dig some more*

Since it is going to be necessary to be environmentally and sociologically *impeccable on paper,* in order to get the mining permits (after that, it's back to the same old ballgame, of course: buy your way), AMAX has pledged to make the Mt. Emmons mine a "model mine development." To that end, they have hired small armies of social engineers, planners, commercial sociologists, consultants on everything from low-cost housing to the proper drainage of bicycle paths, and of course the attendant flanking units of lawyers, three-piece graysuits marching abreast for half a mile or so, enough to make even the Sierra Club say *well sirs let's see what we can work out....* All from the cities, of course: those citadels of variety in life (meaning a twice-weekly change of movies and six-plus channels), small-town sensibility (meaning lots of boutiques and quaint bars with red wallpaper), and rural expertise (meaning SBA loans and FHA grants). They are going to go the ski resort people—of which I have been one—even one better: they are determined to preserve not only all the things the resort people wanted to preserve; they want to preserve the resort atmosphere too. All trailer parks and worker bars will be underground. There will be a community center with night classes in transcendental meditation and android adaptation—simultaneous, for those desirous of developing the whole person for the world of the future. Sign-up sheets for use of the jogging paths. Oh man...I did my small part to lever in civilization into Crested Butte, but I see what a small-time operator I was; my little contribution—a four page funnypaper! —is lost in the cracks between the treads of what's moving in now! (I can only assuage my feelings of relative innocence by reminding myself that, after all, I *was* the right guy in the right place at a critical time; a New York *Times* would have been such obvious overkill it might not have worked.)

Oh travesty...O tempora O mores, oh what the hell....Do you know what I want to do? More than anything in the world? I want to *laugh* about this. I do laugh, dammit. Not a sympathetic chuckle, not a brotherly giggle at being in on the joke, not the hard unfunny bark of commiseration; I want to laugh a laugh I hear so deep in my heart that I have to tear away a thousand generations to get it out. And when I get down to it, what is it, who is it laughing? A caveman, my most ancient and venerated ancestor in Europe, Cro-Magnon growing up in the face of the last great glaciers. Cro-Magnon and the Winter of Würm, the *würm* of winter: he, me, standing at the mouth of a rude shelter and shaking his fist at the ice and the wind and the cold and laughing the laugh of the truly desperate and determined.

I wish he could speak today, that "savage" with his utterly beautiful painted caves deep in the warm womb of that which we've transcended, Mother Earth with all her stifling little rules and limits, and unpredictable beauties and terrors. We always imagine that it would be a real yokel-trip, to bring a caveman into the modern world. Hiding our smiles as he stumbled into the gutter from looking up at tall buildings, watching the look of uncomprehension as he watched the insubstantial image of Johnny Carson flicker across the tube....But I think he would fool us, once past the initial shock of such a total immersion; coming fresh into this pervasive environment called civilization, which we've grown accustomed to in bits and pieces over a mind-numbing duration, I think he would quickly see us much better than we see ourselves.

He would look around the modern world and begin the simple binary categorization of dividing the world into "us" and "them," "ours" and "its." These are the things that are ours, he would say, ours against the winter; and these are the things that are the winter's. The stove with the fire in the middle of the central room is ours; but "central heating" is the winter's. The family that eats together around the table has its back to the winter; but the family that sits down together in front of the tube for recently-thawed dinner invites the winter. The city bus carries fifty souls that could be rubbed together for heat in an emergency, while the car made for six six-footers but occupied by only one small body is a condensation from the distilled cold void between stars.

These are ours, he would say: the family, the tribe, the individual, the gang; and these are the winter's: the committee, the jury, the army, the state, and the nation. Ours is the soul who shakes his fist at the traffic and the TV and the towering urban icescape; but winter loves the soul who gives himself over to this or that National Organization for the (all together now) Shaking of Fists. We hunger and thirst after the variety of life, and the winter of the West gives us the same thing in five different models, six different colors, and a dozen channels. We begin organic, and the winter lures us with plastic immortality.

And he wouldn't need a federal grant and an army of experts to analyze the developing situation on Mount Emmons; one look and he would say, *You're bringing it all full circle: our first act on the edge of awareness was to shake our fists at the winter, and now we're trying to finish its work.* And he would laugh, laugh, laugh.

So laugh along, brethren, laugh at the huge joke on ourselves and *shake those fists!* Laugh at the things that would keep us apart, isolated and alien to each other; laugh at the keepers of the keys and the writers of our schedules; laugh at the experts and engineers and lawyers and demagogues and polygogues and other quacks; laugh in the teeth of the winter and laugh for the light to see by; we proved it before, and from somewhere under the crystallized forms and plastic amorphism of these rich and wretched times, we will come up laughing and shaking our fists at our own part of a winter, to prove it again: *He who laughs lasts!*

The nights were immense. From where we lived, on a night with low-hanging clouds, we would be able to barely see the lights of Crested Butte reflected in the sky. But on a clear and moonless night, the only manmade light we could see was some combination of the lamps from our own cabin; and from the porch, or along the path to the outhouse, the spread of the heavens was magnificent beyond words.

Stepping out of the cabin onto the porch, out of the warm yellow into the night, the eyes are unprepared and see nothing but the darkness at first. The light of a single match, held between oneself and the night, is enough to blot out a majority of the stars. But as the match burns down and goes out, the deep points of light begin coming on flickering like mirages; the soft glow of the Milky Way spreads across the sky like the negative of a cloud; and there seems to be not a spot that doesn't sporadically flash and flicker with some faint distant burning. The lens of the eye opens like a well and light splashes in like a fine mist of rain.

I am not what I would call afraid of the dark. But I do occasionally find myself getting a case of the creeping gooseflesh out in the night for no identifiable reason; I find myself walking faster; I find that a train of thought has been interrupted without being supplanted; and I'm looking around, looking for whatever it is that makes me feel like wanting to look around. But like the man said once, it's only fear when you decide *not* to look around, or slow down. I can handle it by simply turning the matter over to my "better sense." I can make myself come to a full stop, stand there in the midst of the night as if under an umbrella, talk to myself. I remind myself that there is nothing, demonstrably nothing demonstrable, in the night to make a rational being paranoid.

I chant all the unanswered antiphons of rationality: *see, there where the darkness seemed to go so suddenly opaque, it's just the shadow of a tree...right?....The shadow of the tree is of course still accompanied by a tree...aren't you?....See? It's nothing to do with us anyway.* The litany of sanity.

I am not afraid of the dark, but I do admit that occasionally I found the night a bit overwhelming out there. I think of one night in particular—a night in which the night's power was strangely defined, and perhaps abetted, by a funny coincidence.

That was a night in the fall of the third year we were out in the woods, the season I'd finally decided, for the sake of my own future if not the town's, to ease my way out of the ongoing involvements in Crested Butte; I was, as they say in the circus, "between trapezes."

Disenchanted as I was with my life that fall—getting up every morning and driving in to my construction job, listening to the news on the radio (all about a guy named Agnew), cup of coffee slopping into my crotch, like any old suburban plumber heading for the shop in the city—nonetheless I wasn't exactly rushing to change it. Where the ambitious young writer (according to the gospel of *Writer's Digest*) goes straight home from his sustaining job and gets right back to work on the novel, especially if he has a family to provide for, I was more often indulging my natural inclination after a day on the handhammer to go have one or two or half a dozen beers with the old and young men who were not plagued by demon ambition. A lackadaisical demon, mine, that year.

But the evening in point, I'd gone back out to the cabin after a single beer in town. This, even in spite of the fact that I wasn't expected home for supper: Barbara and Sam had gone to a friend's orchard for a few days to pick some apples for winter. Ordinarily, that would have been an almost obligatory evening in town—a hamburger, fourteen beers, bar talk with the roving gallery, the off-chance of a gallop with the twelve-to-two riders of the night, and seven confrontations with Peter Matthiessen's urinal—the one that gurgles *you're pissing your life away.*

But that night, instead of pissing the night away in town, I'd gone back to piss it away in the woods. I was, at the time, trying to write something about forest fires, and fighting them with the Crested Butte Hotshots. But that evening after supper it became quickly apparent that it was going to be one of those up-and-down evenings. Up to turn on the coffeewater...sit back down at the typewriter. Piano of my soul. Wups, there goes the coffeewater boiling: up to make a cup of coffee...sit back down—shit!—bumped the damn cup, up to get a paper towel, clean up the mess. Back down to work...too damn much coffee. Up to go water the skunk cabbage—.

As I stood there, a temporarily captive audience on the edge of the porch, one by one the deep points of light woke up in the darkness; the Milky Way swam into the visible spectrum, slow drift of luminosity....The whole immense night beamed in, indifferent, beautiful, neutral and aloof as a convocation of gods.

For some reason I retreated. Instead of rehearsing the litany of sanity—*magnificent isn't it what scenery what a great place to spend the fall eh?*—I retreated, back into the cabin. That's always a mistake. I let the night have the tempo.

Back inside the cabin, I couldn't get settled down. It was like the nights when the ironclaw owl wakes you up. You lie in the dark with your eyes boring holes in it, thinking about all the things you can't do a damn thing about—at that moment, or ever. The things you did that you wish you hadn't, the things you should be doing that you aren't, the things you have to do that you don't know how to start—all that, that night, and more, and I wasn't even in bed yet. I paced the floor; I imagined the worst about everything; and it all seemed as real as yesterday. It seemed inconceivable that anything in the world was ever going to work out. I was part of nothing, because there was nothing else to be part of. I was a dead man stalking the dead end of a dead civilization. There was some vast presence loose in the world, of which the once-great tangle of wilderness, even the grinding spread of the ice, were only manifestations. More frequently those days, but with special clarity that night, I'd been feeling the same cold mixture of anticipation and inevitability I remembered from my spell in the Army; I knew that down the hall of doorways leading to dreams was a door that opened onto a small bare room, lit with a bare bulb from the ceiling (I hate ceiling lights), and in the center of the room was a small ark, doors shut on the small cold seed whose pale plant, baptized with the right waters, would bear me up and away, up the ramps and out along the edge of the night again—the dark ark of the secret covenant of the walking mad *you can, you know, you can...just get up and walk. And walk and walk.* I peered into the corners of the cabin, and the corners grinned back. *Nobody here but us corners.*

Not sure why—it was something I'd been doing that fall, and it was familiar—I got out the little box with the fifty toothpicks, the *I Ching* text, and the notebook in which I'd been recording my own "book of changes" according to the sporadic hexagrams.

In casting the "lines" of a hexagram, there are actually three casts of the stalks for each of the six lines. You drop the stalks—or toothpicks, or whatever you're using—and then divide them into two piles, approximately equal. The division into two piles is what determines the outcome of the cast: the thumb pushes into the pile, about half the stalks are pushed to one side. One or two kind of roll or slip into the space between the two piles; the fingers flick them one way or the other, into a pile. Cheating—at least on a conscious level—is quite impossible.

The eye would have to count the stalks thumbed aside, the mind calculate which way to push the extras, all in a trice, otherwise you'd know you were cheating—and anyway, who would want to cheat? It's not a game you win or lose.

But when the truly eerie coincidence does occur, the hexagram that so harmonically reflects one's mood (for better or worse), it stops one short: *could* I have cheated somehow without knowing it? Otherwise, how could this be?

The hexagram that emerged that night had *Tui,* the Joyous, the Lake, above, while the lower trigram was, again, *K'an,* the Abysmal. The spring that wells up at the foot of the mountain. The Hexagram called *K'un:* Oppression, Exhaustion...Stuck. The two water symbols: above, the water of the world that we see; below, the subterranean waters that we don't see. "There is no water in the lake," said the text. All pissed away.

But in the fourth place I'd cast a moving line—"old yang" changing to "young yin," tattered banners being furled, a winding-up of old affairs but thinking of catching a nap before anything new....Changing that line at the bottom of the Lake trigram was like pulling a plug: that trigram became the Abysmal as well. The Abyss above, the Abyss below, the hexagram called the Abysmal in fact. The night spread under the door, ran down over the windowsills, brushed up against my ankles like a strange cat.

Years before, on a camping trip down in Mexico, I spent a night in the hills just west of the plain that is mostly covered with Mexico City. *Soon to be a national park* a sign had said at the beginning of the little dirt road turning off the highway, but it wasn't a park yet. I woke up in the middle of a restless night with the realization that there was something moving around outside the tent. Not part of a dream; part of the night. My hair went right up on end, I'm sure. I lay there absolutely paralyzed for—I don't know how long. Then my mind finally started working: *it's probably only a stray dog. Nothing but a goddam stray dog.* Just stick your head out and you'll see it, nothing but a dog, throw something at it or something. I finally did it: stuck out my head, flashed the flashlight around the crowding bushes—and there was a dog. It scurried off into the bushes. You *know* in certain situations that all you have to do is stick your head out of the tent, and sure enough, it'll just be a stray dog. That's not to say it helps. Strayed in from where? Some of those dogs that wander around at night have little black ticks that'll clinch onto your soul and suck it as dry and shriveled as an old rubber hanging off a roadside briar. Leave you good for nothing but a steady job.

Finally that night in the woods I rounded up the resources to edge my way out onto the porch. That little four-by-eight dock between my hundred-watt day and the megavoid night. I drew my reason around me like a thin coat and prepared to scratch the match of my one-candlepower consciousness down across the backside of the night.

But once out there that night, it didn't seem quite necessary to unleash the rational dogs of day right away. It seemed enough for the moment to be secure in the knowledge that if I *needed* to I could always take instant refuge in rationality....It has since occurred to me that the worst cracks in the floor of the mind probably come at moments like that, when, confident in your defense, you relax it. I'm sure it must be the magician's intent to seem "artless" enough to get you to relax, take the infallibility of the senses for granted: his hand cannot be quicker than the eye until the eye relaxes, confident that it can't be fooled.

So I stood under the night, porchant, neither a part nor apart, ready to shed rational light on it all; but for the time being the light was all from the stars. Ancient light, far older than I. I might have grown roots there, but the mind ranged through open doors, loped like a lion along a great ridge, stopping at last on a high escarpment looking over a vast and sunken desert: out of the desert, out in the middle, rose a great rock, only it wasn't a rock but the great broken stump of the bolt-blasted tree that had once carried the deep waters out of the earth up to the sky to run down the branches as numerous as raindrops, onto a land that had bloomed long ago but didn't now. Still, the beauty of the moment was beyond describing, hypnotic, as up from the shattered trunk a seedling began to reach up, reach out, clamber up the night; it spit out a shower of seeds like sparks, meteors against the night, and a great forest began to spread like a shadow across the desert, black against the blue of the night's light, and it reached out, up toward the escarpment—.

I was back, back in time: I was the first man in the world to wake into this night with its majestic dimensions of beauty and strangeness. I was surrounded by giants; they spoke in whispers over my head, far above they whispered, while far away something ground and crashed; I thought *if I'm still I won't be noticed,* but then I had to run, and it seemed that I ran off in all directions, and the trees hid me; I wandered in the darkness calling, as it grew cold and the grinding and crashing seemed to come nearer, or me nearer to it....

The familiar light of my one-candlepower consciousness took the wick and flared, and (like seedhusks slipping and sifting through branches when the grosbeaks come) an uncountable host of attitudes, perceptions, imaginings, fears, legends, and dreams fell away from the shapes of the night before me, joined in a single dark druidic shadow, and slipped back into the receding realm beyond my rational probe. The night gradually became familiar; the shape of the night before me revealed itself to be what poets call, on a sunny day, a tree—the same old tree, the one that stands before the cabin, beautiful to look at, in the way of the sun at ten o'clock, a cause for concern in high winds, a point of contention for use-advocates, home for a jay and two squirrels, occasional station on the way for an owl, a future in firewood....

At present I am a sojourner in civilized life again." We are living in a small-to-medium-size town, two blocks away from a street called Main Street and in most ways typical of that genre, in a modest-size house with a large yard and a white picket fence around it. The house has such features as hot and cold running water, and what Marshall McLuhan would call hot and cold running media. There is a big furnace in the basement, an oil tank outside, registers in every room, and a thermostat on the wall; it's a set-up that is supposed to free me from such mundane tediums as tending the woodburning stove. But for a number of reasons, only one of which is the rising price of oil, we got permission from the landlord to move our stove down from the cabin in the woods and install it in the living room.

We are not very far at all from that cabin—about an hour's drive. In the winter, a forty-minute drive and the familiar old hour-and-a-half to three hours on snow-shoes, depending on the weather and the load. (Once, in town with Sam, we got "snowed out" for two days, and it took me four hours to bust through the new snow with the sled.)

But in the two winters since we moved back away from the edge, I haven't once skiied out to the field station and our cabin. "Our cabin," he says. It isn't our cabin anymore, and that may have something to do with the fact that I haven't skiied out. It's not going home anymore.

We do, however, manage to get up there every so often in the summer, as a family—every so often, but one day in particular, Sarah's birthday. Her birthnight: the biologists working there try to loan us a cabin for that night so we can stay over and we all have a little party together—Sarah wanders through the middle of it, still too young to really know what's up but enjoying it anyway.

She arrived a little after one o'clock in the morning, washed in on that great tide of salt fluids, blood, and slime. Although I was there to help, do whatever a man might do, I had become increasingly, humblingly aware how little there was that I could or should do. As each contraction built, swelled, broke, and subsided, I had begun to feel like an old seawife on the shore listening to the boom and smack of waves rolling in from an offshore storm, knowing (from the tales of survivors) what was happening out there to the old man on the boat, but unable to do a thing about it. One holding a light against the beating darkness, knowing only for sure that at some point this violence rolling and breaking beyond and beneath would yield up—well, would yield up something: in the seawife's case, maybe this time the mute tangle of rope and wood, a broken pot, something facedown and smashed, but with the normal combination of luck and skill—hadn't this happened many times before?—once more the boat and the old man who would require no more than a hand at the last moment, a rope caught, the boat secured and then home for supper...yes, I felt like that old seawife that night.

In our case, everything went more or less as nature apparently intended. Barbara negotiated the storm, I waited the right way in the right place and at the last moment "caught the rope" as it were. It is one of the foolish ironies of our male-oriented society that, on the basis of my service as catcher, I can say that "I delivered my daughter" and not even very many women would laugh.

But I was not without a function that night, as I was to learn. For one thing, there was something of a cleanup job. Which didn't take nearly long enough: she arrived a little after one in the morning, and by a little after two there was nothing left to do. Everything was cleaned up; the bloody sheet rinsed and soaking; mother and child asleep; the cabin warm with wood for the night stacked by; I could have gone to bed myself.

But I wouldn't have slept; I knew that. I would have lain on my back burning holes up through the darkness; and it seemed like a better idea—necessary even—to just sit there in the chair in the loft with them, one light low. It said nothing about that in the books I'd read on the subject; and I hadn't even thought about what might have to be done *after* the event, the event itself had so occupied my mind. But to sit up, keep the fire going, keep my eyes open, my head alert, suddenly seemed to be a desirable, even necessary part of the event; and I put on the coffeepot, put on a sweater (for even though it was August the nights were cold in the mountains), and generally prepared for a night watch.

One o'clock in the morning, two o'clock in the morning. One and two o'clock are nowhere near the morning. There is hardly anything further away from the morning, when you stop (at two o'clock) to think about it.

The night was very quiet: an impressive if neutral silence had settled over the cabin—the kind of silence that isolates, and thereby gives an unnatural emphasis to what small sounds there are, the same way that glass cases direct an unnatural kind of visual attention to objects in a museum. I found myself counting the sounds I could hear, like another man might use the quiet of the night to count his blessings. There was the soft sound of the stove drawing, a sound between a whoosh and a hum; there was the irregular ticking and occasional sharp pop, a cross sound, from the burning wood; there was regular ticking of the old windup alarm clock on the trunk over by the bed; the heavy rhythmic rise-and-fall, swell-and-subside, of Barbara breathing in the bed.

And that was about it. I knew that if I stepped out onto the porch, I would hear the omnidirectional undefinable sound of the "silence that roars." The stream behind the cabin, the distant waterfalls, the cumulative rustle of the teeming night life trying to make no noise down in the weeds and tall grass, the million myriad things in the many degrees of active and passive aspirating oxygenating ventilating...and the slow but steady all-night flow of the cooling air moving down from the high places. But all that was an unfocused sound—more a presence than a noise, really: something allied to the night and nothing to count, as sound or blessing or anything else.

Unlike Barbara's, the baby's was not a sound against the night. Light and quick, her signs of life were more a barely visible flutter than an audible rhythm. Have you ever watched a butterfly sitting on a leaf, at rest, but its wings still worked on by the subtle convective currents we can't even feel? So lightly did life seem to rest on the baby, less than two hours old. It seemed entirely appropriate to say that she wasn't entirely all there yet; she was nothing more than a rallying point for something still straggling in from the night.

Yet her face on emerging—and I'd seen it first, before anyone or anything else in *this* world—had been Buddha-like, cowled with history. . . .

It had grown confused for me at that point—that very critical point, that bad place for confusion. I think I drifted into a kind of mild state of shock at that strangest of sights, the small wrinkly head emergent between the straining legs—and even as I'd looked, amazed, Barbara had pushed again, and a great gush of bloody water had washed out and over the head, not yet a living head. . . . It was a moment that I remember, even now, most of all for its incredible wild beauty, and it pushed me into a brief dopey reverie; I might have been walking over sand dunes and salt grass, topping a rise—to be suddenly confronted with the sea breaking over a desolate and savage piece of coast, pebbled and rocky, and out in the water a ways, a mystery from an earlier world, a carved rock washed and splashed by the inrolling tide, and carved on the rock a faint Buddha-like face, the summary statement of a forgotten world finally seen, even by its own, to have been interesting but ultimately irrelevant. . . *a face covering a history.*

That almost euphoric state of semi-shock couldn't have lasted but a moment, because Barbara didn't remember me lapsing at all. Not that she didn't have other things on her mind. Nevertheless—and the knowledge, that night after it was over, marred the memory of the event for me—I knew my guard was down at that critical moment; and had disaster been looking for a way in. . . .

It was good, in a way though, to have an earlier intuition provisionally confirmed: that disaster probably isn't perfect either, and just like me, just as if human disasters were as human as humans, disaster would miss its chance as often as not even when openly courted or challenged. Why else would insurance companies do so well? They not only *want* us to think that disaster is as perfect and implacable as God; they spend a great deal of the money we give them to actively *persuade* us of it. They establish rate scales whereby policyholders in towns are regarded as "better protected" if the volunteer fire department blows the fire siren every day at noon: the siren howls and the old galvanic juices flow *brother are you covered*? They preach the Gospel of Murphy: *If something can go wrong it will.*

Some doctoral candidate in the social sciences, casting about for a thesis topic, ought to attempt to establish a correlation between the alleged death of God and the ascendance of "the Rock," or the big hands of Allstate cupping the house, car, and family ("He got the whole world, in His hands"). God didn't die, he just reincorporated with a shakeup in the management. Murphy moved up to the right hand.

But disaster just isn't as perfect as they want us to think, as we all find out from time to time, doing something stupid, silly, or dangerous, dropping our guard for a minute, absent-mindedly stepping off the curb against the light...only to wake up a second later finding we didn't get what we deserved. We blew it for a moment, but disaster was asleep, or tripping over its shoelaces, or off in the men's room unzipped, or was just plain too slow.... So I thought, looking at the clock, and noting how slowly it was negotiating the askew quadrant between "a little after two" and "going on two-thirty." It was just barely going on two-thirty.

It was mostly on account of the kids that we left their early home in the woods. Which is to say: if we hadn't had the kids, if it had just been Barbara and me, we might still be in the woods. Or Barbara might be there, or me: it has occurred to us both that the constant daily togetherness of marriage might be a little too much togetherness if we didn't have the kids to shape up, warp, mold, and deform, instead of just each other. We have several friends, or sets of friends—sets including a friend and his or her spouse?—anyway, we know couples who, after a few years of childless marriage, dropped back an intensity-level to the "just good friends" relationship—separate dwellings where they could each indulge their own sloppy habits and peculiarities without being thrown off by the mess of another, but seeing each other for dates, dinners, serving as a dependable couple for small parties, sharing things in the narrow margin of tastes-in-common, and falling back occasionally on the not-to-be-scorned predictable pleasures of a familiar person in the night.

But we had our kids; and if we don't count it a blessing a hundred percent of the time, we aren't heard to be complaining a lot either, and I for one—I'm not supposed to speak for Barbara—am generally pleased with the fact that our *relationship* seems almost to have taken on the nature and character of a third party whose feelings we give as much weight to as our own.

I won't be so...*parental* as to say that we brought our kids out of the woods for *their* sake. We brought them out because it was time for Sam to go to school, and because we were into the years when they were too small to ski six miles but too big to be lugged that far. They would have been perfectly happy, I think, to have stayed there in that cabin and never come to town at all. We could have taught them all the reading, writing, and 'rithmetic they'd need for life there—that much and a little more.

No, it's no good saying we brought them back for their sake; it's closer to the truth to say we brought them back to civilization for civilization's sake. We talked about "the socialization process" as though it were something the kids needed; but now I'm starting to wonder if we weren't just saying that we believed in the American approach to the socialization process (not knowing any other), and were persuaded that the socialization process needed our kids.

It might have been a mistake. A kid is in far less moral peril out in what passes for the woods these days than in the heart of civilization. It's not just the big visible things with wheels that can get you; there's all the little things flying through the air— the flu, television.... Both Sam and Sarah are doing battle with the one-eyed monster these years. The first confrontation with addiction: mustering the effort to think of something else to do instead.

Should we have gone the other way—on into the woods and away from civilization, as far as possible? The question is rhetorical: I wouldn't have been able to, and I know it. I'm too much a part of civilization, civilization is too much a part of me. Maybe I can't love it, not all of it; but I can't leave it either. With the ice, snow, loose rocks, falling trees, and indifferent wilderness one way, and the one-eyed monster, the iron mangle, crime-in-the-streets, and the indifferent city the other way, we chose the latter and the kids had to come along. When they are big enough to leave, if they don't like the choice maybe they can go the other way, all the way. But more likely, they will be as I am, well-grounded in the ways of civilization, so well-grounded that even their dissatisfactions and rebellions will be expressed on and in the proper forms.

Ultimately, I think, parents have to take only a limited responsibility for what happens to, or on account of, their kids. What can we be to them but what we are? We can either give them a distillation of what we ourselves are (*Make hay while the sun shines son*), or we give them nothing but the kind of advice you find on drugstore bookracks. What man, if his son asks for bread, will give him the latest Wonderloaf from this month's pop psychiatrist?

For a few years—I know it's only a few, because I'm already starting to lose it, already starting to get as fatherly as any old Polonius—for a few years, a new father still remembers what it is to be a son. A man is eventually either one or the other: an eternal son until he accepts, or gets stuck with, a father's responsibility. But for awhile, in transition, a man can be something of both and neither.

I can still remember that when I was bothered enough about something to bring it up with my father, I was vaguely disappointed when all I got was *advice*. I could have gotten that in Sunday school. I didn't want to know how I *should* have done it; I just wanted to know if he'd gone through something like the same plagues of uncertainty, agonies of error—I wanted *experience*; I wanted him to say *Well, let me tell you how I blew it when I was your age.*

But then, too, I did want him to be a father, follow the experience with a *However*....What is right? What is truth? Pilate must have been childless, himself a son questioning the son of God, because that is a son's question for testing fathers. A son is a person who knows that there is no "right;" there is only authority, and fathers wield it. And a father is a person who knows what the son knows, that there is no "right;" there is only choice, and fathers make it. The choice made, the father's world becomes the son's world for at least the young years; and the son sets about making the father be a father by constantly forcing a definition of the limits of the world. Like a fly inside a balloon.

I fall back on authority; what else is there? It's not a rational relationship to begin with—did he ask for me? My world? But even as I lecture, warn, and finally whale on his scrawny little butt for pushing too far, I secretly rejoice that my son is mean and independent enough to push me to set these limits, define my world even to myself, then push me to enforce them: he makes me live up to the charge of being a father.

I hope that a father never entirely loses some of the residual, vestigial son in himself. I think it makes me a better father—just as the incipient, embryo father in my son makes so sweet and powerful the moment when, later, after the blowup and the cooling of the mutual rage, we crawl into each other's laps, each other's presence, and know that something has been reaffirmed, almost as if by a ritual.... I forgive him his trespass, as he forgives me my world.

2:30 in the morning. I checked under the covers to see if Barbara was still bleeding. She seemed to be. As gently as possible I lifted her just enough to slip out the old towel, slip in a fresh one, so I'd be able to see how much bleeding there was. An instant trickle glistened down the inner thigh, blotted into the towel. But that may have been from my moving her. How much bleeding is "excessive"? How much blood is there to bleed? I've read statistics on how much water is lost from a dripping faucet—gallons a day, isn't it?

The ten or fifteen different books and chapters of books I'd read on the subject of childbirth all talked about the "normal delivery," "normal bleeding," normal this and that—but I will tell you: for the layman, like myself, the whole event from the first distant swell of contraction is so extraordinary, so extraordinarily powerful, that "normal" has no meaning whatever. You would have to attend fifty birthings before you could start thinking of that tide of blood and fluid in terms of "normal" and "excessive." You might as well talk about the "normal effects of a hurricane of average intensity."

There were so many little things I hadn't known about, comparatively minor details I hadn't even known to ask about. Or *who* to ask about. The afterbirth, for instance. Cleaning up, I'd picked up that package, bagged in plastic and wrapped in newspaper, in heft and feel so much like a package from the meat counter...*what the bloody blazes do you do with the afterbirth*?

I have to remind you here that I wasn't standing in a hospital corridor, surrounded by layer upon layer of insulating civilization, contemplating that strange package—that strange *wonderful* package, a "disposable" unit complex and yet sturdy beyond any combination of mechanical and electronic technology we will ever come up with. I was out on the edge of the woods, and outside was the night, restless with the ebb and flow of the roaring silence; and I didn't want to do anything to offend—anything. So what did one do with something so "spiritually delicate" as this magnificent little inter-world capsule? I didn't want a doctor's advice; I didn't want a scientifically trained modern efficient nurse-midwife to tell me the merely *hygienic* thing to do. I wanted a *real* mid-wife, an old hag veteran of two or three hundred winters, an old lady-shaman so traveled in time and space that her eyes would have a hazy crazy look from trying to remember which two worlds of the many it was that she was "mid" at that moment...such a one would know the *right* and *proper* thing to do with an afterbirth.

I had heard or read somewhere that many primitive people ate (or still eat) the afterbirth, either raw or cooked on a stick over a fire—or perhaps broiled with mushrooms and onions?—

but I would have needed it on good authority from the midwife that that was the right thing to do, and not just part of the solution to a chronic problem of hunger, as I didn't frankly feel hungry, thinking about the afterbirth.

Finally I had put it—not without the gentle and solemn respect due such a package—into the fire, pushing it carefully to the back of the stove in case it smoked. Putting it in the garbage wouldn't have been right. Burying it? Something would have dug it up, carried it off God knows where. Cremation seemed proper.

After rinsing the sheets, I'd thrown the rinse water out over the edge of the porch—only to immediately feel the sinking sense of maybe having done something wrong. I was putting out the scent of blood. Was that excessive advertising?

As I said earlier, there is nothing in the night to make a rational being paranoid. But there's also nothing there to make a paranoid being rational.

I felt around on Barbara's abdomen for the hard knot that was supposed to be there—the uterus reclenching like a miser's fist after its painful release.... My stomach began to contract as I felt carefully around without success in the jellyflab of loose skin that only hours before had been stretched as tight as a drum.... But then there it was, hard little fist. Barbara stirred, moaned quietly, but more like one tired than in pain. How much blood could trickle down into how many towels before the life just simply drained out too?

I hadn't had to worry about that kind of thing the night Sam was born. A winter night that time, but about the same time of the night. I'd been allowed to go into the delivery room and watch, so the events of the actual birth were not that alien and overwhelming that night in the cabin.

But immediately after the birth, Barbara and the baby had been whisked off into a labyrinth of sterile corridors, the baby put into a climate-controlled room where germs were shot on sight by trained nurse-sentries, behind a double pane of bulletproof, fatherproof glass. Everything exuded an air of being Well In Hand, and there didn't seem to be anything for me to do but go look for someone to hand a cigar to. At three o'clock in the morning?

But I was not swaddled in civilization that night; no more was the baby, or Barbara. I did a stupid thing. A friendly doctor in Gunnison had loaned me a big book, a huge tome, that had just about everything man has learned about normal and abnormal birth. He told us what to read in the book—then told us what *not* to read, specifically the section on pathology. Problems and what to do about them. Read that, he said, and you'll just give yourself nightmares about things you won't be able to do a thing about. But, concerned as to whether Barbara's bleeding might be "excessive," I looked in the section on post-natal problems—and quickly began to wish I hadn't. I suppose when you have a true full-fledged hemorrhage on your hands, the question of excessive or not resolves itself; there is simply no question. But while my question was not resolved, I did learn that there wasn't a damn thing I could do if she *was* hemorrhaging. If she were, she was dead: that's all there was to it. Transfusion would be necessary within minutes, and we were an hour plus from the hospital.

It was about then that the enormity—what we were not yet through that night, but only too far into to back out of—hit me. We had never really made a conscious decision not to make the dash into the hospital—finally it was just obviously too late to think about that, and we were into the "emergency childbirth procedure"...for which I had, fortunately, been preparing, most of the day. You could say, I guess, that we had made the decision to be well prepared in case we put off making the decision too long.

Once things were underway, I had been too busy to really think about what we were into. Only afterward, with everything done and the clock going on three, and time to sit down like the sorcerer's apprentice with the forbidden book, only then did it really strike me that we had been—*I* had been—handling lives.

Four out of five births are perfectly normal, we'd heard in a civilized parlor conversation; but the way that echoed in my ears that night in the cabin, one out of five births is not normal, and that sounds awful. Especially if you've just been watching a woman in labor. In her eyes, either in the readable form of resignation or fear, there is the awareness that she is no more in control than she would be if she were rolling off a cliff. If something gets just a little askew, wedged the wrong way, not started the right way—the pushing doesn't stop. Something has to give, give out, give way. When that happens, delicacy has to yield to expediency; doctors go in with forceps like blacksmith's tongs, crowbars and dockhooks, a small charge of dynamite maybe, to break up the jam.

I was one of the one-in-fives myself. I was a ten-pound baby, my mother's first, and I was born feet first, a terrible way to come, a terrible thing to do to one's mother. She told me, many years later, that the last thing she remembered hearing was the doctor saying "he's dead," whereupon she thought she had died too; but the doctor salvaged the whole works. In a cabin in the woods, we would both have died, without question. Sitting there in the cabin that night, I was literally nauseated with the full awareness of what it would have been, to have knelt on the bed watching nature destroy. . . never mind. You get the picture. What had ever possessed us?

On the downside of the clockwise dial, the big hand goes tick-tock tick-tock. On the upside it goes grind-grunt grind-grunt. From two-fifty on over the top to three-oh-one, it goes think-I-can think-I-can.

We wanted to have the baby at the cabin, no question about that. But no one else wanted us to, no question about that either. One doctor wouldn't even talk to us about "emergency childbirth procedure"; he wanted Barbara to spend her last couple of weeks in Gunnison, near the hospital. We found another doctor who was considerably more sympathetic. One of our reasons for wanting to have the baby at home was vulgar money: who can afford hospitals today? But that was not enough of a reason; we had a more philosophical issue behind our desire. We wanted to try to edge in a little closer to the center of our own lives *at a time when the chips were down,* rather than moving to the background as mere onlookers while the trained teams of experts moved in to do the job quickly, carefully, efficiently, and of course expensively.

But it did occur to me that night—rather forcibly, catching me at a bad moment—that it is one thing to take over the maintenance of our own car, or the growing of your own food; something else entirely to literally take your own lives into your own hands. At the very least, it ought to be done with greater decision, a total commitment from the start with no waffling under the barrage of well-meant warning and criticism....

I had to laugh. Looking at the pile of newspapers still stacked there by the bed. If I'd heard it once, I'd heard it a hundred times, the months previous: be sure to have a big pot of boiling water, and a stack of newspapers. The newspapers were for putting under the mother, to soak up the tidal waves.

The pot of water, I decided, was for washing out the sheets when, in the flurry and mystery of the event, you forgot to put the newspapers under the mother.

But—*newspapers*! How could I have put *newspapers* under a woman delivering a baby—my woman, my wife, my baby? What kind of a way is that to start life? Newspapers are for old garbage, fresh fish, puppies, and reading on the bus; but for my wife and child I can wash a sheet.

It had been a sheet with pert little designer-daisies all over it in blue and green—and then in the middle, Jesus great God, how it had looked, that sheet, all those cute little phoney daisies and in the middle that great splashing bloom of rust-crimson...a painting by nature, with Barbara supplying the paint and being the brush. An abstract, rough and marvelous—"Primitive," the critics might say: "Against a formal, almost inconsequentially banal background of stylized daisies, the artist invokes a sense of that dark mythical flower reputed to bloom only once a century, for one night...." I should have stretched that sheet, set it out to dry on a frame in the morning. *Should the morning ever goddammit come.*

Three-fifteen. And it's becoming more clear that time is not something to be used, saved, spent wisely, squandered, or redeemed; time is a vast desert, all washed and cut with gulleys, arroyos and canyons. Space is a gulley or canyon washed out of time, and we live in it, move freely in it, but there's only one way out of it, up onto the high dry plateau from which we might see other spaces in time—including our own space in other parts of time, like tomorrow morning.

For putting under her that night, I would have used the golden fleece, had I known how or where to get it. Silk seems ordinary, almost cheap today—silk sheets sound like something you order out of the small ads in the back pages of *Playboy.* But the golden fleece doesn't sound quite right either, to put under a mother in childbirth. But perhaps...how about this: the uppermost topgallant sail from a clipper ship, fresh from three days of snapping and popping in the clear breeze of a high-pressure front after a good wetting from the forerunning squalls....

So here we are, Henry: sojourners in civilized life again.

Unlike Henry, though, I didn't bring back from the woods an exhortation to "Simplify, simplify!" From me, it would be hypocritical. Henry went to the woods alone, and returned alone; it's easy enough for Henry to talk about simplicity. I went to the woods with my wife and one child, and returned with another child; it was, and is, evident to me that simplicity is not to be my lot.

I only envy Henry the advertised simplicity of his life maybe fifty percent of the time. Maybe even less. I'm reasonably sure I would envy him a lot less if I actually enjoyed his options—I was, after all, a bachelor once myself. I had friends and lovers with whom I broke off relations because they interfered too much with the comparative simplicity of life alone: they brought out what I regarded as the "worst" in me and occasionally they drove me into what I can only term a shamefully bestial rage, a wildness unworthy of a civilized person.

Wildness! What the hell did you know of wildness, Henry! Henry saw a woodchuck crossing his path one night, and "was strongly tempted to seize and devour him raw...for that wildness which he represented." Suppose, instead, that had been a drunk and pissed-off Irishman crossing his path? You can bet that Henry would have had something to say; he always had something to say on the subject of Irishmen (whose shadows, he noted, had no "halo" like his own did); but I doubt that he would have praised the man's wildness. Not even if the man had seized and devoured a woodchuck raw.

Frankly, when I think of Henry in the woods I think of something Henry James said about the state of the English novel, on observing the degree to which "young unmarried ladies" dominated that literary form: "...half of life is a sealed book to young unmarried ladies, and how can a novel be worth anything that deals with only half of life?"

Well, half a life is better than none, I suppose; and it has to be granted that Henry and the Brontë sisters milked more out of their half of life than most old married folk glean from the whole thing.

But out there on the edge between the world and the

woods, where I kept Henry handy by the door for grabbing on the way to the outhouse, I more than once wished Henry were there to defend himself on a few points...wished, for example, that he'd come by our cabin, the way he dropped in on the Irishman John Field and his wife and kids in the "Baker Farm" chapter. To tell us that "if we would live simply, we might all go a-huckleberrying in the summer for our amusement."

I would have taken pleasure in pointing out to Henry the inverse relationship between "living simply" and "wildness" in family life. The *less* wildness, the more *simple* life is. No sooner do you start out a-huckleberrying than the baby shits in her pants and starts crying and scrunching. The delay from diaper-changing makes the four-year-old impatient; he fusses for a minute, then wanders over to the stream and deliberately falls in. Et cetera: some days it's better, some days it's worse, but it's never particularly simple—until a degree of refinement and organization of our basic wildness has been imposed on all parties, by each other. Things get simpler to that degree.

Toilet-training has come in for a certain amount of criticism these years, on the basis of what it allegedly stifles in the natural child. And I suppose one could overdo the job, making a Prussian discipline out of it. But I watched both of my kids jump around in pure joy—well hell, we were *all* jumping around in pure joy—the first few times they remembered in time. It's like the first covenant with society which they initiate themselves; and I'm sure that, whatever they give up of their natural being, they more than gain in a larger world. So far as natural wildness goes, it is probably easier to admire when its principal manifestation in your life is not a little woodchuck filling up the diaper pail every three days.

"Simplify, simplify, I say, let your affairs be as two or three, and not a hundred or a thousand; instead of a million count half-a-dozen, and keep your accounts on your thumbnail." Perhaps if we did have a chance to talk it out, Henry and I would conclude that it comes down to a matter of saying "simplicity in *what*, simplicity *where*?"

I like simplicity in my machines, for example. I have an old pickup truck which I love for its straightforward, large-margin-for-error mechanical simplicity. I have an old Volkswagen which, on the other hand, makes me nervous. I can't fix it with a ten-inch crescent and two sizes of screwdriver. It isn't a simple enough machine for me.

But my standards for people seem to be exactly opposite. An acquaintance is someone I think I understand well enough; a friend is someone I think I'll never understand at all. And my own infinite capacity for complexification of my situation is the worst and best thing in my life. I take a kind of refuge in it: it's the only thing that stands between me and the colossal boredom of perfection. I have no patience with the kind of self-help books so popular in America today: I don't believe there is any difference between the "erroneous zones" and the "edge zones"—and if we pull back from our own edges, how are we going to grow? Better to just get in there like an adult, and thrash it out in the underbrush. Pull back if you have to, into some tidy little well-lighted place where you *always* know what you're doing...but don't call it an achievement.

Simplicity in things mechanical, complexity in things organic—I'd accept that, if Henry would. Let your cylinders be as two or four, and not six or eight; instead of a million dollars count to six thousand, and keep your accounts down to the minimum acceptable by the IRS—but then, then, take the time and the energy you've saved from mechanical preoccupations, and move out into that swamp, the savage swamp where reality is what we manage to pull together in bits and clumps out of the infinitude of natural beauty and terror....Winter simplifies; governments try to simplify (everything else but the government); death simplifies; but from the ancient bog of protozoic slime to the modern bog of psychological chaos, the whole unfolding thrust of life has been to diversify, variegate, complexify, complexify, complexify....

I shook myself awake, not sure why I'd woken, and not clear as to where or why I was sleeping...then the input shuffled in: it was chilly; I was in the chair in the loft, one light low; Barbara stirred again and moaned like a distant wind; the roof creaked and when it creaked the baby stirred and squeaked; and a spider was crawling down the wall above the head of the bed, where Barbara was suddenly restless as if dreaming. I was all but paralyzed for a moment, knowing everything I wanted to do and needed to do, but not what to do first. Nothing moved for a moment but the spider. Then I moved, and took care of business in this order: killed the spider. Lifted the covers to see if Barbara was still bleeding, which she was—maybe less? Ran downstairs to put wood on the almost-out fire. Heard the baby squeak again, and went back upstairs, where the roof creaked again—the night was settling on the cooling cabin, but the stove began to whoosh, warming up once more to the task of pushing back against the night. The cabin became like a small bubble of light and warmth at the bottom of the night.

The baby sneezed, ridiculous little sound but unmistakable. *Gesundheit, God bless.* I read somewhere that when one sneezes the heart stops for just a second, and we say "God bless" on the off-chance that it might not start up again, in which case the person is sent on his or her way with at least one brief blessing. I've never heard of anyone dying in the middle of a sneeze, and I suspect it's just another old wives' tale; nevertheless I still pray *God bless* for those afflicted just in case. Just in case there's a God, just in case the sneeze is fatal. And immediately on my saying it, the baby started to cry.

I picked her up, wrapped in her blanket, and sat down in the rocking chair holding her against my stomach. She cried for just a few minutes, in a half-hearted kind of way, then went back to sleep. I'd be tired too, after a trip like hers that night. The butterfly of life kept its wings folded, stayed in place. By morning, I figured, she would be safely here. Morning.

Morning.

On a cold morning, in the time between early light and sunrise, if I went out on certain slopes and got down low enough to look across the surface of the snow lying on the hillside, I would see a ripply, wavy motion along the surface similar to the watery-looking heat waves rising from a road on a hot afternoon. What it was, was a layer of dense cold air literally flowing down the slopes, seeking the lowest possible level just as water does.

At night, when we turn away from the sun and are exposed to the cold black stare of space, the atmosphere starts to collapse a little as the night sucks off the radiant energy absorbed by the air from the sun all day; and what was an expanding molecular dance under the warmth of the sun begins to slow, wind down, and the air, one might say, starts to fall out of the sky. It's not a wind; it's just a contracting, as when a person surprised by a chill wind folds his arms across his chest and seems to shrivel inward. And where the sinking cold air meets the earth, it piles up in a denser layer of thick and clammy coldness, and where the earth slopes away, the cold air flows down the slope.

If such a morning were the first or second clear morning after a recent snowfall, so that the cliffs of Gothic Mountain still held snow, an interesting almost other-worldly thing would happen in that time between first light and sunrise. Well before the sun would begin beaming directly over the eastern ridge into our valley, it would be moving down across the face of the mountain. And the face of the mountain when coated with snow was like a huge reflecting surface; so much light bounced off its face down into our valley that it was not at all uncommon to see faint *east-facing* shadows on the snow just before the earth finally turned us toward the sun. Because the cliffs were an uneven surface and therefore an inefficient reflector, the light that filled the valley was not like the sun's light, but was a diffuse pinkish light with faint violet shadows: it was more of a glow than a light, as if the air itself had turned luminous.

That impression was only heightened by the fact that the air itself was definitely sparkling, tiny diamond flashes of frozen water vapor darting and bouncing in the "Brownian movement" which was one of man's first real clues to the molecular structure of matter: these tiny flecks of frozen vapor are being bashed and buffeted in a random way by the invisible molecules of air, and so kept "in suspension." Knowing what is causing the flashes of light in the cold air from a scientific point of view adds to, rather than detracts from, the utter. magic of such a moment, when one's morning shadow faces to the east, lavender in a pink light, and the air is flowing down the hills to fill the valleys and is full of diamond facets.

But the unnatural natural beauty of that half-hour or so is balanced off in part by a feeling of dis-ease as one figures out what is actually happening.

Water vapor is freezing and falling out of the air. Everything else that makes up the molecular soup we call air has a freezing point, too—carbon dioxide, oxygen, nitrogen, the works. As the gaseous molecules lose energy, the light molecular dance becomes sedate, goes from a dance to a downhill flow, and if the energy loss continues and continues, the flow becomes lugubrious and dense until at some point a handful of molecules suddenly tumble into a stable relationship and lock together, whereupon others lock on and the phenomenon of structural organization by crystallization spreads throughout, bringing an end to the era of the individual molecule using its energy to avoid structure; henceforth all molecular energy will be directed toward the maintenance of the status quo, proclaims the reich of the night.

Well, to be sure, so long as there is a strong sun and the earth continues to turn to give everything a shot of solar energy, there isn't any danger of it even getting cold enough for the carbon dioxide to fall out in frost flakes, let alone oxygen and nitrogen.

But when viewed in that ultimate perspective, these little darts and flashes of frozen vapor in Brownian suspension are something more than just pretty. Those little flashes of frost glitter on top of the snow too, turning and being turned in molecular currents far too subtle to be felt by me, and although the journey is leisurely and picaresque, the end of the journey for those little flakelets is to lie on the earth until again energized by the sun, sublimated again to vapor in the molecular dance; and when a cold spell stretches out as it can, until the invisible parts of the air begin to "feel" sluggish and the sun looks as though it is shining, or trying to shine, through a pond, I want to start waving my arms and batting at those diamond flashes in the air hurrying on my way to the outhouse in the morning *Come on come on! Stay up, keep it up just a little longer, hang in, hang in! Don't fall now when it's almost here!* Me and my allies, oxygen and nitrogen, trying to keep the air alive till we get to the sun.

The clock said it was four o'clock. Big fucking deal, I said. Look, Mac, said the clock, offended; if you—.

I was startled, distracted by peripheral motion. Knowing immediately, of course, what it was. One of the damn cute little mice that were such a cyclical plague to our life in the woods; it had gone zipping along the floor down where the roof pitch met the wall. I didn't want it there—not that there was much I could do about it. One at a time, those little mice are beautiful, soft tan and white with great liquid black eyes...but those mice apparently breed every three months or so, shit every three minutes or so, and vibrate constantly, twitching and darting and dashing; even when they are still, they quiver and tremble. I think I could have better stood the numbers and the poppy-seed turds, if there hadn't been that constant quivering, that harmonic vibration with some unseen fear.

We trapped mice in the cabin. Not with "snap-traps" but live-traps. When the mouse-cycle was on us, we could fill up four traps a night, and the unlucky mice not in the traps would vibrate around them, looking for a way in, because we baited the traps with peanut butter. In the morning I would take the traps down the road, or across the river, and turn the mice loose. Fiendishly hold them in my hand for a bit, pump up their adrenalin to about 2500 jolts per minute. I was looking for identifying marks, like torn ears, missing eyes, so I would recognize them the next time they found their way to the peanut butter again. Somebody told me once that a prospector up in Alaska—or maybe it was a biologist, same thing, different goals—marked some mice and started taking them further and further from his cabin, after catching them again and again in his live-traps. Five miles, I think, was the record—but the person relaying the information didn't know for sure whether it was the mice or the prospector (or biologist) who quit first.

I am not exactly sure why we didn't kill-trap the mice. I don't think the rationale, or lack of rationale, was entirely humane. I think there was an element of fear. Or fear of fear—because, truly, we had nothing to fear but fear itself, out there. "Good sense." Good sense is the art of transforming fear into "a healthy respect."

Most of us tend to have a fear of rats, or *revulsion* toward rats, which is another transformation by good sense. In our efforts to explain our fear, we emphasize things like the plagues they often carry, how dirty they are, how vicious they are, and all their relatively human qualities. But what bothered me most about the mice out there was the fact that there was no *reason* to be afraid of, or repelled by them. They weren't that dirty or flea-ridden, and they certainly weren't vicious. All they were, was pure naked fear. They *knew*, I think, that they were put there for food; and the fact that they seem to react to everything as if the world were one big mouth is another argument against the concept of a benevolent creator, in my books.

That was what I disliked about those little mice, that constant quivering fear; and I really hated it at night, especially at night, when they infiltrated like little tingling raw nerve endings. Unravelling the sleeve that sleep was trying to knit up. The thought of kill-trapping them was unbearable: every *snapsquish* would be like exploding a little bomb of paranoia right inside the cabin, all that concentrated fear going off in all directions.

There were so many of them. They were not just a species of animal, they were a manifestation of a principle—no: they were the *infestation* of the *absence* of principle; they were the fingerling extensions of the same mindless void that dwells in the depths of the night and the black space between stars and molecules. And at four-fifteen and all's not well, four-fifteen and going to hell, you don't need a mouse in the house.

I wanted to wait for that mouse, leap on it like a weasel and pound its cute little head to a pulp against the side of the stove; I wanted to watch those dear little liquid-ink eyes, as deep as the night is long, fade and go dull, film over. I wanted to offend the night, cut off those invading little tentacles of manifest paranoia, its peculiar vines of silence, its soft weight squatting and pushing against my roof; I wanted to force it to a confrontation, make it congeal itself into a presence even if it were such a presence that one's blood would congeal too, make one go solid as a board with ice in the veins, just as the sight of God is supposed to shrivel one with fire. But that's hardly the way of the night, which tends to serve its victims more like the cat, teasing to death with humiliation and ridicule. The night likes to take old people and babes in the hours from four till false dawn, feeding its blackness first into the gut, so the bladder and colon void themselves and the body goes with an apologetic smile....

Going on four-thirty, and all's about what you'd expect.

I did some rough mathematical calculations: there where I

was in the mountains that night, about midway up through the temperate zone on the turning earth, I was rushing through the night and back around toward the light at an average and presumably constant speed of something around six hundred miles an hour. Ten miles every minute. A kilometer or so for every one of the deep slumbering breaths Barbara continued to take. A handful of short hops in the random day of a butterfly for every flutter of the baby's breathing.

But there are many miles to a night, even in the summer when the nights are shorter. Somewhere between five and seven thousand miles to a night, I suppose—more accurate figures would have been no more encouraging.

It is really impossible to get a sense of the feel of that motion. We can get an illusion of it, lying on our backs and watching clouds pass over until all at once it seems that the clouds are still and we are moving under them. Einstein implied that there is no necessity for developing a sense of that motion: it's as "right" to imagine the world stationary with the universe spinning relative to it, as the other way around.

But either way, we are captive within the motion, and absolutely dependent on its maintenance. We live in a thin geodesic between something and nothing; we are the manifestation of a principle, and about half the time we are peering into the total absence of any principle. One way, we face toward our principle, look into, soak up, the radiant heat and light; the other way, we look down into the cold depths of nothing, a nothingness so deep and vast that suns greater than our own are only pinpricks of aging light. The light of the nearest stars comes from so far away and so long ago that their existence, simultaneous with ours, cannot be proven. We can assume, or hope, that on any given night we are not alone with our sun in the universe; but we can't prove it.

That is a heavy night, the one we look into out there. Its beauty is awesome, but its cold would be terrible; and of its beauty and its coldness, only the latter has a provable continuity. High in the mountains, where only a little over half of the atmosphere remains to insulate us from deep space, you can be looking "up," whatever "up" is, to that night, and still have the feeling of being about to fall in.

Shivering—genuflections to the night—I went in, stuck another piece of wood in the stove, listened as the soft whoosh of its draw picked up. Wood and wind together—*Sun*, the gently penetrating. As is the tree, the fire in the stove is a manifestation of the marriage of opposites, wood and wind.

I went upstairs again to check Barbara. Was it my imagination, or was the bleeding stopped? Was the fact that she seemed to be bleeding less a good sign, or a sign that she was just about out of blood? There is, remember, nothing in the night to make a rational man paranoid.

I remember bartalk from some old bar or another—a fellow was loudly addressing a complaint "to his coy mistress," who wasn't present herself: "She thinks her cunt is a goddam treasure cave." A familiar enough lament. All he wants to do is go in with his flashlight for a quick look-see.

There is a rational effort underway these days to liberate the vagina from mystical connotations. I don't know whether the impetus comes from severely rational men who want women to leave off the "treasure cave" syndrome, or severely rational women who want men to leave off. Probably both. But anyway, the vagina is just another muscle that needs frequent exercise to be healthy and operational, just like the arm or one's pet poodle. We talk about a "healthy sex life" in the same wholesome terms you might expect to see on the side of a *Wheaties* box. People buy books describing variety in sex the way they buy cookbooks for variety on the table. I've heard that in some communities, group sex has replaced square dancing as a number one social activity. It's like recess-time for adults: everybody out on the playground for pump-pump-pullaway.

But being more inclined, myself, to exploration than jogging, I still have to surround the exercise with the old "treasure cave" mystique to keep it interesting. It may not be the best possible metaphor, but it will do until something better comes along. I remember a book I read as a boy, still too young to even suspect anything about treasure caves. It was a book about a boy and a horse. The boy was shipwrecked on some rocks near an island walled by high cliffs. But he found a cave in the cliffs. He entered the cave, and gradually made his way through its labyrinthian darkness, finding in the course of his explorations into various rooms and dead-end passages the skeletons of dead men and other relics. But then he rounded a bend, and there was light ahead; he climbed toward it, and finally emerged from the caves, finding himself past the cliffs and on the edge of a beautiful plateau in the center of the island, and across the grassy plateau surged a herd of wild horses....

According to a little laymen's-level book I have, on the subject of space and the explorations and findings of high-energy astronomers: "Astrophysicists speculate that black holes may be bridges connecting one part of our universe to another."

There is a darkness warm and full and not at all like the night; and sometimes, at rest in that darkness, my mind wanders to those theoretical jars of pennies: the one that the old man said we would never empty, but into which we've just thrown another IOU; and the other, the "talking jar," which still has a fair treasury.

I wonder why we don't just combine those jars, and maybe a few others we aren't even really quite aware of yet. For example, if every time we both simultaneously had the same exact thought and started to speak at the same moment, then stopped, feeling vaguely foolish, we were to take out a penny.... Or every time I successfully moderated my mutton-leg logic, due to seeing the scar jump out anticipating it, we were to take out a penny....

The dailiness of our civilized lives grinds us down. The kids never seem to learn anything, but have to be told twice today what they were twice told yesterday. We have stupid destructive arguments about stupid destructive things like money. Barbara buys the expensive whole-grain, high-protein, organic-aly-grown "natural" foods which I call an unnecessary luxury for the rich; whereupon she points to my beer in the refrigerator and asks if we can afford that. We talk a great deal about money, kids, money, other people, money, what we don't need, money, what we do need, and economy. The depressing truth of the matter is, those things seem to constitute the majority of our conscious world-in-common. A *common* goddam world-in-common: *that's* one thing that we both agree on *all* the time.

But, invisible as the wind and all but unnoticed in the chatter and mutter of our preoccupation with the dailiness of our lives, other potential communications and incipient understandings seem to swirl through our little domestic lives, as insubstantial and elusive to the rational receptors as gnats to a fishnet. That which passed between us that night in the cabin— we never made a conscious verbal decision not to go to the hospital to have the baby, but we did make the decision: a thousand times, a bit at a time, in the seven years between that morning after the night of talking and the night when we didn't even need to speak the decision. Together, we must be *something* more than an executive committee for the organization and distribution of the daily dailiness.

Sometimes I rest in that darkness warm and full, not at all like the night, and my mind wanders off to the first man to ever rub fire from two sticks. If you have ever tried that, you know it takes a discouragingly long time to even get a curl of smoke; and I cannot imagine a person making that kind of discovery entirely by idle chance. I try to imagine what would possess a person to sit down with two dry sticks and rub and rub until "the fire came out." The only possible explanation I can come up with is that he must have been a lonely lover and a latent artist, away from his love and alone under the impersonal weight of the heavy night; driven half frantic with that mixture of hunger and loneliness we all know to some degree or another, he or she picked up two sticks and (like the painter with his images, the writer with his ideas, the sculptor with his forms, the sage with his stalks) symbolically recreated the frictional union of opposites. *Wood and wind, tree and fire, wind and wood, the gently penetrating* just rubbed and rubbed till something came.

Sometimes I rest in that dark and my mind wanders off to that cottage all covered with the vines of silence, and the aged couple within; and I hypothesize that maybe life will prove to be a gradual weaning from the need for rational organization, conscious understanding, self-help and how-to, into a better sense of the many ways in which, as the Psalmist said so long ago:

> *One day speaks to another,*
> *night with night shares its knowledge,*
> *and this without speech or language*
> *or sound of any voice.*

And so we careened or crawled toward the light again. Barbara and the baby slept on, unaware of the night and its slow serpentine length: the one exhausted and vulnerable, the other too new and fragile to be safe; and I felt like one carrying a candle through a fog, where each step sets up a stirring that makes the light gutter and spit, but one doesn't want to stop.

Some years ago—it seemed like another life, that night—a witch gave me a magic capsule. The place was an empty restaurant up near timberline on Loveland Pass, almost atop the Continental Divide. What I was doing there with a witch, and how I knew she was a witch, is all part of another story—"Not that the story need be long," as Henry said once, "but it will take a long while to make it short."

But anyway, she gave me a magic capsule, which had no

sooner got into me than I got into it, and away we went. The full itinerary of the experience would be a travelog of the worst sort, the kind people write when they don't know very much about the places they've been to. But toward the end of the end of that journey, I found myself on the edge of a vast desert, and I was looking eastward across that desert toward the pale translucent blues and cold blue-whites that precede the first blush of dawn. Long night's journey to the edge of day.

I was high up above the floor of the desert, on top of—well, on top of something that towered high above the desert floor. Although I was looking toward the horizon and not at myself, I knew what I looked like: I looked like a monkey carved in stone, some sort of a primate, absolutely motionless, and my long tail was curled into the first smooth cycles of a perfect infolding spiral. Most of the rest of that night, all the strange, the beautiful, the hilarious, the disturbing things, have collapsed in a jumble somewhere in my mind; but that one picture—myself as a monkey, a gargoyle, looking toward the far horizon and the breaking day—is etched on my memory as with acid, in perfect stillness, perfect repose. Nothing moved; the world was dead; but because of whatever it was approaching the horizon, the death was the death-before-life.

It was, and is, a powerful picture to me—one of those things you want to protect from your intelligence; you don't want yourself saying *it means this, it means that*. Some things have to stay unanalyzed, uncategorized, unfiled in the morgue of the mind; because we instinctively know that to say what something means *in terms of what we are* robs it of any power to help make us something else. Maybe you don't want to be anything else. Okay.

But, through what we are wont to call coincidence, other little things began to fall in around that vision.

I was reading Dr. C.G. Jung's memoir one winter—

Memories, Dreams, Reflections. A remarkable book: as necessary for the committed explorer as *Treasure Island* or William Blake.

In one chapter, Jung was describing his experiences traveling in Africa. He reflected on the African dawn:

> The sunrise in these latitudes was a phenomenon that overwhelmed me anew every day.... I formed the habit of taking my camp stool and sitting under an umbrella acacia just before dawn.... At first, the contrasts between light and darkness would be extremely sharp. Then objects would assume contour and emerge into the light which seemed to fill the valley with a compact brightness. The horizon above became radiantly white. Gradually the swelling light seemed to penetrate into the very structure of objects, which became illuminated from within until at last they shone translucently.... At such moments I felt as if I were inside a temple....

But Dr. Jung noticed that he wasn't the only one watching the sunrise. His next words came at me like a crowbar:

> Near my observation point was a high cliff inhabited by big baboons. Every morning they sat quietly, almost motionless, on the ridge of the cliff facing the sun, whereas throughout the rest of the day they ranged noisily through the forest, screeching and chattering. Like me, they seemed to be waiting for the sunrise. They reminded me of the great baboons of the temple of Abu Simbel in Egypt, which perform the gesture of adoration. They tell the same story: for untold ages men have worshipped the great god who redeems the world by rising out of the darkness as a radiant light in the heavens.

There was something else, I knew there was something else, a dim flickering memory that was suddenly aligned with that drug-induced vision and Jung's experience.... I ran for my Larousse *Mythology*, another great outhouse book...thumbed around in the Egyptian section—there: the little picture of the squatting baboon with the orb cupped in a crescent moon on his head, a sculpture from some temple or tomb. "Thoth as a baboon," read the caption..."Worshipped as a lunar deity throughout Egypt, he was believed to take the place of Ra (the sun, sovereign lord of the sky, the creator) in the sky while the latter made his journey through the Underworld during the hours of night...."

Thoth, the dog-faced ape who sat in the sky steering the world through the night and back toward the place where Ra again took over. Thoth, the night shift.

> Endowed with complete knowledge and wisdom, it was Thoth who invented all the arts and sciences: arithmetic, surveying, geography, astronomy, sooth-saying, magic, medicine, surgery, music with wind instruments and strings, drawing and, above all, writing, without which humanity would have run the risk of forgetting his doctrines and of losing the benefit of his discoveries.

Thoth's name was a tribute to his achievements, meaning "three times very, very great." He was adopted into Greek legends with the name translated to "Hermes Trismegistus"—the father of alchemy, which was science before the puffers made science "objective."

Life is a tightrope we walk between taking things too seriously and not seriously enough. I would no more "worship" ancient Thoth or ancient Odin than I would worship ancient Yahweh. Yahweh knew, and gave warning: to name God is to cage God, whereupon God leaves and the faithful worship the cage. Just as there is a *gently penetrating* which is not yet either the root splitting the rock or the wind stirring the limbs, and a *keeping still* which is not yet a mountain, there is something which is not yet this or that old defunct god, this or that old defunct world-idea, this or that old defunct civilization. I have in my deepest memory—down there with the *würm* of winter—a memory, not of God, but of the one who waits for God, the one who dreams of God, and who spends the night inventing all the arts and the sciences while waiting for and dreaming of God. The naked ape on the edge of the night so terrible and beautiful: the edge of night, the edge of day, remembering light, dreaming of light.

Barbara and I had ended up there at the intersection not two hundred feet away to watch the sunrise seven years before that night—jammed together in the front seat of her Volkswagen but not close enough for me; it took years to get that close—and we'd faced east, waiting for the sun, not knowing that the show was on the face of the mountain behind us.

But by that night, on the edge of the morning, I knew what to expect, where to look. Even that first early gray light gets caught by the mountain. That's not an objective light, not a sympathetic light, not the light of day at all but something like an old crotchety bailiff preceding the king, the heir translucent; it just touches the surface, and makes the mountain look old. But I know what's coming, as I crouch by the crib where the baby sleeps and look out the loft window to where the mountain looks old and gray in the harbinger light.

Even as the top of the mountain catches the first stray rays and turns orange, then gold, I see how much light there is already below, and I get up and turn out the light by the chair (although the fire in the stove is still necessary); and in the dim natural light, I see her grow young and complete; she stirs, squirms, and screws up her face as if to sneeze or cry, and at the same moment Barbara stirs as if the umbilica were more than a single severed cord....

I am a sojourner in civilized life again; but where I have

lived the most this past couple of years is not in civilization, but somewhere between civilization and where we lived in the woods. I have lived the most in a little room that we built together, Barbara and I, in the back end of the garage behind the house we rent in the town where we are "sojourning."

It is a room with the ubiquitous (for us) coal-and-wood stove, two work tables, and a single chair. We each use the room half the day: Barbara to carve, me to write—each of us, in our own half-brained way (her right brain and my left would make a powerful mind if ever together), wrestling with memories that mingle with dreams, dreams that seem like memories.

The rest of the day, we each pull our shift in the daily dailiness: taking care of the kids, buying the groceries, doing the wash, cleaning the house, assembling the evidence for our own case in the ongoing daily debates over where will the money come from, where the money is going, how nice it would be to destroy the television, how nice it would be to get the television fixed, and we never talk anymore.

I remember saying to myself, when we moved to the woods, that I wasn't going to write "My Life In The Woods." That shelf is full, I said to myself, and anyway—"After thirty years in the toils and tribulations of Western Civilization, I needed to go out to the unfanged, second-growth, multiple-used, road-laced, over-administered woods to find something to write about"? Yes, my words exactly.

But once I was well into my "life in the woods"...once the woods were well into my life...it began to occur to me that what I had been thinking of as "problems" were more accurately seen as the consequences of a network of *solutions* that weren't working as well as they might have. But underlying all those solutions (with their smokes and smogs and other forms of solution-pollution), were the same old problems, the mysteries, the dragons that are as old as awareness. If we want wilderness, wildness, all we have to do is cancel our solutions, stop our juggernaut (which will eventually run down anyway), and we will have lots and lots of wildness: a tree will grow for every person who dies of starvation, badger violence, and general lostness. If we want predictability, regularity, uniformity, standardization, homogeneity, just remember what the New England farmers said: "The Ice Age isn't over, the glaciers just went back for more rocks."

As it turned out, I gradually came to realize that my real problem, here at the apex of (or maybe just a little past) the greatest of all civilizations so far, was the same basic problem that confronted the oldest of ancient men: How do you put together, out of all this vast potential, something that might work?

All day the sun has shone on the surface of some savage swamp...but now a more dismal and fitting day dawns, and a different race of creatures awakes to express the meaning of Nature there. And in that swamp are many floating islands, reed-rafts and weed-clumps, thrown together, falling apart: "reality" we call the one we're on; we tie two or three together and call it "civilization." A way of doing things. As T.S. Eliot put it: "These fragments I have shored against my ruins." Yes, Henry: "a more dismal and fitting day dawns"—but we might always hope, more fitting than dismal.

I do not say that John or Jonathan will realize all this; but such is the character of that morrow which mere lapse of time can never make to dawn. The light which puts out our eyes is darkness to us. Only that day dawns to which we are awake. There is more day to dawn. The sun is but a morning star.

—Henry, concluding his "Life in the Woods"